The Changing Face of Inequality

The Changing Face of Inequality

Urbanization, Industrial Development, and Immigrants in Detroit, 1880–1920

Olivier Zunz

The University of Chicago Press
Chicago and London

The University of Chicago Press, Chicago 60637
The University of Chicago Press, Ltd., London

Library of Congress Cataloging in Publication Data

Zunz, Olivier.
   The changing face of inequality.

   Includes bibliographical references and index.
   1. Detroit (Mich.)—Industries—History.   2. Alien
labor—Michigan—Detroit—History.   3. Social classes—
Michigan—Detroit—History.   I. Title.
HC108.D6Z86   307.7'64'0977434   82-6986
ISBN 0-226-99457-0   AACR2

For Christine,
Emmanuel, and Sophie

Contents

Illustrations

Tables

Abbreviations

ACD	Americanization Committee of Detroit
BHC	Burton Historical Collection, Detroit Public Library
BLIS	Bureau of Labor and Industrial Statistics, State of Michigan
BPC	Board of Poor Commissioners
DAC	Detroit Association of Charities
DPL	Detroit Public Library
DUL	Detroit Urban League
MHC	Michigan Historical Collections, Bentley Historical Library, University of Michigan
NA	National Archives, Washington, D.C.
WRL	Walter P. Reuther Library, Archives of Labor and Urban Affairs, Wayne State University

Acknowledgments

This study evolved over a period of eight years in three different institutional settings. I wish to thank the University of Michigan's Society of Fellows and its Center for Research on Social Organization and the Centre National de la Recherche Scientifique in Paris for five years of uninterrupted research support. I also extend my heartfelt thanks to the University of Virginia's History Department for giving me release time to complete the manuscript.

Collecting and analyzing large sets of data are costly operations; these were generously supported by the University of Michigan–Ford Foundation Population Development Fund, National Science Foundation grant Soc 76-00277, National Endowment for the Humanities grant R0–00135–79-0516, and the University of Virginia's Research Policy Council. The John M. Munson Fund of the Michigan Department of State's History Division also helped cover part of the mapping costs.

These grants were used primarily to maintain a staff of graduate and undergraduate research assistants who were involved in all levels of the research, from data collection to computer analysis. Some of them had a long-term involvement with the project, especially Charles Gasparovic, who helped assemble the material for 1880, Mary O'Neill and Marc Ness, who contributed to the collection of the 1900 data, Manuel de Uriarte, who helped create the graphic data base, Adeeb R. Fadil, who conducted the building-permit study, Todd Cooper, who assembled most of the material on urban services, and Paul Holoweski, who researched the biographical data on industrial leaders. All shared their many insights with me and contributed much to my own understanding of the material we were gathering.

Archives and libraries have done more than their share to facilitate my research, and it is a pleasure to thank Robert M. Warner and the staff of the University of Michigan's Bentley Historical Library, Philip P. Mason and the staff of Wayne State University's Walter Reuther Library, Alice Dalligan and the staff of the Burton Historical Collection of the Detroit Public Library, Richard Hathaway of the Michigan section of the State Library in Lansing, the staff of the Geography and Map Division of the Library of Congress, and the staff of the Interlibrary Loan Division at the University of Virginia's Alderman Library for their help.

Parts of chapters 1, 2, and 4 appeared in *Social Science History*, *Annales (Economies, Sociétés, Civilisations)*, and the *Journal of Urban History* in 1977. I thank the editors of these journals for their permission to use some of the same material in the book.

Other people were involved in the production of the manuscript. I owe a very special thanks to Patricia R. Schroeder, who edited the manuscript and made my task of writing a book in a second language a truly enjoyable learning experience. I also thank Ella M. Wood, who typed the final manuscript, and Roberta Senechal, who helped prepare the index. The maps in the grey-tone series were prepared by Jim Larson and Michalle Ross of the Center for Cartographic Research and Spatial Analysis of Michigan State University, under the direction of J. Michael Lipsey, and the other maps were drawn by Eugene M. Scheel, mapmaker in Waterford, Virginia. Michael P. Conzen provided essential guidance in the final stages of map preparation. The analysis of the 1920 census manuscript was conducted at the U.S. Bureau of the Census under the direction of Larry W. Carbaugh, of the Data User Services Division.

Many historians shared their expertise with me and helped me pursue specific points of research. Richard Hodas, Mark Coir, Valerie Gerrard Browne, and Sydney Fine gave me many archival leads. Maris Vinovskis and John Knodel suggested important techniques of demographic analysis. John Shy, Raymond Grew, and Theodore Hershberg offered important suggestions at critical junctions. I am also indebted to many of my Parisian friends who kept an active interest in the making of this book despite the geographic distance which separated us, especially Maurice Agulhon, François Furet, Annie Kriegel, Claude Fohlen, and Emmanuel Le Roy Ladurie. In the end, Jean-Marie Apostolidès, Stephen Innes, Robert D. Cross, William H. Harbaugh, Lenard Berlanstein, Theodore Caplow, Kenneth Kusmer, Kathleen Conzen, and John Higham read a complete draft of the manuscript and helped tighten many loose spots.

David D. Bien and Charles Tilly deserve a special note of thanks, not only for reading the manuscript but also for their generous and inspiring friendship, which often stimulated me to pursue the task. I also express my gratitude to

William A. Ericson and Daniel J. Fox, both statisticians, who contributed to the initial sample design and advised me on statistical matters at every stage of the research.

My greatest debt is to my family: my parents Jean and Monique Zunz, who have always encouraged my intellectual pursuits, my wife Christine, to whom I owe the equilibrium of our shared life, and our children Emmanuel and Sophie, who make it all worthwhile.

Needless to say, I assume full responsibility for the content of this book and any error of fact or judgment which remains.

Ann Arbor, Paris, Charlottesville
March 1982

Introduction

DETROIT AND LARGE-SCALE INDUSTRIALIZATION

Central to the formation of modern North American society has been the growth of a vast urban industrial complex, extending from the Eastern Seaboard to the Great Lakes region, which began to develop in the 1870s and reached maturity in the 1920s. In 1920, the United States Bureau of the Census, the nation's official agency for charting demographic change, not only declared that the majority of Americans lived in cities, but also defined metropolitan districts around the large metropolises so as to include the new suburban populations with their core cities.[1] A modern urban world, with new dimensions and a transportation system based on the automobile, was born. Simultaneously, large business corporations accomplished an organizational revolution in mass production and distribution techniques. They formed the new corporate giants that sustained the United States' massive industrial production during the First World War and provided the economic basis for the country's ascent to world power.

Historians have charted in detail the way the United States reached an unprecedented economic and political position of prominence through technological innovation and the accompanying environmental changes. What is less known, however—and the subject of this book—is the way the American social fabric was affected by, and at the same time changed with, these large structural

---

1. U.S., Department of Commerce, Bureau of the Census, *Fourteenth Census of the United States, 1920: Population* (Washington, D.C.: G.P.O., 1921), 1:43; metropolitan districts were first defined in 1910, *Thirteenth Census of the United States, 1910: Population* (Washington, D.C.: G.P.O., 1911), 1:73.

1

changes. A new class of managers, business employees, and salaried personnel—mainly native white Americans—emerged to fill the managerial positions of the new corporate giants. A new industrial labor force of unskilled workers, made up largely of immigrants, poured into coalfields, steel mills, and automobile factories. Southern Blacks, in turn, migrated to northern cities to replace immigrant factory workers when foreign immigration was reduced to a trickle after 1915. In all, a new living environment was created. But in sharp contrast with technological changes, economic transformations, political processes, migration patterns, and the city-building process—all of which have been charted by historians and all of which we understand well—the slow and complex evolutionary social change that accompanied these large-scale structural transformations is still little known.[2]

To examine this social transformation, I selected Detroit in the period 1880–1920. The speed with which Detroit changed between these two dates, after a long period of sluggish growth, and its role in the formation of modern urban America make it an ideal site for the case study on which the historian must ultimately depend to investigate social change in depth. Detroit was actually a very old North American settlement, created by the French in 1701. Located on the Detroit River, which connects Lake Saint Clair to Lake Erie and the Upper Great Lakes to the Lower Great Lakes, Detroit began as an outpost for the fur trade (see map). Its founder, Antoine de la Mothe Cadillac, saw it initially as an ideal location for a large French settlement, and it rapidly grew into a fort and frontier village.[3] Detroit remained French through two-thirds of the eighteenth century but passed into British control in 1763 and to the Americans in 1796. As late as 1810, however, Detroit's population was still as low as 770, and it was not until the 1830s—after the opening of the Erie Canal, improvements in the navigation of the Great Lakes, and later in railroad communications (all factors favoring westward expansion)—that Detroit capitalized on its site and early establishment and became Michigan's largest city. By mid-century, Detroit, already the most important center in the state for the traffic and trade of foodstuffs, also developed a tobacco and cigar industry, a lumber industry, as well as copper smelting and iron making, utilizing Michigan's resources in forestry, copper, and lead, and the Great Lakes transportation network to carry iron ore. For a short while it seemed as though Detroit could

2. For two recent creative syntheses, see Alfred Chandler, *The Visible Hand: The Managerial Revolution in American Business* (Cambridge, Mass.: Harvard University Press, 1977), and Morton Keller, *Affairs of State: Public Life in Late Nineteenth-Century America* (Cambridge, Mass.: Harvard University Press, 1977).

3. C. M. Burton, ed., Cadillac Papers, *Michigan Pioneer and Historical Collections* 33 (1904): 133–51.

become a major commercial and industrial center in the Midwest, but eventually both Chicago and Cleveland took predominance, leaving Detroit behind.[4]

In 1880, then, Detroit was still primarily a commercial center in the Great Lakes system of cities and, with 116,340 inhabitants, ranked only eighteenth in population among American cities. Only forty years later, however, Detroit's landscape was almost totally industrial. Henry Ford had nearly perfected the technique of assembly-line production in his Highland Park Plant, and he had built the Eagle boats of the First World War in his River Rouge Plant. Similarly, General Motors had achieved a model of corporate reorganization in the years immediately following the war. Detroit in 1920, with a population of 993,678, had become the fourth largest city in the United States, and by the early twenties it ranked third (behind New York and Chicago, but ahead of Philadelphia) for its industrial production.[5]

SEVEN PROPOSITIONS

Investigating the sociospatial transformations of Detroit between these two dates, then, allows one to see the way social change affected the lives of Detroiters during the very period of large structural changes in the city's size, economy, and population composition. I shall, throughout the book, argue seven interrelated propositions. These propositions do not deal with separate subjects; rather, they have a telescopic relationship, each proposition emergent from a close study of the previous one:

1. Detroit in 1880 was still a multiethnic city in which class affiliations were secondary to people's ethnic attachments, but by 1920 a silent social revolution brought on a new class consciousness. During the period Detroit certainly, and probably the whole of the United States' northern industrial society, experienced a major restructuring of social relationships: socially diverse but ethnically homogeneous groups broke up as new divisions based on social class grew more important. Ultimately, one's affiliation with a social class came to equal one's attachment to an ethnic group and to have an equal weight in important decisions such as the choice of a marriage partner, the number of children in a family, or the location of a residence.

2. Historians have traditionally explained the loosening of ethnic bonds by a theory of upward social mobility, mobility presumably enhancing a shift from

4. For recent descriptions of mid-nineteenth century Detroit, see John C. Schneider, *Detroit and the Problem of Order, 1830–1880* (Lincoln: University of Nebraska Press, 1980), pp. 3, 14–15; JoEllen Vinyard, *The Irish on the Urban Frontier: Nineteenth Century Detroit* (New York: Arno Press, 1976, pp. 7–19; Melvin G. Holli, ed., *Detroit* (New York: New Viewpoints, 1976), pp. 1–116.

5. Eric Kocher, "Economic and Physical Growth of Detroit, 1701–1935," November 1935, Division of Economics and Statistics, Federal Housing Administration, p. 61 (in MHC).

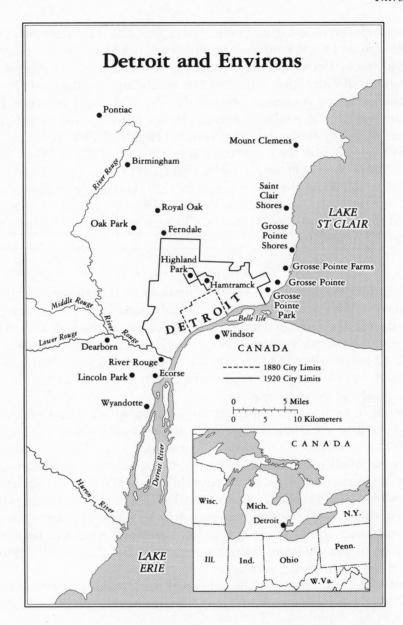

Detroit and Environs

Pontiac

Mount Clemens

Birmingham

Saint
Clair
Shores

*LAKE
ST CLAIR*

Royal Oak

Oak Park

Ferndale

Grosse
Pointe
Shores

Highland
Park

Grosse Pointe Farms

Hamtramck

Grosse Pointe

D E T R O I T

Grosse
Pointe
Park

Belle Isle

Windsor

Dearborn

CANADA

River Rouge

- - - - - - 1880 City Limits

Lincoln Park

Ecorse

———— 1920 City Limits

Wyandotte

0   5 Miles

0   5   10 Kilometers

River Rouge

Middle Rouge

River Rouge

Lower Rouge

Detroit River

Huron River

CANADA

Wisc.

Mich.

Detroit

N.Y.

Penn.

Ill.   Ind.   Ohio

W.Va.

*LAKE
ERIE*

"poverty" to "progress."[6] I want to argue that strong intraethnic group channels
for upward mobility did exist in the nineteenth century and that mobility experienced within one's own group often reinforced ethnic divisions. Intraethnic

6. Stephan Thernstrom, *The Other Bostonians: Poverty and Progress in the American Metropolis, 1880–1970* (Cambridge, Mass.: Harvard University Press, 1973).

group channels for upward mobility largely disappeared, however, with in-dustrialization. In 1880, a German blacksmith could have developed a small carriage factory in the German neighborhood and grown modestly prosperous within his group of origin. Thirty or forty years later, the same ambitious German craftsman could not compete with Ford, Studebaker, or Packard in building an automobile factory or fulfilling war industry contracts. He had to channel his energies toward upward mobility into an opportunity structure no longer controlled by his fellow German citizens but by the native white American establishment. But it was only when native white Americans achieved their dominance over large-scale industrial complexes and became the largest em-ployers in Detroit that this social transformation took shape. By controlling the large industrial complexes which replaced the many smaller shops that relatively recent immigrants usually ran, the native white Americans undermined the possibilities of mobility within a group for a large section of Detroit's work force. Hence, the lessening of ethnic identity was imposed upon all ethnic groups, not only through the passage of time, as traditional assimilation theory phrases it, but through the power of one ethnic group in the industrialization process.

3. Even during this transformation, ethnic divisions remained strong. Cul-tural divisions and behavioral differences between ethnic groups were wide, as evidenced by their different demographic behavior and their different family strategies regarding such matters as work, schooling, income pooling, or the lodging of boarders. Their attitudes also differed toward property ownership, recurring poverty, and more generally the pressures of the economic and political environment. Ethnic groups, whose neighborhoods and institutions (churches, schools, newspapers) had often been original creations and had contributed enormously to the cultural growth of Detroit, maintained a multiethnic city during the industrialization period, despite the many homogenizing forces which played against it.

4. Because ethnic bonds remained so strong during the industrialization pro-cess, the American social structure remained free from the threat of organized class conflicts despite extreme inequality of conditions. Detroit, the most rapidly industrializing city in the country, provides a textbook example of a city in which unionism—the labor historian's usual index of working-class solidarity—hardly penetrated. Labor unions, radical or not, had very little impact in Detroit at the very time when a large class of factory workers was developing. It was only when the shift from ethnicity to class was completed after World War I that the labor movement undertook to organize an existing class of workers. The labor movement, then, postdated the creation of industrial America rather than growing with it and affecting its destiny.

5. The nineteenth-century commercial and early industrial city which his-

torians have traditionally characterized as largely unsegregated—"a jumble of occupations, classes, shops, homes, immigrants, and native Americans"[7]—was in fact segregated along ethnic lines. Its ecology, the distribution of people and activities in space, followed a logic radically different from twentieth-century segregation. What really changed from the nineteenth to the twentieth century was the nature of concentration patterns in the city, not their degree.

6. The map of Detroit, indeed, changed dramatically between 1880 and 1920. Space formerly occupied by self-sufficient ethnic communities was entirely reallocated to specialized uses in the various sections of the growing metropolitan area, as a total industrial landscape, new centers of services, and production and consumption suburbs developed. This spatial redistribution, however, was not a mere functional rearrangement imposed by changes in industrial geography but reflected the fundamental social change which was under way. Cross-class neighborhoods, typical of nineteenth-century ethnic patterns, disappeared to be replaced by more cohesive socioethnic neighborhoods better adapted to the new urban and suburban subdivisions of residences and factories.

7. Blacks were the last group to arrive in large numbers in the industrial city. They experienced a settlement process radically different from that of white ethnic groups, a process which led to the formation of the ghetto. Compared with white ethnic groups, Blacks lived history in reverse: while foreign immigrants ultimately became assimilated into a unified structure dominated by the native white American world and based on rank and social status within it, Blacks were increasingly segregated from whites on the basis of race and irrespective of their social status. The industrialization process, then, in one sphere, contributed to the creation of a culturally homogeneous urban society but in another, in which Blacks were involved, created invidious divisions to a degree which had never before existed.

These seven propositions, which I advance now and shall refine throughout the book in the context of specific hypotheses and particular situations, address some fundamental dimensions of American social change. At times I offer fresh hypotheses; at other times I offer only a new or different angle on topics traditionally studied by historians. Such goes the trade of history, which always requires integrating old and new questions and building on works of others while working toward a comprehensive social analysis. In 1957, at a time when American historians had barely begun to study social history, John Higham, reevaluating his own pathbreaking study of nativism and the variations in the xenophobic impulses of Americans toward immigrants, called for a broad inquiry into the American social structure; as he put it:

7. Sam Bass Warner, Jr., *The Private City* (Philadelphia: University of Pennsylvania Press, 1968), p. 50.

Instead of washing all the specific color out of our ethnic fabric in our fear of propagating stereotypes, let us look for the realities behind them. . . . What I miss, in the most general way, is any serious effort to study historically the structure of American society, to work out, in other words, the interrelations between classes and ethnic groups, taking account of regional and local differences.[8]

Much historical research done in the 1960s was, in practice if not always in intent, an answer to that call. Historians began to probe deep into the structure of American society. Large social history projects were developed in which sources heretofore forgotten, such as the manuscripts of the federal censuses, were exploited. Historians discovered how transient Americans had been, and much of their debate focused on the nature of mass transiency in American society and the relationship between geographic mobility and upward social mobility in the American social system.[9] All historians quickly admitted that transiency was a fundamental feature of American history (although a debate still continues as to its degree), and most historians contended that the road "from the bottom up," although not easily opened, was never entirely closed in American society. And if it was closed somewhere, people could always leave one city to seek success in another. There were no dead ends, only detours. This was a good solution for all Americans; it avoided rebellion while providing manpower. Stephan Thernstrom, for example, forcefully argued in *The Other Bostonians* that mobility was the key to a uniquely open American social system, in which "the availability of superior opportunities for individual self advancement . . . significantly impede the formation of class-based protest movements that sought fundamental alterations in the economic system."[10]

Not all critics share this liberal and optimistic treatment of the American class structure; some argue that mobility merely gave the illusion of advancement and that the American class structure was more rigid than historians and sociologists have traditionally believed. My contention is that the mobility debate was framed in timeless and placeless perspectives, despite its foundations in many case studies of cities of various sizes in different places at various times. Like their sociologist colleagues, historians erred in a vain search for a univer-

8. John Higham, *Send These to Me: Jews and Other Immigrants in Urban America* (New York: Atheneum, 1975), p. 115.

9. Thernstrom, *The Other Bostonians*; Theodore Hershberg, "The Philadelphia Social History Project: A Methodological History" (Ph.D. diss., Stanford University, 1973); Michael B. Katz, Michael J. Doucet, and Mark J. Stern, "Migration and the Social Order in Erie County, New York: 1855," *Journal of Interdisciplinary History* 8 (Spring 1978): 669–701; Clyde Griffen and Sally Griffen, *Natives and Newcomers: The Ordering of Opportunity in Mid-Nineteenth-Century Poughkeepsie* (Cambridge, Mass.: Harvard University Press, 1978).

10. Thernstrom, *The Other Bostonians*, p. 259.

sally valid American model, applicable at all times and places, regardless of sweeping changes in the American economy or in government policies. I will argue in this book that Americans have begun to think in terms of an open and unified class system cutting across all ethnic groups more recently than we have thought and only after there was a fundamental alteration in the relationship between ethnicity and class during the industrialization period. Examples of an open social system in which upward mobility served to assimilate foreigners to an American culture and integrate them into an undifferentiated whole may be found throughout American history; yet such a system is largely the creation of the twentieth century. Its formation was accelerated when Congress, by halting the influx of immigrants in the 1920s, unwittingly loosened the ethnic bonds in urban communities which no longer received an annual fresh supply of newcomers from the old countries.[11] In turn, the modernization of the economy contributed to a structural mobility too often confused with real individual gains. In the new structure and in an economy in which the business sector grew at an unprecedented speed, children of immigrants would work at white-collar occupations more often than their fathers. Then only did a new twentieth-century American class structure emerge.

I propose to test this theory in only one place, an American city where subcultures developed more or less freely, where social conflicts erupted, and where I can investigate social relations in depth. To many social historians involved in the debate over mobility, the city was not a place where social interaction and social conflicts could be observed but merely a discriminating sieve which retained the wealthiest or the more successful of the thousands of transient individuals and families which poured through it. Concurrently with the work of historians involved in what became a vain search for an all too abstract character of the American social structure, other historians, also informed in the methods of social science, opened new frontiers in our knowledge of past social structure. Labor historians and anthropologists, for example, joined forces to probe aspects of working-class subcultures in American society. Social historians and demographers combined their efforts in serious inquiries into family life and demographic behavior within specific ethnic and social groups. Urban historians charted broad processes of spatial and technological changes, involving population redistribution in large areas and major changes in standard of living such as those fostered by the suburbanization process. Other historians produced outstanding studies of specific immigrant groups in specific cities.[12] What was needed, I felt when I began this study in 1973, was

---

11. Higham, *Send These to Me,* pp. 54–58.

12. Herbert G. Gutman, *Work, Culture, and Society in Industrializing America* (New York: Alfred A. Knopf, 1976); Charles Tilly, ed., *Historical Studies of Changing Fertility* (Princeton, N.J.: Princeton University Press, 1978); Warner, *The Private City*; Kathleen N. Conzen, *Im-*

to build on these many disparate studies of sections of the social structure by combining their methods and to study slowly evolving social change, not in the abstract, but in the concrete bedrock of time and place. The time was the industrialization of America, in which I could see the arrival and settlement of all groups which ultimately made up the fabric of American society—native white Americans, old immigrants, new immigrants, and Blacks; the place, Detroit, in which I could study the microunits of life, isolate groups and behavioral differences, and get at the connection between social change and urban organization.

ANALYZING DETROIT FROM 1880 TO 1920

Analyzing a city, I contend, consists of understanding the spatial distribution of the population. Of course, historians and social scientists use categories other than space: the individual, fluid, mobile, migrant; the social class; the ethnoreligious group. The dynamics of people interacting, within and between such categories, constitute the historian's prey when searching for social structure, beyond the boundaries of any one human establishment. But limiting the analysis to an aggregate picture of social groups without spatial differentiation would lead the historian to write a very abstract history of the city, remote from the daily realities of many citizens. Some urbanites had only a limited experience of their city, as the routines of their daily lives involved living and working in only a fraction of it. Others could grasp a larger fraction of the urban universe. But since all people were situated in space, in relationship to each other, the historian can discover how they were distributed in space by locating them on the city map at several points in time. In the twenties, Robert Park laid out the basis of human ecology by stating that "physical distances" were "the indexes of social distances."[13] Spatial distances and spatial divisions do not, however, reflect social divisions equally or uniformly. One major assumption of this book is that spatial units are magnifying mirrors which distort because they amplify. If smaller areas within the city only mirrored well-known characteristics of the aggregate at the local level, they would not be worth studying, but they bring to light the social, economic, ethnic, racial, and religious differences which have traditionally divided American society. What stands out in spatial analysis is the complex interplay of the clustering forces that make some phenomena more apparent than others.

In large sections of this book, then, I shifted the unit of analysis from the individual or even the group to the microenvironment, by concentrating on the

migrant Milwaukee, 1836–1860 (Cambridge, Mass.: Harvard University Press, 1976); Theodore Hershberg, ed., *Philadelphia: Work, Space, Family, and Group Experience in the Nineteenth Century* (New York: Oxford University Press, 1981).

13. Robert E. Park, *Human Communities: The City and Human Ecology* (Glencoe, Ill.: Free Press, 1952), p. 177.

smallest areas of the city in which people daily interacted and in which the processes of social change can be traced. More specifically, from the entire metropolitan area I drew small area samples, most often consisting of a city block and two opposing frontages (see pp. 20–27), in which I studied the nature and degree of ethnic and socioeconomic concentration as well as other social indicators such as types of housing occupancy, rate of home ownership, family organization, and demographic behavior. I also superimposed broader geographic units of analysis on these microunits in order to study the way the different parts of the city were fitted together, and the way citywide changes (such as the development of new industrial sites, or the modernization of urban services) cut across and affected the microunits. In other words, I have tried to trace the changing face of inequality in the metamorphosing urban territory of Detroit. By examining the changing nature of clustering patterns of ethnic, social, and racial groups, I hope to have identified the evolving meanings of ethnicity, class, and race in the making of the industrial metropolis.

The book follows a chronological order, for it rests primarily on the cross-sectional study of Detroit at three stages of development, 1880, 1900, 1920. At each point in time I concentrate on the interaction between social and spatial cleavages. Each such snapshot of the city is based on the linkage of land-use sources in which every house, lot, building, and factory of the city is drawn on maps, with the manuscript door-to-door surveys of the 1880, 1900, and 1920 federal censuses (the still-closed 1920 enumeration being studied by special arrangement with the census bureau; see chap. 13). These three cross-sectional surveys formed the backbone for the book, and provided me with the broad data coverage needed to test the seven propositions I have advanced. But an array of other sources both quantitative and qualitative—city directories, records of building permits, archives of various city departments, case books of social workers, Bureau of Labor Statistics surveys, factory inspections, records of various associations, newspapers, genealogical records, and the like—were added to the study as needed and often directly linked to the basic sources, especially on Detroit at the turn of the century, so as to study processes inaccessible from cross-sectional data alone.

I have chosen three points in time for intensive scrutiny—1880, 1900, and 1920—but I do not give each period equal treatment. The section on 1880 is limited to a detailed study of the city's social geography; this initial description serves to locate Detroit in the urban hierarchy, to establish analytical techniques used throughout the book, and, most importantly, to identify ethnicity as the major factor shaping the distribution of the population. With this baseline established, I devote the better part of the book to the 1890s, when Detroit was gradually becoming a major industrial center. In this section I widen the inquiry from the social geography of the city alone to the city-building process and to a range of forces influencing social history. Relying on a multiplicity of sources, I explain the ways in which autonomous ethnic communities contributed to building Detroit, and I analyze many dimensions of inequality in family life, in the world of work, and in group experiences. Then I conclude with a more limited cross-sectional study of Detroit in 1920 to demonstrate that race and class came to replace ethnicity in dividing and reshaping the mature industrial metropolis. In this span of forty years, Detroit became one of the leading urban centers of America and one of the first to experience the reordering of disparate social segments into a new social order.

1

Detroit in 1880
Space and Society

1

An Open City

Plate 1. Parke, Davis and Company manufacturing plant, Detroit, 1870s.
Courtesy of the Archives of Labor and Urban Affairs, Wayne State University.

DETROIT IN THE NEW INDUSTRIAL BELT

Most American cities witnessed four well-known transformations from the 1870s to the 1920s: cities became bigger, with denser and more diversified populations; the manufacture of industrial goods grew tremendously, as did the amount and types of services produced; government and community organizations changed from relatively simple to more complex structures; and, above all, cities became the prime locus of assimilation for newcomers in American society. This overall transformation of American cities was accelerated by the expansion of new manufacturing centers—Detroit among them—into major metropolises in the urban hierarchy.

The first city whose growth was primarily a result of the expansion of manufactures was Pittsburgh, and its entry into the leading centers of population marked "the beginning of a metropolitan reorganization."[1] In the 1880s, Buffalo and Cleveland followed Pittsburgh's lead and became parts of a new "manufacturing belt," which was completed in the 1890s by Detroit and Milwaukee, the two other major centers on the Great Lakes system. From the 1870s to the 1890s, then, a chain of five new industrial centers—Pittsburgh, Buffalo, Cleveland, Detroit, and Milwaukee—stretched across the territory bounded on the east by the Pennsylvania coalfields and on the west by the iron ore reserves near Lake Superior.

Detroit in 1880 was still a medium-sized city, only beginning to take an active part in this complex metropolitan reorganization. With a population of 116,340, it ranked only eighteenth among American cities, but its potential was great. Detroit was located near a wealth of natural resources in iron, copper, lead, and wood, most of which came from the upper part of the state, and near grindstone quarries and sand for glass. In part because of these nearby resources and in part because of the city's location as a port on the Great Lakes, Detroit had become a regional trading center by 1880. Located between Lake Saint Clair and Lake Erie, the Detroit River was an artery through which the commerce of lakes Superior, Michigan, and Huron was carried on toward Lake Erie and the Eastern Seaboard. In 1880, ten railroads connected Detroit to other parts of Michigan, to the rest of the country via Chicago, Milwaukee, Toledo, Cleveland, Buffalo, Indianapolis, and to the Canadian lines reaching New York and New England.[2]

1. Beverly Duncan and Stanley Lieberson, *Metropolis and Region in Transition* (Beverly Hills: Sage Publications, 1970), p. 71, and Allan R. Pred, *The Spatial Dynamics of United States Urban-Industrial Growth, 1800–1914* (Cambridge, Mass.: M.I.T. Press, 1966); for a recent discussion of urban systems, see Allan R. Pred, *Urban Growth and City-Systems in the United States, 1840–1860* (Cambridge, Mass.: Harvard University Press, 1980).

2. Judith Krass, "Detroit as a Center of Commerce, 1880–1900," (M.A. thesis, Wayne State University, 1965), pp. 15–20, 136; Eric Kocher, "Economic and Physical Growth of Detroit,

Despite the claims of many local boosters, however, Detroit's industrialization was still modest. The manufacturing census for 1880 shows clearly that the largest employers in the city were manufacturing consumer products, clothing, furniture, cigars, food, and carriages. The manufacture of industrial goods— iron and steel and foundry and machine shops—ranked beneath consumer goods in number of employees (table 1.1). The manufacture of railroad cars, which became prominent in Detroit in the eighties and nineties, was still listed under "miscellaneous industries" in 1880.

A more compelling way to see that Detroit was only beginning to be one of the new industrial belt centers is to consider for a moment the largest factories

TABLE 1.1
Mechanical and manufacturing industries, Detroit, 1880

Industrial sector[a]	Number of employees	Number of establishments
Clothing and related	2,166	121
Boot and shoe uppers; boots and shoes including custom work and repairing; clothing, men's; clothing, women's; corsets; hats and caps; shirts		
Lumber and related	1,702	104
Boxes, wooden packing; carpentering; cooperage; furniture; wooden ware; wood, turned and carved		
Tobacco	1,242	63
Tobacco, chewing, smoking and snuff; tobacco, cigars and cigarettes		
Transportation and related	1,152	82
Carriages and wagons; saddlery and harness; wheelwrighting; shipbuilding		
Food	1,100	113
Baking and yeast powders; bread and bakery products; coffee and spices; confectionery; flour and grist-mill products; liquors, malt; slaughtering and meat packing (not including retail butchering establishments)		
Iron and steel	1,095	7
Foundry and machine shop products	1,024	24

SOURCE: U.S., Department of the Interior, Census Office, *Compendium of the Tenth Census, 1880,* 2 vols. (Washington, D.C.: G.P.O., 1888), 2:1058–59.
  a. Seven largest sectors by number of employees.

1701–1935," November 1935, Division of Economics and Statistics, Federal Housing Administration, pp. 15–53 (in MHC); Sidney Glazer, *Detroit: A Study in Urban Development* (New York: Bookman Associates, 1965), pp. 25–49; Melvin G. Holli, ed., *Detroit* (New York: New Viewpoints, 1976), pp. 54–116.

in the city (table 1.2). In 1880 only forty-five companies (or 4.5% of the 919 manufacturing establishments surveyed by the industrial census) had 100 employees or more. In Detroit's immediate vicinity, there were an additional five large factories of 100 employees or more, but they do not appear in the census count of manufactures for Detroit, although one of them, the Detroit Stove Works employing 625 workers, contributed to the reputation of Detroit as a major industrial center.

Of the fifty large companies in Detroit and its immediate surroundings, thirteen were in clothing and related consumer products, like the large factory of boots and shoes of Detroit's future reform mayor Hazen Pingree, which employed 500 workers in 1880. There were seven large tobacco factories. In contrast, one needs to add one freight car company (Peninsular), one passenger car company (Pullman), one car wheel company (Griffin), one stove company (the Detroit Stove Works), three machine shops, and four iron and steel companies to count only twelve large employers involved in metal-related work. Such

TABLE 1.2
Largest industrial establishments, Detroit, 1880

Establishment	Number of workers employed at full capacity[a]	Industrial sector	Location
Pullman Palace Car Co.	736	Railroad	Detroit
Detroit Stove Works	625	Foundry and machine shops	Hamtramck
D.M. Ferry Co.	596	Wholesale seeds	Detroit
Pingree and Smith	500	Clothing and related	Detroit
Heineman Butzel	425	Clothing and related	Detroit
Peninsular Car Co.	325	Railroad	Detroit
Schloss and Brothers	320	Clothing and related	Detroit
Heavenrich Brothers	300	Clothing and related	Detroit
Hayard and Brewser	300	Clothing and related	Detroit
Hargreaves Mfg.	300	Lumber and related	Detroit
Detroit Bridge and Iron Works	290	Iron and steel	Detroit
Richardson Match Co.	265	Matches	Detroit
Ralph L. Polk and Co.	252	Publishing	Detroit
Detroit Wooden Works	250	Wooden wares	Detroit
The Free Press	220	Publishing	Detroit
Buhl Iron Works	220	Iron and steel	Detroit
Scotten, Lovett and Co.	200	Tobacco	Springwells
Detroit Hoop Skirt Co.	200	Clothing	Detroit
E. T. Barnum Fences	200	Iron and steel	Detroit

SOURCE: Tenth Federal Census: Non-population Census Schedules, Products of Industry, manuscript in Michigan State Archives, Lansing, Michigan.
   a. Firms with 200 or more workers.

heavy industrial work was still limited in 1880 Detroit, although it was becoming typical of the new industrial-belt cities geographically equidistant from the mineral wealth of both the Great Lakes region and Pennsylvania.

In this transition toward industrialization, Detroit shared important land use and population features with other emerging industrial metropolises. We can see how Detroit compared with the twenty largest cities in 1880 (all having more than 100,000 inhabitants) by simply examining three variables available in published sources: population density, number of people per dwelling, and percentage of foreign-born population (see table 1.3). From the combination of these measures, which reflect the inflow of population and the space available within the city limits, several distinct types of cities emerge. The first cluster of cities is composed of the crowded places: New York, Boston, and Chicago. They had a high percentage of foreign-born residents, a high rate of occupancy, and a high density. New York scored 39.7% of the population as immigrants, an average of 16.4 people per dwelling, and an average of 46 people per acre.

TABLE 1.3

Immigration and population density in the twenty largest United States cities, 1880

City	Population	Percentage of foreign-born population	Average number of people per dwelling	Average number of people per acre
New York	1,206,299	39.68	16.37	46.01
Philadelphia	847,170	24.12	5.79	10.22
Brooklyn	566,663	31.36	9.11	-
Chicago	503,185	40.71	8.24	22.00
Boston	362,839	31.64	8.26	14.70
St. Louis	350,518	29.96	8.15	8.93
Baltimore	332,313	16.89	6.54	39.37
Cincinnati	255,139	28.01	9.11	16.15
San Francisco	233,959	44.56	6.86	8.67
New Orleans	216,090	19.05	5.95	1.72
Cleveland	160,146	37.10	5.89	8.89
Pittsburgh	156,389	28.52	6.44	8.95
Buffalo	155,134	33.05	6.55	6.25
Washington, D.C.	147,293	9.67	6.11	3.84
Newark	136,508	29.54	7.26	11.63
Louisville	123,758	18.71	6.55	15.62
Jersey City	120,722	32.60	8.59	-
Detroit	116,340	39.23	5.68	11.31
Milwaukee	115,587	39.86	6.17	11.99
Providence	104,857	26.77	7.41	10.78

SOURCES: U.S. Department of the Interior, Census Office, *Compendium of the Tenth Census, 1880*, 2 vols. (Washington, D.C.: G.P.O, 1883), 1:380–405, 456–551; *Tenth Federal Census of the United States, 1880, Population* (Washington, D.C.: G.P.O., 1883), 1:670–71; Roderick D. McKenzie, *The Metropolitan Community* (New York: McGraw-Hill, 1933), pp. 336–39.

Areas of New York reached the world record for population density, with 600 to 800 people per acre in parts of the Lower East Side, and some tenement areas of Chicago reached 400 people per acre. The next group comprised the cities of the new industrial belt: Buffalo, Pittsburgh, Cleveland, Detroit, and Milwaukee, all with a high percentage of immigrants but a generally low density and low rate of occupancy. Detroit had a low average density of 11.3 people per acre, a low rate of 5.7 people per dwelling, and a maximum density of only 80 people per acre. But 39.2% of its population was born in a foreign country, a figure comparable to that of New York or Chicago. Cleveland showed similar characteristics: a low population density of 8.89 people per acre, only 5.89 people per dwelling, and 37.1% of its population foreign born.

Other cities showed different patterns. Cincinnati is an interesting case of a high-density city, 16.15 people per acre on the average, a high rate of dwelling occupancy, 9.11, but a lower proportion of foreign-born population, 28%. New Orleans was an extreme case of underused city with a record low density of 1.72 people per acre, and a "native" city with only 19.05% of its residents being immigrants from foreign countries. Compared with the other large cities of the country, Detroit in 1880 was neither exceptionally physically empty nor disproportionately populated by immigrants. It represented an entire class of newly emerging industrial cities, attracting a diverse labor force, but not yet crowded by the continuous flow of arrivals.

ANALYZING DETROIT IN 1880

A few technical considerations regarding the sampling design and the units of analysis are in order to make clear the steps followed in studying Detroit's socioethnic cleavages in 1880 and in subsequent years. I designed a method of geographic sampling which allowed me to study the city of Detroit in the detail of its land use, in the diversity of its neighborhoods, as well as in its entirety. Broadly speaking, the sample of this study was designed for several purposes: first, to represent geographic clustering in small neighborhoods, in order to study the ways various categories of people gathered in the urban environment and the forms and intensities of their clustering; second, to study the interplay between population characteristics and land-use patterns in order to understand social change in the context of urban growth; and third, to represent the whole city population in terms of demography, ethnicity, and occupation—the three most important sets of variables detailed in the United States census records—in order to study social divisions in Detroit.

Achieving these goals meant combining in the same sample design the study of the city as a whole and the study of its component parts. To examine the relationship of social life to the general form of the city, the sample had to cover the whole territory. Working on that scale, however, a researcher ordinarily sacrifices detail to achieve coverage. But to examine the constraints and the routines which are part of everyday experience, a sample must provide that very detail—intensive observations of small area subpopulations. The researcher who embraces such detail, however, ordinarily sacrifices the attempt to achieve coverage of the city as a whole. The two goals have thus seemed mutually exclusive in any single sampling design, and the historical study of the American city has often followed two distinct lines of approach: either gross patterns in urban land use have been investigated to understand aspects of the city's change, its dynamics of growth, and the development of suburbanization, for example; or the experience of neighborhoods or single ethnic or social groups have been studied intensively.[3]

My sampling scheme was conceived to study the city of Detroit in the late nineteenth century both in the diversity of its neighborhoods and in its entirety. So many complex and often hidden patterns develop in a multiethnic city of immigrants that only a fine-grain analysis permits one to distinguish overlapping phenomena with different boundaries. Given the diversity of the urban environment, there is no predetermined area unit which would best permit one to study all types of inhabitants and areas simultaneously. Students of neighborhood activities have long recognized that there are no simple, "natural," geographic boundaries. Those boundaries defining an ethnic concentration are not the same as those defining a given social class area, which in turn overlap with boundaries of nonresidential spaces. In addition, the concept of "neighborhood" is necessarily imprecise; it connotes relative concentration, relative cohesiveness, social interaction, and commonality of institutions rather than a closed space with well-defined borders. To define neighborhoods in advance as a unit of measurement is therefore hazardous, because geographic boundaries are vague, defined simultaneously by objective criteria, the perception of the inhabitants, and physical boundaries.

Given these problems, many scholars examine administrative or electoral units, a study made easier because official data is accessible and already aggregated at the census tract or the ward level. The units, however, are often artificial; the nineteenth-century electoral wards were large, and their boundaries changed from one election to another. In Detroit, ward boundaries were changed in 1881 precisely to break up neighborhood homogeneity. It is, there-

3. For example, Sam Bass Warner, Jr., *Streetcar Suburbs* (Cambridge, Mass.: Harvard University Press, 1962); Moses Rischin, *The Promised City: New York's Jews, 1870–1914* (Cambridge, Mass.: Harvard University Press, 1962).

fore, not surprising that indices used to measure segregation at the ward level revealed that immigrants of all groups lived in all wards, and one is tempted to conclude too quickly that residential areas were integrated.[4]

If one goes to the other extreme and studies smaller geographic units such as the block, other problems arise, for even city blocks often include widely different realities. On the same block, the front on the main street is often different from the fronts on the small streets, or the outside of the block differs from the inside. As two prominent ecologists have noted: "If all non-whites resided on alleyways and all whites in street-front structures, then even a block index would fail to reveal the high degree of segregation."[5] If one chooses an even smaller unit, such as the block front, one misses concentration patterns that clearly appear only in larger areas; this is especially true in a city like Detroit with a generally low population density.

Clearly a unit larger in size than the block but smaller than the ethnic neighborhood or administrative unit is needed. I have tried to solve this problem by selecting as a sampling unit a cluster of six block frontages as represented in figure 1.1. This unit includes all fronts in one randomly selected square block plus two randomly selected fronts across the street and allows the grid plan typical of the American city to serve as a natural sampling frame. The block front—one side of a four sided block—is its smallest geographic component; a very flexible unit, the block front is easily drawn on a map along one street from one corner of the block to the other. When several frontages are linked, one creates a reconstruction of several urban forms: a block, a street, or a larger cluster.

The sampling unit can thus be divided into three separate units for purposes of analysis: the front, the block, or the larger cluster of six fronts. I chose the triple unit of front, block, and cluster to catch subtle patterns of concentration and scattered patterns of dominance. The addition to the primary block of two randomly selected opposing fronts permits me to represent streets on both sides without including all opposite fronts. The triple unit also offers the possibility of changing units of study for different analyses and/or comparing the same analysis at several geographic levels. The front can be used, for example, for a fine survey of the housing pattern. The block is more appropriate for questions related to urban densities. The cluster, containing a mean of 123 inhabitants in the 1880 final sample, is a large enough unit to represent accurately dominance patterns at a small neighborhood level. Using the three levels consecutively

---

4. JoEllen Vinyard, *The Irish on the Urban Frontier: Nineteenth Century Detroit* (New York: Arno Press, 1976), pp. 174–75.

5. Otis D. Duncan and Beverly Duncan, "A Methodological Analysis of Segregation Indexes," *American Sociological Review* 20 (April 1955): 216.

FIG. 1.1

A Cluster of Six Block Frontages

permits me to measure geographic variations in clustering patterns of different ethnic groups, social classes, age groups, and other population variables or to measure geographic variations in the continuity of residences and nonresidential activities.

The chances of measuring changing neighborhood activities are increased by selecting such a geographic unit well fitted to the grid plan and by sampling a large number of those units rather than by artificially delineating the boundaries. The analysis of the same phenomenon in units of different sizes, the analysis of sets of units in specific parts of the city, and the addition of all units together will permit me to study many questions related to the geography of the city and the distribution of demographic, ethnic, and social patterns: Detroit's land use in this chapter, ethnic and socioeconomic concentrations in the next, then the relationship between population distribution and demographic behavior in the third chapter, and a general assessment of social relations in 1880 in the fourth.

All the complex technical aspects of the sampling are presented in Appendix 1; it is important to note here, however, that a dense net of clusters was cast over the entire territory and that two main data sources were used to collect detailed information on the land use and the demographic, socioeconomic, and ethnic occupancy of each cluster. One hundred twenty-seven clusters were selected from the twenty plates covering Detroit in the Robinson-Pidgeon *Atlas of the City of Detroit.*[6] These 127 clusters, spread over Detroit's entire territory, are displayed on the map of the 1880 sample (map 1.1). With the city atlas providing a detailed set of maps which identified not only block fronts but also their lots, buildings, and house numbers (information which I complemented with city directory data on commercial and industrial land uses), and with the manuscript schedules of the federal census providing demographic and socioeconomic data for the listed individuals along with their addresses, a reasonably accurate picture of the clusters was reconstructed: on the one hand, the lots and buildings; on the other, the population.[7]

To be sure, there are many holes in the map of the sample. It may be that areas not sampled were significantly different from those that were and that important concentrations were missed, but this is unlikely because the sample was taken from each of the twenty plates of the atlas to insure geographic coverage. Each plate was classified into one of three density classes in order to sample more intensely in the more populated areas. Each block of the city was also classified in one of four land-use categories—primarily residential, primarily nonresidential, primarily vacant, or mixed—in order to use different sampling fractions for different land uses in different density zones. Based on an exhaustive search in the manuscript census, the final sample includes 12,185 people, comprising 2,410 households on 721 frontages, or 127 clusters. Of these, 353 frontages were actually inhabited, and the others were nonresidential. A full land-use and population census has been taken of each unit.

The degree of accuracy with which the sample represents Detroit can be judged by checking to see how known population characteristics (from published census figures) are estimated from this sample. Figure 1.2 displays the sample estimate for each of ten population ratios. A range of two standard errors above and below the sample estimate is also indicated. Finally, the true population value from the published census is also indicated on the graph. It is clear from the comparison of known population ratios with corresponding sample estimates that, taken together, the sample area units provide a description of the overall urban territory. They are, of course, representative of the city's microenvironment. In them one can observe the population's demographic, social, and ethnic

6. Elisha Robinson and Roger H. Pidgeon, *Atlas of the City of Detroit and Suburbs Embracing Portions of Hamtramck, Springwells, and Greenfield Townships* (New York, 1885).

7. For the 1880 census, see "Instructions to Enumerators," in Carroll D. Wright, *The History and Growth of the United States Census* (Washington, D.C.: G.P.O., 1900), pp. 167–77; *Detroit City Directory for 1880* (Detroit: J. W. Weeks & Co., 1880).

MAP 1.1

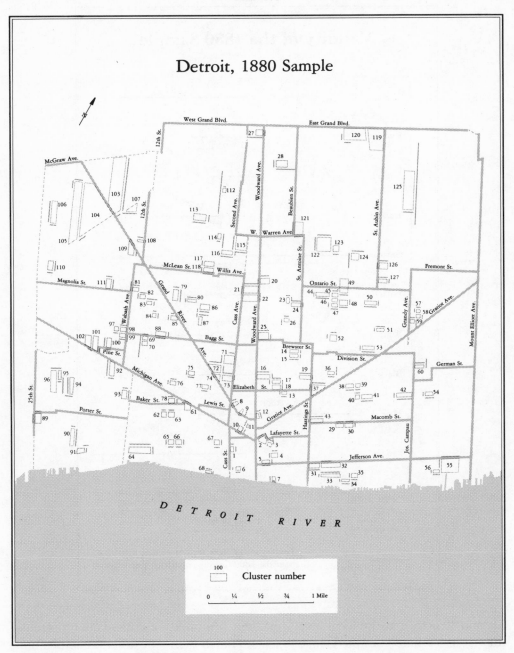

Detroit, 1880 Sample

FIG. 1.2

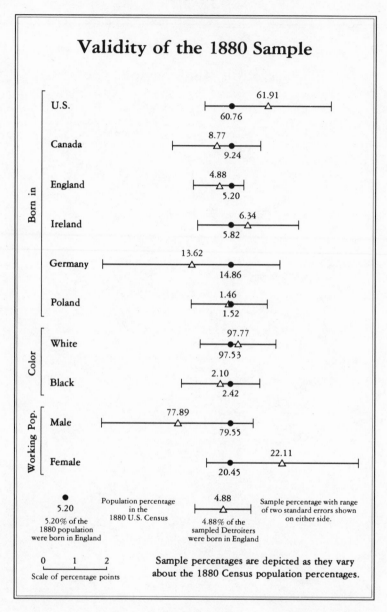

Validity of the 1880 Sample

life and structure at the local level, but their combination effectively represents the city as a whole. Sampled clusters, useful for showing the diverse composition of neighborhoods, aggregate into a sample of the entire city. In this way, the randomly chosen lesser parts of the city are easily compared and studied in relationship to their sum. It becomes possible to measure the diversity of local life in the light of a general picture of the city.

A LOW DENSITY CITY

When this sample is put into use, it becomes clear from Detroit's geography that large-scale economic transformations were only in their infancy in 1880. Detroit was still spatially small; the distance from the river in the south to the northern boundary was only three and one-half miles along Woodward Avenue. Several of the characteristics of land use revealed by our sample of clusters are particularly intriguing: all economic activities were still concentrated in Detroit's center. In contrast to this great concentration in a small area, half of the outer city was simply empty. In between the busy center and the large vacant peripheral zone, residences clustered around the city center. Despite the compactness of the residential settlement around the center, the population density was generally low (see map 1.2).

The chief characteristics of the city center were both the diversity and the numerical concentration of activities at its hub, the intersection of the river and Woodward Avenue. Warehouses and wholesale establishments crowded near the riverfront and the railroad terminals. Mixed with them were many factories fronting the river, with its jumble of shipyards, freightyards, and repair docks. In fact, George Pullman's railroad passenger-car shop employing 736 workers (the single largest factory in Detroit) was located at the intersection of Croghan and Dequindre, just north of the east-side railroad terminal. A half-mile north on Woodward Avenue were the better retail establishments near Campus Martius. This concentration of all Detroit's economic activity in the smallest section of the city stands out sharply on the land-use map. Each "solid" cluster contained at least five of the following land uses: heavy industry, light industry, craft shops, wholesale stores, retail stores, bars and saloons, businesses, professional offices, public services, churches, parks, and recreation lots. Block fronts comprised an accumulation and juxtaposition of industries, crafts, wholesale and retail outlets, professional and public buildings, as well as hotels and residences. As an example of a typical downtown street front, one block front on Monroe Street in 1880 included six retail stores, three saloons, three businesses, three professional offices, one public service office, and two industrial establishments. The hub of Detroit had not yet become specialized into a modern downtown of business firms without residents or industries.

The center, however, was no longer an area of family residences as it had been earlier in the century. It was densely populated, but inhabited by an unusually large number of young male bachelors in the hotels and boardinghouses

MAP 1.2

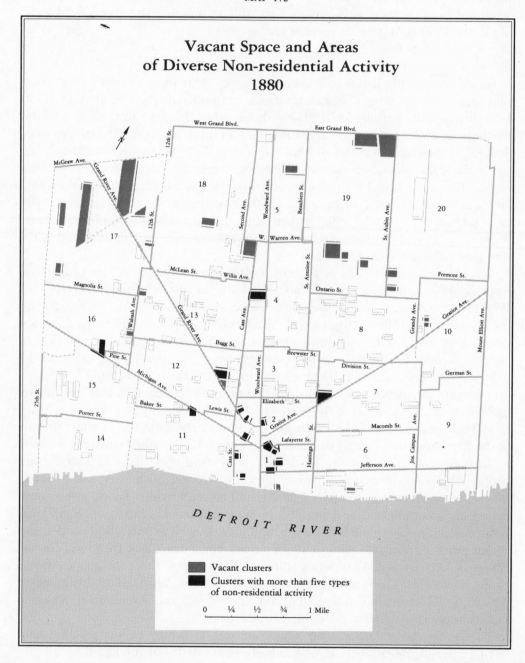

Vacant Space and Areas
of Diverse Non-residential Activity
1880

(map 1.3). The diversity of activities found there catered to the needs of the "young bachelor" population of the center and also provided jobs for workers throughout the city. Reflecting this mixture, the sample units that contained hotels and boardinghouses in 1880 also contained 42% of the heavy industry, 80% of the light industry, 68% of the craft shops, 95% of the wholesale commerce, 57% of the retail stores, 60% of the bars and saloons, 97% of the businesses, 68% of the professional offices, and 75% of the public services.

Dispersion of activities was beginning in 1880, but it was limited to a few blocks along the main thoroughfares of residential areas: Woodward, Gratiot,

MAP 1.3

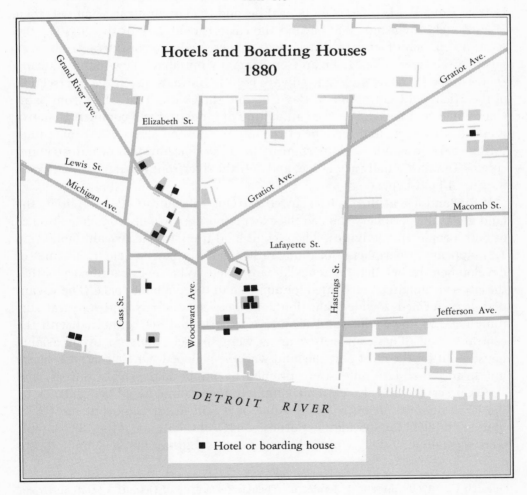

**Hotels and Boarding Houses
1880**

■ Hotel or boarding house

Grand River, and Michigan, to which some activities of the center leapfrogged. This was especially the case for some small industrial companies in the clothing, furniture, and cigar businesses, some craft shops and retail stores, and some bars and saloons, especially in the residential sections of the near east side, where more light industries and craft activities were intermingled with residences. The only real extension of heavy industrial activities outside the center, however, was on the riverfront. Industries had begun to spread along the river in the 1860s, in a narrow strip bounded by the railroads, parallel to the river. Manufacturers installed their own private railroad cars along the river as a means of transferring goods to and from the regular railroad tracks. By 1880, the riverfront had become a long industrial strip, and some companies, like the Detroit Stove Works, had even moved beyond the city limits in what was then Hamtramck Township, just beyond the eastern boundary of the city. On the west, a new manufacturing district was also created at a considerable distance north of the river. The Michigan Car Company initiated a new manufacturing center in the 1870s by building railway shops in Springwells, at the intersection of the Michigan Central line to Bay City and the Grand Trunk line from Saint Clair River to Toledo.[8] But the catapulting of industrial and commercial activities into the residential sections of the city or into the new western manufacturing center was not yet important in 1880. Deconcentration of industry and commerce was virtually negligible, and only the riverfront was a part of Detroit's industrial landscape.

If the land use at the center showed extreme concentration of activities, the land use at the periphery showed the exact opposite: virtually complete absence of both people and activities. The second land-use variable, vacant land (map 1.2), appears in peripheral locations rather than in the city center, in zones of development rather than in zones already filled. What is extraordinary is that the city's vacant areas accounted for almost half the available space. The vacant periphery formed a wide transition zone between the city and its rural surroundings, its townships, and its future suburbs not yet connected with the central region. These underused areas were sparsely built up by occasional houses, but for the most part the land was undeveloped. Of Detroit's 16 square miles, only 6 square miles were drained by public and private sewers, and streetcar service was also extremely limited. One cannot avoid being struck by the large quantity of open space, some of it still in farmland but most of it unused and held for speculative purposes: 44% of the fronts of the 1880 sample were partially or totally empty. Not only was suburban life very limited, but

8. Silas Farmer, *The History of Detroit and Michigan* (Detroit: S. Farmer & Co., 1890; Gale Research Co., 1969), pp. 802–4; Jerome G. Thomas, "The City of Detroit: A Study in Urban Geography" (Ph.D. diss., University of Michigan, 1928), pp. 113–15.

the used city was only a fraction of the space available within its legal boundaries.

Family residences were to be found elsewhere, in between the two extremes of land use. Of course, some residences existed in all parts of the city, even intermingled with industrial activities and spread out in the vacant areas, but a large concentric zone around the center and well inside the vacant periphery constituted the main residential region. Such residential sections of Detroit were by no means uniform or undifferentiated, but most sampled clusters rated low or medium in the land-use variables for which diversity of activities reflected central location, and vacancy, peripheral location. With the residential areas crowded around the center, Detroit was still a compact city of the type familiar in most of the nineteenth century, often termed the "walking" or pedestrian city because most employment and industry was concentrated in a central urban location, and most urban dwellers lived within walking distance of it.[9] That Detroit was still a physically compact city becomes readily apparent when one mentally subtracts the vacant areas from the map.

In 1880, population density was generally low and no noticeable crowding existed despite the compactness of the residential settlement. It is generally accepted as a law in urban geography that, for large cities, residential population density declines in a negatively exponential manner as the distance from the city center increases.[10] This decline in density was more abrupt in the earlier pedestrian city, dropping off sharply beyond reasonable walking distances to employment downtown. Up to a 1.3-mile limit from the intersection of the river and Woodward, the center of Detroit, of course, had the highest density of the city population, with a maximum of 60 people per acre. Beyond this distance there was a dramatic decline in density, reaching the vacancy level at about 2 miles from the river. The density was still 14 people per acre at 1.8 miles, but there was hardly one person per acre at 2.5 miles, still one mile inside the city limits (fig. 1.3).

Since the density curve represents an average density on each density gradient (see Appendix 5), one could expect some empty or nonresidential blocks to balance out more densely populated residential blocks. Yet most blocks were only partially filled in 1880; residential or nonresidential structures rarely filled an entire block, and the density was similarly low in mixed or purely residential blocks. At all points in Detroit, including the dense city center, many clusters

9. On the "walking city," see Kenneth Jackson, "Urban Deconcentration in the Nineteenth Century: A Statistical Inquiry," in *The New Urban History*, ed. Leo F. Schnore (Princeton, N.J.: Princeton University Press, 1975), pp. 110–44, and David Ward, *Cities and Immigrants* (New York: Oxford University Press, 1971), pp. 132–33.

10. Jackson, "Urban Deconcentration," pp. 117–23; Colin Clark, "Urban Population Densities," *Journal of the Royal Statistical Society*, Series A, 114 (1951): 490–96.

FIG. 1.3

Density Decline from the
Center to the Periphery
1880

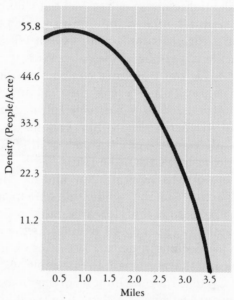

of six fronts had several fronts with vacant lots. Within the same blocks, nonresidential buildings could coexist with dwellings without affecting the density pattern. In other words, the space occupied by a commercial establishment, a public service building, or a church generally did not affect the block density.

A major factor which accounts for the generally low population density is that Detroit was a city of single-family homes. In 1880, 92.6% of Detroit's homes were inhabited by only one family, 6.5% by two families, and not even 1% by more than two families. There were no tenements and no crowding. If we exclude hotels and boardinghouses, each dwelling unit was occupied by an average of 4.9 people. To describe Detroit as a city of low density and single-family homes certainly sounds familiar. The same words are used to describe Detroit today, or Los Angeles in our own era of automobiles and urban sprawl. What is striking is that Detroit had those characteristics in an early era, when it was still a walking city, then lost and eventually regained them. A good way to describe Detroit in 1880 is to call it an open city: unused space existed in abundance within the city limits, but it also existed in the more densely populated city center. The urbanites of 1880, all of whom lived around the center, did not feel crowded in their single-family dwellings of partially built blocks. Rather, they were surrounded by empty land, in and around their neighborhoods.

Such spatial openness in the city made it possible for a large number of immigrants to settle in Detroit without producing the crowded conditions already familiar in cities like New York and popularized in the writings of social workers and journalists like Jacob Riis.[11] Newcomers could rent a dwelling in or near the downtown area, move to newly developed areas of the city, or even find spots to settle on undeveloped land. In open cities like Detroit, the ample availability of space provided people with some freedom of choice as to where they would live: newcomers could take advantage of the looseness of the settlement, decide to settle just about anywhere, and still be within walking distances of places of work. Hence the residential location of Detroiters can be interpreted as reflecting their primary association, either toward their ethnic group of origin or their socioeconomic group.

ETHNICITY AND SOCIAL STRUCTURE: PRELIMINARY HYPOTHESES

The great demographic changes that affected industrial cities in the Gilded Age were only beginning in 1880 Detroit. The city was still mainly populated by native white Americans and by members of well-established immigrant groups, including Canadians, English, Irish, and Germans. Very few people from eastern European countries lived in Detroit; the Poles had just recently started to move in; and only a small fraction of the population was Black. But Detroit's social structure was far more complex than these facts might make it seem. By turning to the combination of social, ethnic, and demographic characteristics, we can define broad patterns of social cleavage, beginning at the aggregate level of the city's population and then comparing these figures with those of different city sections. In this way we can analyze the interweaving of ethnic and socioeconomic categories in 1880 Detroit.

Throughout this analysis of Detroit in 1880—only the first step in a study of the social dynamics of industrialization—my analytical categories are limited by the sets of variables available in the 1880 census. As long as I am observing Detroit at only one point in time, in a static view, I will purposely limit my investigation to the combination of the two large documents used to design the sample, the 1880 census and the city atlas. Such an approach permits broad coverage of the entire social and urban fabric, and will serve as a baseline for

11. Jacob Riis, *How the Other Half Lives* (New York: Scribners & Sons, 1890).

studying change. The categories derived from the census are not perfect: ethnicity is defined by the place of birth of each individual and of his/her two
parents, without including religion; census occupational titles say next to nothing
about income or working conditions.[12] All historians working with census data
have been painfully aware of their limitations. Later in this book it will become
possible to refine the categories and to add depth to broad coverage. The study
of religious affiliation and of institutional life will broaden our understanding
of ethnicity. In turn, a close look at elite groups at one end of the social spectrum,
and at the lives of the very poor at the other, will help us to grasp the dynamics
of class affiliation in a changing social structure. But for an overall description
of social cleavages in 1880 the two primary sets of source material—census and
atlas—alone provide enough information to divide the population according to
major sociological and demographic characteristics and to identify the groups'
distribution in the industrializing city's space.

In 1880, Detroit was populated by five major groups. First, 28% of Detroit's
households were headed by an immigrant from Germany. Next to the German-
headed households, 19% of Detroit's households were headed by native-born
white Americans of native-born parents—that is, at least third-generation
Americans—whom I will cite henceforth as "native white Americans." Next
came the Irish (12.3%), the British (9.7%), and then the Canadians (4.3%).
These five groups alone comprised 73% of Detroit's households. Detroit was
thus a city of immigrants and native white Americans. Very few members of
the second generation—native-born of foreign parents—were heads of households: only 2.2% of Detroit's households were headed by a native-born offspring
of German parents, 2.1% had Irish parents, 1.2% British parents, and only
0.4% Canadian parents. Adding the second generation to the first group brings
to 80% the proportion of households in the five major groups. Despite the fact
that the Germans and the Irish had been coming to Detroit for almost half a
century (the first Irish Catholic Church of Detroit was founded in 1834) there
were few second-generation households in a community composed of newcomers. In 1880 most native residents born of foreign parents were simply
children living in their parents' homes (see table 1.4).

Many Detroiters had arrived only recently. The Germans came mainly from
Prussia, a few from Bavaria, Baden, Saxony, Würtemberg, Hesse, and Meck-
lenburg; the overwhelming majority of their children (91.5%) were born in
Michigan, although a few were born on the way to Detroit, in New York or
in Ohio. Sixty-seven percent of the British came from England, 31% from
Scotland, and 1.6% from Wales. Other groups, such as the Canadians, had only

12. "Instructions to Enumerators," in Wright, *United States Census*, pp. 167–77.

TABLE 1.4
Ethnicity of heads of households, Detroit, 1880

Ethnic group	Number in sample	Percentage
Native white American[a]	452	18.7
Black and mulatto	59	2.5
Canadian[b]	103	4.3
Canadian American[c]	9	.4
British Canadian[d]	37	1.5
Irish Canadian[e]	26	1.1
British	233	9.7
British American	30	1.2
Irish	297	12.3
Irish American	50	2.1
German	658	27.3
German American	53	2.2
Polish	61	2.5
Swiss	20	.8
French	37	1.5
Belgian, Dutch, and Luxembourger	27	1.1
Russian	4	.2
Austro-Hungarian	26	1.1
Italian	6	.3
Norwegian, Swedish, and Danish	6	.3
Other	216	8.9
Total	2,410	100.0

SOURCE: 1880 sample.
  a. Born in the U.S. of two U.S.-born parents.
  b. Born in Canada of two Canadian parents, born in Great Britain of two British parents, etc.
  c. Born in the U.S. of two Canadian parents, born in the U.S of two British parents, etc.
  d. Born in Canada of two British parents.
  e. Born in Canada of two Irish parents.

the Detroit River to cross to work or live in the United States; thus, the presence of a large Canadian community, especially English Canadians, was a permanent feature of Detroit.

Two other groups, although still small in numbers, made up a sizable fraction of Detroit's population: the Poles and the Blacks. The Poles were of recent arrival. There was no official Poland in 1880, so a number of the Poles probably listed themselves as Germans or Russians in the census, but self-identified Poles made up 2.6% of the heads of households in 1880. Newcomers to Detroit in 1880, the Poles were to become a very large group by the late nineteenth century. In contrast, Blacks had lived in Detroit almost from the city's founding but always in small numbers, and their fraction of the population in fact decreased until about 1910. If we add together the native-born Blacks (74% of the Blacks), the Canadian-born Blacks, and the mulattoes, Blacks formed only 2.4% of

Detroit's households in 1880. Fifty-six percent of the American-born Blacks were born in northern states (35% in Michigan), and the others came from the South, especially Virginia (17.5%) and Kentucky (15.8%).

None of the other groups living in Detroit in 1880 exceeded 2% of the total number of households: the French (1.6%), the Belgians (1.1%), the Austrians and Hungarians (1.1%). There were a handful of Italians (0.3%!), a few Russian Jews, and, of course, many households whose head was native-born of mixed foreign parentage, or who had one parent native white American and the other immigrant. Altogether, these smaller groups accounted for 10% of Detroit's households with two major groups among them, the Canadian-born of British parentage (1.6%) and the Canadian-born of Irish parentage (1.1%).

It is illuminating to see the ways the members of these different ethnic groups were distributed on the occupational ladder. Popular writing is replete with success stories of a few individuals, freshly arrived from the old country, who achieved the status of prominent citizens. Such people did exist. Popular views also express the many stereotypes in which everybody stays in place: the German immigrant as craftsman, carpenter, or blacksmith; the native white American as white-collar office worker; the Pole as unskilled industrial laborer; the Irish or Canadian woman as domestic servant; the Jew as street peddler; the Black as porter. Like the success-story hero, these stereotypes would not persist in the collective memory if they, too, did not correspond to some reality. The occupational distribution of Detroit's population was quite complex, however, and only a more analytic approach, the cross tabulation of ethnic categories with occupational groups, can reveal its main tendencies (table 1.5).

Very significant differences in the world of work appear among the ethnic groups in Detroit; native white Americans, Germans, Canadians, English, and Irish held different positions in the work forces. At one level of analysis, the working population of Detroit was divided along a relatively simple cleavage: on one side an Anglo-Saxon city of white-collar workers, running most businesses and industries; on the other a labor force mainly of Celtic and German origin. The native white Americans were the only group with more than half of its working members (54%) in white-collar occupations. The British lagged behind with 28%, then the Irish (17%), and the Canadians (17%), while the Germans, numerically the most important group of workers in Detroit, counted only 14% of its work force in white-collar positions. If we are more selective in our criterion and look at the small category of high white-collar professionals—the businessmen, merchants, and important manufacturers—we find only the native white Americans with as many as 10% of their work force in this group. Again the British followed, but they were far behind, with 3%.

TABLE 1.5
Ethnicity versus occupational status, Detroit, 1880[a]

| Ethnic group | Occupational group | | | |
	High white-collar	Low white-collar	Skilled	Semiskilled or unskilled
Native white American[b]	78	335	182	167
Ethnic group (%)	10.2	44.0	23.9	21.9
Occupational group (%)	72.9	50.4	19.7	14.8
Black and mulatto	1	8	33	88
Ethnic group (%)	.8	6.2	25.4	67.1
Occupational group (%)	.9	1.2	3.6	7.8
Canadian[c]	3	39	78	125
Ethnic group (%)	1.2	15.9	31.8	51.0
Occupational group (%)	2.8	5.9	8.4	11.1
British	10	81	138	99
Ethnic group (%)	3.0	24.7	42.1	30.2
Occupational group (%)	9.0	12.2	14.9	8.8
Irish	3	67	94	236
Ethnic group (%)	.8	16.8	23.5	59.0
Occupational group (%)	2.8	10.1	10.2	20.9
German	11	109	384	371
Ethnic group (%)	1.3	12.5	43.9	42.4
Occupational group (%)	10.3	16.4	41.6	32.9
Polish	1	26	15	43
Ethnic group (%)	1.2	30.6	17.6	50.6
Occupational group (%)	.9	3.9	1.6	3.8

SOURCE: 1880 sample.
  a. Total work force in selected ethnic groups.
  b. Born in the U.S. of two U.S.-born parents.
  c. Born in Canada of two Canadian parents, born in Great Britain of two British parents, etc.

Among the Irish, only 0.8% were high white-collar workers. The Germans, on the other hand, could boast a significant 1.3% of their labor force among this upper stratum. In fact, native white Americans made up 73% of the upper stratum of workers, followed by the Germans who, because of their size as a group, accounted for 10% of it. At the other extreme of the occupational distribution, 59% of the Irish and 51% of the Canadian workers were unskilled laborers. The majority of the Germans (44%) were skilled craftsmen and almost as many (42%) were semiskilled or unskilled workers.

   Among the smaller groups, the Poles were heavily concentrated in unspecified factory day labor, although some were craftsmen, and a few Russian Poles were peddlers. The Blacks were heavily concentrated in unskilled and semiskilled work and were found in personal service as barbers, cooks, waiters, coachmen, and servants. In Detroit, as in other cities, the number of skilled Black workers was very limited and had probably declined proportionately since the 1850s, and there were only a handful of Black professionals.[13]

But at another level of analysis, this interpretation of the socioeconomic distribution of ethnic groups which stresses the economic dominance of native white American white-collar workers is misleading because it obscures the economic autonomy of large sections of ethnic communities. If instead of looking at the occupational distribution in categories reflecting socioeconomic status, we turn to specific work sectors, other differences emerge (table 1.6). Different segments of the population dominated different industries. For example, in 1880 the Germans were overrepresented in the tobacco industry, in marble and stone work, and to a lesser extent, in the food and metallurgy industries; they also ran the majority of saloons. The Americans and English tended to run the printing shops and teach in the schools. They also ran hotels and boarding-houses, held the majority of jobs in railroad work, did plastering and painting. Canadians and Irish, without numerically dominating any sector, were fairly well represented in the wood and transportation industries. These ethnic groups dominated sectors of industry not only with large numbers of skilled workers and general laborers but also with workers in the better positions of manufac-turers and wholesalers, as JoEllen Vinyard documented for Detroit's Irish.[14] Other estimates from the 1880 sample indicate that, for example, 25% of the city's tobacco manufacturers were Germans, another 25% British, and another 12.5% Canadians, leaving only 37.5% for the native white Americans. All marble and stone dealers of the sample were Germans, and Germans also held important positions in other industrial sectors since 7% of the textile dealers and 11% of the food dealers were Germans. Unfortunately, it is impossible to determine from census data alone the proportion of German skilled craftsmen who were independent workers and the proportion who worked in factories, but the very presence of both German employers and German artisans shows that at least a significant part of the German community was independent economically. Detroit's German community of 1880 probably resembled the Milwaukee community of some twenty years earlier, which Kathleen Conzen described as "sufficiently diverse to include both employers and employees, skilled and unskilled, cultured and unlettered" and which "could therefore supply its own leaders, provide for most of the needs of its members—economic, social, cultural—within its bounds, and contain the upwardly mobile."[15] In

13. David M. Katzman, *Before the Ghetto: Black Detroit in the Nineteenth Century* (Urbana: University of Illinois Press, 1973), p. 113; Stephan Thernstrom, ed., *Harvard Encyclopedia of American Ethnic Groups* (Cambridge, Mass.: Harvard University Press, 1980), pp. 14, 21.

14. Vinyard, *The Irish on the Urban Frontier*, pp. 142–45.

15. Kathleen N. Conzen, *Immigrant Milwaukee, 1836–1860* (Cambridge, Mass.: Harvard University Press, 1976), p. 225.

TABLE 1.6

Heads of households of selected groups in selected work sectors, Detroit, 1880

Sector	Native white American[a] (%)	Canadian[b] (%)	British (%)	Irish (%)	German (%)	Polish (%)
Clothing and related	21.9	9.7	10.8	9.0	44.8	3.8
Lumber and related	21.1	10.1	15.6	10.6	41.3	1.4
Tobacco	11.9	1.5	9.0	4.5	61.2	11.9
Land transportation	26.5	12.0	10.8	24.1	24.1	2.4
Water transportation	33.8	28.2	15.5	11.3	11.3	0
Construction	45.6	3.5	19.3	5.3	24.6	1.8
Marble and stone	16.3	0	10.2	20.4	53.1	0
Chemical and drug	22.9	8.5	13.7	15.7	39.2	0
Foundry and machine shop	21.2	9.3	16.9	15.3	35.6	1.7
Iron and steel	49.5	4.5	10.4	19.4	14.9	1.5
Printing	58.5	0	20.8	3.8	13.2	3.8
Education	83.6	1.5	4.5	3.0	7.5	0
Boardinghouse	40.3	11.7	10.4	11.7	26.0	0
Bar and saloon	15.6	2.2	6.7	11.1	62.2	2.2
Domestic service	15.5	20.0	12.8	26.9	23.1	1.7
Ethnic distribution[c]	26.3	5.9	12.9	15.0	36.7	3.2

SOURCE: 1880 sample.

a. Born in the U.S. of two U.S.-born parents.

b. Born in Canada of two Canadian parents, born in Great Britain of two British parents, etc.

c. Limited to the heads of households of these ethnic groups and work sectors.

short, it was a community which could live in almost complete autonomy—a city within the city—with its members distributed at all levels of the social structure.

The task before us, then, is to understand the complex relationship between ethnicity and class in the open city. The American scholars' fascination with mobility has impeded the study of social structures on which we must now focus. By reducing the problem of mobility to an abstract race of individuals on a vertical ladder of occupations, historians have unfortunately also reduced the meaning of ethnic affiliations to no more than mere labels on the racers' shirts. And by generally implying that mobility fostered assimilation into the dominant native white American group—hence the continuous creation of a unified open class structure—historians have simply obscured the fundamental question of ethnic cohesiveness in American society. I will therefore depart from the traditional historical approach and turn to new indexes of ethnic and social affiliations. I will turn to the way people were distributed in the residential sections of Detroit to see whether Detroiters established neighborhoods with fellows of the same ethnic group instead of the same social group. Residential location in the open city serves as an independent test of the relative strength of ethnicity and class in dividing the city.

2

Concentration, Dispersion, and Dominance

Plate 2. Workers paving Monroe Street as people pass by, c. 1880.
Courtesy of the Burton Historical Collection, Detroit Public Library.

I dentifying the clustering patterns of the different groups of urbanites and understanding the way ethnic and social cleavages combined to divide the still loosely populated territory of Detroit into recognizable areas are necessary steps toward grasping the profound social forces behind such divisions. Unfortunately, most of our understanding of the urban past and many generalizations about it come from observations of cities that have little in common with Detroit in 1880. Historians have most often studied the commercial walking city of the early nineteenth-century Eastern Seaboard or the crowded giant industrial metropolis of the twentieth century. But the midwestern industrial metropolis in its infancy, with its peculiar combination of smallness, open space, and multiethnic population, is almost terra incognita. It has more often been defined by what it was not than by what, in fact, it was.[1]

THE MELTING POT OR THE GHETTO?

Historians generally agree that the history of the American city is the history of increasing segregation. They have presented an interesting argument, derived primarily from large-scale observations of the city's sociospatial structure, that social divisions did not readily translate into spatial divisions through most of the nineteenth century. From the pioneer communities of the founding fathers to the walking cities of the mid-nineteenth century, no great specialization of land use, residential or otherwise, existed. The "old" immigration, Sam Bass Warner and Colin Burke argued, "never sustained ghettos except in an occasional city for a brief period."[2] Cities were spatially integrated, and historians saw them as melting pots.

Beginning in the late nineteenth century, however, many factors combined to end spatial integration and make social divisions more visible in urban space: large-scale industrialization, the transformation of the walking city into a giant metropolis, the increased immmigration of unskilled labor into the city (especially the massive migration of eastern Europeans and of southern Blacks), and the development of outlying areas inhabited by the well-to-do. The increasing differentiation among residential areas, then, involved a redistribution of the population within the expanding metropolitan area, and the formation of the ghetto.

1. For recent reviews of historical studies of residential segregation, see Kathleen N. Conzen, "Immigrants, Immigrant Neighborhoods, and Ethnic Identity: Historical Issues," *Journal of American History* 66 (December 1979): 603–15; Olivier Zunz, "Residential Segregation in the American Metropolis: Concentration, Dispersion and Dominance," in *Urban History Yearbook, 1980*, ed. David Reeder (Leicester: Leicester University Press, 1980), pp. 23–33.

2. Sam Bass Warner, Jr., and Colin B. Burke, "Cultural Change and the Ghetto," *Journal of Contemporary History* 4 (October 1969): 182; Howard P. Chudacoff, "A New Look at Ethnic Neighborhoods: Residential Dispersion and the Concept of Visibility in a Medium-Sized City," *Journal of American History* 60 (June 1973): 79–93.

This shift from the earlier, socially intermixed "big city" to the "separated society" of the industrial metropolis has been well documented.[3] First, there was an increasing specialization of land use, with residential areas becoming more residential, nonresidential areas more nonresidential, and fewer areas devoted to a mixed land use. Second, the residential areas themselves became more segregated along class lines, with increasing differentiation between the ghetto, the "zone of emergence" out of the ghetto, and the residential suburbs.[4] The redistribution of the population in the growing metropolitan area is usually described as a class-selective process, in which those who could afford it were the first to move out of the city.

The argument that segregation increased over time may not be accurate, but it carries a great deal of emotional appeal. With large Black ghettos now existing in all major cities, experts and lay citizens alike agree that Americans live in a "separated society." The universal concern about the magnitude of today's segregation makes the historical debate intriguing. Was it once different? Was there a time when cities were integrated? At some time in the past, many believe, American cities were better places in which to live; hence, we should strive to recover our lost community.

The most influential description of this general process of social and ethnic redistribution in the American metropolis is certainly the model of population succession which Ernest Burgess, of the University of Chicago, first defined in 1923 in a pilot project on the city of Chicago.[5] Burgess divided Chicago into physical zones, each of them representing a step in the assimilation process of immigrants. He depicted the city in five concentric circles with powerfully related social and spatial divisions: the central business district, the zone of transition, the zone of independent workingmen's homes, the zone of better residences, and the commuters' zone. Burgess depicted immigrants as settling first in an area of confinement near the center and then dispersing throughout the city as their occupations, incomes, educational levels, and the composition of their families came to resemble those of the population as a whole. This model of invasion/succession assumed that most newcomers lived in areas of the city center which had been abandoned to them by others, in houses vacated by previous settlers who had moved toward more peripheral, cosmopolitan

3. Sam Bass Warner, Jr., *The Urban Wilderness* (New York: Harper & Row, 1972), pp. 55–152; Michael N. Danielson, *The Politics of Exclusion* (New York: Columbia University Press, 1976), pp. 1–26.

4. Robert A. Woods and Albert J. Kennedy, *The Zone of Emergence* (Cambridge, Mass.: M.I.T. Press, 1962).

5. Ernest W. Burgess, "The Growth of the City," in *The City*, ed. Ernest W. Burgess and Roderick D. McKenzie (Chicago: University of Chicago Press, 1925), pp. 47–62.

zones of the city. As members of ethnic groups became better assimilated to American society, they were leaving the zone of transition to move gradually toward cosmopolitan areas.

Louis Wirth, another pioneer of urban sociology at the University of Chicago, defined the zone of transition as "the ghetto," and presented the new Chicago model as universal, applicable to all groups in the city. Wirth insisted that:

> The Jews drift into the ghetto . . . for the same reasons that the Italians live in Little Sicily, the Negroes in the black belt, and the Chinese in Chinatowns. The various areas that compose the urban community attract the type of population whose economic status and cultural tradition is more nearly adapted to the physical and social characteristics to be found in each. As each new increment is added to the population it does not at random locate itself just anywhere, but it brings about a resifting of the whole mass of human beings, resulting finally in the anchoring of each to a milieu that, if not most desirable, is at any rate least undesirable.[6]

Fifteen years after Burgess had formalized the Chicago model, Paul Cressey developed its most precise definition:

> Immigrant stocks follow a regular sequence of settlement in successive areas of increasing stability and status. . . . An immigrant group on its arrival settles in a compact colony in a low rent industrial area usually located in the transitional zone near the center of the city. . . . These congested areas of first settlement are characterized by the perpetuation of many European cultural traits. After some years of residence in such an area, the group is not so closely concentrated physically, there is less cultural solidarity, and more American standards of living are adopted. Subsequent areas of settlement may develop in some cases, but the last stage in this series of movements is one of gradual dispersion through cosmopolitan residential districts. This diffusion marks the disintegration of the group and the absorption of the individuals into the general American population. The relative concentration or dispersion of various immigrant groups furnishes an excellent indication of the length of residence in the city and the general degree of assimilation which has taken place.[7]

The "ghetto" is thus the area of first settlement for each immigrant group. According to Wirth, Burgess, and Cressey, it is a zone of transition, located in the dense center of the urban community, populated by ethnic minorities, and vividly contrasting with the residential neighborhoods of the majority, the single-

6. Louis Wirth, *The Ghetto*, 2d ed. (Chicago: University of Chicago Press, 1956), p. 283.
7. Paul F. Cressey, "Population Succession in Chicago, 1898–1930," *American Journal of Sociology* 4 (July 1938): 61.

family homes and green suburbs of the middle class. The ghetto was, of course, a slum where living conditions were degrading. Many social workers visited ghetto families from the 1880s onward and published accounts of their visits; they ran up and down the filthy stairways of crowded tenements, surveying the conditions of immigrant life, appalled by their findings. Because their objective was to touch the nation's sense of moral responsibility, they focused on the most extreme cases of poverty, overcrowding, and deterioration found in the ghetto. They were inspired by the social gospel, not by the credo of social science, and so their surveys, although certainly accurate, were never serious attempts at representing the "statistical" reality. Yet, social workers described impressive cases of deterioration. Jane Addams's story of the suicide of a talented craftsman whose family was among those helped at Hull-House is a good example:

> A Bohemian, whose little girl attended classes at Hull-House, in one of his periodic drunken spells had literally almost choked her to death, and later had committed suicide when in delirium tremens. His poor wife . . . one day showed me a gold ring which her husband had made for their betrothal. It exhibited the most exquisite workmanship, and she said that although in the old country he had been a goldsmith, in America he had for twenty years shoveled coal in a furnace room of a large manufacturing plant. . . . Why had we never been told? Why had our interest in the remarkable musical ability of his child, blinded us to the hidden artistic ability of the father?[8]

In the ghetto the combined effects of immigration and discrimination crystallized. The ghetto was a closed unchanging space, symbol of immigrant isolation for a few months, a few years, or life. Elsewhere lived the majority, atomized in multiple communities where institutions—local government, schools, churches—orchestrated the rhythms of private life. The concepts of the ghetto coexisting with a separate native white American community and the shift from one to the other with upward social mobility are pervasive, well-anchored images in American culture, reappearing constantly in the ethnic literature of the 1930s, for example. When Studs Lonigan finishes primary school at Saint Patrick's Catholic School in an Irish section of Chicago, "old man Lonigan," one who was called "pig pen Irish, shanty Irish . . . the kind of Irishman that slept with the pigs back in the old country," simply says: "I got the money and we can send the lad *any place* we want to."[9]

Over the years, the Chicago model was often criticized in its details, but it

8. Jane Addams, *Twenty Years at Hull-House* (New York: Macmillan, 1949), pp. 246–47.
9. James T. Farrell, *Studs Lonigan* (New York: Vanguard Press, 1938), pp. 13, 25 .

has remained unchallenged in its basic assumptions.[10] Its great strength is consistency to an overall theory of assimilation into American society, the same theory prevalent in most studies of upward social mobility. Immigrants started at the bottom economically and suffered from cultural and geographic isolation. With time, or from one generation to another, they improved their situation, moved away from the zone of transition, and became assimilated into an undefined middle-class America. The Chicago sociologists, Burgess, Wirth, and, of course, Robert Park, created this attractive model of urban assimilation, in which the ecological, social, cultural, and eventually national levels of assimilation fit together nicely. As John Higham pointed out, Park's scheme of assimilation, very influential in casting the model, was

> an improved version of the classic American ideal of assimilation, now extended, as only a few radicals had done before, to include Negroes as well as immigrants. Park defined prejudice not as an exceptional or especially irrational phenomenon but simply as a kind of conservatism, a way of keeping what is strange and unfamiliar at a distance. Yet modern urban life inevitably throws people together. . . . It widens their horizons while loosening their customary ties. In the long run assimilation usually occurs.[11]

In the past twenty years, historians have either uncritically applied the model of the ghetto to the past or criticized it without offering an alternative. Some historians stressed the difference between the slum and the ghetto, justly pointing out that the two were not necessarily the same; others insisted on the great fluidity of population in immigrant quarters, thus questioning the very possibility of a ghetto culture; yet others reacted against the breakdown thesis implied in many social workers' observations on ghetto life. Some historians pushed the criticism of the ghetto model to the extreme and denied its validity altogether. Instead, they proposed to extend the model of the early nineteenth-century residential mixture all the way into the twentieth century, arguing that only

10. C. D. Harris and E. L. Ullman, "The Nature of Cities," *Annals of the American Academy of Political and Social Science* 242 (November 1945): 7–17; Homer Hoyt, *The Structure and Growth of Residential Neighborhoods in American Cities* (Washington, D.C.: Federal Housing Administration, 1939); Beverly Duncan, "Variables in Urban Morphology," in Ernest W. Burgess and Donald J. Bogue, eds., *Urban Sociology*, abridged ed. (Chicago: University of Chicago Press, 1967), pp. 17–30; Otis D. Duncan and Stanley Lieberson, "Ethnic Segregation and Assimilation," *American Journal of Sociology* 64 (January 1959): 364–74; Stanley Lieberson, *Ethnic Patterns in American Cities* (New York: Free Press of Glencoe, 1963); Charles Tilly, "Metropolitan Boston's Social Structure," in Charles Tilly, ed., *An Urban World* (Boston: Little, Brown, 1974), pp. 250–73.

11. John Higham, *Send These to Me* (New York: Atheneum, 1975), p. 215.

Blacks ever experienced the "real" ghetto.[12] The "ghetto" and the "residential melting pot" have been very powerful concepts because they correspond to two different, although not necessarily mutually exclusive, visions of American society. Finding a residential melting pot suggests that ethnic conflicts were never very strong, at least not strong enough to be translated into conflicts for space, and possibly less important than the class conflicts readily apparent in otherwise ethnically mixed cities. Finding the ghetto suggests great ethnic differences in American society, but it also implies that they are temporary. The two realities are contradictory only in appearance. We are finding but another example of the close relationship between the melting pot and the ghetto, which are, in fact, two sides of one coin.

The situation in Detroit did not resemble either model. Still a walking city with most activities concentrated in the center and everybody living within a mile and a half of the center, Detroit could appear to be a spatially integrated city, but it was not. A growing multiethnic city, Detroit could appear to be a ghetto, but it was not that either. Detroit's neighborhoods had strong ethnic dominances, although the lines of division between them were often subtle, and the transitions from one neighborhood to another were evidence of complex interaction among different groups. Still, the analysis of Detroit's concentration patterns in 1880 reveals that ethnicity played a dominant role in the process of population concentration and that ethnic dominance was more apparent over large areas than was class dominance.

The problems that arise in defining 1880 Detroit stem from the frequent misuse of the concepts of concentration and dispersion by historians and sociologists alike; they have too often dealt only with obvious clustering or obvious mixture, thus creating only two alternatives, the ghetto or the residential melting pot. Considering the ethnic diversity of Detroit, one expects to find a strong ethnic communal life based on "similarities of the external appearance or customs or both, or on memories of common migration," as Max Weber once defined it.[13] What occurred in Detroit, however, was neither extreme ghettolike concentration nor melting-pot dispersion, but more subtle forms of dominance

12. Uncritical acceptance of the model of the ghetto is illustrated by Oscar Handlin, *The Uprooted* (Boston: Little, Brown, 1951); criticisms of the model are best expressed in David Ward, *Cities and Immigrants: A Geography of Change in Nineteenth Century America* (New York: Oxford University Press, 1971), pp. 105–24; Stephan Thernstrom, "Reflections on the New Urban History," *Daedalus* 100 (Spring 1971): 367; and most recently James Borchert, *Alley Life in Washington: Family, Community, Religion, and Folklife in the City, 1850–1970* (Urbana: University of Illinois Press, 1980). The most extreme criticism is in Warner and Burke, "Cultural Change," and for Detroit in JoEllen Vinyard, *The Irish on the Urban Frontier: Nineteenth Century Detroit, 1850–1880* (New York: Arno Press, 1976), pp. 174–75.

13. Max Weber, *Economie et société* (Paris: Librairie Plon, 1971), p. 416.

which, without being necessarily dramatic, were nonetheless important and tenacious. The concept of dominance, by which I mean simply the threshold at which geographic concentration is significant for a given group in a given area, is more appropriate than that of either concentration or dispersion in measuring segregation. Dominance is not determined by a rigid numerical criterion applicable in all instances, but by the complex interplay of the variables which caused geographic concentration and dispersion. By including the more subtle forms of clustering found in the emerging ethnic city, the concept of dominance is useful for those who wish to grasp the complexity of the immigrants' urban experience in industrial America.[14]

DOMINANCE: CONCEPT AND MEASUREMENT

It is often difficult to translate complex concepts into practical analysis of data. Measuring dominance in 1880 Detroit becomes a relatively straightforward task, however, since I designed my sample of 127 clusters distributed across the urban territory to that end. In order to assess the relative degree of concentration of different ethnic groups, occupational groups, and socioethnic groups, the areas of abnormal concentration must first be located. Usually a group dominated an area or several small areas within a larger region of the city, though members of other groups, related or not, lived there too. Two related aspects of dominance must be considered in defining these abnormal concentrations. First, the proportion of people in one area from one ethnic or occupational group indicates how dominant a given group is in that area. Second, the proportion of an ethnic group or occupational group in a single area, compared with those from that group in the total population of Detroit, reveals how important a particular area is for the group. Often these two figures appear similar, yet they may indicate substantially different conditions. For instance, it is conceivable that while a group may make up only 20% of any block in a region of the city, 90% of this group might live in this region.

The analysis covers the 2,410 sampled heads of households distributed among 2,180 houses in the 104 inhabited clusters of the sample. I limited the analysis to heads of households so that other members of the households (the rest of the family, boarders, and servants) do not unnecessarily blur the picture by adding intrafamily variability. I divided the sample into ethnic, occupational, and socioethnic categories according to the characteristics of the heads of households. Of the sixty-six ethnic combinations of the census respondent's place of birth and that of his/her two parents, I selected the six most frequent responses for

14. Theodore Hershberg defined "dominance" as "the proportion of an area's total population accounted for by a single group" in "The Philadelphia Social History Project: A Methodological History" (Ph.D. diss., Stanford University, 1973), p. 293.

the statistical analysis of geographic distribution: native white Americans (452), and immigrants from Canada (103), Great Britain (233), Ireland (297), Germany (658), and Poland (61) (in all cases with both parents born in the same country). These six categories comprise 1,804 heads of households. The remaining 606 heads of households fall into smaller categories: Blacks born in the United States and in Canada (45 Blacks and 14 mulattoes), whites born in the United States (or in Canada) of immigrant parents, European immigrants born in Austria, Hungary, Bohemia, Italy, Switzerland, France, Belgium, Luxembourg, the Netherlands, Sweden, Finland, and Denmark, and some special cases.

I next analyzed the heads of households according to occupational categories. The sample contained over 600 occupational titles which serve as broad indicators of social class; in later chapters, we can refine these observations with data on income and working conditions. The 2,003 working heads of households were classified into four large categories: high white-collar (mostly the professionals, the more important merchants, and industrialists: 91); low white-collar (especially business employees and retailers: 520), skilled craftsmen and workers (829), and semiskilled and unskilled workers (563). This classification allowed me to determine whether craftsmen had a tendency to be concentrated in the same region, if the proletariat was either dispersed or concentrated into slum areas, and if the lower middle class still lived in the downtown, to mention a few possibilities. The 407 heads of households not included in one of the four categories did not have occupations listed in the census: 236 female heads of households did not report an occupation; 31 of the 171 men without occupation were over sixty-five years of age.

I also grouped the heads of households into 15 socioethnic categories (table 2.1) by combining ethnic and occupational groups. I limited this grouping to the first 5 ethnic categories—native white Americans, Canadians, British, Irish, and Germans—and I reduced the four occupational categories to three by combining high white-collar and low white-collar into a "white-collar" category. This limited the number of heads of households to 1,449, distributed over 15 groups. By excluding the Poles and thereby reducing the number of ethnic categories and by consolidating two occupational categories, I was able to avoid creating very small socioethnic groups, difficult to analyze statistically.

The sample unit of the cluster of six fronts was especially conceived for this spatial analysis. Particularly helpful is the flexibility of the sampling unit: it is perfectly conceivable, for example, that too few Irish lived on a front for a concentration pattern to appear; when adding several other such fronts at the level of the block or the cluster, however, the presence of Irish households would become significant. It may also be that in heavily populated Irish areas, a concentration pattern would be readily apparent at the front level. This plas-

TABLE 2.1
Socioethnic distribution of heads of households, Detroit, 1880

Socioethnic group	Number in sample	Percentage
High and low white-collar native white American[a]	206	14.21
Skilled native white American	108	7.45
Unskilled native white American	54	3.72
High and low white-collar Canadian[b]	25	1.72
Skilled Canadian	41	2.82
Unskilled Canadian	27	1.86
High and low white-collar British	69	4.76
Skilled British	90	6.21
Unskilled British	37	2.55
High and low white-collar Irish	53	3.65
Skilled Irish	63	4.34
Unskilled Irish	102	7.03
High and low white-collar German	88	6.07
Skilled German	299	20.63
Unskilled German	187	12.90
Total	1,449	100.00

SOURCE: 1880 sample.
a. Born in the U.S. of two U.S.-born parents.
b. Born in Canada of two Canadian parents, born in Great Britain of two British parents, etc.

ticity, of course, is useful not only for comparing concentration levels of one group, but also for comparing several groups or different types of groups; it becomes possible to determine whether, in some areas, ethnic concentration is more readily apparent than occupational concentration, or vice versa. In the end, by combining several clusters together, we can define larger zones in the city, and by combining all clusters, we can compare the different socioethnic groups in the city as a whole.

It is, of course, essential to devise a statistical device which allows for such flexibility of measurement. One needs an index of concentration that will work not only when measuring concentration patterns of many groups (as many as 15 socioethnic groups) in the small geographic units of the sample, but also when adding the sampled fronts, blocks, and clusters, and comparing concentration patterns of different categories in the city as a whole. This is a highly challenging problem, which I discuss in detail in Appendix 4. Suffice it to say here that I constructed such an index, based on a standardization of the chi-square statistic (a natural measure of the departure of observed from expected frequencies under various hypotheses). Theoretically, if the population of Detroit were distributed at random over the urban territory, we should observe in each geographic unit a distribution of inhabitants across the different categories similar to that of the city as a whole. If, for example, the Germans made up

36% of the city's households, we "expect" to find 36% of the households of each sampled cluster to be headed by a German. If this is indeed what we "observe," the index would be zero. And as the differences between the "expected" and the "observed" values in each geographic unit—front, block, or cluster depending on the level of analysis—rise, so does the index.

The technique actually involves the computing of two indexes. The first index, computed for the city as a whole, indicates the existence of ethnic or occupational concentrations and their relative importance. This citywide index is the standardized sum of a second index, computed for each cluster separately, which reveals the precise clusters where abnormal concentrations existed (see Appendix 4). The results of this complex analysis are very revealing, and well worth this elaborate sifting of the data. By using the global index first, we can test for randomness of the spatial distribution of ethnic, occupational, and socioethnic groups (rejected if the index is above 1.65 at the significance level of 5% or less), and we can identify the main factors accounting for concentration patterns among categories and geographic levels.

THE SPATIAL DISTRIBUTION OF ETHNIC AND OCCUPATIONAL GROUPS

Not surprisingly, the indexes for the three categories at the three geographic levels allow us to reject the hypothesis of randomness. Important ethnic, occupational, and socioethnic concentrations existed in Detroit in 1880, regardless of the unit of measurement—front, block, or cluster. Furthermore, the index is systematically higher (at all three geographic levels) for ethnic categories than for either occupational or socioethnic categories. The difference between ethnic and occupational clustering appears most pronounced at the level of the cluster, with an index of 39.13 for ethnic categories but only 9.12 for occupational categories (see table 2.2). Clearly, then, ethnic affiliation played the dominant role in the process of population concentration.

Ethnic and occupational concentrations took different forms in the city, as

TABLE 2.2
Citywide index of concentration, Detroit, 1880[a]

Geographic unit	Ethnic groups	Occupational groups	Socioethnic groups
Front	12.23	4.30	-
Block	25.31	8.49	-
Cluster	39.13	9.12	3.80

SOURCE: 1880 sample.

a. x_s^2 (standardized values); see Appendix 4.

expressed by the varying fluctuations of the indexes from front to block and
from block to cluster. For the occupational categories, the index moves from
4.3 at the front level up to 8.49 at the block level, but then stays there, reaching
only a value of 9.42 at the cluster level. The differences are more striking for
ethnic groups: the index starts at 12.23 at the front level, moves to 25.31 at the
block level, and reaches 39.13 at the cluster level. The concentrations associated
with occupational categories, then, were relatively uniform, regular, and limited
in space. In contrast, the concentration patterns of ethnic groups stand out best
at the larger geographic level of the cluster, although they certainly existed too
at the front level. It seems likely that a number of fronts would appear ethnically
heterogeneous when observed in isolation, but would turn up homogeneous
when joined to adjacent fronts of the same block and beyond. The dominance
pattern of ethnic groups shows up most clearly in strong concentrations scattered
in the urban territory, often spreading from one street to another but varied in
importance according to the group and the neighborhood. The index for socioethnic categories (which combine ethnic and occupational categories) shows
a much lower value (3.8) at the cluster level, indicating that the two phenomena
of ethnic and occupational concentration could be mutually exclusive. At least
they were not identical, since the concentrations associated with ethnic groups
were not necessarily also associated with occupational categories.

Using this information, I was able to analyze each geographic unit separately
and by sets of units. Since it is clear that the concentration of the various groups
is best expressed at the level of the cluster, I particularly examined the index
computed for each cluster, rather than the indexes for the blocks or the fronts.
Selecting 2.7 as the index value above which the hypothesis of randomness can
be rejected (a value of 2.7 corresponds to at least 86.3% certainty, a value of
5 corresponds to at least 96% certainty, etc.; see Appendix 4), I identified 33
clusters with the ethnic index, 33 with the occupational index, and 23 with the
socioethnic index; from there, I grouped them for closer scrutiny. In addition
to the index, I had two additional sets of information for each cluster: first, the
number of households within each category and, second, the geographic location
of the cluster. The index values and the proportions of heads of households in
each category formed the basis for the two maps of ethnic concentration and
occupational concentration in 1880 Detroit presented here. For each cluster with
an index value above 2.7, the map displays the dominant category if it included
at least 60% of the households, or the two dominant categories if none reached
60% (see maps 2.1 and 2.2).

The combination of these three sources of information—index, proportion,
situation—clearly depicts the distribution of zones of concentration and zones
of dispersion and the distribution of the categories identified in the statistical

MAP 2.1

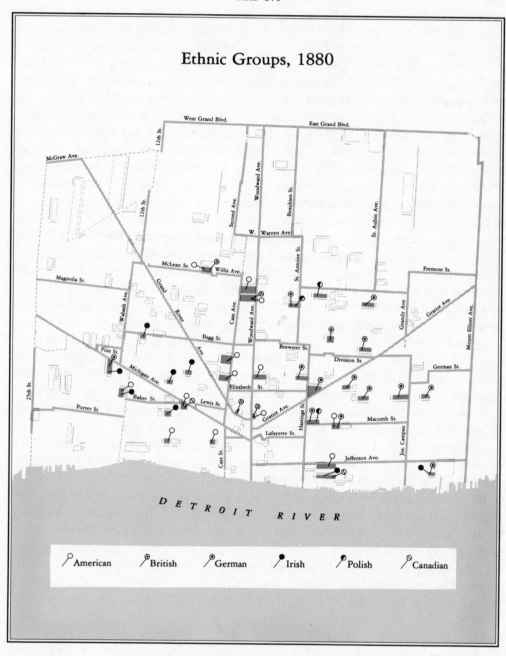

Ethnic Groups, 1880

MAP 2.2

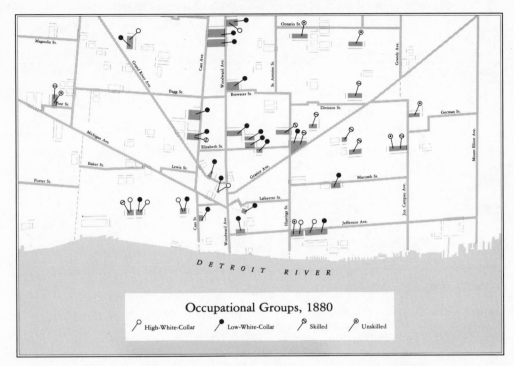

Occupational Groups, 1880

High-White-Collar   Low-White-Collar   Skilled   Unskilled

analysis; the two maps neatly summarize the information. Four clearly distinguished ethnic zones emerge: a native white American center located above the city center of activities which we have already defined; a large German quarter in the east; an Irish zone, Corktown, in the west; and, in addition, a small Polish enclave in the northeast. It seems that there were few concentrations of British and Canadians. In contrast to the diversity of ethnic zones, only two occupational categories formed large spatial concentrations: the lower middle-class (the low white-collar workers of the center) and the skilled workers in the east. There were only a few groupings of exclusively unskilled workers, and these too few to be statistically important. The 33 clusters identified by the ethnic index (above 2.7) comprised 53.99% (974 out of 1,804) of the heads of households of the ethnic categories, and the 33 revealed by the occupational index comprised 42.38% (849 out of 2,003) of those of occupational categories.

The percentages of households of different categories in zones of concentration or zones of dispersion varied from one group to another (table 2.3). Among ethnic groups, 37.61% of the native white Americans were living in clusters

TABLE 2.3
Clusters with ethnic and occupational dominances, Detroit, 1880[a]

Ethnic and occupational groups	Dominated clusters	Number of households in dominated clusters	in sample	Percentage of households in dominated clusters
Native white American[b]	9, 12, 16, 21, 22, 29, 32, 61, 65, 67, 71, 73, 93, 118	170	452	37.61
Canadian[c]	33, 61	18	103	17.48
British	9, 12, 22, 118	32	233	13.73
Irish	33, 56, 63, 69, 75, 76	121	297	40.74
German	19, 24, 29, 37, 38, 41, 42, 43, 50 52, 53, 54, 56, 92	345	658	52.43
Polish	24, 43, 44	43	61	70.49
High white-collar	11, 20, 31, 32, 65, 66	37	91	40.66
Low white-collar	1, 3, 5, 9, 11, 13, 16, 17, 18, 20, 21, 22, 25, 32, 37, 66, 67, 71, 73, 79	233	520	44.81
Skilled	19, 30, 36, 37, 39, 41, 42, 53, 73, 100	257	829	31.00
Unskilled	31, 42, 44, 50, 60, 100	105	563	18.65

SOURCE: 1880 sample.

a. Clusters with significant indexes of concentration; single dominance if 60% or more of the household heads are of one group; dual dominance if no group reaches 60%.

b. Born in the U.S. of two U.S.-born parents.

c. Born in Canada of two Canadian parents, born in Great Britain of two British parents, etc.

which they dominated, and this was the case for over 40% of the Irish households, over 52% of the German households, and over 70% of the Polish households. Among occupational groups, the highest percentages were due to the concentration of white-collar workers, with over 40% of high white-collar workers in clusters which they dominated, and almost 45% of low white-collar workers in such self-dominated clusters.

Many of the clusters populating the other half of the city did not appear on the maps. They constituted a background upon which the population seems to have been distributed at random. Among them, of course, were the clusters of the city center proper, which we have already identified as the zone of hotels and boardinghouses, with few families. There was no particular concentration in the loosely populated periphery either (where 23 uninhabited clusters have not been included in the computations of the indexes).

Reading the two maps of ethnic and occupational distribution, one could schematically divide Detroit into four zones: the German and Polish east side, where many skilled workers lived; the lower middle-class American center; the Anglo-Saxon west, except for the Irish neighborhood; and the large mixed low-density periphery. But can we really talk about the combination of Germans and skilled craftsmen in the east side, or is this too diagrammatic a view, one that distorts reality? Do the ethnic and occupational indexes reveal one concentration with the same ethnic background and the same occupational category, or different and independent concentrations? Looking at the three indexes simultaneously can answer this question. Among the 23 clusters with a socioethnic index above 2.7, 6 showed households headed by native white American white-collar workers (60% or more), and 4 showed households headed by German skilled workers (60% or more). In some cases, then, there was clearly an interaction between ethnicity and occupation. But often the ethnic and occupational factors did not coincide, as appears clearly when we compare the ethnic and occupational indexes on a scatter plot (see fig. 2.1). Whenever ethnic dominance was clear, occupational concentration was less evident, and vice versa. Some clusters had comparable values on both indexes (around 3, 4.5, and 9), but more often the clusters with high values on the ethnic index were different from the clusters with high values on the occupational index.

These results indicate that a cleavage existed between ethnic affiliation and socioeconomic categories. This division was not absolute, since the two indexes often reveal the same clusters, but it was real, as their inverse values confirm. In other words, Detroit was made up largely of cross-class ethnic communities. The social mix in some sections of ethnic neighborhoods reflected the fact that ethnic communities kept many of their upwardly mobile members within their boundaries. Other sections in which ethnic and occupational indexes coincided reflected the socioeconomic positions of the majority of the group's members. Only in rare instances (no more than 3% of the German families, for example, lived in native white American clusters) was this coincidence accounted for by the movement of upwardly mobile members of east-side groups into Anglo-Saxon middle-class sections of the west side.

That neighborhoods were persistently ethnically dominated is also clear from

FIG. 2.1

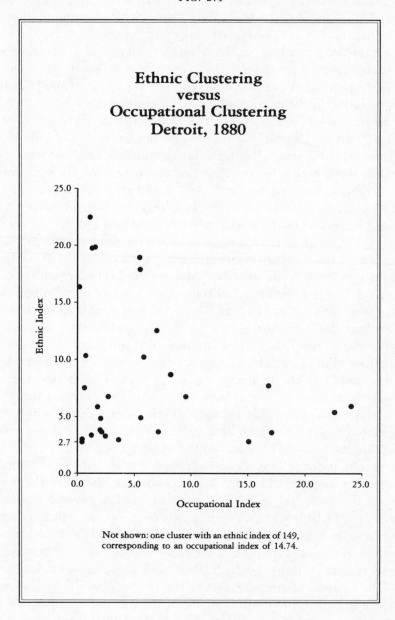

**Ethnic Clustering
versus
Occupational Clustering
Detroit, 1880**

Not shown: one cluster with an ethnic index of 149,
corresponding to an occupational index of 14.74.

the complementary analysis of households headed by native residents born of
foreign parents, too few in numbers to be included as separate categories in the

computation of the indexes. It appears clear that, at least for the major ethnic groups, the second generation did not break away from the first. The majority of households headed by native residents born of German parents were in the German east side (37 out of 54). The native household heads born of Irish parents also lived in the Irish quarter on the west side (34 out of 50), as did those born in Canada of Irish parents (11 out of 14).

The only exception to this pattern of mutually exclusive zones of ethnic concentration—and the exception which makes it so difficult to identify such a pattern—is that Detroit's east side also functioned as a port of entry for many small groups of immigrants, not numerous enough to carve a niche of their own. This was the case of the Blacks and also of many small groups of immigrants from Austria, Hungary, Bohemia, Italy, Switzerland, France, Belgium, Luxembourg, the Netherlands, Sweden, Finland, and Denmark. These small groups infiltrated sections of the east side, the main working-class district of Detroit, in a way similar to that described by Burgess, Wirth, and Cressey in their classic model of ghetto formation. This process of the pouring of a few immigrants into the near east side was, however, too limited to alter the balance of basically independent ethnic neighborhoods. Still, these small groups intruded on ethnic homogeneity by creating small pockets of concentration or transitional zones within the predominantly German area.

Particularly interesting is the case of the Blacks and the mulattoes. Nearly all families headed by a Black or a mulatto lived in the German-dominated east side (only 2 out of 59 lived on the west side). Generally, there were one or two Black households in clusters otherwise dominated by German or Polish families. In only two small sections of town did the Blacks either share the cluster equally with the Germans or slightly dominate it: around Kentucky Street near Saint Antoine between Brewster and Ontario, and along Division Street, especially at its intersection with Joseph Campau.[15]

The distribution in Detroit of the members of the many small groups makes the contrast between the east and the west sides of town even more apparent. In the east, near or mixed with the Germans and the Poles, lived most members of the small European groups who did not speak English: 3 out of 4 Russians in the sample, 6 out of 6 Italians; 17 out of 20 Swiss; 33 out of 37 French; 33 out of 37 Belgians, Luxembourgers, and Netherlanders; and 2 out of 6 Scandinavians.

15. David Katzman, *Before the Ghetto: Black Detroit in the Nineteenth Century* (Urbana: University of Illinois Press, 1973), p. 79; Donald R. Deskins, Jr., *Residential Mobility of Negroes in Detroit, 1837–1965* (Ann Arbor: University of Michigan, Department of Geography, 1972), pp. 68–69, 102–3.

This analysis of the ethnic and occupational concentration and dominance patterns which allows us to locate each group in the city is also helpful in understanding the nature of the concentrations and in estimating the size of each group considered. If we compare our results with the informed description of a local historian writing in the early 1880s, we see that we have not only confirmed some of the known characteristics of late nineteenth-century Detroit, but also added some important new dimensions to the picture. Not only was Silas Farmer, who first published his *History of Detroit* in 1884, a city biographer, he also drew up some of the finest maps of Detroit in his day; he was therefore an expert in the local geography of Detroit and noted population characteristics while describing the more mundane matters of "streets and street-paving." He reported that:

The nationality and characteristics of the people congregated in certain parts of the city have given rise to peculiar designations for such localities. Thus the larger portion of the territory on Fifth and Sixth Streets, for several blocks east side of Michigan Avenue, is called Corktown, because chiefly occupied by people from the Emerald Isle. The eastern part of the city, for several blocks on each side of Gratiot Avenue beyond Brush Street, for similar reasons is often spoken of as Dutchtown, or the German quarter. That part of the city lying a few blocks north of High Street and between Brush and Hastings, is known as Kentucky, from the number of colored people living there. A walk of a few blocks east and north of this locality terminates in the heart of Polacktown, where many Poles reside. That portion of the city just west of Woodward Avenue and North of Grand River Avenue, forming part of the old Fifth Ward, is sometimes designated as Piety Hill; for the reason that it is largely occupied by well-to-do citizens, who are supposed to largely represent the moral and religious portion of the community.

Peddlers' Point is a name frequently applied to a part of Grand River Avenue near Twelfth Street. The intersection of several streets at that place forms a pointed block, which locality is a favorite place for itinerant hucksters to intercept and purchase supplies from the farmers coming on the Grand River Road.

Swill Point is the not very euphonious appellation sometimes given to a portion of Larned Street near Second because of a distillery formerly located near by. Atwater and Franklin Streets, for several blocks east of Brush Street, are frequently designated as the Potomac. This locality is near the river. . . . The Heights is a name applied to a region near the westerly end of Fort Street East, occupied in part by former denizens of the Potomac quarter. This last region being on lower ground, a removal to Fort Street was spoken of as a removal to the "Heights," possibly the fact that "high old times" have been frequent in this locality has also had something to do with the particular designation. These last localities have numbered among their inhabitants the worst classes of both sexes.

Woodward Avenue, with one end at the river's edge, and the other reaching indefinitely into the country, has no superior on the continent. The elegant stores, residences, and churches that mark its route, the beautiful parks and private grounds that lie on either side, win universal admiration.

Griswold Street, running from the river to the High School, is the financial artery of the city. On its courts, lawyers, and banks abound.[16]

It is reassuring to see that our statistical analysis of a probability sample is in basic agreement with the firsthand observations of a contemporary cartographer and local historian; it is also interesting to note that Farmer subtly shifted from ethnic to occupational categories, depending on which characteristic was dominant in the part of the city he described. Here, too, our statistical analysis confirms his informed judgment. In turn, we are now able to go far beyond Farmer's description. We can recapitulate the geographic distribution, in all its complexity, of Detroit's inhabitants in 1880, distributed among ethnic and occupational categories, not only by identifying and circumscribing the zones of concentration but especially by measuring their numerical importance and the distribution of individuals among the concentrated and dispersed areas. We are also able to grasp the nature of the relationships of small groups to large groups, and the respective importance of ethnic and occupational categories in determining concentration patterns.

The residential distribution of 1880 Detroit, then, did not conform to any stage of the process set forth by the traditional sociological succession theory. What I found does not resemble the neat succession of concentric circles defined by Burgess, but neither does it resemble the integration of the walking city. In still loosely populated Detroit, the inhabitants were distributed according to an irregular system of dominance, with an abundance of single-family dwellings even in modest neighborhoods, and few traces of ghetto formation. The next task, then, is to evaluate the extent to which the city's segmentation into distinct ethnic neighborhoods reflected important cultural and behavioral differences in Detroit's society.

16. Silas Farmer, *The History of Detroit and Michigan* (Detroit: S. Farmer & Co., 1890; Gale Research Co., 1969), p. 938.

3

Spatial Bonds:
Ethnicity, Class, and Fertility

Plate 3. Black street sweepers, 1880s.
Courtesy of the Burton Historical Collection, Detroit Public Library.

E thnicity and class are two interwoven forces in American history, and it may be artificial to try to separate them. During the period of intense immigration in the late nineteenth century, immigrant life always comprised two complementary spheres of influence. In one, life involved the family and a community of friends and neighbors in an environment where kinship and cultural ties were free to develop. In the other, life depended on economic forces, working conditions, and job opportunities unequally distributed throughout the city. Although the community and the world of work were organized according to different principles, the two aspects of life were closely related and probably considered together in every decision that had to be made. Often, in fact, the two worlds converged, as the hiring practices of large employers in the preunion era encouraged workers to bring in some of their family members to work in the factory.[1]

Our study of two indicators of ethnicity and class—place of birth and occupation—has shown some ways in which the two factors are often entwined and how difficult it is to separate them. My analysis of ethnic and occupational bonds, however, did reveal areas of 1880 Detroit where the two types of concentration did not significantly overlap. In several parts of Detroit, the ethnic factor stood out clearly, without competitor. In contrast, the city center was unique in its total absence of ethnic concentration.

SOCIAL CLASS AND CENTER CITY

The city center was the one populated area of Detroit without significant concentrations of ethnic groups; its dense concentration of people and activities and its heterogeneity contrasted vividly with the residential zones around it. No sampled clusters in the central area defined by Cass Street, Lafayette, Hastings, and the river showed an abnormal concentration of any ethnic group. The concentrations of native white Americans began to take shape only in the upper center at the intersection of the main arteries, Michigan, Grand River, Woodward, and Gratiot. Residentially, the center appeared to be a mix of all ethnic groups but showed a noticeable concentration of white-collar workers, especially established merchants, lawyers, and physicians, living close to the many downtown offices. Wealthy citizens were still anchored, at least in part, in the heart of the city in 1880.

While the center had its share of the wealthy, it also had its share of the very

---

1. Tamara K. Hareven, "The Dynamics of Kin in an Industrial Community," in *Turning Points: Historical and Sociological Essays on the Family*, ed. John Demos and Sarane S. Boocock (Chicago: University of Chicago Press, 1978), pp. 151–82, supplement, 1978, to vol. 84 of the *American Journal of Sociology*; see also Edward O. Laumann, *Bonds of Pluralism: The Form and Substance of Urban Social Networks* (New York: John Wiley & Sons, 1973).

poor. The Detroit Association of Charities investigated "the homes of the poorest classes" in Detroit in 1883 and proclaimed that "seventy per cent of the cases reported by district committees were found on the east side of Woodward Avenue from a line drawn from the River, east of Brush street to the northern limits; 30% were found west of Woodward Avenue to the western limits of the city."[2] The Association of Charities, in fact, located 11% of the poor of the city (or rather 102 of the 946 families which they investigated in 1883) in the city center, or an area which they defined between Saint Antoine in the east, Third Street in the west, Adams Avenue, and the river. In general, the association had no kind word for the city center. According to the report,

> the central district embraces within its eastern border from the river, between Brush and Antoine Streets, as far as Illinois Street, some of the worst dens of infamy existing in Detroit—the purlieus of vice and de- bauchery and the resort of criminals . . . places resorted to by the most dangerous of the criminal class and their concomitant depraved women.[3]

The report also describes the living conditions of the poor in Detroit's center:

> There are no regular large crowded tenement houses here. A close in- spection of the dwellings of the poor in the eastern and central districts shows that nearly all are of one-story wood, generally occupied by two families, averaging twelve to fifteen souls. A considerable number of these tenements are located in alleys; three-fourths of the entire number are in bad condition: these are located on the lower streets and otherwise as mentioned. As a rule the poorest class of colored people are found in the worst class of tenements. . . . The average rent demanded from each family is $1.25 a week, and the landlords are invariably represented as exacting.[4]

The city center received many newcomers, but not all of them were patrons of the "purlieus of vice." Many dwelled in a variety of boardinghouses. Over 25% of the boardinghouse residents sampled were native white Americans, and another 28% were native-born Americans with at least one parent born in the United States. Next were the Canadians and the British (7.7% each) and then the Irish and the Germans (4.2% each). These percentages show a tendency for bachelor members of groups with strong ethnic neighborhoods to avoid the center if possible. But the lack of a strong ethnic concentration did not nec- essarily indicate strong occupational bonds; in fact, boarders of the hotels and boardinghouses were employed in all varieties of jobs. Many were clerical

2. DAC, *Fourth Annual Report of the Central Committee* (Detroit: Chas. M. Rousseau's Printing House, 1883), p. 13.

3. Ibid., p. 13–14.

4. Ibid., p. 13.

workers, bookkeepers, telegraph operators, railroad or steamboat agents; others worked in small shops as bookbinders, printers, piano tuners, or tailors; still others were industrial workers.[5]

Some of the newcomers, albeit only a small fraction of them, were channeled into different parts of the city after they entered Detroit through the center. This was often the case for the women who came to town to find employment and boarded for a while in the Young Woman's Home, one of the many boardinghouses of downtown Detroit. Although societies for working women had been in existence since the 1830s in the United States, such agencies had functioned primarily to encourage domestic service and had acted as employment agencies for the benefit of employers. It was not until several decades later that concern for employees emerged in the form of benevolent reform societies to aid working women. Stimulated by the success of such organizations in other cities, a group of women in Detroit formed the Working Woman's Home Association in 1877,

> for the purpose of protecting, elevating, and encouraging our young women. This association shall have as a primary object the establishing of a home for women where strangers in our city in search of work may come and register their names; also be boarded at a small cost until situations are procured. This home shall also be open to girls of good moral character who are from any cause unable to find employment, and if unable to pay for their board, shall be kept until furnished with a situation, by agreeing to give an' equivalent in labor. This home shall be open for our industrious women, who are employed in our factories and workshops, without relatives or friends with whom they can live, and who are in receipt of small wages and unable to secure comfortable and respectable homes.[6]

The first activity of the association was to set up an employment bureau, which predated the actual opening of the home; it was announced in the *Detroit Free Press* on 29 March 1877, that girls in want of work "May register free of charge on Friday and Saturday between the hours of 9 and 11 A.M. and 3 and 6 P.M., at Room 4, over Preston's Bank."[7] Preston's Bank was only a temporary location, and after the home opened, the employment bureau operated on the first floor of the home, located originally at 270 Jefferson Avenue and, then at 41 Congress Street West. After one year, the employment bureau reported a great deal of activity: "The number of applicants for work during the ten months

---

5. For an examination of the "bachelor-transient subculture," see John C. Schneider, *Detroit and the Problem of Order, 1830–1880* (Lincoln: University of Nebraska Press, 1980), pp. 36–45.

6. Richard Hodas, "A History of the Young Woman's Home Association of Detroit" (1973), p. 2, copy at MHC.

7. *Detroit Free Press*, 29 March 1877.

the Home has been open was 1,714. The number applying for servants was 1,350."[8]

In 1878, women from 43 towns outside Detroit applied for jobs through the Young Woman's Home. Many of these young women who applied to the home's employment office boarded upstairs for a while; in fact, the employment register for 1880 reveals that 62 women, or 12.8% of the applicants for that year, were residents of the home. The women who resided at the home ranged in age from 16 to 55, but 65% were below 25 years of age. They had diverse backgrounds, although a few nationality groups dominated: Canadian Protestant girls made up 35.5% or 22 of the 62 residents of the home in 1880, reflecting the continuous flow of women immigrants coming into Detroit through Windsor. Next were Irish Catholics (10 women), then native white American Protestants (6), Canadian Catholics (6), German Protestants (5), and other young women of varied ethnic and religious backgrounds (13). They usually sought domestic service, most wanting just "general work," with a few specifying "cook," or work in "upstairs," or "laundress." To these young women, the "Home" was the port of entry into Detroit.[9]

If the center showed an ethnic and socioeconomic mixture unusual elsewhere in Detroit, it is because the center was only partially an area of family residences. The peculiar characteristics of the city center clearly stand out when we examine the demographic structure of each front where hotels and boardinghouses were standing and compare the age and sex profiles of the population of the hotels and boardinghouses with those of the other houses of the same fronts. Sixty-three percent of the residents of hotels and boardinghouses were men. In contrast, other houses on the same fronts had a balanced sex ratio. Seventy-one percent of the population of the hotels and boardinghouses was between the ages of 17 and 40 as opposed to only 47% in the other houses of the same fronts. The hotels and boardinghouses received a disproportionate share of young male bachelors of diverse backgrounds, which made the center a demographically incomplete area.

The city center also maintained great diversity of social classes. Next to some of the finest homes in Detroit were some of the worst alleys. On one side of a particular block stood an elegant hotel, staffed by a dozen Black servants; on another, some dilapidated houses where some of the poorest Blacks lived; on yet another stood a brothel patronized by stevedores and longshoremen. The

8. Hodas, "History of the Young Woman's Home," p. 6.
9. Statistical analysis of the 1880 Employment Register of the Young Woman's Home Association, which includes name, address, age, nationality, religion, and work wanted for each woman, as well as whether her parents were living or dead; original in possession of Mr. Richard Hodas, copy at MHC; see also Valerie Gerrard Browne, "The Employment Bureau of Detroit's Working Woman's Home Association" (1978), in my possession.

center did not belong to any one group in particular; it was, rather, a conglomerate of all that existed in Detroit.

It is common practice in statistical analysis to isolate that which appears to be special in order to understand better that which appears to be general; by treating Detroit's unique city center separately, then, we gain greater insight into the respective roles of ethnic and socioeconomic factors in shaping the city as a whole. More specifically, by "controlling for" the center, I can once again test for the factors that most accounted for the clustering of the different groups of urbanites.

I first divided Detroit into two large zones: the center and the "rest" of the city. The center is defined as a half-circle with a one mile radius from the intersection of Woodward and the river; this area, which included 27.1% of the sampled inhabitants, was the highest density zone on the density curve, and so this definition is clearly independent of our prior knowledge of ethnic and socioeconomic concentrations. I then divided the "rest" of the city into two regions, one east of Woodward, the other west of Woodward. What I analyzed is the probability of living in one of these regions, depending on ethnicity or occupation. Once again I worked with variables that act as proxies for the basic cleavages I wanted to uncover: the places of birth of the individuals and of their two parents to define ethnicity, and census occupational titles to define occupational status. I limited the analysis not only to the heads of households—as I had done before to avoid intrafamily variability—but to the heads of households for which I have ethnic *and* occupational information. I excluded the Poles once again because of their very small numbers in the white-collar categories. The analysis, therefore, centers on the native white Americans, the Canadians, the British, the Irish, and the Germans, in the four previously defined occupational categories.

My statistical test consisted of predicting central location by two independent variables: ethnicity and occupational status. The final equation reveals that the category of high white-collar was the only strong predictor of central location in 1880 Detroit (table 3.1). It is followed closely by low white-collar, although the regression coefficient is significantly lower. Only one ethnic group, the Canadians, appear to have been positively related to central location. In contrast, being a skilled worker, an unskilled worker, an Irish or a German immigrant was negatively related to central location. These results are quite startling in that ethnicity, which in previous analyses explained most of the clustering patterns throughout the city, hardly counts in this analysis. Central location was best predicted by high social status in Detroit in 1880, not by ethnicity (see Appendix 5).

Another important function of the analysis is to compute the probability for the average citizen, the average craftsman, the average Irishman, the average

TABLE 3.1

Dichotomous regression: Predicting central location, Detroit, 1880[a]

Ethnic and occupational categories	Regression coefficient	Sample proportion	Probability of living in the center	95% confidence limits	
Native white American[b]	.46	.275	.271	.228	.318
Canadian[c]	.74	.063	.328	.293	.432
British	.16	.131	.216	.163	.279
Irish	−.04	.145	.182	.135	.242
German	−.50	.383	.123	.098	.154
High white-collar	1.11	.048	.415	.305	.535
Low white-collar	.72	.250	.324	.277	.376
Skilled	−.27	.413	.150	.123	.181
Unskilled	−.42	.287	.132	.102	.168

SOURCE: 1880 sample.

a. See Appendix 5; R^2 = 10%: 7.9% for occupational categories; 2.1% for ethnic categories.

b. Born in the U.S. of two U.S.-born parents.

c. Born in Canada of two Canadian parents, born in Great Britain of two British parents, etc.

high white-collar professional to live in this small circumscribed area which I have arbitrarily defined as the center of the city; table 3.1 displays the results. We learn that in 1880 Detroit, the likelihood of living in the center varied greatly depending on one's affiliation with one group or another. Although the high white-collar workers made up only 4.88% of our sample, 41.5% of them were likely to live in the center (between 30.5 and 53.5%). The low white-collar workers made up 25% of the sample, but 32.4% of all low white-collar workers were likely to live in the center. Inversely, the percentages for the skilled and unskilled workers were 41% and 28%, respectively, for the sample, and only 15% and 13.2% of them were likely to live in the center. Among the ethnic categories, which have proven already to be a poor indicator of central location, only the Canadians and the British had a relatively high probability of central residence.

But if I now rerun the same analysis, suppressing the center of town, to predict location in the east side, the results are extremely revealing. This time, ethnicity stands out as the great predictor of residential location. Not surprisingly, the only factors that positively predict eastern location are German ethnic affiliation (1.37) and skilled craftsmen occupations (.23). Occupational categories hardly contribute at all in predicting eastern location, once we control for the city center. Needless to say, the probability of living in the east was very high for the Germans, 80% (from 76.5% to 83.6%), though they made up only 43.36% of the sample overall. In contrast, the western section of town was largely Anglo-Saxon and Celtic. Table 3.2 reveals a high probability of 37% for Amer-

TABLE 3.2
Dichotomous regression: Predicting eastern location, Detroit, 1880[a]

Ethnic and occupational categories	Regression coefficient	Sample proportion	Probability of living in the east	95% confidence limits	
Native white American[b]	−.55	.232	.373	.315	.435
Canadian[c]	−.24	.054	.447	.330	.571
British	−1.07	.126	.261	.196	.338
Irish	−2.07	.152	.115	.075	.172
German	1.37	.433	.803	.765	.836
High white-collar	−.07	.031	.489	.318	.663
Low white-collar	−.33	.201	.425	.350	.503
Skilled	.23	.448	.566	.514	.617
Unskilled	−.10	.318	.481	.419	.544

SOURCE: 1880 sample.
  a. See Apendix 5; R^2 = 31%: 27.4% for ethnic categories; 3.6% for occupational categories.
  b. Born in the U.S. of two U.S.-born parents.
  c. Born in Canada of two Canadian parents, born in Great Britain of two British parents, etc.

icans living in the east, but this unexpected concentration is easy to explain since our dividing line between east and west is Woodward Avenue, on both sides of which existed the native white American neighborhoods.

The point of this analysis is not so much to determine the exact location of ethnic and occupational groups, but to define the distinction between the center and the residential zones, a distinction which also corresponds to a cleavage between social status and ethnicity. A high social status as well as the means of and desire for easy access to the city center were important in determining residential location in this otherwise mixed area. Of course, the center was not numerically dominated by higher classes; what I have measured here is another phenomenon, the high probability of members of the upper class living in the center. The center also served a variegated young population, but most bachelors never lived in the boardinghouses of the center, boarding instead in the private residences of the American, German, or Irish neighborhoods. Many newcomers, if they themselves formed a family, also avoided the center, and immediately joined one of the residential neighborhoods. As soon as one left this geographically limited center, class distinctions faded out and residential location was neatly and almost exclusively organized around ethnicity.

HOUSEHOLD ORGANIZATION, FERTILITY, AND THE NEIGHBORHOOD

Ethnicity, then, was the primary organizing principle of Detroit's territory. In a multiethnic city, the newcomers and their children had more to gain by staying together than by dispersing throughout the city. The fact that people with similar backgrounds lived together was obviously not fortuitous, but the extent to which ethnic clustering represented cultural cohesiveness is, however, still in question. Ethnicity certainly seems to have had a profound impact on church membership. Ralph Janis recently discovered, from studying membership of 67 churches in Detroit in and around 1880, that

> Yankees [white Anglo-Protestants] almost never prayed with Germans or members of any other ethnic group, even if they shared similar or identical religious beliefs. . . . And the same held true for Germans, whether Protestant, Catholic, or Jewish, and for Irish and French Detroiters. The only exception to this universal religious ethnocentrism were a few of the city's younger churchgoers.[10]

Later in this book I will take up the question of religious affiliation in Detroit, its relationship to ethnicity, to marriage, and to the institutional life of the city. At the moment, I wish only to point out the cohesiveness of Detroit's neighborhoods, using indicators which present a good intuitive understanding of the differences in everyday life.

Ethnicity is an ascribed status; one can adapt it to circumstances, even deny it, but one cannot change it: "An Irishman is always an Irishman, a Jew always a Jew. Irishman or Jew is born; citizen, lawyer or church member is made," once wrote Horace Kallen.[11] Occupation is ascribed to a lesser degree, only inasmuch as the parents' status translates somewhat into the children's status. There is, of course, a clear shift from ascribed to achieved status in the career of many individuals, both in upward and in downward directions. In turn, the organization of one's family, demographic behavior in particular, provides good indicators of the lifestyle people wanted and/or could afford—the lifestyle which they chose rather than that into which they were simply born. In studying some of the demographic characteristics of the population in 1880 Detroit, I want to determine whether the demography of each group coincides with the geographic patterns of ethnic dominance which I have uncovered, and if clustering can in part be explained by some of the less tangible cultural attributes which influence demographic behavior. Some differences in the ethnic groups' demographic profiles simply reflected the existence of successive waves of arrival. The German and Irish communities, for example, comprised a greater number of elderly people than the Polish community: in 1880, 25% of the Irish-born immigrants and 21% of the German-born immigrants were over fifty years of age, as opposed

10. Ralph Janis, "Ethnic Mixture and the Persistence of Cultural Pluralism in the Church Communities of Detroit, 1880–1940," *Mid-America: A Historical Review* 61 (April–July 1979): 102.

11. Horace Kallen, *The Structure of Lasting Peace* (Boston: Marshall Jones Co., 1918), p. 31.

to 9.4% of the Poles. But other demographic differences, such as differences in family organization and fertility, were more profound and suggest that a variety of family patterns existed in the city.

Many dynamic and structural elements combined to contribute to the organization of the household; as a result, it is difficult to isolate with any precision the effects of ethnicity and class on household structure, which also depends on the stage of the family's life cycle. For example, bachelors, young and old, are likely to be found living alone, whereas 70% to 80% of the families in any one enumeration are likely to be nuclear. The nuclear family itself can be extended in two basic ways: a simple expansion to relatives up, across, or down the family tree (father, brother, nephew, for instance), or the formation of a second-kin nucleus, making a multiple family. Key moments in the life cycle also play a part, dictating when a family extension is most likely to be necessary: when one of the two parents of either spouse dies and the widow or widower moves into her/his child's home; when a child gets married and temporarily lives with her/his spouse in one of their parents' homes. The family unit may also be extended to unrelated members, most frequently boarders, often bachelors, and sometimes married couples. This form of extension is also likely to happen at key moments, especially when some children leave the parental home and vacant rooms can be rented to boarders.[12]

While these important differences due to stages in the life cycle operated across all ethnic and socioeconomic groups in 1880 Detroit, family and household compositions were also somewhat affected by independent ethnic and socioeconomic forces. Among immigrant groups most families were nuclear: 82% of the Irish, 86% of the Germans, 93% of the Poles. The extended family was frequent only among the native white Americans (around 21%), who were more likely than anybody else in the city to live near kin and, at one or several points in their family history, to provide a roof for relatives. Only about 11% of Irish and German families were extended; immigrants married and had children, of course, but generally few other kin members were available in Detroit for family extension (table 3.3). Family sizes also differed. Nuclear German, Irish, and Polish families were generally more numerous—up to 5 people—than American families—about 4 people. Thus, there were two extremes: on the one hand, large nuclear families of immigrants and, on the other, extended American families with a smaller primary nucleus. The Black family, however, was of a third type, with as little extension as immigrant families but an even smaller

12. Tamara K. Hareven, ed., *Transitions: The Family and the Life Course in Historical Perspective* (New York: Academic Press, 1978), pp. 1–98; Michael B. Katz, *The People of Hamilton, Canada West: Family and Class in a Mid-Nineteenth-Century City* (Cambridge, Mass.: Harvard University Press, 1975), pp. 209–308.

TABLE 3.3

Family structure for selected ethnic and occupational groups, Detroit, 1880[a]

Ethnic and occupational group	Solitary		Coresident		Nuclear[b]		Extended[c]		Multiple[d]	
	(n)	(%)	(n)	(%)	(n)	(%)	(n)	(%)	(n)	(%)
Native white American[e]	16	3.9	4	1.0	305	74.4	54	13.2	31	7.6
Black and mulatto	2	3.5	-	-	49	86.0	2	3.5	4	7.0
Canadian[f]	2	2.1	3	3.2	72	76.6	12	12.8	5	5.3
British	4	1.8	-	-	178	79.8	31	13.9	10	4.5
Irish	8	2.9	5	1.8	226	82.5	24	8.8	11	4.0
German	16	2.5	4	.6	554	86.4	49	7.6	18	2.8
Polish	-	-	-	-	56	93.3	-	-	4	6.7
High white-collar	1	1.3	1	1.3	56	70.9	14	17.7	7	8.9
Low white-colar	12	2.5	7	1.5	375	78.3	56	11.7	29	6.1
Skilled	12	1.5	8	1.0	684	85.9	68	8.5	24	3.0
Unskilled	16	2.9	5	.9	473	86.3	41	7.5	13	2.4

SOURCE: 1880 sample.

   a. Kin-related members of the household only.

   b. Married couples, or married couples with children, or single parent with children.

   c. Extension of relatives up, across and down the family tree, without forming a second nucleus.

   d. Extension leading to the formation to two or more nuclei in the same family (married parents, married children, etc.).

   e. Born in the U.S. of two U.S.-born parents.

   f. Born in Canada of two Canadian parents, born in Great Britain of two British parents, etc.

size than that of the native white Americans, with an average of only 3.7 people (table 3.4).

These variations in family structure were often further complicated by the presence of boarders and servants in the household. Eleven percent of Detroit's households had boarders in 1880, although boarding was still "a migrant rather than a foreign immigrant practice."[13] The largest group of boarders were native white Americans: in 1880, 36% of the boarders were native white Americans, 22% were Germans, 16% Irish, and 15% English, and 40% of the boarders lived in native white Americans households. Usually the boarder was of the same ethnic group as the receiving family: this happened in 75% of the cases involving native white American households, 74% and 70% of the cases involving Irish and German households. Canadian and English boarders were more dispersed among several groups. Very few Polish or Black families received boarders (tables 3.4 and 3.5). As for the servants, 12% of Detroit's households included domestic helpers in 1880. Not unexpectedly, German, Irish, and Ca-

13. John Modell and Tamara K. Hareven, "Urbanization and the Malleable Household: An Examination of Boarding and Lodging in American Families," *Journal of Marriage and the Family* 35 (August 1973): 471.

TABLE 3.4

Family and household sizes for selected ethnic and occupational groups, Detroit, 1880[a]

Ethnic and occupational group	Number in sample	Minimum	Maximum	Mean	Standard deviation
Native white American[b]					
Household size	421	1.00	15.00	4.78	2.35
Family size	421	1.00	14.00	4.02	1.90
Black and mulatto					
Household size	58	1.00	10.00	3.86	2.01
Family size	58	1.00	10.00	3.76	1.99
Canadian[c]					
Household size	97	1.00	13.00	5.50	2.50
Family size	97	1.00	13.00	5.21	2.52
British					
Household size	228	1.00	12.00	4.85	2.20
Family size	228	1.00	11.00	4.38	1.97
Irish					
Household size	281	1.00	13.00	5.23	2.47
Family	281	1.00	13.00	5.01	2.42
German					
Household size	648	1.00	16.00	5.00	2.20
Family size	648	1.00	16.00	4.86	2.15
Polish					
Household size	60	2.00	11.00	5.12	2.31
Family size	60	2.00	10.00	5.02	2.21
High white-collar					
Household size	82	2.00	15.00	6.06	2.50
Family size	82	1.00	12.00	4.84	2.06
Low white-collar					
Household size	487	1.00	13.00	5.08	2.38
Family size	487	1.00	13.00	4.50	2.14
Skilled					
Household size	811	1.00	16.00	4.92	2.26
Family size	811	1.00	16.00	4.72	2.21
Unskilled					
Household size	552	1.00	13.00	4.79	2.19
Family size	552	1.00	13.00	4.61	2.17

SOURCE: 1880 sample.

a. Family: kin-related members of the household only; household: all member of the household unit. Hotels, boardinghouses and institutions not included.

b. Born in the U.S. of two U.S.-born parents.

c. Born in Canada of two Canadian parents, born in Great Britain of two British parents, etc.

nadian girls and women furnished over half of the domestics employed, for the most part, in native white American and English households. Sixty percent of the servants were employed in households headed by a native white American and another 13% in households headed by a British immigrant (tables 3.4 and 3.5).

TABLE 3.5
Ethnicity of servants and boarders, Detroit, 1880

Ethnic group	Servants		Boarders	
	(n)	(%)	(n)	(%)
Native white American[a]	25	7.2	119	27.7
Black and mulatto	15	4.3	2	.5
Canadian[b]	35	10.1	31	7.2
Canadian American[c]	3	.9	6	1.4
British Canadian[d]	19	5.5	3	.7
Irish Canadian[e]	11	3.2	7	1.6
British	23	6.6	41	9.5
British American	5	1.4	10	2.3
Irish	51	14.7	36	8.4
Irish American	15	4.3	21	4.9
German	44	12.7	43	10.0
German American	44	12.7	18	4.2
Polish	2	.6	2	.5
Swiss	-	-	1	.2
French	2	.6	5	1.2
Belgian, Dutch, and Luxembourger	3	.9	1	.2
Austro-Hungarian	1	.3	-	-
Other	49	14.1	85	19.8
Total	347	100.0	430	100.0

SOURCE: 1880 sample.
  a. Born in the U.S of two U.S.-born parents.
  b. Born in Canada of two Canadian parents, born in Great Britain of two British parents, etc.
  c. Born in the U.S. of two Canadian parents, born in the U.S. of two British parents, etc.
  d. Born in Canada of two British parents.
  e. Born in Canada of two Irish parents.

Ethnicity aside, the proportion of extended families was directly proportional to social status, from 27% of the families headed by high white-collar workers being extended to only 10% among the unskilled workers (table 3.3).

These differences in household organization reflect a complex interplay of ethnicity, social status, and age, all interwoven realities in the social structure. The form which a household takes is naturally flexible, however, adaptable to changing circumstances and not necessarily reflecting any pervasive cultural values which would permanently mark a particular ethnic group with a particular household composition. In fact, each ethnic neighborhood exhibited a great variety of household arrangements within the broad tendencies which I have uncovered, and household organization, finally, remains too susceptible to too many different influences to reflect cultural and behavioral differences among groups with much precision. This is not the case, however, with fertility: in my study of marital fertility, the ambiguous relationship between ethnicity, class, and life cycle cleared up, and ethnicity stood out again as the key factor in explaining fertility differentials. Not only were the differences in fertility rates much more dramatic among ethnic groups than they were among occupational groups, but also the map of fertility differentials almost duplicates that of the ethnic concentrations in 1880 Detroit.

Fertility, better than any other variable currently available, reveals important sociocultural differences among ethnic groups and areas of the city, because men and women control it *together*. Fertility is in part a function of the mortality level—how many children are expected to survive birth, hence how many are needed to achieve a certain family size; it is also a function of the relative cost of children weighed against their usefulness in the context of the family economy. Fertility is also related to the status of women and their role in the work force; and fertility is further influenced by religion and by moral codes regarding the secular, rational attitude toward birth control. There is no simple explanation of the determinants of fertility. Demographers who have studied the long-term fertility decline from the late eighteenth century to the present warn us that there is no "universally valid model or generalized description" of the determinants of fertility.[14] But fertility reflects the complex sets of attitudes of the parent couple and its general outlook on life: whether birth control is an acceptable practice, whether many children are needed to assure the family's survival, whether one can better educate fewer children, for some examples. Fertility also reflects conditions partially or wholly outside the control of individuals at any particular time, especially the educational level and more generally what sociologists like to call the opportunity structure. A fertility rate thus combines many otherwise immeasurable factors. In itself, it may be a fairly abstract quantity, but the differences among groups' fertility rates indicate significant sociocultural distances.

Constructing a fertility index from the 1880 census is a fairly straightforward matter, as several historical demographers have already shown.[15] The child to woman ratio measuring the number of children under 5 years of age per thousand married women is a good estimator of marital fertility. I limited the in-

14. Ansley J. Coale, "The Decline of Fertility in Europe from the French Revolution to World War II," in *Fertility and Family Planning*, ed. S. J. Behrman, Leslie Corsa, Jr., and Ronald Freeman (Ann Arbor: University of Michigan Press, 1969), pp. 4, 18; see also Evelyn M. Kitagawa and Philip M. Hauser, "Trends in Differential Fertility and Mortality in a Metropolis—Chicago," in Ernest W. Burgess and Donald J. Bogue, eds., *Urban Sociology* (Chicago: University of Chicago Press, 1964), p. 32.

15. Tamara K. Hareven and Maris A. Vinovskis, "Marital Fertility, Ethnicity, and Occupation in Urban Families: An Analysis of South Boston and the South End in 1880," *Journal of Social History* 8 (March 1975): 69–93; Maris A. Vinovskis, *Demographic History and the World Population Crisis* (Worcester, Mass.: Clark University Press, 1976), pp. 44–50.

vestigation here to marital fertility (as opposed to overall fertility) to keep a tighter control over the results. The index is standardized to account for the variation in age of women from one group to another, and both standardized and unstandardized values are presented in the tables and graphs.

The differences between the different groups of Detroiters were striking. Native white American women and British women had the lowest rates of fertility, around 500 children under 5 years of age per thousand married women aged 20–49. In contrast, Irish, German, and Polish women had a record high fertility—from 900 to 1,100. Canadian women scored somewhere in between, perhaps due to the lack of distinction between French and English Canadians in the 1880 United States census (see table 3.6). The variation for women reclassified by occupational status of their husbands is also clear, but not so dramatic as that among ethnic groups. The minimum and the maximum ratios are closer to one another, from 530 for the wives of high white-collar workers to 846 for the wives of unskilled workers. The fertility rate of the women was thus inversely proportional to the occupational status of their husbands.

The ratios by age groups show additional striking differences (fig. 3.1). Of course Irish, German, and Polish women in each age group had more children, but, more importantly, they bore children even past their thirty-fifth birthday. For them, the childbearing period extended through 40 years of age, but for the

TABLE 3.6
Marital fertility for selected ethnic and occupational groups, Detroit, 1880

Ethnic and occupational groups[a]	Number of families	Child-woman ratio standardized for age distribution[b]
Native white American[c]	391	470.12
Canadian[d]	78	764.94
British	115	536.28
Irish	171	934.19
German	407	944.68
Polish	48	1,058
High white-collar	76	530.83
Low white-collar	451	598.05
Skilled	709	794.01
Unskilled	442	846.78

SOURCE: 1880 sample.
   a. Ethnicity of the mother, occupation of the father.
   b. Number of children under the age of 5 per 1,000 married women aged 20–49.
   c. Born in the U.S. of two U.S.-born parents.
   d. Born in Canada of two Canadian parents, born in Great Britain of two British parents, etc.

FIG. 3.1

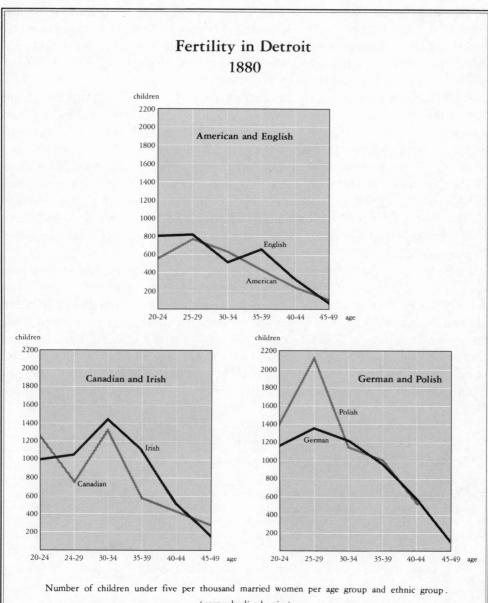

Fertility in Detroit
1880

Number of children under five per thousand married women per age group and ethnic group.
(unstandardized ratios)

native white American women, the childbearing period clearly stopped earlier.
Here is a fundamental difference in demographic behavior between native white
Americans and the three major immigrant groups in Detroit. Such clear distinction did not appear, however, among occupational categories: generally the
childbearing period extended through 40 years of age, for all four occupational
categories, with only the wives of high white-collar workers tending to have
all their children before age 30.

While we see a clear-cut rise in fertility from Americans to Poles and from
high white-collar to unskilled workers, the index computed for the combined
socioethnic categories cannot be interpreted so neatly, showing that socioeconomic status was secondary to ethnicity in explaining the differentials. Native
white American women tended to be fertile at a uniformly low level, regardless
of the occupational status of their husbands. The British women had a low
fertility in the aggregate, but more children in the families of skilled and unskilled workers. The Irish, German, and Polish women, in turn, had uniformly
high fertility rates with little clear variations among occupational categories
(see table 3.7).

Considering these differences among groups, it is quite normal to find that
such sharp differences in fertility were also printed onto the city's space. Map
3.1 represents the fertility ratio in each cluster of the sample in one of three
classes: up to 400 children under age 5 per thousand married women aged
20–49, from 401 to 800, and above 800. Not surprisingly, the fertility map
reproduces almost exactly the map of ethnic groups. The superimposition is,
of course, not perfect, largely because of the medium fertility rate of Canadian
women, which blurs the picture a little. The fertility ratio was very low in the

TABLE 3.7
Marital fertility for selected socioethnic groups, Detroit, 1880

Ethnic group	High white-collar		Low white-collar		Skilled		Unskilled	
	n	ratio[a]	n	ratio	n	ratio	n	ratio
Native white American[b]	43	505.29	155	416.86	100	541.18	64	393.29
Canadian[c]	1	0	9	1,266.70	34	746.89	27	591.67
British	4	70.00	31	294.67	53	699.86	21	747.17
Irish	1	440.00	30	949.94	58	825.07	71	988.01
German	5	0	48	756.24	204	957.34	128	1,009.90
Polish	1	0	18	897.08	5	635.00	24	1,067.30

SOURCE: 1880 sample.

a. Child-woman ratio standardized for age distribution: number of children under the age of 5 per 1,000
women aged 20–49.

b. Born in the U.S. of two U.S.-born parents.

c. Born in Canada of two Canadian parents, born in Great Britian of two British parents, etc.

MAP 3.1

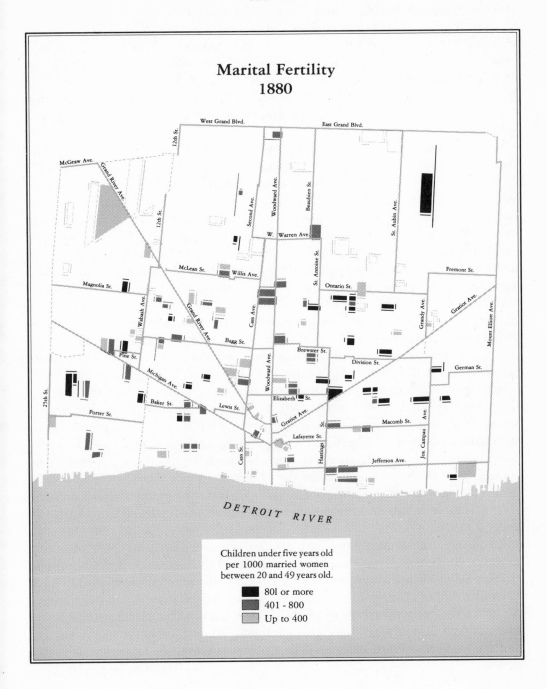

**Marital Fertility
1880**

West Grand Blvd. East Grand Blvd.

McGraw Ave.

Grand River Ave.

12th St.

12th St.

Woodward Ave.

Second Ave.

Beaubien St.

St. Aubin Ave.

W. Warren Ave.

McLean St. Willis Ave.

St. Antoine St.

Fremont St.

Magnolia St.

Wabash Ave.

Grand River Ave.

Cass Ave.

Ontario St.

Grandy Ave.

Gratiot Ave.

Mount Elliott Ave.

Bagg St.

Brewster St.

Woodward Ave.

Division St.

German St.

Pine St.

Michigan Ave.

25th St.

Baker St.

Lewis St.

Elizabeth St.

Gratiot Ave.

Macomb St.

Jos. Campau Ave.

Porter St.

Cass St.

Lafayette St.

Hastings St.

Jefferson Ave.

DETROIT RIVER

Children under five years old
per 1000 married women
between 20 and 49 years old.

■ 801 or more
■ 401 - 800
□ Up to 400

very center of the city as well as in the periphery, but once more the Irish neighborhood on the west and the German and Polish east side stand out sharply. The fertility of the Polish neighborhood was soon to become legendary; a journalist interviewing a Polish doctor in 1896 reported: "When Dr. Kwieciński who had spent his life in the Polish quarter was asked why it was that the Polish people had such very large families, he shook his head as though there had been suggested to him a profound and inexplicable problem."[16] Contrasting with these zones of high fertility, the American residential upper center showed a low to medium rate of fertility.

The profound demographic differences between native white Americans and most immigrant groups confirm our analysis of Detroit as an ethnically divided city. On the one hand, there was an Anglo-Saxon city, with a low fertility rate, with families often headed by white-collar workers, often extended by boarders, and often employing servants. On the other hand, there was a fertile German and Celtic city, of large primarily working-class but also middle-class families.

Fertility, then, is a solid indicator of deep differences between the groups and areas of Detroit. But what happened when members of an ethnic group parted from the neighborhood of their fellow countrymen? What happened when they settled elsewhere? The sample design allows me to explore a very subtle form of dominance and dispersion within the different ethnic groups, by distinguishing between the members of an ethnic group who were spatially concentrated and those who were dispersed. When such a distinction is made, it becomes possible to test the theory that residential integration is a sign of assimilation. The extent to which the spatially concentrated members of an ethnic group differ from those scattered throughout the city is a question of cardinal importance: Is the sense of community best expressed within a spatial context? Does it survive without one? The shift from spatial to nonspatial bonds is a complex one, and an ambiguous relationship exists between the members of a group who remain close to the core culture of the group and those who do not. Does the geographic process of concentration and dispersion correspond to a sociocultural shift of ethnic bonds to occupational bonds and to a concomitant change in general attitudes?

To answer these questions, perhaps too schematically, members of ethnic groups could live in one of three types of areas in 1880 Detroit: in a neighborhood dominated by their own group, in an area where the population seemed to have been distributed at random, or in a neighborhood dominated by another group. Many factors played a role in choosing a residential location; ethnicity and occupational status were only two of them. Among other factors were the shifting locations of industries and other places of work, the expansion of urban

16. *Detroit Sunday News-Tribune*, 6 September 1896.

services, the availability of vacant land for building new neighborhoods, and the quality and price of the available housing. Considering the interaction among such factors and the continuous flow of people in and out of the city, it is quite normal to expect to find a significant proportion of members of an ethnic group residentially dispersed and an equally significant proportion residentially clustered on the basis of ethnic origin. What difference did it then make to settle in a mixed or a clustered area? Only the Germans were numerous enough in 1880 Detroit to be well represented among all three types of areas in the sample—in German clusters, of course, but also in "random" clusters and in clusters dominated by other groups. Indeed, if we compare the fertility ratios for German women living in the three types of areas—in German-dominated clusters, in random clusters, and in native white American-dominated clusters—only in the third case do we notice a clear change in behavior. In German-dominated clusters, the (age-standardized) fertility index of German women was 942: it was just about the same, 980, in clusters where no apparent patterns of concentrations existed. But it fell to 411 for the German women living in clusters dominated by native white Americans, slightly below the fertility of the American women, 490, in their own clusters.

Dispersion alone evidently did not play a role in reducing intergroup differences. If assimilation existed, it was not in an undefined middle ground. In contrast, clear differences existed for those few families who left their neighborhood of origin and penetrated a stranger's environment. Ethnic neighborhoods exemplified the characteristics of the group as a whole, but residential mixture was by no means a sure indication that the assimilation process had started. Only in the third case, with people holding minority status in an area dominated by a different group, is there a reason to expect a clear rupture between them and their fellow immigrants. In some instances, like the Poles in the German neighborhood, the first settlers of a group were simply using another group's neighborhood as a port of entry. In an opposite instance, the few Germans who had settled in native white areas were probably breaking away from their fellow countrymen. Their fertility decline did not simply reflect a rise in socioeconomic status, which they could also have experienced in their own neighborhood, then, but a more complete assimilation into the mores of the other half.

One could have thought that the shock of the migration and the Atlantic adventure would have levelled the differences, that the divisions were mainly temporary cleavages of identity, not necessarily reflective of deep behavioral distinctions. The different groups could have separately, silently, adopted the same overall demographic practices. In fact, the attitudes toward life remained fundamentally different, and these differences were translated into the city's space.

4

The Urban Quilt:
Unequal Autonomy

Plate 4. The neighborhood store: T. Harms, hardware and
tinware, at the southwest corner of Fort West and Springwells
Avenue since 1887, with family and clerk boarding at location.
Courtesy of the Detroit Historical Museum.

Two sets of competing forces divided Detroit's society on the eve of the city's large-scale industrialization. At one level, the ability of ethnic communities to retain their successful members (small manufacturers, small entrepreneurs, shopkeepers, and even white-collar workers and professionals), combined with the communities' sociocultural homogeneity, fostered the maintenance of many semiautonomous enclaves in the city. But at another level, the unequal distribution of wealth and status was reflected in Detroit's geography and accounted for the occupations typical of the majority of neighborhoods' residents. In other words, the degree of socioeconomic mix that existed even in recent immigrant areas must not obscure the basic lines of inequality that divided the city. The remarkable cohesiveness of ethnic communities suggests, however, that the forces behind their autonomy effectively compensated them for the persistent social inequality they faced outside their own neighborhoods. Just about every Detroiter had his roots in one visible ethnic community, as demonstrated by the brief analysis of the neighborhoods' sociocultural homogeneity which concludes our first survey of Detroit.

One can visualize the grid of Detroit in 1880 as a quilt with a few primary colors and many secondary shades. The areas of primary colors were inhabited by people who were similar enough across a series of variables to give an area a distinct tone: a typical "German" neighborhood of the nineteenth century, in which many heads of households were craftsmen living in homes inhabited by a single family with a large number of young children, would be an example of a "primary color." Another example would be a typical "low white-collar" neighborhood, inhabited primarily by native white Americans, with medium-sized families, and with households often extended by the presence of one or several servants and/or boarders. Each of the primary-color areas of the urban quilt would reflect a crystallization of socioeconomic, ethnic, and demographic characteristics. In other areas of the city, the various shades would be less distinct. For example, a small area might be characteristic of an age group but would not reflect any strong social and/or ethnic clustering. Other areas might be integrated. Which areas of the city qualified for the primary colors of the quilt in 1880 Detroit, and which for the many intermediate shades? An answer to this question tells us how and to what degree spatial clusters reflected social divisions and, in turn, reflects the importance of these divisions in the late nineteenth-century urban environment.

Until now, we looked at sets of variables independent of each other to discover the existence of geographic cleavages and their correspondence to social divisions. We divided the city into land use zones, into areas of ethnic concentration and of occupational concentration; we also defined several demographic regions. Some of the complexity of the urban fabric began to make sense. Some of the interconnected networks and combinations of characteristics began to appear but, to the amateur puzzle solver, the ways in which these different zones fit together remains a most intriguing question. It is time to conclude this socio-spatial survey of Detroit in 1880 by pulling the variables together in a multi-variate analysis. I began this analysis by first determining if people who lived in geographic proximity shared none, only one, or perhaps several common characteristics, and whether or not the confluence of these characteristics created distinct urban areas. I proceeded to examine land-use, socioethnic, and de-mographic variables together rather than independently, in order to see whether homogeneous clusters existed in the urban environment of the late nineteenth century. In other words, where were the primary colors of the urban quilt of Detroit in 1880?

A MULTIDIMENSIONAL SCALE

In designing this composite analysis, I selected the most telling factors from each of my previous, independent analyses. I chose two land-use variables: the diversity of nonresidential activities and the amount of vacant space per sampled unit. These variables, which I used in chapter 1, permit me to locate each sample unit in the texture of the late nineteenth-century city and to indicate with some accuracy whether the land use of an area was of the central type, a peripheral type, or a mixed type found very often in residential areas. I sought particularly the diversity of activities in an area rather than the numerical concentration of activities, since the chief characteristic of the "central" type was the accumulation and juxtaposition on block fronts of many land uses. The second land-use variable, vacant land, points to an opposite pattern: peripheral location rather than centrality. A sample unit of six fronts with several fronts having vacant lots was likely to be located in the low-density areas of the periphery, with few inhabitants and few activities. Family residences were to be found elsewhere, in units that rate low and medium on the two land-use variables that I selected.

Two other variables, the standardized chi-squared indexes computed for each cluster in chapter 2, enabled me to capture residential clustering on the basis of ethnicity and occupational status. Since ethnic origin and occupational status are structural variables which only suggest behavioral differences, I also looked at fertility for a more direct reflection of fundamental behavioral differences between groups in the society, as explained in chapter 3.

A cluster analysis was used to group similar units on different branches of a hierarchical tree (see Appendix 5 for a technical discussion of hierarchical clustering techniques and the formula for the computation of the euclidean distance). Each sampled unit received a value for each of the 5 variables included in the analysis, ranging as follows: (1) from 0 to 10 different types of nonresidential activities; (2) from 0 to 6 fronts with vacant lots; (3) an index value per unit for ethnic clustering; (4) an index value for occupational clustering; (5) from 0 to 1,875 children under 5 per thousand women aged 20–49. The range of these variables was then reduced by categorizing them into two or three classes, two for ethnic and occupational clustering (with or without), and three classes (low, medium, high) for the other three variables—nonresidential activities, vacancy, and fertility. The variables were then weighted to balance land-use pattern, socioethnic clustering, and demographic behavior equally (see table 4.1).

The units were then classified according to their similarity across the five variables; that is, I computed the euclidean distance of each unit (which would be zero if the units were strictly similar on the multidimensional scale). For example, all units ranging high in the number of nonresidential activities, low in the amount of vacant land, positive on ethnic and occupational clustering, and, say, low on the fertility measure would be clustered together because they were similar. To interpret the results, I examined the characteristics of the groups of units that were rated positive on the ethnic and/or occupational concentration variables. I completed my information by looking at the dominant ethnic and occupational status group (or the two dominant groups if none counted more than 60% of the families) in each unit.

SIX TYPES OF NEIGHBORHOODS

The clustering analysis enables me to classify the sampled units into six groups that I can define geographically (see map 4.1):

TABLE 4.1
Variables in cluster analysis, Detroit, 1880

Ethnic concentration	Occupational concentration	Diversity of nonresidential activities		Number of fronts with vacant land		Fertility	
no	no	0		0		0–400	
yes[a]	yes	1–4		1–3		401–800	
-	-	5–10		4–6		800	
0	0	0	0	0	0	0	0
1	1	1	0	1	0	1	0
-	-	1	1	1	1	1	1
2[b]	2	1	1	1	1	2	2

SOURCE: 1880 sample.
  a. Cluster with significant index of concentration (see chap. 2 and Appendix 4).
  b. Weight.

MAP 4.1

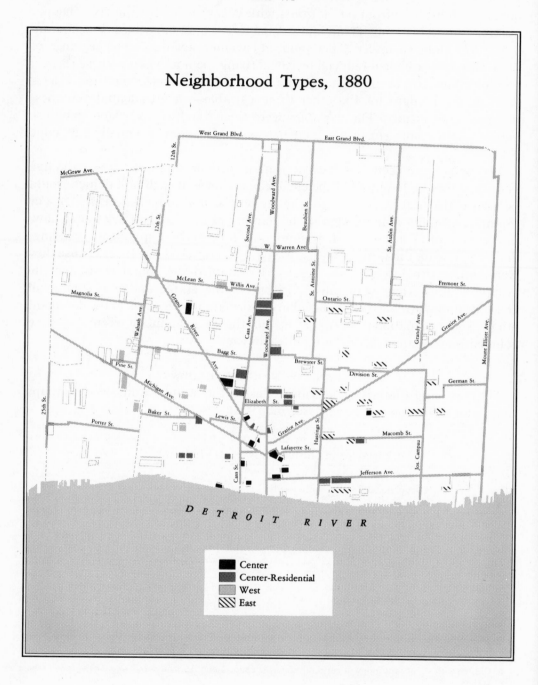

Neighborhood Types, 1880

First, the central type, comprising 1,579 or 13% of the sampled inhabitants in thirteen clusters, was characterized by many types of nonresidential activities (with a mean of 5.7 types of activities per cluster). There was little vacant land (only 20% of one front per unit of six fronts with vacant land, on the average); no ethnic concentration; and only five of the thirteen units had a concentration of white-collar workers. Low fertility was also typical of the central type (with a mean of 315 children under 5 years of age per thousand married women per cluster).

The second type, the residential center, comprised 2,647 or 21.7% of the sampled inhabitants, distributed over nineteen clusters around the center, mostly north of the center but also near the river. The residential center rated low or medium in activities (mean of 2.7 types of nonresidential activities per cluster). The clusters usually had some vacant land (mean of 1.3 fronts per unit with vacant land). The residential center was characterized by the concentration of native white American and British households (showing only eight units without ethnic clustering), and by the concentration of both high white-collar and low white-collar workers (showing only two units without such clustering). Fertility was either low or medium (mean of 514 children under 5 years of age per thousand married women).

The east side type made up a third distinct grouping in the multidimensional analysis, including 3,793 or 31% of the sampled inhabitants in eighteen units. These clusters rated either low or medium in the number of activities with a mean of 1.9 types of activities. There was some land available in each cluster (1.8 fronts with some vacant land). The east side was, of course, populated mainly by Germans, by Poles in the upper area, and by many skilled and unskilled workers; it was a region of high fertility (mean of 953 children under 5 years of age per thousand married women).

The west side type, the fourth grouping on the multidimensional scale, comprised 1,404 or 11.5% of the sampled inhabitants of Detroit in eight clusters. It had many of the characteristics of the east side in diversity of nonresidential activities (a medium average rate of 1.25 per cluster), in vacancy (one front with vacant land on the average), in fertility (a child to woman ratio of 854 per thousand), and in concentration of skilled and unskilled workers, but it merits a distinct fourth type because of its strong Irish character.

The background or peripheral type, the fifth group, comprised 2,754 or 22.6% of the sampled inhabitants spread over forty-four units or a third of those sampled. There were few nonresidential activities, only one type of activity per cluster on the average. Vacant land, however, was abundant (3.04 fronts per unit). There was neither ethnic concentration nor occupational concentration, and fertility was medium with a mean of 567 children under 5 per thousand married women).

The vacant clusters made up the sixth or last category, twenty-five clusters of the sample altogether.

This cluster analysis clarifies a number of points about 1880 Detroit. First, far from being spatially integrated, this medium-sized midwestern city was unequivocally divided. Seventy-seven percent of the population lived in one of the four primary colors, the four types that were represented either in the center, the upper center, or sections of the east and west sides of the city. These areas make up less than half the sampled units, but include more than two-thirds of their population in 1880 Detroit. The forty-four units in the background or peripheral category, 34% of the sampled units, accounted for only 23% of the population.

Second, different group characteristics were reflected in these different areas. All the aggregate characteristics of Germans, Poles, and Irish were reproduced at the neighborhood level. They tended to crystallize in each unit, showing a high degree of geographic cohesiveness. The native white Americans also appeared to have a high degree of cohesiveness in the near center. Canadians and English were more dispersed, and their aggregate characteristics less consolidated in the microenvironment. The distance between the three main immigrant groups—Irish, Germans, and Poles—and the native white Americans was significant. Canadians, coming into Detroit from the nearby country across the river, and the British, essentially low white-collar workers, were more easily integrated into the various parts of the city.

These territorial types showed distinct differences in land uses, ethnic and occupational structures, and fertility patterns. The two areas that showed remarkably little socioethnic concentration, the dense city center and the relatively vacant periphery, were both demographically incomplete areas. Beyond the relative simplicity of the land use and the statistical uniformity of single family housing, a complex system of networks existed. With its large supply of available land within the city, Detroit in 1880 was an underused city, with no unusual crowding. But this did not prevent it from being highly differentiated and unequal. Detroit was also a heterogeneous city, stratified at a variety of overlapping levels. Often the various strata combined and reinforced each other, making differences even more visible in the city. Such a combination of characteristics, combining ethnic background, socioeconomic status, and the organization of the family, transformed this simple semiempty midwestern city into the maze of small neighborhoods which we have begun to uncover. The primary colors of the quilt represented pervasive ethnic and class differentials, which were confirmed by demographic differences; in turn, the many shades reflected the constant permeability, the easing of divisions, and the leveling of differences. The multidimensional analysis of small areas shows how cohesive neighborhoods actually were and how characteristic of the divisions that existed in American society.

CITY, ETHNICITY, AND CLASS

Several theoretically relevant comments are in order at the end of this preliminary survey of Detroit in 1880. The concept of ethnicity has been most often reduced to two strong images, well rooted in American consciousness: the ghetto, symbol of segregation, fixity, and poverty; or upward social mobility, symbol of movement and progress. These two contradictory images are in fact complementary if one reduces the problem of assimilation to a mechanistic cycle, detailing the slow movement from minority to majority, the parting from one's group for the individual fusion into the whole.

My analyses of Detroit in 1880 do not support such an artificially satisfying model of linear progression from minority to majority, however. The ethnic neighborhoods did not represent temporary living arrangements, but deep divisions in the social and cultural fabric of the city. Housing was organized around the major ethnic groups, and the smaller groups inserted themselves within the dominance patterns of the larger groups. The organization of the city seemed to reflect stability of associations, not transition. I believe that it is from the diversity of these subcultures that modern industrial urban America was born, not from their integration into an undifferentiated whole. Detroit was a genuinely multiethnic city with little crossover from one group to the next. The task before us is to move beyond the cross-sectional study of the city's social geography at only one point in time, to study processes and change, to widen the inquiry into the city-building process and the whole range of forces that influence social history. This will allow me not only to describe what it was like to live in the various areas of Detroit, but also to explain what caused the pattern of unequal autonomy that I have identified and its consequences for such important matters as Detroit's political life, work organization, and institutional networks. The most important and intriguing task, however, is to find out whether and how large-scale societal changes such as industrialization, urbanization, and migration either reinforced existing cleavages or diluted them to impose new ones of a different nature. I will try to grasp and explain social changes in Detroit from 1880 to 1900 in three ways: by studying the formation of neighborhoods in relation to the city-building process and industrialization; by analyzing in detail the demographic structure of ethnoreligious groups; and by turning to a reevaluation of Detroit's social structure at the turn of the century.

City, ethnicity, and class are the three key words of my analysis. I observed ethnic and social groups not in the abstract but in the bounded territory of their living environment, because the building of a city and the relationship between the host society and the newcomers are not independent ventures. It is on the same territory, itself transformed, that people settle, produce and exchange goods and services, face each other and integrate one group rather than another. In this first picture of Detroit, I have tried to capture the whole community and identify social cleavages. I can now study the ways in which such cleavages evolved and eventually changed in the growing industrial metropolis.

2

The City-Building Process and the Neighborhood

5

Urban Growth and the Unequal Distribution of Services

Plate 5. Woodward Avenue, looking north from Jefferson Avenue, c. 1900.
Courtesy of the Archives of Labor and Urban Affairs, Wayne State University.

Detroit in the late nineteenth century followed the lead of other rapidly growing manufacturing centers of the new industrial belt—especially Cleveland, Buffalo, and Pittsburgh—and completed its transformation from a modest industrial center to an industrial metropolis. The new Detroit redistributed its expanding activities and growing population over a widening territory, and in the process the three interdependent elements of the ecological complex— territory, activities, and population—were all transformed.[1] It took many organizations and thousands of actors to shape the expanding city. Growing industries changed their locations in the urban territory, drawing with them thousands of workers. Utility companies, street-railway companies, and realtors also had a tremendous interest in growth; they were, in fact, in the growth business. The city government likewise began to take an active role in regulating growth. And, of course, the people of Detroit, divided into ethnoreligious groups and social classes, had some say in deciding where to live in the metropolis.

But how much of a say did people really have when special interest groups and the city government sought to build a unified metropolis? Could ethnic autonomy withstand growth that was controlled, coordinated, and ordered from industries, from real estate offices, from street-railway companies, and from city hall? To begin answering this question, I will first describe the broad directions of change in late nineteenth-century Detroit; I will then concentrate on the ways in which the metropolis was equipped, especially on the unequal distribution of important city services (water, sewers, pavement, transportation) among the different groups of urbanites, before studying (in the next chapter) the role of ethnic communities in the city-building process. The question of who benefitted from improved services is not a simple one, and it must be answered in the context of the problems faced by the various parties who had a stake in the growth business.

A NEW SAMPLE

In studying Detroit in 1880, I had cast a net of 127 clusters over the city, and I combined sociodemographic and land-use data from the federal census manuscript of 1880 and the Robinson-Pidgeon atlas of 1885. To study the growth of Detroit from modest city to metropolis, I have replicated the 1880 sample for the year 1900, and enlarged it to include additional sample clusters in areas that first became a part of the city between 1880 and 1900. The new sample comprises 178 clusters across Detroit's territory (map 5.1). Many large vacant blocks of the 1880 sample, most of them on the periphery of the city, were subdivided into smaller blocks by 1900. Because the replication of the 1880 sample for 1900 gave a good coverage of the empty fringe areas of the 1880

1. Charles Tilly, *An Urban World* (Boston: Little, Brown, 1974), pp. 18–20.

MAP 5.1

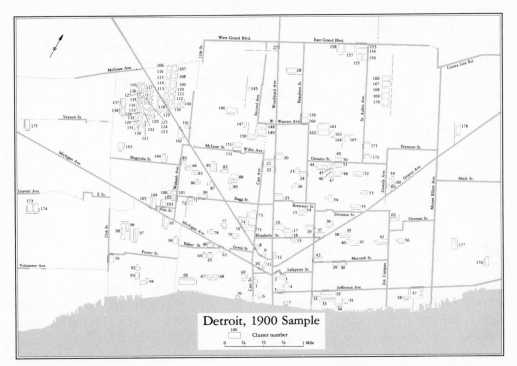

Detroit, 1900 Sample

city, it was not necessary to sample intensely in the areas newly annexed in 1900. Only five new clusters were selected as test cases outside the 1880 city limits.

Replicating the 1880 sample for 1900 offers the great advantage of showing how established areas of the city had changed during this period of great transformation of the urban fabric. One recalls that the 1880 sample was designed to study the city in its entirety as well as in the diversity of the microenvironment, with the sampled units adding to a description of the city as a whole. The same holds true for the 1900 sample, with an appropriate weighting scheme to balance the sampled units since, due to the replication, some parts of the city are better represented than others (see Appendix 1). The information on the city in 1900 comes from two major sources of sociodemographic and land use information, similar to those used for 1880: the manuscript of the federal census for 1900, and the Sanborn-Perris real estate atlases of 1897.[2] In the 178 sampled clusters

2. For an introduction to the manuscript of the United States Census for 1900, see U.S., Department of the Interior, Census Office, *Instructions to Enumerators: Twelfth Census of the United States* (Washington, D.C.: G.P.O., 1900); Sanborn Map Company, *Insurance Maps of Detroit, Michigan*, 6 vols. (New York: Sanborn-Perris Map Co., 1897).

lived 26,181 people, and I recorded their census characteristics as well as the characteristics of 8,132 houses and buildings standing in those clusters. In addition to these two large data sets, I consulted other sources of information when necessary. For instance, knowing the religion of the sampled people was fundamental to understanding the ethnic divisions of the city, but, unfortunately for the historian, religion was not recorded by the federal census; to obtain this information, then, I studied the marriage licenses of Wayne County to discover the religious affiliation of one subset of families from the 1900 sample.[3] I also used numerous maps and the records of several city departments to study the distribution of street railways and services throughout the city, especially water, sewers, and pavement in the 1890s.[4] Thus, the two primary samples of 1880 and 1900 permitted me to cover the entire sociophysical fabric of the city at two points in time, with additional sources used to study the growth and distribution of services in between these dates.

DIRECTIONS OF CHANGE: TERRITORY, ACTIVITIES, AND
POPULATION

In the late nineteenth century urban growth included the annexation of new territory, and what would typically be called "suburbanization" still took place within the city limits.[5] Because Detroit kept expanding its jurisdiction over the surrounding communities, it absorbed all population growth without a competitor. Outlying areas were constantly integrated into the city as they became populated, so independent suburbs did not develop to compete for a share of the expanding population. In 1900, surrounding communities maintained 33,963 people around a city of 285,704. All were rural townships except the industrial satellite of Wyandotte, a town of 5,183, which comprised a large share of the peripheral inhabitants. The townships of Springwells (Delray Village), Ecorse (River Rouge Village), Greenfield (Highland Park), Hamtramck, and Grosse Pointe were not yet suburbs in the modern sense. Hamtramck, for example, became an incorporated village within Wayne County only in 1901 and did not attain the status of city before 1922.[6]

3. The marriage licenses are available in the city-county building in Detroit. The 1900 census gives the number of years each couple has been married. It is therefore relatively simple to develop a strategy to find the marriage licenses which are kept by years. Starting with the year 1900, I ended the search at 1887. For this thirteen-year span, I found that half of the couples married in the U.S. and living in Detroit in 1900 had been married in Wayne County.

4. Detroit, *Annual Report of the Board of Public Works of the City of Detroit*, reports 18–26 (Detroit, 1892–1900); Detroit, *Annual Report of the Board of Water Commissioners of the City of Detroit*, reports 40–48 (Detroit: Detroit Free Press Printing Co., 1892–1900).

5. This process has been described by Sam Bass Warner, Jr., *Streetcar Suburbs* (Cambridge, Mass.: Harvard University Press, 1962).

6. U.S., Department of the Interior, Census Office, *Twelfth Census of the United States, 1900: Population* (Washington, D.C.: G.P.O., 1901), 1:214.

Construction within the city of Detroit paralleled the national building boom of the 1880s and early 1890s. But despite the depression of 1893, building activity remained substantial in the 1890s. According to the official statistics, the number of housing units added to the city between 1880 and 1900 increased city dwellings by 154%. Twenty-four hundred new dwellings were built in 1892; 1,900 in 1893, 1,200 in 1894, and construction remained at 1,200 new dwellings per year for the rest of the 1890s.[7] In short, the building industry suffered somewhat from the depression, but continued healthy through the decade along with those other industries, such as street railways and utilities, directly linked to urban growth.

As we have seen, half of Detroit's area was still vacant and unequipped in 1880, and the city was built only to about 1.5 miles from city hall. By 1900, however, massive immigration had swelled the city's population by 146%, and, despite large annexations of new territory in 1885 and 1891, the area of the city had grown by only 76%. The area between 1.5 and 2 miles from city hall was built up in the early 1880s, the next half-mile circle in the late 1880s, and the construction beyond 2.5 miles from the center mostly in the 1890s. New buildings filled the vacant lots. On a block where 40 people had dwelt twenty years earlier, 80 lived in 1900. Large empty blocks were divided and built up, especially along Grand Boulevard. The regions of low use had been pushed nearly one mile further from the city center (see map 5.2). In 1900 there were virtually no empty zones as the city experienced the unprecedented phenomenon of filling up the empty spots, incorporating the empty zones into the zones of residences, which now extended to the city limits.

Thus, by 1900, the three distinct zones of Detroit, that is, center, zone of residences, and vacant periphery, had been reduced to two, with the vacant periphery no longer vacant. Because of this increase in residential areas, the city center became even more exclusively nonresidential than it had been in 1880: 62% of the center-city buildings were now exclusively nonresidential and another 14.3% had mixed residential and nonresidential uses, leaving only 23.6% of the buildings for residences. Since 1880, the center had experienced a decline of 54% in the number of its residential structures while, of course, gaining a very large number of new nonresidential buildings.

With the expansion and diversification of the metropolis, a number of activities were relocated outside the center. This deconcentration of activities involved a movement from the center along previously existing axes, a diversification

7. Detroit, *Twenty-Sixth Annual Report of the Fire Commission* (Detroit: Detroit Free Press Printing Co., 1893), p. 70; Detroit, *Twenty-Seventh Annual Report of the Fire Commission* (Detroit: James Martin, 1895), p. 76; Detroit, *Twenty-Eighth Annual Report of the Fire Commission* (Detroit: James Martin, 1896), p. 71; Detroit, *Thirty-Third Annual Report of the Fire Commission* (Detroit: Geo. W. Mattie, 1900), p. 9.

MAP 5.2

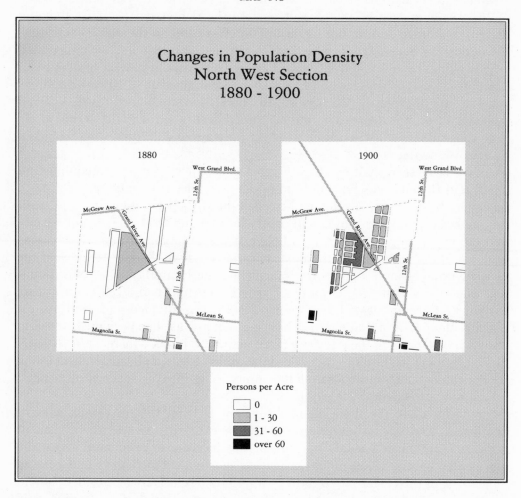

Changes in Population Density
North West Section
1880 - 1900

of some of the newly built neighborhoods, and a redefinition of the relationship between work and residence. As Hans Blumenfeld describes it,

> the competition for space, both within the center and on the transportation facilities, leads to a displacement from the center of all those uses which require relatively much space and can also function elsewhere. There are primarily those dealing with goods, manufacturing and warehouses, but also retail stores, consumer services and residences.[8]

8. H. Blumenfeld, "The Urban Pattern," *Annals of the American Academy of Political and Social Science* 352 (March 1964): 74–83.

This process was well under way in Detroit at the turn of the century. Following the trend of expansion and diversification, hotels and boardinghouses leap-frogged outside the city center into the near residential zone. By 1900 craft shops had been numerous on the east side of Detroit for some time, and they remained there, outside the city center. Many retail stores were also built in the newly developed neighborhoods, together with churches, schools, bars and saloons to cater to the needs of a large city which could no longer rely exclusively on the center.

As the city expanded, the industrial landscape changed considerably. In 1880, there had been few large employers in metal-related work. Foundry and machine shop products had appeared in seventh position in the manufacturing census in order of number of workers employed, but by 1900 they became the single largest employers. The pharmaceutical industry, not even listed as a separate category in the 1880 census of manufactures, appeared as the sixth largest employer in 1904 (see table 5.1).[9] Many industrial establishments were recent creations. In 1900, when the Michigan Bureau of Labor and Industrial Statistics inspected 1,588 factories in Detroit to enforce laws regarding child labor and safety standards, the surveyors reported that a full 42% of the factories they visited had begun operation since 1895.[10] With these many recently opened factories, industry was booming in 1900 Detroit. The surveyors reported that the 1,588 inspected factories were averaging 9.7 hours work per day, 26.8 days per month, and 11.6 months per year. And the average Detroit factory employed 36.6 workers in 1900. This average covers, of course, a great variety of situations. The bureau visited many small downtown shops, with only a few workers. They also visited 23 companies with more than 300 workers each in iron and steel, foundry, and railroad manufacturing. These large manufacturers, fewer in number and employing large pools of workers, typify the emerging industrial giants of the late nineteenth century. Among the large employers in Detroit, screened by the labor bureau's factory inspections from 1897 through 1900, the combined sectors of transportation-related industries (including railroad equipment, wheels, shipbuilding, automobiles, and carriages), of pharmaceutical and chemical products, of industrial goods, and of metal-related work (including casting, brass work, and stoves) far outdistanced in number of employees the traditional consumer industries, for example, food, clothing,

9. Many large companies were still run as partnerships even if they were incorporated; see Thomas R. Navin and Marian V. Sears, "The Rise of a Market for Industrial Securities, 1887–1902," *Business History Review* 29 (June 1955): 109.

10. Michigan, "State Factory Inspection," appendix to *Eighteenth Annual Report of the Bureau of Labor and Industrial Statistics* (Lansing: Wynkoop Hallenbeck Crawford Co., State Printers, 1901), p. 38.

TABLE 5.1

Mechanical and manufacturing industries, Detroit, 1900 and 1904

Industrial sector	Number of employees		Number of establishments	
	1900	1904	1900	1904
Foundry and machine shop	6,544	4,212	74	89
Clothing and related	6,359	4,284	585	66
Construction	4,649	-ᵃ	505	-ᵃ
Tobacco	4,037	4,517	192	225
Lumber and related	3,411	3,528	137	77
Food and beverages	2,952	3,777	284	243
Printing and publishing	2,277	2,539	136	152
Druggists' preparations	2,155	2,809	9	14
Iron and steel	1,630	1,659	12	14
Transportation and related	838	1,317	139	39
Automobiles	-	1,191	-	19

SOURCES: U.S., Department of the Interior, Census Office, *Twelfth Census of the United States, 1900, Manufactures,* 4 vols. (Washington, D.C.: G.P.O, 1902) 2:427–431; U.S., Department of Commerce and Labor, Bureau of the Census, *Census of Manufactures, 1904* (Washington, D.C.: G.P.O., 1905), pp. 24–27. The table includes "every establishment of mechanical or manufacturing industry . . . having had a year product of five hundred dollars or more in value." The general categories of enumeration were defined somewhat differently in 1900 and 1904. The specific numbered categories selected from census tables to create the larger categories compared here are:

Foundry and machine shop	1900: 43
	1904: 37
Clothing and related	1900: 8, 9, 24, 25, 26, 27, 32, 53, 54, 68, 93
	1904: 10, 22, 23, 45, 46
Construction	1900: 16, 18, 64, 65, 73, 75, 77, 82, 84, 88
Tobacco	1900: 99, 100
	1904: 84, 85
Lumber and related	1900: 13, 31, 46, 47, 61, 62, 106
	1904: 13, 26, 39, 52, 91
Food and beverages	1900: 3, 10, 15, 22, 28, 30, 41, 42, 58, 63, 69, 81, 94, 95
	1904: 15, 25, 35, 36, 50, 53, 56, 65, 76, 77
Printing and publishing	1900: 7, 85, 86
	1904: 9, 68, 69
Druggist preparation	1900: 33
	1904: 28
Iron and steel	1900: 56, 47
	1904: 47, 82
Transportation and related	1900: 5, 20, 21, 89, 92
	1904: 19, 20, 21, 72, 74
Automobile	1904: 4, 5
a. Incomplete data.	

furniture, and tobacco, which had dominated the scene in 1880. The large employers of Detroit now employed 21,437 workers in the first group, only 13,678 in the second (table 5.2).

A few industrial giants were already emerging in the transportation industry,

TABLE 5.2

Largest industrial establishments, Detroit, 1897–1900

Industrial Sector	Employees		Establishments	
	(N)	(%)	(N)	(%)
Transportation and related Automobiles, wheels, shipbuilding, carriages and saddlery, railroad equipment	4,380	11.3	12	9.0
Pharmaceutical and chemical Drugs, paints, varnish and matches	3,835	9.9	12	9.0
Industrial goods Motors, shipping and packing goods, hardware	2,145	5.5	9	6.8
Metal and related Casting, brass, copper and brass, iron, steel, stoves and boilers	11,077	28.6	35	26.3
Food	1,490	3.8	8	6.0
Clothing and related	5,880	15.2	21	15.7
Tobacco	3,697	9.5	10	7.5
Lumber and furniture	2,611	6.7	12	9.0
Miscellaneous Wholesale grain, publishing, decorating, laundry, street-railway repair shop	3,534	9.1	14	10.5
Total	38,649	100.0	133	100.0

SOURCES: "State Factory Inspection," appendix to the *Fifteenth, Sixteenth, Seventeenth,* and *Eighteenth Annual Report of the Bureau of Labor and Industrial Statistics* (Lansing, Michigan: 1898–1901): firms with 100 or more workers from the 1900 inspection (published in 1901), and firms with 200 or more workers from the 1897–1899 inspections.

especially in the manufacture of railroad cars; American Car and Foundry, employing 2,200 workers, was the largest employer in the city in 1900. The Detroit branch of Pullman closed in 1897, but other large railroad shops and wheel factories employed several hundred workers each. Shipbuilding was also growing in Detroit, with the Detroit Shipbuilding Company employing over 500 workers. In addition to these large transportation firms, Detroit boasted numerous other firms specializing in industrial hardware, valves, pipes, nuts and bolts, and tools. Similarly, all aspects of casting, brass works, copper works, iron work, sheet metal, and steel were represented by large firms in Detroit, such as Detroit Steel and Spring Company with 500 workers.

This combination of giant new industrial companies in transportation and metalwork (typical of the new industrial belt) with the traditional Michigan lumber companies and carriage manufacturing shops supplied the perfect conditions to promote the automobile industry in Detroit: the diversified expertise, the labor force, and the capital were all there; the variety of necessary components, from traditional carriage seats to new engine works, were also available. In 1900 the first automobile manufacturer of the city, Ransom Olds, moved from East Lansing to Detroit and created Olds's motor works at the corner of Jefferson and Concord, employing 165 workers. The Oldsmobile was thus the first commercially built car, just six years after Charles King and five years after Henry Ford had driven their own gasoline cars in Detroit, but one year before the creation of the first Henry Ford Automobile Company, and three years before the creation of Cadillac Company by Henry Leland. A number of enterprising people of Detroit, attuned to the industrial conditions, were ready to move into the automobile manufacturing business in 1900. When Ford built his first car in 1896, he was still an engineer in the Edison Company. Leland, who built the engines for Olds' new factory, had been running a machine shop with Robert Falconer. Henry Russel, a corporate lawyer for the Michigan Central Railroad, and C. S. Smith, who had made a fortune in the brass industry, invested the necessary capital in Olds. David Buick was in the plumbing business in 1900—the Buick and Sherwood Manufacturing Company—until a few years later, he joined with William Durant in creating General Motors.[11]

Other industries likewise contributed to Detroit's growing investment in manufactures. The traditional stove industry was now one of the largest employers in the city: the Detroit Stove Works employed 1,150 workers, the Michigan Stove Company 1,000, and Peninsular Stove 800. Within the growing pharmaceutical industry, the factory inspection reveals that Parke, Davis and Company was the giant employing 1,350 workers, seconded by Frederick Stearns with 400 workers, and followed by four other sizable companies. In addition, the industries already well established in 1880—tobacco, clothing, furniture, food, and other consumer goods—continued to grow and included some of the largest employers of Detroit: Pingree's shoe firm with 700 workers, William Brothers and Charbonneau preserves with 500 workers, Scotten tobacco factory with almost a thousand workers, and D. M. Ferry Seed with 900 workers to process and sell agricultural implements.

In 1900, the manufacturing establishments of Detroit formed an almost perfect half circle, with the river as diameter and with the railroad lines encircling the built-up sections of the 1880 city (see map 5.3). In 1880, the city center had still accommodated most plants, while a few large concerns crowded the riverfront near the railroad terminals. Only a handful of companies had moved

11. John B. Rae, *American Automobile Manufacturers* (Philadelphia: Chilton Co., 1959); Thomas J. Ticknor, "Motor City: The Impact of the Automobile Industry upon Detroit, 1900–1975" (Ph.D. diss., University of Michigan, 1978); Clarence M. Burton, ed., *The City of Detroit, Michigan, 1701–1922*, 5 vols. (Detroit: S. J. Clarke Publishing Co., 1922), 1:530–614.

away, some further east on the riverfront. During the 1880s, however, two new
industrial sites emerged at the crossing of railroads. The first one, West Detroit,
was at the crossing of the Michigan Central Railroad (from Detroit to Bay City)
and the Grand Trunk Railroad (from the Saint Clair River to Toledo). The
intersection of these two railroads became the center of the Michigan Railroad
Car Company; soon other railway shops and large metal shops (like Detroit
Steel and Spring Company) moved there. These two railroads—Michigan Central and Grand Trunk—crossed a third, the Detroit and Milwaukee Railroad,
just east of Woodward Avenue in the northern section of town, where the second
industrial center, the Lake Shore and Milwaukee Junction, developed. Large
companies, including the Peninsular Car Company (later merged into American
Car and Foundry) and the American Radiator Company, built factories there.
Subsequent industrial development in Detroit expanded these two concentrations along the railroad lines themselves. In the late eighties, the Michigan
Central built a belt line encircling Detroit and added a new line joining the
northeastern section of town to the old manufacturers' line on the riverfront.
Similarly, manufactures on the riverfront expanded down the river toward
Delray Village in the west.

Some of the older concerns in Detroit—D. M. Ferry Seed, D. Scotten tobacco,
Pullman—were still near the city center, reflecting the territorial organization
of the past. The communication firms (such as printing) were also located
downtown, as well as most traditional industries manufacturing consumer products, food, clothing, tobacco, and furniture. Two large clothing factories, Standard and Pearl Button, remained in the midtown section of the east side, but
other factories moved toward the city's fringes: Murphy and Wasey, a large
furniture factory, moved to the Lake Shore and Milwaukee Junction; Williams
Brothers and Charbonneau, the largest food factory, was located along Michigan, toward West Detroit. And the map of Detroit's largest employers shows
clearly that most large industrial enterprises involved in the production of iron
and steel, other metalworks, stoves, railroad equipment, and railroad cars, as
well as chemicals and drugs were now invariably located either along the river,
on both east and west sides, toward the periphery of the city, or at the railroad
intersections.

The increase in industry from 1880 to 1900 and the availability of residential
space formed an attractive combination to a large immigrant population, and
newcomers continued to enter growing industrial Detroit in increasing numbers.
The concept of ethnic groups being well-bounded minorities in late nineteenth-
century Detroit is unrealistic, as their combined proportion of the population
in the period of heavy immigration shows. As much as 78.64% of the entire

MAP 5.3

Large Employers, 1897–1900

■ Clothing   • Food   ◈ Stove and boilermakers,
▣ Printing   + Tobacco   foundries, and machine shops
▢ Transportation   ✳ Lumber   ▨ Drugs and Chemicals
          ◉ Iron and steel   ◦ Brass and other metals

Shown are factories employing 200 or more workers; factories
employing 400 or more workers are named.

SOURCE: Factory Inspections, Bureau of Labor and Industrial Statistics, 1898–1901.

```
0      ¼      ½      ¾      1                      2
━━━━━━━━━━━━━━━━━━━━━━━━━━━━━━━━━━━━━━━━━━━━━━━━━━━━━
                    MILES

0             1              2             3
━━━━━━━━━━━━━━━━━━━━━━━━━━━━━━━━━━━━━━━━━━━━
            KILOMETERS
```

OSTON ST.

OLBROOK

ST.

AVE.

OAKLAND

ST. AUBIN

CITY LIMITS

1900

LAY ST. Milwaukee Junction GRAND TRUNK R.R.

OULEVARD

CITY LIMITS   1880

DIVISION

ICHIGAN

R.R. SOUTHERN ST.

◈ AMERICAN RADIATOR CO.
(MICHIGAN PLANT)

✳ MURPHY, WASEY & CO.

Lake Shore Junction

▢ AMERICAN CAR AND FOUNDRY ST.

FERRY

HARPER

R.R.

AVE.

AVE.

ST.

AVE.

1900

MILWAUKEE

FOREST

AVE.

BOULEVARD

R.R.

BOULEVARD

1885

■ STANDARD PEARL BUTTON

E.

GRAND HAVEN

MACK

GRATIOT ST.

1880

AVE.

ST.

MACK

ST.

VENA ST.

RUSSELL

DETROIT AVE.

CHENE ST.

ELMWOOD

MT. ELLIOTT

CITY LIMITS

CENTRAL LINE

MICHIGAN BELT

BOULEVARD

KERCHEVAL

CITY LIMITS

VAN DYKE

McCLELLAN

CADILLAC

CITY LIMITS

ST.

BRUSH

GRATIOT

HASTINGS

SHERMAN

ST.

McDOUGALL

ST.

AVE.

• D.M. FERRY

✳+

▢ PULLMAN PALACE CAR CO.

CHAMPLAIN

◦

ST.

AMERICAN
LADY CORSET

HAMILTON
CARHARTT

DETROIT SHIPBUILDING

JEFFERSON

MICHIGAN
STOVE CO.

◈ FREDERICK STEARNS CO.

◈ DETROIT STOVE WORKS

◉ IDEAL MFG.

BUHL
MALLEABLE

◈ IRELAND AND MATHEWS MFG. CO.

ATWATER ST.

▢ ▢ ▨ PARKE, DAVIS & CO.

◈ AMERICAN
RADIATOR CO.
(DETROIT PLANT)

R.R. FERRY

FERRY

River

UNITED STATES
CANADA

Belle Isle

population of Detroit in 1900 could be classified as ethnic, that is, either foreign-born, having at least one foreign-born parent, or belonging to the very small Black community (table 5.3).

TABLE 5.3
Ethnic groups, Detroit, 1900

Ethnicity	Population[a]	Percentage
Native white American[b]	60,904	21.36
Native black American	2,604	.91
Foreign-born Black	1,707	.60
Native-born white of mixed American and foreign parentage	37,030	12.99
Canadian (English)[c]	10,694	3.75
Canadian American (English)[d]	4,939	1.73
Canadian (French)	2,823	.99
Canadian American (French)	1,976	.69
British	7,916	2.78
British American	5,319	1.87
Irish	6,316	2.22
Irish American	8,561	3.04
German	30,903	10.84
German American	38,436	13.48
Polish	12,177	4.27
Polish American	12,799	4.49
Russian	1,637	.57
Russian American	1,155	.41
Austro-Hungarian	596	.21
Austro-Hungarian American	599	.21
Italian	734	.26
Italian American	463	.16
Swiss	337	.12
Swiss American	132	.05
French	427	.15
French American	620	.22
Belgian, Dutch, and Luxembourger	1,083	.38
Belgian, Dutch, and Luxembourger American	554	.19
Norwegian, Swedish, and Danish	394	.14
Norwegian, Swedish, and Danish American	116	.04
Other foreign-born European	118	.04
Other European American	7	.00
Oriental	23	.01
Native-born white of mixed foreign parentage	10,834	3.80
Foreign-born white of mixed foreign parentage	20,095	7.05

SOURCE: 1900 sample.
    a. Estimated number from weighted sample data.
    b. Born in the U.S. of two U.S.-born parents.
    c. Born in English-speaking Canada of two Canadian parents, born in French-speaking Canada of two Canadian parents, born in Great Britain of two British parents, etc.
    d. Born in the U.S. of two parents born in English-speaking Canada, etc.

Throughout the period of intense immigration and new settlement in Detroit (from 1850 through 1920) some foreign groups increased their share of the population while some others declined (see table 5.4). The Canadians, most of them English Canadians having crossed the river from their neighboring country, always made up a fairly large and stable share of the foreign-born population: around 20%, with a peak of 30% in 1900. The percentage of immigrants from Great Britain (not including Ireland) decreased from 1850 through 1920 from 17.32% to 8.52% but always remained a sizable figure. The Irish-born population, however, the most important foreign-born group in 1850, steadily declined in proportion to other groups to become a small minority by 1920. The single largest group of immigrants throughout the nineteenth century was the Germans, with a peak population of 43% in 1890. At the turn of the century and on into the twenties, the population of Poles, Russians, and Hungarians, which constituted only tiny minorities in the seventies and eighties, grew in importance to make up 40% of the foreign-born population of Detroit by 1920. The evolution of the foreign-born populations in Detroit, then, follows the national urban trend of a relative decrease of "old" immigrant groups and an increase of new groups from eastern Europe.

Geographic origin is an essential determinant for identifying someone with an ethnic group, but people from a similar origin may differ in religious affiliation, a distinction that may be very important in shaping the ethnic map of Detroit: 64% of the native white Americans were Protestant, as were 79.5% of the English Canadian immigrants, 83.3% of the English immigrants, and 65.4% of the German immigrants. Similarly, 85% of the French Canadians, 81.9% of the Irish immigrants, and all of the Poles whose religion I could identify were Catholic. Only 1.04% of the Germans were Jews, whereas most of the Russians, 88%, were Jewish (table 5.5).

To be sure, the Protestant denominations differed from one nationality group to another, and within the Protestant population some denominations were better represented than others. The most important were the Episcopalians (14.9% of the Protestant population), the Methodists (15.23%), the Presbyterians (11.27%), and the Lutherans (23.52%). Native white American Protestants were very well represented among the Episcopalians (60.89% were Americans), the Methodists (39.16%), and the Presbyterians (27.26%). The English Canadians comprised 31.13% of the Methodist congregations. The largest group of Presbyterians (37.16%) were from Great Britain; of these, 72.2% were Scottish, as could be expected. Thus these three denominations, Episcopalian, Methodist, and Presbyterian, were composed primarily of Americans, British immigrants, and English Canadians. Two other major Protestant denominations, German Evangelical and Lutheran, were heavily German, 68.17% and 92.01%, respectively (table 5.6).

TABLE 5.4

Foreign-born population, Detroit, 1850–1920

Ethnic group		1850	1860	1870	1880	1890	1900	1910	1920
Canadian (English)[a]	(%)	-	-	-	-	-	26.32	-	-
Canadian (unspecified)	(%)	-	14.46	21.83	23.56	23.00	-	24.55	19.13
Canadian (French)	(%)	-	-	-	-	-	3.67	2.64	1.27
British	(%)	17.32	16.49	14.03	13.28	11.88	9.27	7.95	8.52
Irish	(%)	33.13	28.08	19.70	14.84	9.11	6.64	3.54	2.42
German	(%)	28.66	33.82	35.75	37.69	43.42	33.19	28.36	10.48
Austrian Empire (without Hungary)[b]	(%)	.07	-	1.98	1.50	1.44	1.12	8.99	6.13
Hungarian	(%)	-	-	.15	.14	.14	.09	3.77	4.69
Russian	(%)	-	-	.25	.17	.82	3.18	11.83	9.43
Polish[c]	(%)	-	-	.81	3.88	6.55	14.12	-	19.57
Norwegian, Swedish, and Danish	(%)	-	-	.15	.34	.53	.59	.82	2.35
Belgian, Dutch, and Luxembourger	(%)	-	-	1.53	1.31	.91	1.11	1.79	2.82
French	(%)	2.84	2.92	2.15	1.58	.98	.61	.40	.60
Italian	(%)	.04	-	.10	.28	.41	.94	3.63	5.60
Greek	(%)	-	-	<.01	<.01	<.01	.02	.37	1.60
Other Europeans	(%)	.04	-	1.32	.96	.53	.56	1.15	4.00
All others	(%)	18.65	4.23	.19	.24	.51	.28	.26	1.42
Foreign-born population	(N)	9,927	21,349	35,381	45,645	81,709	96,503	153,534	289,297
Total population	(N)	21,019	45,619	79,603	116,340	205,876	285,704	465,766	993,678
Foreign-born population	(%)	47.22	46.79	44.44	39.23	39.68	33.77	32.96	29.11

SOURCE: U.S., Census, 1850–1920, published *Population* volumes.

a. Born in English-speaking Canada of two Canadian parents; born in French-speaking Canada of two British parents; born in Great Britain of two British parents, etc. The enumeration of Canadian varied from year to year. In some years they were categorized by province and in other years more generally as English or French Canadians. For the year 1850, most "All others" were Canadians.

b. The Austro-Hungarian Empire was composed of the kingdoms of Austria, Hungary, and Bohemia until 1918. In the tabulation here, the immigrant populations of Bohemia (in 1870–1900), Czechoslovakia (1920), and Yugoslavia (1920) have been included with the Austrians for convenience.

c. In 1910, Polish immigrants were listed with Russians, Germans, or Austrians according to which country the respondents chose. Only in 1900, the census recorded Poland Austria, Poland Germany, Poland Russia, Poland unspecified. In 1917, Poland reestablished its political sovereignty.

TABLE 5.5
Major religious denominations for selected ethnic groups, Detroit, 1900

Ethnicity	Protestant (%)	Catholic (%)	Jewish (%)
Native white American[a]	64.75	34.85	.39
Canadian (English)[b]	79.51	20.49	-
Canadian (French)	14.50	85.50	-
British	83.37	15.52	1.12
Irish	18.04	81.96	-
Irish American	25.47	74.53	-
German	65.43	33.54	1.04
German American	66.91	30.21	2.88
Polish	-	100.00	-
Polish American	-	100.00	-
Russian	-	11.59	88.41

SOURCES: 1900 sample, weighted percentages based on data obtained from the linkage of the 1900 census manuscript population schedules with the marriage licenses of couples married in Wayne County between 1887 and 1900. Estimates of less than 1% should not be considered reliable.

a. Born in the U.S. of two U.S.-born parents.

b. Born in English-speaking Canada of two Canadian parents; born in French-speaking Canada of two Canadian parents; born in Great Britain of two British parents, etc.

Two general observations can be made on this ethnoreligious distribution. First, the percentage of Catholics in Detroit's population, 39%, exceeded by far the average figures for the Midwest or for the country at large, both at around 17%. Like other large industrializing cities, Detroit was receiving a disproportionate share of the Catholic immigration. Second, if one aggregates the population of the more ritualistic Protestant denominations, such as the Lutheran, to the Catholic population, it is easy to see that Detroit was inhabited primarily by immigrants from Germany, Poland, and Ireland, ritualistic in religion and, as several studies have shown, likely to be attached to the Democratic party.[12] It was along these dividing ethnoreligious political lines that most issues, especially temperance and observing the Sabbath, were fought in late nineteenth-century Detroit. Two different clusters of denominations, pietists and ritualists, emphasized different dimensions of life, which led their adherents to different political commitments. In the words of Paul Kleppner, to the pietist, the duty of government, no less than that of the individual, was to eradicate sin, while the ritualists "compartmentalized their lives into the sacred and the profane. . . . To the Catholic, drinking in itself was no sin, although excessive drinking

12. Richard Jensen, *The Winning of the Midwest* (Chicago: University of Chicago Press, 1971), pp. 58–88; Paul Kleppner, *The Third Electoral System, 1853–1892* (Chapel Hill: University of North Carolina Press, 1979), pp. 143–197; Paul Kleppner, *The Cross of Culture* (New York: Free Press, 1970), pp. 35–91.

TABLE 5.6

Major Protestant denominations for selected ethnic groups, Detroit, 1900

Ethnicity	Baptist (%)	Christian (%)	Congrega-tional (%)	Episcopalian (%)	German Evangelical (%)	Lutheran (%)	Methodist (%)	Presbyterian (%)	Reformed German (%)
Native white American[a]	72.09	60.80	73.43	60.89	23.11	7.04	39.16	27.25	4.63
Black and mulatto	11.94	-	-	-	-	-	4.70	7.10	-
Canadian (English)[b]	-	10.06	7.63	13.09	1.78	-	31.13	15.90	13.54
Canadian (French)	-	-	-	-	-	.94	-	1.96	-
British	12.09	20.91	14.59	14.51	6.93	-	14.42	37.16	-
Irish	-	-	-	2.85	-	-	3.54	5.04	-
German	3.86	8.17	4.33	8.63	68.17	92.01	7.02	5.55	81.82
Total	100.00	100.00	100.00	100.00	100.00	100.00	100.00	100.00	100.00
All denominations (%)	4.65	2.20	4.15	14.90	16.99	23.52	15.23	11.27	4.23

SOURCE: 1900 sample, weighted percentages based on data obtained from the linkage of the 1900 census manuscript population schedules with the marriage licenses of couples married in Wayne County between 1887 and 1900.

a. Born in the U.S of two U.S.-born parents.

b. Born in English-speaking Canada of two Canadian parents; born in French-speaking Canada of two Canadian parents; born in Great Britain of two British parents, etc.

might be. It might be desirable to encourage individuals to abstain, but it was surely no violation of God's law should they fail to do so."[13] Yet as political rhetoric periodically readdressed these moral themes, new debates directly linked to the ways the changing environment of Detroit affected the urbanites gradually took predominance.

OLD AND NEW DEBATES

Many political debates in Detroit still focused on the old partisan lines of liquor and corruption; the issues at stake during the campaigns conducted every other year for Detroit's offices of mayor, city clerk, city attorney, and alderman on the board of the common council often revolved around temperance. The Republicans, who controlled the mayoralty and the common council through 1887, were the "prohibition party"; against them, the Democrats represented the liquor interests. The Democratic candidate for mayor in 1883, Marvin H. Chamberlain, was president of a wholesale wine and liquor company, and the Republicans were quick to call the Democratic convention, "the liquor dealers' convention." It was common for Democratic aldermen to be saloonkeepers, like Alois Deimel, who owned a popular tavern on Cadillac Square. In 1897, the *Free Press* identified ten saloonkeepers among the thirty-four aldermen of the council.[14] The Republicans drew consistent support from the west side, inhabited by the more pietist groups, while the Democrats systematically carried the east side. John Pridgeon, Jr., the Democratic nominee for mayor in 1887, won the election over Dr. Yemans, his Republican opponent, a victory which he owed to the abstention of many of the west side voters, dry Republicans alienated by Yemans's bid to gain the pro-liquor German vote. Kleppner, who analyzed the presidential election of 1888 in Detroit, observed a similar connection between ethnoreligious affiliation, residential location, and voting: "the strongest Democratic ward, the seventh, contained a large proportion of Polish voters and was the most heavily Catholic ward in the city. The second ward, which ranked sixteenth in Democratic percentage strength, but was also a strongly working-class ward, ranked second in its percentage of native voters and was one of the city's most heavily Protestant wards."[15]

While the Democrats stressed local ward-based politics, the Republicans systematically tried to promote known personalities who could be elected by the city population at large. To this end, Mayor Thompson in 1881 attempted to break the social and ethnic homogeneity of the wards by dividing Detroit into long thin strips running south-north from the river to the city limits and

13. Kleppner, *Third Electoral System*, pp. 194–95.
14. Jack D. Elenbaas, "The Democrats in Detroit, 1880–1900" (M.A. thesis, Wayne State University, 1964), p. 10.
15. Kleppner, *Cross of Culture*, p. 21.

including in each new ward "a portion of the residence, manufacturing and river districts."[16] The Republican administration also tried to impart gradually more authority to the short-lived (lasting only from 1881 to 1887) Board of Councilmen, composed of twelve members elected at large, over the aldermen of the common council who were elected by ward.[17] To the Republicans, personalities known to the entire city were more desirable than local tavernkeepers. Hazen Pingree, a prominent manufacturer of Detroit, was a perfect candidate to run for mayor on the Republican ticket in 1889 and defeat the Democrats. He represented Detroit's manufacturing establishment, politically controlled by the Michigan Club, the Republican organization created by railroad car magnate Senator James McMillan. Pingree himself, a shoe manufacturer, was one of the largest employers in the city. Pingree became the candidate of good government, running against Democratic corruption. Of course, the Democrats did not have the monopoly on municipal corruption; they themselves had used the theme against the Republicans in 1887, but in 1889 a grand jury revealed unorthodox deals between Democratic aldermen and paving contractors. Corruption in Mayor Pridgeon's administration became the focus of the Republican campaign; Hazen Pingree "promised to redeem the city from Democratic political sins committed against the citizens of Detroit . . . [and] offered a policy of wise spending, careful planning, simple honesty, and nonpartisan administration."[18] Pingree easily won the election, even in the east side. It is likely that the German Lutherans, although liturgical in religion, were sensitive to the growing acceptance by the Michigan Club of urban immigrant voters and were willing to emphasize their distance from the Catholics; they probably acted as a swing group and secured the Republican victory.[19]

But political rhetoric underwent a dramatic transformation during the latter part of the nineteenth century as the people of Detroit became more and more concerned with their total environment. Both the city and private interests consciously engaged in the business of equipping the metropolis and controlling its growth. Charles Tilly once remarked in regard to urbanization that "even cities become more urban."[20] In Detroit, this meant meeting the transportation, communication, energy, and sanitation needs of more industries, more businesses, and more people, in a greater space than ever before. It meant laying out miles of new railroad tracks to provide for the transportation of people and

16. Silas Farmer, *History of Detroit and Wayne County and Early Michigan* (Detroit: Silas Farmer & Co., 1890; Gale Research Co., 1969), pp. 147–48.

17. Ibid., pp. 137–38.

18. Jack D. Elenbaas, "Detroit and the Progressive Era" (Ph.D. diss., Wayne State University, 1968), pp. 22–23.

19. Kleppner, *Cross of Culture*, pp. 47–48, 82–83, 128.

20. Charles Tilly, *The Vendée* (Cambridge, Mass.: Harvard University Press, 1964), p. 18.

goods. It meant laying out miles of new water and sewer pipes to accommodate the metropolis. Urban governments had long been in the business of controlling the city's environment, but the challenges of the old commercial city were not comparable to the new challenges of the growing metropolis.[21]

Once Pingree was elected, he soon recognized that the problems of Detroit were of a much greater magnitude than the party platform on which he ran had ever recognized. An honest man, coming from the manufacturing leadership of the city, running under the banner of good government, Pingree was soon to discover that morality was only part of the story. To the amazement of his early supporters, he rose above mere party politics and dealt directly with all issues that affected the people of Detroit. In the campaign of 1889, issues other than booze and graft had already begun to appear in the press. For instance, Samuel Goldwater, a Jewish immigrant from Poland, cigar maker, and activist in the trade union movement, "condemned Mayor Pridgeon for his failure to enforce the eight hour day among city workers."[22] Once elected, Pingree took a hard look at the whole range of governmental activities, from taxation to the distribution of services, especially transportation and utilities; mayor during the depression of 1893, he also confronted poverty. Pingree is known as one of the first major urban reformers, able to combine prominent structural reforms with social goals in a spirit of social justice.

Nobody understood the necessity for the city to engineer growth better than Pingree. He saw the providing of services as the key role of his administration and moved to exert tighter control over the private companies that provided services to the community, particularly in his long battle with the streetcar companies over rates and quality of service. Although municipal ownership of transit services became a reality only in 1920, Pingree's administration marks the beginning of the city's involvement in rapid transit. Pingree also initiated municipal ownership of an electric plant, tightened the city's control of the telephone and other companies, and worked at improving services traditionally offered by city hall and paid for out of bonds and tax revenues.[23] Many problems common to major cities faced the new mayor, and Detroit simply did not have the "in-house" expertise to implement the organization, control, and regulation of utilities and services. In most cases, the technology was so new that most who knew about it were out in the field making money and not working for the city. Detroit was unable, for instance, to deal effectively with the public

21. Jon C. Teaford, *The Municipal Revolution in America* (Chicago: University of Chicago Press, 1975).

22. Elenbaas, "Democrats in Detroit," p. 63.

23. Melvin G. Holli, *Reform in Detroit* (New York: Oxford University Press, 1969), pp. 33, 42–61, 74–100.

service problems presented by the electric light industry, problems such as expensive duplication of service in the same area, lack of standardization in the industry, and instability caused by intense competition. In fact, Pingree launched a war against the electric companies in Detroit, trying to regulate the setting of poles in the streets. He complained in 1893: "For years all corporations setting poles in the streets have done so at their own sweet will, regardless of the rights or comforts of citizens, or of whether such poles would interfere with public improvements."[24] Pingree conducted a survey of ninety-two cities and concluded that if Detroit had its own electric plant, the cost to consumers of street lighting would be reduced by half. Ultimately, the city won and opened its own plant in 1895, leaving only private lighting to Detroit Edison, although the Public Lighting Commission was never sure that the new plant had effectively saved money for the taxpayers.[25]

In addition to the problems caused by the technological gap between the city and the industries, the laws that governed incorporation and regulation of companies were clumsily written and replete with loopholes, and the loose laws facilitated corruption, fraud, and abuses. Often the state legislature placed the city at a disadvantage. In his fight for a municipally owned electric plant, for example, Pingree reported in his annual address of 1893 that "private interests secured the passage of a law at the last session of the legislature which prohibits cities in this state of more than 25,000 inhabitants from doing their own lighting."[26] The city was eventually able to overcome this obstacle, but it was not so successful with the street railways, fighting and eventually losing a lengthy court battle over the right to grant, terminate, and regulate charters and franchises in street-railway service. The case involving Detroit's termination of the operating rights of Detroit's Citizens Street Railway Company was eventually decided by a federal court of appeals, where Detroit lost. Nor could Detroit effectively control the rates of phone services judged unreasonable by the mayor's office.[27]

Detroit under Pingree came to the realization that directing urban growth was a priority issue, but even so this realization led to only partial success. In overseeing services for an expanding territory, the city did overcome its initial lack of expertise, but despite the city's involvement, services were never equally distributed throughout the city. Because many parties were involved—city hall, interest groups, and the taxpayers of Detroit, on whom the cost of improving

24. Detroit, *Annual Address of Hazen S. Pingree, Mayor of the City of Detroit, Delivered January 10, 1893* (Detroit: Thos. Smith Printing Co., City Printers, 1893), p. 10.

25. Detroit, *Second Annual Report of the Public Lighting Commission* (Detroit: Press of the Richmond & Backus Co., 1897), p. 26.

26. Detroit, *Annual Address of Hazen S. Pingree*, p. 16.

27. Holli, *Reform in Detroit*, pp. 46–47, 97–98.

services ultimately rested—there was no unified view of how things should be done. Streetcar and electric companies, for example, changed the urban landscape; they had as their objective "to make unlimited profit; only secondarily if at all, did they consider the public aspect of the venture."[28] Mediating this logic of profit, engineers working for the city or the private companies constituted a new class of professionals, a new "strategic elite," which imposed its own view of how to equip the metropolis.[29] These engineers dealt with the city as a physical entity, and their recommendations were motivated by technological considerations (such as how to pump water) or by the geography of the urban territory. To them, natural obstacles were more important than political boundaries, tax assessments, or ward-based politics. Political and social pressures coming from all sections of the metropolis also influenced decisions, as interest groups pressured city hall or the state legislature for charter amendments. Even ordinary citizens could affect decisions by refusing special tax assessments linked to services, since owners of abutting property shared the costs of street improvements, or by boycotting the street railway when the rates were too high. Within city hall itself, many internal dissensions had to be resolved. It is amid these many conflicts and through the attempts to solve the problems of the metropolis of the late nineteenth century that different groups of Detroiters received an unequal share of Detroit's new services.

EQUIPPING THE METROPOLIS

Three services directly controlled by city hall and affecting all citizens in all parts of the city—water, sewers, and pavements—were vital for the maintenance and expansion of the metropolis. No part of the city could really exist without some source of water. Indeed, new water pipes were constantly laid throughout Detroit, but the quality of water service varied greatly from one section of the city to another. Sewers, less indispensable in some ways (since privy vault cesspools were still in use in many sections of 1890s Detroit), were nonetheless vital to the hygiene of the city in all densely populated areas. And paved streets not only facilitated communications but also helped reduce disease by eliminating stagnant water. Knowing how these services were provided for,

28. Glen E. Holt, "The Changing Perception of Urban Pathology," in *Cities in American History*, ed. Kenneth T. Jackson and Stanley K. Schultz (New York: Alfred A. Knopf, 1972), p. 325.

29. Stanley K. Schultz and Clay McShane, "To Engineer the Metropolis: Sewers, Sanitation, and City Planning in Late Nineteenth Century America," *Journal of American History* 65 (September 1978): 389–411; Stanley K. Schultz and Clay McShane, "Pollution and Political Reform in Urban America: The Role of Municipal Engineers, 1840–1920," in *Pollution and Reform in American Cities, 1870–1930*, ed. Martin V. Melosi (Austin: University of Texas Press, 1980), pp. 155–72.

how good they were, and how available they were in different sections of the city will contribute not only to our understanding of the city-building process, but will enable us to discover just how equitably services were distributed.

Water pipes, sewers, and pavements followed the growth pattern of the metropolis. If we analyze the distribution of new services built between 1891 and 1900 by distance from city hall, in concentric circles of half a mile each, we see that the city was equipped as it grew. Most construction of new services in the 1890s happened when or before new housing was built, usually 2–3 miles from the city center. Table 5.7 sums up the information collected from the city's

TABLE 5.7

Density of city services (linear feet per acre) by concentric rings from city center, Detroit, 1891–1899

Distance from city center[a]	New paving	Repaving	Lateral sewers[b]	Public sewers[c]	Water feeder system[d]
From 0 to .5 miles	15.53	192.87	6.94	16.68	56.50
From .5 to 1.0 miles	35.64	85.90	5.66	10.15	49.32
From 1.0 to 1.5 miles	57.38	43.90	5.08	4.96	21.71
From 1.5 to 2.0 miles	78.61	21.99	18.75	3.91	17.52
West side	85.06	31.02	12.70	6.22	13.69
East side	74.04	14.04	25.27	1.70	21.95
From 2.0 to 2.5 miles	54.27	7.04	44.96	8.77	19.15
West side	53.40	11.58	29.62	8.04	25.50
East side	56.44	2.67	60.29	4.68	13.26
From 2.5 to 3.0 miles	37.91	2.04	68.76	15.33	10.76
West side	44.25	3.73	84.87	14.31	10.65
East side	32.40	.45	52.66	16.72	11.13
Above 3.0 miles	20.99	.71	56.60	18.75	10.28
From 3.0 miles to western city limit	22.04	2.42	82.96	19.88	10.16
From 3.0 to 3.5 miles on east side	15.85	-	53.88	24.23	10.73
From 3.5 miles to eastern city limit	8.73	-	16.21	16.24	6.90
North above 3.0 miles[e]	34.24	.66	69.48	13.70	12.23

SOURCES: *Fortieth, Forty-first, Forty-second, Forty-third, Forty-fourth, Forty-fifth, Forty-sixth, Forty-seventh,* and *Forty-eighth Annual Report of the Board of Water Commissioners to the Common Council of the City of Detroit* (Detroit: The Detroit Free Press Printing Company, 1892–1900); *Eighteenth, Nineteenth, Twentieth, Twenty-first, Twenty-second, Twenty-third, Twenty-fourth, Twenty-fifth,* and *Twenty-sixth Annual Report of the Board of Public Works to the Common Council of the City of Detroit* (Detroit, 1892–1900).

  a. Intersection of Michigan and Woodward.

  b. Sewers placed in alleys behind houses.

  c. Large capacity sewers draining lateral sewers.

  d. Water pipes 8 inches or larger in diameter.

  e. Between St. Aubin and Oakland on the east, 12th on the west, and north of Bethune, Hamlin, and Custer streets.

annual reports: in the 1890s the water feeder system was improved at the two geographic extremes of the metropolis, downtown and at the periphery, 3 miles away from downtown. In the 1890s the Board of Water Commissioners laid an average of 56.5 feet of feeder pipe per acre of land in the downtown section of the city in order to keep up with the increased use of water in industrial shops. At the same time, the density of new feeder pipe at the periphery was still above 10 feet per acre, as water was needed to service existing or anticipated houses on Detroit's fringes. The statistics for public sewers follow somewhat the same trend of downtown renovation and new construction at the periphery, with 16.6 feet per acre downtown but almost as much, 15.33, between 2.5 and 3 miles from city hall, and 18.75 feet per acre of land beyond 3 miles from city hall. The laying of lateral sewers, connecting houses to public sewers, naturally followed the rhythm of construction of houses in the city. Only 5.08 feet of lateral sewers were laid per acre of land in the area from 1 to 1.5 miles from city hall, but this figure increased to 18.75 from 1.5 to 2 miles, and 44.96 in the next half circle from 2 to 2.5 miles from city hall. The ratio of lateral sewer per acre went up to 68.76 from 2.5 to 3 miles and to 56.6 above 3 miles, in the regions of the city built mostly during the 1890s. Generally speaking, water was the first service installed, followed by sewers. Pavement was last and often came a few years after the other services. Thus the midtown area was paved in the 1890s, with 78 feet of new pavement per acre of land in the concentric zone from 1.5 to 2 miles from city hall. But paving slowed down beyond three miles of city hall, despite the increased building activity. Repaving was undertaken mostly in the city center in the 1890s, following the improvement of the water and sewer systems.

In the 1890s, then, the city reequipped its center and also equipped the periphery which was being developed in response to demographic pressure. Work went on even during the depression of 1893, when city departments made a point of hiring as many unemployed workers as they could to help alleviate the city's unemployment rate. This neat order of concentric circles representing Detroit's growth, well matched by the construction of new services, may be a reformer's dream. What appears to be true for the aggregate, however, takes on a different meaning when we study more closely the operation of each city's department as well as the areas improved. At this more local level we discover that the basic cleavages which we uncovered for 1880 and their translation into the city's space constituted a base for a differential rate of development of services in the 1890s.

A close look at the water system in the city and at the operation of the Board of Water Commissioners illustrates some of the many problems which the city faced in providing services, as well as a bias in favor of speculators and against the working class of Detroit. The city had owned and operated the previously privately owned water system since 1836. In 1857, the city built a reservoir at its upper limit (at the intersection of Erskine and Orleans), with water pumped to the reservoir from the river and redistributed in the city by pipe. By 1870, the reservoir system was proving to be inadequate for the city's needs. Water pressure was especially low in the west section of expanding downtown. In order to increase pressure downtown, a section of 24-inch pipe was laid from the water pumps themselves, at Orleans and the river, to the city center in 1872. This created a dual system by which part of the city's water was supplied by direct pressure from the pumps, and the rest from the reservoir by way of a gravity drain system. This dual system, however, did not have the expected effect. It drained water away from the northeastern areas of the city to the southwestern area with a corresponding loss of water pressure in the northeast and too much pressure in the southwest. To remedy this problem, in the 1870s the city built a new water works near Grosse Pointe and laid feeder pipes to link it with the old city system and to extend the system in the northern sections. By 1885, the feeder system reached 1.5 miles from city hall, about the limits of the inhabited city. Between 1885 and the early 1890s, pipage was extended into the areas annexed east, west, and north of Grand Boulevard, while many feeder pipes throughout the city were upgraded from generally 6 inches in diameter to anywhere between 8 and 45 inches, the very large mains built in the hope of equalizing water pressure throughout the city. Unfortunately, in 1893 the water commissioners reported that water pressure in Detroit was "as low as the lowest in any city of the United States."[30] The strategy of laying bigger feeders from the reservoirs to all parts of the city was simply not doing the job, and the board chairman admitted: "with the very limited knowledge of engineering that I possessed, or was had by any of the then employees of the Board, it was impossible to arrive at the true cause that was producing this unhealthy condition, and not knowing the cause, it was impossible to cure it."[31] The board reported that water pressure around Cass and Woodward near North Boulevard was 75% lower than it should have been; "Those living in the northern sections of Cass and Woodward were oftentimes unable to get water into second story bathrooms."[32] In the area of Gratiot from Hastings north and east, the highest part of the city, the water pressure was often "insufficient for the needs of the manufacturing establishments there."[33] The board also admitted that the water pressure was "too low to satisfy the demands of our population

30. Detroit, *Forty-Second Annual Report of the Board of Water Commissioners* (1894), p. 41.
31. Ibid., p. 9.
32. Ibid., p. 41.
33. Ibid., p. 44.

for several years past and what had been available has been very unfortunately distributed."[34] It was only in the face of such problems that the board for the first time hired a civil engineer whose task was to redirect the water flow in various ways so as to alleviate the problem of uneven pressure. The early nineties thus represent the turning point, the professionalization, on technical grounds, of the Board of Water Commissioners.

While the board worked toward a better flow of water through the underground, it also faced numerous managerial and organizational problems, some of them reflecting the feuds which went on within city hall as to how to engineer the metropolis. The Board of Water Commissioners was practically independent of the mayor and the city council. Once its members had been selected by the mayor and approved by the council, the board had the authority to issue new bonds and to administer its own revenue from water rates. In fact, the city charter required only that the board assess each lot in front of which water pipes were laid with a small "annual tax or assessment of three cents per lineal foot of frontage of such lot or lots."[35] Thus, the board relied almost exclusively on bonds and on water revenues, not on tax from the abutting property. City assessors recorded the use of each building (residential, commercial), the number of families within a building, and the different types of bathrooms and kitchen facilities within each home; all these factors were added into an assessed fee for water. But users often wasted water because of leaks in the pipes. If a discovered leak was not fixed by the user, the water was shut off until the leak was repaired. During 1891/92, water was shut off in 321 residences. In order to discourage continued use of leaky plumbing and thereby control usage better, the board began to replace estimated assessments of water usage with meters counting the actual consumption, especially on livery stables, laundries, breweries, and other manufacturing establishments. This indeed helped to limit water waste and better redistribute water pressure. The Board of Public Health, however, complained that this more economical use of water, by restricting its quantity and flow into sewers, prevented a normal removal of the accretions therein and was directly responsible for the prevalence of diptheria and other diseases.[36]

In addition to the water commissioners' many technical problems and limited expertise in solving them, they fell under heavy fire from the mayor's office for their political independence as well. Pingree, in his annual address of 1895/96, advised that the water board, "with its independent organization beyond the common council, should be wiped out" and its functions incorporated under

34. Ibid., p. 41.
35. Detroit, *The Charter of the City of Detroit* (Detroit: Thos. Smith Printing Co., City Printers, 1893), chap. 21, sections 517, 527, 532.
36. Detroit, *Forty-Second Annual Report of the Board of Water Commissioners*, p. 17–18.

the Department of Public Works.[37] In other instances, Pingree attacked members of the board for bribing members of the state legislature to defeat a change in the city charter. Pingree saw the development of the water system as strictly linked to taxation. He called for abolishing water rates, dismissing the "army of water assessors," and advised setting aside tax revenue for water, letting the property past which a water line runs pay for that line regardless of the number of inhabitants. The mayor made the point that

> vast sums have been levied upon the homes, the manufactures and the business houses, while the thousands of acres of unimproved real estate within the city limits, held for speculative purposes, and the value of which is being constantly enhanced by the water rates levied on the industrial classes, did not contribute a cent.[38]

It is clear that by laying pipes in newly opened streets for a nominal fee, the city joined the real estate interests in the growth business. The new pipes of the still uninhabited sections of town were good quality large iron pipes, while the east side of town, which I have characterized as the port of entry for immigrants and as the working class section of the city, was still equipped in the 1890s with small wooden pipes, 2.25–3 inches in diameter (see map 5.4). Most of these small wooden pipes had been replaced by 6–8-inch iron pipes elsewhere in the city in the 1880s. In 1892, the east side was using 78% of the 44,772 feet of wooden pipes still existing in the city, the bulk of them within a triangle of 404 acres on a line from the intersection of Willis and John R. to the intersection of Waterloo and MacDougall. Theoretically, water was accessible everywhere in Detroit; practically, the service was hampered by many technical problems which were slowly being resolved by the professionalization of the department. But a basic social inequality persisted, as uninhabited land received priority over the working-class sectors of the city for the distribution and improvement of services.

The commissioners's policy of actually favoring the undeveloped areas of Detroit over the districts of the poor was in fact standard practice in Detroit's government, as illustrated by the policy and debate revolving around the creation and paving of Detroit's major artery, Grand Boulevard. The Grand Boulevard project was authorized by the legislature in 1879 by "an act to provide for the establishment and maintenance of a broad street or Boulevard about the limits of the city of Detroit and through portions of the townships of Ham-

---

37. Detroit, *Sixth Annual Message of Mayor Hazen S. Pingree to the Common Council of the City of Detroit, Delivered January 8, 1895* (Detroit: Thos. Smith Printing Co., City Printers, 1895), p. 29.

38. Ibid., p. 28.

tramck, Greenfield, and Springwells in the county of Wayne."[39] The Board of Boulevard Commissioners was appointed to administer the provisions of the act. The land for the boulevard itself, which was to become the major artery encircling Detroit, was actually donated to the city by the landowners, but the common council was unwilling to commit a great deal of money to the paving and improvement of the road.

In the 1880s Mayor Thompson and Mayor Chamberlain were in favor of taxing the abutting property for the improvements that needed to be made, as Chamberlain explained in the *Detroit Tribune* in 1887:

> On and in the vicinity of the Boulevard, values have been enhanced several hundred percent. It stands to reason that that property should pay a larger proportion of the cost of the improvement than other property two or three miles removed which has not been increased in value five per cent.[40]

The property owners and new homeowners along the boulevard, of course, resisted this view. Some were among the wealthier citizens of Detroit with interests in real estate, like Bella Hubbard, a wealthy landowner who had invested heavily in the west side. James Randall, a politician and businessman who owned several newspapers and had large interests in the railroads, campaigned for increasing the city's bonded indebtedness to improve the boulevard. Randall argued that "unless it is decided to bond the city for its completion, [the boulevard] will never be more than a dirt road";[41] he also argued that the boulevard was not a mere road but rather a park which would benefit Detroit as much as Belle Isle would, and therefore the improvement of the boulevard should be linked with that of the newly acquired island. In 1888, the *Evening News* bitterly attacked Randall's plan:

> Nearly a quarter of a million people visited the Island Park last summer. These are the people who demand the improvement of the island. How many people visited the Boulevard? All around its dreary length one could drive on any pleasant Sunday without meeting more than a dozen vehicles and not a single pedestrian. Who demands the improvement of the boulevard? A few big real estate owners who are trying to make fortunes at the public cost.[42]

39. Michigan, *Local Acts of the Legislature of the State of Michigan, 1879*, vol. 2, Act no. 374, p. 177; see also Donald Z. Danuloff, "The Acquisition of Belle Isle and the Grand Boulevard Project" (M.A. thesis, Wayne State University, 1966), p. 41.

40. *Detroit Tribune*, 4 January 1887, cited by Danuloff "Acquisition of Belle Isle," p. 46.

41. Danuloff, "Acquisition of Belle Isle," p. 46.

42. *Detroit Evening News*, 13 April 1888, cited by Danuloff, "Acquisition of Belle Isle," p. 50.

MAP 5.4

Wooden Pipes, 2½ inches in Diameter, 1891

SOURCE: *Fortieth Annual Report of the Board of Water Commissioners to the Common Council of the City of Detroit, 1891* (Detroit, 1892).

0   ¼   ½   ¾   1   2
MILES

0   1   2   3
KILOMETERS

TON ST.

1900

AVE.

BROOK

OAKLAND

ST. AUBIN AVE.

R.R.

CITY LIMITS

ST.

Milwaukee Junction

GRAND TRUNK R.R.

EVARD

CITY LIMITS

1880

AVE.

DIVISION)

HIGAN

ST.

SOUTHERN

ST.

AVE.

AVE.

HARPER

R.R.

AVE.

1900

ST.

Lake Shore Junction

BOULEVARD

R.R.

FERRY

ST.

BOULEVARD

MILWAUKEE

1885

FOREST

E.

AVE.

GRATIOT

1880

MACK

ST.

MACK

GRAND HAVEN

ST.

CITY LIMITS

CENTRAL LINE

CITY LIMITS

CITY LIMITS

RUSSELL

BRUSH

GRATIOT

HASTINGS

DETROIT

AVE.

CHENE

ST.

ELMWOOD

MT. ELLIOTT ST.

MICHIGAN BELT

BOULEVARD

KERCHEVAL

ST.

VAN DYKE

McCLELLAN ST.

CADILLAC

AVE.

McDOUGALL

SHERMAN

CHAMPLAIN

JEFFERSON

ATWATER   ST.

R.R. FERRY

FERRY

iver

UNITED STATES
CANADA

Belle Isle

Actually, little had been achieved for Belle Isle in the 1880s. Detroit's common council had hired the noted landscape architect, Frederick Law Olmsted, famous for his designs of New York's Central Park and Chicago's Riverside, to design a plan for Detroit's Belle Isle in 1881. Too expensive, the plan was set aside and not much had been done since to improve the island.[43] Randall, who was leader of the Democratic minority in the state legislature in 1889, saw to the passing of an act empowering the common council of Detroit to borrow $500,000 for the improvement of the boulevard, another $400,000 for the improvement of Belle Isle, and the formation of a new body, the Commissioners of Parks and Boulevards, combining two previously separate boards.[44] This was but one more instance in which the city—in this case the Democratic administration which preceded Pingree—had favored spreading the cost of improving unopened land over all taxpayers of the city rather than assigning the burden to the people who would benefit from large speculative gains.

Pingree could not control the Board of Water Commissioners, but he had more authority with the Board of Public Works, which reported directly to the common council. The Board of Public Works was responsible for laying out sewers and for opening and paving streets. Much work needed to be done in the 1890s, and the Board of Public Works operated from a variety of funds, some from general taxation, some from the sale of bonds, some from special taxation on the abutting property benefiting from improved services. While some cities were constructing separate sewer systems, one system to "remove excremental matters from the household speedily," and the other designed to handle storm water, Detroit maintained a combined system of sewer mains.[45] During Pingree's administration, the board moved to build better quality sewers, and the mayor launched a well-publicized campaign against contractors who had provided low quality cement. The city also equipped many blocks with lateral sewers made of vitrified crock or brick to join houses to sewer mains and replace unsanitary privy vault cesspools throughout the city. The board of Public Works was also in charge of paving and repaving streets, which, by all accounts, were in wretched condition in 1890. It was not until 1893 that the Board finally convinced the common council that all street paving material— cedar, brick, or asphalt—had to be placed on a bed of concrete rather than on a cheap sand foundation. The board was also involved in constant battles with the water commissioners and Detroit's gas company to prevent their tearing up the streets it had recently paved in order to lay water or gas pipes. The board

43. Danuloff, "Acquisition of Belle Isle," pp. 37–39; Burton, *City of Detroit*, pp. 429–62.
44. Danuloff, "Acquisition of Belle Isle," pp. 51–52.
45. Joel A. Tarr, "The Separate vs. Combined Sewer Problem," *Journal of Urban History* 5 (May 1979): 308–9.

also tried to regulate the setting of poles in the street for the purpose of running electrical, phone, and other wires, and it tried to enforce the ordinance requiring street-railway companies to maintain the streets over which their tracks ran. Thus the Board of Public Works considerably tightened its control of contractors throughout the decade.[46]

As we have seen, the independent water commissioners had left the working-class east side underequipped in the 1890s. Despite the mayor's rhetoric, the Board of Public Works did not do much better when it came to sewers and pavements, and the east side lagged far behind the west side. In the 1890s, east-side streets from 1.5 to 2.5 miles from city hall were paved and sewers installed, long after houses had been built. In contrast, much activity went on in the west side beyond 2.5 miles from city hall simultaneously with or in anticipation of new housing development. In the 1890s, the west side between 2.5 and 3 miles from city hall received 84.87 feet of lateral sewer per acre of land compared with 52.66 in the east; and the difference between west and east was of the same magnitude between 3 and 3.5 miles from city hall. Similar differences existed for pavements (see table 5.7), as substantially more pavement was laid on the west side where the middle-class native white Americans lived. In the east side, on the other hand, the streets running from Riopelle on the west to Joseph Campau on the east and between Canfield and Scott were still without pavement in 1900. This 176 acre area was mostly the home of Germans and Poles.

City departments trying to cope with urban growth and technological change succeeded partially, but they neglected large sections of the city, notably the east side, in favor of others. Private companies, in the business of providing services to the city, also neglected the east side of town. Street railways, often described as the major pulling force toward the suburbs, had indeed served the western section of Detroit well, but they almost completely neglected the east which grew, despite this blatant lack of services, during the last two decades of the nineteenth century.[47] Three companies operated horse-drawn railways in Detroit in 1880: the Detroit City Railway, the Fort Wayne and Elmwood

46. Holli, *Reform in Detroit*, pp. 24–27, 92.

47. W. B. Scott, *Street Railways of Detroit* (New York: Knickerbocker Press, 1895); Jack E. Schramm and William H. Henning, *Detroit's Street Railways*, vol. 1: *1863–1922*, Bulletin 117 (Chicago: Central Electric Railfans Association, 1978); Graeme O'Geran, *A History of the Detroit Street Railways* (Detroit: Conover Press, 1931); for additional information see *Detroit City Directory for 1880*, and for the years 1881–84 (Detroit: J. W. Weeks & Co., 1880–84); *J. W. Weeks and Co.'s Detroit City Directory for 1885* (Detroit: R. L. Polk & Co., 1885); *Detroit City and Wayne County Directory for 1886* (Detroit: R. L. Polk & Co., 1886); *Detroit City Directory for 1887*, and for the years 1888–91 (Detroit: R. L. Polk & Co., 1887–91); *Detroit City Directory for the Year Commencing August 1st, 1892*, and for the years 1893–1900 (Detroit: R. L. Polk & Co., 1892–1900).

Railway, and the Grand River Street Railway. In 1880, 72% of their combined trackage was in the west side, and only 28% in the east. In the 1880s, many workmen had no alternative to walking or bicycling to work, although some could board a train a few times a day at a small station near Woodward Avenue, at the intersection of the Grand Trunk Railway, the Lake Shore and Michigan Southern, and the Detroit and Bay City Railway. It was only in 1886 that a street-railway line following Brush, Ohio, Saint Antoine, Farnsworth, Russell, and Ferry connected the city center to the industrial Lake Shore and Milwaukee Junction, and only in 1890 that another line along Chene Street cut across the entire east side from the river to the north. The situation of the east side became better with the construction of the Belt Line by the Michigan Central Railroad in 1889 (see map 5.5). Immediately, real estate firms promoted subdivisions near the Lake Shore and Milwaukee Junction, pointing to the proximity to the new street railway and railroad lines. In the *Real Estate Advertiser* of 1890 Harrah's Real Estate Exchange advertised such a subdivision with seventy-two lots for sale,

> [one] end of it being only two blocks distant from both a belt line station and the terminus of the Chene Street Car line, which runs up from the Detroit River. The other end is within two blocks of the point where the Belt Line crosses the Grand Trunk and Bay City Railways; and as all trains must come to a full stop there, passengers are enabled to get on and off, as at a regular station. The advantages offered by a subdivision so situated, one from which lines of railway run in three directions, should be readily seen and appreciated. From it, by rapid transit, the great factory districts existing, as well as those being opened up, may be reached.[48]

Such opportunities were the exception rather than the rule, however, as we can see from the chronological map of street-railway development: street railways equipped the east side after it was built and populated, not in anticipation of future developments. Although the east side had 44% of the city's street railway trackage in 1890, most of it was accounted for by three lines built in 1888 on the three streets above Jefferson, running east-west, mainly serving the downtown and the river area. In the 1890s, Mayor Pingree and the transit companies engaged in a well-publicized war over prices, with Pingree campaigning for a three-cent fare which the workingman could afford. Melvin Holli, Pingree's biographer, hailed the mayor for having led "a nationwide fight for low fares," including the creation in 1894 of a new company, the Detroit Railway, to compete with and break the near monopoly of the Detroit Citizens Railway (which had bought the Detroit City Railway).[49]

48. Harrah's Real Estate Exchange, Detroit *Real Estate Advertiser* 1 (April 1890): 30.
49. Holli, *Reform in Detroit*, pp. 101–24.

The many aspects of the struggle between the reform mayor and the street railway companies are well known, including the constant battles between the city and the companies over the technology of street-railway electrification, safety standards, and the problems posed by the breaking of water pipes from the discharge of electricity into the ground along the railway lines. More important for our purpose is the conclusion that transportation was not the leading factor of Detroit's development. It is clear that the street-railway companies had not fulfilled their outspoken claim, echoed by a Detroit real estate publication of 1892, that rapid transit

> had solved the problem of city life. It is fast abolishing the horrors of the crowded tenements. It is shortening the hours of labor. It makes the poor a land owner. It is doing more to put down socialism, in this country at least, than all other things combined.[50]

Such claims and the advertisements for a few well-located subdivisions must not obscure the basic fact that the street-railway companies, primarily motivated by profit, had largely neglected the working-class sections of Detroit.

Street railways did not play a major part in Detroit's expansion during the last two decades of the nineteenth century, when the city grew and expanded its housing from 1.5 miles past city hall to the fringes beyond 3 miles from city hall. At least half of the city did without the street railways. In the west, white-collar Americans had been provided with transportation to their new subdivisions as they opened. In the east, working-class immigrants could not count on it. If Detroit in 1880 was a profoundly divided city, it remained so as it grew, and technological change did not cut across social cleavages but rather adapted to them. A casual observer of the map of street railways, applying the accepted urban planning theory that urban development usually follows improvements in transportation, could conclude that substantial sections of the east side were not developed in the 1890s; yet this was not the case. The east-side inhabitants did without city services to a large extent, but their lack of a technologically developed environment did not prevent them from developing a unique urban culture and contributing to the city's growth. When we compare the chronology of housing development to that of services, it becomes clear that through an opportune combination of private and public interests, only one half of Detroit benefited from services as soon as houses were built. The other half had to wait a long time for vital connections to the city's systems of service. This inequality was blatant, regardless of the type of service or how it was financed, whether entirely by city revenues (for water), partially through taxes paid by beneficiaries (for sewer and pavement), or through business ventures of private companies

50. Shelley and Simpson, Detroit *Real Estate Review* 1 (June 1892): 1.

MAP 5.5

Street Railways, 1880 – 1900

All merged to form the Detroit United Railway by 31 December 1900.

[1]The Detroit City Railway, founded in 1863, became the Detroit Street
Railway in 1890, the Detroit Citizens Street Railway in 1891, and the
Detroit Traction Company in 1894.

[2]The Detroit Railway, founded in 1894, became the Detroit Electric
Railway in 1896.

[3]The Fort Wayne and Elmwood Railway, founded in 1871, became the
Fort Wayne and Belle Isle Railway in 1892.

[4]The Cadillac line was acquired in 1889 and abandoned in 1891.

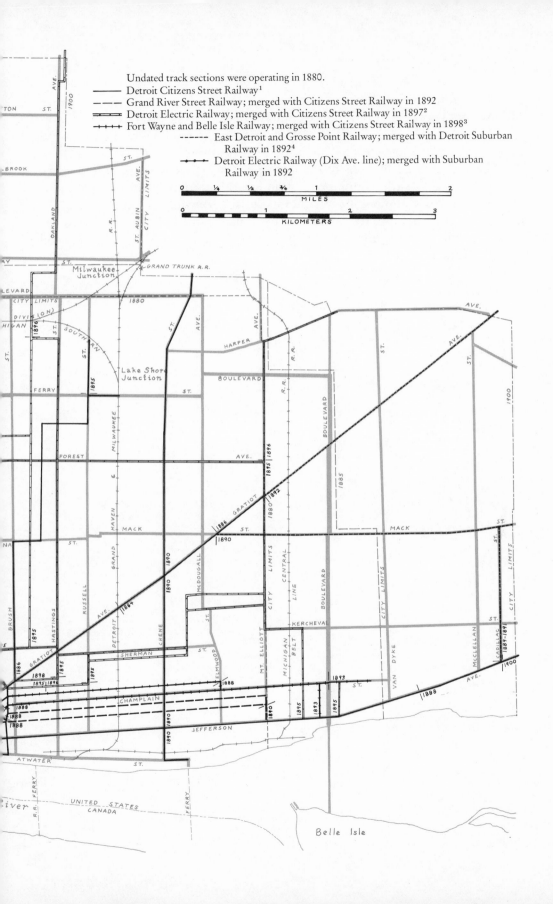

Undated track sections were operating in 1880.

——— Detroit Citizens Street Railway[1]

– – – Grand River Street Railway; merged with Citizens Street Railway in 1892

═══ Detroit Electric Railway; merged with Citizens Street Railway in 1897[2]

+++ Fort Wayne and Belle Isle Railway; merged with Citizens Street Railway in 1898[3]

------ East Detroit and Grosse Point Railway; merged with Detroit Suburban Railway in 1892[4]

•—•— Detroit Electric Railway (Dix Ave. line); merged with Suburban Railway in 1892 (for street railways). What we do not know, however, is the extent to which this uneven treatment of different sections of the city reflected the discrimination imposed upon the poorer sections of town, seen as poor investments, by the public and private agencies in the business of equipping the metropolis. It may have been that large sections of the metropolis were left without amenities not entirely because of discrimination, although this undoubtedly played a part, but because their autonomous inhabitants resisted the unification imposed upon the urban territory by city engineers and businessmen. This is the problem which I will now examine by analyzing the ways Detroit's neighborhoods evolved from 1880 to 1900.

6

Neighborhoods, Homes, and the Dual Housing Market

Plate 6. The home of Mayor Hazen S. Pingree, 990 Woodward Avenue, Detroit, c. 1900. Courtesy of the Archives of Labor and Urban Affairs, Wayne State University.

All groups of urbanites contributed to Detroit's multidimensional growth, albeit in a variety of ways and with widely different interests at stake. The workings of the various interest groups produced a maze of different neighborhoods, as some sections of the city were built through the speculative ventures of well-established real estate firms and others through informal channels of neighborhood collaboration. Given the availability of vacant spaces in the city itself, near job opportunities, and given the importance and cohesiveness of Detroit's ethnic neighborhoods in 1880, it is reasonable to expect that newcomers to Detroit would not settle in dilapidated downtown houses left to them by previous occupants, but would rather enlarge existing communities and participate in the city's expansion.[1] By so doing, newcomers played an important role in the unique experience of simultaneous deconcentration and filling up of open spaces which preceded massive suburbanization.

In order to understand the ways in which different groups of urbanites contributed to the city-building process, I will attempt to define their goals, to outline their strategies, and to describe the outcome of their efforts—the residential neighborhoods of Detroit at the turn of the century. I will first look at the changes in the ethnic map of Detroit from 1880 to 1900; I will then examine the broad differences in residential land uses in several major sections of the city; finally, I will examine patterns of homeownership among Detroit's ethnic groups and the variety of operations of the housing markets within the city.

A CHANGING ETHNIC MAP

A comparison of ethnic residential patterns for 1880 and 1900 reveals radical changes in ethnic group location during the twenty-year period. Nine ethnic groups—Americans, English Canadians, French Canadians, British, Irish, Germans, Poles, Russians (almost all Jewish), and Blacks—were selected for computing the index of ethnic dominance; four occupational categories—high white-collar, low white-collar, skilled, semiskilled and unskilled workers—were used for computing the index of occupational dominance. Many important differences in the detail of the ethnic arrangement of the city emerge from this observation of changing neighborhoods, but the fact that stands out is that most ethnic groups participated in the city-building process by expanding toward previously undeveloped areas of the city. A review of each ethnic group of the city shows that most groups moved toward the new subdivisions of the periphery while also maintaining some of their members in their area of initial settlement in the walking city. This was clearly the case for native white Americans,

---

1. In contrast to the familiar post–World War II city, where space is available mostly in suburbs, see William Alonso, "The Historic and Structural Theories of Urban Form: Their Implications for Urban Renewal," *Journal of Land Economics* 40 (1964): 227–31

British, and English Canadians, but this was also the case for the working-class groups of German and Polish immigrants. This process of population expansion, deconcentration, and relocation in newer areas of the city, however, involved sets of constraints for the Anglo-Saxon population different from those for the Germans and the Poles—constraints I will examine in detail. Other groups, such as the Russian Jews, the Blacks, the French Canadians, and some other minorities like the Italians (not included in the computation of the index because of their small numbers in the city), remained clustered near the downtown area, although each group clustered in different ways. Another group, the Irish, experienced yet another process, which was neither expansion to new land nor concentration in the center but rather relative decline. How did each group contribute to the city-building process? Answering this question will disclose a great deal about the role of ethnicity in the making of the industrial metropolis. Nine maps comparing the 1880 and 1900 samples will begin to answer the question by demonstrating the changing composition and location of ethnic groups in the city. Since ethnicity was the dominant factor accounting for the clustering of urbanites in the late nineteenth-century city, I will concentrate on the changing ethnic distribution in the clusters of the two samples, using individual maps depicting concentrations of one ethnic group or a combination of two ethnic groups, but I will complete the information by including a general map of occupational concentration (see maps 6.1–6.9).

Leaving the city center and taking Woodward Avenue north, one would have entered a residential zone inhabited largely by families headed by white-collar, working, native white Americans. In 1880, this area was primarily confined to a region along Woodward Avenue, starting approximately three-quarters of a mile from the river. Outside this "central residential" area, there were also some concentrations of native white Americans on the west side in 1880, mainly around the Irish-dominated settlement of Corktown. In some blocks, Americans were mixing with Irish and with Canadians. Some heavily residential blocks inhabited by American families were also located on the west side near the river and on the east side south of Jefferson, often adjacent to blocks of much poorer and ethnically mixed people. In 1880, close to 40% of the households headed by a native white American were in these American central areas. Twenty years later, the native white Americans remained anchored in the original neighborhoods of the "walking city," but they also expanded in five directions: moving up north along Woodward Avenue, moving into the vacant areas of the west side, settling along Grand Boulevard, settling along the river on the east side in newly acquired land, and consolidating their position in the traditionally Irish-dominated area. In 1900, 51.5% of the native white American families were located in areas that they dominated numerically (see map 6.1).

MAP 6.1

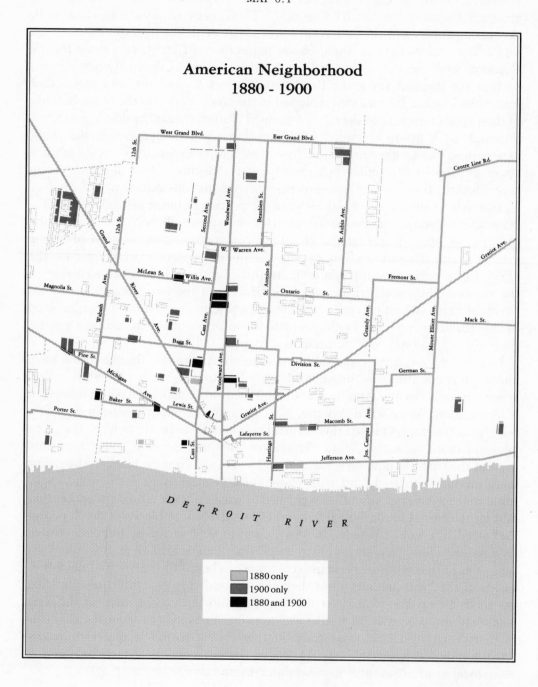

American Neighborhood
1880 - 1900

DETROIT RIVER

1880 only
1900 only
1880 and 1900

American families were thus solidly clustered in their neighborhoods. They were mostly middle-class white-collar workers and most often Episcopalians, Methodists, or Presbyterians. Yet the native white Americans shared their neighborhoods with other English-speaking groups, especially English Canadians and immigrants from England, usually Protestants, and frequently white-collar workers. This mixing developed especially in the move toward the new neighborhoods of the expanding city (see maps 6.2 and 6.3). Except in these American-dominated sections, Canadian and British immigrants were not heavily clustered in identifiable areas—only about 17% of the Canadians and 14% of the British were clustered in such areas in 1880 or 1900—but when they did cluster they joined lower-middle-class American workers.

Of the traditionally working-class districts of the west, the one most rapidly changing was Corktown, the old Irish Catholic neighborhood in this otherwise Anglo-Saxon–dominated section. Centered around the first Irish church of Detroit, Most Holy Trinity, Corktown in 1880 included 40% of those households headed by one Irish immigrant. The number of Irish people concentrated in parts of the city in 1900 remained about 40%, but more and more of the Irish shared their blocks with other groups (see map 6.4). Although Corktown maintained a strong Irish tone, it became more and more native white American and Protestant. One can see here the complex and intriguing process of one ethnoreligious group, the Irish Catholics of Corktown, slowly losing some of its importance in the area, largely because the percentage of Irish-born inhabitants in Detroit's population decreased substantially throughout the second half of the nineteenth century. As the Irish community was growing old, receiving fewer new immigrants from Ireland, the area was also losing some of its ethnic cohesiveness as it became progressively invaded by Protestant native white Americans. The diminishing numbers of Irish who remained in their own neighborhood eventually had to open it to other groups, especially Americans but also Germans; and they did not move as a group into newly built sections of the city.

Detroit's east side, a large area east of Woodward Avenue, bordered by Grand Boulevard, and divided diagonally by Gratiot Avenue, was the main German area of the city in 1880 and remained so in 1900: 52% of the households headed by a German lived there in 1880, 58% in 1900. From 1880 to 1900, however, the enterprising Germans, while remaining in the old east side, expanded and consolidated their positions in other sections of the city, particularly in the midtown section of the east side, north of Division Street, and on the fringes of the east side, in recently incorporated sections of the city where they shared clusters with native white Americans. In the west, Germans settled in and

MAP 6.2

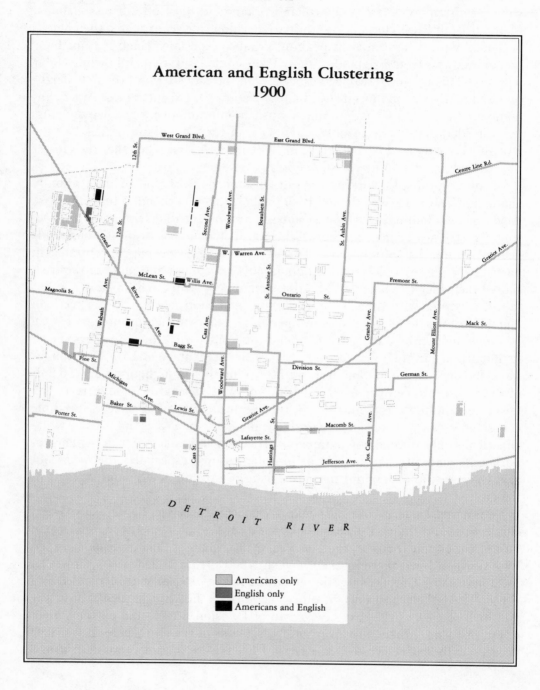

**American and English Clustering
1900**

Americans only
English only
Americans and English

MAP 6.3

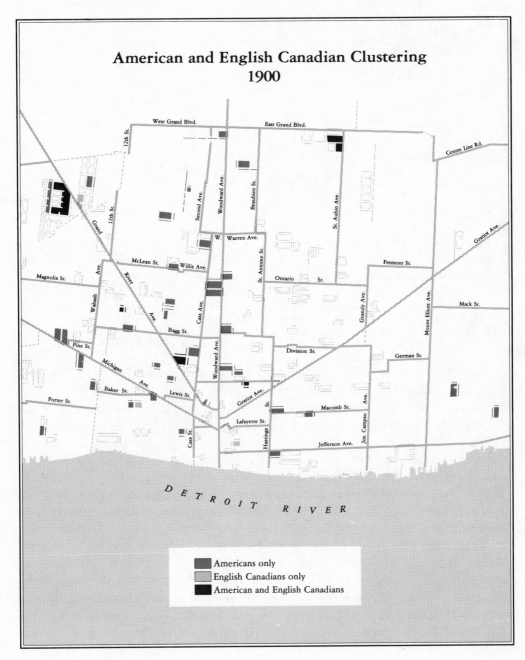

American and English Canadian Clustering 1900

MAP 6.4

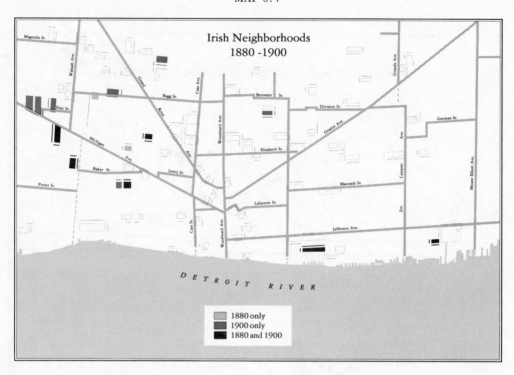

around previously Irish-dominated clusters along Michigan Avenue. The Germans also jumped over the native white American neighborhoods of the west to initiate a new settlement near the city limits, north of Michigan Avenue, sharing some of these new western clusters with Polish families (see map 6.5).

The building of the Polish neighborhood provides an intriguing example of the way in which some immigrant groups entered Detroit through the German-dominated east side. In 1880, only a handful of Polish families had settled in Detroit, and they lived among the Germans. As their numbers grew, the Poles moved further north to locate around Russell Street, Saint Aubin Avenue, and the Catholic Church of the Sweetest Heart of Mary (see maps 6.6). By 1900, the developing Polish neighborhood had become established and cohesive, containing approximately 82% of the Polish population of the city. What is remarkable about the growth of the Polish neighborhood is that the bulk of the newcomers settled in the new east side, beyond the 1.5 mile limit from the city center which was developed in 1880. In other words, Polish immigrants in the 1880s and 1890s reached out toward the periphery of the city, moving into

MAP 6.5

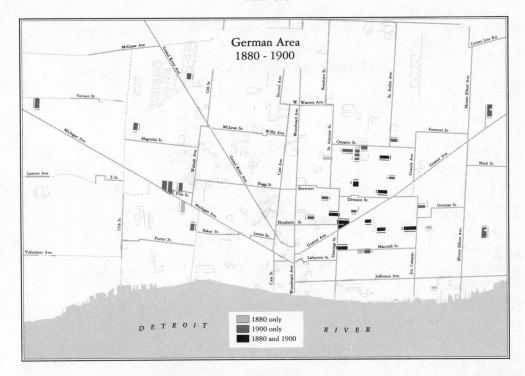

underdeveloped areas neglected by the street railways and ill-equipped with city services. Poles also began a move toward the new subdivisions of the west side, settled near the city limits, and built a church, but the Polish community of west Detroit did not grow large before the twentieth century.

Not only did the old east side house the main German community of the city in 1880 and 1900 as well as the growing Polish settlement, it also included several smaller immigrant groups: French Canadians, Russian Jews, Italians, and immigrants from Austria, Hungary, Belgium, the Netherlands, and Scandinavia. The east side continued to serve as the port of entry to many immigrant families and continued to foster the growth of the early and small Black community. Not all groups of the east side, however, had initiated a move toward the new sections of the city by 1900. Certainly, the French Canadians, the Italians, Austrians, Belgians, and Netherlanders remained scattered among German clusters, sometimes concentrated in small pockets. Only the Russian Jews were numerous enough among the recent immigrants to dominate a few blocks of the business thoroughfares of the old east side, around Gratiot and

MAP 6.6

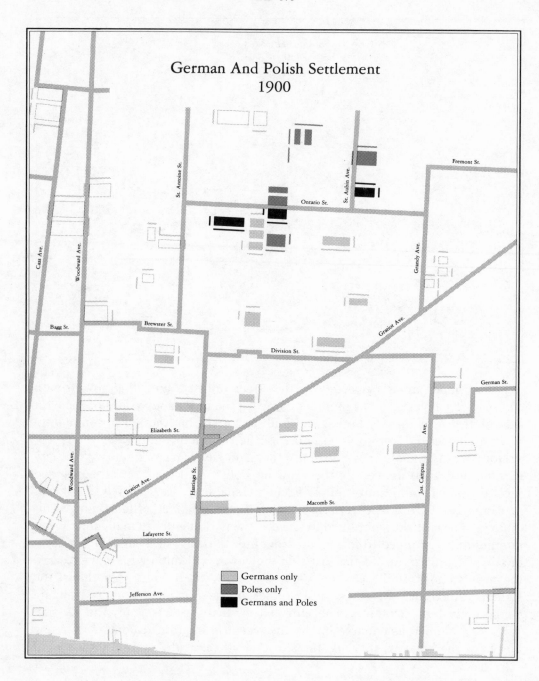

German And Polish Settlement
1900

Germans only
Poles only
Germans and Poles

Hastings. Just as the Poles had originally settled among German Catholics, the Russian Jews often shared blocks with German Jews of the near east side (see map 6.7).

In contrast to the recently arrived Russian Jews, the Blacks had been settling in Detroit for a long time, many of them filling service occupations, working as barbers, waiters, hotel porters, or servants. But at the turn of the century, the Black population constituted only 1.5% of the population of Detroit, a decline since 1880. No cluster sampled on the east side was dominated entirely by Blacks; in fact, only three clusters of the sample showed a distinct pattern of Black dominance: one cluster shared with working-class, native white Americans, Germans, and French Canadians near the riverfront; one located in a German section of the old east side; and a third shared with Russian Jews along Gratiot. It was not rare to see one or two Black families on German and Russian fronts of the east side, many in single family homes, but many in rented apartments. It was not for another decade and a half that the Blacks would grow in number and occupy a significant space in the city (see map 6.8).

Although ethnic groups moved within the growing city and although most of them settled in new areas, the comparison of the indexes of dominance for 1880 and 1900 still reveals intriguing similarities in the nature of socioethnic clustering. Higher index values for 1900 reflect a greater population density in the city than in 1880 and a greater clustering of similar urbanites in the sampled clusters, but the results also suggest that the relationship between ethnicity and social status remained strikingly stable from 1880 to 1900. The values of the indexes for ethnic and occupational concentrations in 1880 was 39.13 for the ethnic categories and 9.12 for the occupational categories (remember that the index is significant at the .05 level if above 1.65; see chap. 2). For 1900, the indexes soared to 98.49 and 56.24, respectively, indicating a strengthening of ethnic and occupational concentrations. As in 1880, however, the relationship between ethnic and occupational concentration was somewhat complex. In some clusters inhabited by native white American white-collar workers, or German skilled craftsmen, or Polish unskilled workers, ethnicity and occupational status were clearly linked (see map 6.9). In many clusters, however, important cross-class ethnic concentrations appeared; many concentrations of German households comprised members of all occupational statuses in the same cluster. There is no need to repeat now the lengthy analysis of the 1880 pattern using 1900 figures, since the two analyses coincide so neatly; it is important to note, however, that the similarity in the concentration and dominance patterns at the two points in time suggests the importance, tenacity, and durability of the neighborhoods in late nineteenth-century Detroit.

MAP 6.7

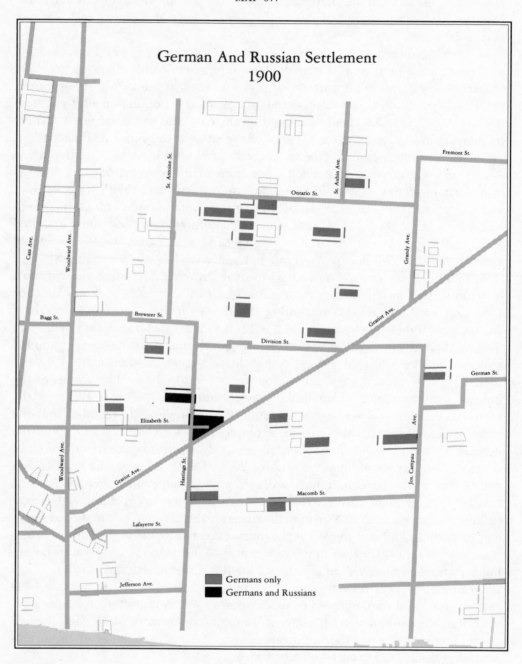

German And Russian Settlement
1900

Germans only
Germans and Russians

MAP 6.8

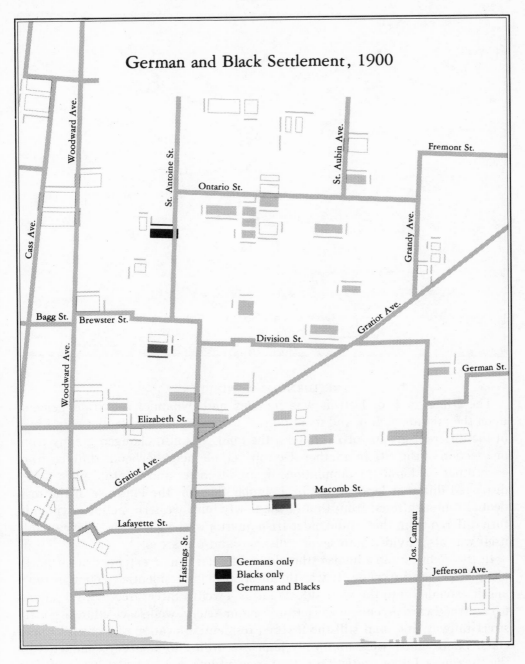

German and Black Settlement, 1900

Germans only
Blacks only
Germans and Blacks

MAP 6.9

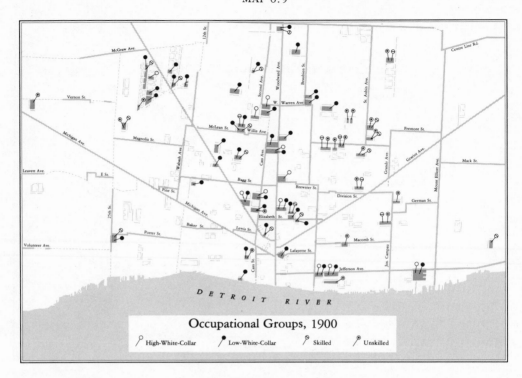

Occupational Groups, 1900

High-White-Collar   Low-White-Collar   Skilled   Unskilled

RESIDENTIAL LAND USES

The ethnic map of Detroit was complex and dynamic, heavily dependent upon the migratory flow and its impulses. Following the residential clusterings of the different groups of Detroiters, the land uses also changed greatly from one section of the city to another. Detroit's ethnic neighborhoods differed from each other in dominant population, in architecture, and in atmosphere; they displayed different landscapes. In a similar fashion, the land use of the residential center differed from that of the newly built western sections, which in turn differed from that of the older Irish quarter of the west side. The east side itself was also divided into several distinct land-use areas.

In the eighties and nineties, the old residential center extended itself north along Woodward Avenue. It was the most spacious residential section of town and it extended into the west side as far as Twelfth Street (see maps 6.10 and 6.11). Woodward Avenue was Detroit's major artery, well serviced by a central street-railway line, and still the favored residential location of Detroit's upper class. Land values were uniformly high. According to a survey conducted by the Bureau of Labor Statistics in 1891, vacant lots of about 12,500 square feet on Woodward Avenue or adjacent streets such as Palmer or Ferry, about 2 miles from city hall, ranged in price (converted to 1912) from $3,700 to $7,800.[2] While the area of high land values extended only through a couple of blocks east of Woodward, it covered about ten blocks west through Trumbull, Commonwealth, or Avery, with a fine graduation from lots worth $1,500 to $2,500 two or three blocks west of Woodward to lots worth between $1,300 and $1,800 on the fringes of the neighborhood.

Houses in these areas of the old residential center and its extension along Woodward were very large and often made of brick. In 1900, as many as 16.23% of the American houses of the city were made of brick, most of them in the "residential center," while houses in the newly developed zones were built of wood. The land use was almost totally residential, with large backyards and stables in each lot. Often a church was built at the intersection of Woodward and a side street. The population density was relatively low: an average of 48.02 people per acre and only 4.6 people lived in these spacious houses (table 6.1).

This section of town boasted the most expensive houses in the city, as the advertisements of real estate dealers clearly show. The Hannan Real Estate Exchange, a firm listing over 12% of its houses priced above $10,000, handled many expensive homes in this section. On the front page of its listing for January 1889, the firm described three houses on Woodward Avenue for $68,500, $43,740, and $40,500 (in 1912 value). One was

> a corner property on the finest portion of this leading avenue; handsome and substantially-built brick residence, stone foundation . . . , three stories, contains eighteen apartments [meaning rooms], is heated by steam, supplied with every modern convenience, and is handsomely finished throughout. Lot 90 × 158.

The second one was advertised as "expensively finished in oak, ash, bird's eye maple," and the third contained "upwards of 14 apartments of palatial finish."[3] Other firms less specialized in luxurious homes—like the Harrah's Real Estate Exchange, which devoted only 2% of its business to homes above $10,000— listed their expensive homes in the same area. In 1890 Harrah's listed a house on Watson Street for $20,000:

> a very desirable two-and-a-half story brick residence having every modern convenience, twelve apartments and a large attic, heated by steam, several

---

2. Michigan, *Ninth Annual Report of the Bureau of Labor and Industrial Statistics* (Lansing, 1892), pp. 280–301.

3. Hannan Real Estate Exchange, *W. W. Hannan's Real Estate Record* (Detroit) 1 (January 1889): 1.

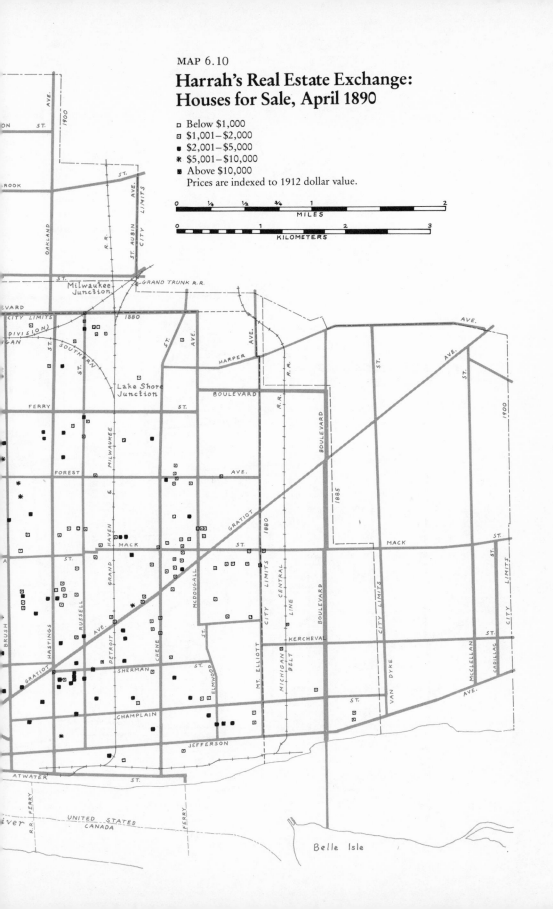

MAP 6.10

Harrah's Real Estate Exchange:
Houses for Sale, April 1890

▫ Below $1,000
▣ $1,001–$2,000
▪ $2,001–$5,000
✳ $5,001–$10,000
◼ Above $10,000
Prices are indexed to 1912 dollar value.

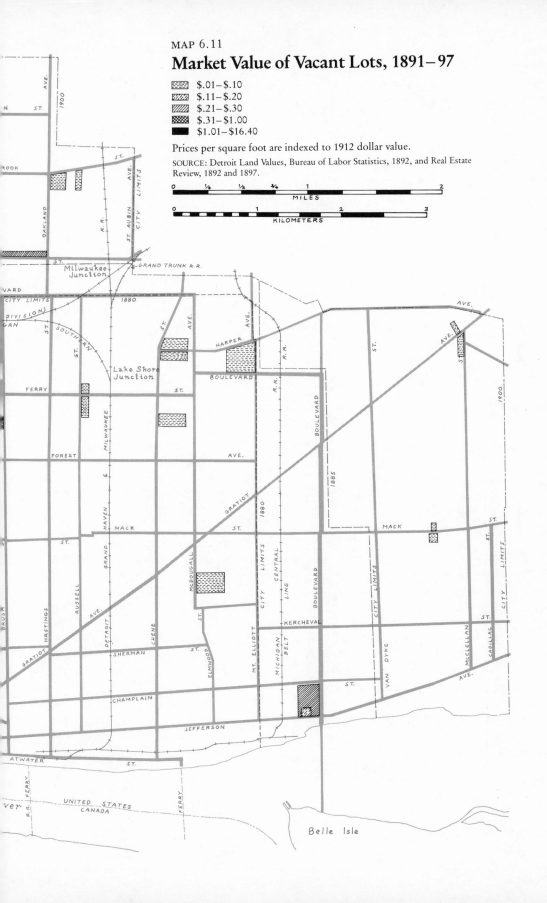

MAP 6.11
Market Value of Vacant Lots, 1891–97

▦ $.01–$.10
▨ $.11–$.20
▧ $.21–$.30
▩ $.31–$1.00
■ $1.01–$16.40

Prices per square foot are indexed to 1912 dollar value.

SOURCE: Detroit Land Values, Bureau of Labor Statistics, 1892, and Real Estate Review, 1892 and 1897.

TABLE 6.1

Building material, building occupancy, and neighborhood density for selected ethnic neighborhoods, Detroit, 1900[a]

Ethnicity	Mean number of people per house[b]	Mean number of stories per house[b]	Mean number of people per acre		Building material[b]				
					Brick	Wood	Stone	Brick and wood	Other combinations
Native white American	4.60	1.47	48.02	(%)	18.30	73.30	0.10	7.90	0.40
Irish	4.62	1.32	54.45	(%)	6.40	88.10	0.00	5.50	0.00
German	4.99	1.20	62.83	(%)	7.50	88.00	0.00	4.40	0.00
Polish	5.95	1.08	72.30	(%)	0.00	96.60	0.00	3.40	0.00

SOURCES: 1900 sample, manuscript schedules of the 1900 population census and *Insurance Maps of Detroit*, 6 vols. (New York: Sanborn-Perris Map Co., 1897).

a. Each neighborhood was identified by locating a high concentration of the population belonging to the particular ethnic group (see maps 6.1, 6.4–6.6). These neighborhood figures include all the houses of the neighborhood, not just houses of the dominant ethnic group.

b. Single-family dwellings.

grates with handsome mantels; hardwood floors, plate glass windows; electric bells throughout. Laundry with stationary tubs; large cellar. Lot 59 × 129; splendid brick barn.[4]

Still luxurious but less expensive homes, in the $5,000 to $10,000 range, were for sale in the same general area of the residential center (see map 6.10). Real estate listings include houses such as one on Rowena Street for $8,200:

near Woodward Avenue, a two-and-a-half story brick dwelling, built on a stone foundation; contains eight apartments, large reception hall, handsome hardwood stairway, principal rooms finished in hardwood; attic suitable for a billiard room. Boynton furnace, modern conveniences, basement lathed and plastered. Lot 25 × 145.

Most such houses were for sale on the near west side through Third Street and Fourth, but some were found as far west as Twelfth Street, such as one advertised for $5,500 between Perry and Bagg streets:

two story frame dwelling, containing twelve apartments exclusive of bath rooms, all nicely finished and papered; high ceilings, hot and cold water; good cellar. Lot 74 × 195. Barn with stabling for six horses. Fruit and shade trees.[5]

The most exclusive residential section of Detroit, then, was in the midtown area, from Woodward toward Twelfth Street on the west side. The real estate market was especially active in the 1880s and 1890s immediately above this exclusive area, in the previously vacant northwest sections of town which were now subdivided and transformed into residential neighborhoods inhabited primarily by native white Americans, British, and English Canadians. Once again the real estate surveys provide us with almost a carbon copy of the picture derived from our concentration indexes on the sampled clusters of the west side.

The overwhelming majority of houses in the middle-class bracket, worth from $2,000 to $5,000, were located on the new west side, in the areas being taken over by the native white Americans, the British, and the English Canadians, although some houses in this price range were also located near the city center, south of Michigan in the west and south of Gratiot in the east. These houses were frame, less luxurious than those in the residential center, but comfortable and typical of the new residential areas of the middle class. For example, on Hancock Avenue West between Seventh Street and Crawford, a house listed for $4,500 was described as a "two story frame dwelling—eight rooms and bath; interior finish oiled pine; one grate and mantel, good cellar.

4. Harrah's Real Estate Exchange, *Real Estate Advertiser* (Detroit) 1 (April 1890): 1.
5. Ibid., pp. 3, 5.

Lot 40 × 110." Or one could find for $2,400 a "spacious new cottage" containing seven rooms on a lot 30 × 115 on Perry Street between Trumbull and National Avenue.[6] Most of these houses were close to the city limits on the west side, where the bulk of the real estate business was located. The 1890 listing of Harrah's real estate exchange comprised 431 entries, 41% of them for houses between $2,000 and $5,000. One 1889 listing of Hannan's exchange also offered 41% of its 1,120 houses for sale in that price range.[7] Many houses of these new subdivisions were still surrounded by empty lots in the 1890s, as realtors continued to divide and plat many subdivisions and sell the lots individually or in bulk to investors. According to the 1891 survey of the Bureau of Labor Statistics, vacant lots were worth about $350 around the boulevard on the west side of town, many of them for sale in this still loosely built, but rapidly developing, area of the city (see map 6.11).

In contrast to this relatively empty middle-class area, other parts of the west side, like Corktown, still maintained a very compact land use, with houses packed one against another on street fronts. The Irish houses were medium-sized structures, 88% of them built of wood. Although the building density was very high, the population density was only moderate, with 54.45 people per acre in 1900 and an average of 4.62 people per house—the same figure then as for the Americans, although the Irish had smaller houses (table 6.1). In the 1890s, however, more substantial houses were built in the area as it became progressively inhabited by larger numbers of native white Americans and slowly integrated into the larger west side.

Things were very different in the east side, where land use differed from the pattern typical of Detroit at large. "The East Side has an environment all its own," wrote the *Detroit Sunday News-Tribune* in 1896:

> It has the churches, the synagogues, the breweries and the beer gardens that for elegance and desirability cannot be excelled in any other portion of the city; but while this is true, the fact remains that there are also on the east side certain sections with environments especially their own as to make them striking examples of foreign customs transported to American soil.[8]

In most of Detroit, residential areas were usually separate from craft and industrial activities, but in the east side many industrial activities intermingled with residences, resulting in a pattern of intensive land use. The Germans who populated the east side formed the backbone of Detroit's working class. Num-

6. Ibid., p. 7.
7. Ibid., pp. 6–16; Hannan, *Real Estate Record* 1:13–30.
8. *Detroit Sunday News-Tribune,* 6 September 1896.

bers of them worked in factories and shops of the east side, in such occupations as the tobacco industry, marble and stone work, textiles, and to a lesser extent the food and metallurgy industries. Others, self-employed or artisans working in small shops, were cabinetmakers, carpenters, blacksmiths, shoemakers, tailors, bakers, brewers, or saloonkeepers.

The east side intermingling of land uses reflected not only the diversity of activities in this section of town, but also the religious diversity of the population. Like other large industrializing cities, Detroit was receiving a large share of Catholic immigration, and over 30% of the German immigrants were Catholics. German Protestant immigrants were also well represented in denominations like the German Lutherans, the German Evangelicals, and the Reformed Germans, so Catholic and Protestant churches were located close to one another. The modest Lutheran churches contrasted with the expensive brick and stone Catholic buildings, and further emphasized the diversity of life in the east side.

East side houses—most of them frame—tended to be smaller than homes of the Irish neighborhood, yet they housed an average of 5 people as opposed to the 4.6 American and Irish figure, with a general density in the neighborhood of about 64 people per acre. Real estate firms were selling a number of houses ranging in price from $1,000 to $2,000 on the east-side main arteries, primarily along Gratiot and on the blocks adjacent to it (see map 6.11). These were the best houses of the east side. Harrah's listed a house on Joseph Campau between Saint Joseph and Illinois for $1,850, "a frame dwelling, one and a half story, bay window, six rooms, usual closets, cellar. Lot 32 × 100, shed and good barn with workshop above."[9] But most of the houses in this price range were too expensive for the great majority of east-side inhabitants, and very few such houses were for sale in the areas newly settled by German and Polish workers.

Newer sections of the east side did not have this mixture of residential and nonresidential activities; the new Polish neighborhood, in the upper east side, for example, was entirely residential. Houses there were very small—97% of them frame and only one story high—yet they housed an average of 5.95 people. The frame cottages of the Polish laborers were neatly packed on crowded streets, and the density of the neighborhood was 72.3 people per acre, the highest in Detroit (table 6.1). In contrast to the very modest houses, the tall steeples of the richly ornamented Catholic churches stood out and contributed to the neighborhood's unique appearance of a complete, compact village within the city.

The old sections of the east side, especially the areas inhabited by Blacks, Italians, French Canadians, and Jews, were very crowded, combining multiple-family dwellings, shops, and stores on busy streets. The *Detroit Sunday News-*

9. Harrah's *Real Estate Advertiser* 1:17.

Tribune in 1896 described the Jewish quarter, for example, as one of the busiest sections of the old east side:

> In a rectangle formed by four streets, Monroe, Watson, Brush and Orleans, the larger portions, by far, of all the Jews in Detroit, have made their homes. Of this whole district Hastings Street is the business thoroughfare. Around that street and those that adjoin it pretty much all that is orthodox and distinctive of the Jewish race in Detroit clusters.[10]

The intense activity of the Jewish quarter and its varied land use was confirmed by the census taker who canvassed this area of town for the 1900 census. He reported many "Russian" peddlers working there and living in crowded multiple-family dwellings.

Such were the various residences of Detroit in the late nineteenth century, from the very spacious homes of the wealthiest native white Americans to the modest cottages of Detroit's Polonia. There were, of course, many variations within this pattern. The newly developed parts of the east side's periphery, where Germans shared clusters with working-class or lower-middle-class Americans, more closely resembled the northwestern developments of town than the nearby Polish neighborhoods. Yet other fringe developments, like the new western subdivisions of German and Polish day laborers, were also built of modest frame cottages compactly settled on the block. We can now deepen our inquiry, investigate those who owned or rented these homes, and determine how many families usually occupied them in the various sections of town which we have defined. After locating the peoples of Detroit in their changing environment and describing their residences, we can begin to uncover the larger forces at work in the building of Detroit's neighborhoods, especially the role each community played in giving the environment its special tone.

HOME OWNERSHIP AND HOME OCCUPANCY

Some factors immediately stand out in an analysis of housing statistics for Detroit in 1900. The first striking feature of the housing statistics is that working-class immigrants owned their homes proportionately more often than middle-class, native white Americans. Generally speaking, many people owned a home in Detroit; 35.5% of the heads of households above twenty years of age reported to the census takers that they owned their home (free of encumbrance or not). But 55% of the Germans owned their homes, 44% of the Poles, 46% of the Irish, and only 27% of the native white Americans (table 6.2). If we divide the same population of adult heads of households by occupational categories, we find that approximately the same percentage (35%) of each occupational group,

10. *Detroit Sunday News-Tribune*, 13 September 1896.

TABLE 6.2

Home ownership for selected ethnic and occupational groups, Detroit, 1900

Ethnic and occupational group		Owned[a]	Mortgaged	Rented
Native white American[b]	(%)	18.2	8.9	72.9
Black	(%)	14.0	7.9	78.1
Canadian (English)[c]	(%)	7.8	9.3	82.8
Canadian (French)	(%)	14.9	10.8	74.3
British	(%)	28.3	11.7	59.9
Irish	(%)	32.4	13.3	54.4
German	(%)	38.4	16.3	45.2
Polish	(%)	21.4	22.4	56.2
Russian	(%)	7.9	6.6	85.5
High white-collar	(%)	26.5	11.0	62.5
Low white-collar	(%)	20.7	12.1	67.2
Skilled	(%)	22.4	12.5	65.1
Unskilled	(%)	20.4	13.6	66.0

SOURCE: 1900 sample.

a. Owned free or unspecified.

b. Ethnicity of head of household: born in the U.S. of two U.S.-born parents.

c. Born in English-speaking Canada of two Canadian parents; born in French-speaking Canada of two Canadian parents, born in Great Britain of two British parents, etc.

that is, high white-collar professionals, low white-collar workers, skilled workers, and semiskilled and unskilled workers, owned their homes. Today lawmakers and the general public alike consider home ownership as a sign of entrance into the middle class, but the reality of home ownership at the turn of the century was evidently quite different. Some historians have already argued that home ownership at the turn of the century was neither particularly middle class nor American. Stephan Thernstrom suggested in his study of Newburyport that Irish immigrants were acquiring homes at the expense of their children's education; Daniel Luria showed that in Boston "home ownership was probably an investment inferior to most" and that the middle class made a better return on their bonds than on their investment in real estate.[11]

The Detroit census statistics, revealing uniformity of home ownership among occupational categories but substantial differences among ethnic groups, suggest that home ownership in the multiethnic city of the turn of the century was a part of a larger organization of ethnic groups into the neighborhoods which we have described. That owning one's home was more an ethnocultural phenomenon than one of class is clear when we examine more closely the patterns of

11. Stephan Thernstrom, *Poverty and Progress: Social Mobility in a Nineteenth-Century City* (Cambridge, Mass.: Harvard University Press, 1964), p. 201; Daniel D. Luria, "Wealth, Capital, and Power: The Social Meaning of Home Ownership," *Journal of Interdisciplinary History* 7 (Autumn 1976): 278.

home ownership among the working class. Every year since 1884, the Michigan Bureau of Labor Statistics has surveyed factory workers in Detroit and published reports on various industries. In six of these reports, the bureau actually published the raw data, the survey of individual workers, providing information on ethnicity, ownership, and age, among other variables. The reports vary in depth and scope: in 1890, the bureau reported on furniture factories with interviews of 848 workers; in 1891 on metal industries with 3,899 interviews; in 1894 on the railroad employees of Michigan, with 839 cases from Detroit; in 1896 on street railway employees with 600 surveyed workers, and on the employees of hack and bus lines with 147 respondents; in 1897, on the vehicle-making industry with 402 workers.[12] As we follow the surveyors of the Bureau of Labor Statistics from one year to the next, from one industry to the next, and from one company to the next, we find, of course, a great deal of diversity and many special situations. But in all reports, one figure stands out sharply: native white American workers owned their homes substantially less often than immigrants employed in the same occupation and of the same age group. What is important here is the magnitude of the difference between extremes rather than exact percentage points, since we do not know how the samples of factories were originally drawn by the Bureau of Labor Statistics and since we have to assume that these factories were indeed representative of the industries. To complicate matters further, the bureau changed its definition of ethnicity after 1892, recording only the birthplace of the individual worker and no longer that of the parents. But despite these inconsistencies, the results of the surveys reveal several sharp cleavages. Only 11% of the native white American furniture makers owned their homes, compared with 37% of the German furniture makers. In some occupations within the furniture industry (for example, machine hand) the difference was as great as from 16.7% to 41.5%. In the metal industries, subject of the largest bureau report, only 14% of the Americans, 14.9% of the Canadians, 25.4% of the British owned their homes, but the percentages jumped as high as 30.7% for the Irish, 39.7% for the Germans and 32.2% for the Poles. Within the metal industry, the contrast stands out even more sharply when we look at specific occupations. At the bottom of the scale (unspecified daily labor) only 4.8% of the American metal-working laborers were home-owners, compared with 36% of the Poles and 41% of the Germans. The other

12. Michigan, *Seventh Annual Report of the Bureau of Labor and Industrial Statistics* (Lansing, 1890), pp. 150–81; *Eighth Annual Report of the Bureau of Labor and Industrial Statistics* (Lansing, 1891), pp. 2–151; *Eleventh Annual Report of the Bureau of Labor and Industrial Statistics* (Lansing, 1894), pp. 1–385; *Thirteenth Annual Report of the Bureau of Labor and Industrial Statistics* (Lansing, 1896), pp. 1–65, 86–91; *Fourteenth Annual Report of the Bureau of Labor and Industrial Statistics* (Lansing, 1897), pp. 6–169.

reports all show variations on this theme. Among railroad workers, 65% of the Germans but only 21.8% of the native-born laborers owned their homes; in the vehicle industry, 71% of the Germans as opposed to 27.6% of the native-born were homeowners. Employees of hack and bus lines, essentially service workers such as teamsters and delivery men, generally owned few homes, but 26.5% of the Germans did while only 5.6% of the adult native-born owned a home. Only the street-railway employees (conductors, drivers, linemen) showed less contrast between the two groups, with 31.4% and 21.6%, respectively (table 6.3). Such important differences were, of course, reflected in the clusters of the 1900 sample. Not many of the houses in American-dominated clusters were owned by their occupants: only 37% of the single-family dwellings in American-

TABLE 6.3

Home ownership and home values for selected groups of workers, Detroit, 1890–1897

Industry	Homeowners and home values, by ethnicity of workers[a]					
	Native white American (%)	Canadian (%)	British (%)	Irish (%)	German (%)	Polish (%)
1890 Furniture						
Machine hands	16.7	20.0	-	-	41.5	-
Cabinetmakers	-	-	50.0	-	43.6	-
All workers	11.4	20.0	30.8	-	37.4	-
1891 Metal						
Laborers	4.8	18.2	7.1	23.9	40.7	35.6
All workers	14.1	14.9	25.4	30.7	39.7	32.2
Mean home values[b] (all workers)	$1,642	$1,589	$1,763	$1,725	$1,054	$786
	Homeowners, by place of birth of workers					
	United States (%)	Canada (%)	Great Britain (%)	Ireland (%)	Germany (%)	Poland (%)
1894 Railroad						
All workers	21.8	18.0	37.3	27.3	64.5	-
1896 Street railways						
All workers	21.6	23.0	31.3	29.6	31.4	-
1896 Hack and bus lines						
All workers	5.6	-	-	-	26.5	-
1897 Vehicle manufacturing						
All workers	27.6	25.0	-	-	71.4	-

SOURCES: Michigan, *Seventh Annual Report of the Bureau of Labor and Industrial Statistics* (Lansing, 1890), pp. 150–181; *Eighth Annual Report of the Bureau of Labor and Industrial Statistics* (Lansing, 1891); pp. 2–151; *Eleventh Annual Report of the Bureau of Labor and Industrial Statistics* (Lansing, 1896), pp. 1–65, 89–91; *Fourteenth Annual Report of the Bureau of Labor and Industrial Statistics* (Lansing, 1897), pp. 6–169.

a. Born in the U.S. of two U.S.-born parents; born in Canada of two Canadian parents, etc.; workers above 20 years of age.

b. Indexed 1910–1914.

dominated clusters were occupied by the owner, compared with 49% in the German neighborhood, and 67% in the Polish neighborhood (table 6.4).

A second factor that stands out in a general study of housing in Detroit at the turn of the century is that Detroit was a city of single-family dwellings. We have already observed that, in 1880, only 7.3% of the population lived in houses divided into two or more apartments. By 1900, this proportion had risen to only 13.3%, despite the tremendous pressure on the city's housing market caused by the continuous inflow of newcomers and the slowdown of the housing industry in 1893 (table 6.5). In Detroit, far from New York and the tenements of the lower east side, workingmen and recent immigrants were not crowded into filthy "railroad" tenements or throwing garbage into the airshafts of the dumb-bells. In fact, Robert DeForest and Lawrence Veiller noted in their survey of housing problems in twenty-five large American cities at the turn of the century that Detroit was free of the tenement-house evil. In their widely acclaimed exhibit on tenements, DeForest and Veiller examined what was wrong with New York and explained what was right with Detroit:

> Although the city of Detroit has a population of 285,704, yet it has no housing problem at all and tenement houses are unknown. The homes of the majority of the workingmen and poor people of the city are for the most part thoroughly comfortable, and most of the people live in separate houses, there being very few houses throughout the city where there are as many as three families in one building, and only a small number of cases where there are two families living in the same house. There are no block buildings or tenements. A few of the very poorest people live in old houses, which have formerly been used as residences of the rich, but which are now abandoned. In this class of buildings are usually to be found two or three families. The great majority of the workingmen, however, own their own homes, which are usually one or two story cottages, worth from

TABLE 6.4
Home ownership for selected ethnic neighborhoods, Detroit, 1900[a]

Ethnicity		Own[b]	Mortgage	Rent
Native white American	(%)	26.20	10.40	63.40
Irish	(%)	24.60	6.90	68.50
German	(%)	35.60	13.10	51.20
Polish	(%)	41.30	25.40	33.30

SOURCE: 1900 sample.

a. Each neighborhood was identified by locating a high concentration of the population belonging to the particular ethnic group (see maps 6.1, 6.4–6.6). These neighborhood figures include all the inhabitants of the neighborhood living in single-family dwellings.

b. Owned free or unspecified.

TABLE 6.5

Dwelling types for selected ethnic groups, Detroit, 1900

Ethnicity		Single-family dwelling	Multiple-family dwelling
Native white American[a]	(%)	77.47	22.53
Black	(%)	70.34	29.66
Canadian (English)[b]	(%)	78.80	21.20
Canadian (French)	(%)	70.89	29.11
British	(%)	86.28	13.72
Irish	(%)	86.91	13.09
German	(%)	74.33	25.67
Polish	(%)	30.99	69.01
Russian	(%)	51.00	49.00

SOURCE: 1900 sample.

  a. Ethnicity of head of household: born in the U.S. of two U.S.-born parents.

  b. Born in English-speaking Canada of two Canadian parents; born in Great Britain of two British parents, etc.

$800 to $2,000. The average rent paid by the ordinary workingman is from $8 to $10 a month for a whole house, containing six good-sized rooms, with water in the kitchen.[13]

Clearly DeForest and Veiller overlooked some of the crowding which characterized certain sections of Detroit, but they were correct in their overall assessment of the situation. This becomes clear if we examine carefully some of the multifamily houses which did exist in Detroit. The Poles, the ethnic group maintaining the highest proportion of families living in multifamily dwellings, also maintained an extremely high rate of home ownership. As we look at the multifamily dwellings of the Polish neighborhood closely, we find that they were rarely rented by absentee owners to unknown tenants. More often the owner of the house rented a part of it (often the better part, like the front parlor) to a second family. This additional income helped pay for the house, and the prospect of home ownership compensated for the temporary inconvenience of doubling up.[14] A few figures easily demonstrate this pattern: while only 31% of the Detroit Poles lived in single-family dwellings, these were overwhelmingly owners. In fact, the Poles had the highest rate of home ownership of all groups (74%) when we consider single-family dwellings only. The rest of the Polish

13. Robert W. DeForest and Lawrence Veiller, *The Tenement House Problem*, 2 vols. (New York: Macmillan Co., 1903), 1:146–47.

14. Sister Mary R. Napolska, "The Polish Immigrant in Detroit to 1914," *Annals of the Polish Roman Catholic Union Archives and Museum* 10 (1946): 67; Roger D. Simon, "The City-Building Process: Housing and Services in New Milwaukee Neighborhoods 1880–1910," *Transactions of the American Philosophical Society* 68 (July 1978): 19.

population of Detroit, or 69% of the Polish families, lived in multiple dwellings, most of them inhabited by two families (see map 6.12). Forty percent of the Poles living in two-family dwellings were owners living on the spot, which means that most of the second families were renting from an owner who lived on the premises. In the few cases of three-family dwellings occupied by Poles, 30% of the families were owners also living on the spot. In most cases, the second and third families were also Polish; in 91.5% of the cases involving two families, Polish families occupied both apartments in the dwelling. The same pattern occurred in 75% of the cases involving German families, but in only 42% of the cases involving American families in other sections of town.

As a result of the high rate of home ownership and the plethora of single-family dwellings, only limited sections of Detroit resembled the physical ghettos—downtown areas inhabited by minority-group members who rented dilapidated homes from absentee owners—described by Louis Wirth and Ernest Burgess. The Russian Jews came closest to living in ghetto conditions; in fact, a reporter for the *Detroit Sunday News-Tribune*, who investigated the Jewish quarter in 1896, labelled it "a ghetto" in his article.[15] The Russian Jews were concentrated in small sections along otherwise industrial and commercial streets. They lived next to Stroh's brewery on Gratiot Avenue, for example, and on business thoroughfares around Gratiot. In one cluster of the sample—on Hastings, Saint Antoine, High, and Montcalm, in the heart of the Jewish quarter— 299 people lived in 1900 (cluster 19). The cluster included 58 people born in Russia, 38 born in the United States of Russian parents, 37 born in Germany, 48 born in the United States of German parents, 46 white Americans, 14 Blacks, and some people of mixed foreign parentage. Inhabitants of the cluster held a variety of jobs also typical of the urban ghetto with peddlers of various goods predominating, followed by semiskilled textile workers, and a few community leaders such as a rabbi.

This Russian-Jewish quarter differed significantly from the classic ghetto, however, in its housing. A close examination of the area reveals that many Russian Jews lived in small, newly built tenement houses, not in the dilapidated houses abandoned by previous occupants typical of the urban ghetto. In fact, building activity flourished in this cluster of the near east side: of the 53 houses standing in 1900, at least 26 were built between 1880 and 1900. The records of the building permits reveal that two-story brick duplexes, often combining stores and apartments, were built by German architects, builders, contractors, and carpenters who invested in the area and rented the structures to the Jews

15. *Detroit Sunday News-Tribune*, 13 September 1896.

MAP 6.12

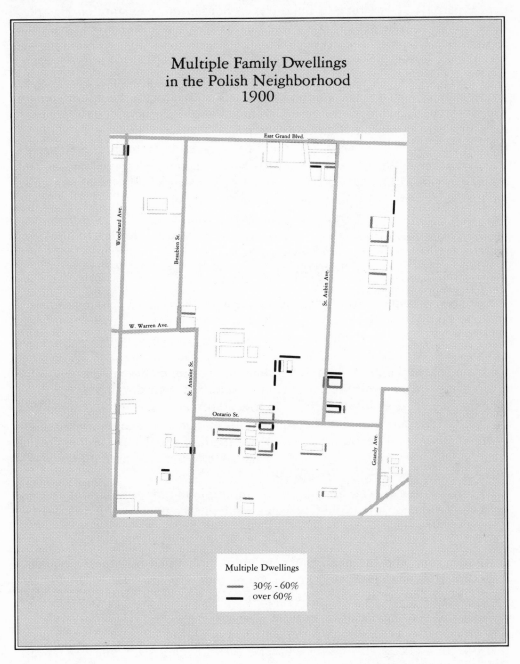

Multiple Family Dwellings
in the Polish Neighborhood
1900

and to some Blacks.[16] One German mason, Ferdinand D. Scheiner, obtained twelve permits at one time to build eleven houses and one store on Hastings Street in 1897. Whether Scheiner was the investor himself or building for yet another investor, we do not know. The important point, however, is that the new houses were all rented at the time of the 1900 census: one to a Russian-Jewish dry goods peddler; one divided into two parts, half rented to a Russian-Jewish painter who had his painting store on the spot, and the other to a German widow. Around the block, the same German mason, Scheiner, built twelve two-story brick dwellings on High Street in 1897. One was rented to the rabbi of the community and his family, another one was divided into three apartments rented to three families headed by a Russian capmaker, a clothing peddler, and a junk peddler. Other German contractors invested in the same block, building for themselves or for other absentee owners, and collected the rent from the recent immigrants living in these dense areas of merchandizing and peddling. So although the Russian-Jewish blocks of the near east side clearly formed a rental zone owned by German investors, with occasional multifamily units, the buildings there were new investments rather than the left-over remnants of a better time.

The only examples of old tenement houses rented to recent immigrants by absentee landlords in Detroit were located in a handful of blocks of the old east side shared by poor Germans, Blacks, and Italians. In two clusters of the 1900 sample, one dominated by Blacks (cluster 30), and one where Italians and Germans shared dominance, most families rented from an absentee owner; 30% of the houses were multifamily dwellings, some of them housing as many as four families. In the Black cluster, on Macomb, one tenement was inhabited by two Black families and one Russian family, and on Croghan, one was rented to three Black families and one French-Canadian family. According to the records of the fire marshal, there were hardly any building activities in these clusters in the twenty years before 1900.

As this housing survey has shown, the multiple-family dwellings of Detroit were not for the most part old tenements rented to the poor by greedy absentee landlords. This traditional type of multiple dwelling—the notorious railroad tenements of Manhattan—existed in Detroit but only in limited sections of the downtown area and the near center, primarily inhabited by Blacks, Italians, a handful of Russian Jews, and French Canadians. Beyond these isolated pockets, Detroit was a city of single-family homes, or of multiple dwellings inhabited by their owners such as those in the Polish neighborhood. And Detroit was a

16. Mark Coir, "A Manual for the Use of the Building Permits as Issued by the Fire Marshal 1880–1908" (1977); Detroit, Department of Building and Safety, "Fire Marshal Building Permits, 1881–1901" (manuscript at BHC).

city of homeowners; the analyses of both surveys of the Bureau of Labor Statistics and of the federal census interview schedules showed that owning a home at the turn of the century was not a middle-class phenomenon, nor was it a sign of any movement into the middle class. Considering the large number of day laborers owning a home, it may well have been a brake to mobility. In fact, home ownership was more an emblem of immigrant working-class culture than of the established middle-class native white American culture. While twentieth-century lawmakers talk of home ownership as a birthright of Americans, this tradition seems to have taken its roots in the ethnic neighborhoods of American industrial cities. This phenomenon brings a question immediately to mind: how could day laborers, often with unsteady employment, in fact become homeowners? The answer to this question will not only illuminate the home-building process in the city but also cast some light on the nature of ethnic communities in urban industrial America. I will argue that at least two separate housing markets existed in Detroit in the late nineteenth century. One was formal, operated through professionals from their downtown offices. It produced expensive homes for the native white American community, many of them for rent. The other market was informal, highly localized, controlled from within the ethnic communities and designed to fit their means. It was this second housing market that produced the owner-occupied cottages of the working class.

THE FORMAL HOUSING MARKET

An expanding city with plenty of vacant space, expanding street railways, and expanding city services is a dream come true for real estate dealers and speculators. Another look at the map of houses for sale in 1890, however, shows that real estate agents—Harrah's was in this respect typical of the other firms for which we also have listings—neglected large sections of Detroit. The real estate listings almost duplicated the findings of our samples for the west side, as the pattern of fine gradation in quality and price of the houses for sale by realtors confirmed many of our findings on socioethnic clustering. In contrast, realtors were active on the east side only along main arteries, selling houses in the $1,000 to $2,000 price range which were too expensive for the great majority of east-side inhabitants. Realtors had only a handful of small cottages to offer in the price range below $1,000, and most such houses were in the west side. Harrah's listed only 6% of its houses for sale in this low price range, and Hannan's 3%.[17] For the professionals of the real estate business, the newly developing sections of German and Polish concentration (mostly in the east, but also in the west) were not attractive areas.

17. Harrah's *Real Estate Advertiser* 1:22; Hannan, *Real Estate Record* 1:30–34.

This neglect of immigrant neighborhoods is understandable when we examine in detail the ways in which the professional realtors operated. Real estate specialists and builders were more involved in the city-building process than anybody else, and in late nineteenth-century Detroit they were seemingly active in all aspects of city building. They participated in political struggles siding with the street-railway companies against the city on policy issues. They convinced railroad companies to expand trackage into new areas, believing the construction of the Belt Line by the Michigan Central in 1889 to be a major victory for their interests.[18] Real estate specialists tried to cater to all the needs of their clients, but they selected their clients carefully; they served best either large investors or people who could afford expensive homes.

Realtors were in the business of selling vacant land—platted and unplatted, by lot or by entire subdivision—as well as homes, and they arranged mortgage loans for their selected customers. Harrah's real estate exchange, for example, advertised in 1890 that they would arrange mortgage loans for their customers, at the lowest rate of interest, while promising "Gilt Edge mortgages" to the largest real estate investors.[19] Harrah's and other realtors turned to state-chartered banks and private mortgage firms such as building and loan associations to obtain loans for their clients.[20] Most commonly the purchaser had to pay a large down payment (often over a third of the total price), and repay the loan over a relatively short period of time, often five years. In 1896, there were only six building and loan associations in Detroit, and these were not directed to or controlled by the working class.[21] They were rather under the control of the business, financial, and industrial establishment of the city. In Detroit, the largest association was the National Loan and Investment Company and its subsidiary, the Industrial Building and Loan Association. Silas Coleman, the president of both firms in 1896, was also a vice president of the Detroit United Bank and occupied a position of prominence in financial circles of the city. He succeeded Francis F. Palms in the job, who had himself succeeded his father who "for many years was the president and the largest stockholder in the People's Savings Bank and in the Michigan Stove Company and was also connected with the Galvin Brass and Iron Company, the Union Iron Company, the Vulcan Furnace and the Peninsular Land Company. His largest railroad

18. Shelley and Simpson, *Real Estate Review* 1 (April 1892): 2, 4–5.

19. Harrah's *Real Estate Advertiser* 1:6.

20. Howard P. Chudacoff, *Mobile Americans* (New York: Oxford University Press, 1972), p. 117; H. Morton Bodfish, ed., *History of Building and Loan in the United States* (Chicago: United States Building and Loan League, 1931); Jules Tygiel, "Housing in Late Nineteenth-Century American Cities: Suggestions for Research," *Historical Methods* 12 (Spring 1979): 84–97.

21. Bodfish, *Building and Loan*, pp. 442–47; *State of Michigan Report on Building and Loan Associations* (Lansing, 1897).

investment was in the Detroit, Mackinac and Marquette Road of which he was vice president and a director."[22] In the late eighties the Palms made massive investments in Detroit city property and constructed a large number of business blocks; their interest in building associations was, therefore, a vested one.

Realtors made a special effort to promote many outlying subdivisions. Land was initially purchased by acres, platted, and then individual lots were sold at retail to prospective homeowners or in bulk to investors. The *Real Estate Review*, for example, reported large sales on the northern section of Woodward in April of 1892:

> Among the large sales for the past week, was one by Homer Warren to E. T. Barnum, of twenty acres on Woodward Avenue for $40,000, for J. B. McKay and others. The piece adjoins the twenty acres sold by the same parties a short time since, at the same price, also to Mr. Barnum. These forty acres were bought less than three years ago by Mr. McKay and others for about $1,000 an acre, and makes them a nice profit of about $40,000 in that time, and yet the 'croakers' said they would lose money when they bought. Shelley and Simpson bought the twenty acres south of this piece, less than two years ago, and paid $1,200 an acre. They platted 'Buena Vista' subdivision of 100 large lots, and sold same at retail in less than one year, making a profit of over $20,000.[23]

Most realtors promoted the new subdivisions with low prices and "easy terms." They advertised lots, costing usually around $250, for $25 down and the balance due in quarterly payments of $25, with substantial discounts for investors. Many realtors advertised upgraded services as an incentive to buy; they pointed to the continuous system of rapid transit, "the extension of sewer," "the repaving of Woodward Avenue."[24] In fact, many realtors invested in unimproved vacant properties, improved the land by platting it and petitioning for the extension of city services, and then sold improved areas at retail price. Most of the new subdivisions created in the 1890s and advertised in real estate publications were located in areas which our dominance indexes have revealed to be later inhabited by white Anglo-Saxon Protestants of the middle and lower-middle classes. These were the subdivisions like Collins, Woodbridge, Avery, or Sibley in the new northwest, Alger Place or Kiefer in the northern periphery, Oakwood in the new southwest, Mills or Gamble in the new east side along the river, or Van Dyke on Gratiot extended. Very few of these new subdivisions advertised in

22. Clarence M. Burton and M. Agnes Burton, eds., *History of Wayne County and Detroit, Michigan,* 5 vols. (Chicago: S. J. Clarke, 1930), 3:79; Clarence M. Burton, ed., *The City of Detroit, Michigan, 1701–1922,* 5 vols. (Detroit: S. J. Clarke Publishing Co., 1922), 3:29.

23. Shelley and Simpson, *Real Estate Review* 1:5.

24. Ibid., p. 6.

real estate publications were located in working-class sections of Detroit. Only two of the many subdivisions advertised in the real estate journals were clearly aimed at workingmen, located in working-class areas, and advertised as close to new factories.[25]

Realtors went beyond the mere sale of property; they manipulated the development of areas by offering their customers a variety of additional services, including exchange of property and rental. As one agent put it:

> We transact a general real estate business. That is, we buy, sell, exchange and rent properties for clients on commission; take charge of estates, attending to the leasing, rent collecting, payment of taxes and assessments, necessary improvements and repairs, insurance, etc. Executor, Trustees and others who wish to be relieved of the anxiety of the charge and annoyance of the details incident to the care of properties, would experience satisfaction if they entrusted us with such work. We also loan money on first mortgage security, attend sales for mortgages, and may be engaged to make investments and guard the interests of the investors.[26]

Needless to say, realtors were committed to playing their traditional role of gatekeeper to keep undesirables out of particular neighborhoods. For example, Shelley and Simpson advertised lots on Monterey Avenue in 1892 in the following unambiguous terms:

> The lots are fifty feet front, and with ample depth for fine residences and beautiful lawns. And in keeping with our policy to make this the most desirable residence property in Detroit, it will be stipulated in terms of sale that no house shall be built to cost less than $2,000, nor shall stand less than twenty feet from the street. This will make our avenues 100 feet from house to house. We also restrict that only one house shall be built upon a lot and that it shall never be used for other than residence purposes. These restrictions will keep away all undesirable and one-story cheap houses, and guarantee that if you build your ideal home no one will put up near you something that will damage your property.[27]

Other realtors used more subtle language; they advertised lots in Avery and Van Husen subdivisions, as part of the "northwestern part of the city, all under building restrictions" or in Woodbridge specifying that "the building restrictions in the northwestern part of the city will cause this property to advance in value rapidly."[28] The formal housing market was thus consciously practicing one of its oldest functions: neighborhood steering.

25. Harrah's *Real Estate Advertiser* 1:30; Hannan, *Real Estate Record* 1:67–68, 70, 72–77.
26. Harrah's *Real Estate Advertiser* 1:4.
27. Shelley and Simpson, *Real Estate Review* 1:7.
28. Hannan, *Real Estate Record* 1:70, 75.

One gains an even better insight into the workings of the formal housing market by looking beyond the advertisements of real estate companies. Down at the level of the sampled clusters, we can study in detail two vital aspects of the market: first, the home-building industry—the process of building a new home on a vacant lot—and second, the laying out of services in relationship to the creation of new homes. In order to study these processes, I had to use new sets of sources. The records of the building permits issued by the fire marshal yielded much information on the houses of the sampled clusters: the dates when the houses were built, their dimensions, their estimated prices, and most important, the name of the person who secured the permit, most often the builder or contractor responsible for building the house. In turn, city directories and census data provided key biographical information on each applicant granted a permit: his occupation, his ethnicity, his address in the city before and after the house was built. All this constituted a very complex record linkage operation, but a multiplicity of sources was necessary to understand the workings of the home-building industry.[29]

To follow the growth of services to new housing areas, I searched through the annual reports of the Board of Water Commissioners and of the Board of Public Works for information on when water pipes, sewers, and pavements were laid along the clusters selected for the intensive study.[30] Every year the city reports record an exact description of all work done in the city, with specific address and location, the size of the pipes, the material used for construction, the name of the contractor, and other pertinent information; from them we were able to assemble a complete chronology of services on our sampled clusters and compare it with a chronology of housing construction. I will begin by examining some of the native white American clusters of the sample.

If we look at four clusters dominated by native white Americans, one near the old city center (79), one in the elegant area of Woodward Avenue (21), one in the northern section of Woodward Avenue (28), and one in the new subdivisions of the northwest (127), we find exactly what we expected from the formal housing market: most permit takers were professional builders—architects, builders, contractors, realtors. Together they made up 61% of the "permit takers," and carpenters alone made up another 18.6%. That 79% of the building activity was certainly in the hands of professionals is absolutely remarkable compared with the percentages of other sections of the city. Most of these

29. Detroit, "Fire Marshal Building Permits"; on this record linkage, see Appendix 7. For the use of the Recorder of Deeds Archives for the study of the purchase of already built houses, see John Bodnar, Roger Simon, and Michael Weber, *Lives of Their Own: Blacks, Italians, and Poles in Pittsburgh, 1900–1960* (Urbana: University of Illinois Press, 1982), pp. 154–83.

30. Previously cited, see chap. 5, note 4.

professionals were native white Americans, Canadians, or English. Most of them had downtown offices and built houses for customers who could afford to put a brand new house on their property. Prices estimated in the permits averaged $2,826 for the house alone (i.e., not including the lot) but in the blocks of the old residential center the typical new house was estimated at $6,000 (see table 6.6).

TABLE 6.6

The home-building process in selected clusters, Detroit, 1900

Permit-takers	Native white American[a]		German[b]		Polish[c]	
	(n)	(%)	(n)	(%)	(n)	(%)
Ethnicity						
Native white American[d]	12	38.7	-	-	-	-
Native-born white of American and British parentage	1	3.2	-	-	-	-
Native-born white of American and Irish parentage	2	6.5	-	-	-	-
Native-born white of mixed (or unknown) foreign parentage	4	12.9	3	13.0	-	-
Canadian (English)[e]	5	16.1	2	8.7	-	-
Canadian (French)	-	-	1	4.3	-	-
British	1	3.2	-	-	-	-
British American	2	6.5	-	-	-	-
German	2	6.5	13	56.5	6	31.6
German American	2	6.5	3	13.0	2	10.5
Polish (unspecified)	-	-	-	-	8	42.1
Polish (Russian Poland)	-	-	1	4.3	1	5.3
Polish (German Poland)	-	-	-	-	2	10.5
Total	31	100.0	23	100.0	19	100.0
Missing data	35		28		41	
Grand total	66		51		60	
Occupation						
Professional builder[f]	36	61.0	8	18.6	-	-
Carpenter	11	18.6	16	37.2	17	45.9
White-collar worker	4	6.8	3	7.0	2	5.4
Skilled or semiskilled worker	5	8.5	6	14.0	6	16.2
Unskilled worker	3	5.1	10	23.3	12	32.4
Total	59	100.0	43	100.0	37	100.0
Mising data	7		8		23	
Grand total	66		51		60	
Distance of permit-takers' residence from construction site						

TABLE 6.6 (*Continued*)

Permit-takers	Native white American[a]		German[b]		Polish[c]	
	(n)	(%)	(n)	(%)	(n)	(%)
None (within the cluster)	6	15.8	5	15.2	10	29.4
Within ¼ of a mile	3	7.9	7	21.2	3	8.8
Between ¼ and ½ a mile	2	5.3	4	12.1	7	20.5
Between ½ and 1 mile	10	26.3	6	18.2	6	17.6
Above 1 mile	17	44.7	11	33.2	8	23.5
Total	38	100.0	33	100.0	34	100.0
Missing data	28		18		26	
Grand total	66		51		60	
Number of permit-takers						
For personal residence	6	12.5	16	39.0	14	28.5
For other residences	39	81.3	25	61.0	32	65.3
For both	3	6.3	-	-	3	6.1
Total	48	100.0	41	100.0	49	100.0
Missing data	18		10		11	
Grand total	66		51		60	
Number of permits per taker						
1	39	76.5	35	83.3	44	89.8
2	5	9.8	4	9.5	3	6.1
3	3	5.9	1	2.4	1	2.0
4	1	2.0	1	2.4	-	-
5	1	2.0	1	2.4	-	-
6 or more	2	3.9	-	-	1	2.0
Total	51	100.0	42	100.0	49	100.0
Missing data	15		9		11	
Grand total	66		51		60	
Number of permits taken for homes, 1880–1900[g]	101		77		82	
Average value per home (indexed 1910–1914)	$2,826		$716		$576	
Minimum value	$350		$246		$233	
Maximum value	$20,400[h]		$1,640		$1,892	

SOURCES: Detroit, Department of Building and Safety, Fire Marshal Building Permits, 1881–1901, BHC; manuscript schedules of the 1900 population census; Detroit City Directories 1881–1901.

a. Native white American clusters 21, 28, 79, 127.

b. German cluster 42; German-Polish cluster 175; German-American cluster 177.

c. Polish clusters 49, 50, 164, 165, 171.

d. Born in the U.S. of two U.S.-born parents.

e. Born in English-speaking Canada of two Canadian parents; born in French-speaking Canada of two Canadian parents; born in Great Britain of two British parents, etc.

f. Includes architect, builder, contractor, and realtor.

g. Not including a $38,500 apartment house and a $6,150 church built in cluster 21, a $19,550 school built in cluster 42, and a $28,880 school built in cluster 171; in the native white American clusters 77 houses were actually built, 54 in the German clusters, and 67 in the Polish clusters.

h. The next highest value was $9,840.

A few examples give a good idea of the building activity in the old American residential center. The cluster defined by Woodward, Alexandrine, Selden, and Cass (21), in the upper residential center, was a rather exclusive area, inhabited primarily by professionals in 1900: one physician, two dentists, two lawyers, two real estate men, several engineers, several high-ranking city employees, several merchants, and other businessmen lived there. This was clearly an upper middle-class area, as evidenced not only by the high concentration of high white-collar professionals but also of domestics employed in their homes: the 1900 census counted 31 maids and cooks, 5 coachmen, and some livery stable boys among the 291 inhabitants of the cluster. In 1900, 64 houses were standing in this cluster, 20 of them built in the preceding twenty years. An apartment building and a church were also built in this cluster in the 1890s. This rapid construction of new homes was undertaken mostly at the hands of architects. In 1882, Almon C. Varney, an architect with his firm located in the Bank Building downtown, built a two-story home on 691 Cass for Edgar McCurdy, at an estimated value of $9,720. By 1900, the home had changed hands and belonged to Edward D. Peck, a sixty-year-old native white American who lived there with his wife, three children, and a maid. Also in 1882, Henry Knowles, a contractor and builder, built a home next door, 693 Cass, for D. M. Odena. In 1890, Adam Gray, a carpenter, built a second story to the house which had changed hands and now belonged to Josephius Chambers. Chambers, a native white American in the cigar business, had a mortgage on the home; he still lived there in 1900 with his wife, his daughter, and a maid. Across the street, Joseph E. Mills, an architect with his office in the Chamber of Commerce, built a brick two-story home for an estimated cost of $6,160 in 1899 for William R. McLaren. In 1900, the house was rented to a young dentist, Joseph Lathrop, who lived and practiced there, sharing the house with his immediate family, a wife and two young children, two nurses and a cook. The same architect, Mills, also built the house next door, 700 Cass, at the same time and for the same price, for William Hill, a forty-seven-year-old native white American manufacturer who owned the home with a mortgage and lived in it with his household of three. Around the block, Albert E. French, another architect with a downtown office on Griswold in 1892, built a two-story brick home on 60 Selden for $2,280 for Joseph Sumonds. In 1900, the home was rented to William Irving, a native-born American of British parents who worked in the advertising business and lived at this address with a household of eight. In the 1880s and 1890s, then, usually expensive, well-built, brick homes designed by architects were built in this cluster, some inhabited by their owners and some rented to other members of the middle class. The area was sufficiently close to the downtown area for Copeland H. Coldwell, a real estate firm located on 143 Grand River, to build an apartment building, the Alberta Flat, on 37 Alexandrine West in 1894. Twelve families rented apartments in this seven-story, $55,000 brick structure, and a thirteenth apartment was used by the janitor. The tenants were middle-class professionals and employees, an optician, several salesmen, a cashier, a bookkeeper, and other office workers who enjoyed the proximity to the downtown area as well as residence in one of the first luxury apartment buildings in an exclusive neighborhood of Detroit.

Most builders could build only one or two houses in the blocks of the old residential center; on the fringes of the city, however, builders and realtors developed entire blocks. A cluster typical of the new subdivisions of the westward expansion is cluster 127 in the 1900 sample, delimited by Maybury Grand, Warren, Williams, and Hudson; in 1880 it was empty but in 1900, 154 people lived there in 45 houses. Most heads of households were white-collar, native white Americans—including one bookkeeper, one civil engineer, one dentist, two dry goods clerks, one salesman, two lumber dealers, one plumber, and one pharmacist—but only two households employed servants. Over 60% of the residents of this cluster rented their homes. All the homes had been built recently, although we could locate building permits for only 27 of the 45 houses standing in 1900—all frame houses with an average value of $1,300. Although we cannot say who the absentee owners were in 1900, we can assume that they were either real estate firms themselves or independent investors who hired contractors and builders to develop the blocks. On Kirby Street West (a small dead-end street in mid-cluster), Peter McDougall, an English-Canadian contractor and builder, built 6 homes on the odd side of the street in 1900. Two years before he had built 4 houses around the block, rented by 4 native white American families in 1900; one family was headed by a dry goods clerk, one by a hotel keeper, one by a grocer, and one by a clerk employed in the wholesaling of shoes. Similarly, most of Maybury Grand, the largest avenue of the cluster, had been developed between 1891 and 1896 by Arthur E. Howlett and William H. Sherman, two partners in the contracting and building business, and all houses were rented.

These new houses were usually provided with services as they were built, unless services had already been installed in the street in anticipation of the construction. Water was provided ahead of time through new, large 6-inch pipes, but other services were installed too. For example, in the new northwest where the bulk of the construction activity took place in the mid 1890s, lateral sewers were laid in 1894–95. In one cluster (127) 81% of the linked addresses had access to sewers when built. Paving of some streets followed the next year.

In the adjacent cluster (117), all houses built between 1891 and 1900 had lateral sewers at the time they were built, water pipes laid at the time of construction, and streets paved the following years.

THE INFORMAL HOUSING MARKET

The formal housing market, then, operated by professionals from their downtown offices, produced expensive homes and rentals for middle-class Americans but largely neglected the newly developing German and Polish settlements. Yet these ethnic communities had the highest rate of home ownership in the city. A completely different housing market existed for the working-class immigrant, and this informal market of the ethnic communities produced the tenant-owned cottages of the working class. Realtors were guaranteeing their prospective customers that no houses costing less than $2,000 would be built in the new western subdivisions, but houses of the workers never reached such prices anyway. The mean value of the homes of the metalworkers surveyed by the Bureau of Labor Statistics in 1890 was $1,287. For those few native white American metalworkers who owned their homes, the mean value was $1,642; but for the Germans it was $1,054 and for the Poles, $786. The average house of the day laborer was worth about $900 (table 6.3).

Not only were the owner-occupied cottages of the ethnic communities bought on a different market, they were financed in a different way. The workers surveyed by the Bureau of Labor Statistics did not favor the kind of financing offered by the real estate firms. An amazing 63% of those homeowners among the surveyed street-railway employees, 54% among the vehicle workers, and 54% among the railroad workers declared that they owned their homes free of encumbrance. When these homeowners were in debt for their houses, they were usually under contract with a builder who charged them 7% interest; for example, 67% of the street railway workers who owed money on their homes were under contract.[31] Nor is there evidence that local workmen's building and loan associations sprang up in Detroit, as they did in Philadelphia. In Philadelphia, such associations helped workingmen finance the purchase of homes already built, often row houses; in Detroit, working-class immigrants built new, separate homes on individual lots.[32]

If so many German and Polish workers of Detroit owned their homes, and if so many owned them free of encumbrance, it is because they built them

31. Statistical analysis of surveys in Michigan, *Eleventh, Thirteenth,* and *Fourteenth Annual Report of the Bureau of Labor and Industrial Statistics.*

32. U.S., Congress, House, Industrial Commission, *Report of the Industrial Commission on the Relations and Conditions of Capital and Labor Employed in Manufactures and General Business,* 57th Cong., 1st sess., 1901, H. Doc. 183, pp. 595–603.

themselves. They were builder-owners. Not only did they invest their savings—past and future—in putting a roof over their heads and providing shelter for the family, they also invested their time. Building a home was a neighborhood business, a community affair, since workers could not rely on the formal home-building industry to build houses for them. It is probably because the industry responded so little to their needs that working class immigrants built for themselves in order to become homeowners in an environment which they could control. Thus the neighborhood became the locus of an economic investment as well as of an emotional one.

From the records of building permits issued by the fire marshal, we can again observe the construction of new homes in selected clusters of the sample. Discussing the German and Polish neighborhood in general is too abstract, and so we will concentrate on four test areas.

First, the old east side. Looking at a typical cluster of the old German neighborhood (where 406 people lived in 82 houses in 1900), the statistics of home ownership are quite revealing: 58% of the houses (whether single-family or multiple-family homes) were occupied by their owners. Seventy percent of the homes were single-family homes and as many as 57% of the households living in such single-family dwellings owned them. This was a wholly working-class area, inhabited by many day laborers (about 30 on the block), a few cabinetmakers, a few cigar makers, a few beer peddlers, a pattern fitter, a printer, a stove molder, and a handful of clerks (cluster 42).

Second, the new east side. This neighborhood was also heavily populated by Germans, but it was located in an area annexed by the city between 1880 and 1900, and it included some American families. When we move to this newly incorporated part of the city, we also find a predominantly working-class pattern, although a few clerical employees and a couple of professionals mixed with the scores of day laborers. In a cluster of 48 houses with 234 people at the time of the 1900 census enumeration, 65% of the houses were occupied by their owners, and 75% of them were single-family homes (cluster 177).

Third, the new west side. This was a suburban extension of a German and Polish working-class neighborhood, newly incorporated by 1900. This area of the city had not been settled by Germans and Poles before, since the west side tended to be primarily native white American and Anglo-Saxon. Here is an example of a high concentration of day laborers and industrial workers of specific industries—brassworkers, ironworkers—located in a new outlying working-class subdivision. Again, the rate of absentee ownership was only 20%, and 67% of the homes were single-family dwellings (cluster 175).

Fourth, the Polish neighborhood which developed in the 1880s and 1890s north of the German old east side. This was a solid working-class neighborhood with dozens of day laborers, from unskilled workers such as tobacco strippers and cigar rollers to skilled workers such as brass finishers, molders, and polishers. Looking at five key clusters in the Polish area the figures are startling; in this community the rate of absentee ownership was extraordinarily low, ranging from 16 to 25%. On the average, then, 80% of the houses were occupied by their owners even if (and it was often the case) many families doubled up, or even tripled up, to meet financial needs. In the Polish neighborhood, only 17% of the homes were single-family dwellings, but all the owners lived on the spot, even if they had to share their roof for an indefinite period of time (clusters 49, 50, 164, 165, 171).

A pattern of "local" building activity prevailed in the three test areas for the German clusters, although it was not uniform. One builder was an architect; there were a few established builders, a number of carpenters and masons, as well as many day laborers and other workers. Most individuals seeking permits to build homes were neighborhood people; of the 23 permit applicants we could trace in the census, 13 were born in Germany, one in Poland, and only 3 in the United States. These figures reflect a building activity by and for neighborhood people, but there were interesting variations in the three German areas. In the old German section, 86% of the permits were issued to first or second-generation Germans, of whom 75% were professional builders or carpenters, indicating that neighborhood professionals operated in the old east side. John Schaefer, for instance, a German carpenter who lived on Mack Avenue, built a house in 1893 at 391 Sherman for Watko Simon, a fifty-eight-year-old native born of German parents, a bellmaker who owned the $1,400 two-story dwelling and still lived there in 1900 with his family of three. Frank Whitman, another German carpenter living on Antietam, built a home in 1892 at 397 Sherman for Charles Manzelman, a thirty-year-old German broommaker who still lived there in 1900 with his family of four. In this part of town—well incorporated into the city in the 1890s, and part of the traditional German east side—the home industry operated mainly in the hands of local professionals, not in the hands of downtown real estate firms or architects.

The number of German "professionals" dropped substantially in the newer subdivisions of town. Among the permit applicants, only 40% in the east and 47% in the west were professionals, with as many day laborers taking permits as established carpenters. Our test cluster of the new west side (175) is the perfect example of an outlying working-class settlement in a new subdivision. It was dominated by German laborers, but also inhabited by some Polish families; in 1900, there were 470 people living in this cluster, 160 born in Germany, 166 born in the United States of German parents, 64 born in Poland, and 71 born in the United States of Polish parents. The working population comprised

131 day laborers and only a handful of skilled workers—one brass molder, three iron molders, one machinist, two conductors. Of the 69 houses standing in 1900, we could locate the building permits of only 23 of them, an indication of how little the city controlled the building activity in this outlying area. As many as 21 "builders" built these 23 cheap (averaging $550) one-story frame cottages; only seven were carpenters; most of the other builders were simply day laborers.

The analysis of the construction process in the Polish neighborhood reveals an even more startling trend. In the Polish quarter homes were sometimes built by carpenters, but the majority of them were built by other workers—day laborers, machine hands, bricklayers, blacksmiths. Sixty-five percent of the builders were born in Poland, the rest in Germany, and depending on the cluster, from 30% to 60% of the builders lived in the cluster where the house was built, or within half a mile. Only one cluster reflected the intense activity of one carpenter, Joseph Gutow, listed as born in Prussia in the 1880 census, but most likely a Pole (perhaps his name was Gutowski); he built fourteen houses in one cluster. Most other builders, professionals or nonprofessionals, built only at one address, and between 30% and 50% of them (depending on the cluster) built only a home for themselves. Occasionally, a professional builder appeared on these streets to build community buildings, like Frank P. Lorkowski, a Polish builder, who built the Saint Albertus school house at 871 Saint Aubin in 1892.

In the Polish neighborhood, the process of building for oneself is best exemplified through numerous examples. John Kreft, a Polish day laborer, built his home in 1887, a one-and-a-half story frame home at 807 Riopelle for an estimated cost of $340. In 1887, Kreft was a brewer working for the Detroit Brewery Company. In 1900, at age forty-six, he was a day laborer, still owning his home, parts of which he rented to two other Polish laborers, Anthony Koss and August Fichta, and their families; thirteen people altogether lived in this small house in 1900. On the next block Joseph Landowski, a Polish mason, built a house worth $233 at 829 Riopelle, also in 1887. In 1900 Landowski, listed as a day laborer, still lived in the house; he had a mortgage on it, and rented one part of it to his son, John Landowski, a cigar maker, and another part to Wladislaus Worwakowski, another Polish cigar maker. In all, 11 people lived in the house. This building activity, then, led to some exceptionally packed living arrangements: at 573 Canfield East, Mary Kosicki, Polish widow of Casimir Kosicki, owned the house which she and her husband had built a few years before, but in 1900 she shared it with 28 people! This house had only one-and-a-half stories, but it also had a full basement and two sheds (or small unnumbered buildings) on the lot; it is therefore conceivable that it was divided into at least five semi-independent dwelling units. Listed as renters at 573

Canfield East were Peter Ranz, John Browalski, and Anthony Hermanowski, Polish day laborers and their families; D. P. Bartels, a machinist, a native born of German parents; Josephine Kolch, a Polish woman listed without occupation; and Minnie Edwards, an American born of German parents, also without occupation.

In native white American sections of towns, the establishment of essential services often preceded the construction of houses, since realtors were willing to improve the vacant lots before selling them at retail. This simply never happened in the new German and Polish sections. Of course, most houses were built in areas with water running through the street. We have no reason to suspect that houses were not connected to these pipes, but we know that the water pressure in the Polish neighborhood was extremely low (probably the worst in the city), for several reasons. The pipes which existed in the Polish quarter built in the eighties and nineties were still the small 2.5-inch wooden pipes; this section of town was also the highest in altitude, which further reduced water pressure. The cost of city services was also a problem for these working-class homeowners. Water was paid for by the users according to an assessment of the number of fixtures in the house; little was charged to the owners of the land for the initial laying of the pipe. Pavements and sewers, on the other hand, were in part paid for by the abutting taxpayers, so in the German and Polish working-class clusters, most new owners chose to delay services at least until the house was completed, and sometimes longer in order to keep expenses down. In the Polish clusters built in the early eighties, lateral sewers were installed only near the end of that decade. In others built mostly in the late 1880s lateral sewers were not installed before the mid-nineties. In the new sections of the east side built in the early nineties, lateral sewers were laid in 1895 only, and pavements from 1893 to 1898; by this time half of the addresses had already been built. If we look again at the new west side, built mainly between 1890 and 1895 and dominated by German and Polish day laborers, we are looking at the largest concentration of day laborers in the city, settling on newly opened land. While houses were built on fronts equipped with 6-inch water pipes, public sewers did not reach the area until 1896/97, and only then were lateral sewers built. Of course, none of the streets were paved by 1900. Delaying services, buying unimproved land, building with local help, and doubling or tripling up were all parts of the overall strategy of becoming homeowners.

To be sure, the modest frame cottages of the working-class owner-occupants were not worth much. In the building permits the prices of the houses (given as an estimate of the construction costs) ranged from $400 to $600 in the Polish neighborhood, to about $750 in the German neighborhoods; houses in most American neighborhoods averaged between $1,400 and $2,400, while in some blocks of the old residential center, the average new house was worth around $6,000. Land itself was also generally cheap in these areas of working-class construction: several sections of the east side were included in the 1891 survey of land values by the Michigan Bureau of Labor Statistics, and their estimated market prices were the lowest in the city, averaging about $200 for a lot (see map 6.11). These prices do not reflect the total price of the finished house and the lot, but they are consistent with the prices we have already found in our survey of the real estate market and of worker-owners. The formal market simply was not in the business of building such cheap homes. They were left to the informal procedures of local construction.

These differences between the formal and the informal housing markets do not mean that the two were always absolutely separate. Most areas of the city were indeed built by either one or the other, but a few areas combined both. This was especially the case in transitional neighborhoods like the old Irish Corktown, where local Irish carpenters were still active but competing with the agents of the native white Americans who moved into the neighborhood. Other small areas were inhabited by a mixture of German skilled craftsmen and American lower-middle-class workers, or of German and American laborers and American lower white-collar workers; these clusters cannot be easily classified into one or the other type. Generally, however, the evidence clearly bears out the peculiarity of the home-building process in the immigrant neighborhoods. As opposed to the middle-class American neighborhoods where the business was almost exclusively in the hands of professionals—architects, established builders and contractors, realtors (who outnumbered all other professionals, including the carpenters)—construction in Polish and German neighborhoods was often carried out by the owners and for themselves, with the help of other neighborhood nonprofessionals. And when professionals were involved, they came from within the community. The available evidence did not reveal who was paid what to build the homes, and one can speculate about the role and remuneration of the nonprofessionals involved in the building process. To assume that they provided cheap labor is quite reasonable in view of the fact that most workers surveyed by the Bureau of Labor Statistics declared that they owned their homes free of encumbrance.

For the working-class immigrants, owning a home was perhaps the only way of gaining some security, of earning some stability. But this stability could only be gained within the framework of one's own ethnic group, in the urban neighborhood. Maybe the Polish laborer's small cottage did not resemble Adam's house in paradise; after all, on his earthly corner of Detroit, such a cottage was worth only the price of a barn in some more exclusive neighborhood. It was, however, a home built by himself or his fellow countrymen, in his own universe.

In their quest for home ownership, the main foreign-born groups of Detroit, the Germans and the Poles, contributed to the complex city-building process. Instead of settling in downtown ghettos in dilapidated houses, as they did in New York where no land was available, the immigrants reached out and built their own neighborhoods. In so doing they managed a *tour de force*: they transformed inequality into an advantage. After all, they were free to build. They did it where they could afford it and in the way they could afford it. Transportation and services were not readily available, but ownership, which provided a basis for community organization, was worth the gamble of tying up their assets to create a world of their own.

7

The Completeness of the Immigrant Working Class Neighborhood

Plate 7. German Detroit and Polish Detroit in the 1890s, *a*. Saint Joseph Catholic Church, consecrated in 1873 (photo by Paul Holoweski); *b*. Ekhardt and Becker Brewery, at Winder and Orleans, built around 1891; *c*. 448 Montcalm (146 before 1921), a building in the German style built before 1889; *d*. Sweetest Heart of Mary, consecrated in 1893 (photo by Paul Holoweski); *e*. 1356 Leland (232 before 1921), a house on a German-Polish frontage, built around 1890, destroyed 1978; *f*. another house on Leland, built around 1890, destroyed 1978.

TRANSIENCE, STABILITY, AND WORK

Within each neighborhood, working-class immigrants shared a common ethnic background, a common set of customs, and common institutions with fellow countrymen. But the neighborhood did not evolve in isolation from the rest of the city; the suburbanization of the working class and the branching out of ethnic neighborhoods into newly developed areas of Detroit, for example, took place simultaneously with the diffusion of factories toward the city's periphery, and this mutual movement was no mere coincidence. To what extent, then, were the lives of immigrant workers and their families influenced by the new industrial order which was being constructed in the city and imposed upon them? Was the special environment of the urban neighborhood—where kinship and cultural ties were free to develop—endangered by the reordering of job opportunities in different sections of the city?

Historians of the late nineteenth century have often described processes of urbanization which do not conform to my description of immigrant neighborhoods in late nineteenth-century Detroit. I have insisted that ethnic neighborhoods were the spatial anchor of the communities, the primary colors of the urban quilt. I have stressed ethnicity as the major force behind clustering and presented immigrants as actors building their own communities with their own labor and sweat on their own soil. I have also argued that home ownership provided the basis for community organization. But other historians have emphasized the location of factories in determining the settlement and shape of immigrant neighborhoods.[1] If ethnic neighborhoods were organized primarily around work sites, such neighborhoods could not possibly provide a stable environment, certainly not an environment worth the type of building investment I have described; instead, they would be merely temporary arrangements produced by the changing spatial distribution of factories and the irregularity of the business cycle. As Theodore Hershberg reminded us, work was rarely stable in the late nineteenth century, and in the absence of cheap available means of transportation for the laboring classes, "frequent layoffs, seasonal fluctuation, little job security and the lack of institutional supports such as unemployment insurance meant that workers had to change residences when the location of their employment shifted substantially."[2]

Workers certainly had to move around in the city to remain employed, but

---

1. Caroline Golab, *Immigrant Destinations* (Philadelphia: Temple University Press, 1977), pp. 116–17.

2. Theodore Hershberg, et al., "The 'Journey-to-Work': An Empirical Investigation of Work, Residence, and Transportation, Philadelphia, 1850 and 1880," in *Philadelphia: Work, Space, Family, and Group Experience in the Nineteenth Century,* ed. Theodore Hershberg (New York: Oxford University Press, 1981), p. 166.

they did not stop at the city limits. Intracity mobility was just one part of a larger movement of people in search of jobs, moving from one city on to the next. Historians have justly described the late nineteenth-century society as extremely fluid; immigrants entered cities by the thousands, worked there for a while, and then moved on toward new destinations. In this process, historians argued, the city acted as an intelligent sieve, retaining the more successful and letting the unsuccessful and poor go. Stephan Thernstrom, whose studies of geographic and occupational mobility initiated over a decade of historical research in the late 1960s, went as far in his interpretation of mobility as to deny the very existence of immigrant neighborhoods; as he explained it: "If there was anything like 'a culture of poverty' in the American city, it lacked deep local roots, for most of the people exposed to it were incessantly on the move from place to place."[3] Following Thernstrom's lead, historians documented the great turnover of population throughout urban America. They identified the poorer laboring classes as the most mobile of all in this seething milieu. Michael Katz, another leading historian of mobility and social structure, concluded the decade of research opened by Thernstrom very simply: "When Victorians sought a symbol of progress, they often chose the steam engine; had they wanted a metaphor for their cities, they could have found none more apt than the railroad station."[4] It would be easy to deduce from such sketches of American urban life in the 1880s and 1890s that the lower crust of the population never had a chance to settle anywhere. The large segment of common laborers seemed, rather, to live without continuity, following a rootless existence subject to the vicissitudes of economic forces. The poor and the working class thus became ensnared in a system that made a worthwhile community life nearly impossible.

Busy documenting the great moves of Americans from one place to another, however, many historians dismissed the importance of spatial structures within the cities themselves. They did not recognize the importance of place in a fluid, volatile, and ascending society. They, too, often treated the city as a whole without descending to the level of the neighborhood. They neglected to assess the impact of mobility—which they were otherwise measuring—on institutions, or on the workings of communities within the metropolis.[5]

How, then, to reconcile a vision of stable ethnic neighborhoods of home-owners, typical of late nineteenth-century urban subcultures, with the image

3. Stephan Thernstrom, "Reflections on the New Urban History," *Daedalus* 100 (Spring 1971): 367.

4. Michael B. Katz, Michael J. Doucet, and Mark J. Stern, "Migration and the Social Order in Erie County, New York, 1855," *Journal of Interdisciplinary History* 8 (Spring 1978): 669.

5. Unlike the Chicago ecologists who had promoted the model of the ghetto; see Robert E. Park, *Human Communities: The City and Human Ecology* (New York: Free Press, 1952), p. 177.

of the poor always on the move, only temporarily clustering around places of work? Apparent paradoxes are usually just that—apparent but not real. Mobility and fixity are not necessarily mutually exclusive, but more likely functionally complementary when a core of settled people maintains a community which serves many transients. All available indicators suggest that in Detroit the deconcentration of factories did not in itself contribute significantly to the creation of working-class neighborhoods. Remaining in their own neighborhoods, immigrant workers did not settle temporarily, but rather made long-term commitments to the place.

In the first phase of large-scale industrialization in Detroit, industries and residences intersected in a way which did not seriously impede neighborhood autonomy. Without records providing the addresses of workers of specific factories, I can only approximate the distance workers lived from their place of work by overlaying two independent surveys of work and residence—the Bureau of Labor and Industrial Statistics factory inspection for 1900 on my sample of 178 clusters spread on all areas of the city—but even incomplete information shows that the new factories did not create a mill-town area around them.[6]

All industrial sectors of Detroit followed a pattern of concentration of most firms in the city center (see chap. 5), and expansion of some firms along the main thoroughfares and along the river or near railroad intersections (see map 5.3). With the deconcentration of large factories, Detroit's industrial district began to form a crescent around the city, connected between the two tips by the industrial strip along the river. Many factories located or relocated on sections of this industrial belt, and a few factories in clothing, food (breweries especially), and tobacco penetrated deeper into the east side. In 1900, the highest concentration of large firms in Detroit was on the long east-west side industrial strip along the river, approximately one mile wide, which also comprised the city center. In addition, some large factories were located at the intersection of key railroad lines. The largest employers at the time of the 1900 factory inspections were the American Car and Foundry Company, which built railroad cars and employed 2,200 workers; Parke-Davis, with 1,350 workers to manufacture drugs; Ideal Manufacturing Company, a plumbing company, with 1,100 workers; the Michigan Stove Company, with 1,000; while 22 firms had more than 300 employees, and 137 firms more than 100. Despite its growth, the city still had a radius of only 3.5 miles from city hall in 1900. With the deconcentration of many large factories, then, Detroit was not large enough for any worker to live extremely far from a possible place of employment. By 1900,

6. Michigan, "State Factory Inspection," appendix to *Eighteenth Annual Report of the Bureau of Labor and Industrial Statistics* (Lansing: Wynkoop Hallenbeck Crawford Co., State Printers, 1901), pp. 6–37.

most working-class neighborhoods were located between several manufacturing districts and the distance to at least two important work sites ranged from half a mile to 2.5 miles, in most cases.

I will look first at the residential distribution of the large pool of unskilled workers in 1900, listed in the 1900 census as day laborers or factory workers, before turning to specific subsectors of industrial production. I consider a distance of one mile from home to work as walking distance. Distances beyond one mile show a clear separation between residence and work. Conversely, distances shorter than one mile, especially half a mile or less, indicate a close association between the two, possibly a mill-town effect, with many workers concentrating immediately around a few mills. If we look at the residences of unskilled laborers, it is clear that the large factories, calling on a large pool of laborers, did not stimulate the building of workers' houses around themselves. Heavy concentrations of day laborers were not organized around specific work sites in 1900 Detroit: only 21% of the unskilled industrial laborers of the population sample were living in the main mile-wide industrial strip along the river. In contrast, 42% of them were to be found in a relatively small area, at the heart of the old residential east side, about a mile north of the main industrial strip. Another 23% of the day laborers were located in the new peripheral neighborhoods of the west side.

The laborers near the heart of the residential east side were in fact well situated in relation to work sites. They were relatively far from the river industrial area, but close to the Lake Shore and Milwaukee Junction where several large factories clustered in the 1880s and 1890s. The Polish neighborhood, however, had developed in this region before the factories arrived. The Peninsular Car Company, for example, which later merged into the American Car and Foundry, built its works on Ferry Avenue, near the Lake Shore junction only in 1885, by which time the formation of the Polish neighborhood was well underway; Saint Albertus, the first Polish church, was built in 1871, and the Poles simply continued to settle where they started to in the 1870s and continued to throughout the 1880s. In the 1890s unskilled German and Polish laborers also settled in new peripheral neighborhoods of the west side, where they built homes. The new zones of residential settlement were more than a mile away from West Detroit and the large industrial section along the Michigan Central Railroad, and at least two miles away from the closest industrial spot on the river.

The pattern of relative separation between work and residence emerges even more clearly when we turn to specific industries and specific groups of workers. In the iron and steel sector, 39% of the firms were located in the city center. They usually employed less than ten workers and specialized in decorative ironwork. In all, these central shops employed only 3% of the labor force. The seven larger iron and steel firms listed in the 1900 inspection, however, ranging in size from 100 to 500 workers, employed 75% of the labor force. Because iron and steel firms were thus divided between the center and the other industrial districts, no ironworkers and steelworkers lived very far from a possible place of work. But no large residential concentration of specialized workers existed immediately around iron and steel factories; only 22% of ironworkers and steel-workers of the residential sample lived within half a mile of such firms.

If we turn to the stove industry, only 46% of the stove workers of the sample lived within a mile of any stove factories which we could identify from the 1900 factory inspection. A special Bureau of Labor and Industrial Statistics survey of 1890 on metal industries included two large stove firms of Detroit, the Michigan Stove Company with 645 workers and the Detroit Stove Works with 296 workers.[7] Fifty-one percent of Michigan Stove's workers were Germans, 15% Irish, and 9% Polish. The Detroit Stove Works had proportionately a few more Germans, 58%, and 12% Irish and 5% Poles. These two giants of the new stove industry, both located on the river at the eastern boundary of the city, were far beyond one mile from where most Germans, Irish, and Poles, who made up the bulk of their labor force, lived in the city.

We find even less evidence that work determined residence to any great extent if we turn to workers in the brass industry. Twenty-six percent of the brass foundries in the 1900 factory inspection had fewer than 10 employees. Seventy-four percent of the factories had more than 30 workers, including a few factories with 500 workers. But no brassworker of the residential sample was recorded as living within a half-mile or less from any brass firm. Instead, the largest concentration of brassworkers (55% of them) was in the old residential east side, more than two miles away from the major brass firms.

If the heavy industries typical of the new industrial order did not reorganize the residential patterns, it may simply have been that urban neighborhoods were already organized around traditional industries. But this was not the case either. For purposes of brevity, I shall limit my analysis to two industries, furniture making and tobacco. The furniture industry was a part of the large "lumber and related" sector, which ranked fifth in the city in number of workers in 1900. Here again the location of most factories was limited to the dense industrial center, the industrial strip along the river, and the intersection of railroad lines. In the case of furniture makers, however, some large factories of 50–100 workers were spread along the main thoroughfares, Gratiot Avenue

7. Michigan, *Seventh Annual Report of the Bureau of Labor and Industrial Statistics* (Lansing, 1890), pp. 150–81.

in the east and Michigan Avenue in the west. Because of this extension of some factories into the residential areas, no furniture workers of the sample lived beyond one mile from a possible place of employment, and 53% lived within half a mile of a factory. But relatively few workers of the east side worked in the generally small neighborhood factories; the bulk of the workers had to travel longer distances to work.

The tobacco industry also provides an interesting example of this split between place of residence and place of work. Traditionally a large industry in Detroit, it still comprised 8% of the labor force in 1900—including many women, often daughters of German and Polish workers. Tobacco workers were divided into two groups: the tobacco strippers and handlers, and the cigar makers. The strippers worked in large factories: 92% of them worked in factories with more than 100 employees, and a few small factories existed. The cigar makers, on the other hand, could find employment in scores of small cigar-making shops, although there were some larger factories as well. All shops and factories were heavily concentrated in the city center, although the smaller cigar shops spread along Gratiot Avenue, the main thoroughfare of the working-class east side. Where did most workers live? Not around the factories. In fact, only 5% of tobacco workers lived within one mile of any tobacco-handling firm. And only 5.5% of the cigar workers lived within a mile of the city center where most firms were located.

Similar examples abound; they all show variations of the same theme: separation between the factories and the residences of the working class. But who did live around the factories if not the workers? A more specific way of asking the question is: who lived around the city center and the riverfront where employment (industrial or not) was still largely concentrated in Detroit in 1900? Who filled the geographic gap between the city center and the working-class neighborhoods? The answer is simple: almost 50% of the white-collar employees in the residential sample lived within a mile radius of the city center, in contrast with only 12% of the general laborers. Many white-collar workers kept a strong foothold in and around the city center where they were employed, while others moved into newer, suburban areas of the west side. The immigrant worker, however, was not willing to live in just any shelter, merely to be near a place of employment. If land was too expensive around the center to build a decent house and become a homeowner, the German and Polish workers opted to stay farther away. Yet Detroit's industrial geography helped the working classes along the way. The factories progressively encircled the city, and immigrant neighborhoods became the midpoint between several types of industries. Their location, near no particular factory but not too distant from any, was an asset in the context of the family economy where men, women, parents, and children parted to work in different directions. From the houses around Saint Albertus or Saint Joseph, it was not very far for a Polish or a German laborer to reach American Car and Foundry at the Lake Shore and Milwaukee Junction. It was a longer distance—up to 2.5 miles, which is usually considered beyond walking distance—to reach Parke, Davis and Company or the Michigan Stove Works along the river, but employment there was still feasible; and the son of the same Polish or German laborer may have been working in a printing shop downtown, or in an east side brewery, while a daughter could have been employed as a tobacco stripper or a seamstress in or near a downtown area. Detroit had become industrialized in such a way that the geography of work did not seriously interfere with the creation of autonomous neighborhoods.

That many Detroiters were either transients or recent arrivals is obvious from the growth rate of the city, which counted 116,340 inhabitants in 1880 and 287,704 in 1900. But despite the tremendous flow of people in and out of the city, transience did not threaten community organization. The recent mobility studies do show high turnover in cities, especially among laboring classes, but it does not necessarily follow that such classes were bereft of a meaningful community.[8] Such studies never examine the workers' actual living space to see what was happening there. My limited purpose, therefore, is not to repeat what has already been well established by historians, but—avoiding the depiction of social reality only from images—to document the existence of a group of persisters at the level of Detroit's immigrant working-class neighborhoods. Of course, determining that a core of persisters existed in even the poorest neighborhoods does not in itself insure that the group provided the continuity, norms, and spirit that are essential for a sense of community, but it at least lays the groundwork for documenting the existence of a vital community life.

Since we have sample clusters in Detroit categorized according to ethnicity—clusters that include specific house addresses—we can examine every house in selected clusters to discover changes among its residents from one year to the next at least since 1888, when the Detroit City Directory began to include a street guide. Every Detroit street is listed alphabetically in the guide, and every house on most streets, along with the head of household, is included. All that remained to do, then, was to compile a twelve-year record. I limited the analysis to three native white American clusters of the residential center (28, 21, and 79) as well as one American cluster in a newly annexed area of the city (176),

8. Stephan Thernstrom, *The Other Bostonians: Poverty and Progress in the American Metropolis, 1880–1970* (Cambridge, Mass.: Harvard University Press, 1973); Michael B. Katz, *The People of Hamilton, Canada West: Family and Class in a Mid-Nineteenth-Century City* (Cambridge, Mass.: Harvard University Press, 1975).

and to three clusters of the Polish neighborhood (51, 164, and 171). In this way I explored opposite types of neighborhoods, one of relatively wealthy white-collar workers and professionals, and one neighborhood of unskilled workers. For each street of the clusters, I computed the maximum length of residency in each house from 1888 to 1900. Not all houses standing in 1900 were built in 1888 so I measured persistence at intervals of three, six, nine, and twelve years, including in each bracket only the houses standing during the entire period, from 1888 to 1891, from 1888 to 1894, from 1888 to 1897, and from 1888 to 1900 (see table 7.1). If a house was inhabited by several families, I selected the most stable family since the test was aimed at documenting the existence of persisters.

The results are as clear as the method is simple. In the three native white American clusters of the residential center, between 27% and 38% of the houses were inhabited by the same family for a twelve-year period. In constrast, the Polish clusters showed a remarkably higher rate of persistence among the inhabitants, a rate that could have been predicted from the high incidence of home ownership: 45% of the houses in one cluster were inhabited by the same family for twelve years, 65% in the second, and 69% of the houses in the third! The neighborhood was inhabited by a core of stable residents regardless of the number of transients who were employed only for a few months in Detroit's factories. The neighborhood certainly had the stablity which the factories lacked.

TABLE 7.1
Continuous residency in houses standing in 1900 (by construction year)[a]

Cluster	1897–1900 (%)	1894–1900 (%)	1891–1900 (%)	1888–1900 (%)
Native white American				
21[b]	62.7	51.0	40.8	28.6
28	56.0	49.0	45.0	37.0
79	47.6	31.0	28.6	27.5
176	64.0	50.0	-	-
Polish				
51	71.4	60.0	51.4	65.2
164	88.0	84.0	81.0	69.0
171	70.7	60.0	52.9	45.0

SOURCES: *Detroit City Directory for 1888, 1889, 1890, 1891* (Detroit: R. L. Polk and Co., 1887–1891); *Detroit City Directory for the Year Commencing August 1st, 1892, 1893, 1894, 1895, 1896, 1897, 1898, 1899, 1900* (Detroit: R. L. Polk and Co., 1892–1900).

a. Houses standing at each end of the three-, six-, nine- and twelve-year intervals.

b. Not including one apartment building.

NEIGHBORHOOD COHESIVENESS

What was life like, then, in Detroit's east side among German and Polish workers? The neighborhood was all that many immigrants knew of Detroit. A simple measure of the degree of isolation that members of ethnic groups may have experienced in ethnic neighborhoods is reflected in their ability or inability to speak English. In 1900, as many as 15% of the German-born immigrants over ten years of age and 36% of the Polish natives over ten did not speak English. The neighborhood had to provide a diversified environment to accommodate a sizable part of its population otherwise unable to deal with the society at large. Of the immigrants unable to speak English, the majority were women: 67% of the Germans who could not speak English and 58% of the Poles who could not speak English were females. Among foreign speakers, social interaction was most likely limited to the family and to the neighborhood's social networks.

Many specialized institutions existed in the east side, especially designed to meet the needs of the immigrant population. At times, conflicts along class lines divided immigrant associations, but these institutions for the most part served to cement the ethnic communities. Early in the history of their settlement in Detroit, the socially active Germans organized a number of voluntary associations, some of them intended to help working people and their families in time of need. In 1875, the *Michigan Journal* counted 73 German organizations in the city, comprising 20 relief and aid societies, 11 secret lodges, 8 singing societies, 17 miscellaneous organizations, and 3 Catholic, 11 Protestant, and 3 Jewish congregations.[9] Arbeiter Halle, for example, the home of the German's Workingmen's Aid Society (Arbeiter Unterstützungverein) was built in 1868 at the northeast corner of Russell and Catherine Street "on the plan of many an old country halle, with a 'garten' outside where one could eat and drink in pleasant weather, with halls for meetings."[10] The Arbeiter Society provided many services to its members; for instance, in 1877, upon the death of a member, the widow or orphans received $351, while a sick member received $5 per week.[11]

In addition to insurance benefits, the voluntary associations provided the east side population with social gatherings. Arbeiter Halle, often a center for rallies, was also rented to outside organizations for dances and parties. The Detroit Socialer Turnverein, founded in 1853, represented the Turner or athletic movement, promoting "physical training, the furthering of free thought on the basis

9. *Detroit Free Press*, 14 March 1875.
10. *Detroit Saturday Night*, 12 February 1927.
11. *Detroit Free Press*, 8 August 1872.

of modern intelligence, and the promotion of social life."[12] Another society, the Harmonie Society, was the most popular of numerous musical groups.[13] All these societies met in annual parades through the east side, representing all the trades, occupations, and industries that Germans pursued. In 1891 the *Detroit News* reported that on parade day most of Detroit's large companies—the Detroit Stove Works, the Delta Lumber Company, the Michigan Stove Company, the Peninsular Stove Company, Calvert Lithographing Company, Pingree and Smith, Russel Wheel and Foundry Company—"either permitted their German employees to parade or else shut down at noon and gave their men a half holiday."[14]

An example of the strength of ethnic bonds in the city and the ways in which they pervaded all aspects of life is provided by the organization of social and communal life in Detroit's Polish neighborhood. The Polish laborer's investment in his home looks pale compared with his investment in neighborhood institutions, especially the local church. In 1907, a Polish immigrant, Wincenty Smołczyński, published a business directory of the Polish community together with the first history of the Polish settlement in Detroit.[15] Smołczyński had fought in the Polish uprising of 1863–64. After their defeat by the Russians, he moved to Austria and worked for a while as a cook at various hotels. While in Austria, he participated in public life and was nominated as a Polish reprsentative to the Council in Vienna. He came to the United States and to Detroit in 1902 with his wife and two children, where "he worked physically to earn his bread." In his *History of the Polish Settlement and Religious Community* in Detroit, Smołczyński insisted that the first activity of the Poles in America, in Detroit and elsewhere, was to establish their churches:

> Wherever it was possible, Poles organized religious communities, built their Polish churches and schools, though on many an occasion it was very difficult for them to do so. Very often, they had nothing to eat, but they gathered their last strength to build a church, or even a small chapel. Often, very often, they not only lacked funds but also moral support and personal example on the part of those who were supposed to come to their help, and that is why they experienced bitter disappointment and discouragement. There were many settlements where a hundred, a hundred-

12. Ibid., 2 September 1894.
13. Ibid., 28 May 1899.
14. *Detroit News*, 5 October 1891; on the German press in Detroit see Mark O. Kistler, "The German Language Press in Michigan, A Survey and Bibliography," *Michigan History* 44 (1960): 303–23.
15. Wincenty Smołczyński, *Przewodnik Adresowy i Historya Osady Polskiej w Detroit, Mich.* (Detroit, 1907). I wish to thank Gennady Shkliarevsky for his translation of this directory, and Richard Hodas for this reference; a copy of *Przewodnik Adresowy* is available at MHC.

and-fifty or two-hundred families got together, and—well motivated—they decided, provided there was time, to organize a Polish religious community and build a Polish church. A committee was then elected and sent to a bishop with a request to send a Polish priest to lead the organized community. The bishop, an Irish or sometimes a German, who are biased against Poles, would tell the Poles that in their locality there was already an Irish or German church and Poles could belong to that one. Irish and German bishops wanted to keep the Poles, who were arriving at that time in large masses, from building their own churches, and thus their own society, but rather to mix them up with representatives of other religious communities, and give respect to the church hierarchy, the Irish or the Germans, so that while mixing in the community with other nationalities, the Poles would lose their own identity. Notwithstanding this, the Polish peasant had decided to praise God in America; as Poles do, he did not feel calm until he reached his goal. Aryan bishops put numerous obstacles in his way, which were hard to overcome, but the Polish peasant was persistent and proved his own.[16]

Poles focused their energy on the church. A national church was needed in America not only to structure the community internally, so as to insure its religious independence from the German and Irish Catholic hierarchy, but also to reunify a partitioned Poland, to bring together the Prusak, the Rosjanin, the Galicijak, and the Kashub in a new country.[17] In 1900, the overwhelming majority of Detroit's Poles, 86%, came from German Poland, 13% from Russian Poland, and only 1% from Austrian Poland. But the adult Pole, aged thirty to forty, had been living in the United States for an average of only fourteen years. Most adults, then, had spent a fair share of their childhood under either Prussian or Russian rule. To them, the church was instrumental in recreating a common past.

By 1900, Detroit's Polish community had six churches, five on the east side and one on the west side. The first one, Saint Albertus, was founded in 1871 and located on Saint Aubin between Winter and Fremont. With the creation of Saint Albertus, the Poles could for the first time worship in their own church, under the spiritual leadership of Father Wieczorek, and did not have to attend the German Catholic church, Saint Joseph. A modest frame church was initially built for $5,500, but in 1884 the church was rebuilt for $61,000. Saint Casimir,

---

16. Ibid., pp. 8–9.
17. Thaddeus C. Radzialowski and Donald Binkowski, "Polish-Americans in Detroit Politics," in *Ethnic Politics in Urban America*, ed. Angela T. Pienkos (Chicago: Polish Historical Association, 1978), pp. 40–65; Thaddeus Radzialowski, "The View from a Polish Ghetto: Some Observations on the First One Hundred Years in Detroit," *Ethnicity* 1 (1974): 125–50.

on the west side, at Twenty-third and Myrtle, opened in 1882. There, too, the initial church was modest, costing only $7,500, but was rebuilt in 1887–90, modeled after Saint Peter's of Rome, for $126,000. The Polish community did not experience enough growth for the construction of a second church on the west side, but four more churches were built on the east side before 1900. Saint Francis of Assisi was first built in 1888 and rebuilt in 1896–97 for $145,000, the organ itself costing $6,000, and the stations of the cross $1,400, coming from France. Sweetest Heart of Mary was initially built in 1888–89 on Canfield and Russell, and rebuilt in the early nineties for vast sums of money, the value of the church being assessed at $214,000 in 1897. Saint Josaphat was built in 1889–90 at the intersection of Canfield and Hastings for $100,000. The only modest Polish church standing in 1900 was Saint Stanislas, created in 1898, and still located in the initial German Lutheran frame church on Dubois Street which the community bought for $16,000.[18]

Next to each church a school was invariably built, and often a presbytery and a community hall as well, sometimes adding a $50,000 to $60,000 price tag to the already expensive church building. How could modest Polish day laborers afford such expenses while they were doubling or tripling up in their small cottages in order to meet daily expenses? Usually a committee of parishioners was organized, no more than ten people, in charge of raising money for acquiring the land and building the church. Saint Josaphat, for example, was built about 1890; Tomasz Żółtowski, a grocer and brewer who had lived in Detroit since the 1870s, donated the land. Of the $100,000 construction costs, the committee raised $50,000 from the community and borrowed $50,000 from a bank. In 1907, when Wincenty Smołczyński wrote his *History*, $15,000 was already paid back to the bank.[19]

The building of Sweetest Heart of Mary and the controversy that surrounded it provides a perfect example of the Poles' difficulties with the hierarchy and of their dedication to their churches. It also sheds light on internal dissensions within the Polish community, between those willing to abide by the bishop's authority, and those (priests and parishioners alike) preferring a uniquely Polish-American church which would leave some decisions to the laity. In 1886, Bishop Borgess dismissed Father Kolasiński from his pastorate at Saint Albertus when, amidst other charges of disobedience, he refused to submit his financial books to the bishop for audit. His popularity among his parishioners, however, was such that many of Saint Albertus's congregants violently protested their pastor's

18. Smołczyński, *Przewodnik Adresowy*, pp. 67, 74, 78, 84, 87.
19. Ibid., p. 84.

dismissal.[20] A crowd of women initially forbade entrance to the church to the new pastor, Father Dąbrowski, the founder of the Polish seminary, and this was only one in a series of violent incidents which divided the Polish community over the degree of autonomy of the Polish-American church. Kolasiński's supporters went as far as severing their ties from the diocese and waited for Kolasiński's return to Detroit in December 1888 to build a new church of their own, Sweetest Heart of Mary, without the bishop's consent, just a few blocks away from Saint Albertus.

In retaliation, the bishop excommunicated all Kolasiński's parishioners, and the new church was not dedicated until December 1893, when the dispute was finally resolved and Kolasiński publicly reconciled with the hierarchy. In the meantime, a group of Poles managed to break away from the Catholic hierarchy to keep their priest on the job; they bought the land for a new church for $13,600, and built church, school, and presbytery for another $13,700. A few years later, the parishioners started a fund-raising drive for a new church building, and in 1897, Sweetest Heart of Mary was estimated to be the most expensive church building of the Polish community. That year, however, the community defaulted on its debt. American Savings Bank refused to extend the repayment period and took the case to court. The community tried to settle the dispute by paying the interest of the debt or $7,700; Potrzuski, a butcher on Riopelle, alone gave $2,800. This sum, however, did not settle the dispute; the case was tried and the church sold at a public auction for $30,000, to a lawyer, Mr. McGravie. The Polish community took the case to a higher court, charging that a property appraised at $214,000 could not be sold for $30,000. The court granted a new auction, but in the meantime community leaders managed to get a new loan for $65,000 from London Bank in Montreal, which many community members guaranteed by mortgaging their homes, and bought off the church from McGravie.[21] This dramatic story of a church built by excommunicated parishioners against the orders of church hierarchy, so expensive that the community defaulted, and yet a church that the parishioners managed to buy a second time with money secured by new mortgages on their homes, clearly demonstrates the communal strength of Detroit's Polonia.

20. Radzialowski and Binkowski, "Polish-Americans"; Radzialowski, "View from a Polish Ghetto," pp. 127–28; Edward Adam Skendzel, *The Kolasiński Story* (Grand Rapids: Littleshield Press, 1979); Lawrence D. Orton, *Polish Detroit and the Kolasiński Affair* (Detroit: Wayne State University Press, 1981); the best treatment of this affair is Leslie Woodcock Tentler, "Who Is the Church? Conflict in a Polish Immigrant Parish in Late Nineteenth Century Detroit" (1981); for similar conflicts in Chicago see Victor R. Greene, "For God and Country: The Origins of Slavic Catholic Self-Consciousness in America," *Church History* 35 (December 1966): 446–60.

21. Smolczyński, *Przewodnik Adresowy*, pp. 78–80.

So many aspects of life in the Polish community revolved around the church that, to the Pole, keeping the church going was worth many sacrifices. The church organized a curriculum of education from primary school to higher education. Each parish had its own schoolhouse. In 1900, Polish schools, taught by Felician Sisters, had an estimated enrollment of 4,313: 1,420 children at Saint Albertus, 636 at Saint Casimir, 785 at Sweetest Heart of Mary, 650 at Saint Josaphat, 644 at Saint Francis, 178 at Saint Stanislas. The Polish curriculum, drafted by Father Dąbrowski, comprised an eighth-grade elementary school and a four-year high school.[22] The exact number of children of Polish families attending the parish schools and the number attending one of the four public schools which bordered the Polish quarter is, unfortunately, impossible to estimate with the available data, but it is clear that the Poles had the largest organization of private schools in the city. Instruction in these schools was conducted both in Polish and in English. The sisters who taught there were trained in the Seminary of the Felician Sisters in Detroit. Detroit also had a Polish seminary for the priesthood, Saints Cyril and Methodius Seminary at Saint Aubin and Forest Avenue, founded in 1885 by Father Dąbrowski. In order to provide teachers for the seminary, the best students were sent to Rome to study at the Gregorian University. In 1907, the seminary counted over 250 students and had already graduated 42 priests.[23]

The churches of Detroit's Polonia set the rhythm of life. Smołczyński reports that, in 1907, Saint Albertus comprised 15 brotherhoods counting several hundred members each, such as the brotherhood of Saint Stanislas, or the Brotherhood of the Holy Rosary. In 1907 Saint Casimir also had 15 brotherhoods, Sweetest Heart of Mary 19, Saint Josaphat 12, Saint Francis 9, and Saint Stanislas also 9. Many of these brotherhoods were in fact incorporated under Michigan law, with a board of trustees, a treasurer, a secretary, and different committees or members responsible for particular activities: a choir director, a standard bearer, a committee for the care of orphans. Some brotherhoods were dedicated to a saint, others to the Kashubian Knights or the Polish Knights, or to the Kósciuszko Legion. Some were only for men; some included women and children. Church brotherhoods coordinated community activities, provided channels for fund-raising efforts to finance school extensions or new church buildings; most brotherhoods also provided sickness and death benefits to their members, since the Polish day laborers were without other protection. In addition to church brotherhoods, Saint Albertus, the oldest parish, also

22. Sister Mary R. Napolska, "The Polish Immigrant in Detroit to 1914," *Annals of the Polish Roman Catholic Union Archives and Museum* 10 (1945–46): 87–92.
23. Smołczyński, *Przewodnik Adresowy*, pp. 26–37.

controlled communitywide associations such as the Society of Polish–Roman Catholics under the Protection of the Holy Trinity, an association with 4,201 members in 1907 divided into 43 groups.[24]

Nonchurch associations also existed in Detroit's Polonia, often branches of national Polish-American associations. Some of them were part of the group of Detroit's Polish Associations, created in Detroit in 1894 by Piotr Leszczyński; among them were the Association of Polish Sons, the Sons of the Polish Crown, the Polish Dramatic Society, the Society of Brotherly Assistance of Polish Artisans, the Polish Eagle Society, the Association of the Polish Family, the Nest of Freedom, and the Polish Banner. Often members of the associations wore golden enameled buttons or other signs of their affiliation with the group. Other associations provided a basis for social organization. The Polish Falcons, for example, was essentially an athletic club under the appearance of a paramilitary organization; the Nest also had a drama circle, and the Falcons spent as much time rehearsing plays as drilling. In 1907, the Detroit's Nest of the Falcons had 97 members.[25]

The Polish press played the role that most foreign language papers played in immigrant neighborhoods; it served to maintain community cohesion, but it also helped establish a connection between the neighborhood and the larger world. Six of the eight Polish newspapers that appeared before 1900 were a part of one church institution or another. The *Polish Catholic Newspaper* was first published in 1874 but lasted only a few weeks. In 1885, the Reverend Gutowski started the publication of the *Polish Pilgrim*, which lasted until 1888, when it was replaced by *Prawda*, edited by Dr. Laskowski, a professor of the Polish seminary. *Niedziela*, founded in 1891, was a popular literary weekly, also published by the Polish seminary. *Swoboda*, another paper that appeared, sometimes weekly and sometimes daily, between 1896 and 1898, was edited by Dr. Howiecki, a former collaborator of *Prawda* at the seminary. And *Polonia*, which began its publication in 1898, was the organ of the Society of Polish–Roman Catholics under the Protection of Holy Trinity. Only two papers were not directly controlled by the church or a church organization: one was a socialist paper, *Gazeta Narodowa*, which lasted only a short period of time in the late 1870s or early 1880s, and the *Gwiazda*, published between 1889 and 1897. It was only in 1904 that the *Polish Daily* was first published and that the Polish community of Detroit had a large paper, published by a staff of professional journalists. Before that, the churches and related associations printed the news of interest to the Poles: in 1907, *Polonia* was published every Saturday,

24. Ibid., pp. 105–19.
25. Ibid., pp. 120–35.

advertised as "the only publication devoted to Polish interests," and the *Polish Daily* claimed to provide up-to-date news, always to write the truth, to print several instructive articles every day on various aspects of human life, as well as to make publications available cheaply and, of course, to provide the best place for advertisements.[26]

When the census takers visited the Polish neighborhood in 1900 and recorded the occupations of the working population, 65% of those recorded held unskilled occupations, 31% were engaged in skilled work, and only 5% could be classified as white collar. In fact, 48% of working Poles were simply day laborers or unspecified factory workers. The skilled workers held occupations such as stove molders or iron molders, blacksmiths, or carpenters; the handful of white-collar workers were essentially small businessmen and small proprietors, grocers, saloonkeepers, undertakers, or contractors, with few teachers or professionals. Seven years after the census was taken, Smołczyński wrote biograhical sketches of Detroit's prominent Poles in his history; he counted 63 personalities, including himself! The Poles celebrated in this history and community directory were the rectors of the different Polish parishes and the many small businessmen who made up the commercial elite in this community of industrial laborers. Men like Piotr Leszczyński were typical. Piotr was born in America in 1866, his father having migrated from Galicia. He was educated at Saint Albertus parish school, and then in public school, and in 1893 he opened a clothing shop at the corner of Russell and Canfield streets; in addition to his business activities, Piotr actively participated in Polish public life, organizing a singing society and a chapter of the Organization of the Polish People. Kazimierz Mioskowski, another prominent local businessman, was born in Prussia in 1863; he arrived in Detroit in 1891 and worked as a shoemaker in various firms before opening his own shop in 1900 on Canfield. Tomasz Żółtowski, yet another successful local merchant, was born in Prussia; he worked as a cartwright before founding a grocery shop and a brewery in Detroit. With the local mercantile elite, the directory also listed the few Poles who became professionals, men like Leopold Kosciński, who became a lawyer after attending the Polish seminary and then the Detroit College of Law, or like Stanisław Lachajewski, who also graduated from the seminary and then studied medicine in the Detroit Medical College. Stanisław was a city doctor, but he also owned a drugstore on Saint Aubin. Other notable Poles kept their roots in the community while holding a city job. Antoni Treppa, whose family settled in Detroit as early as 1859, was an inspector of public schools, but he owned a grocery store and a warehouse of vodkas and

---

26. Ibid., pp. 63–65; for a larger view see Edmund G. Olszyk, *The Polish Press in America* (Milwaukee, Wis.: Marquette University Press, 1940).

wines in the neighborhood. All the saloonkeepers made Smolczyński's list of prominent citizens, and all of them were active in church affairs.[27] Men met at the saloon not only to drink but also to read the paper, to argue over important community issues, such as raising money to save Sweetest Heart of Mary, or occasionally to arrange for sending money to the old country through the saloonkeeper, who often took on the additional jobs of transferring money and performing notary duties. The local elite set the tone for life. Merchants provided most necessities—clothes, shoes, foods, baked goods, hardware, furniture, coal, drugs (including "curing wine" from Częstochowa, "the best treatment for anemia and weakness")—which could be bought locally; they also provided the few luxuries of life which the laborer could afford only once in a while, an icon, a religious statuette, a harmonica or another musical instrument, so much desired for family and church reunions.[28]

The important point in all these details of Polish community life is that the Polish neighborhood was not inhabited solely by poor Poles. Our concentration indexes revealed, and Smolczyński's *History of the Polish Settlement* confirmed, that the small percentage (5% of the Polish population) who made up the elite, the clergy, the few professionals, the commercial class, all stayed within the community and contributed to its development. They were the ones who gave the largest sums of money to build churches and schools, although the scores of day laborers contributed to the effort too. The predominantly working-class Polish neighborhood was built, at least in part, by the upper social stratum of the ethnic group. All members of this upper occupational stratum had experienced a classic form of upward mobility, their biographies reveal, from day labor to economic independence as shopkeepers and small proprietors. But success was achieved within the community; consequently, they did not leave their area of initial settlement to join native white Americans. Instead, social mobility was reinvested in the community and used as a means to reinforce ethnic identity.

The strength of the Polish community at the turn of the century did not necessarily reflect the experience of other groups in Detroit, since the intensity of communal life was partly a question of numbers. The Germans and Poles who formed the backbone of the working class were numerous at the turn of the century. The Germans, who had been settled in Detroit for a long time, had a more complex social structure as well as more diversified cultural and religious organizations than the Poles, who could all rally under the banner of the Catholic church. The Irish, who once had been the largest foreign-born

27. Smolczyński, *Przewodnik Adresowy*, pp. 138–40, 144, 149, 150–53.
28. Ibid., p. 174.

group in Detroit, were on the decline at the turn of the century; while Polish institutions were flourishing, the Hibernian Hall building, the home of the Hibernian Benevolent Society on Michigan Avenue, in the heart of Corktown, was sold in 1908.[29] At the turn of the century, Russian Jews, Italians, and Hungarians were still too few in number in the German near east side to have developed an ethnic organization on the scale of the Polish community. Their institutions, as well as those of the Blacks, took on new dimensions during the first two decades of the twentieth century.

I selected the Polish community at the turn of the century for an intensive study of neighborhood institutions because of their exemplary character and because of the deep social meaning of their neighborhood social organization. The Poles were builders of homes, of churches, of schools, and evidently made a long-term commitment to their new country; a large majority of Polish immigrants living in Detroit in 1900 were naturalized; 60% were already citizens and another 20% were in the process of becoming citizens. But they intended to be assimilated separately into the American reality. The urban neighborhood provided them with a space where they could be autonomous and isolated citizens in an environment of their own.

29. Detroit, *Annual Report of the City Historiographer* (Detroit, 1908), p. 30.

3

Structures of Inequality

Ethnicity and Social Class at the Turn of the Century

8

The Leaders of Detroit's Industrialization

Plate 8. A businessman (possibly Daniel Scotten) on Michigan Avenue.
Courtesy of the Burton Historical Collection, Detroit Public Library.

Affiliation with a single lesser community within the multiethnic city caused tension in the everyday lives of many Detroiters at the turn of the century. For working-class immigrants, living face to face in a smaller ethnic community was more important than living in a large and continuously growing city. But to the industrialists who built Detroit's larger factories, Detroit was only one city. While ethnic diversity divided Detroit into isolated segments, continuous industrialization unified the urban scene. The men who led Detroit's industrial transformation, creating and expanding large enterprises, shared a common interest in cutting across the microunits of the city to secure a large pool of factory workers hired from an ethnically diverse and geographically divided population.

From 1880 to 1900, the population of Detroit increased 2.4 times, but the number of workers employed in large industrial establishments (over 200 workers) increased 10 times, an indication of the sustained transformation of Detroit's work scene. In 1880, a German blacksmith could have developed a small carriage factory in the German neighborhood and grown modestly prosperous within his group of origin. While this opportunity still existed in 1900, the growth of larger concerns made it increasingly difficult for local shops to compete with new industrial giants. With industrialization, channels for upward mobility within ethnic groups were severely limited, as leading industrialists gained greater control of the opportunity structure by hiring an ever increasing number of workers, technicians, and white-collar help, as well as by branching out into the marketing of their product.[1]

The last two decades of the nineteenth century saw not only the development of larger factories but also major transformations in the management structure of these industrial establishments. In the 1880s few establishments were incorporated; the only large industrial securities were the railroads, and many investors preferred to put their money into real estate rather than business. Partnership organizations still predominated, allowing for the transfer of ownership only if the firm was dissolved and reestablished. But the market for industrial securities developed greatly in the 1880s and 1890s, when industrialists needed more capital to finance heavy equipment and structural transformations; by 1900, most industrial establishments were incorporated, even if most of these incorporated companies were still run as partnerships. Incorporation offered a more flexible legal structure for bringing in of new capital and also more security against personal liability.[2]

1. Alfred D. Chandler, Jr., *The Visible Hand* (Cambridge, Mass: Harvard University Press, 1977), pp. 287–314.

2. Thomas R. Navin and Marian V. Sears, "The Rise of a Market for Industrial Securities, 1887–1902," *Business History Review* 29 (June 1955): 105–38.

By investigating the origins and careers of these newly incorporated companies' presidents, we can identify the men who either built or inherited firms and so contributed to Detroit's transmutation into a manufacturing center of the new industrial belt. I will pursue, then, the analysis of Detroit's society not from the bottom up but rather from the top down, looking again at the issues of unity and diversity in American urban society, but this time from the perspective of those few who held positions of economic leadership. By studying those who penetrated the ranks of the manufacturing elite, we can determine the extent to which and the ways in which some ethnic groups came to be represented at the top level of the social structure while others remained barred from it. This chapter and the three succeeding ones attempt to broaden our understanding of class divisions in the industrializing city by exploring sections of the social structure in greater depth than can be gained from the uses of standard socioeconomic indicators. With the elite, we concentrate on the people who promoted economic growth in key sectors. We will then turn to the living conditions of selected groups of workers, to the relationship between demographic behavior and socioeconomic status, and to the fate of the growing class of poor in the industrializing city.

Detroit in 1900 was a new manufacturing center but an old urban establishment, populated by the French in the eighteenth century and transformed into a Great Lakes mercantile center in the nineteenth. To determine which citizens were responsible for Detroit's industrialization—the old families of the mercantile elite or the newcomers or both—I decided to cast a large net over all important industrial establishments of the city at the turn of the century, either in the traditional consumer-related industries or in the new iron and steel complex of the industrial belt. From the 1900 factory inspection, I isolated all factories employing at least 100 workers when running at full capacity; in order to include most large employers of the city, I also selected all factories employing at least 200 workers, not visited by the Labor Bureau in 1900 but visited instead in the 1897, 1898, and 1899 inspections. This procedure yielded a total of 133 large factories visited once or several times during those four years.[3]

FACTORIES AND INDUSTRIALISTS: THE DATA

The 133 industrial establishments represented all sectors of production (see table 5.2). Twelve factories in the transportation sector specialized in railroad

3. Michigan, "State Factory Inspection," appendix to *Fifteenth Annual Report of the Bureau of Labor and Industrial Statistics* (Lansing, 1898), pp. 31–55; appendix to *Sixteenth Annual Report of the Bureau of Labor and Industrial Statistics* (Lansing, 1899), pp. 8–37; appendix to *Seventeenth Annual Report of the Bureau of Labor and Industrial Statistics* (Lansing, 1900), pp. 6–37; and appendix to *Eighteenth Annual Report of the Bureau of Labor and Industrial Statistics* (Lansing, 1901), pp. 6–37.

cars and equipment, shipbuilding, automobiles, and carriages. Another 12 firms specialized in one or another form of chemical product, either drugs, paints, varnishes, or matches. There were 27 firms in metal-related work—casting, brass works, copper works, and, of course, iron and steel. The inspections also listed a variety of consumer industries: of the 59 large factories in this sector, 8 were food factories, 21 clothing factories, 10 furniture shops, 10 tobacco firms, one silverware factory, one spectacle-making factory, and 8 factories of stoves and boilers, the latter producing both consumer products and industrial goods. A few other, miscellaneous firms had more than 100 workers in 1900: 2 construction firms and 2 lumber firms, 4 publishing firms, 3 service enterprises (such as a laundry), one decorating firm, the repair shop of the Detroit Citizens Street Railway Company, the machine shop of the Detroit, Grand Haven and Milwaukee Railroad, and also a large company processing seeds and agricultural products.

The 133 selected factories yielded a list of 121 industrialists for whom I sought biographic information; 83 of them were presidents of one (and sometimes several) corporations, and 38 others were either sole owners of their firms or a partner (see Appendix 6). James McMillan, for example, was president of 2 listed companies—Seamless Steel Tube and Fulton Iron and Engine Works— as well as chairman of American Car and Foundry. Others, like Hazen and Frank Pingree, George Peck, and John Howarth, were among the multiple partners of one firm only. For intensive study, I selected all partners, owners, and presidents, but excluded vice-presidents and board members of incorporated companies, as well as managers of large branch firms whose central offices operated outside Detroit. Men like H. L. Spaulding, general manager of Pullman's Detroit plant (which closed in 1897/98), were thus not included, despite the importance of the firm, because Pullman's central operation was located elsewhere.

My study, then, does not include all industrial leaders, nor does it include bankers, realtors, and other nonmanufacturing businessmen other than those selected industrialists who were also involved in such business ventures. My purpose is not to reconstruct a portrait of the business elite in its diversity and in the complexity of interlocking relationships, but rather to conduct an investigation into the lives of the prominent manufacturers—selected not because of their extraordinary wealth or extensive business holdings, but because they were the largest employers in Detroit.

The search for biographical information on the 121 industrialists yielded enough information to draw a collective portrait of the manufacturing leaders, but the quality of the information varied greatly from one case to another (see Appendix 6). Local historians like Clarence Burton and Silas Farmer wrote many biographies of local business leaders, all useful but rarely carrying the same information systematically from one manufacturer to another and always presenting these businessmen with a local optimistic boosterism rather than with a critical eye for those social differences among them that I was seeking. In many other cases no biographies had been written, and I was forced to rely on as little as a short newspaper article, an obituary, or just the individual census record for 1900. I was able to locate 115 of the 121 manufacturing leaders in the 1900 census, and so for them I have consistent information on their own place of birth and those of their parents (the latter being rarely given in biographies), but I was able to identify the political affiliation of only 49 of them.

FACTORIES AND INDUSTRIALISTS: THE MEN

Using this uneven and partial data, and thus with caution, I will draw a picture of the manufacturing leaders of turn-of-the-century Detroit. Many historians have already argued, sometimes passionately, over the origins of the American business elite, as some set out to deny the rags-to-riches myth while others tried to demonstrate its reality.[4] Beyond the surface argument, however, scholars have reached some agreement and developed a set of balanced answers. Opportunities for entering the ranks of the business elite increased, it seems, in developing cities but decreased as the cities grew bigger and older. A recent study of Chicago's business elite conducted by Jocelyn Maynard Ghent and Frederic Cople Jaher, which included not only manufacturers but also bankers, realtors, and merchants, concluded that "leading Chicago business men became less Algeristic in origins with each successive birth cohort."[5] In another study limited to steel manufacturers but including several cities, John Ingham persuasively argued that the social system was more open in cities of the new manufacturing belt like Pittsburgh and Cleveland than in older cities like Philadelphia, where the typical iron and steel manufacturer of the gilded age came from a successful family established in this country since the seventeenth or eighteenth century, of Northern Irish, English, Scottish, or Welsh ancestry, either Presbyterian or Episcopalian. Although the situation was more open in newer cities, Ingham still concluded that "maufacturers generally were not alien men operating on foreign soil, but came from the 'first families' of their communities."[6]

---

4. Herbert G. Gutman, *Work, Culture, and Society in Industrializing America* (New York: Alfred A. Knopf, 1976), pp. 211–33.

5. Jocelyn M. Ghent and Frederic C. Jaher, "The Chicago Business Elite: 1830–1930," *Business History Review* 50 (Autumn 1976): 328.

6. John N. Ingham, "Rags to Riches Revisited: The Effect of City Size and Related Factors on the Recruitment of Business Leaders," *Journal of American History* 63 (December 1976): 637.

The most significant point revealed by my study is that the similarities between Detroit's manufacturers stand out more sharply than their differences.
There were different levels of wealth and importance within this manufacturing
group, and a smaller group of leaders clearly dominated the economic scene by
being president and/or board member of several companies at once (26% of the
industrialists were on the boards of other manufacturing establishments and
27% on the boards of banks). This smaller group constituted an elite within the
elite, but overall they were typical of the group as a whole. Most men of industry
were alike politically and religiously, 71% being Republicans and 87% being
Protestants, mostly Episcopalians and Presbyterians. Many inherited wealth
and control of the company's economy (no more than 20% of the industrialists
came from poor families), and they reached prominent positions young, with
68% becoming presidents, senior partners, or owners before reaching the age
of thirty-five. Most of these industrialists were well-educated people; as many
as 31% of them had attended college at a time when less than 5% of the
population did so. Most met in exclusive clubs such as the Detroit Club (organized in 1882, and enrolling 65% of the industrialists studied), the Detroit
Boat Club, the Yondotega Country Club, the Grosse Pointe Country Club, the
Detroit Athletic Club, the Sons of the American Revolution, and also the Masonic lodges (see tables 8.1–8.4).

This politically, religiously, and socially homogeneous group was open to
newcomers, but only if they were of Anglo-Saxon origins. Almost 85% of the
industrialists shared a common Anglo-Saxon background, although many had
only recently settled in Detroit. Despite the fact that most industrialists were

TABLE 8.1
Religious affiliation of Detroit's industrialists, 1897–1900

Religion	Number in sample	Percentage
Episcopalian	10	26.3
Congregational	8	21.1
Presbyterian	8	21.1
Unitarian	2	5.3
Methodist	2	5.3
Baptist	2	5.3
Lutheran	1	2.6
Roman Catholic	4	10.5
Jewish	1	2.6
Total	38	100.0
Missing data	83	-
Grand total	121	-

SOURCE: See Appendix 6.

TABLE 8.2

Route to directing firm, Detroit's industrialists, 1897–1900

Method	Number in sample	Percentage
Inherited	17	20.2
Founded alone	36	42.9
Cofounder; organizer	14	16.7
Investor	14	16.7
Rose through ranks	3	3.5
Total	84	100.0
Missing data	37	-
Grand total	121	-

SOURCE: See Appendix 6.

a. This table reflects the ways the industrialists became presidents, owners or senior partners of their establishments. It does not refer to their sources of capital; a founder may have acquired wealth prior to becoming an industrialist.

born in the United States, only 44% of them were native-born of native parents. Quite a few were immigrants, 9% from England, 5% from Germany, another 2% from English Canada. Many more were first-generation Americans, 4% native-born of British parents, 5% native-born of German parents, 3% native-born of Irish parents; there were a few isolated immigrants from other countries, including one Irishman, one Frenchman, one Netherlander, and two Belgians; some had mixed backgrounds, born in Canada of English parents, or of Irish parents, or born in the United States of mixed British and English-Canadian parents. Eight of the industrialists were identified only as born in the United States and another three as born in Canada, with no reference to the birthplaces of their parents (see table 8.5). By looking at each of these ethnic groups sep-

TABLE 8.3

Age on becoming head of firm, Detroit's industrialists, 1897–1900

Age	Number in sample	Percentage
16–20	2	3.3
21–25	9	15.0
26–30	18	30.0
31–35	12	20.0
36–40	13	21.7
41–45	2	3.3
46–50	4	6.7
Total	60	100.00
Missing data	61	-
Grand total	121	-

SOURCE: See Appendix 6.

TABLE 8.4

Clubs with at least five industrialists as members, Detroit, 1897–1900[a]

Club Name	Number in sample
Detroit Club	31
Masonic lodges	21
Detroit Boat Club	17
Old Club	12
Country Club	12
Detroit Athletic Club	9
Sons of the American Revolution	9
Yondotega Club	5

SOURCE: See Appendix 6.

a. We found sixty-seven industrialists belonging to a total of 85 clubs which we could identify.

arately, we can gain a clearer insight into the differences among the industrialists from different origins.

THE NATIVE WHITE AMERICANS

Fifty-one (or 44% of the industrialists) were native white Americans: 10 were born in Detroit, another 11 in Michigan, 5 came from other states of the old northwest (especially Ohio and Indiana), 11 from New England (especially Connecticut but also from Maine, Massachusetts, Rhode Island, and New Hampshire), and another 14 came from mid-Atlantic states (especially New York and Pennsylvania). Although I could identify the birthplace of most industrialists, I could trace with some accuracy the careers of only 38 of the 51 native white Americans. These 38 men attained to the ownership, partnership, or presidency of a large industrial establishment by one of five ways: 5 inherited the firms from their fathers; another 8 bought into existing firms; 15 were the sole founders of a firm; 9 were cofounders; and only one industrialist rose through the ranks of the establishment in which he was employed.

Of the 5 presidents who inherited their firms from their fathers, 4 were born in Detroit and another came to Detroit as a child. They were all born into the wealthy mercantile and industrial elite and remained a part of it. John Bagley, president of a tobacco firm which his father had founded in 1853, employed 160 workers in 1900. Bagley's father had served as governor of Michigan from 1873 to 1877; the family, of English ancestry, had come to Massachusetts in the seventeenth century. John attended school in Detroit, studied at the Michigan Military Academy and in Germany before becoming president of the firm at age twenty-three, in 1883. He was Unitarian, Republican, and belonged to several exclusive clubs of the business elite—the Detroit Club, the Yondotega

TABLE 8.5

Ethnic origins of Detroit's industrialists, 1897–1900

| | Place of Birth | | | |
Person	First parent	Second parent	Number in sample	Percentage
United States[a]	United States	United States	51	44.3
English Canada	English Canada	English Canada	2	1.7
English Canada	Great Britain[b]	Great Britain	2	1.7
English Canada	English Canada	Great Britain	1	.9
English Canada	Ireland	Ireland	1	.9
English Canada	United States	Ireland	1	.9
English Canada	-	-	3	2.6
Great Britain[c]	Great Britain	Great Britain	10	8.7
United States	Great Britain[d]	Great Britain	5	4.3
Germany	Germany	Germany	6	5.2
United States	Germany	Germany	6	5.2
Ireland	Ireland	Ireland	1	.9
United States	Ireland	Ireland	4	3.5
France	France	France	1	.9
Netherlands	Netherlands	Netherlands	1	.9
Belgium	Belgium	Belgium	2	1.7
United States	Switzerland	Switzerland	1	.9
United States	United States	Great Britain	2	1.7
United States	United States	French Canada	2	1.7
United States	United States	Germany	2	1.7
United States	Canada	Ireland	1	.9
United States	Great Britain	-	2	1.7
United States	-	-	8	7.0
Total			115	100.0
Missing data			6	
Grand total			121	

SOURCE: See Appendix 6.

　a. Place of birth in the United States: Detroit, 11; Michigan, 10; New York, 13; Connecticut, 5; Maine, 3; Vermont, 2; Pennsylvania, 2; Ohio, 3; Indiana, 2.

　b. Including one couple from Scotland, the other unknown.

　c. Place of birth in Great Britain: Scotland, 5; England, 3; Wales, 2.

　d. Including three couples from England, the other two unknown.

Country Club, the Detroit Boat Club, and others. William Barbour, the president of the Detroit Stove Works, is another native Detroiter who inherited a large firm (1,150 workers). The Barbours were from Collinsville, Connecticut, also descended from an English family which had settled in New England in the seventeenth century. Edwin Barbour had come to Detroit in the 1830s and worked in the dry goods business; after marrying Ella Tefft, the daughter of one of the founders of the Detroit Stove Works, he became secretary and then president (in 1884) of the stove company, a position he held until his death in 1894. Another member of the Barbour family, George, also came from Collinsville to Detroit in 1872, and in 1900, at age fifty-six, was one of the leading businessmen of Detroit, president of the brass firm Ireland and Matthews, vice-president and general manager of Michigan Stove (which he helped to create), and also vice-president of two banks and an insurance company. William Barbour, Edwin's son, attended Phillips Academy in Andover after graduating from Detroit School and before becoming president of one of Detroit's largest enterprises in 1897, at age twenty. In 1902, William married Margaret Chittenden, the daughter of a Detroit lumber magnate.

Other Detroiters who inherited their firms included Charles Hammond, who became president of a large meat company at age thirty; he was one of the best-educated members of the manufacturing elite, with an engineering degree from MIT and two years at Harvard Law School. Or Merrill Mills, one of the wealthiest citizens of Detroit, who succeeded his father as president of the Banner Cigar Tobacco Company and vice president of Michigan Stove and later became a board member of several other establishments. Or Frederick Stearns, who, although born in Buffalo, was raised in Detroit, where his family moved when he was an infant. After attending the University of Michigan, Stearns entered his father's pharmaceutical business, became the president at age thirty-three, and soon transformed the firm into a giant of the pharmaceutical industry. A Republican, Stearns was active in many aspects of Detroit life: he was president of the Detroit Baseball Club in 1885 and 1887, and one of the founders of the Detroit Athletic Club.

Those others who did not inherit a manufacturing establishment but bought into a firm also came from wealthy backgrounds; often they first invested in a firm and then became its president. Most of these men, Detroiters or not, were born into the political, professional, and commercial elite of the antebellum period. Truman Newberry, for example, president of Detroit Steel and Spring, was a native Detroiter, son of a lawyer, politician, and industrialist who founded the Michigan Car Company with James McMillan. Truman was educated at Yale, became president of Detroit Steel and Spring at age twenty-three, and was active in Detroit social circles as vice-president of the Detroit Club and of the Yondotega Country Club. He later served as secretary of the navy in Theodore Roosevelt's administration and eventually entered the United States Senate. Another investor-turned-president was Fordyce Rodgers, also born in Detroit, who purchased the Detroit White Lead works in 1880; he came from a mercantile family in Pontiac and acquired extensive business experience in New York and California before returning to Michigan and investing in Detroit's industry. Or William Chittenden, who came to Detroit at age eighteen, the son of a lawyer and congressman; his primary interest was in the hotel business as the owner of the Russell House, but he invested in manufacturing establishments and by 1900 was the president of two important firms, Hargreaver Manufacturing, employing 326 workers, and the Michigan Wire Cloth Company, employing 110 workers. Theodore Buhl, one of the most prominent Detroit manufacturers in 1900, was the son of former Detroit mayor Christian Buhl (who was born in Pennsylvania of German parents, moved to Detroit with his family in the 1830s, and built a large hardware business) and the nephew of former Detroit mayor Frederick Buhl. Theodore began his business career as a partner in the family hardware firm at age twenty-one. In 1900, at age fifty-six, he was the president of Buhl Stamping (specialized in tinware), Buhl malleable (specialized in casting) as well as president of Parke, Davis and Co., the largest drug company in Detroit.

Most of the men who created new firms instead of investing in existing ones were also born with wealth, power, and social prominence, and through their business enterprises maintained their positions in the industrial city. The available information does not prove conclusively that all were wealthy, but most were well educated and came from backgrounds with business interests and business connections. George Russel, born in Detroit and founder of Russel Wheel, was the son of a leading surgeon in the city. Frederick Smith, also born in Detroit and founder of a large lumber company, Wolverine Manufacturing with 350 workers, was the son of a businessman and leading educator in Detroit. Fred Moran succeeded his brother to the presidency of the Peninsular Stove Company, after contributing to its creation with his brother and James Dwyer; he was the son of Charles Moran, judge in the territorial court and member of the first Michigan constitution convention and of the state legislature. Other founders and cofounders of manufacturing establishments came from business backgrounds. John Dyar, who created the American Radiator Company, had started in his father's mercantile establishment in Romeo, Michigan. Dyar died in 1898 but his business continued to flourish; in 1900 American Radiator Company had two plants, employing 912 workers between them. Abner Larned, who came to Detroit from Genesee County, Michigan, at age nineteen, was the son of a businessman in Fenton; he created Larned and Carter, a clothing company employing 125 workers. Hamilton Carhartt came to Detroit at age twenty-three from Jackson; he used the capital from a family wholesale firm to build a large cotton manufacturing plant employing 535 people. Dexter Ferry, president of the largest seed-processing company in the Detroit area (employing 900 workers), came to Detroit at age nineteen from New York. His father was identified only as a wagon maker, but his maternal grandfather was a representative in the Massachusetts legislature and his paternal grandfather prosperous in agriculture.

Only four of the thirty-eight industrialists, native-born of native-born parents, for whom the business career is known with some accuracy came from modest backgrounds. Only one senior partner of a firm in 1900 achieved his business status by rising through the ranks of the firm. This was James Lee, who came to Detroit at age eighteen after a high school education in Brighton, Michigan; as Clarence Burton, his biographer, sums it up, "he secured a situation with James Nall and Company and subsequently entered the employ of Charles Root and Company, Wholesale Dry Goods Merchants. He devoted every energy to learning the business, faithfully performing each task assigned him, and was advanced from one position to another of greater importance and responsibility until he became the junior member of the firm in 1880. Upon the death of Mr. Root four months later the firm of Strong, Lee, and Company was organized."[7] But this story of promotion through the ranks, although it may sound familiar, was the exception in Detroit. Indeed, only three other native-born industrialists of native parents rose from such humble beginnings. Hazen Pingree and his brother Frank were the children of a poor New England farmer and both learned the trade of shoecutter as young apprentices. Hazen enlisted in the First Massachusetts Regiment at age twenty, came to Detroit shortly after his discharge in 1865 at age twenty-three, and, after working for a short time for a boot and shoe factory, started his own with C. H. Smith, employing only eight people. In 1900, after Pingree had become mayor of Detroit and governor of Michigan, the firm employed 700 people. Pingree's brother Frank had joined Hazen in 1868 and become a senior partner in 1883. The sole other manufacturer of modest origin in this native group was Thomas Wadsworth, the owner-founder of the Western Cigar Box Manufacture, employing 100 workers in 1900. The son of a ship's carpenter, he started as a mechanic in the employ of another manufacturer of cigar boxes before engaging in business for himself.

These native businessmen were alike in remaining or becoming active in local affairs and municipal politics. Theodore Buhl came from this municipal milieu, since both his father and his uncle had been mayors of Detroit. Pingree was the hope of the manufacturing establishment when he was elected mayor; many of the business elite simply forgot that he was, in fact, the exception among them. He was Republican certainly, and Protestant, but his modest background had brought him closer to the sorrows and problems of the working class than the

---

7. Clarence M. Burton, ed., *The City of Detroit, Michigan, 1701–1922*, 5 vols. (Detroit: S. J. Clarke Publishing Co., 1922), 4:97.

other members of the manufacturing establishment realized. Many other industrialists were also involved in city affairs: George Barbour was at one point president of the City Council; Dexter Ferry and Frederick Smith were on the Board of Estimates; Hamilton Carhartt served on the Public Lighting Commission, W. J. Chittenden on the Board of the Detroit House of Correction, Frank Kirby as a water commissioner; others, like William Sherwood, who served as commissioner of banking, were involved in state affairs; and of course many manufacturers, including W. J. Chittenden, Truman Newberry, Frederick Smith, Marvin Stanton, Edwin Thompson, and James Wright, served on the Board of Trade (which became the Board of Commerce in 1903).

These native white industrialists, overwhelmingly Republican (72%), overwhelmingly Protestant, either Episcopalian, Congregationalist, or Presbyterian (there was only one known Catholic), operated within all sectors of industry in Detroit. A few of these men were very active in Republican politics; men like Darius Thorp, involved in publishing the *State Republican*, or James Wright, the treasurer of the state central committee. They formed an active elite who controlled not only the city's factories but also other aspects of the economy, since almost 40% of them were on the boards of banks. Their social life revolved around the handsome mansions of Woodward Avenue, the west side, Jefferson Avenue, and, in the summer, mansions of Grosse Pointe; and most met in the Detroit Club, or the Detroit Boat Club, or the Detroit Athletic Club, or the Yondotega Country Club, or at the Masonic Lodge.

BRITISH AND ENGLISH-CANADIAN INDUSTRIALISTS

The manufacturers who were native-born of native parents were a homogeneous group, but they made up only half of the manufacturing leaders. All other manufacturers had at least one foreign-born parent and many were foreign-born themselves, but in all other ways they differed remarkably little from the native group. The ranks of leading manufacturers were indeed open to newcomers, but only if they were of English, Scottish, or English-Canadian origin. Twenty-six of the manufacturers were part of what we could call an Anglo-Saxon mix, including 10 men born in England, 7 born in the United States of English parents, and 5 with a variety of mixed parentage, either American, English, or Canadian. We can probably add to this list 8 born in the United States and 3 born in Canada of unknown parentage, but who were Protestants, Republicans, and likely of Anglo-Saxon origin; I did not include them in this Anglo-Saxon group since the data on their national origin is incomplete. Given the typical picture of humble immigrant life, we could expect to find more success stories in this group of immigrant and first-generation American industrial leaders than among the native white Americans, but this was not the case. As many as 6 out of 26 of these predominantly foreign-born manufacturers inherited their firms, while only 2 rose through the ranks. Only 6 out of the 22 industrialists for whom we could identify the father's social status came from poor backgrounds.

Without reviewing the careers of all manufacturers, I can provide a few examples to illustrate who these men were and where they came from. Some born in Great Britain had moved to the United States with their parents when they were still young, and little difference existed between them and the native-born Americans of British parents. Several inherited their firms: John Gray, born in Edinburgh, inherited the candy manufacturing company of Gray, Toynton, and Fox, which his father had created in Detroit; he employed 250 workers in 1900. A millionaire through his wide business investments, Gray also backed Henry Ford and became the first president of the Ford Motor Company. John Harvey, born in Glasgow, also emigrated from Scotland as a child. He inherited a foundry, Andrew Harvey and Sons, from his father (the foundry employed 200 workers in 1900), and also developed a prosperous drug business. Presbyterian in religion, Harvey was known among the charitable circles for being the superintendent of the Mission Sunday School of the Detroit Industrial School for Destitute Children. Other inheritors include Harry Hodge, born in the United States, who inherited the presidency of his father's large foundry. The Scotten brothers, William and Oren, one president of the Scotten, Dillon, and Company tobacco firm (employing 125 workers), the other president of Daniel Scotten Company (employing 976 workers), both inherited their positions from their uncle, Daniel Scotten, born in 1819 in England of a Scottish family, who had built the largest tobacco firm in Detroit.

Others created their own firms but were born into business families. Annis Newton was the son of a tobacco wholesale dealer, who was also involved in the fur trade; Annis created his own fur company, building on his father's experience as well as working for Frederick Buhl. Joseph Berry, whose father had built a tannery, developed extensive business holdings around the Detroit-based varnish factory which he founded.

A vivid illustration of how little difference there was between native white Americans and immigrants of British origins is that the most influential businessman in late nineteenth-century Detroit, James McMillan, was born in Ontario of Scottish parents. James was born in the sleepy little town of Hamilton in 1838, son of a businessman who had invested in the Great Western Railway. At age eighteen James moved to Detroit, where he built a manufacturing and political empire. By 1900, when McMillan was sixty-two years old, he represented Michigan in the United States Senate; he had for ten years (from 1886 to 1896) headed the State Republican Central Committee; and he was the leading force of the powerful Republican Michigan Club, which had initially backed Pingree. Although by 1900 most of his business holdings were handled by his elder sons, Hugh and William, James was chairman of American Car and Foundry, the product of a merger between his own Michigan Car Company (which he had founded in 1864) and several other car companies. He was also president of Seamless Steel Tube, of Fulton Iron and Engine Works, and a board member of no less than twenty-two other industrial establishments. McMillan's influence extended even beyond the business and political spheres, since he was founder, president, or board member of several exclusive social clubs. A Presbyterian Republican like his native-born counterparts, McMillan was not himself a native Detroiter; that his influence was so widespread despite his British-Canadian origins indicates clearly that foreign birth mattered little to Detroit's business elite. What mattered instead was an Anglo-Saxon background, the right religion, the right politics, and an initial means of wealth.

Among Anglo-Saxon immigrants and their children, the manufacturers from modest backgrounds were clearly the exception. One native American of British parentage, John B. Howarth, rose through the ranks at Pingree and Smith until he became a senior partner in a shoe firm directed by a group of self-made men. Among the English-Canadian immigrants, only Joseph Boyer was of modest origins; he contributed to the creation of the Burroughs Business Machine Corporation in Chicago before creating his own foundry and machine company in Detroit. A few British immigrants were also self-made men. David Buick, for example, had settled in Detroit as a child. After working on a farm as a teenager, Buick became an apprentice in the brass-finishing trade at age thirteen and a foreman only twelve years later. He began his own business in 1881 and started tinkering with a gasoline engine in 1895. By 1900, he was the president of Buick and Sherwood, an iron and plumbing firm employing 300 workers. Buick eventually sold his iron and steel plumbing business, developed a car, and became associated with Durant's General Motors in 1908; in 1909 he organized his own automobile firm which collapsed, and Buick died in near poverty. Not all British immigrants had the same misfortune, however. James Scripps, the son of an English bookbinder, became the powerful president of the Evening News Association. Perhaps the best success story among the immigrants was that of Alexander McVittie from Scotland, a mechanic when he first came to Detroit at age twenty-five. In 1900, at age fifty-eight, he was president of Detroit Shipbuilding (employing 500 workers), of Detroit Sheet Metal and Brass (employing 325 workers) and of Detroit Dry Docks (with 300 workers). Methodist in religion, prohibitionist in politics, he represented the class of Scottish immigrants who contributed most to the legend of the self-made man in large American industry.[8]

THE OTHER INDUSTRIALISTS

The backgrounds of these Anglo-Saxon immigrants and first-generation Americans was close enough to that of native white American industrialists to permit their entry into the elite class of Detroit, but what about those industrialists who came from other horizons? Fort Pontchartrain du Detroit was created by the French in 1703 and remained exclusively French through most of the eighteenth century, but few French families retained important positions after the British and then the Americans took over the city. By 1900 the manufacturing elite was so dominated by the Anglo-Saxon group that only one native Detroiter of French-Canadian ancestry, George Ducharme, was president of a large firm. George's father, Charles Ducharme, was born in Montreal, came to Detroit in 1838, and engaged in the hardware business with Christian Buhl. Ducharme was among the organizers of Michigan Stove and served as its president until his death in 1873. He had married an American woman from New York and had two sons, George, president of the U.S. Heater Company, and Charles Albert, secretary of Michigan Stove. The Ducharme brothers were forty and forty-two, respectively, in 1900, had inherited their positions in the ranks of the leading industrialists, and, unlike their French counterparts, were members of all the exclusive clubs of the city.

The Irish made up the largest immigrant community in 1850, but by 1900 they had not entered the ranks of the manufacturing elite. Jeremiah Dwyer, who at age sixty-three in 1900 was president of Michigan Stove (a post where he succeeded Ducharme, Palms, and Mills), has often been cited by historians—together with his brother James, also in the stove industry—as an example and symbol of Irish achievement in Detroit.[9] It is true that Jeremiah and James were born into an Irish Catholic family of Detroit; their father had settled first in Brooklyn but then moved to Springwells, just outside Detroit, where he was a farmer. Young Jeremiah possessed limited means at his father's death and learned the trade of molding at the Hydraulic Iron Works. He then worked as a journeyman in several eastern stove foundries before returning to Detroit and opening a stove foundry in about 1861. Two years later Tefft and Mills bought into the firm, which became the Detroit Stove Works, and Dwyer became the general manager. A few years later, Jeremiah sold his interest to his brother

8. On Andrew Carnegie, see Matthew Josephson, *The Robber Barons* (New York: Harcourt Brace Jovanovich, 1962; reprint of 1934 edition), pp. 41–44.

9. JoEllen Vinyard, *The Irish on the Urban Frontier* (New York: Arno Press, 1976), pp. 156–62.

when he traveled south for his health. Upon his return to Detroit in 1871, he founded the Michigan Stove Company with Mills, Ducharme, Barbour, Long, and Palms. The Dwyer brothers, then, did manage to break through the ethnic barrier and achieve the status of leading industrialists, but only through their unique technical expertise and their association with a group of Anglo-Saxon business leaders.

The other Irish among the leading industrialists were also atypical of the Irish community. Only one Irish immigrant, Thomas Murphy, built and owned a factory, the Murphy Iron Works, which employed 100 workers in 1900. Murphy was a Congregationalist, hence a member of the Protestant Irish minority who made up only about 20% of the predominantly Catholic Irish community. Only three other native-born Americans of Irish parents were among the leading industrialists. George Brown, born in Ohio, came to Detroit at age thirty-seven after living in Ontario; he employed 675 people in his tobacco business. Frank Howard, a second-generation Irish Catholic banker, held interests in the lumber business and the farm implement business and in 1900, at age sixty, was president of Pearl Button, a clothing factory employing 240 workers. Edwin Armstrong, the Presbyterian owner of a saddlery firm employing 150 people, married the daughter of the president of Dimes Savings Bank and also became very much a member of the Anglo-Saxon world. Only four native Americans of Irish parents, one Irish immigrant, and one native American of French-Canadian ancestry, then, were among the manufacturing leaders, but they were the exceptions to the French-Canadian or Irish communities of Detroit, the few who had integrated the world of the Anglo-Saxon elite.

Of the remaining manufacturers of Detroit, six were German immigrants, six native-born Americans of German parents, two native-born men of mixed German-American parentage, one Alsatian, two Belgians, one immigrant from the Netherlands, and one son of Swiss immigrants. Despite the fact that the Germans were the single largest foreign-born group living in Detroit in the 1890s, very few German immigrants or their children had attained a leading position among the industrialists of Detroit, and even fewer had integrated the social world of the industrial elite. We know little of the social origins of these few non–Anglo-Saxon industrial leaders, but only in this group of predominantly German manufacturers did I find some exceptions to the profile of the typical Detroit industrialist. While half of these newcomers had become assimilated into the Protestant Republican establishment of the city, the other half, representing the few large local east side manufacturers, had not.

Among those who joined the Protestant establishment were men like William Pungs, born a French citizen in Alsace in 1849, who came to Detroit at age three. At age fifty-four in 1900, Pungs was president of a carriage factory and an ardent prohibitionist who changed payday from Saturday to Monday to save workingmen from the saloon over the weekend. Among the Germans, Jacob Siegel came to the United States in 1876, founded American Lady Corset, a firm which he still owned in 1900 at age fifty-nine and which then employed 555 workers. Siegel had clearly parted from the German quarter since, like Pungs, he lived in an elegant mansion of the upper residential center. Frank Hubel, another German, came to Detroit at age sixteen, took chemistry courses at the University of Michigan before entering the capsule manufacturing business and selling his pharmaceutical products to Parke, Davis and Co. Three native-born Americans of German parents had also definitely entered the social milieu of the Anglo-Saxon manufacturing elite, men like Edward Schmidt, who had inherited his father's large tannery in 1897, or like Christian Haberkorn, owner of a large furniture factory and member of the First Congregational Church, as well as of all the exclusive clubs of Detroit. The most striking example of the integration of a handful of first- or second-generation Germans into the manufacturing elite was Frank Hecker, the president of American Car and Foundry (its chairman was James McMillan). Hecker was born in Washtenaw County of German parents; a veteran of both the Civil War and the Spanish-American War, he started his career on the railroad in the 1870s as a division superintendent, then created the Michigan Peninsular Company, which ultimately merged with American Car and Foundry. Involved in other businesses as director of the People's State Bank, Hecker was also a board member of Union Trust, of Detroit Copper and Brass Rolling Mills, and of Detroit Lumber Company. He built a lavish mansion in the French Renaissance style on Woodward Avenue and, of course, belonged to all the exclusive local clubs— the Detroit Club, the Old Club, the Yondotega Country Club, the Detroit Boat Club, and others.

In contrast to these few German manufacturers who had entered the social world of the Anglo-Saxon business elite, a few other manufacturers (with 100 employees or more) operated primarily in the east-side neighborhoods and stayed within their ethnic community—men like S. Marx, a German immigrant who was the owner of a large spectacle factory employing 119 workers (Michigan Optical) and had come to Detroit at age twenty-three. In 1900, he still lived on Gratiot Avenue, in the heart of the German quarter; he was the largest stockholder of the *Arbeiter Zeitung* (a labor paper), the founder of the Harmonie Society, and he organized the first German band in Detroit. Others, like Charles Goldsmith, who owned a large clothing factory, also lived on Gratiot in the heart of the east side. Bernard Stroh, a native Detroiter of German parents, inherited his father's brewery; although he eventually established his residence in the upper section of Woodward Avenue near the city limits, he remained active in many east-side German organizations and became one of the few businessmen who maintained affiliations with both the German community and his business peers in a city where almost all had to choose one or the other. A few other immigrant manufacturers were similarly successful, but remained local and operated socially within the confines of their original community. Emmanuel Schloss, for example, a clothier employing 200 workers, was the only large manufacturer I could identify as a Jew, and his wife was active in several east-side Jewish charities. The Posselius brothers, Alphonse and John Cornelius, inherited their furniture firm from their father (who had come from Belgium and settled in Detroit in the late 1850s) and also counted among the large east-side employers; all their lives, they lived in the east side near their furniture firm on Gratiot, as did Leonard Laurense, who came from Holland· and established a molding company at the foot of Leib Street.

Detroit in 1900 was, then, economically dominated by an elite of industrialists which, beyond its apparent openness to newcomers, was culturally and socially homogeneous. Only a handful of non–Anglo-Saxon immigrants or their children were large employers, and even fewer had penetrated the social network of the other manufacturers. Most of the large German employers who produced mostly consumer products such as beer, clothing, or furniture operated within the confines of the east side only, not in the city at large. Although the ranks of the leading industrialists seemed open, allowing a large number of immigrants or first-generation Americans to enter them, these newcomers were of Anglo-Saxon Protestant backgrounds and did not pose a threat to the social order and ideology of the establishment. It was not native birth as opposed to foreign birth that enabled an individual to become a leader in Detroit, but rather the combination of the right cultural background and an initial means of wealth. Those English Canadians and British immigrants and their children who met these conditions made up almost half of the leading manufacturers at the turn of the century. Anglo-Saxon immigrants were already sharing the old west-side neighborhoods and the new subdivisions with the native white Americans. By cutting across the city's internal boundaries to create a large industrial labor force, this homogeneous group of industrialists came to regulate the work lives of many Detroiters, inevitably pressuring the various ethnic communities into a more uniform economic and social system. Late nineteenth-century industrialization had not yet reordered the hierarchy of residence and work for the majority of Detroiters, but the cohesiveness of the leading industrialists and the growing number of their large factories signaled the possible reversal of Detroit's ethnically based sociospatial arrangement.

9

Ethnic Fragmentation of the Working Class

Plate 9. Packard Automobile Company before the moving assembly line; car frames were assembled on sawhorses, c. 1910.
Courtesy of the Archives of Labor and Urban Affairs, Wayne State University.

I n late nineteenth-century Detroit, some ethnic groups were spread across the entire social spectrum, with their members distributed among all socio-economic categories, while other groups were little represented in certain sections of the social structure, either being cut off from the top level of society completely, or entering the ranks of even the middle class only marginally. In this context, the growth of an industrial labor force—largely made up of recent immigrants—could unite previously distinct ethnic groups into one working class. But despite widespread inequality, the working class remained fragmented during the industrialization of the 1890s, developing little working-class solidarity and posing little threat to the established social order.

Historians have observed a similar apparent acceptance of social imbalance in other cities and explained it by the combined effects of closed ethnic subcultures and upward mobility outside their boundaries. They have generally viewed the American working class as too fragmented by ethnic loyalties to join forces in challenging the economic and social establishment.[1] And they have argued that a revolutionary labor movement was effectively prevented by manifold opportunities for advancement in American society. Historians have portrayed most immigrants to nineteenth-century cities as experiencing enough upward mobility to fulfill their expectations and to enter the mainstream of American life if they were willing to work hard and move from one city to another in search of better opportunities. Barriers on the road from poverty to progress were not easily surmounted but never unscalable; if they seemed to be closed in one city, people could always leave to seek success in another. There were no deadends, only detours, and this freedom of movement avoided rebellion while providing manpower throughout the country.[2] But the social historian's dichotomy, which envisions the upwardly mobile immigrants leaving (thus weakening) the ethnic community and being assimilated into the native white American world and their unsuccessful fellows physically departing from the city and hence abandoning their base for class action, fails to account for the complexity of local situations. This dichotomy, while supported by solid

1. See, for example, John R. Commons, et al., *History of Labor in the United States*, 2 vols. (New York: Macmillan, 1918), 1:9–10, 488. Herbert Gutman has insisted on the persistence of the "first generation" experience over more than a century of American life; see his *Work, Culture, and Society in Industrializing America* (New York: Alfred A. Knopf, 1976), pp. 43–46; David Montgomery makes the point that the phrase "workers' control" entered the vocabulary of the American labor movement only around the end of World War I, with "new styles of struggle in a unique industrial and political environment"; see his *Worker's Control in America: Studies in the History of Work, Technology, and Labor Struggles* (Cambridge: Cambridge University Press, 1979), p. 27.

2. This view is best expressed in Stephan Thernstrom, *The Other Bostonians: Poverty and Progress in the American Metropolis, 1880–1970* (Cambridge, Mass.: Harvard University Press, 1973), pp. 256–261.

evidence concerning geographic mobility, remains mere speculation when used to explain the lives of the working-class immigrants who stayed within their original communities.

At least two other important social processes contributed to reinforcing ethnic bonds and preventing working-class solidarity in Detroit: first, opportunities for mobility within the group continued during the industrialization period, thus maintaining a dual opportunity structure that reinforced existing ethnic bonds; second, economic constraints forced most working-class families to develop strategies of pooling members' income to make ends meet, which also helped strengthen ethnic bonds and so weaken working-class solidarity.

TWO COMPETING SOCIAL SYSTEMS

The key to the social equilibrium that characterized Detroit at the turn of the century was not the loosening bonds of ethnic affiliation but rather the strength of the ethnic communities. We have seen that neighborhoods were organized around patterns of ethnic dominance, but included a mixture of immigrants of all statuses. That a significant segment of the immigrant population or their children were employed in white-collar occupations attests to the real mobility of many immigrants, but access to low white-collar jobs was by no means a sure sign of entry into the Anglo-Saxon world. Immigrants did experience some mobility, but as professionals, manufacturers, dealers, or white-collar office workers, many could operate within their own ethnic community, which provided them with ample patrons. (See, for example, biographies of Polish shopkeepers and professionals in chap. 7.) Actually, two competing social systems existed, one in which immigrants or children of immigrants succeeded within the ethnic community, experiencing upward mobility and access to white-collar work, and one in which a more complex intergroup relationship was involved. The possibilities were manifold: a German white-collar worker could work in a German-owned firm, and his life—including the language he most often spoke, the press he read, the food he ate, and the builder of his home—would revolve around the German community; but another German white-collar worker could work instead in a downtown bank, part of the Anglo-Saxon world, and experience a greater demarcation between home and work.

Anglo-Saxon groups had the largest share of the more prestigious professional and white-collar jobs in the city in 1900: 55% of the native white American heads of households were white-collar workers (10% high white-collar workers and 45% low white-collar workers), and the Americans made up 60% of the high white-collar workers in the city (see table 9.1). No other group, even among the Anglo-Saxons, included such a high percentage of white-collar workers,

TABLE 9.1
Ethnicity versus occupational status, Detroit, 1900[a]

Ethnic group	Occupational group			
	High white-collar	Low white-collar	Skilled	Semiskilled or unskilled
Native white American[b]	94	407	266	130
Ethnic group (%)	10.5	45.4	29.7	14.5
Occupational group (%)	60.3	42.6	20.0	11.1
Black	-	7	21	73
Ethnic group (%)	-	6.9	20.8	72.3
Occupational group (%)	-	.1	1.6	6.2
Canadian (English)[c]	10	63	68	51
Ethnic group (%)	5.2	32.8	35.4	26.6
Occupational group (%)	6.4	6.6	5.1	4.4
Canadian (French)	1	14	39	17
Ethnic group (%)	1.4	19.7	54.9	23.9
Occupational group (%)	.6	1.5	2.9	1.5
British	8	81	128	61
Ethnic group (%)	2.9	29.1	46.0	21.9
Occupational group (%)	5.1	8.5	9.6	5.2
British American	9	41	41	9
Ethnic group (%)	9.0	41.0	41.0	9.0
Occupational group (%)	5.8	4.3	3.1	.8
Irish	4	28	37	87
Ethnic group (%)	2.6	17.9	23.7	55.8
Occupational group (%)	2.6	2.9	2.8	7.4
Irish American	4	45	65	42
Ethnic group (%)	2.6	28.8	41.7	26.9
Occupational group (%)	2.6	4.7	4.9	3.6
German	11	141	389	368
Ethnic group (%)	1.2	15.5	42.8	40.5
Occupational group (%)	7.1	14.8	29.2	31.5
German American	12	91	145	97
Ethnic group (%)	3.5	26.4	42.0	28.1
Occupational group (%)	7.7	9.5	10.9	8.3
Polish	-	19	109	207
Ethnic group (%)	-	5.7	32.5	61.8
Occupational group (%)	-	2.0	8.2	17.7
Russian	3	18	23	28
Ethnic group (%)	4.2	25.0	31.9	38.9
Occupational group (%)	1.9	1.9	1.7	2.4

SOURCE: 1900 sample.
 a. Heads of households.
 b. Born in the U.S. of two U.S.-born parents.
 c. Born in English-speaking Canada of two Canadian parents; born in French-speaking Canada of two Canadian parents; born in Great Britain of two British parents, etc.

although British immigrants had 32%, English Canadians 38%, and native Americans of British parents 50%.

Among the other groups, the percentage of white-collar workers was always significant, ranging from 6% to 30%. German immigrants had 17% of their households heads in the white-collar category (including 1.2% of high white-collar workers), and the Irish had 20%. The children born in the United States of Irish or German parents who were heads of households in 1900 fared a little better, with generally 30% in the white-collar group. Other small groups such as the French Canadians and the Russian Jews had 21% and 30% of their heads of households in the white-collar category. Only the Poles and the Blacks had a small but not negligible percentage of 6%.

Most Anglo-Saxon white-collar workers, and to some extent the children of immigrants who faced no language barrier, entered office work and teaching professions: 68.7% of the low white-collar Americans were in business-related occupations specializing in bookkeeping, stenography, clerical, or sales work; another 11.5% were in education; and only 16.7% in sectors such as store owner, manager, or even building contractor. In contrast, the majority of immigrants from other horizons who worked at white-collar occupations were generally shopkeepers or small entrepreneurs who worked within their own community, together with the professional and intellectual elite—the few doctors, priests or pastors or rabbis, and journalists—who also worked in the community. The distribution of German immigrants in white-collar jobs was opposite that of their American counterparts, with less than 5% teachers, only 42.8% in office work, while 46.9% were grocers, store owners, saloonkeepers and various retail commercial operators (see table 9.2). The balance was somewhat reestablished in favor of office work among the children of German immigrants, with 65.2% of the white-collar workers in that sector—many of them also employed in their own ethnic community—27.5% engaged in retail or commercial ventures, and only 3.1% in education.

In the skilled worker category, native white Americans counted only 30% of their heads of households, while English Canadians counted 35% and British immigrants 46%. These three groups had an even lower percentage of unskilled workers, 14% among the native white Americans, 22% for the British immigrants, and 27% for the English Canadians. In contrast, the Irish had 56% of their families headed by an unskilled worker; the Germans were more evenly distributed than the Irish among skilled and unskilled workers with 43% and 40%, respectively. But even though non–Anglo-Saxon groups were more generally employed in skilled or unskilled occupations than were their English-speaking counterparts, they did not necessarily work in the factories owned or run by the Anglo-Saxon establishment either. Heads of households born in the

TABLE 9.2
White-collar workers for selected ethnic groups, Detroit, 1900[a]

Occupational group	Native white American[b] (%)	Canadian[c] (English) (%)	British (%)	Irish American (%)	German (%)	German American (%)
Manufacturer	1.2	.6	3.4	.8	2.8	2.2
Owner or proprietor	.7	1.1	1.7	-	3.1	.7
Manager	1.4	.6	1.7	1.5	3.5	1.2
Keeper	4.0	4.0	5.9	3.8	12.0	6.9
Wholesaler	.2	-	-	1.5	1.4	-
Dealer	4.2	5.1	9.2	4.6	8.9	7.7
Builder	2.0	1.7	10.1	3.8	6.9	1.9
Technician	3.0	5.1	4.2	4.6	8.3	6.9
Educator	11.5	6.3	3.4	9.9	4.8	3.1
Artist	3.3	2.3	4.2	1.5	5.5	3.8
Superintendent	1.2	-	-	2.3	.7	1.8
Bookkeeper	12.6	14.3	8.4	8.4	2.8	6.5
Agent	6.1	5.7	8.4	4.6	6.2	3.3
Salesman	13.6	14.3	6.7	12.2	11.7	13.4
Clerk	31.9	38.9	27.7	33.6	20.7	39.0
Government worker	2.6	-	3.4	3.8	.7	1.2
Inspector	.7	-	1.7	3.1	-	-
All office work and related	68.7	73.2	56.3	68.0	42.8	65.2
Number in sample	891	175	119	131	145	261

SOURCE: 1900 sample.

a. Total work force.

b. Born in the U.S. of two U.S.-born parents.

c. Born in English-speaking Canada of two Canadian parents; born in Great Britain of two British parents, etc.

United States of Irish or German parents were more often employed at skilled occupations (about 42%) than at unskilled occupations (27%). Other numerically important groups of heads of households—the French Canadians, the Poles, the Russian Jews, and the Blacks—all counted mostly skilled and unskilled workers, but with interesting variations. The French Canadians were mostly skilled workers (55%); the Russian Jews were almost evenly divided between skilled and unskilled (32% and 40%). Only the Poles and the Blacks were heavily grouped in unskilled jobs (62% and 71%), although many were skilled workers (32% and 24%). Unskilled Russian Jews were almost evenly divided between factory work and peddling or street vending; Poles instead were almost all factory workers, while the Blacks were employed in the same variety of service occupations, such as barbers, waiters, or hotel porters, that they held in most cities.

Among the skilled and unskilled workers, the Germans were the most likely to be employed within their own community. They occupied every variety of skilled position, many working for large industrial concerns but as many being independent craftsmen, often employing a few men of their own. The Bureau of Labor's factory inspection reports are filled with these small east-side shops run by Germans—the small hat factory with five workers, or the local newspaper with a work force of four, or the small bookbindery, or the jewelry or fabric store, or the small cigar factory.[3] Some German entrepreneurs would hire only German employees, but some would also hire Polish workers or Russian-Jewish cigar makers, thus economically dominating other ethnic groups.

THE FAILURE OF THE LABOR MOVEMENT

In this fragmented world, no one institution could effectively cut across ethnic boundaries and unify the different segments of society. The failure of the labor movement in Detroit is a case in point. Inequality was rampant, but the labor movement was unable to transcend the differences among workers and create a durable working-class subculture. Throughout the late nineteenth century and until the 1930s, Detroit was the least unionized major city in the country. There had been a sudden upsurge of unionization in the mid-1880s, as workers' frustrations crystallized for a moment around the Knights of Labor and the eight-hour day movement (headed in Detroit by Joseph Labadie), but after the tragedy of Haymarket, the movement disintegrated as quickly as it had risen, following the rapid nationwide decline of the Knights of Labor. Labor historian Richard Oestreicher estimated the number of unionized workers in Detroit to be 4,000 in 1882; it rose to an all-time high of 13,000 or about 20% of the labor force in 1886, but dropped to 7,000 or 8,000 in 1887 and remained at that level for the rest of the century. The sheer decline in union membership was remarkable throughout the 1890s. In 1892 only 8.2% of the labor force was unionized, in 1901 only 6.2%.[4]

The success of the Knights in the mid-eighties resulted from their ability to transcend the fragmentation of the working class and to create a unique—albeit short-lived—"subculture of opposition."[5] The Michigan Bureau of Labor's report on a bricklayers' strike in Springwells (just outside Detroit) in 1886 describes just how this subculture operated:

3. See, for example, Michigan, "State Factory Inspection," appendix to *Eighteenth Annual Report of the Bureau of Labor and Industrial Statistics* (Lansing, 1901), pp. 6–37.

4. Richard J. Oestreicher, "Solidarity and Fragmentation: Working People and Class Consciousness in Detroit, 1877–1895" (Ph.D. diss., Michigan State University, 1979), pp. 522, 524; idem, "Changing Patterns of Class Relations in Detroit, 1880–1900," *Detroit in Perspective: A Journal of Regional History* 3 (Spring 1979): 145–65.

5. Oestreicher, "Solidarity and Fragmentation," pp. 233–37.

In close proximity to the brickyards were noticed a large number of saloons, said to be fifty to sixty; among them, one prominent resort, having a public hall in the second story. At this hall large gatherings were frequent on Sunday, and at these Sunday meetings beer was said to flow freely, and many exciting speeches were listened to. For a few weeks prior to the strike these meetings were addressed by men from Detroit, and their theme was that the brickworkers were receiving too low wages, that by unitedly stopping work the men would force the employers to pay, at least, $2.00 per day. Taking the statement of the strikers as our authority, this advice was generally fringed with talk of a socialistic nature, if not strongly communistic.[6]

The Knights of Labor was the only labor organization to have attracted successfully the unskilled workers into the ranks of the labor movement; speakers at labor rallies made a point of addressing the workers not only in English but also in German and Polish in an effort to reach all workers. But the American Federation of Labor, which focused on organizing specific groups of skilled workers, failed to keep up the precarious unity achieved by the Knights. In Detroit in the 1890s three independent trades councils were attached to the Michigan Federation of Labor (created in 1889): the Council of Trade and Labor Unions representing 69 unions, the Central Labor Union (exclusively German) representing 9 unions, and the Building Trades Council representing 8 unions.[7] While the Knights had emphasized ethnic and racial solidarity, the unions of the 1890s were divided along ethnic and racial lines. There were two separate locals of the Journeymen Bakers' International Union, one German, with 78 members in 1896, and the other English, with 27 members; among the printers' unions were also some exclusively German groups, like Typographia No. 21 with 36 members in 1896. While the Knights of Labor Longshoremen's Association had a large Black membership in the 1880s, in the 1890s there were separate white (with 150 members) and Black (with 100 members) locals under the Council of Trade and Labor Unions.[8]

 The degree of unionization varied greatly from one industry to another, and within each industry from one occupation to another. Some industries were well unionized. The Amalgamated Association of Street Car Employees, for example, had a membership of 895 in Detroit alone in 1896; the preceding year the Bureau of Labor, inspecting 600 workers of the Citizen's Street Railway

6. Michigan, *Third Annual Report of the Bureau of Labor and Industrial Statistics* (Lansing, 1886), p. 89.

7. Michigan, *Thirteenth Annual Report of the Bureau of Labor and Industrial Statistics* (Lansing, 1896), pp. 238, 241.

8. Ibid., pp. 247–57.

Company, the Detroit Railway Company, and the Fort Wayne and Belle Isle Railway Company, reported a high rate of unionization among street-railway workers, with wages uniformly high, and with virtually no child labor in the industry. Many of the building trades, which were grouped under their own trade council, were also well unionized, with 28% belonging to one union in 1893, although this percentage varied greatly from one building occupation to another. In some occupations most were union members, including 85% of the bricklayers, 73% of the stair builders, 69% of the hod carriers, and 52% of the stonemasons. But among carpenters, who made up 32% of the building trade labor force, only 7% were union members, and only 5% of the paperhangers, and none of the grainers, marble cutters, brick strippers, or mantel settlers belonged to a trade union.[9]

But street-railway workers and these few well-unionized building trades were the exceptions in Detroit. Only 22 of the 1,066 railroad-car shop workers interviewed by the Bureau of Labor in 1893 belonged to a labor organization, and only 6 of 398 workers of the vehicle industry interviewed in 1897 were union members.[10] In 1893 the bureau interviewed railroad workers in Michigan and published the individual level data including the question on union membership. This is the sole Bureau of Labor report from which we can abstract some characteristics typical of union members. Overall, 13% of railroad workers based in Detroit were unionized, and most of them worked for the Michigan Central Railroad. Most of these union members clustered in a few highly skilled and well-paid occupations: 15 of the 27 engineers interviewed, 17 of the 38 firemen, 31 of the 54 switchmen, but only 8 of the 88 freight handlers. In contrast to the Street Railway Unions, which concentrated on securing strike funds, these railroad unions carried sick and death benefits. Over half of their membership was made up of native-born workers: although German immigrants made up 19% of railroad workers, only 6% of them were unionized.[11]

9. Ibid., pp. 1–65 (statistical analysis of street-railway workers), and p. 252; also *Tenth Annual Report of the Bureau of Labor and Industrial Statistics* (Lansing, 1893), p. 737.

10. *Tenth Annual Report*, p. 737; and statistical analysis of vehicle workers, from Michigan, *Fourteenth Annual Report of the Bureau of Labor and Industrial Statistics* (Lansing, 1897), pp. 6–169.

11. Statistical analysis of railroad workers, from Michigan, *Eleventh Annual Report of the Bureau of Labor and Industrial Statistics* (Lansing, 1894), pp. 1–385; other employers were the Wabash Railroad, and then the Detroit, Lansing and Northern Railroad, the Duluth, South Shore and Atlantic Railway, the Flint and Pere Marquette Railroad, the Grand Trunk Railroad, and the Lake Shore and Michigan Southern Railway. The unions most often mentioned were the Brotherhood of Locomotive Engineers, the Brotherhood of Locomotive Firemen, the Brotherhood of Locomotive Trainmen, the Freight Handler's Aid Association, the International Association of American Machinists, the Order of Railroad Telegraphers, the Order of Railway Conductors, and the Switchmen's Mutual Aid Association.

With union membership so low and exclusive, it is not surprising that there were few instances of labor unrest in Detroit in the 1890s, and even fewer conducted by unions. In the year 1892/93 the Bureau of Labor recorded only 8 instances of strikes in Detroit, then a large city; all were short-lived, and only half of them were conducted by the unions.[12]

THE FAMILY ECONOMY

Between the employer's vigorous opposition to the labor movement and the movement's effort to expand primarily into skilled occupations, most workers of the open-shop era could not count on labor organizations to provide security in their lives. They relied instead on the ethnic community, and within it on their immediate kin. Reliance on the immediate family rather than on working-class institutions made work and family very close to each other—a part of a more general communal experience which reinforced Detroit's fragmentation along ethnic lines. It was primarily through kinship and a familywide economy that most Detroit workers survived difficult winters, took care of the sick and the elderly, and generally carved their niche in Detroit's environment.[13]

Rarely could one income support a family in the late nineteenth century as the hierarchy of income clearly shows. Middle-class white-collar occupations often paid over $1,000 a year in the 1890s.[14] Key officials in Detroit's city government such as city comptroller, city treasurer, or member of the board of public works, for example, were paid $2,280 per year. The next echelon, with occupations such as tax assessor, city attorney, or city engineer, carried an annual salary of $1,900; in turn, jobs like bookkeeper or superintendent paid $1,003, and the average clerk working for the city made $916 (table 9.3). Lower echelons of white-collar workers were often paid somewhere between $1,000 and $500 but rarely less than that; railroad clerks, for instance, made about $500 a year.[15]

12. *Tenth Annual Report*, pp. 1211–13.

13. For comparable studies of Philadelphia, see Michael R. Haines, "Poverty, Economic Stress, and the Family in the Late Nineteenth-Century American City," and Claudia Goldin, "Family Strategies and the Family Economy in the Late Nineteenth Century: The Role of the Secondary Workers," in *Philadelphia: Work, Space, Family, and Group Experience in the Nineteenth Century*, ed. Theodore Hershberg (New York: Oxford University Press, 1981), pp. 240–76, 277–310; also on Philadelphia, Eudice Glassberg, "Work, Wages, and the Cost of Living, Ethnic Differences, and the Poverty Line, Philadelphia, 1880," *Pennsylvania History* 66 (January 1979): 17–58; on Manchester, New Hampshire, see Tamara K. Hareven, "The Dynamics of Kin in an Industrial Community," in *Turning Points: Historical and Sociological Essays on the Family*, ed. John Demos and Sarane Spence Boocock (Chicago: University of Chicago Press, 1978), pp. 151–82.

14. All money figures, taken from various surveys of the 1890s have been indexed to 1910–14 value for purposes of comparison. See George F. Warren and Frank A. Pearson, *Prices* (New York: John Wiley & Sons, 1933) pp. 24–26, 197.

15. Statistical analysis of railroad workers, from *Eleventh Annual Report*, pp. 1–385.

TABLE 9.3
Annual income of selected city employees, Detroit, 1893[a]

Occupation	Average pay	Highest pay	Lowest pay
City Comptroller	$2,280	-	-
City Treasurer	2,280	-	-
Member Board of Public Works	2,280	-	-
Assessor	1,900	-	-
City Attorney	1,900	-	-
City Engineer	1,900	-	-
Deputy or assistant	1,375	$2,280	$760
Superintendent	1,030	1,368	692
Bookkeeper	1,003	-	-
Clerk	916	2,660	527
Engineer	886	1,900	547
Inspector	707	1,216	593
Janitor	654	786	534
Alderman	456	-	-
Messenger	187	228	114

SOURCE: Michigan, *Tenth Annual Report of the Bureau of Labor and Industrial Statistics* (Lansing, 1893), p. 990.

a. Dollar values indexed to 1910–1914.

In contrast to the more comfortable wages paid to white-collar workers, very few adult industrial workers over twenty years of age made more than $500 a year, although income varied greatly by industry and occupation. In the furniture industry, most workers made about $370 a year as machine hands or finishers, while a cabinetmaker was paid a little better, $397 on the average. Workers in the vehicle-manufacturing industry, such as blacksmiths, trimmers, and woodworkers, were also paid around $370 a year. Street-railway workers were paid somewhat better, between $400 and $430 a year as conductors, drivers, linemen, or motormen. In the metal-related industries such as foundries, stove works, and machine shops, unskilled day laborers—the bulk of the labor force in most industries—made only $290 a year, while the better-paid skilled positions carried an annual pay of $457 for a molder and $596 for a pattern-maker. Among railroad workers, the pay varied from $301 for the freight handler, $338 for the laborer, $463 for the brakeman, $439 for the carpenter, $503 for the machinist, $521 for the fireman, $609 for the switchman, and $853 for the engineer.

For some skilled occupations, adult pay continued to increase with age; a cabinetmaker, for example, made $458 on the average after age forty, or $60 more than one between twenty-one and forty; a molder's pay went as high as $595, and an older patternmaker's pay as high as $616. But only a handful of occupations had a pay scale proportional to age within the adult group (see table 9.4).

Workers thus turned to their children to supplement the family income, but workers under twenty years of age were paid much less than their adult counterparts in the same occupation. In the furniture industry, a young cabinetmaker twenty or younger made $229 a year, a finisher or a machine hand only $148 a year; a laborer in the metal industries no more than $157 per year and a young molder or patternmaker about $270. Broadly speaking, it usually took two teenaged boys to earn the same income as one adult household head (table 9.4).

Many young women joined their brothers on the work force; in 1891 the Bureau of Labor interviewed no less than 6,000 young women working in Detroit, 95% of them single, 84% still living with their parents, and 63% aged twenty or younger. The industry with most women workers was the tobacco industry, where 25% of Detroit's working women were employed; the most frequent occupation within this industry was that of tobacco stripper, carrying a salary of $117 per year on the average. Women, however, were reported working in forty-one different industries with a great variety of income. In the tobacco industry, the lowest annual income was that of box packers for $101 a year, while a few highly paid hand workers reported an annual income of $648 a year. In boot and shoe factories, a press feeder made only $104 a year but a machine operator $277; in capsule factories, a capsule joiner earned only $166 but the forelady was paid $394. The income of women working in laundries varied from $73 for a roller to $215 for an ironer and $235 for a washer (table 9.5).

In addition to young adults, many younger children under fourteen worked in Detroit's factories. According to the law, no child under ten was allowed to work at all; no child under fourteen could work unless he had attended a qualified school for at least four months of the preceding twelve months; and no child under eighteen could work in a factory for a period exceeding an average of ten hours per day or sixty hours per week.[16] Actually the law was openly violated; the Bureau of Labor reported children from seven to fourteen in 69 different types of factories at an average daily pay of $.29 to boys and $.24 to girls for an average ten hour workday. Children probably did not work every day, but some were reported to make as much as $.72 a week in tobacco factories (table 9.6).

There were usually no significant differences in pay among the various ethnic groups of workers within the same age groups and for a comparable length of

16. Michigan, *Second Annual Report of the Bureau of Labor and Industrial Statistics* (Lansing, 1885), p. 91.

TABLE 9.4

Annual income of selected workers, by occupation, age, and ethnicity, Detroit, 1891–1897[a]

Occupation by industry	Below 21 years of age						Native white American
	All workers	Native white American[b]	Canadian[c]	German	Polish	All workers	
Furniture							
Machine hand	$169	-	-	$170	-	$381	$422
Finisher	148	-	-	164	-	367	-
Cabinetmaker	229	-	-	-	-	398	-
Vehicle							
Painter	226	-	-	-	-	319	321
Blacksmith	97	-	-	-	-	366	396
Woodworker	177	-	-	-	-	376	378
Street railways							
Conductor	371	-	-	-	-	428	427
Motorman	-	-	-	-	-	434	418
Driver	-	-	-	-	-	398	409
Metal							
Laborer	157	$170	$170	159	$160	288	283
Machinist	249	277	-	-	-	531	547
Molder	270	-	-	258	-	458	498
Railroad							
Clerk	297	284	-	-	-	500	489
Freight handler	287	-	-	-	-	302	311
Carpenter	-	-	-	-	-	440	-
Switchman	-	-	-	-	-	610	618

SOURCES: Michigan, *Seventh Annual Report of the Bureau of Labor and Industrial Statistics* (Lansing, 1890), pp. 150–181; *Eighth Annual Report of the Bureau of Labor and Industrial Statistics* (lansing, 1894), pp. 1–385; *Eleventh Annual Report of the Bureau of Labor and Industrial Statistics* (Lansing, 1894), pp. 1–385; *Thirteenth Annual Report of Bureau of Labor and Industrial Statistics* (Lansing, 1896), pp. 1–65; *Fourteenth Annual Report of the Bureau of Labor and Industrial Statistics* (Lansing, 1897), pp. 6–169.

time worked, but a few exceptions illustrate both the weak position of the Poles, who had joined the industrial labor force only recently, and the discriminatory employment practices of some employers.[17] The comprehensive Bureau of Labor Statistics survey of metal trades in 1890 covered 3,899 workers in 69 factories and 145 occupations. This year 1890 was a good one in Detroit; the factories worked at full capacity and workers were fully employed. The average length of employment for the 3,899 workers interviewed was 45.3 weeks for the year, with very little variation from one skill to another or from one ethnic group to another. Most of the workers interviewed were German immigrants or children

17. On the relative parity of wages, see Robert Higgs, "Race, Skills, and Earnings: American Immigrants in 1909," *Journal of Economic History* 31 (June 1971): 420–28; Peter J. Hill, "Relative Skill and Income Levels of Native and Foreign Born Workers in the United States," *Explorations in Economic History* 12 (January 1975): 47–60.

21 to 40 years of age					Above 40 years of age				
Canadian	British	Irish	German	Polish	All workers	Native white American	British	Irish	German
-	-	-	$387	-	$384	-	-	-	-
-	-	-	380	-	370	-	-	-	-
-	-	-	370	-	458	-	-	-	$453
-	-	-	-	-	300	-	-	-	-
-	-	-	-	-	436	-	-	-	-
-	-	-	-	-	336	-	-	-	-
$441	$422	$443	417	-	441	$438	-	-	-
473	-	422	448	-	457	-	-	-	-
-	-	-	-	-	409	-	-	-	-
262	-	308	291	$278	296	-	-	$308	290
530	522	-	553	-	554	558	$561	-	-
504	547	501	-	-	595	-	594	632	-
492	-	-	-	-	491	-	-	-	-
315	-	287	-	-	319	-	-	-	-
-	-	-	421	-	450	-	-	-	448
581	-	-	-	-	585	-	-	-	-

a. All cells include more than 10 cases; dollar values indexed to 1910–1914.
b. Born in the U.S. of two U.S.-born parents.
c. Born in Canada of two Canadian parents; born in Great Britain of two British parents, etc.

of German immigrants (46%), while Americans, Canadians, British, and Irish ranged from 9% to 14% of this labor force. The Poles, however, made up only 5% of this large pool of industrial workers, and in all shops were concentrated in unskilled positions. Only at Michigan Stove, where 645 workers were interviewed, were the Polish workers evenly distributed between day laborers and molders, but while the average pay for the molder was $457 a year, the Poles made only $344; they were admittedly better paid than unskilled workers, but still paid less than the rate for German or American molders.[18] Such pay practices obviously reinforced the already deep divisions that existed in an ethnically segmented working class.

18. Michigan, *Eighth Annual Report of the Bureau of Labor and Industrial Statistics* (Lansing, 1891), pp. 2–151.

TABLE 9.5

Women's annual income in selected occupations, by industry, Detroit, 1892[a]

Industry	Most frequent occupation		Highest-paid occupation		Lowest-paid occupation	
Tobacco	Stripper	$117	Hand worker	$648	Box Packer	$101
Clothing	Parts maker	198	Cap cutter	410	Thread trimmer	75
Chemical	Laboratory worker	228	Stenographer	494	Table worker	125
Boot and shoe	Shoe fitter	250	Operator	227	Press feeder	104
Laundry	Ironer	215	Washer	235	Roller	73
Capsule	Capsule maker	207	Forelady	394	Capsule joiner	166

SOURCE: Michigan, *Ninth Annual Report of the Bureau of Labor and Industrial Statistics* (Lansing, 1892), pp. 139–181.

a. Dollar values indexed to 1910–1914.

That a working-class family needed several wage earners is clear from the few contemporary budget studies that we have. A laborer interviewed by the Bureau of Labor in 1892 reported an average monthly income of $23.67 but an average monthly expense of $26.33 for his small family of only himself, a wife, and a four-month old baby. In November 1891 they spent $28.01: the largest sum, $9.02, went to pay the rent, then $6.51 for food, $3.61 for furniture, $3.32 for taxes and insurance, $2.94 for utilities, $1.09 for sundries, $.66 for tobacco, $.29 for medicine, $.21 for clothing, $.16 for dry goods, $.10 for postage, $.08 for transportation, and $.02 for literature. Of the $6.50 spent on food, $1.29 was spent on meat, $.84 on bread, $.71 on sugar, $.70 on fruits and vegetables, $.64 on butter, $.55 on milk, $.47 on poultry, $.44 on fish, $.39 on eggs, $.29 on coffee, and $.21 on tea. This native white American laborer was spending more than he earned, a salary which did not permit him to support even a small family. He was not, however, without any capital, as his house contained some objects of value which he could possibly sell in case of necessity. His household effect of highest value was the stove, worth $56, followed by sundry furnishings worth $49, then $48 worth of watches, $42 of chairs, $39 of jewelry and ornaments, $38 of carpets, $23 of bedding, $23 of pictures, $9 of curtains, $8 of rings, and $2 of brooches.

A carpenter slightly better off, with a monthly income of $32.75, reported expenses of $30.42 in a month without any extraordinary purchases. He, too, had only a wife and a little girl to support. He spent less on rent ($7.60) and less on utilities (49 cents) than the laborer, but more on food ($9.56) and more on transportation ($8.44). By and large his household was quite precarious; while the value of household effects reached $337 for the laborer just mentioned, that of the carpenter did not even reach $200. The carpenter apparently lived on his budget, but the only luxury of his household was $11 worth of musical instruments, $4 worth of rings, and one brooch valued at one dollar.

TABLE 9.6
Children's weekly income in selected industries, Detroit, 1886[a]

Industry	Average pay	Highest pay	Lowest pay
Tobacco	$ .72	$1.64	$ .21
Chair factor	.27	1.64	.24
Lithographing	2.46	-	-
Dry goods, retail	.26	.34	.21
Stove works	.41	-	-
Knitting	.73	1.23	.14

SOURCE: Michigan, *Fourth Annual Report of the Bureau of Labor and Industrial Statistics* (Lansing, 1887), p. 253.
   a. Children 10–15 years old; dollar values indexed to 1910–1914.

In contrast to these hand-to-mouth budgets, the expense record of a professional accountant gives a glimpse of what was the still modest but decent life of a lower white-collar worker employed in a bank and reporting an income of $608 a year in salary and $190 from other sources. He was married without children but supported his mother. His monthly budget varied from $43 to $72, double or triple the monthly budget of the laborer or the carpenter. In January 1892, a month in which he spent only $43, he spent $13.22 on food, $9.88 on rent, $7.11 on taxes and insurance, $4.99 in utilities, $2.45 in dry goods, $2.10 in sundries, $1.71 in transportation, $.53 in literature, $.42 in liquor and tobacco, $.30 in furniture, $.27 in medical expenses, and $.19 in clothing. Overall, his household goods were valued at $931, including $266 worth of musical instruments, $46 worth of rings, and $11 worth of brooches.[19]

Most large working-class families, then, had to pool incomes from a variety of sources to make ends meet, but the particular combination of wage earners in the family varied from one ethnic group to another. In all groups the male heads of households usually worked and the married women did not: 87% of the heads of households reported one occupation at the 1900 census and little variation existed by status, ethnicity, or color. Only 2.3% of the married women worked, the lowest percentage being among the Poles (.6%) and the highest percentage among the Blacks (still with only 5.4%). It seems that wives generally worked only when the added income of a child's wages was not available.[20]

The burden of supplementing the father's income, then, rested on the children, and the ways in which children contributed to the family support exemplify the wide variations among ethnic groups. The reliance on children's income was, of course, inversely proportional to the socioeconomic status of the head of the

19. *Tenth Annual Report*, pp. 1043–47; all prices again indexed to 1910–14.
20. Leslie Woodcock Tentler, *Wage Earning Women: Industrial Work and Family Life in the United States, 1900–1930* (New York: Oxford University Press, 1979), pp. 137–38.

household, but at every level of the occupational structure, children of German and Polish families worked proportionately more often than their counterparts in native white American families, the differences being even more pronounced for daughters than for sons. Thirty-five percent of the sons aged twelve to twenty and 10% of the daughters of native white American families worked if their father was a lower white-collar worker; in the same socioeconomic category the percentages were 42% for boys and 28% for girls in German-headed families, and 37% and 25% among the Poles. Among families of native white American unskilled workers, fully 43% of the boys worked but only 16% of the girls; the percentages of children employed among families of German unskilled workers were as high as 66% of the boys and 43% of the girls; among the Poles, 68% and 56%, respectively (see table 9.7 for statistics by ethnic groups).

Conversely, while 55% of the American children aged twelve to twenty were sent to school, only 29% and 26% of children of the same age born into German and Polish families were reported at school. While most other groups stayed within these two extremes, showing only small differences between rates of attendance for boys and girls, the Russian Jews made a clear exception by deliberately sending their sons to school and their daughters to work. Only 30% of the boys between twelve and twenty living with their parents worked, while 53%, a figure comparable to that of the Americans, went to school; in contrast, a full 60% of the daughters born into Russian-Jewish families were busy working, not only to help bring home food and necessities but also to pay for their brothers' education (table 9.7).

TABLE 9.7
Children's status in selected ethnic groups, Detroit, 1900[a]

Ethnicity		Sons 12–20			Daughters 12–20		
		School	Work	Home	School	Work	Home
Native white American[b]	(%)	54.7	40.4	4.9	56.1	16.9	27.0
Black	(%)	50.0	50.0	0.0	45.5	40.9	13.6
Canadian (English)[c]	(%)	54.7	39.6	5.7	40.7	27.8	31.5
Canadian (French)	(%)	46.2	48.7	5.1	28.2	43.6	28.2
British	(%)	45.0	49.2	5.8	53.4	27.1	19.5
Irish	(%)	43.2	48.6	8.1	43.2	39.8	17.0
German	(%)	30.5	59.5	10.0	29.2	45.1	25.8
Polish	(%)	26.4	63.5	10.1	26.1	56.2	17.6
Russian	(%)	53.3	30.0	16.7	17.4	60.9	21.7

SOURCE: 1900 sample.

a. Ethnicity for heads of households.

b. Born in the U.S. of two U.S.-born parents.

c. Born in English-speaking Canada of two Canadian parents; born in French-speaking Canada of two Canadian parents; born in Great Britain of two British parents, etc.

The working-class immigrant family, then, relied on children's income to a much greater extent than did families of native white workers. Whenever a family needed additional income, the solution was to put the children to work, even at the expense of their schooling. While this was also common practice among many native white American families, an alternative which was widespread among them, but not among immigrant families, was to take boarders and lodgers into the house in exchange for a monthly room and board fee. In 1900 there was one boarder for every four American households, but only one for every twelve German households. If only a modest amount of money was needed and if there was room in the house, boarders often provided financial relief for American lower white-collar or working-class families and spared the children from working. Most immigrant families, however, did not have the space to house a boarder and needed more additional income than one boarder alone could provide.

To see how family members combined incomes to make a decent living, we can attach income figures (not originally provided in the census) to the occupational titles of the 1900 sample; these income figures are derived from the many labor surveys I have used so far and vary with age and ethnicity.

The 1900 sample counted 491 families headed by a day laborer from one of the main ethnic groups; 18 were native white Americans, 17 English Canadians, 9 French Canadians, 11 British, 24 Irish, 215 Germans, 184 Poles; there were also 12 Blacks and one Russian Jew. Of the families with teenagers, 33% of American families, 33% of English-Canadian families, 50% of Black families, 67% of French-Canadian families, 71% of English families, 74% of German families, 75% of Irish families, 81% of Polish families and the lone Russian-Jewish family sent one or more of their teenagers to work. The majority of teenaged children labored in unskilled jobs; only among the Irish were a quarter of the teenagers employed in low white-collar jobs, with the rest evenly split between skilled and unskilled jobs; a narrow majority of American workers held skilled jobs, with the remainder in unskilled jobs.

The general pattern for families headed by German laborers was to send children to school between the ages of six and thirteen and then put them to work at age fourteen. A German laborer in his thirties usually made $282 a year, but his income could double with the family economy. In eight of the nine cases of families headed by a German immigrant aged between thirty-six and forty, the wife did not work. In one case, one sixteen-year-old daughter did housework, which increased the family income to $393; in another four families, a fourteen- or fifteen-year-old son worked as a laborer, which brought the total income to $433. In another family two sons, fifteen and years sixteen of age, worked as laborers, which brought an estimated family income of $561. In one case the added income from a daughter working as a dressmaker and in another from the wife's working as a washing laborer and a sixteen-year-old son laborer brought the family totals to $448 and $657. In three instances the families were extended, one by a nonworking father-in-law and two by adult brothers-in-law, in the two families where the children were still too young to work. With one other adult working as a laborer, the estimated family income rose to $566.

The German heads of households who were a little older (between forty-one and forty-five) had more children entering the labor force and hence a higher income. In the cases of ten families with wives not working, the annual income ranged from $413 to $922; the higher incomes were a result of two daughters employed as cigar makers in two families and one son employed as an upholsterer and two daughters working as knitters in another (table 9.8). After the head of household reached the age of forty-five, children began to leave home; few families took in newly wed children and the family income began to decline. No German families with the head above forty-five earned a family income above $840.

Other groups of workers followed a pattern similar to that of the Germans, with a few group nuances. Polish workers tended to send their children to school somewhat later than the Germans but had them enter the labor force as early;

TABLE 9.8

Estimated annual income of selected families headed by a German laborer age 41–45,

Head of household's income		$274		$274		$274		$274
Children's status and income by age	Son	Daughter	Son	Daughter	Son	Daughter	Son	Daughter
1–2		Home	H					
3–4		H						H
5–6			H			H		
7–8				S	S			S
9–10					S			
11–12		School	S				S	
13–14	$139[b]						$150[b]	
15–16					$150[b]			
17–18			$139[b]					
Above 18								
Total children's income		$139		$139		$150		$150
Wife's income		-		-		-		-
Family's income		$413		$413		$424		$424

SOURCES: Household data from 1900 sample; income data from *First* to *Eighteenth Annual Report of the Bureau of Labor and Industrial Statistics* (Lansing, 1884–1901).

a. All dollar values indexed to 1910–1914.

b. Laborer; income figures vary slightly with industry.

most sons worked as day laborers and daughters as cigar makers or tobacco strippers (table 9.9). Among the Irish there were more instances of multiple families, especially when the head was over fifty, than among either Germans and Poles, who kept only unwed children at home.

The family economy was practiced not only by the unskilled workers but also by skilled workers, following a similar trend of increasing family income as children entered the labor force and decreasing again when they left the parental home; since skilled occupations were generally better paid, the total family income could add up to a comfortable sum of money. In the case of German carpenters, for example, the income of a lone head wage earner about forty years of age would have been $390 per year, but with a sixteen-year-old son working as a hatmaker, the income could reach $544, and with a twenty-year-old son working as a patternmaker, the income could be as high as $642. In one family the head, aged fifty, was a carpenter; three children lived at home and worked, a twenty-year-old daughter, as a wireworker, and two sons, as molders, one nineteen and the other twenty-one, producing a comfortable combined family income of $1,428. Similar examples abound for most skilled trades, for the trend among German and Polish families was to put the children to work as soon as they were able to perform on the job. Eighty percent of the

Detroit, 1900[a]

$274		$274		$274		$274		$274		$274	
Son	Daughter	Son	Daughter	Son	Daughter	Son	Daughter	Son	Daughter	Son	Daughter
								H	H		
				H			H				
		H				H		H	H		
					S	S			S		
				S							
		$139[b]	S				S				
	$100[c]	$139[b]					$132[e]	S			
$170[b]				$150[b]			$132[e]	$324[f]			
				$150[b]		$356[d]		$324[f]		$324[f]	
										$324[f]	
	$270		$278		$300		$620		$648		$648
	-		-		-		-		-		-
	$544		$552		$574		$894		$922		$922

c. Feeder.
d. Upholsterer.
e. Knitter.
f. Cigar maker.

TABLE 9.9

Estimated annual income of selected families headed by a Polish laborer age 41–45,

Head of household's income	$279		$279		$279		$279		$279		$279	
Children's status and income by age	Son	Daugh-ter	Son	Daugh-ter	Son	Daugh-ter	Son	Daugh-ter	Son	Daugh-ter	Son	Daugh-ter
1–2	Home				H		H	H				
3–4				H		H		H				
5–6		H	H		H	H	H		H			S
7–8						S	H		S			
9–10			School	S	S						S	
11–12					S		S			S		
13–14	S			H	$125b				$115b		$125b	
15–16		H					$115b		$115b			$117c
17–18			$125b				$115b					
Above 18	$115b									H		
Total children's income	$115		$125		$125		$230		$230		$242	
Wife's income	-		-		-		-		-		-	
Family's income	$394		$404		$404		$509		$509		$521	

SOURCES: Household data from 1900 sample; income data from *First* to *Eighteenth Annual Report of the Bureau of Labor and Industrial Statistics* (Lansing, 1884–1901).

a. All dollar values indexed to 1910–1914.

b. Laborer; income figures vary slightly with industry.

c. Tobacco stripper.

German and Polish carpenters put at least some of their teenagers to work, and the percentage was the same in families headed by molders or stove mounters, for example.

Native white American workers, however, were somewhat more hesitant to sacrifice their children's schooling. If we look at skilled trades dominated by native white American workers like machinists or railroad conductors, we see that they relied less on the family economy than did the German skilled workers. Only 33% of the families headed by machinists in the American and English-Canadian groups who had teenagers sent at least some of them to work. American machinists earned around $550 a year and supported children who went to school, including fourteen to sixteen-year-old children who would have worked had they been born into a German or Polish family. The children who did work were often in their early twenties—their machinist fathers in their late forties or fifties—and were employed in a variety of occupations including such white-collar jobs as school teacher; in these families, the father's income was

Detroit, 1900[a]

$279		$279		$279		$279		$279		$279		$279		$279	
Son	Daugh-ter	Son	Daugh-ter	Son	Daugh-ter	Son	Daugh-ter	Son	Daugh-ter	Son	Daugh-ter	Son	Daugh-ter	Son	Daugh-ter
H	H			H		H			H			H	H		H
														H	
	H	H				H	H					H	H		H
	S					H						H	H		S
H		S											H		
S		S											S		
	$125[b]												$117[h]		$115[b]
	$149[e]														
				$324[f]		$350[g]		$350[g]			$324[f]		$350[g]		$115[b]
$263[d]															
	$263		$274		$324		$350		$350	$125[b]					
											$449		$467		$230
-		-		-		-		-		-		-			$257[b]
$542		$553		$603		$629		$629		$728		$746		$766	

d. Stove molder.
e. Brass finisher.
f. Cigar maker.
g. Cigar roller.
h. Cigar stripper.

nearly doubled by that of his children. In the families headed by railroad conductors, a highly paid, skilled occupation (carrying an annual income over $800), rarely did the children work. It was not uncommon for a railroad conductor to support not only his wife and children through school, but also an elderly father or mother at home.

The family economy practiced among immigrant families was an absolute necessity not only for the bare survival of the family unit but also for the development of the ethnic communities, which I have described. The same immigrants who relied so much on their children's income were the home builders of Detroit; they were also supporting churches and patronizing many community institutions. This ethnic autonomy required the cash that only a firm strategy of pooled incomes could bring, but the obvious and heavy toll for economic well-being within the community was a brake on the children's education, a price that many native white American workers were unwilling to pay.

The family economy, then, reinforced ethnic fragmentation by integrating the children early into the work force, most often in the footsteps of the parents, and thus limiting the prospects for the children to move out of the community of their birth. But the largest ethnic communities, certainly the Irish since the 1850s, the Germans in the 1880s and the 1890s, the Poles at the turn of the century, and to some extent the Russian Jews, were both large enough and diversified enough to provide opportunity for growth and upward mobility to their own people. While the family economy effectively prevented many children from advancing socially through education, the opportunities that existed in the community they lived in provided them with an alternative, albeit incomplete, system of mobility.

10

Ethnic Endogamy and the
Survival Cycle

Plate 10. A worker's family in their log cabin near the city limits of Detroit, early 1900s. Courtesy of the Archives of Labor and Urban Affairs, Wayne State University.

Perhaps the greatest inequality among Detroit's ethnic and social groups appears in their relative abilities to give life and to prevent premature death. Demographic behavior in 1880 varied little by socioeconomic status within the same ethnic group (as we have seen in chap. 3). In 1900, however, ethnic communities' demographic behavior was less distinctive, as the realities of working-class life penetrated deeper into all ethnic groups. What did it mean, then, for an infant to be born in Detroit of German parents, or of Polish parents, or of Black parents, or of native white American parents? What was a newborn's chance of surviving the first few months of life? The vital events—births and deaths—which mark the course of life affected the organization of Detroit's households, and both the differences in household arrangements and in vital events reflected the cultural and social distances that separated the ethnic groups of Detroit.

Sociologists who have studied the variety of household arrangements in modern societies have long considered the nuclear family a sign of modernization and progress.

> [They] argue that, as societies modernize, many activities performed by an extended family are assumed by other institutions and in this way the family becomes structurally more differentiated from other institutions. Economic production is removed from the home, children are sent to schools, and welfare institutions are created to care for the indigent and the elderly. The nuclear family that evolves is a more specialized unit, one devoted primarily to the expressive and child-rearing functions. This unit was described as isolated, in the sense that it is cut off from other pivotal institutions in the society.

Neil Smelser and Sydney Halpern thus summarize the prevailing sociological theory of a " 'fit' between industrial economies, necessitating a geographically and socially mobile labor force, and a small nuclear family unencumbered by primary commitments to a broader kinship network."[1]

More than a decade of research, however, has led historians to correct the sociologists' perspective and prove that the nuclear household has long been the traditional form of residential organization. The thrust of most studies of living arrangements in western communities, including the United States, has been to stress the predominance of nuclear households in the past. Tamara Hareven and Maris Vinovskis report that

1. Neil J. Smelser and Sydney Halpern, "The Historical Triangulation of Family, Economy, and Education," in *Turning Points: Historical and Sociological Essays on the Family*, ed. John Demos and Sarane Spence Boocock (Chicago: University of Chicago Press, 1978), p. 289.

in American communities throughout the second half of the nineteenth century, indeed, the dominant pattern of household structure appears to have been nuclear. This pattern varied slightly across rural-urban or ethnic lines. Approximately seventy-five to eighty percent of all households were nuclear, approximately twelve to fifteen percent were extended, and about three to five percent were single-member households.[2]

Both the sociologists' insistence on the "modernization" of the family and the historians' emphasis on structural descriptions of past household arrangements have unfortunately obscured the fundamental question of the relationships between household organization, vital events, and social structure. What were the differences between the households of the rich and of the poor, of the native and of the newcomer? I propose to show that, at the turn of the century, the socioethnic groups in Detroit with the most diversified household structures— including a significant fraction of extended families—also experienced a balanced set of vital events, controlling birth and experiencing a moderate rate of infant mortality. The extended structure of many of their households was not a relic of another epoch; family members—elderly parents or newly wed children—were available in the city and these households had the means of receiving them under the common roof. In contrast, groups who had the largest proportion of nuclear households were fighting a tough demographic struggle, which I call the survival cycle. It involved high fertility and high mortality simultaneously, as women had to give birth to several children to keep one alive. Nuclearity, in their case, was more the sign of limited opportunities than of modernization.

The diversity of Detroit's population in 1900 (conveyed by the 1900 sample), combined with the detailed demographic information of the 1900 manuscript census, allows for a finer demographic survey for 1900 than for 1880. Not only does the census provide the age of each household member and each member's relationship to the head (wife, son, cousin, boarder, etc.)—facts which are needed to study household composition and to compute the child-woman ratio (our indicator of fertility)—the 1900 census also carried information on the number of years people were married and on the number of children born and the number surviving in each household. I used these last two items to estimate infant mortality and life expectancy. Since marriage patterns among ethnic groups determine, to a large extent, the structure of the households, I began by studying these marital patterns before turning to an analysis of household composition and vital events.

---

2. Tamara K. Hareven and Maris A. Vinovskis, eds., *Family and Population in Nineteenth-Century America* (Princeton, N.J.: Princeton University Press, 1978), pp. 14–15.

MARRIAGE

A family begins with a marriage. When a man and a woman join for life, they almost always establish an independent household, live as a conjugal unit, and preside over the destiny of their children for a long period of time. At the turn of the century, this pattern of separate conjugal units was followed by and large by all ethnic groups and included clearly defined roles for both husbands and wives. As we have seen, the husband of the unit worked as the breadwinner, while the wife stayed home, raising children. But even if most married couples still conformed to the pattern of separate conjugal units and to the Victorian roles for husbands and wives, married life and the organization of the family differed greatly from one ethnic group to another in Detroit at the turn of the century. Since men generally married women of the same ethnic group, ethnic endogamy became the basis for family organization, and several different types of family life arose along ethnic lines.

The degree to which members of a group selected their mates from within their own group depended, of course, on the availability of mates of a compatible age. At times, mate selection within the group was difficult simply because of a larger number of marriageable males or females in certain age groups, and at these times intermarriage was more likely. It is unfortunately very difficult to know exactly what percentage of the population thus needed to rely on intermarriage in Detroit, because only a fraction of Detroit's population married within the city: only 32% of the Detroiters who had married in the 1890s had married in Wayne County, leaving 68% who married in other locations, in communities where they may have experienced different conditions regarding mate availability. But if members of endogamous groups did occasionally break with the accepted behavior and select marriage mates outside the group, which groups were more likely to do so, and what were the consequences of such choices?

I limited this study of marriage patterns to the selection of wives by men of the nine major ethnic groups in the city—native white Americans, French and English immigrants from Canada, immigrants from Great Britain, (without Ireland), Ireland, Germany, Poland, and Russia, and also Black Americans. To be included in the subsample, these men had to be married residents of Detroit in 1900 and had to have married within the United States in the 1890s. Thus, only those immigrants whose marriage followed their entry into the United States in the ten years preceding the census and the natives of the United States were included in the study; the wives came from all ethnic origins, not from the nine major groups only (see table 10.1).

The analysis of marriage patterns deepens our understanding of ethnic life in Detroit. Generally the groups that had a high degree of geographic cohesiveness also had a high level of endogamy, whereas members of the more geographically dispersed groups were the more likely to intermarry. The foreign-born groups with the most tight-knit communities thus had the highest percentages of endogamous marriages: 78.4% of German-born males who married in the United States in the 1890s married either German-born women (51.3%) or the daughters of German immigrants (27.1%); 86% of the Polish men and 72% of the Russians also married endogamously. Next to these groups with an exceptionally high percentage of endogamy came the Irish, still a close-knit ethnic group despite the relative decline of the Irish community: 64% of Irish men who married in the United States in the 1890s married either Irish women (44.4%) or the daughters of Irish immigrants (19.4%).

The native white Americans were the most diverse. Only 52.9% of them married within their group, but this percentage, lower than that of most immigrant groups, was to be expected. Native white Americans made up the largest group of marriageable people and, by virtue of more frequent contact outside their own group, were more likely to select mates outside the group; some native white Americans also had grandparents who were immigrants, so they could easily associate with certain ethnic groups, especially Anglo-Saxon Protestant British and English Canadians.

Only three ethnic groups among the white groups reviewed had a low rate of endogamy in the 1890s, and these same three groups had not developed their own neighborhoods, either: 19.7% of the British immigrants, 21.4% of the English Canadians, and 31.3% of the French Canadians married within their own group, but the majority searched elsewhere for their marriage companions.

Whatever complex marriage patterns may have existed among the ethnic groups of Detroit, they never affected the Black community. The Blacks were scattered across the German east side in a few pockets of concentration, but there were virtually no mixed marriages (the 1900 sample includes only three such mixed marriages in the 1890s) between Blacks and whites.

These marriage patterns generally held true at every level of the social structure, for rich and poor alike; white-collar Polish employees had the same endogamous pattern as their fellow industrial workers. Among the Irish, likewise, the percentage of exogamous marriages was not clearly linked to socioeconomic status, since 40% of the skilled workers but only 33% of the white-collar workers married outside the group. Only among the Germans was there a tendency for the white-collar workers to intermarry with other ethnic groups more often than the skilled or unskilled workers; 37% of the white-collar German workers selected their wives outside the group, but only 22% of the skilled workers and 14% of the unskilled workers selected non-German wives.

These simple differences in percentage points tell a good deal of the story,

TABLE 10.1

Choice of wives by men of selected ethnic groups, Detroit, 1900[a]

Wife's ethnic group	Husband's ethnic group								
	Native white American (%)	Black (%)	Canadian (English) (%)	Canadian (French) (%)	British (%)	Irish (%)	German (%)	Polish (%)	Russian (%)
Native white American[b]	52.9	4.7[e]	29.3	25.0	18.3	5.6	5.5	-	-
Black	.2[d]	95.3	-	-	-	-	-	-	-
Canadian (English)[c]	5.4	-	18.7	6.3	2.8	2.8	2.0	-	-
Canadian American (English)	1.8	-	2.7	6.3	4.2	-	-	-	-
Canadian (French)	1.1	-	-	25.0	-	-	-	-	-
Canadian American (French)	.2	-	-	6.3	-	-	-	-	-
British	2.7	-	2.7	-	14.1	2.8	-	-	-
British American	2.7	-	5.3	-	5.6	-	1.0	-	-
Irish	.9	-	1.3	-	1.4	44.4	.5	-	-
Irish American	2.0	-	2.7	12.5	2.8	19.4	.5	-	-
German	2.3	-	1.3	-	2.8	2.8	51.3	8.4	12.5
German American	4.5	-	5.3	6.3	14.1	-	27.1	2.8	6.3
Polish	-	-	-	-	-	-	-	70.1	-
Polish American	-	-	-	-	-	-	-	15.9	-
Russian	-	-	-	-	-	-	.5	-	59.4
Russian American	-	-	-	-	-	-	.5	-	12.5
Other	23.1	-	30.7	12.5	33.8	22.2	11.1	2.8	9.4

SOURCE: 1900 sample.

a. Couples married in the U.S. in the 1890s and living in Detroit in 1900.

b. Born in the U.S of two U.S.-born parents.

c. Born in English-speaking Canada of two Canadian parents; born in the U.S. of two parents born in English-speaking Canada; born in French-speaking Canada of two Canadian parents, etc.

d. 1 case in the sample.

e. 2 cases in the sample.

but not all of it; they tell only what actually happened without providing a yardstick to measure the facts against what could have happened if the selection of a marriage mate were a random event. A simple technique—the Rogoff ratio—has been designed to provide just such a measurement; it consists of dividing the observed number of marriages between two groups by the expected number, which is computed on the basis of potential mates in the overall population.[3] In our case (as in most cases), the Rogoff ratios ought to be interpreted cautiously, since we do not know whether those couples who married outside Detroit faced conditions in age and sex ratios similar to those existing in Detroit; despite this limitation, however, we can use the ratios to get a general sense of the departures from expected marriage patterns. If the ratio is one to one, the observed number being the same as the expected number, then the marriage pattern between two groups is almost random; a higher ratio shows strong attraction between two groups while a lower ratio shows, of course, little attraction.

Looking first at the endogamous marriages (and defining immigrant groups strictly, without mixing generations), we see the highest ratios among Russian Jews (55:1) and Blacks (47:1), indicating the extraordinary rate of endogamy in these two groups considering the small numbers of available mates in their limited populations. The lowest ratio was for native white Americans (2.16:1); considering the high availability of marriage mates for them in the population, their 55% intramarriage rate is not unexpected. The Germans, who had a lower (51%) rate of endogamy (when only immigrants are counted), had a higher ratio of 5.52:1. The Poles, in turn, had a ratio of 15:1, indicating very strong endogamous tendencies. And surprisingly, the British immigrants, the English Canadians, and the French Canadians, who intermarried substantially, also married endogamously, the ratios of 7:1, 5:1, and 20:1 revealed, more than could have been expected on the basis of their numbers.

The high rate of endogamy brought out by this statistical device is not the most remarkable result of this study of marriage patterns; more interesting is the absence of a clear pattern of exogamy between any one ethnic group and native white Americans. We learn from the Rogoff ratios—which, below one,

3. Richard M. Bernard and John B. Sharpless, "Analyzing Structural Influence on Social History Data," *Historical Methods* 11 (Summer 1978): 113–17. This is a critique of the Rogoff ratios, but it provides a clear explanation of how they are computed. Considering the severe limits of the data, there is no point in using more sophisticated techniques here. See also an important discussion of intermarriage statistics in Josef J. Barton, *Peasants and Strangers: Italians, Rumanians, and Slovaks in an American City, 1890–1950* (Cambridge, Mass.: Harvard University Press, 1975), pp. 197–98 and note; for a general discussion of intermarriage see Stephan Thernstrom, ed., *Harvard Encyclopedia of American Ethnic Groups* (Cambridge, Mass.: Harvard University Press, 1980), pp. 513–21.

indicate fewer intermarriages than expected on the basis of the availability of partners in the population—that no group felt particularly attracted by any other group; we learn that the British or the English Canadians, for example, married significantly less often with native white Americans than could have been expected on the basis of their available numbers in the 1890s. British grooms and native white American brides had a ratio of .0004:1; English Canadian grooms and native white American brides had a ratio of .0006:1; the ratio dropped even further, to .0001:1, between Irish and native white Americans and between Germans and native white Americans. In other words, intermarrying in 1900 was more a consequence of the imbalances of age and sex in the community than the result of any strong attraction to a particular receiving group; that the native white Americans were largely a receiving group was more a function of their numbers in the community than of choice. The English-Canadian males who married in the 1890s in the United States and resided in Detroit in 1900 provide a good example of what happened. Only 21.4% of them married other English Canadians or women born in the United States of English-Canadian parents. Of the English-Canadian men 29.3% did marry native white American women, certainly a sizeable percentage of all marriages, but half of the English Canadians married outside these two groups in many directions: some married women from Great Britain, Ireland, Germany, Scandinavia, Switzerland, or the Netherlands; others married native-born women of foreign parentage. To a group with a high rate of intermarriage, marrying outside the group was not necessarily a move toward assimilation into the native white American world. It was not a one-dimensional movement but rather one that reflected the many directions available for finding a marriage partner when one was not readily available within one's own group.

THE FAMILY

Marriage, then, made the family the primary cell of ethnic life in the city, but we must now turn to the family and the household to study the different living arrangements and demographic behavior of the ethnic groups of Detroit. As in chapter 3, I use the word "family" to describe the blood relatives living under the same roof and sharing the same table and the word "household" to refer to all the individuals under that roof, not only the blood relatives. A household, then, comprises a family, sometimes augmented by boarders and/or servants. The distinction is essentially technical, but it is useful in classifying households as different groups afforded different combinations of kin and non-kin members. A family may be a solitary resident, or may comprise kin-related coresidents (siblings, for example), or be a nuclear family (a married couple, a married couple with children, or a single parent with children); a family may be extended up, across, or down the family tree (father, brother, nephew for instance). Such an extended family—in which the extension does not create a second nucleus—is distinct from the multiple family, in which at least two nuclei exist. A family comprising a second nucleus (father and mother, brother and sister-in-law, married children, for instance) in addition to the primary nucleus, is a multiple family. Such are the main headings of my family classification scheme.[4] If only kin-related members lived under one roof, then the family and the household were equivalent, but any type of family—single resident and coresidents, nuclear, extended, or multiple—could have been augmented by boarders and/or servants.

Limiting the study of family life to the residential unit (in other words, to the living arrangements) of Detroit's citizens at one point in time seriously restricts the scope of investigation; such an approach would be too limited if one wanted to grasp the complex web of family relations outside the constraints of one roof, such as the processes of chain migration due to kinship, or if one wanted to study "the developmental process of the family cycle."[5] But if the census does not provide observations for everything that is worth studying about the family, it does provide a snapshot view of all of the households of Detroit at once, in the context of the daily routine of the home. By sorting the households not only by ethnicity or socioeconomic status of the head of the household but also by his or her age, we can analyze comparable households, effectively controlling for changes due to different positions in the life cycle; and by using what demographers call indirect techniques of estimation, we can measure such vital events as fertility and mortality among the various groups of Detroit residents.

Households headed by native white Americans showed the most diversity in organization. While 73.6% of the families were nuclear, 10.2% were either single residents or blood-related coresidents (many of them young siblings, in their twenties); 11.5% of the families were extended (most often laterally or upward), and 4.8% were multiple families (most often downward, with married children). In addition to the blood relatives, many American-headed households received boarders; there was one boarder for every four American households. Many boarders were considered a part of the receiving family; as Michael Katz reminded us, "people in times past used the words family and household loosely and interchangeably, too imprecisely in fact to make discrimination between the two possible." The American household often served as a "surrogate family"

---

4. This is derived from Peter Laslett's pioneering studies of the demography of residential units, in Peter Laslett, ed., *Household and Family in Past Time* (Cambridge: Cambridge University Press, 1972), pp. 1–73.

5. Tamara K. Hareven, ed., *Transitions: The Family and the Life Course in Historical Perspective* (New York: Academic Press, 1978), pp. 1–16.

to the many young boarders, also native white Americans who, for a while, lived in a state of "semi-autonomy," in a stranger's household, before establishing their own, fully independent households (see table 10.2).[6]

Despite these added numbers of boarders, native white Americans had the smallest families and households of all white groups (3.45 and 3.95 people on the average); and native white American women had the lowest fertility rate in the city, with a child-woman ratio of 386 children under five per 1,000 married women aged twenty to forty-nine (see table 10.3). Most native white Americans were Protestants (65%), and it is clear from a comparison of fertility ratios by religious affiliation that American Protestants controlled birth quite effectively. As John and Robin Haller indicate, "Most Protestant church leaders ignored the question of contraception altogether. While condemning feticide, they seldom dealt with the problem of prevention, preferring to leave the matter to private conscience. . . . The Catholic clergy, on the other hand, was united

TABLE 10.2

Family structure for selected ethnic and occupational groups, Detroit, 1900[a]

Ethnic and occupational group		Solitary and coresident	Nuclear[b]	Extended[c]	Multiple[d]
Native white American[e]	(%)	10.2	73.6	11.5	4.8
Black	(%)	16.3	66.3	12.8	4.7
Canadian (English)[f]	(%)	7.7	76.1	10.0	6.2
Canadian (French)	(%)	5.1	82.1	3.8	9.0
British	(%)	7.9	80.3	7.1	4.7
Irish	(%)	10.5	73.2	11.7	4.6
German	(%)	3.3	84.8	7.4	4.4
Polish	(%)	2.9	88.1	7.4	1.6
Russian	(%)	3.8	87.5	6.3	2.5
High white-collar	(%)	9.8	74.1	10.2	5.9
Low white-collar	(%)	5.9	76.9	12.6	4.7
Skilled	(%)	5.1	81.9	10.0	3.0
Unskilled	(%)	4.8	81.6	9.5	4.2

SOURCE: 1900 sample.

a. Kin-related members of household only.

b. Married couples, or married couples with children, or single parents.

c. Extension of relatives up, across and down the family tree, without forming a second nucleus.

d. Extension leading to the formation of two or more nuclei in the same family (married parents, married children, etc.).

e. Born in the U.S. of two U.S.-born parents.

f. Born in English-speaking Canada of two Canadian parents; born in French-speaking Canada of two Canadian parents, born in Great Britain of two British parents, etc.

6. Michael B. Katz, *The People of Hamilton, Canada West: Family and Class in a Mid-Nineteenth-Century City* (Cambridge, Mass.: Harvard University Press, 1975), p. 215.

TABLE 10.3

Marital fertility for selected ethnic and occupational groups, Detroit, 1900[a]

Ethnic and occupational group	Child-woman ratio standardized for age distribution[b]
Native white American[c]	386.93
Black	415.04
Canadian (English)[d]	543.87
Canadian (French)	600.85
British	428.89
Irish	855.86
German	958.12
Polish	1,264.70
Russian	1,016.70
High white-collar	538.90
Low white-collar	430.87
Skilled	679.23
Unskilled	904.02

SOURCE: 1900 sample.

   a. Ethnicity of the mother, occupation of the father.

   b. Number of children under the age of 5 per 1,000 married women aged 20–49.

   c. Born in the U.S. of two U.S.-born parents.

   d. Born in English-speaking Canada of two Canadian parents; born in French-speaking Canada of two Canadian parents, etc.

in its condemnation."[7] We can estimate the fertility of both Protestant and Catholic native white American women in Detroit based on the religious information from their marriage licenses: the Protestants had a child-woman ratio of 506 children per 1,000 married women aged twenty to forty-nine, while the Catholics reached a ratio of 1,227.[8]

Effectively controlling birth was a part of a more complex process. Those fewer children born to American women had a better than average chance of survival. In 1900, an infant's surviving the first few days or even the first few months of life was not at all a sure prospect. The question was sufficiently important for the federal census to ask each mother how many children she had borne, and how many had died. Often fathers rather than mothers answered the census takers and were more likely to forget a few dead children! But even if we cannot check for consistency in the answers, this information contained in the 1900 census proved to be extremely useful in estimating infant mortality

   7. John S. Haller and Robin M. Haller, *The Physician and Sexuality in Victorian America* (Urbana: University of Illinois Press, 1974), p. 121.

   8. Since there were no women over the age of forty in the subsample, this was a younger group than that included in the overall index. Thus even the age-standardized child-woman ratio was higher than would be shown in an overall index.

and life expectancy. The demographic technique consists of locating each group at its appropriate level of the life tables depending on the number of surviving children per age group.[9] Indeed, the native white Americans had the lowest rate of infant mortality and the highest life expectancy in the city: 12.4% of the infants born of native white American mothers were likely to die in their first year, but of those who survived the first year, only 6.7% were likely to die between age one and age five. Having reached age five, an American child could expect to live another fifty-five years (see table 10.4).

German and Polish households differed in almost every respect from native white American households. We could have expected immigrants to have a more diversified family structure than Americans simply because they had an excess of adults and a somewhat unbalanced sex ratio; 54% of the foreign-born population of Detroit were between the ages of twenty and forty-four against only 39% of the native white Americans. While Americans and Germans had a relatively balanced sex ratio (around 50% each for the adults aged twenty-one to fifty), the Poles in that age group had a 4% excess of males. Despite the greater imbalance of age and sex, however, the immigrant families had fewer adults living as solitaries, fewer extensions, and fewer households receiving boarders.

The overwhelming majority of German and Polish families were simple nuclear families (84.8 and 88.1%, respectively); only a handful were solitaries or coresidents (about 3%), most of the solitaries being older widows or widowers and not young people living outside the nuclear family. Unlike the Americans, Germans and Poles kept their adult, unmarried children at home. Few families were extended (7.4%). While the Germans had the same percentage of multiple families as the Americans (4.4%, with mainly newly wed children still temporarily under parental roof), only 1.6% of the Polish families were in this category. In 1900, there was only one boarder for every twelve German house-

9. I have computed here the Sullivan estimates. On indirect techniques for estimating mortality, see William Brass, et al., *The Demography of Tropical Africa* (Princeton, N.J.: Princeton University Press, 1968); Jeremiah Sullivan, "Models for the Estimation of the Probability of Dying between Birth and Exact Ages of Early Childhood," *Population Studies* 26 (March 1972): 79–97; James Trussell, "A Reestimation of the Multiplying Factors for the Brass Technique for Determining Childhood Survivorship Rates," *Population Studies* 29 (March 1975): 97–107; Kenneth Hill and James Trussell, "Further Developments in Indirect Mortality Estimation," *Population Studies* 31 (July 1977): 313–33; see also James A. Palmore, "Measuring Mortality: A Self-Teaching Guide to Elementary Measures," *Papers of the East-West Population Institute* 15 (May 1971; revised June 1973, reprinted March 1975); on mortality in cities, see Gretchen A. Condran and Eileen Crimmins-Gardner, "Public Health Measures and Mortality in U.S. Cities in the Late Nineteenth Century," *Human Ecology* 6 (March 1978): 27–54. I am indebted to John Knodel, who provided me with advice and a computer program for these computations.

TABLE 10.4

Infant mortality and life expectancy for selected ethnic and occupational groups, Detroit, 1900[a]

Ethnic and occupational group	Life expectancy at birth e_0	Life expectancy after age 5 e_5	Probability of dying before age 1 $1q_0$	Probability of dying between the ages of 1 and 5 $4q_1$
Native white American[b]	49.38	55.25	.1243	.0672
German[c]	46.36	53.52	.1416	.0813
Polish	40.75	50.16	.1778	.1073
White-collar workers	53.48	57.57	.1020	.0501
Blue-collar workers	48.24	54.61	.1308	.0725

SOURCE: 1900 sample.

  a. Ethnicity of the mother, occupation of the father.

  b. Born in the U.S. of two U.S.-born parents.

  c. Born in Germany of two German parents, etc.

holds, and one for every seven Polish households, in contrast to the one-in-four figure of the Americans.

Generally speaking, German and Polish families, although simpler in composition, were much larger than the American families. The Germans had an average of 4.76 persons per family (4.89 in the household), and the Poles had the highest family size in the city (5.18 on the average; 5.33 for the household). German and Polish women had very high fertility ratios; the child-woman ratio was 958 children under five per 1,000 married German women aged twenty to forty-nine, and it was 1,264 for the Poles. These groups certainly did not practice the birth control techniques of the Americans. All Poles were Catholics; but among the Germans, who were 65% Protestants and 34% Catholics, little or no difference—in contrast to the separation of native white Americans into religious groups—existed in fertility rates along religious lines.[10]

German and Polish parents had more somber prospects than the Americans for seeing their children survive the first few months or years of life. Fourteen percent of the babies born of German mothers were likely to die in the first year of their existence, and another 8.1% of the survivors between age one and age five. The Poles were losing almost 17.7% of their children in the first year of their life and another 10.7% of the survivors during the following four years. And life expectancy at time of birth for an American-born infant and a Polish-born infant was about nine years apart. At birth, the Polish infant could expect

10. The fertility rate being around 1,170 for both Catholic and Protestant groups, for married women up to age thirty-nine.

to live for only forty-one years. At age five, life expectancy among the Polish children was still trailing five years behind the Americans.

After highly endogamous marriages, then, native white Americans, Germans, and Poles developed different sorts of households. Two different patterns clearly emerge. The first typified native white American families, whose diversified and rather complex household structure translated into a variety of family situations. American families often took in newly wed children, or elderly parents, or other kin in need of a roof, and they often included boarders within the household. They practiced birth control effectively and experienced moderate infant mortality. The contrast with the simplicity and uniformity of the immigrant family is striking. As a matter of choice, Germans and Poles stuck to the nuclear family; they kept their children under the parental roof for a longer time than the Americans, domestic service being the only channel by which unmarried daughters (especially Germans) could leave their parents' households. And the large immigrant family struck a precarious balance between the fragility of the newborn infant and his questionable survival.

The strength of the nuclear family among German and Polish immigrants shows up even more clearly if, instead of looking at familial arrangements, we turn to the population of hotels and boardinghouses. We have seen that the young unmarried German or Pole stayed within the confines of his/her family as a matter of rule, but that often the young American did not. Often the young American left his parental household to live as boarder in another household, to establish his own independent household, or to live in a hotel or a boardinghouse near the downtown area. Young Americans made up almost half of the population of hotels and boardinghouses of the city center in 1900, the other half comprising representatives of all other groups. They were most often clerical employees—clerks in stores or bookkeepers—in their twenties and early thirties and had severed their ties with their parental home, a move which fewer German or Polish young adults had made.

Ethnic differences in family life certainly appeared to be profound; yet critics may argue that such differences simply reflect the class differences between native white Americans and immigrants. Since most native white American heads of households were white-collar workers and most German and Polish immigrants skilled and unskilled workers it may very well be that what I have labeled ethnic differences were really differences resulting from socioeconomic status. Indeed, the extended family was more characteristic of the middle class than of the working class; indeed, fertility and infant mortality tended to increase inversely with social status; and indeed, life expectancy was lower for the poor than for the rich. Yet the profound differences that existed between the three ethnic groups that we have compared persisted even after controlling for socioeconomic status. For example, among the white-collar workers, 72% of the American families were nuclear, in contrast to 78% among the Germans and 84% among the Poles. The percentage of nuclear families rose to 79% for the American unskilled workers, but that of the Germans and the Poles similarly rose to 88%. And while the fertility ratio for the American unskilled workers was 511 children under five per 1,000 married women between twenty and forty-nine, a higher ratio than for the group at large, it was still less than half that of the German and Polish wives of unskilled workers with ratios reaching 1,200 (see table 10.5).

The organization of the household is also a function of the life cycle. Some of the differences I have stressed may simply have reflected differences in age groups between the heads of households in different ethnic communities. For instance, Polish heads of households may have been too young to have children getting married and living in their parents' households, or too young to have to take in elderly parents, while native white American heads of households, being significantly older, would be more ready for a family or a household extension while children left the parental home. But the mean age for American heads of households in 1900 Detroit was forty-four, between the average of forty-eight years for the Germans and that of forty-two years for the Poles. And within each age group, ethnic differences in household composition and vital rates persisted. For example, in the twenty-one to thirty age group, the percentage of nuclear families for the Americans was 74.3%, but 91% for the

TABLE 10.5

Marital fertility for selected socioethnic groups, Detroit, 1900[a]

Ethnic group	High white-collar	Low white-collar	Skilled	Unskilled
		Occupational group		
Native white American[b]	561.04	258.76	521.60	511.83
Black	-	43.87	289.79	401.70
Canadian (English)[c]	580.63	418.29	479.26	753.76
Canadian (French)	-	100.00	556.34	470.08
British	170.00	820.46	300.04	307.36
Irish	-	137.73	788.92	1,052.40
German	271.17	679.03	848.23	1,125.60
Polish	-	1,035.09	1,329.40	1,201.90
Russian	440.00	547.28	917.04	1,290.40

SOURCE: 1900 sample.

a. Child-woman ratio standardized for age distribution, computed as the number of children under the age of 5 per 1,000 married women aged 20–49; ethnicity of the mother, occupation of the father.

b. Born in the U.S. of two U.S.-born parents.

c. Born in English-speaking Canada of two Canadian parents; born in French-speaking Canada of two Canadian parents; born in Great Britain of two British parents, etc.

Germans and 89% for the Poles; in the forty to fifty age group, the percentages were, respectively, 77%, 81.4%, and 89.4%. It was most often after the household head reached forty that upward or downward multiple families appeared. In the forty to fifty age group, 4.6% of the American families were multiple, 2.5% of the Germans and none of the Polish families. In the fifty to sixty age group, the Americans had 8.3% such families, but the Germans and the Poles only 4.3% and 2%, respectively.

Almost all groups of Detroit fitted into one of the two types which I have described, but correct measurements of the smaller groups are difficult to capture. Even our large sample for 1900 becomes small when subdivided into ethnoreligious groups and social groups and then further broken down by age. I have not computed the mortality estimates for the small groups because their low numbers preclude statistical accuracy, but the figures on household composition and fertility are solid enough to allow us to fit the smaller groups into Detroit's overall framework. The groups that most resembled the native white Americans were the British immigrants (without Ireland) and the English Canadians. Both groups had a few more nuclear families than the Americans, and the English Canadians had more extended and multiple families than the British, but their overall situations were comparable. Both groups had a high percentage of young solitaries, like the Americans, and both groups took in quite a few boarders; the English Canadians had one boarder in every three households, the British one in every five, while the Americans had one in every four. Women had a higher fertility rate than that of the Americans—428 for the British and 543 for the English Canadians—but lower than all other white groups. Demographically, then, English Canadians and British were a part of the native white American world.

On the other side of town the other groups more closely resembled the Germans and the Poles than the Americans. The Russian-Jewish pattern was closest to the German and Polish pattern with strong nuclear character (88%), very few solitaries and coresidents (4%), and few extensions to other kin-related members, with a high overall fertility ratio of 1,016. The French Canadians had many of the same characteristics, including strong nuclear tendencies and keeping the young at home, but they had more multiple families (9%), maybe a sign of the greater availability of kin to Detroit's Canadians. The Irish, in turn, were also closer to the immigrant pattern than to the native white American pattern, despite their diversified family structure, with only 71.5% nuclear families and 11% solitaries or coresidents. Almost all the Irish solitaries were older people, in contrast to the younger independent American solitaries; and Irish women had a fertility ratio of 855, significantly higher than that of the American women, but lower than the German or Polish women.

The one group in Detroit that did not fit either model was the small Black community, which showed yet another variant of family life. Despite the recent effort by historians to revise W. E. B. DuBois or Franklin Frazier's descriptions of the unstable Black urban household, the data for Detroit show the extent to which Blacks suffered from their low socioeconomic status.[11] The data revealed the absence of consistent family strategies as well as a serious inability to give birth (points on which I will expand in chap. 14). Blacks had a very diversified family structure, a diversity which did not reflect an adaptability to different pressures but rather an inability to establish one type of household or another. Blacks had the highest percentage of solitaries (16%), a large fraction of extension (12.8%), the smallest percentage of nuclear families (66.3%), and a large number of boarders, one per 2.5 households. When Black families were extended, they did not have the completeness of the native white American family; often a married couple or a widow kept a grandchild without the parents, or a single parent with children lived with a distant blood relative. Nor did the Black nuclear family have the strength of numbers of the immigrant nuclear family; in fact, the majority (60%) of the Black nuclear families were either childless couples or single parents rather than complete families with both parents and the children present.

Blacks had the lowest family and household sizes in Detroit (3.1 and 3.6 on the average), and a low child-woman ratio of 415. There are good indications in the data that such a low fertility ratio was due to sterility rather than effective birth control. As Reynolds Farley put it, discussing the characteristics of the Black population: "if a high proportion bore no children, it may reflect high rates of sterility, and if many women had five or more children, we probably have a good indication that effective birth control techniques were not used."[12] In Detroit in 1900, the significant number of childless couples suggest indeed a high level of sterility resulting from tuberculosis (indeed, 22.2% of deaths among Blacks in 1890 were due to tuberculosis, in contrast to only 7.6% among whites), while an equally significant number of large families also suggests the absence of birth control.[13]

11. Franklin E. Frazier, *The Negro Family in the United States* (Chicago: University of Chicago Press, 1939); and critique by Herbert G. Gutman, "Persistent Myths about the Afro-American Family," *Journal of Interdisciplinary History* 6 (Autumn 1975): 181–210; idem, *The Black Family in Slavery and Freedom, 1750–1925* (New York: Pantheon Books, 1976), pp. 432–60.

12. Reynolds Farley, *Growth of the Black Population* (Chicago: Markham Publishing Co., 1970), p. 109.

13. For a critique of Farley, particularly his conclusions on venereal disease, see Joseph A. McFalls, Jr., "Impact of V.D. on the Fertility of the U.S. Black Population, 1880–1950," *Social Biology* 20 (March 1973): 2–18. For statistics on causes of mortality, see U.S., Department of Interior, Census Office, *Report on Vital and Social Statistics in the United States at the Eleventh Census: 1890*, 2 vols. (Washington, D.C.: G.P.O., 1896), 1:570–73, 2:219–77; see also general statements on Black mortality in Elizabeth H. Pleck, *Black Migration and Poverty: Boston, 1865–1900* (New York: Academic Press, 1979), pp. 34–36, 178–81.

That the Blacks of Detroit had the least stable family organization of all groups is further demonstrated by the large percentage of families headed by the mother. In Detroit at large, only 14% of the households were headed by females in 1900, but Blacks—in this respect, similar to the Irish—had a number of female heads (27%). Where the missing fathers were is always a difficult question to answer. As Andrew Greeley remarked about the Irish, "they may have been dead, they may have been off working on the canals or the railroads, they may have deserted the families, or been in jails or hospitals for drunkenness."[14] All of this was possible, as seen in the list of responses female applicants gave to the Detroit Association of Charities in 1891. When asked where their husbands were, 58% of the women declared their husbands dead; but 25% confessed they did not know, and another 9% declared their husbands still in Detroit or in Wayne County, implicitly admitting desertion. Other responses varied; to some the husband was in Ohio or in Ontario; to others he was in a city like Chicago or Grand Rapids; and to yet others he was in prison in Jackson. The 1900 census—which included all female heads of households, not only the applicants to charities—reported a much higher rate of widows, 86% for the Irish, 80% for the Blacks. It may be that a large number of women declared themselves widows to avoid the stigma of desertion. The claim of widowhood was, however, plausible for the Irish female heads whose average age was about sixty, and even for the Black women, who were only ten years younger on the average (see table 11.4).

The households of Detroit were, then, divided into three groups. Some, best represented by the native white Americans, enjoyed a diversified household structure and a good control over their biological environment. Others, best represented by German and Poles, experienced high nuclearity and a survival cycle of both high fertility and high mortality. Yet a third type, exemplified by the small Black community, showed not even the strength of the immigrant nuclear family but rather many signs of the scarcity of a stable family life. These differences in family life and perspectives on birth and death fit the image which we have already drawn of a geographically divided Detroit, one side of it built of spacious and well-equipped homes primarily inhabited by Anglo-Saxon groups, the other side built of smaller homes, often crowded, and often lacking the most essential services of abundant running water, sewers, and pavement. In the small space of the immigrant cottage, there was neither room nor time for family extension; mothers were trapped in a cycle of numerous pregnancies while poor sanitation took the lives of many babies. Establishing a large nuclear family, in which older children were available to contribute to childrearing and family support, was the only choice most immigrants had.

14. Andrew M. Greeley, *That Most Distressful Nation: The Taming of the American Irish* (Chicago: Quadrangle Books, 1972), p. 101.

11

Poverty
Ideology and Reality

Plate 11. Unemployed foreign workers around 1905.
Courtesy of the Detroit Historical Museum.

An important way to appreciate the extent to which Detroit was still ethnically divided in the late nineteenth century is to examine the circumstances of the very poor who could not make it on their own. Did they belong to their own ethnic communities or did they rather belong to a floating underclass, dependent on the largess of welfare agencies dominated by middle-class Protestants? The question is important because it may have been through welfare agencies—and their related means of social control—that the Protestant establishment finally penetrated otherwise autonomous ethnic communities.

Poverty was a part of the everyday scene in late nineteenth-century Detroit. As a large industrializing city receiving thousands of newcomers from all backgrounds, Detroit produced the conditions that foster poverty. Workers were quickly hired when employment was abundant but just as quickly laid off, facing temporary or long-lasting hardship. The ranks of the poor comprised an astonishing variety of people: the temporarily laid-off worker, the vagrant, the deserted wife, the elderly person, the abandoned child. But even more amazing than the diversity of people who made up the ranks of the poor was the extreme simplicity of judgment with which the middle class confronted this complex social reality. The middle class cast a moral judgment on the poor, assuming their poverty to be somehow of their own making; they saw the poor not as they really were but as makers of a social evil, and their ideological view of poverty prevented their seeing its reality.

That an industrial society would generate a great amount of poverty was only a recently accepted fact in the late nineteenth century. The first American industrialists who had founded the textile mills of Lowell and hired the daughters of New England farmers as textile operatives had dreamed of an industrial society without poverty. In those early years, it seemed that the dream had come true. When Michel Chevalier visited Lowell in 1834, he compared it with the British capital of cotton manufacture. Observing the young women operatives, he remarked:

> On seeing them pass through the streets in the morning and evening and at their meal-hour, neatly dressed; on finding their scarfs, and shawls, and green silk hoods which they wear as a shelter from the sun and dust (for Lowell is not yet paved), hanging up in the factories amidst the flowers and shrubs, which they cultivate, I said to myself, this, then, is not Manchester; and when I was informed of the rate of their wages, I understood that it was not at all like Manchester.[1]

But reality quickly changed. As the once abundant job opportunities in industrial labor were filled to overflowing by an ever growing supply of poor hands—

---

1. Michel Chevalier, *Society, Manners, and Politics in the United States* (Boston: Weeks, Jordan & Co., 1839), p. 137.

the immigrants to America—poverty entered the industrial scene to stay. But industrialists and middle-class observers who all witnessed poverty spreading from one manufacturing town to another contended that poverty in the new world was only a temporary condition. The able-bodied poor would soon rise to a better condition.[2]

The dominant theory regarding the United States' poor at the turn of the century is well known. The middle-class Protestant charity workers pronounced the poor inferior and attributed destitution to personal failings such as idleness, intemperance, or simply ignorance. They sought to single out the "deserving poor," destitute through no fault of their own. But they never defined such "deserving" individuals other than as exceptions to the legions of undeserving paupers. This harsh view of the poor was most directly propagated by members of the Charity Organization Movement, which administered most of the relief in America's urban areas.[3] But just about everybody who played a part in helping the poor in late nineteenth-century cities looked at the poor from a middle-class Protestant perspective. Even the more liberal social workers who did not believe in "the survival of the fittest" theories—people like Jane Addams at Chicago's Hull-House or Robert Woods and Albert Kennedy, who opened settlement houses in Boston—saw in their roles a chance to offer the poor a model of middle-class life.[4] Even prominent Black leaders like Booker T. Washington, the man who entitled his autobiography *Up from Slavery*, had little sympathy for the poor. On a visit to Detroit, Washington "publicly argued that the northern black lower-class workers were victims of their own failure to acquire a trade and that they were insufficiently thrifty or industrious."[5]

This stern view of the poor did not recede when severe economic depressions struck American cities, forcing many unemployed people into poverty. Despite repeated periods of depression in the 1870s, 1880s, and 1890s, the privately run charity organization movement in the country forcefully argued for an end to public "outdoor" relief to the poor, declaring that public funds should be channeled only to poorhouses and institutions and not be used to give relief to the poor in their own homes. In some instances this view was echoed by public

2. Thomas Bender, *Towards an Urban Vision: Ideas and Institutions in Nineteenth-Century America* (Lexington: University Press of Kentucky, 1975), pp. 113–14.

3. Paul Boyer, *Urban Masses and Moral Order in America, 1820–1920* (Cambridge, Mass.: Harvard University Press, 1978), p. 144; see also James Leiby, *A History of Social Welfare and Social Work in the United States* (New York: Columbia University Press, 1978); and also Kenneth L. Kusmer, "The Functions of Organized Charity in the Progressive Era: Chicago as a Case Study," *Journal of American History* 60 (December 1973): 657–78.

4. Sam Bass Warner, Jr., "Preface," in *The Zone of Emergence*, ed. Robert A. Woods and Albert J. Kennedy (Cambridge, Mass.: M.I.T. Press, 1962), pp. 2–27.

5. David M. Katzman, *Before the Ghetto: Black Detroit in the Nineteenth Century* (Urbana: University of Illinois Press, 1973), p. 169.

officials, who felt it was not the place of the government to engage in relief
operations. During the midst of the depression of 1893 Governor Flower of
New York turned down a proposal for a public works program for fear of
establishing "a dangerous precedent for the future, justifying paternal legislation
of all kinds and encouraging prodigal extravagance."[6] With this government
acquiescence, the charity movement was often successful at reducing public
involvement in charitable activities; according to a survey made in 1900, ten
of the twenty-one United States cities with a population over 200,000 gave
virtually no public relief in people's homes, and two more gave very little.[7] In
general, the charity movement in America campaigned against any donation,
even if it was private, outside its own controlled channels. When two New
York city newspapers, the *Herald* and the *World*, raised money during the
depression of 1893 to distribute clothing and food, a charity organization worker
retorted in the *Journal of Social Science*:

> But to offer free meals and lodgings, or meals and lodgings at so low a
> rate that every man was sure to get enough to pay, whether he worked or
> not, to encourage a mass of homeless men to come into and remain in New
> York, daily losing more and more of their manhood, was an injury to every
> man who was fed and lodged, and to the whole city.[8]

The success of the private charities in controlling most outdoor relief in urban
America was not apparent in turn-of-the-century Detroit, however, where both
public and private relief agencies attended to the needs of the poor. Detroit had
a strong tradition of public support of the poor, a system which in fact helped
more cases of poor families than all the private charities combined. Rather than
seeking the abolition of public support of the poor as its counterparts in other
industrial cities had done, the Detroit charity movement cooperated with the
city and managed to reorient some of its activities. As a result both private and
public efforts shared in the same vision of the poor and worked from the same
premises. But despite their similar intentions, differences between the private
and the public welfare sectors evolved, and the two sectors developed different
clients among the poor.

6. Samuel Rezneck, "Unemployment, Unrest, and Relief in the United States during the
Depression of 1893–97," *Journal of Political Economy* 61 (August 1953): 332.
   7. Raymond A. Mohl, "The Abolition of Public Relief, 1870–1900: A Critique of the Piven-
Cloward Thesis," in *Social Welfare or Social Control?* ed. Walter I. Trattner (Knoxville: University
of Tennessee Press, 1983).
   8. C. R. Lowell, "The Unemployment in New York City, 1893–94," *Journal of Social Science*
32 (November 1894): 21.

THE CHARITY MOVEMENT: PRIVATE AND PUBLIC
RELIEF FOR THE POOR

In Detroit, the private charity movement crystallized with the creation in 1879 of the Detroit Association of Charities (DAC). Like its counterparts in other large cities, the movement rested on three assumptions: that the poor person was responsible for his/her own condition; that it was important to bring the poor person to recognize his/her own deficiencies and correct them; and that this could only be achieved by cooperation between the various charitable organizations.[9] The first chairman of the DAC council, Levi L. Barbour, clearly stated the goal of the young association in 1881:

Let it be understood, however, that it is by no means the object of the Association to stop the flow of private charity. We rather seek to foster than repress the spirit of charity, only let it be administered discriminately. Let it flow, if you will, through the agencies the Association has established for sifting out and separating the worthy from the undeserving, with the full assurance that your alms will be wisely given to the first and as wisely withheld from the last, unless it accompanies evidence of reformation.[10]

Officially the aims of the association were

To bring the various public and private charitable agencies of the City of Detroit into communication and co-operation with each other.
To investigate cases of applicants for charitable relief, and place the information thus acquired at the disposal of the public.
To prevent indiscriminate and duplicate giving.
To refer deserving cases of destitution to charitable organizations or individuals, or to the Board of Poor Commissioners.
To secure the community from imposture.
To reduce vagrancy and pauperism, by making employment the basis of relief.[11]

Behind the DAC stood the wealthy establishment of Detroit. Among the various lists of donors that the association published, one finds many of the familiar names of the manufacturing leaders of Detroit either making donations to the association or taking an active part in its committee work. Men like James McMillan, chairman of American Car and Foundry (the largest employer

---

9. Boyer, *Urban Masses*, p. 144.
10. DAC, *Proceedings of the Second Annual Meeting* (Detroit: O. S. Gulley Printing House, 1882), p. 8.
11. DAC, Constitution of the Detroit Association of Charities, in *Proceedings*, p. 25.

in Detroit) and a leading figure of the Republican party, were on the council of the association. Frank Hecker, president of American Car and Foundry, Theodore Buhl, president of Parke, Davis and Co., F. A. Hubel and Frederick Stearns, other leaders of the pharmaceutical industry, G. H. Barbour, one of the founders of Michigan Stove, John Gray, the manufacturer who later financed Henry Ford, the Pingrees and their associates, and many other well-known manufacturers were members of the association.[12] Two hundred and fourteen individuals and companies made donations to the association in 1890; most were prominent citizens, part of the manufacturing elite with its political and financial ramifications, Protestant in religion and Republican in politics.

The DAC was created to work as a central clearinghouse for the different charities, hospitals, and other agencies of various denominations which could all rely on its file of investigation to provide aid to the poor. By 1900, ten hospitals, five homes for women, eight child-related institutions, and thirteen other agencies including homes for discharged prisoners, homes for the elderly, and visiting organizations to families, took an active part in the affairs of the DAC.[13] In addition, many ministers throughout the city constantly referred charity applicants to one of the DAC district offices for investigation. The DAC objective was to facilitate the distribution of aid by the various private charities to the deserving needy, hence the need to distinguish him or her from the undeserving poor.

When individuals approached one of the many associated charities, they were sent to a DAC district office. There they were often given a very small amount of relief such as a small grocery order or a lodging ticket for one night without investigation, but any aid for more than one day, which the DAC referred to as "non-immediate" relief, required a thorough investigation. In pursuing thorough investigations of applicants, the Detroit establishment worked in ways similar to charity organizations in other cities where information on individual poor applicants was systematically accumulated and stored in central files. In the district offices, the life history of each applicant was entered in two different books. In one book, one page per applicant contained a description of the household, including basic employment and income data, basic information on living conditions and rent, and basic information on various sources of aid already available to the family, if any. This form also registered whom the applicant was sent by and included a general statement by the district inves-

12. DAC, *Twelfth Annual Report of the Board of Trustees of the Detroit Association of Charities* (Detroit: Ostler Printing Co., 1891), pp. 45–47.

13. DAC, *Twenty-Second Annual Report of the Board of Trustees of the Detroit Association of Charities* (Detroit, 1901), pp. 10–27.

tigator on the case. In another book, the same items for each applicant were covered in greater detail. The questionnaire included lines for every family member, and if a woman applied, she was inevitably asked where her husband was, how long it had been since he left her, when she last heard from him, if friends knew his whereabouts, and if he had sent anything for support. The questionnaire reviewed in detail each applicant's ethnic background, location in the city, length of residence at present address, length of residence in the city, place of residence before settling in Detroit, the occupation, income, and reason for being out of work of each family member, as well as the age and educational level of every family member. The questionnaire also detailed the family medical history. Inquiries were made regarding nearest friends and relatives, church affiliation, membership in benevolent societies. The investigators also looked into the amount of indebtedness, number of pawn tickets, arrears due on the rent, and other items such as literacy and military status. [14]

Depending on the outcome of the investigation, the DAC issued one of three recommendations to the charity which had originally referred the applicant: the individual deserved relief and the DAC specified the type and the amount; the individual required work rather than relief and was referred to the DAC's labor bureau; the individual did not deserve or require relief. Though the recommendations were not binding, the charities usually adhered to them. If a charity declined or was unable to offer aid to a recommended applicant, the DAC office referred him or her to other institutions. The aid given was most often in kind, rarely in cash; for example, the DAC would recommend that the applicant receive fifty or one hundred pounds of flour, or half a cord of wood, or a grocery order of a certain amount, or meal tickets, or clothing. Sometimes the DAC recommended the applicant for money to pay the rent. Some applicants were sent to institutions for indoor help in hospitals or poorhouses; some were given transportation to leave the city; yet others were denied aid simply because they had a bad reputation or were intemperate. [15]

While the DAC issued food and lodging tickets to the "deserving" destitute, the DAC believed that pauperism should be extinguished by making work the basis of relief and emphasized the demoralizing tendencies of outdoor relief. Consequently, the organization operated a labor bureau which functioned as an employment agency for the destitute. When applicants for relief were sent to the labor bureau or when individuals approached the DAC directly for employment, their names, whereabouts, and occupational history were added to

14. DAC case files, United Community Services Collection, WRL. We have coded the records of investigations without recording names. I wish to thank Philip Mason for his help in gaining access to this closed collection.
15. Ibid.

the bureau's employment file, and employers were requested to fill job vacancies with individuals on file.[16]

Only exceptionally did a family receive help for any length of time. In 1889/ 90, a year when an influenza epidemic had naturally taken its heaviest toll among the poor, the DAC proceeded with its usual caution. The report noted the severe impact of the epidemic but warned against those who could take advantage of the situation:

> There was scarcely a family but one or more of the breadwinners became its victims, thus inducing many to make application for aid who had never done so before. At the same time, there is no doubt, it furnished an excuse or cloak for several undeserving and not needy persons to apply for assistance.
>
> The whole number of families applying for relief in some form or other, during the year ending September 30th, 1890, was 1,453. Of these 143 were recurrent cases, that is, cases that have applied at least once before, and some of them several times, and whose names and investigations were already on our records. These recurrent cases were disposed as follows: 2 were recommended for continuous relief, 75 for temporary relief, 2 for indoor relief, and those remaining were found to be undeserving or not needing help. Of the 1,310 new cases investigated, continuous relief was recommended for 17, temporary relief for 620, considered as needing work rather than relief 401, decided as requiring indoor relief 16, 208 cases as not needing, and unworthy 48.[17]

A central actor of the charity movement in Detroit, as in other large cities, was the "friendly visitor," often a middle-class woman, a volunteer who not only visited the needy families but worked toward their moral transformation. As Kenneth Kusmer remarks, "charity workers glorified the friendly visitor as the key to the regeneration of American society."[18] Some of the DAC's hints and suggestions to visitors set the tone of the visit. The first recommendation was to

> Conduct your intercourse with the poor on the basis of honest simple *friendship*, especially avoiding the appearance of anything like condescension or patronage.

16. DAC, *Fourth Annual Report of the Central Council of the Detroit Association of Charities* (Detroit: Chas. M. Rousseau's Printing House, 1884), p. 11.

17. DAC, *Eleventh Annual Report of the Board of Trustees of the Detroit Association of Charities* (Detroit: J. W. Morrison & Co., 1890), pp. 7–8.

18. Kusmer, "Functions of Organized Charity," p. 669; see also Boyer, *Urban Masses*, pp. 150–51.

Quickly, however, visitors were warned to be alert and ready to respond to possible attempts to deceive them:

> Be always on your guard against being deceived, whether by appearances, simulation, direct falsehood or the natural love of romancing; at the same time avoid wounding the feelings by showing distrust or suspicion unnecessarily.

Visitors were instructed to uplift the poor to middle-class standards of behavior, especially in such matters as keeping the house clean, eating a balanced diet, and sending the children to school:

> Whenever you perceive a want of *personal cleanliness*, or a neglect of proper ventilation, take an opportunity of advising, and even urging the importance of improvement, and *keep urging* it until a change is made.
>
> When you can, without offense, communicate any simple recipes for cooking, or suggestions for the greater comfort of the table or the house, or suggestions as to economic housekeeping, the cheapest and most nutritious articles of food, and the least expensive and most durable articles of clothing, etc.
>
> Encourage and urge the attendance of children at schools, as far as practicable.
>
> Endeavor to foster the *"pride of home,"* by helping to make the dwelling bright and cheerful, with the gift of such articles as cannot possibly pauperize, but will elevate and refine the taste.

Some of this friendly counsel was, of course, totally out of place when it advised near destitute families to save money or to live in a better neighborhood:

> Do all you can to encourage the formation of *provident habits*, and urge the saving and laying by of something out of the earnings even of the very poor, when it is at all practicable.
>
> Where families are being contaminated by vicious surroundings, endeavor to persuade them to remove to another dwelling, or to a better neighborhood.

The visitor was instructed to behave as a friend, not as a detective, but to report on his friendly investigation immediately to the DAC district office, especially on "the social and moral condition of the family," and "on the character of the surroundings."[19]

Despite all these activities, the rhetoric of charity workers, and the support of the city's manufacturing elite, the DAC never replaced the city as the larger

---

19. DAC, *Proceedings*, pp. 33–35.

relief agency. The charity movement did, however, play a key role in reorganizing public welfare, since it was under pressure from the DAC that the state legislature passed a charter amendment in 1880 to create the Board of Poor Commissioners (BPC). The establishment of the BPC was a success for the charity movement, which had sought to replace the old system under which city funds had been dispensed for the poor. Under the old system, the director of the poor was an elected official, and according to the charities' spokesmen "money intended for the assistance of worthy and necessitous people was diverted from its benevolent purposes, and wasted upon unworthy recipients under the dictation of party influence in particular wards of the city."[20] Under the new system, BPC members were appointed by the common council on nomination of the mayor and served in an advisory capacity without remuneration for their services. The commission had a small staff of people in charge of investigating welfare cases and keeping a record of all persons receiving aid, pretty much along the lines of the DAC system. Actually, the BPC, whose mission was "to supply provisions, fuel and medical aid to the needy worthy poor of Detroit at their homes, and make contacts with hospitals for the care of the sick; to provide for the burial of the poor and to give transportation to poor desiring to leave the city," was one of the associated charities.[21] BPC staff members had access to DAC files and conversely the DAC made a point of avoiding duplicate aid between the public and the private charities. In Detroit, then, the private charity organization movement, which did not campaign to abolish public outdoor relief, had managed to align the practices of public welfare to its own.

Once the BPC was established, however, its activities increasingly overshadowed those of the DAC. Whereas for the year 1890/91 the Board of Poor Commissioners already aided approximately 39% more cases than the DAC reviewed, by the year 1896/97 the BPC was aiding more than four times as many cases as the DAC was reviewing. That year the city reported helping 5,575 families; in contrast the DAC reviewed 1,250 families and did not help them all (see table 11.1).

Through the BPC, the city launched a large relief program of food coupons (redeemable in most groceries in the city), fuel coupons (redeemable in wood yards), and distribution of clothing. No provision had been made in the charter amendment for rent, and the city could provide shelter for the poor only in the Wayne County House; often city investigators sent applicants in need of rent

20. Leone Garrity, "The Story of the Poor Commission of Detroit: 1880–1918" (M.A. thesis, Wayne University, 1940), pp. 1–2.
21. DAC, Constitution, *Proceedings*, p. 26.

TABLE 11.1
DAC and BPC recipients, Detroit, 1891–1901[a]

Year	DAC		BPC	
	(n)	(%)	(n)	(%)
1890–1891	1,010	41.9	1,398	58.1
1891–1892	983	38.7	1,558	61.3
1892–1893	978	37.6	1,621	62.4
1893–1894	-	-	6,379	-
1894–1895	-	-	4,489	-
1895–1896	817	29.7	1,930	70.3
1896–1897	1,250	18.3	5,575	81.7
1897–1898	714	23.3	2,348	76.7
1898–1899	-	-	1,945	-
1899–1900	-	-	1,803	-
1900–1901[b]	745	-	-	-

SOURCES: Detroit Association of Charities, *Twelfth, Thirteenth, Fourteenth, Seventeenth, Eighteenth, Nineteenth*, and *Twenty-second Annual Report of the Board of Trustees of the Detroit Associations of Charities* (Detroit, 1891–1893, 1896–1898, 1901); *Eleventh, Twelfth, Thirteenth, Fourteenth, Fifteenth, Sixteenth, Seventeenth, Eighteenth, Nineteenth*, and *Twentieth Annual Report of the Board of Poor Commissioners to the Common Council of the City of Detroit* (Detroit: Thomas Smith Press, 1891–1900).

a. Number of households.
b. To replace 1898–1900.

money to the Harmonie Society and to other private charities which could cover this expense. The city also had a large program for the care of the sick poor in various hospitals, and the city supported five city physicians to answer the call of poor people in need of medical service. Applicants registered at the downtown office of the commission, which was located just above the central police station; there they were interviewed by the commission's staff and soon were visited at home.[22]

Though resentment of public funding of relief activities prevented public outdoor relief in large metropolises like New York, this movement clearly failed in Detroit, where public outdoor relief dramatically increased in the 1890s. The city, under the leadership of Pingree, reacted forcefully to the depression of 1893, which by some accounts had put a third of the labor force out of work.[23] During the winter of 1893/94, when the poor commission was absorbing an additional 250 welfare cases per day, the mayor campaigned to show that many of the poor were unemployed through no desire of their own and adopted a diversified relief policy aimed at alleviating immediate needs and putting people

22. Garrity, "Poor Commission," pp. 50, 52.
23. Melvin G. Holli, *Reform in Detroit* (New York: Oxford University Press, 1969), pp. 64, 68–70.

back to work. One of Pingree's most original ideas was to allow the poor to grow food for themselves on the empty land at the city's perimeter.[24] Pingree's potato patches plan, as it was called, was quite popular; the city provided qualified applicants with tools, seeds, and one-half acre plots for cultivation so that they could grow food for their families.

A PROFILE OF THE POOR

Why public welfare was bigger than the private effort to help the poor in Detroit is an important question, the answer to which does not lie in the agencies' principles but rather in their practices. A close examination of the DAC and BPC records reveals the most striking development in their history: the two agencies simply did not help the same poor. The Protestant groups, including the Blacks, made up the lion's share of the DAC applicants. Throughout the decade of the 1890s, native born whites made up 35.5% of the DAC's cases but only 18.1% of the BPC's. Blacks made up 11.3% of the private charities applicants, only 4.4% of the city's. Canadian and British immigrants were also better represented among the private charities' applicants (15% and 11%, respectively) than on the rolls of public relief (8.74% and 4.5%). Only the Irish among the Catholics were equally represented with the private charities (7.9%) and with the city (7.2%). In contrast, Germans, Poles, and Russians filled the rolls of the poor commission and clearly avoided the private charities as much as possible. Germans made up 15.3% of all DAC applicants, but 23.8% of all city applicants. Poles and Russians combined made up only 1.5% of the charities applicants but 27.2% of the city applicants (table 11.2).

According to their written programs, both agencies should have received the same type of poor. The 1880 charter amendment specified that the commission had to keep a record of each and every applicant, including the cause of aid. In practice, however, the poor commission operated with limited personnel. There were only two investigators, and during times of crisis the entire staff of the downtown office—the two investigators and two clerical workers—had to work extra hours just to handle all the applications and to process cases.[25] It was clearly impossible to complete a thorough investigation of all the applications. The Anglo-Saxon Protestant groups and the Blacks were probably more disposed to accept the practice of a thorough investigation and went to the DAC district offices, while the Catholics, Jews, and generally non–English-speaking groups were more suspicious and avoided the private charities altogether when they could. The Catholic immigrants especially shunned the private charities,

24. Detroit, *Sixth Annual Message of Mayor Hazen S. Pingree* (Detroit: Thos. Smith Printing Co., 1895), p. 45.

25. Garrity, "Poor Commission," pp. 43, 51.

TABLE 11.2

DAC and BPC recipients by place of birth, Detroit, 1891–1901[a]

Place of birth	DAC		BPC	
	(N)	(%)	(N)	(%)
United States	2,305.5	35.5	5,267	18.1
Black[b]	733.5	11.3	1,280	4.4
Canada	977.5	15.0	2,540	8.7
Great Britain	719.5	11.1	1,315	4.5
Ireland	515.5	7.9	2,093	7.2
Germany	991	15.3	6,916	23.8
Poland[c]	98	1.5	7,890	27.2
Russia	-	-	707	2.4
France[d]	45.5	.7	185	.6
Belgium	-	-	75	.3
Netherlands	13	.2	80	.3
Sweden[e]	30	.5	25	.1
Norway	-	-	10	[g]
Denmark	-	-	32	.1
Italy	19	.3	118	.4
Switzerland	18.5	.3	108	.4
Austro-Hungary	7	.1	309	1.1
Spain[f]	2	[g]	2	[g]
Other	6.5	.1	146	.4
Total	6,482	100.0	29,098	100.0

SOURCES: Detroit Association of Charities, *Twelfth, Thirteenth, Fourteenth, Seventeenth, Eighteenth, Nineteenth,* and *Twenty-second Annual Report of the Board of Trustees of the Detroit Associations of Charities* (Detroit, 1891–93, 1896–98, 1901); Detroit, *Eleventh, Twelfth, Thirteenth, Fourteenth, Fifteenth, Sixteenth, Seventeenth, Eighteenth, Nineteenth,* and *Twentieth Annual Report of the Board of Poor Commissioners to the Common Council of the City of Detroit* (Detroit: Thomas Smith Press, 1891–1900).

a. In number of households, in case of intermarriage, the DAC divided households in halves.
b. Blacks born in the United States and Canada.
c. DAC combined Poland and Russia.
d. DAC combined France and Belgium
e. DAC combined Sweden, Norway and Denmark.
f. DAC combined Spain and Portugal.
g. Less than .1%.

partially because of a deep-seated mutual distrust between the Catholic and Protestant churches and partially because intemperance—commonly accepted among Catholic immigrants—was a special target of DAC workers, to whom intemperate behavior was intolerable.

The group that most carefully avoided the Protestant charities and relied most fully on the city was the Poles. The Polish laborer had every reason to fear the Protestant middle-class investigator: he did not speak English; he was most likely drinking; he was also a good Catholic. Had he sought advice of the priest, he had most likely been sent to the city, not to the Protestant network. Among the city physicians working for the commission, one was a Pole who also referred many needy families to the downtown office. Since lack of personnel prevented the city from enforcing its own rules of investigation, the poor who were in need of physical help but in no need of redemption by the friendly visitor avoided the private charities.

Beyond obvious differences in ethnic and religious affiliations, were there real differences among the poor who sought aid from different agencies? Who were these people seeking aid? What do we know of them besides the fact that they were poor? In order to answer these questions, I developed a detailed profile of the poor by analyzing the DAC case investigations for 1891. I found 341 family records for that year, a year of relative economic stability before the depression of 1893. As the aggregate statistics for the 1890s demonstrated, many more native-born and Protestant poor than foreign-born Catholic poor made up the clientele of the charities in this smaller set of cases. For 1891, the cases were distributed as follows: 24% whites born in the United States, 20% Blacks born in the United States, 12% Canadian whites, 4% Canadian Blacks, 6% immigrants from England, and 4% immigrants from Scotland. The remaining 7% comprised poor coming from Belgium, Bohemia, Denmark, Holland, Italy, Poland, Switzerland, and France; in this whole year, the file contained investigations of only two Polish families.

Most applicants (67%) were Protestants. They were Episcopalians (12.4%), Methodists (25.7%), Presbyterians (8.6%), and Congregationalists (1.2%), denominations dominated by native white Americans, English Canadians, or British immigrants. Another 6.2% were Baptists, predominantly Blacks, and 6.8% Lutherans, predominantly Germans. Catholic poor made up about 32% of the applicants investigated by the association in 1891; again, they were mostly native-born white Americans (8.6%), and then only Irish (8.3%), German (5.3%), and Canadian (4.4%). Only a handful of cases (1.5%) were Jewish despite the fact that two Jewish charities, Beth El Hebrew Relief Society and the Society for the Relief of the Hebrew, were listed as participating organizations on the DAC roster.

If we were to plot on a map the addresses of the people investigated, we would see that few lived in the heart of the German, Polish, or Russian neighborhoods. Only the Black sections of the east side were well known to DAC visitors. DAC visitors were also familiar with Corktown on the west side, where most of the poor Irish were still located (although a few of the destitute Irish families lived on the east-side riverfront, between the docks and the railroad tracks). Most other poor, native white Americans, Canadians, English, or Scots lived on the fringes of the city center, in the east or west sides, or scattered in different parts of the city. The Protestant middle-class visitors could call on many poor families and yet rarely enter the German, Polish, or Russian strong-holds of Detroit.

The charities wanted to help the deserving poor, laborers temporarily out of work through no fault of their own. But if charity workers had coolly analyzed the data they so vigilantly collected, they would have discovered that by their own criteria the deserving poor did not exist. The DAC dealt mostly with a class of permanent poor. Of all investigated households 62% were headed by men; the great majority of the heads of households (82%) were between the ages of nineteen and forty-five, the very age of productive work. Yet despite the relative youth of these men, many had been unemployed for years: Blacks showed a mean of 9.5 years of unemployment, Germans 10.5 years, English 13.2 years, Irish 16.6 years, and native white Americans, 20.8 years—extremely long periods of unemployment for men in the prime years of their lives. Racial prejudice in hiring practices may explain the rate of Black unemployment, but it was the lowest among the applicants, and Blacks accounted for only 24% of all cases investigated. Furthermore, of the ninety-three cases containing infor-mation on why the individual was out of work, only 27% were unemployed because sickness, injury, or accident left them physically unfit to work (table 11.3). Clearly, these men represent not the hardworking poor forced by an unexpected misfortune to seek temporary aid, but the chronic poor, the per-manent burdens on society that the DAC despised and claimed not to assist.

The association's council repeatedly complained that the very transiency of the poor made it very difficult to control poverty:

> From its geographical position Detroit, like other seaport and frontier cities, has to contend with a floating population, largely partaking of the poorer classes, and more or less transient. Organized and intelligent plans designed as efforts for the betterment of the condition of the poor, find here this difficulty to contend with which neutralizes the result desired. Similar efforts would, no doubt, prove more successful in inland localities with a fixed and growing population.[26]

But the charities own case files reveal that the poor were not newcomers to the city or vagrants passing through Detroit. The average number of years the visited poor lived in Detroit ranged from 8.5 years for native whites to 16.5 years for the Irish. According to the DAC's own standards, these men had been in the city long enough to recognize its job opportunities and to secure employment.

Of all DAC's investigated cases in 1891, 38% were women heads of house-

26. DAC, *Fourth Annual Report*, p. 9.

TABLE 11.3

Male heads of household helped by the DAC, Detroit, 1891

Place of birth	Number	Mean age	Mean number of years in Detroit	Mean number of years at same address	Mean number of chidren per family	Number of people employed	Mean number of years unemployed	Causes for leaving employ				
								Number	No work[a] (%)	Worked only part time[b] (%)	Injury[c] (%)	Not paid (%)
United States (White)	55	38.9	7.9	1.5	2.9	13	20.8	28	46.4	7.1	42.9	3.6
United States (Black)	41	45.1	15.5	1.5	2.0	9	9.5	13	53.8	15.4	23.1	7.7
Canada (White)	20	40.7	9.8	1.9	4.6	15	12.2	11	81.8	9.1	9.1	–
Canada (Black)	11	36.9	9.6	.7	2.7	10	10.6	2	–	50.0	50.0	–
England	15	43.4	8.1	.8	3.3	15	13.2	8	62.5	–	37.5	–
Scotland	7	44.3	10.5	.9	3.1	7	12.0	6	50.0	16.7	33.3	–
Ireland	22	47.4	15.3	1.3	5.2	22	16.6	12	83.3	16.7	16.7	–
Germany	27	49.1	8.8	1.4	4.0	26	10.5	7	85.7	–	14.3	–

SOURCE: Case files of the Detroit Association of Charities, United Community Services Collection, WRL.

a. Or discharged, company out of business.

b. Or was only substitute worker, works occasionally, works when able, works when there is any.

c. Or accident, sickness.

holds, either widowed or deserted wives. Unless these women remarried a man able to support them, they were likely to remain permanent charity recipients, first to support their children and later in their old age. Most of these women heads of households had been without husbands for many years, 7.5 years on the average. Seventy-eight percent of them declared absolutely no source of income, and only 10% said they could rely on some help from friends (table 11.4).

Despite their protestations to the contrary, then, the DAC was dealing with a class of long-term poor. Many of the investigated heads of houehold were illiterate; 19% could neither read nor write, 11% could only read. For the Blacks, these percentages of illiteracy rose to 33 and 15, respectively. Many were sick; in 172 cases out of 211 where husbands and wives lived together, the wife was found with one form or another of sickness or declared to be "sickly." Many of these poor were crowded in dismal quarters; the average household size (with both husband and wife present) was 4.7 (and as high as 5.8 for the Irish), but the average number of rooms per dwelling was only 2.9. Many of these families were restless. They stayed in the city, but they only lived at the same address for an average of 1.5 years since they periodically faced landlord problems: two-thirds of the cases investigated owed an average of $7 worth of unpaid rent and were forced to move from one tenement or shack to another when they could not pay. These DAC cases were not a result of sudden misfortune, requiring only temporary help. They were truly the chronic poor, but the association, unwilling or unable to understand the meaning of the information it collected from the applicants, did not offer real help but rather piecemeal and inconsistent temporary relief.

To what extent does this portrait of the poor also apply to the poor helped by the BPC? Unfortunately, records of individual investigations do not exist for the poor commission and we must rely on aggregate published statistics for a description of BPC applicants. Even with limited information, however, the comparison of the two groups of poor suggests wide differences between them. There is no doubt from the BPC published reports that many applicants were also women heads of households, since 25% of the applicants during the 1890s reported washing as a profession, 3% sewing, and another 1% knitting, while only 52% declared they were laborers; some reported such crafts as carpentry (2.7%) or such work as peddling (2%), painting (1.7%), and other professions (less than 1% of the applicants each). But these percentages varied greatly by ethnic group: Among BPC applicants the native white Americans had 44% of their applicants in the washing, sewing, knitting group, the Blacks 45%, the British 42%, and the Irish 50%; in contrast the Germans had only 27% of their applicants in this group, the Poles only 15%, and the Russians only 11%.

TABLE 11.4

Female heads of household helped by the DAC, Detroit, 1891

Place of birth	Number	Mean age	Mean number of years in Detroit	Mean number of years at address	Mean number of children at home	Mean number of years alone	Location of husband			
							Deceased (%)	Detroit Wayne County (%)	Other[a] (%)	Unknown (%)
United States (White)	28	37.8	9.6	.8	2.0	4.7	40.7	-	11.2	48.1
United States (Black)	27	49.7	16.2	2.1	1.3	8.2	70.4	7.4	7.4	14.8
Canada (White)	22	41.0	7.8	1.4	1.7	7.0	59.1	13.6	13.7	13.6
England	7	57.3	26.4	6.9	1.9	5.8	57.1	28.6	-	14.3
Scotland	6	56.0	13.3	1.6	.7	13.4	66.7	-	16.6	16.7
Ireland	16	55.6	18.3	1.1	1.2	11.5	86.7	6.7	-	6.7
Germany	15	52.9	16.7	2.3	2.2	8.6	46.7	33.3	-	20.0

SOURCE: Case files of the Detroit Association of Charities, United Community Services Collection, WRL.

a. Grand River, Michigan; Chicago; Ohio; Ontario; and Jackson Prison, Michigan.

German applicants were predominantly day laborers (59%) and as many as 3.8% were carpenters; in turn 80% of the Polish applicants were laborers and the Russians were divided between laborers (26%) and peddlers (51%) (table 11.5).

German and Polish workers made up the bulk of factory labor in the city. They were often relegated to the lowest paying jobs, hence often on the brink of poverty. Thus the Germans and Poles applying to the BPC for assistance might not represent a class of chronically unemployed men and women, as was the case with many of the poor applying to the DAC for aid; they came instead from self-supporting households which, because of very low factory wages, were occasionally forced to seek aid to get through emergencies. The percentages of Germans and Poles seeking relief during the depression years from 1893 to 1897 fluctuated greatly. Depending on the circumstances, their number on the public rolls could increase or decrease up to seven times from one year to the next, while the number of Irish or Blacks remained relatively constant. Moreover, years of high enrollments of the Poles at the BPC were not accompanied by a significant upsurge of Poles at the DAC (table 11.6). Clearly, then, most Poles seeking relief throughout the 1890s in Detroit were not chronically poor.[27] Rather, they were people whose jobs were subject to the instability of economic conditions, and so were occasionally forced to seek temporary relief from the BPC.

My overall profile of Detroit's charity recipients suggests that the poor in Detroit came from a variety of backgrounds and variety of circumstances, under conditions frequently misunderstood by the Protestant establishment. In fact, by making sure that they were helping only the right people, the DAC may very well have alienated from the start those they precisely claimed they wanted to help and were thus left with no choice but to help those whom they despised. The differences between the DAC and the BPC were practical and not ideological, as virtually everybody shared in the principles of the DAC, but the board never had the investigative means—based on volunteer work—of the association. The duality of institutions and the matter-of-fact differences between them permitted the poor to choose, at least partially, their relief agency. Their choice reflected the strong ideological and cultural differences that divided Detroit. Even in the deep hole of misery caused by hunger, or marital disso-

27. The economic situation improved in Detroit only in 1897, as indicated by the increase in building permits. See Detroit, *Thirty-Third Annual Report of the Fire Commission* (Detroit: Geo. W. Mattice, 1900) p. 9; for a general treatment of the economic crisis of 1893 see Charles Hoffmann, "The Depression of the Nineties," *Journal of Economic History* 16 (June 1956): 137–64.

TABLE 11.5

BPC recipients by ethnicity and occupation, Detroit, 1891–1900[a]

Occupational group	United States (White) (N)	(%)	United States (Black) (N)	(%)	Canada (N)	(%)	Great Britain (N)	(%)	Ireland (N)	(%)	Germany (N)	(%)	Poland (N)	(%)	Russia (N)	(%)	Total (N)	(%)
Carpenter	204	4.07	-	-	168	6.52	49	3.72	21	1.00	260	3.78	74	.94	9	1.27	768	2.68
Cook	-	-	32	2.51	-	-	-	-	-	-	-	-	-	-	-	-	32	-[b]
Laborer	1,867	37.27	511	40.22	926	35.92	450	34.17	795	37.98	4,010	58.36	6,322	80.13	183	25.88	15,096	51.55
Molder	-	-	-	-	-	-	-	-	-	-	-	-	53	.67	-	-	53	-[b]
Painter	199	3.97	-	-	64	2.48	40	3.04	29	1.39	115	1.67	33	.42	8	1.13	493	1.68
Peddler	60	1.20	13	1.02	24	.93	22	1.67	20	.97	73	1.06	24	.29	360	50.92	592	2.02
Shoemaker	42	.84	-	-	18	.70	19	1.44	28	1.34	51	.74	19	.24	23	3.25	203	.69
Tailor	-	-	-	-	-	-	-	-	-	-	55	-[b]	-	-	19	2.69	74	-[b]
Teamster	-	-	9	.70	-	-	-	-	-	-	-	-	-	-	-	-	9	-[b]
Knitter	39	.78	-	-	18	.70	11	.84	35	1.67	141	2.05	50	.63	6	.85	307	1.05
Seamstress	317	6.33	-	-	174	6.75	71	5.38	114	5.45	173	2.52	54	.67	18	2.55	944	3.22
Washer	1,845	36.83	576	45.11	910	35.30	467	35.46	881	42.09	1,551	22.57	1,100	13.94	52	7.36	7,380	25.20

SOURCES: Detroit, *Eleventh, Twelfth, Thirteenth, Fourteenth, Fifteenth, Sixteenth, Seventeenth, Eighteenth, Nineteenth,* and *Twentieth Annual Report of the Board of Poor Commissioners to the Common Council of the City of Detroit* (Detroit: Thomas Smith Press, 1891–1900).

a. Several occupations (machinist, barber, baker, teacher, and attorney) were not included because of the small number of cases.

b. Less than .1%.

lution, or other misfortunes, the Catholic Germans and Poles learned how to keep their distance from the Protestant Anglo-Saxon institutions. The poor in need of help beyond what their peers could offer turned to the city government, and so maintained the basic cultural cleavages of this genuinely multiethnic society.

TABLE 11.6

DAC and BPC recipients by place of birth and year, Detroit, 1891–1901

Year and charitable organization		United States (White)	Black[a]	Canada (White)	Great Britain	Ireland	Germany	Poland[b]	Russia	Other
						Place of birth				
1890–1891										
DAC	(%)	13.27	17.92	12.38	11.78	10.19	13.56	1.63	-	19.27
BPC	(%)	18.60	7.58	8.44	6.08	17.17	19.98	15.95	2.43	3.77
1891–1892										
DAC	(%)	33.37	12.21	14.85	12.31	10.43	12.92	1.48	-	2.43
BPC	(%)	17.97	8.47	10.98	6.87	14.31	19.38	14.89	2.76	4.37
1892–1893										
DAC	(%)	31.80	11.35	15.90	11.35	8.49	16.56	3.27	-	1.28
BPC	(%)	19.37	5.80	12.40	6.60	11.84	19.86	17.27	2.84	4.02
1893–1894										
DAC	(%)	-	-	-	-	-	-	-	-	-
BPC.	(%)	16.60	2.65	7.92	4.06	5.55	28.37	27.83	3.14	3.88
1894–1895										
DAC	(%)	-	-	-	-	-	-	-	-	-
BPC	(%)	15.66	3.05	7.11	3.43	4.01	25.80	35.29	2.58	3.07
1895–1896										
DAC	(%)	41.13	9.67	14.93	9.30	4.90	16.89	.98	-	2.20
BPC	(%)	22.44	6.11	11.04	5.54	7.56	26.99	14.51	3.01	2.80
1896–1897										
DAC	(%)	37.28	7.92	14.28	10.24	6.28	20.40	1.44	-	2.16
BPC	(%)	14.31	2.92	6.37	3.14	4.61	20.11	40.79	1.20	6.55
1897–1898										
DAC	(%)	41.11	11.97	15.76	9.59	5.67	12.45	.70	-	2.75
BPC	(%)	21.55	5.83	10.86	5.24	7.58	14.78	22.66	2.56	8.94
1898–1899										
DAC	(%)	-	-	-	-	-	-	-	-	-
BPC	(%)	24.22	5.35	11.36	5.09	8.48	21.29	19.02	2.37	2.82
1899–1900										
DAC	(%)	-	-	-	-	-	-	-	-	-
BPC	(%)	24.57	6.66	10.09	6.05	8.76	20.41	18.86	2.05	2.55
1900–1901[c]										
DAC	(%)	35.57	7.79	18.66	12.89	9.13	11.14	.54	-	4.28

SOURCES: Detroit Association of Charities, *Twelfth, Thirteenth, Fourteenth, Seventeenth, Eighteenth, Nineteenth, and Twenty-second Annual Report of the Board of Trustees of the Detroit Association of Charities* (Detroit: 1891–1893, 1896–1898, 1901); Detroit, *Eleventh, Twelfth, Thirteenth, Fourteenth, Fifteenth, Sixteenth, Seventeenth, Eighteenth, Nineteenth, and Twentieth Annual Report of the Board of Poor Commissioners to the Common Council of the City of Detroit* (Detroit: Thomas Smith Press, 1891–1900).

a. Blacks born in the United States and Canada.

b. DAC combined Poland and Russia.

c. DAC only, to replace 1898–1900.

4

Detroit in 1920

A New City, Another Society?

12

New Dimensions for a Metropolis and the Dream of a New Society

Plate 12. Part of the Ford Motor Company Highland Park factory near the end of its construction (Albert Kahn, architect) at Highland Park, Michigan, 1918.
Courtesy of Albert Kahn Associates.

B y 1920, Detroit had become a mature industrial metropolis, altogether
different from the burgeoning industrial city of the turn of the century.
Detroit retained its nineteenth-century diversified industrial base, but the extraordinary growth of the automobile industry—employing 45.4% of the manufacturing labor force in 1919—and the increased industrial production during
World War I fostered the growth of this industrial giant. By 1916, Detroit had
reached fourth place in the nation for the dollar value of its manufactured
products, and in the early 1920s moved to third, after New York and Chicago,
leaving Philadelphia behind.[1]

The population also grew phenomenally. There were 993,678 inhabitants
within the city limits and another 171,475 in the surrounding metropolitan
district (as defined by the 1920 census). The thirteenth most populated city in
1900, Detroit jumped to fourth in 1920, behind New York, Chicago, and Philadelphia. This population increase caused the city to take on new physical
dimensions: it almost tripled in size between 1900 and 1920, by which time the
city itself had reached 79.6 square miles. With so many people distributed over
such a wide territory, spatial differentiation became more pronounced than ever
before. City and suburb were increasingly separated, and the landscape became
almost totally industrial.[2]

As a result of this phenomenal growth in size and production, an entirely
new society emerged in Detroit in the 1910s. The industrial magnates became
active social leaders during this period, as they began consciously to define and
outspokenly to advocate a new social order based on a unified work force. Using
the industrial image of the melting pot, these leaders proposed a model of
American life to the new industrial worker, presenting a vision of society in
which ethnic affiliation would give way to a new, unifying American identity.
Was this vision realistic, and was imposing it justifiable? Before we can answer
these questions, we must first understand the conditions that made this vision
desirable to the industrialists, as well as the social distances that impeded its
realization. To that end, in this chapter I will first describe the changes that

1. Eric Kocher, "Economic and Physical Growth of Detroit, 1701–1935," November 1935,
Division of Economics and Statistics, Federal Housing Administration, p. 61 (in MHC); Thomas
James Ticknor, "Motor City: The Impact of the Automobile Industry upon Detroit, 1900–1975"
(Ph.D. diss., University of Michigan, 1978); Thomas L. Munger, *Detroit and World Trade: A
Survey of the City's Present and Potential Foreign Trade and Seaboard Traffic, and the Facilities
Therefor, with Special Reference to the Proposed St. Lawrence Deep Waterway to the Sea* (Detroit:
Detroit Board of Commerce, 1920); Detroit, City Plan Commission, *Master Plan Reports: The
Economic Base of Detroit* (Detroit, 1944), p. 13.

2. U.S., Department of Commerce, Bureau of the Census, *Fourteenth Census of the United
States, 1920: Population* (Washington, D.C.: G.P.O., 1921), 1:76–77; Kocher, "Growth of De-
troit"; Leonard S. Wilson, "Functional Areas of Detroit, 1890–1933," *Papers of the Michigan
Academy of Science, Arts and Letters* 22 (1939): 397–409.

took place between 1900 and 1920—changes in industrial organization and in ethnic and racial configurations—before undertaking, in chapters 13 and 14, a more fully documented empirical investigation of social relations in 1920.

NEW DIMENSIONS FOR A METROPOLIS

Detroit's population growth was caused primarily by migration to the city: of the 528,000 people added to the city population between 1910 and 1920, 412,000 were migrants. Natural increase accounted for 109,000 new inhabitants (with an average birth rate of 32 per 1,000 and a death rate of 15 per 1,000), and annexation of new territory to the city brought only 7,000 new people into the expanded city limits during the decade.[3]

This flow of immigrants came from American farms, from the lumber camps or mines, from the rural South, and from an ever growing number of foreign countries.[4] By and large the percentage of foreign-born Detroiters slowly decreased decade by decade: in 1850, 47.22% were foreign-born; in 1900, 33.77%; in 1920, only 29.27%, but with more different countries than ever contributing to Detroit's population. The single largest group of foreign-born Detroiters in 1920 were now the Poles (19.57%), followed by English Canadians (19.13%), Germans (10.42%), Russians (9.43%), British (8.52%), Austrians (6.13%), Italians (5.6%), and Hungarians (4.69%). A few other groups contributed in smaller proportions: the combined percentages of foreign-born Detroiters from Holland, Belgium, and Luxembourg was 2.82% of the total number of foreign-born people; Scandinavians made up another 2.35%; the Irish, who in 1850 made up 33% of the foreign-born population, now accounted for only 2.42%, the Greeks for 1.6%, and the French Canadians for 1.27% (see table 5.4).

As the percentage of foreign-born immigrants decreased in the population, that of their children increased dramatically. In 1920, native-born whites of foreign parentage made up 24.86% of the population, and those of mixed parentage added another 10.24%. In contrast, native-born whites of native parentage accounted for only 31.6% of Detroit's population.

During World War I, foreign immigration was reduced to a trickle; no more than 1.1% of the foreign immigrants who lived in Detroit in 1920 had arrived in 1917, and only 0.8% in 1918.[5] Southern Blacks, however, had been arriving in increasing numbers since 1910 to work in Detroit's factories. Their numbers swelled during the war, and by 1920, Blacks made up 4.11% of the total city

3. Ticknor, "Motor City," p. 162; Detroit, City Plan Commission, *Master Plan Reports: The People of Detroit* (Detroit, 1946), pp. 5, 11–12.

4. For a vivid description of lumberjacks and Detroit, see Robert Conot, *American Odyssey* (New York: Bantam Books, 1974), pp. 1–5.

5. Bureau of the Census, *Fourteenth Census* 2:788–95.

population. In 1900, only 4,111 Blacks lived in the city; twenty years later the figure was 40,838, a smaller number than the 56,926 Polish immigrants but more than the 30,310 immigrants from Britain (Ireland excluded).[6]

We have no records of how many foreign immigrants arrived every day in Detroit by way of other American or Canadian ports of entry, and we do not know how many lumberjacks and miners were leaving the lumber camps or copper mines of the Upper Peninsula to find jobs in Detroit's factories, but we do have some estimates of how many Blacks arrived from the South by the month, the week, or the day. Forrester B. Washington, the first head of the Detroit branch of the Urban League, reported that "1,000 Negroes a month were arriving in the city" in May, June, and July of 1917. By 1920, Washington estimated that the figure was over 1,000 per week. During the summer of 1920, he sent an Urban League worker to meet the three trains which daily brought the majority of the migrants, and the count at the train station resulted in the following chart:[7]

Monday	May 3, 1920	. . . .	216 Negro migrants
Tuesday	May 4, 1920	. . . .	245
Wednesday	May 5, 1920	. . . .	215
Thursday	May 6, 1920	. . . .	274
Friday	May 7, 1920	. . . .	272
Saturday	May 8, 1920	. . . .	217
Sunday	May 9, 1920	. . . .	371

1,809

The continuous flow of migrants to Detroit greatly disrupted the demographic balance of the city, as we can see from the comparison of age/sex pyramids for 1900 and 1920 (see figure 12.1). Detroit in 1900 still had a balanced demographic structure, close to that of the entire country, with children under ten as the largest age group, forming the base of the pyramid. The only imbalance in 1900 was caused by a slight excess of females aged twenty to twenty-five, reflecting the arrival of many young women from Canada and the neighboring countryside who came to Detroit to work as servants. Writing in the 1890s, the demographer Adna Weber imputed this superfluity of females in cities to the higher mortality rate among males both at birth but also as adults, a difference which he attributed to their occupations and to the "vice, crime and excesses of various

6. Ibid., 2:47–49.
7. Forrester B. Washington, "The Negro in Detroit: A Survey of the Conditions of a Negro Group in a Northern Industrial Center during the War Prosperity Period" (Detroit, 1920), chap. 5, part A of section, "The Historical Background of the Negro in Detroit from 1800 to 1920," BHC.

FIG. 12.1

Age and Sex Composition

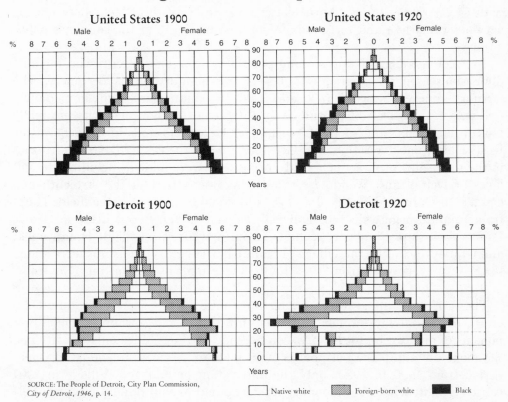

SOURCE: The People of Detroit, City Plan Commission,
City of Detroit, 1946, p. 14.

☐ Native white   ▨ Foreign-born white   ■ Black

kinds which shorten life."[8] The male to female ratio for Detroit in 1900 was indeed 94.7 men for every 100 women, but apart from this relatively minor imbalance, Detroit was a city of families (see figure 12.1).

In 1920, however, markedly fewer children and adolescents lived in the city than did adults between twenty and thirty-five years of age. The largest excess was among male industrial workers: males in the twenty-five to twenty-nine age group made up 8% of Detroit's population, which can be compared with 4.5% in the country at large in 1920. In contrast, male children between ten and fourteen made up only 3.5% of Detroit's population, a smaller percentage than their 5% in 1900 Detroit or 5% in the nation in 1920. In 1920, the male

8. Adna Ferrin Weber, *The Growth of Cities in the Nineteenth Century: A Study in Statistics* (Ithaca, N.Y.: Cornell University Press, 1967), pp. 285–300; U.S., Department of Commerce, Bureau of the Census, *Fourteenth Census*, 2:115–16, 129; City Plan Commission, *The People of Detroit*, pp. 12, 14–15.

to female ratio of 119.1 men for every 100 women in Detroit marked a distinct change from 1900 and reflected this new influx of male industrial workers. Not surprisingly, the ratio was 137 for Blacks and 140.7 for foreign-born whites, with 54.2% of the foreign-born whites and 50.1% of the Blacks between the ages of twenty-five and forty-four in contrast to 39.4% of the country's population.[9]

To accommodate this burgeoning population, the city grew to considerable dimensions as it systematically annexed new territory on its periphery. The territory annexed between 1880 and 1900 was platted and built immediately (see map 5.2), as Detroit continued its outward expansion. The city gradually took in larger portions of the townships of Greenfield and Springwells in the west, Hamtramck, Gratiot, and Grosse Pointe in the east. In 1905, territories in the townships of Greenfield and Springwells were added, including the villages of Delray and Woodmere, which became a part of the sixteenth and eighteenth wards of the city. In 1907, additional territory in Greenfield, Hamtramck, and Springwells was annexed, as well as Fairview Village in Grosse Pointe Township. Similarly, sections of Springwells, Greenfield, Hamtramck, and Gratiot (including the village of Saint Clair Heights) townships were added to the city every year from 1915 to 1918 (see map of Detroit and Environs, p. 4).[10]

The process of integrating new territory into the city went smoothly. Generally, but not always, annexation was ratified by a referendum in which proponents of annexation to the city won by wide margins, since only the city had the money to equip the peripheries with modern services. In the twenty-year period from 1900 to 1920, only the annexation of Fairview Village in 1907 caused a fight, when the saloonkeepers, who had to shut down their profitable slot machines after the village became a part of the city, opposed the annexation bill. Fairview was badly in need of a sewer system, however, which, at an estimated installation cost of $260,000, the villagers could not afford; the city health commissioner thus advised the city that the sewerage work and hence annexation of the village was necessary "to preserve the health of the citizens of Detroit."[11]

Most of this annexed area was farmland. Nine-tenths of Gratiot, Hamtramck, and Greenfield townships were rural, where the only platted residential areas

9. Bureau of the Census, *Fourteenth Census*, 2:293, 365.
10. Michigan, *Local Acts of the Legislature of the State of Michigan, Passed at the Regular Session of 1905* (Lansing, 1905), pp. 1068–73, 1144; *Regular Session of 1907*, pp. 355–58, 940–42; *Regular Session of 1913*, pp. 55–56; *Regular Session of 1917*, pp. 32–41; *Regular Session of 1919*, pp. 43–44. Jon C. Teaford, *City and Suburb: The Political Fragmentation of Metropolitan America, 1850–1970* (Baltimore: Johns Hopkins University Press, 1979), pp. 62, 87.
11. *Detroit Free Press*, 27, 28 March, 1 May 1907.

were immediately adjacent to the city limits. Many of these border lots were already built upon and were simply awaiting their incorporation into the city; it was difficult to say where Detroit really ended and where the suburbs began.

Despite the trend toward annexation, however, distinct territories in and around Detroit were well populated and important economically, but not part of the city proper. Fifty-five percent of the 171,475 census metropolitan district inhabitants were concentrated in two independent cities within the city of Detroit: Hamtramck, which had grown from a village of a few hundred in 1900 to a city of 48,615 around the Dodge Plant in 1920, and Highland Park, which had similarly grown to a city of 46,499 around the Ford Motor Company.[12] These cities, built around industrial giants, were better off with their independent government, free from Detroit's taxes and directly controlled by industrial interests. In one instance, James Couzens, vice president of Ford Motor Company, took the city of Detroit to court and won permission to empty Highland Park sewerage into Detroit's sewer system; it was not until Couzens himself became mayor of Detroit in 1918 that he discovered he had created a major problem for the city.[13] Other independent production suburbs included the southern section of Springwells Township, site of Ford's River Rouge Plant, which was to become the major industrial complex of the 1920s. Springwells was the most diversified suburban area of 1920 Detroit; it had working-class houses near the Ford plant, large brick-making concerns (in operation since the 1890s), and farms throughout the township.[14]

The only exclusively upper-class residential suburbs in 1920 were the Grosse Pointe villages, along the river at the eastern tip of the city. As Detroit's city directory for 1920 proudly stated, subdivisions in Grosse Pointe Park Village "are of the highest class with high restrictions, which will make the village of Grosse Pointe Park the beauty spot of all the property adjacent to the city of Detroit."[15]

With the uninterrupted flow of immigrants, even these vast tracts of added territory did not suffice to keep Detroit a low-density city. The number of newly built buildings, having reached an all-time high of 16,489 in 1916, went down to 12,109 in 1917 and to 7,011 in 1918. Although the figure rose again to 21,473 in 1919, the wartime decline in housing construction added to the crowding caused by increasing immigration.[16] While half of Detroit within the city limits

12. Bureau of the Census, *Fourteenth Census,* 2:66.

13. John M. T. Chavis, "James Couzens: Mayor of Detroit, 1919–1922" (Ph.D. diss., Michigan State University, 1970), p. 15.

14. G. William Baist, *Real Estate Atlas of Surveys of Detroit and Suburbs,* 2 vols. (Philadelphia, 1918).

15. Thomas L. Munger, *Detroit Today* (Detroit: R. L. Polk & Co., 1921), p. 57.

16. Kocher, "Growth of Detroit," p. 77.

was almost empty in 1880 and the highest density—at the center—was on the order of 55 people per acre, in 1920 the city was completely occupied, and densities of about 50 people per acre were common also on the city's peripheries (see map 12.1).[17] In the central part of the city, west-side districts often had densities of 100 people per acre, and some sections even held up to 200. The east side had the highest density of the city, with between 100 and 200 people per acre along Gratiot, between 200 and 300 in several residential districts, and a pocket of over 300 people per acre near the downtown area. In 1918, Black sociologist George Haynes visited this high-density section where many Blacks lived and reported that some rooms were so crowded that "the most convenient way to dress was to stand in the middle of the bed."[18] Detroit in 1920, then, was exhibiting the crowded districts which had been typical of sections of New York and Chicago for decades but which had not formed in Detroit until the great transformation of the city's terrain into a total industrial landscape.

THE TOTAL INDUSTRIAL LANDSCAPE

Detroit's spectacular rise to prominence on the industrial scene was a direct result of the automobile industry. In 1900 Detroit produced only 4,192 passenger cars (see chap. 5), but twenty years later the motor city produced 1,905,560 passenger cars and 321,789 trucks. Detroit, which had employed 17% of the auto workers, nationwide, in 1904, gave work to 47% in 1914. Between 1909 and 1914, 85% of the national growth in the automobile industry occurred in Detroit.[19]

At the turn of the century, Detroit's auto plants were usually operated by small-scale designers and assemblers rather than manufacturers, and they relied for parts on a complex of local suppliers. Relatively little capital was involved in the creation of an auto plant; Ford, for example, began production with only $28,000. But by 1920 a score of small companies had folded, and automobile production was concentrated in the larger manufacturing companies that had survived. Lincoln, for example, spent $6,000,000 in tools and machinery after

17. Maps of the 1920 census enumeration districts are available in the National Archives, Washington, D.C., but they are too damaged to be useful. The archives hold, however, a list of Detroit's 659 enumeration districts, with descriptions of their exact boundaries and reports of their population totals. Preparing the density map was then just a matter of tracing boundaries on a good city map, computing areas and then tabulating the density of each enumeration district.

18. George Edmund Haynes, *Negro Newcomers in Detroit, Michigan: A Challenge to Christian Statesmanship; A Preliminary Survey* (New York: Home Missions Council, 1918; Arno Press and the New York Times, 1969), p. 21.

19. Kocher, "Growth of Detroit," p. 81; Ticknor, "Motor City," p. 92; Melvin G. Holli, "The Impact of Automobile Manufacturing upon Detroit," *Detroit in Perspective: A Journal of Regional History* 2 (Spring 1976): 176–88.

World War I before producing a single car.[20] In 1920 the Detroit Board of Commerce reported that there were 29 distinct automobile companies in the Detroit district, manufacturing 30 different makes of passenger cars, trucks, and tractors; 120 companies for parts and accessories; and, of course, scores of small shops that worked on contract, making parts, stampings, castings, and forgings.[21]

The automobile plants employed about 135,000 workers in 1920. Ford alone employed 40,000 workers, his enormous success stemming from the popularity of the Model T. Ford produced only 248,000 cars in 1914, but the figure rose to over two million cars and trucks in 1923, almost half of Detroit's total production at that time, when Ford's Highland Park Plant maintained an average of 62,000 production workers. General Motors, the merger by William Durant of a number of independent companies including Buick, Cadillac, Olds, and Chevrolet, was only partially based in Detroit, but established its headquarters in the city and employed about 12% of the city's auto workers in 1920. Other major employers in 1920 were Studebaker (the Indiana-based corporation which bought EMF), Hudson, Packard, Maxwell, and Dodge. Walter P. Chrysler, the former president of Buick and the first vice-president of General Motors, merged Maxwell and Dodge in 1923 to form the nucleus of the Chrysler Corporation.[22]

The newly created automobile industry provided a natural base for the United States' massive effort in war industrialization: Lincoln, Ford, Dodge, and Packard manufactured the Liberty airplane motors; Ford built Eagle boats in the new River Rouge Plant; Dodge Brothers built recoil mechanisms for French howitzers; and the Fisher Body Company assembled airplanes. In addition, scores of smaller Detroit factories produced shells and ammunitions, as well as army trucks.[23]

Under the impetus of such industrial growth, Detroit experienced a complete reordering of production techniques. New automobile plants often contained more than a million square feet of floor space on sites of fifty acres or more. Albert Kahn, the leading industrial architect of the time, first designed the Packard Plant on East Grand Boulevard in 1903. Built of reinforced concrete

20. Ticknor, "Motor City," pp. 98–99, 105, 110; John B. Rae, *American Automobile Manufacturers: The First Forty Years* (Phildelphia: Chilton Co., 1959), pp. 128–49.

21. Munger, *Detroit and World Trade*, p. 57.

22. Sydney Fine, *The Automobile under the Blue Eagle: Labor, Management, and the Automobile Manufacturing Code* (Ann Arbor: University of Michigan Press, 1963), pp. 2–4; Munger, *Detroit and World Trade*, p. 57; Donald F. Davis, "Studebaker Stumbles into Detroit," *Detroit in Perspective: A Journal of Regional History* 4 (Fall 1979): 16–35.

23. Munger, *Detroit and World Trade*, pp. 28–30.

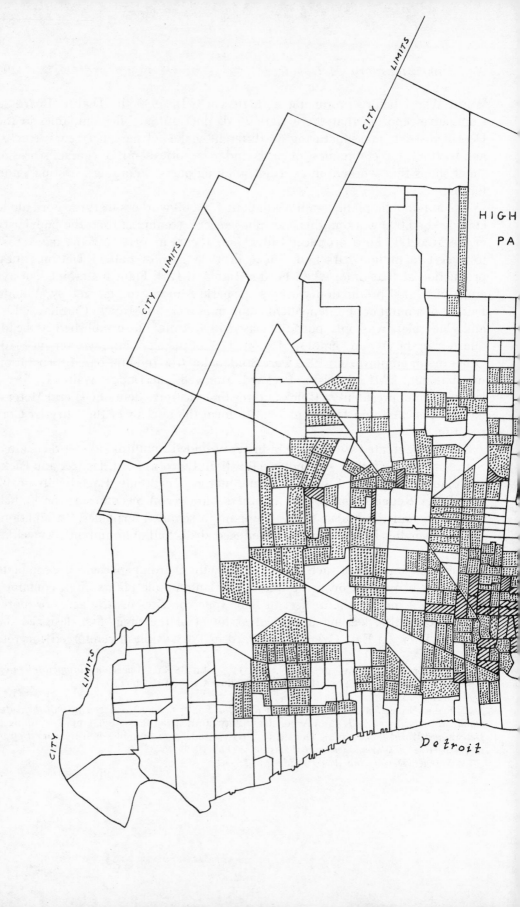

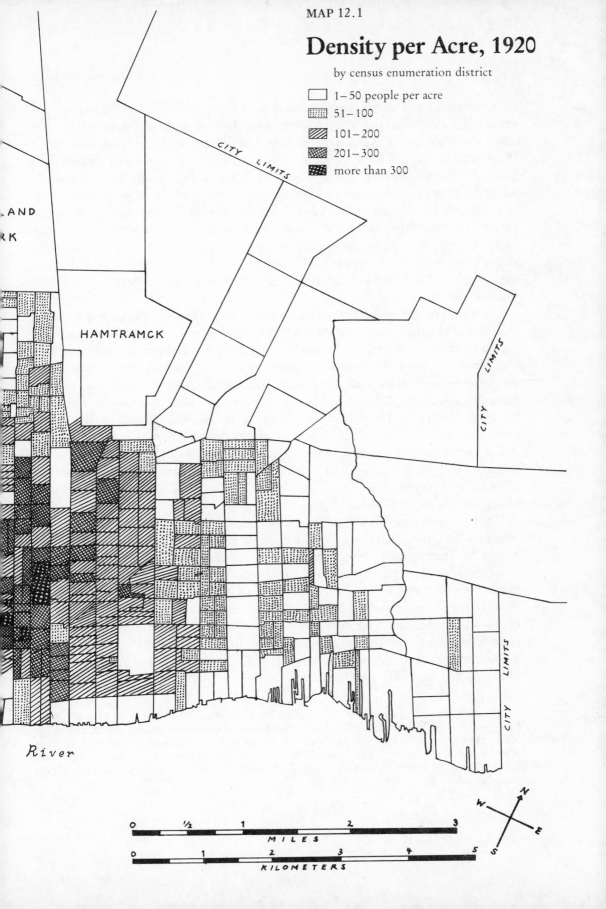

MAP 12.1

Density per Acre, 1920

by census enumeration district

☐	1–50 people per acre
▦	51–100
▨	101–200
▩	201–300
▦	more than 300

CITY LIMITS

CITY LIMITS

HAMTRAMCK

...AND ...RK

CITY LIMITS

CITY LIMITS

River

0	½	1	2	3

MILES

0	1	2	3	4	5

KILOMETERS

N
W E
S

to limit the danger of fire and designed with vast windows and widely spaced supporting columns, the plant was a large hollow square conceived for the assembly line process. Kahn also built the Ford Highland Park Plant, the Dodge Plant, the Cadillac Plant, and the new Ford River Rouge Plant designed to build the Eagle boats. These new plants, coupled with production on a scale never achieved before, required major restructuring of work shifts and intensified industrial discipline. As labor historian David Montgomery notes, "the process of converting skilled workers into toolmakers or supervisors, so that production itself could be assigned to untrained operatives, performing minutely subdivided tasks, was carried to its ultimate development in Ford's Highland Park plant."[24] Ford could claim in 1922 that 85% of his labor force required less than two weeks of training.

Locating the automobile factories on the map of Detroit, together with other factories of the transportation industry (tires and wheels, shipbuilding, railroad cars, airplanes—see map 12.2), shows that Detroit's industrial landscape was organized in semicircular districts, with variations according to periods of development and type of industry. A large number of the first automobile plants, basically assembly plants, were located along the riverfront and the tracks of the inner Belt Line. These first automobile factories, rather small in size, made use of the existing physical equipment as well as the proximity to many suppliers. A few larger factories were also built within or near the old industrial crescent: Studebaker and Timken Detroit Axle on the riverfront, Studebaker at the Milwaukee Junction near American Car and Foundry, Cadillac and Northway along the Michigan Central.

One by one, however, the larger factories established themselves beyond the limits of the inner Belt Line: Packard on Grand Boulevard East, Dodge and Briggs in Hamtramck, Hupp in between Packard and Dodge. Some of the plants were built even farther away, on the peripheries, where land values and taxes were low and where there was room to expand. Lincoln and the Kelsey Wheel Company appeared on the Pere Marquette and other secondary railroads of the west side, and four concentrations of factories developed on the outer railway system of the Detroit terminal railroad, in a half-circle about six miles away from city hall: one on the far east side, close to Jefferson Avenue, where Hudson, Continental, and Chalmers built new plants immediately after the

24. David Montgomery, *Workers' Control in America: Studies in the History of Work, Technology, and Labor Struggles* (Cambridge: Cambridge University Press, 1979), p. 119; Alfred D. Chandler, Jr., *The Visible Hand: The Managerial Revolution in American Business* (Cambridge, Mass.: Harvard University Press, 1977), p. 280; Daniel Nelson, *Managers and Workers: Origins of the New Factory System in the United States, 1880–1920* (Madison: University of Wisconsin Press, 1975) p. 16, 24–25; W. Hawkins Ferry, *The Buildings of Detroit: A History* (Detroit: Wayne State University Press, 1968), pp. 178–88.

railway was put through; Ford's Highland Park Plant at the center; Paige and Savon at the extreme west; and of course the new River Rouge complex, which Ford built for manufacturing the Eagle boats (see map 12.2).

Metalwork factories, industrial goods factories, and plants specialized in chemicals, fuels, and construction materials also show the new distribution of factories between the old industrial crescent and the outer areas, although the deconcentration pattern is less obvious in these industries than in the transportation sector. Only a handful of metalwork factories were located along Gratiot on the east side. Most were spread along the riverfront, a site which the large stove works and foundries (Michigan Stove Works, Detroit Stove Works, Peninsular Stove Works) had established in the 1870s. Many factories also settled on the railroad lines that encircled the 1880 city limits, along the Michigan Central on the west (Buhl Stamping, Railway Steel), at the Milwaukee Junction (Art Stove Works), and along the tracks of the Michigan Central near Grand Boulevard East. But metalworks proliferated beyond the boundaries of the 1880 city. There was a movement of factories down the river around and beyond Fort Wayne, Delray Village, and toward River Rouge, as indicated by the location of Michigan Copper and Brass and Michigan Malleable. In the northeast, factories such as Russel Wheel and Foundry and Ajax Pattern Works settled into the industrial enclave of Hamtramck; in the east, some factories (like Michigan Stamping Company) established along the outermost recent railroad line encircling the city, the Detroit Terminal Railroad.

Among industrial goods, while Burroughs Business Machines and Buhl Malleable were located at different points on the old industrial crescent, Detroit Sulphite Pulp and Paper Company was near the River Rouge, Detroit Seamless Steel Tube Company on the western side of the Detroit Terminal Railroad, and American Motor Castings Company and Detroit Wire Spring Company along Hamtramck city limits. The location of chemicals, fuels, and construction shows a similar pattern of some expansion into newer industrial areas; the two giant concerns of the drug industry, Parke, Davis and Company (by then the largest drug company in the world) and Frederick Stearns, had retained their sites along the riverfront within the 1880 city limits, but the Solvay Process was at the foot of Fort Wayne and the Michigan Carbon Works on the River Rouge, while Edison Illuminating Company was at the eastern terminal of the Detroit Terminal Railroad, near the intersection of the city limits and the river (see maps 12.3–12.5).

Only the manufacturers of consumer goods—food products, furniture, tobacco, publications, and miscellaneous products such as soap, leather goods, and woodwork—were still located primarily in the inner city (see map 12.6). Some were heavily concentrated at the city center itself; others followed the

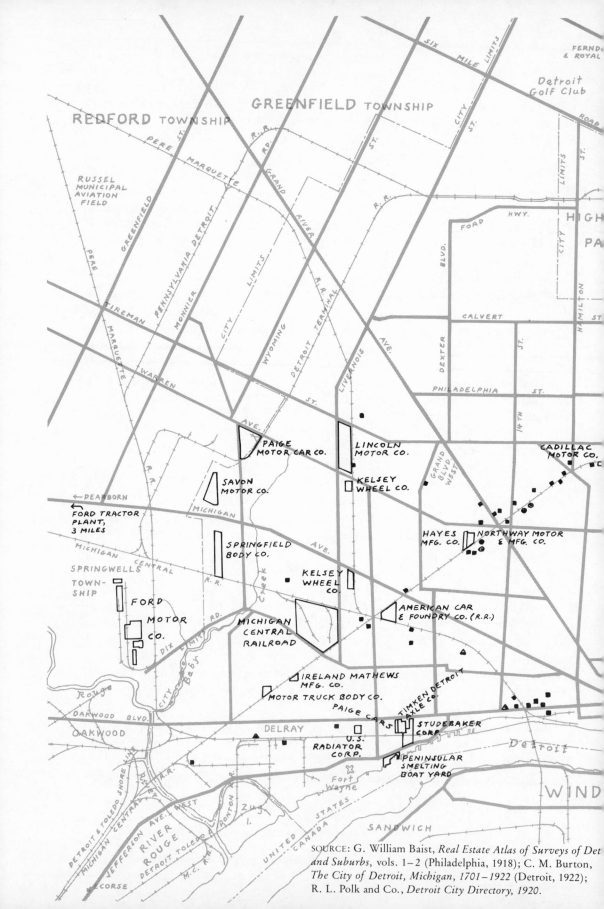

SOURCE: G. William Baist, *Real Estate Atlas of Surveys of Det* and *Suburbs*, vols. 1–2 (Philadelphia, 1918); C. M. Burton, *The City of Detroit, Michigan, 1701–1922* (Detroit, 1922); R. L. Polk and Co., *Detroit City Directory, 1920.*

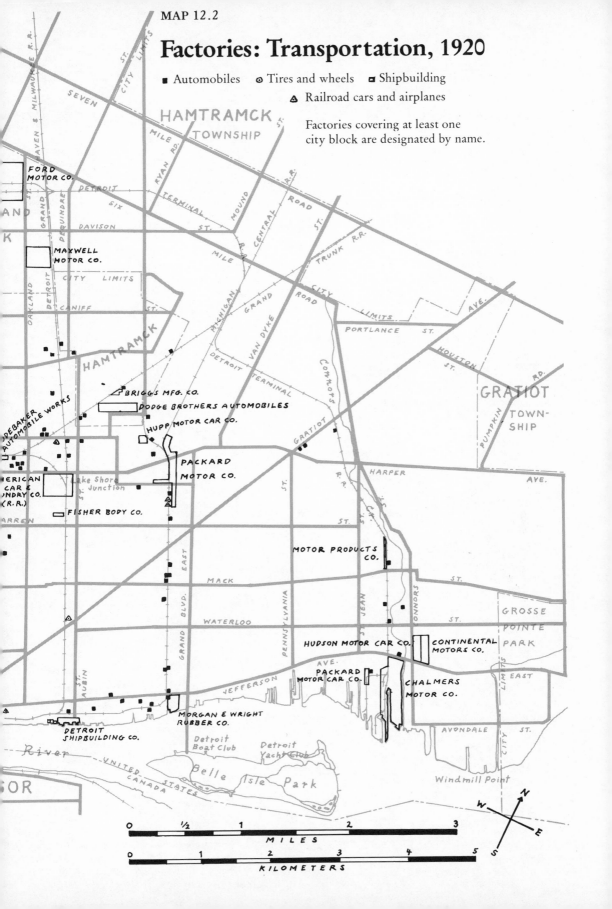

MAP 12.2

Factories: Transportation, 1920

■ Automobiles   ⊙ Tires and wheels   ⊡ Shipbuilding

△ Railroad cars and airplanes

Factories covering at least one
city block are designated by name.

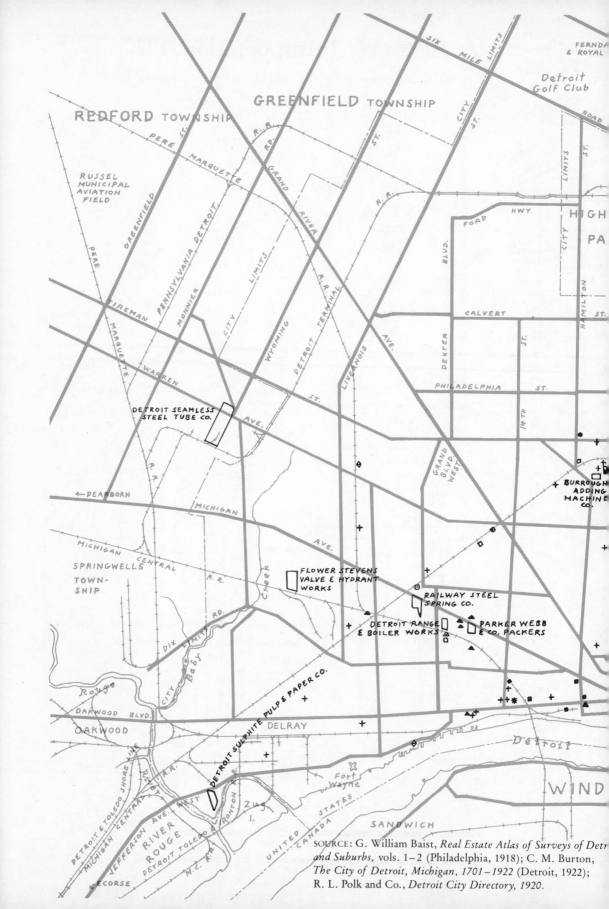

SOURCE: G. William Baist, *Real Estate Atlas of Surveys of Detr* *and Suburbs*, vols. 1–2 (Philadelphia, 1918); C. M. Burton, *The City of Detroit, Michigan, 1701–1922* (Detroit, 1922); R. L. Polk and Co., *Detroit City Directory, 1920*.

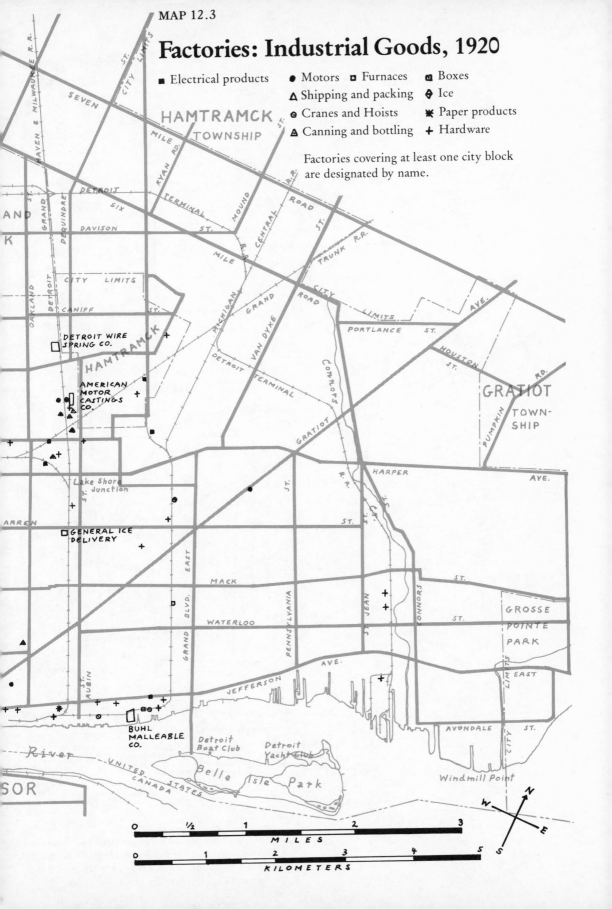

MAP 12.3

Factories: Industrial Goods, 1920

■ Electrical products   ● Motors   ▫ Furnaces   ▣ Boxes

▲ Shipping and packing   ◈ Ice

◉ Cranes and Hoists   ✳ Paper products

△ Canning and bottling   ✛ Hardware

Factories covering at least one city block
are designated by name.

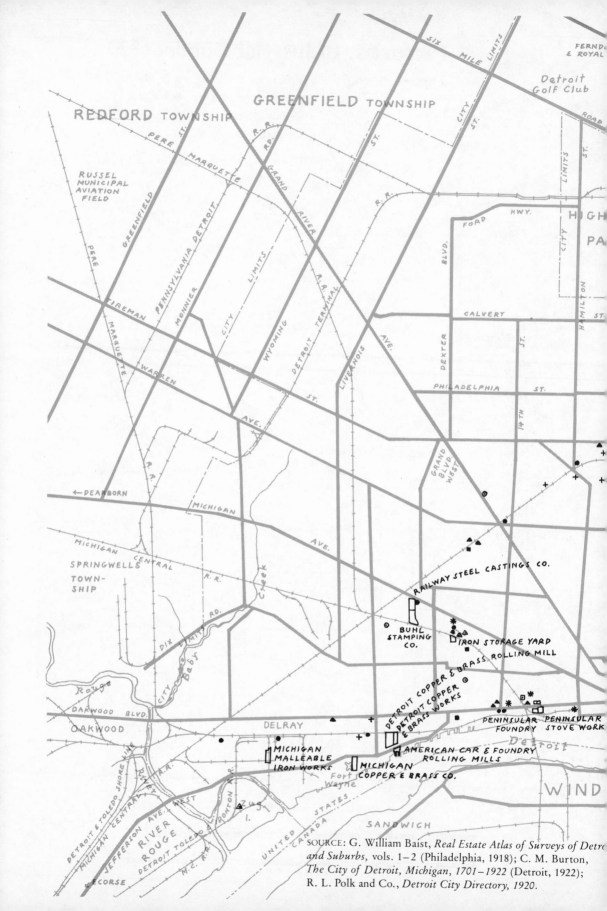

SOURCE: G. William Baist, *Real Estate Atlas of Surveys of Detroit and Suburbs*, vols. 1–2 (Philadelphia, 1918); C. M. Burton, *The City of Detroit, Michigan, 1701–1922* (Detroit, 1922); R. L. Polk and Co., *Detroit City Directory, 1920*.

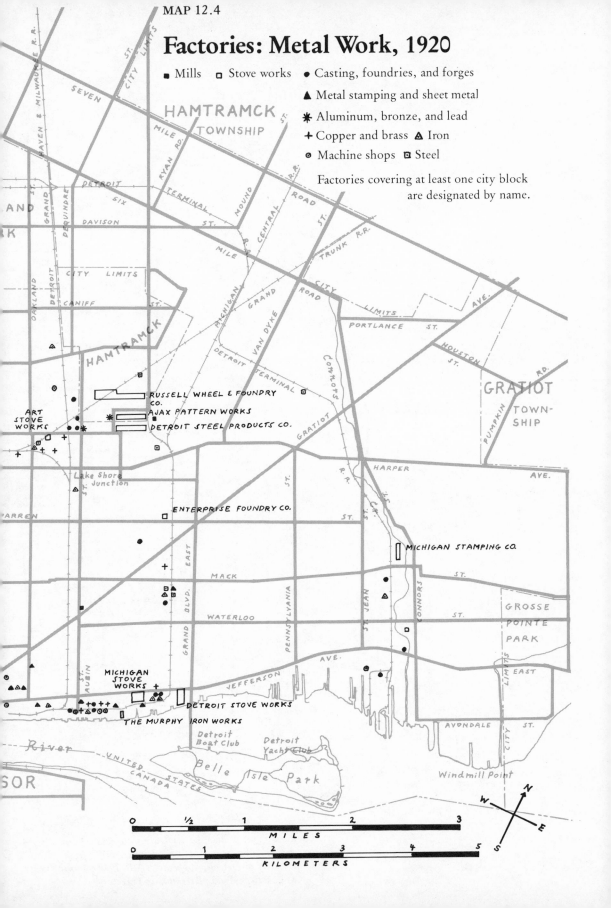

MAP 12.4

Factories: Metal Work, 1920

- ■ Mills □ Stove works • Casting, foundries, and forges
- ▲ Metal stamping and sheet metal
- ✳ Aluminum, bronze, and lead
- + Copper and brass ▲ Iron
- ⊙ Machine shops ▣ Steel

Factories covering at least one city block
are designated by name.

RUSSELL WHEEL & FOUNDRY CO.

AJAX PATTERN WORKS

DETROIT STEEL PRODUCTS CO.

ART STOVE WORKS

ENTERPRISE FOUNDRY CO.

MICHIGAN STAMPING CO.

MICHIGAN STOVE WORKS

DETROIT STOVE WORKS

THE MURPHY IRON WORKS

GRATIOT TOWNSHIP

GROSSE POINTE PARK

Detroit Boat Club

Detroit Yacht Club

Belle Isle Park

Windmill Point

River

UNITED STATES
CANADA

| 0 | 1/2 | 1 | | 2 | | 3 |
MILES

| 0 | | 1 | | 2 | | 3 | | 4 | | 5 |
KILOMETERS

N
W   E
S

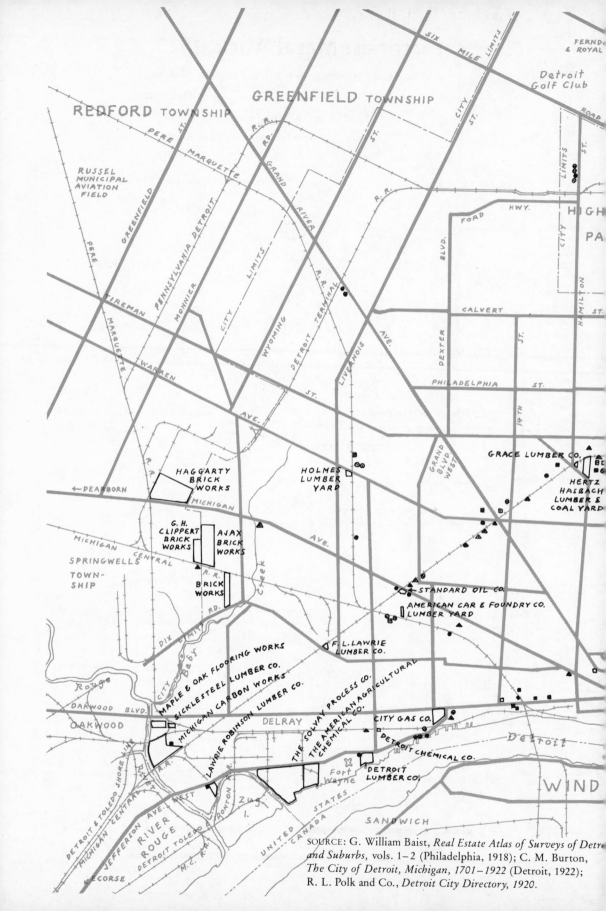

SOURCE: G. William Baist, *Real Estate Atlas of Surveys of Detroit and Suburbs,* vols. 1–2 (Philadelphia, 1918); C. M. Burton, *The City of Detroit, Michigan, 1701–1922* (Detroit, 1922); R. L. Polk and Co., *Detroit City Directory, 1920.*

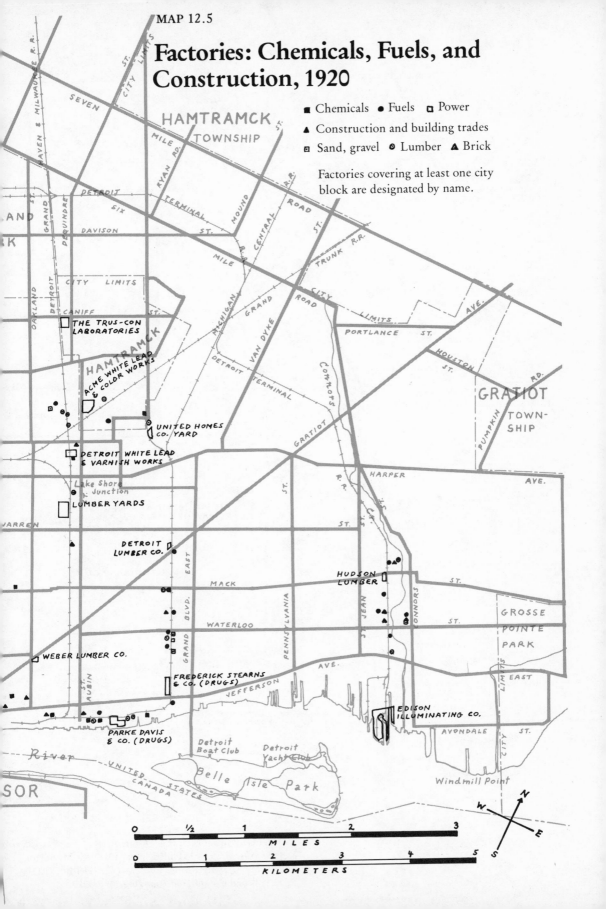

MAP 12.5

Factories: Chemicals, Fuels, and Construction, 1920

■ Chemicals ● Fuels ▫ Power
▲ Construction and building trades
▣ Sand, gravel ◉ Lumber ▲ Brick

Factories covering at least one city block are designated by name.

REDFORD TOWNSHIP

GREENFIELD TOWNSHIP

Detroit
Golf Club

FERNDA
& ROYAL

RUSSEL
MUNICIPAL
AVIATION
FIELD

HIGH
PA

SPRINGWELLS
TOWN-
SHIP

THE WILLIAMS PICKLE
& PRESERVATIVE FACTORY

AMERICAN MALTING
WORKS

CORCORAN LAMP CO.

OAKWOOD

DELRAY

SCOTTEN & CO.
TOBACCO WORKS

Fort
Wayne

WIND

SANDWICH

SOURCE: G. William Baist, *Real Estate Atlas of Surveys of Detro
and Suburbs*, vols. 1–2 (Philadelphia, 1918); C. M. Burton,
The City of Detroit, Michigan, 1701–1922 (Detroit, 1922);
R. L. Polk and Co., *Detroit City Directory, 1920.*

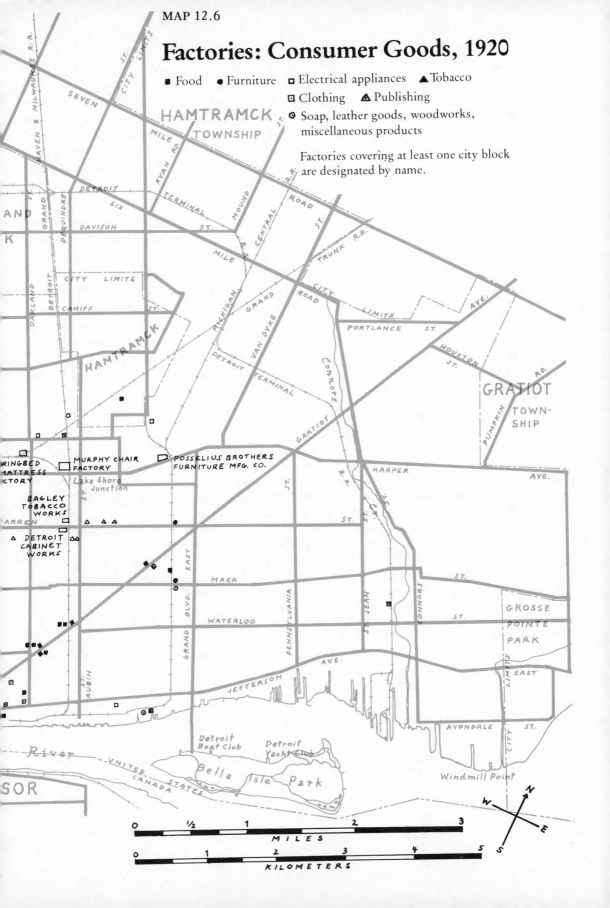

MAP 12.6

Factories: Consumer Goods, 1920

■ Food   ● Furniture   ▫ Electrical appliances   ▲ Tobacco
▣ Clothing   ◬ Publishing
◉ Soap, leather goods, woodworks, miscellaneous products

Factories covering at least one city block
are designated by name.

riverfront on the east and west sides, as far west as the Scotten and Company Tobacco Works. Clothing firms, tobacco firms, and food factories also penetrated the city's interior along the main avenues (Michigan Avenue, Grand River, and Gratiot), while the larger factories encircled the 1880 city limits, along the tracks of the Michigan Central Railroad, and the Milwaukee Railroad Junction on the east side (Murphy Chair Factory, Springbed and Mattress Factory, Bagley Tobacco Works, and Detroit Cabinet Works).

With all these industries combined, the spread of factories over Detroit and their density along main axes, in the industrial crescent, and along the concentric circles of the new railroad axes is simply staggering; only the major factories represented in land-use atlases are reproduced on these maps, but scores of small industrial shops added to the existing densities or filled in the blank spaces. In 1920, although industrial growth had followed the directions set forth by nineteenth-century industrialization, the density of factories was such that the city appeared to have a totally industrial landscape; the relative separation of the immigrant neighborhood from large industrial work sites which still existed in the late nineteenth century had simply disappeared. The 1920/21 edition of the Detroit city directory echoed the general opinion that:

> A peculiar situation has developed in Detroit during the last decade with regard to the location of industries throughout the city. There are no well-defined factory districts, such as are found in most cities. Instead the plants are to be found in every section. The rapid increase in population since 1910 has caused the city to spread out, so the many large plants, which only a few years ago were located far outside the city limits, now are found in the center of some otherwise pleasant residence district, or even far downtown in the neighborhood of office buildings, shops and theaters. The railroads in nearly every case penetrate close to the center of the city, coming from all directions, and the factories naturally have retained their sites along these tracks. Even the Detroit Terminal Railroad makes a circle that is from one to five miles inside the city limits.[25]

Detroit's growth into an industrial giant and the subsequent extension of the city's space also fostered a shift from a city with one center only—around city hall, at the intersection of Woodward Avenue and the river—to a modern multiple-nucleus city. In the first two decades of the twentieth century, skyscrapers took over parts of the old city center. The Hotel Pontchartrain, where most important executives met, was erected on the site of the old Russell House in 1907. D. H. Burnham built the Ford Building in 1909 and the Dime Building

---

25. Munger, *Detroit Today*, p. 37; Jerome Gale Thomas, "The City of Detroit: A Study in Urban Geography" (Ph.D. diss., University of Michigan, 1928), pp. 116–20.

in 1910 in the Chicago tradition; and Albert Kahn, who built large auto plants around the city, built the Detroit News Building and the Detroit Athletic Club downtown. Soon, however, the city's tertiary functions were in part relocated, following a movement similar to that of the factories. It was along Grand Boulevard, in the geographic center of the new metropolis, that General Motors established its large four-wing headquarters which Albert Kahn completed in 1922, soon to be followed by the Fisher Building. And it was on Woodward Avenue, midway between the old downtown and the new tertiary center of the boulevard, that the city began to create its new cultural center when architect Cass Gilbert completed the Detroit Public Library in 1921.[26]

With its scores of factories, its centers of tertiary activities, its port and railroad terminals, its well-separated production and consumption suburbs, its giant territory, and its diverse population, Detroit in 1920 had become a symbol of urban-industrial America.

THE MELTING POT

Detroit's industrialization fostered drastic changes in the city's physical landscape and population distribution, but it affected even more profoundly the daily life of every Detroit citizen. In human terms, Detroit was a place where— more than in any other place in the United States—the industrial society was changing the way people lived. There were 495 man-hours needed to build an automobile in 1920, and the definition of a person's workday, family life, and hopes rested very much on what specific task of this complex process he or she could perform.[27] Naturally, the way in which Detroit grew into America's third industrial center in a span of twenty years and the social model envisioned by the industrialists were closely related. Industrialists were staunch advocates of a new social order which they tried to promote through large programs of welfare capitalism. On the one hand, they tried to put some order in the metropolis and insure better productivity; on the other, they dreamed of a new society in which everybody would share the same values, so they began an all-out effort to promote a new ideology—the melting pot—using an appropriate industrial image popularized by Israel Zangwill's 1908 Broadway play.[28] They defined an American system which struck a balance of moral qualities, orderly work, and prosperity, and joined under the banner of "Americanization"— through language classes, industrial education, and training in citizenship—to unify a variegated labor force. When World War I broke out, industrialists had

26. Ferry, *The Buildings of Detroit*, pp. 240, 242; Kocher, "Growth of Detroit," pp. 56, 65–66.
27. City Plan Commission, *The Economic Base of Detroit*, p. 8.
28. John Higham, *Send These to Me: Jews and Other Immigrants in Urban America* (New York: Atheneum, 1975), pp. 203, 238–39.

a chance to combine their own self-interests with the interest of America at large, since the war simultaneously accelerated Detroit's industrialization and applied pressures for national allegiance that supposed a single American identity. The industrialists' programs, initially aimed at controlling workers, now became phrased in terms of national duty.[29]

The primary condition necessary for Detroit's employers to impose their views successfully was freedom from pressures from workers' organizations, and Detroit justly acquired the reputation of being the "graveyard of organizers."[30] The Employers' Association, an organization created in part under the leadership of Henry Leland, founder of Cadillac, effectively maintained the open shop. The automobile industry provides a major case in point. The American Federation of Labor's policy of unionizing only skilled workers and only in their traditional trades prevented their forming a comprehensive auto workers' union. In 1918, the Carriage, Wagon, and Automobile Workers' International Union, which attempted to form such a comprehensive union, was suspended from the American Federation of Labor because the union refused to abide by the federation's rule. But the union persisted in taking membership away from skilled unions in the automobile industry and refused to drop the word "automobile" from its name. The union reorganized under the name of the United Automobile, Aircraft, and Vehicle Workers of America (more generally known as Auto Workers' Union) and was dedicated to the principle of industrial unionism as opposed to the federation craft unionism; but its 1919 membership in Detroit did not exceed 7,000 out of some 200,000 auto workers. In turn, the International Association of Machinists, the logical group in the American Federation of Labor to interest itself in the unionization of auto workers, gained most of its membership in the metal-trades branches of the automobile industry. As late as 1933, the American Federation of Labor had unionized only a few craftsmen in the automobile industry (patternmakers, molders, and metal polishers) and had failed entirely to unionize the unskilled and semiskilled production workers. More radical unions also failed in Detroit; the Industrial Workers of the World had conducted a major offensive in 1913 among auto workers by leading 6,000 workers to strike at Studebaker, but the strike failed and the union was left with only 200 members. The IWW was suppressed during the war and many of its members defected to the new communist parties in 1919, leaving only a handful of Wobblies still distributing literature among striking yardmen in 1919. Similarly, the Workers' International Industrial Union (which grew out of a

29. John Higham, *Strangers in the Land: Patterns of American Nativism, 1865–1925* (New Brunswick, N.J.: Rutgers University Press, 1955), pp. 234–63; Howard C. Hill, "The Americanization Movement," *American Journal of Sociology* 24 (May, 1919): 609–42.
    30. Fine, *The Automobile under the Blue Eagle*, p. 21.

split within the IWW in 1908) published the monthly *Industrial Union News*
and the *First of May Magazine* from Hamtramck to campaign for one great
industrial union, but had only five small locals in Detroit in 1915.[31]

Since laborers had no union to negotiate for them, management took free rein
in reorganizing both factories and urban life. The Ford Motor Company led
the way in defining large programs of welfare capitalism aimed at improving
productivity and at transforming American society. The immediate problem
was practical: as thousands of workers passed through the city, it became
increasingly difficult for employers to maintain a stable labor force. Between
50,000 and 60,000 workers passed through Ford's employment office in 1913
when the number of employees was only 13,600; the company needed to hire
between 40% and 60% of its labor force every month just to maintain it. These
workers composed the diverse and ever changing work force supposed to perform methodical work on the assembly line in a coordinated and efficient fashion. When Henry Ford announced on 12 January 1914 that during the ensuing
year the company would share $10,000,000 of its profits with employees through
a pay plan of five dollars a day, part of it given as wage and part of it as profit
sharing, a complete reorganization of Ford's personnel was at stake. To be
eligible for the profit-sharing program workers not only had to perform well on
the job but also had to make a commitment to the community. According to
the company's own claim, "The idea Mr. Ford had in mind was to help the
men to a LIFE—not a mere LIVING."[32] The company selected the workers who
could earn the extra money according to certain criteria, sometimes specific,
more often vague, but which combined to produce a definition of the melting
pot by American industrialists. The first condition was, of course, to speak
English. Ford set up an English school and made attendance compulsory. As
a company spokesman clearly stated:

31. Robert W. Dunn, *Labor and Automobiles* (New York: International Publishers, 1929), pp.
183–84; Fred Yonce, "The Big Red Scare in Detroit, 1919–1920" (1963, in the possession of
Sidney Fine, University of Michigan), pp. 13–16; Roger Keeran, *The Communist Party and the
Auto Workers Unions* (Bloomington: Indiana University Press, 1980), p. 29; Joyce Shaw Peterson,
"A Social History of Automobile Workers before Unionization, 1900–1933" (Ph.D. diss., Uni-
versity of Wisconsin, 1976), pp. 24, 223–92.

32. Jonathan Schwartz, "Henry Ford's Melting Pot," in *Ethnic Groups in the City: Culture,
Institutions, and Power*, ed. Otto Feinstein (Lexington, Mass.: Heath Lexington Books, D.C.
Heath & Co., 1971), pp. 191–98; Stephen Meyer, "Adapting the Immigrant to the Line: Amer-
icanization in the Ford Factory, 1914–1921," *Journal of Social History* 14 (Fall 1980): 69; idem,
*The Five Dollar Day: Labor Management and Social Control in the Ford Motor Company,
1908–1921* (Albany: State University of New York Press, 1981); John R. Lee, "The So-Called
Profit Sharing System in the Ford Plant," *Annals of the American Academy of Political and Social
Science* 65 (May 1916): 302–9; Ford Motor Company, *Ford Factory Facts* (Detroit: Ford Motor
Co., 1915), pp. 42, 47–51.

If a man declines to go to school, the advantages of the training are carefully
explained to him. If he still hesitates, he is laid off and given a chance for
uninterrupted meditation and reconsideration. He seldom fails to change
his mind. There are over fifty nationalities in the factory and there may
be as many nationalities in each class as there are men present, for we
make no attempt to group them according to language and race. The fact
is we prefer that classes be mixed as to race and country, for our one great
aim is to impress these men that they are, or should be, Americans, and
that former racial, national, and linguistic differences are to be forgotten.[33]

The graduation ceremony illustrated the metamorphosis of the immigrant
worker into an American. As the company reported:

Commencement exercises were held in the largest hall in the city. On the
stage was represented an immigrant ship. In front of it was a huge melting
pot. Down the gang plank came the members of the class dressed in their
national garbs and carrying luggage such as they carried when they landed
in this country. Down they poured into the Ford melting pot and disappeared. Then the teachers began to stir the contents of the pot with long
ladles. Presently the pot began to boil over and out came the men dressed
in their best American clothes and waving American flags.[34]

Knowing English was not enough, however, to make one eligible for the five
dollars a day. Ford men were evaluated by a corps of about 200 "sociologists"
of the Ford Sociology Department, "picked for their peculiar fitness as judges
of human nature." These investigators looked for evidence of "manhood and
thrift," the two qualities which were needed to qualify for the "American" pay.
The men had to live a clean and constructive life: if married they had to be
living with and taking good care of the family; if single and above twenty-two
years of age, they had to prove that they were "thrifty and of good habits."
Men younger than twenty-two were eligible for profit sharing only if they were
the sole support of relatives. To determine degrees of manhood and thrift,
investigators consulted every available source of information—churches, fra-
ternal organizations, the government, passports, family Bibles. They were instructed to explain, through an interpreter if necessary, the joy and healthful
advantages of cleanliness and order, and to impress this fact especially upon
the housewife. They encouraged bank deposits, and—without realizing that
they were often talking to Polish workers who already dreamed of owning their
homes—they explained the advantages of home ownership. They encouraged
uncrowded living conditions and looked down on the bad habit of taking in

33. Schwartz, "Henry Ford's Melting Pot," p. 192.
34. Ibid., p. 193.

boarders and lodgers, who cramped living quarters and disrupted family life.[35]

The Ford Americanization movement was not an isolated or eccentric phenomenon, but rather a well-publicized symptom of a general trend in Detroit. In 1915, the Board of Commerce's committees on education and on immigrants merged into the Detroit Americanization Committee with this official purpose:

> to promote and inculcate in both native and foreign born residents of the metropolitan district including and surrounding the city of Detroit, the principles of American institutions and good citizenship, to the end of encouraging and assisting immigrants to learn the English language, the history, laws and government of the United States, the rights and duties of citizenship; and in becoming intelligent Americans.[36]

That same year the National Americanization Committee was also formed, under the leadership of Frances Kellor, with the more limited goal of celebrating national Independence Day by bringing together "all Americans, wherever born."[37]

The Detroit Americanization movement was initially controlled by the large employers. Six of the eleven members of the Board of Commerce's education committee were representatives of Detroit's big corporations: Henry W. Hoyt, vice-president of the Great Lakes Engineering Company; F. S. Bigler, president of Michigan Bolt and Nut Company; Ernest L. Lloyd, president of Lloyd Construction Company; John R. Lee, director of the Ford Sociological Department; Horace Rackham, an attorney and "capitalist" who was Ford's legal counsel; and W. E. Scripps, of the Scripps Motor Company, Scripps-Booth Cycle Car Company, and the *Detroit News*. To this committee of businessmen were added a few key administrative officials needed to make the idea work: Frank D. Cody, assistant superintendent of the city schools, since the school system was to play a major role in the English class program; A. J. Tuttle, judge on the U.S. District Court, and Thomas J. Farrell, county clerk, both instrumental regarding immigration matters; A. G. Studer, another important community member and general secretary of the Y.M.C.A. And Detroit's mayor, Oscar B. Marx, was asked to join. Marx was himself an industrialist, the president of Michigan Optical Company, founded by his German father who had remained close to the German community all his life (see chap. 8); the son, however, had broadened the family's social and economic horizons by serving

---

35. Ibid., pp. 193–96.

36. *Articles of Association of the Americanization Committee of Detroit*, Art. I, sec. 2 (1925), ACD Papers.

37. Higham, *Strangers in the Land*, pp. 243–46; Hill, "The Americanization Movement," p. 617.

as mayor and as treasurer and vice-president of two construction and real estate companies.[38]

The Detroit committee began by issuing a report on the condition of the immigrant in Detroit, completed in 1915 by Raymond E. Cole, and proceeded to pursue the ambitious night school program initiated by the Committee on Education. In May 1915, the committee informed all large employers of Detroit that the school superintendent, Dr. Charles E. Chadsey, had agreed to double the appropriation for conducting night schools for non–English-speaking foreigners. The committee urged the employers to help secure the attendance of their non–English-speaking workers at these classes. The employers responded by impressing on foreign workers that the non–English-speaking foreigner was usually the first to be laid off and the last to be taken back when business was slack, implying that many of their troubles were caused by their failure to speak or understand English.[39]

The committee was quite conscious of its mission, the language course being only one practical way toward the grander goal of educating men in something called citizenship. Assistant Superintendent Cody, for example, proposed

> placing a red, white and blue light upon each of the public schools open in the evening for the instruction of foreigners in English. . . . Such a light would enable the prospective pupil to quickly locate the schools and would be a constant reminder to passers-by of the work being done in connection with the Americanization movement in Detroit.

The committee heartily endorsed the plan and commended Mr. Cody for the originality of the idea.[40]

Evening classes were widely advertised in the communities, at employers' expense. In January 1916, for instance, automobiles were furnished by the Hupp Motor Company, Saxon Motor Company, Chalmers Motor Company, Maxwell Motor Car Company, and the King Motor Car Company for distributing handbills at factories. In addition to handbills, the committee used slide shows in the motion picture houses in immigrant sections of the city and placed a notice in the bulletin of the Michigan Workmen's Compensation Mutual Insurance Company to advertise the classes. It worked through the library, which agreed to distribute to foreigner patrons "a pamphlet printed in several languages describing the advantages of attending night school"; it worked also

38. Members of the Education Committee of the Detroit Board of Commerce to Corporation Executives, May 1915, ACD Papers.
39. Raymond E. Cole, "The Immigrant in Detroit," May 1915, ACD Papers.
40. Minutes, 15 June 1916, ACD Papers.

through the Recreation Commission, which distributed cards to children at city playgrounds.[41]

The Americanization committee's initial strategy was to concentrate its efforts on Detroit's largest employers, asking them to cooperate in the venture. In June 1916, the committee had collected data on thirty-nine large firms and estimated that, for example, Dodge Brothers had 3,000 non–English-speaking workers out of 9,400 employees, but only 157 attended school; Studebaker had 1,200 non–English-speaking workers out of a work force of 6,800, but only 97 attended school.[42] These large Detroit firms were the targets of the committee, whose efforts proved successful as many companies decided to follow Ford's example and make class attendance virtually compulsory. Here is Packard's strategy, according to a company spokesman:

> We asked the foreman of each department to furnish us with a list of all those in his department who could not speak, read or write the English language, and we did not inform the foremen at that time as to what purpose this list would be used for. After this was done, we held group meetings with proper interpreters, and told all of these men that their job depended on whether or not they attended night school. We found that we had about one thousand employees who could not speak, read or write English. These men were instructed to enroll in the evening schools at once. They were told that each week they must bring in their attendance card and turn it over to the foreman of their department who would, in turn, hand the cards over to the Welfare Department, have them checked off with the list, returning the cards to the men to whom they belonged. The first complaint that we received was that the teachers did not always give the men attendance cards. The manner in which we are checking up these cards at present is to put opposite each department the total number of foreigners, and each week the attendance cards from each department are checked off with the list. If a department has twenty foreigners, and hands in only fifteen attendance cards, we put it to the foreman to find out who the five men are that have not handed in cards.[43]

Most employers, seeing a chance to further their own interests, agreed to promote night schools. Of all factories contacted, only two employers did not fully endorse the program. The American Blower Company complained "that it was impossible to get the most ignorant and unskilled workmen, truckmen,

41. Minutes, Committee on Education, 6 January 1916; Minutes, 10 August 1916, ACD Papers.
42. "Information for the Committee on Education," 17 January 1916; List of large firms, 1 June 1916, ACD Papers.
43. "Plan of Factory Co-operation," 14 June 1916, ACD Papers.

etc., to go to night school. Many of them threatened to quit their jobs rather than go, and it is impossible to fill the jobs with English speaking men, as such men will not do this work"; and Dodge refused to endorse the program because evening classes conflicted with its night shift. Generally speaking, however, the program was successful in large factories, to the point that after several years, some employers—Ford and Packard in particular—reported that evening classes were no longer necessary because nearly all workers now knew the English language.[44]

Having succeeded with large employers, the committee sought to reach smaller employers and also to integrate representatives of ethnic communities into its ranks. From its inception, the committee had kept in touch with ethnic leaders. Most ethnic leaders endorsed the program but not always uncritically; in December 1915, Alexander Jasienski, an organizer of Polish lodges and an editor of the *Polish Daily Record*,

> assured the committee of the support of his paper. He further stated that he had heard a great deal from his people about the lessons taught in the schools, and that he was convinced that they were effective but that they were entirely too exaggerated. He endorsed the dramatic method, but suggested that it would be better for the teacher to draw a picture of a cow on the blackboard, than to go on all fours before the class in an effort to dramatize the antics of the animal. The Polish people talked a great deal in their homes about the antics of the teachers, and this detracted a great deal from the value of the lesson.[45]

By 1917 the committee enlarged its limited and exclusive membership of 1915 to include less notable but needed citizens, often middle-rank officials or workers in educational and cultural fields as well as representatives of ethnic communities, editors of ethnic presses, priests, and rabbis. In 1917, for instance, the list of committee members icluded names such as Adam Strohm, librarian of the Detroit Public Library, and Anton Feder, publisher of the *Magyar Hirlap*. By 1922, it included men like Ellis G. Van Deventer, superintendent of Hamtramck High School; George Kemeny, an editor of the Hungarian Press; George Laskeris, who ran a Greek-American Printing Company; the Reverend Joseph Ciarrochi, editor of *La Voce del Popolo*; the Reverend John C. Vismara, teacher at the Sacred Heart Seminary; Rabbi M. Hershman; the Reverend Stanley Skrzyski; the Reverend Francis A. Bawja, pastor of Saint Hyacinth's Roman

44. "Information for the Committee on Education," 17 January 1916; "Information for the Committee on Education," 10 January 1916; Minutes, 9 October 1917, ACD Papers.
45. Minutes, Committee on Education, 16 December 1915, ACD Papers.

Catholic Church; and Dr. Roman Sadowski, a Polish physician and a notable in the Polish community.[46]

Concurrently the Americanization committee turned to small firms, and starting in 1917, moved many classes from public schools to factories in order to reach the workers who did not make it to the school buildings. Public school classes were also maintained, but often for a new target population, including the workers' families as well as the workers themselves. By 1920, sixteen mothers' classes were underway with a total attendance of about 450; in connection with the mothers' classes, the Americanization committee published for distribution 10,000 handbills in English, Italian, Hungarian, Polish, and Yiddish.[47]

Teaching English classes was only one activity of the Americanization campaign; the Americanization committee also worked toward facilitating naturalization of immigrants. In April 1916, for example, the committee arranged for the chief naturalization examiner from Chicago to visit several Detroit plants—Morgan and Wright, American Blower Company, General Aluminum and Brass Manufacturing Company, the Studebaker Corporation, Packard Motor Car Company, C. R. Wilson Body Company, Timken Detroit Axle Company, and the Murphy Chair Company. Following such visits, "at several of the plants the employment manager arranged to take the applicants for citizenship papers down to the government offices in automobiles at the expense of the company, and on the company's time."[48] Along with such activities, the committee distributed pamphlets on citizenship and organized classes in naturalization. Some of these classes were directed at specific groups; the committee, for example, sought the collaboration of Jewish Charities in urging all Jewish men to learn the English language and to obtain their naturalization papers. Similarly, they made a special effort—seeking the help of the Solvay Company—to penetrate the Delray area where many Hungarians lived, and organized a free information bureau staffed by Hungarian Americans.[49]

With America's involvement in the world war, the committee recast its rhetoric in terms of emergency national duty. What had been a self-serving movement among employers who sought better workers through the semiphilanthropic framework of Americanization became in 1917 a first-priority duty under the

46. Minutes, 5 December 1917; Annual Report, 1 April 1921 to 31 March 1922, ACD Papers; *Detroit Saturday Night*, 15 December 1917.
47. Annual Report, 31 March 1920, ACD Papers.
48. Minutes, Committee on Education, 3 April 1916, ACD Papers.
49. Minutes, Committee on Education, 9 April 1916; Minutes, 20 November 1916; Minutes, 4 June 1917; Minutes, 20 August 1917; Minutes, 10 September 1917; Annual Report, 31 March 1920, ACD Papers.

pressures of the war. For the first time in America, it was imperative to forego any sign of dual allegiance; in several places in the country, Germans of dubious patriotism suffered discrimination, even lynching, and the ethnic presses had to submit an English translation of every article to a postmaster for advance approval.[50] The United States Chamber of Commerce organized a meeting in New York City to warn employers that they would "at once have to face practical decisions as to attitude and policy toward foreign born workmen of certain races."[51]

Detroit was the center of the war economy, and the Detroit Americanization Committee clearly stated:

> If the United States is to win the war the foreigner must be made an American and a dependable labor supply . . . in the present crisis many of our industries strategic in national defense are largely manned by immigrants. Industrial difficulties with these men, now due to the misunderstandings that go with lack of Americanization, may mean national difficulty of great magnitude.

The committee, then, proceeded to establish alien information bureaus for "authentic information on draft regulations, naturalization, liberty bonds, war laws, and learning English" and against "German propaganda and misinformation, lies, disloyalty, spying, distrust and intrigue."[52]

THE COLOR LINE

Even though industrial leaders and their spokesmen on the Detroit Board of Commerce were convinced that they could make America a melting pot of prosperous industrial workers, they were clearly at a loss when faced with the continuous flow of southern Blacks into the city. The migration of Blacks to the city and its factories was a daily reality which employers not only experienced but often fostered, and yet there was no satisfactory place for Blacks in the new society. In its 1920 report, the Americanization committee, aware of the overcrowded and dilapidated conditions of houses inhabited by Blacks, reported that "the Negro housing situation in Detroit . . . was serious and that some action should be taken to relieve it." The committee met with John Dancy of the Urban League and began an inquiry in the housing question in the Black

50. Frederick C. Luebke, *Bonds of Loyalty: German Americans and World War I* (De Kalb: Northern Illinois University Press, 1974), pp. 3, 23–24; Mark O. Kistler, "The German Language Press in Michigan: A Survey and Bibliography," *Michigan History* 64 (1960): 318–19; Robert E. Park, *The Immigrant Press and Its Control* (New York: Harper & Bros., 1922), pp. 433–44.

51. Minutes, 19 March 1917, ACD Papers.

52. Henry W. Hoyt, "A Plea for State Alien Information," *Detroit Saturday Night*, 22 December 1917, ACD Papers.

ghetto, but dropped the matter soon "because the Negroes are all native-born, full American citizens, whose entire culture is derived in America and it was not deemed proper to imply in any degree that the Negroes were not all Americans."[53]

The job of inquiring into the condition of the Blacks and relieving some of the tensions in the Black community was left to the few Black scholars trained in sociology and social work, and eventually led to the founding of the Urban League and its Detroit branch. In 1910 Columbia sociologist George Haynes founded the Committee on Urban Conditions among Negroes in New York City, which became the National Urban League on Urban Conditions among Negroes, and later the Urban League.[54] In Detroit, Eugene Kinkle Jones, Haynes' first assistant, carefully followed the Urban League's strategy of co-operating with white agencies. Since Blacks had traditionally applied for welfare through the Associated Charities (formerly the Detroit Association of Charities; see chap. 11), Jones went to a wealthy Detroit citizen, Henry G. Stevens, vice-president of Detroit's Associated Charities and persuaded him to fund the Detroit local office of the Urban League.[55] Jones's efforts to obtain community support paid off: the league opened its first Detroit office in 1915. Soon the Detroit Employers' Association—already behind the Americanization movement— agreed to fund the new Urban League's employment bureau.[56] Although these alliances with white city groups caused a few Blacks to oppose the newly formed league, calling it "the 'white' Urban League on 'Negro Conditions,' " the league soon became the city's only powerful social work agency among the Blacks.[57]

In June 1916, Forrester B. Washington became the first head of the Urban League's Detroit branch, a post he held for two years before becoming district supervisor for Michigan and Illinois in the Division of Negro Economics of the U.S. Department of Labor and being replaced at the Urban League post by John C. Dancy. Like Haynes, Washington and Dancy were trained sociologists. While in Detroit, Washington was working toward a master's degree in social

53. Annual Report, 31 March 1920, ACD Papers; *Detroiter*, 15 December 1919.

54. *Guide to the Microfilm Edition of the Detroit Urban League Papers* (Ann Arbor: Michigan Historical Collection, Bentley Historical Library, University of Michigan, 1974), pp. 1–6; Nancy J. Weiss, *The National Urban League, 1910–1940* (New York: Oxford University Press, 1974), pp. 29–34, 40–46; David Allen Levine, *Internal Combustion: The Races in Detroit, 1915–1926* (Westport, Conn.: Greenwood Press, 1976) pp. 43–45, 50, 124–28; Lester Brooks and Guichard Parris, *Blacks in the City: A History of the National Urban League* (Boston: Little, Brown & Co., 1971) p. 141.

55. Levine, *Internal Combustion*, pp. 72–73; Weiss, *The National Urban League*, p. 44.

56. Levine, *Internal Combustion*, p. 81; August Meier and Elliott Rudwick, *Black Detroit and the Rise of the UAW* (New York: Oxford University Press, 1979), p. 18.

57. J. H. Porter, Chairman, Good Citizenship League, to Officers and Members of Detroit Board of Commerce, 11 March 1918, Executive Secretary's General File, DUL Papers.

work at Columbia; Dancy had received graduate training at the University of Pennsylvania.[58] The Urban League also maintained extensive contacts with Arthur Woods and other faculty members of the sociology department at the University of Michigan in Ann Arbor.[59] In 1918, Haynes published a survey, *Negro-Newcomers in Detroit*, based partly on data assembled by Washington in 1917, and in 1920 Washington himself compiled a (still unpublished) survey of the Black community.[60] The quality of both observations and estimates in each survey shows the high professional standards of these social workers: Washington, for example, estimated the population size of the Detroit Black community to be 40,000 in 1920; shortly thereafter, the U.S. Census Bureau released its figure of 40,838. Other estimates in Washington's report, such as the age of the Black population (75% over twenty years of age), its sex ratio (70% males), and its lack of families (40% of the Blacks were single males) also fell in line with census tabulations released only later.[61]

Both Haynes and Washington conveyed many firsthand observations on the Detroit Black community. Although they often lacked historical and comparative perspectives and were often unable to explain important processes to which they pointed, their insights are worth taking seriously. Both presented a cautiously optimistic view of the Great Migration, pointing to the opportunities for Blacks to enter industrial jobs never available to them before; at the same time, both presented a dim view of the conditions of "Negro Life" in the new environment of Detroit. The very growth of the Black community was an irreversible check to the industrialists' dream of a unified society.

Writing in 1918 and idealizing the past, Haynes dated the formation of the ghetto from about 1908:

> For many years preceding 1915, Detroit had a small Negro population. It consisted mainly of families of a high grade both in intelligence and well-being. They lived in various parts of the city, self-respecting and respected for their intelligence and moral character. Some of them held responsible places in the business, professional and community life of the city.
>
> About ten years ago, the crusade in other sections of the Country against race-tracks and the popularity of a race-track at Windsor, Canada, just across the river from Detroit, brought many Negroes of the undesirable

58. Levine, *Internal Combustion*, pp. 85–86, 114–15; John C. Dancy, *Sand against the Wind: The Memoirs of John C. Dancy* (Detroit: Wayne State University Press, 1966), pp. 76–78.

59. Report, section on employment, 14 August 1919, Board of Directors Minutes and Reports, DUL Papers.

60. Haynes, *Negro Newcomers in Detroit*; Washington, "The Negro in Detroit," BHC.

61. Washington, "The Negro in Detroit," part A of section, "The Identification of the Negro in Detroit," BHC.

type to the city. The freedom from police interference caused Detroit to be known as a "wide-open town." Disreputable characters of other kinds than those who follow the race-track were drawn from other large cities. The beginning of a Negro ghetto in the region of St. Antoine and Hastings Streets and Adams Avenue was made.

Then came the Great War. The industrial demands of Detroit for laborers became imperative. Negroes were drawn to the city by the hundreds daily. These newcomers were usually of the honest, industrious type who were seeking conditions better than those under which they were living. They were for the most part unskilled and with little education but were seeking better things.[62]

Better things came in terms of jobs; the Urban League reported that between 2 July and 23 December 1917, its employment office received calls for 5,542 male and 317 female workers, the overwhelming majority for unskilled labor in auto factories, a large proportion for domestic and personal servants, but also a significant number (about 600) for men in skilled or semiskilled positions.[63] As Forrester B. Washington reported in 1920:

The most surprising feature of the investigation into the industrial status of the Negro in Detroit is the variety of occupations into which he has entered during the past five years. The narrow limits of porter, elevator-operator and waiter within which the Negro was practically confined up until 1915 have been extended to include carmaker, engineer, millwright, moulder, toolmaker, riveter, dairyworker, chipper, grinder, welder, punch-press operator, heat treater, galvanizer, chassis and frame assembler, crane operator, timekeeper, cigar stripper, paint mixer, varnish cooker and so on to 179 different occupations discovered by this survey.[64]

But this optimism, marking both the entry of the Blacks into the industrial labor force and their small foothold in skilled positions was tempered by the recognition of the intense racial segregation which existed within factories. Washington reported that Black workers were systematically excluded from the social life of factories, the bowling leagues, the baseball teams, the dances and picnics, and he also reported—without mentioning company names—that

Certain companies not only have not tried to develop better relationships between their white and colored workers but have actually taken active steps to increase the gap between the two groups of workers and aggravate the social situation. For instance, one of the largest factories in the city

62. Haynes, *Negro Newcomers in Detroit*, pp. 8–9.
63. Ibid., p. 13.
64. Washington, "The Negro in Detroit," chap. 2, part B of section, "The Negro in the Industries of Detroit," BHC.

separated its colored employees from its white employees in its lunch-room with a large iron chain. There are other factories which have attempted to enforce segregation in their wash-rooms and toilets by posting signs reading "This side for whites," "this side for negroes."[65]

Actually, Black women workers were even more segregated than their male counterparts; not only were they ostracized from factory social events, but in some factories they also worked at separate benches, in separate rooms, or even at separate occupations.[66]

The Urban League was conscious that Black workers were competing for jobs with foreign-born workers. When Washington addressed a group of employers in New York City in January 1918, he sought to reassure employers by comparing Black workers with foreigners:

> The Companies that are employing these Negroes are generally satisfied so far as I can learn. They are a good, fair average of unskilled workmen. As a matter of fact, some of the leaders testify that they are superior to the Foreign element that are coming into Detroit. In the first place, a Negro's physique is superior to the physique of the South European, and where you want muscular labor, you can get more of it for your money than you do of any other nationality. In addition to that the Negro is docile, tractable, teachable, good natured and fairly intelligent, very frequently highly so. And he is an American.[67]

Keenly aware of the fragility of their newly acquired industrial situation—and having clearly assimilated the employers' demands—the Black leaders circulated tracts in factories to warn Black workers of the stiff competition they were to expect and to impress the realities of industrial discipline on them:

WHY HE FAILED

He watched the clock,
He was always behind hand.
He asked too many questions.
His stock excuse was "I forgot."
He was not ready for the next step.
He did not put his heart in his work.
He learned nothing from his blunders.
He was contented to be a second rater.

65. Ibid., chap. 6 of section, "The Negro in the Industries of Detroit."
66. Ibid., chap. 7, part E of section, "The Negro in the Industries of Detroit."
67. Speech presented before Conference of National Urban League, New York, January 1918, Executive Secretary's General File, DUL Papers.

He didn't learn that the best part of his
salary was not in his pay envelope—SUCCESS
    Note: By not paying strict attention to the
    above details you may not be able to
    keep your job after the war is ended
    and foreign labor is again available.[68]

CONFLICT IN A MATURE INDUSTRIAL SOCIETY

By the end of the war Detroit's factories had been running at full capacity
for several years, and they had attracted a diverse multiethnic and multiracial
labor force. For the previous decade industrial leaders had aimed at putting
some order in this vast array of men and machines distributed over this huge
checkerboard of houses and factories, and by 1918 they had strengthened their
control not only of the labor force within factories but also of the city itself by
sponsoring a new city charter. Through the Detroit Citizens League, the Detroit
Bureau of Governmental Research, and the Detroit Board of Commerce, Detroit's businessmen developed a plan for a new city charter that would strengthen
the authority of the mayor and lessen the influence of working-class, immigrant,
ward-based organizations. The Detroit Citizens League—which identified its
enemies clearly in poolrooms, dance halls, saloons, and houses of prostitution—
was organized in 1912 under the guidance of Henry Leland, founder of Cadillac
Motor Company. The bureau, created in 1916, was a nonpartisan agency designed to bring efficiency—the reformers' keynote—into the city government;
it conducted surveys in administrative matters and published a journal, *Public
Business.* The Board of Commerce was generally concerned with municipal
expansion and fostering a climate favorable to good business. It was in 1918
that the new charter—providing for the at-large elections of the mayor and the
councilmen and large appointive powers to the mayor—went into effect. The
first mayor of the new regime was James Couzens, formerly vice-president of
the Ford Motor Company, a logical choice when it came time to run the city
as a corporation.[69] This new legal instrument for urban government was only
one victory of the lobbying efforts of business organizations. For several years,

68. Ibid.
69. Chavis, "James Couzens: Mayor of Detroit, 1919–1922," pp. 37, 44–45, 48, 50; Sidney
Fine, *Frank Murphy: The Detroit Years* (Ann Arbor: University of Michigan Press, 1975), pp.
91–92; Detroit, *Charter of the City of Detroit* (1918), title II, chapter II; title III, chapter I; title
IV, chapter I; Raymond R. Fragnoli, "Progressive Coalitions and Municipal Reform: Charter
Revision in Detroit, 1912–1918," *Detroit in Perspective: A Journal of Regional History* 4 (Spring
1980): 119–42; for a recent overview of urban reform, see Martin J. Schiesl, *The Politics of
Efficiency: Municipal Administration and Reform in America, 1880–1920* (Berkeley: University
of California Press, 1977).

the Detroit Citizens League had supported prohibition—including endorsing Billy Sunday's visit to Detroit in 1916—when it came to Michigan in 1918; ridden with anxiety over what was foreign and generally beyond control, Detroit joined the unhappy national experience in prohibition.[70]

But the two years immediately following the war were a period of readjustment and industrial contraction. About 35,000 workers out of an estimated industrial labor force of 308,520 were unemployed in January 1919. In 1920, the industrial labor force was down to about 250,000, or at the 1916 level. In 1918 and 1919, the number of cars and trucks manufactured in Detroit dropped from 1,873,949 to 1,170,686.[71] In this context of recession, the industrialists' efforts to sift newcomers according to degrees of manhood and thrift, to gain control over city affairs, and to impose their view of what American society ought to be was under serious challenge; the war was over, and Detroit faced the daily routines of a mature industrial society. Prohibition could never be enforced in Detroit where "blind pigs" quickly replaced licensed saloons. For all the talk of Americanization and despite the employers' strong hand on the labor movement, the fear of radicals flourished. The year 1919 was one of labor unrest through the country. In Detroit a rash of small strikes reached a peak in May but did not spread. Yet the red scare struck in Detroit as in other large cities. Mayor Couzens, who tried to hold on to a policy of free speech, could not prevent his police department from collaborating with Attorney General Palmer's raids on the House of the Masses, Detroit's communist center, and other hotbeds of radicalism; suspects were arrested and often deported.[72] The white Protestant establishment feared Russian Jewish communists; whites in general tried to keep the Blacks in place by loosely organized urban terrorism.[73] As early as 1919, bombing and mob threats discouraged Blacks from moving into white neighborhoods, and by 1925, when Dr. Ossian Sweet and his family went on trial in a nationally publicized case of Blacks accused of murder in resistance to mob action, the Ku Klux Klan was well established in Detroit, and the KKK write-in candidate for mayor, Charles Bowles, had almost won.[74]

70. Larry Daniel Engelman, "O, Whiskey: The History of Prohibition in Michigan" (Ph.D. diss., University of Michigan, 1971) pp. 2–3, 263–64; Fine, *Frank Murphy*, pp. 91–92; for an overview of Prohibition, see Norman H. Clark, *Deliver Us from Evil: An Interpretation of American Prohibition* (New York: W. W. Norton, 1976).

71. Kocher, "Growth of Detroit," p. 81; Yonce, "The Big Red Scare in Detroit," p. 8.

72. Yonce, "The Big Red Scare in Detroit," pp. 19–24.

73. See chap. 14.

74. Levine, *Internal Combustion*, pp. 3–4, 167–90; Dancy, *Sand against the Wind*, pp. 21–34; Kenneth T. Jackson, *The Ku Klux Klan in the City, 1915–1930* (New York: Oxford University Press, 1967), pp. 127–43.

It is to the analysis of the interrelations between ethnic, racial, and class cleavages in this complex city which I will now turn by conducting a new cross-sectional study of the city's space and inhabitants in 1920—a survey similar to those for 1880 and 1900. Did the 1920 society reflect some fusion of the various ethnic segments into one more unified society, a society in which the industrialists' melting pot had worked? Or was it still the multiethnic society of the late nineteenth century? With the growth of the Black community, what role did race play in shaping the new industrial metropolis? My survey of Detroit in 1920 will take on many of George Haynes' or Forrester B. Washington's questions, present alternative findings, and compare Detroit's Blacks with its other ethnic groups rather than study them in isolation. In the late nineteenth century, social class appeared to be less important a cleavage dividing the society than ethnicity; how did social class interact with ethnic and racial bonds in 1920 in defining Detroit's residential patterns, and more generally its inhabitants' jobs, family life, and mores?

13

Social and Spatial Cleavages

Plate 13. A Russian family, just as they stepped off the train in Detroit, 1917. Courtesy of the Henry Ford Museum, the Edison Institute.

Profound changes had affected Detroit since 1900, especially in the ways the city's space was divided along ethnic, racial, and socioeconomic lines. In contrast to late nineteenth-century Detroit, with its cross-class ethnic communities, the 1920 city exhibited zones of ethnic clustering in a much narrower occupational range. Previously socially mixed ethnic neighborhoods were fragmented into primarily working-class ethnic communities, and the growth of the Black ghetto added yet a third, a racial dimension to the city's spatial cleavages. In short, the growth of Detroit into a leading industrial metropolis brought with it many modern divisions still familiar to today's observers.

It was rather simple to predict the spatial configuration of Detroit in 1900 from our cross-sectional study of the city in 1880; although the city expanded greatly in the last twenty years of the nineteenth century, it grew in a way that reinforced the already existing ethnic bonds. Predicting the 1920 sociospatial configuration from the 1900 situation was, however, impossible, because Detroit shifted from a multiethnic city made up of somewhat impermeable zones (such as the German east side and the Anglo-Saxon west side) into a modern industrial metropolis where class and race each began to play as important a role as ethnicity in shaping the urban territory. By 1920, the ethnic groups were divided along class lines in a way not known before, a way linked directly to the economic transformations of the city and to the ensuing reorganization of the urban territory.

For the first time, Detroit's spatial arrangement began to resemble the classic zones of successive settlement—which newcomers entered in a set order—described by the Chicago sociologists (Robert Park, Ernest Burgess, Roderick McKenzie, Louis Wirth, Paul Cressey) in their general model of assimilation to American society (see chap. 2). According to the Chicago sociologists, newcomers, often speaking a foreign language or of Black complexion, "naturally" settled in a ghetto in the dense center of the urban territory; gradually, however, they moved out of the center while experiencing upward social mobility and adapting to new American mores, and they finally reached the peripheral cosmopolitan areas of the metropolis. While a model is always a simplification of a multifaceted reality, evidence from 1920 Detroit corroborates many astute observations made by these sociologists about the first industrial metropolises.[1] To be sure, some areas such as the Hungarian village of Delray—a zone of first settlement on the city's periphery instead of in its center—were exceptions, but such exceptions are in fact accounted for in the many revisions of the Chicago

1. See, for example, James F. Short, ed., *The Social Fabric of the Metropolis: Contributions of the Chicago School of Urban Sociology* (Chicago: University of Chicago Press, 1971).

model.[2] A number of Detroit's zones, indeed, resembled the zones of initial settlement with their tight socioethnic homogeneity of factory workers; others, not so close to factories, looked like transitional zones; still others had features of cosmopolitan zones.

The Chicago sociologists were pioneers in their days, good social observers, and sympathetic to the lives of the people they described. It may be that the divergences from the model I uncovered for 1880 and 1900 Detroit arose because these sociologists presented a special case—the industrial metropolis of the 1920s, or in Chicago's case of earlier industrialization, of the 1910s—as a universal model; they built too quickly a long-range history from their recent observations, and historians followed them in projecting their model back into the past. But I want to go beyond the descriptive limitations of the Chicago model, and I will treat in detail two key components of the sociospatial transformation: first, the new relationship between ethnicity and social class in shaping the industrial metropolis; and second, the different ways in which white ethnic groups and Blacks entered and settled into the giant metropolis. This chapter will deal primarily with the issue of residential concentration, and the next will compare housing, family organization, and work patterns among selected Black and white communities. By describing the new spatial arrangements and contrasting them to the previous ones which I have described in detail, I want to show how modern, how new, and how different from nineteenth-century Detroit the 1920 city has become.

ANATOMY OF A METROPOLIS: THE 1920 SAMPLE

Considering Detroit's dimensions in 1920, it was necessary to design a whole new sample to represent its population and neighborhoods accurately. For purposes of comparison, the 1920 sample would have to match up with the 1880 and 1900 samples, in which individual family members were carefully mapped out in the city and coded on a house-by-house basis in the microenvironments of the block front, the city block, and the cluster of six fronts. The United States Bureau of the Census agreed to collaborate on this study by coding a sample of Detroit's respondents from the still closed (until 1992) 1920 census survey and by providing aggregate statistics for city blocks (see Appendix 2,

2. See Chauncy D. Harris and Edward L. Ullman, "The Nature of Cities," *Annals of the American Academy of Political and Social Science* 242 (November 1945): 7–17; Homer Hoyt, *The Structure and Growth of Residential Neighborhoods in American Cities* (Washington, D.C.: Federal Housing Administration, 1939); Beverly Duncan, "Variables in Urban Morphology," in *Contributions to Urban Sociology*, ed. Ernest W. Burgess and Donald J. Bogue (Chicago: University of Chicago Press, 1964), pp. 17–30; and especially Otis D. Duncan and Stanley Lieberson "Ethnic Segregation and Assimilation," *American Journal of Sociology* 64 (January 1959): 364–74; Stanley Lieberson, *Ethnic Patterns in American Cities* (New York: Free Press of Glencoe, 1963).

which details the agreement with the census bureau and explains the sampling design). Aggregating data at the block level—which was simpler than at the cluster level—would work well for 1920, when population density was sufficiently high for the block to serve as a large enough geographic unit in which to measure residential clustering.

It was imperative to keep the 1920 sample large enough to maintain the detailed analysis of many small areas in all density classes distributed across the city—such as those for 1880 and 1900—and to maintain reasonably low standard errors of estimates. At the same time, it was important for economic reasons to keep the sample limited; while I had been able to afford proportionately larger samples for 1880 and 1900, it was obvious that with almost one million inhabitants in the city I could sample only a smaller proportion of the population for 1920. In addition, any accurate description of Detroit in 1920 would have to include the newly formed suburbs, an obligation which did not exist for the prior decades.

The final sampling design included every third head of household in randomly selected blocks distributed in all areas of the city and in all density classes. The design insured that every head of household in Detroit had roughly the same probability of being selected. The sampling actually yielded 4,864 heads of households in 272 city blocks (see map 13.1 and Appendix 2). The decision to restrict the survey to heads of households had two limiting effects: first, groups with a large proportion of their adult population as boarders would be underrepresented, a likely occurrence for those groups providing a large share of the male adult factory labor force, such as the Poles, the Hungarians, and the Blacks; second, it prevented the duplication for 1920 of the fine-grained demographic analysis which I had conducted for 1880 and 1900, when I included other household members in the sample. This survey, however, served to cover the entire urban territory at once; it allowed me to study the intersections of ethnic, racial, and social cleavages; to identify and locate the areas of highest concentration for each of these groups; and then to go back to specific blocks in a second stage, taking a total enumeration of the characteristics of their entire population, in order to conduct a finer housing and demographic survey of a few key areas in Detroit (see chap. 14).

In addition to this "equal probability" sample of heads of households in selected city blocks, I also drew independent systematic samples of heads of households in eight selected suburban areas of Detroit. Each of the eight areas selected corresponds to one or more civil divisions immediately adjacent to Detroit. On the east side, Gratiot Township and Hamtramck Township were eliminated because they were still predominantly rural townships; the various Grosse Pointe townships, however, made up one area. In the north, Ferndale

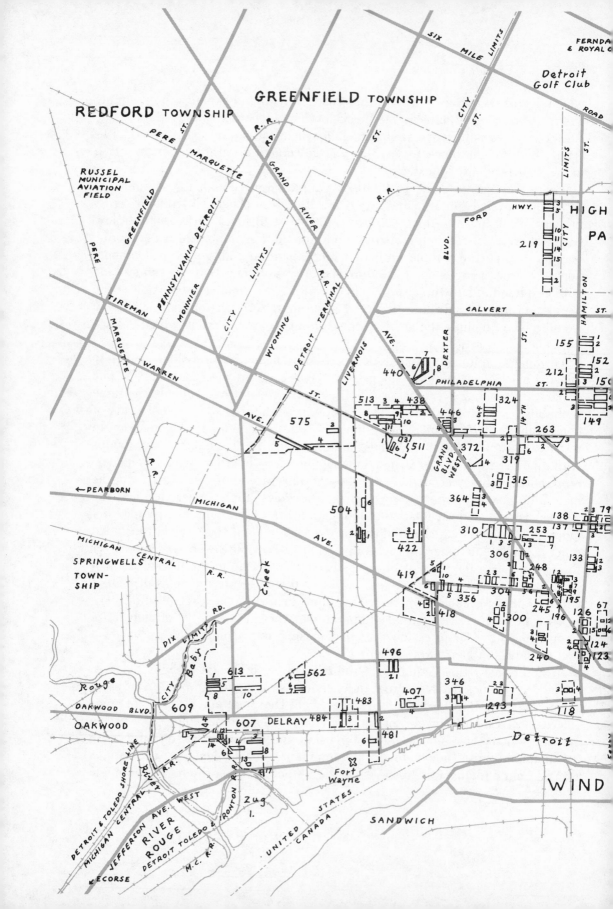

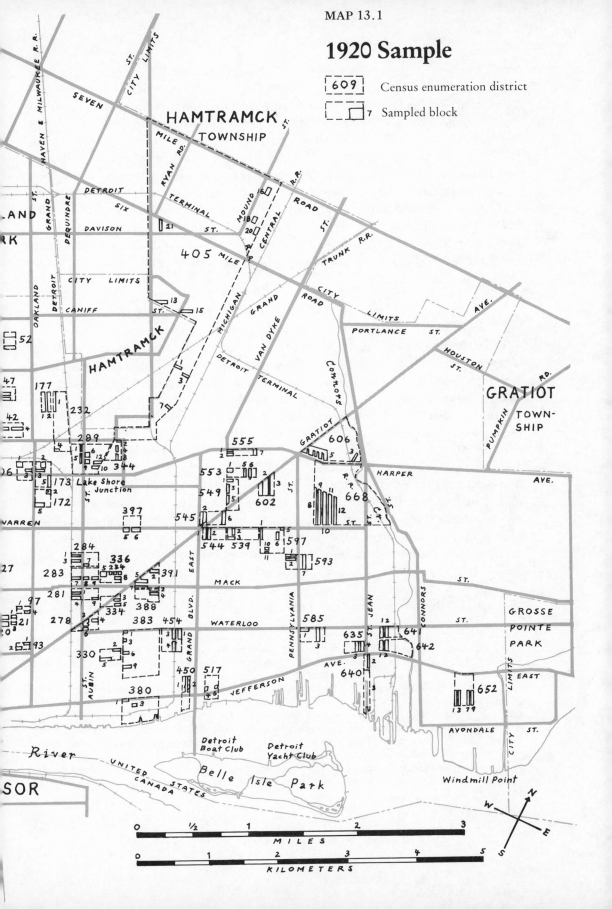

MAP 13.1

1920 Sample

609 Census enumeration district

7 Sampled block

Village and Royal Oak (township and village) combined to form another sampled area. I sampled heads of households in Greenfield Township in the west, in Springwells Township farther south, and still farther south along the river in the combined area of Oakwood Village, River Rouge Village, Ecorse Village, and Ecorse Township. Immediately beyond these western suburbs, I also took a sample of heads of households in Dearborn, where the Ford industrial empire had begun to expand with a new Ford tractor plant. In addition, I drew samples in the industrial enclaves of Highland Park and Hamtramck. Altogether, 1,391 heads of households were sampled over eight suburban and satellite areas, thus completing our statistical picture of the fourth largest United States metropolis in 1920.

CLASS, ETHNICITY, AND RACE: CATEGORIES AND
INDEXES

When it comes to quantitative analysis of social indicators, we must rely on categorical variables which only approximate the more profound social qualities we want to uncover. This momentary reduction of complex realities into measurable quantities is necessary to understand the sociospatial cleavages of the metropolis. For the turn of the century, we had been able to dwell on a variety of sources to understand the significance of ethnic and class affiliations beyond the administrative categories of the census. The 1920 survey, however (like the 1880 survey), rests on the linkage of only two sources, the manuscript census and land use atlases. The place of birth and mother tongue of the respondent and of his/her parents, as well as the respondent's occupation, will serve again as indicators of ethnicity and class. Similarly, residential concentration will be, once again, our indicator of the groups' cohesiveness and of the extent to which group members shared common values and behaviors.

The complex mix of places of birth, skin colors, mother tongues, and generations of immigrants to Detroit was well represented in the sample.[3] Of the sampled heads of households, 29.6% were native white Americans (95% of

3. A special effort was made to record the ethnic and racial characteristics of the population in the 1920 census; color or race was of course recorded: White, Black, Mulatto, Indian, Chinese, Japanese, Filipino, Hindu, Korean or "other." The census also recorded the place of birth and the mother tongue of each individual and of the two parents. As in previous censuses, religion was not recorded, but it is easy to identify at least the Jews in 1920, with mother tongue listed as Yiddish or Hebrew. Because European political geography changed greatly following the territorial reorganization of the Versailles Treaty, census-takers were instructed to record the city of birth of respondents who were not sure in which country or province they were born. In Detroit, however, only in the Hungarian section of Delray were these instructions followed; scores of names of small Hungarian villages were recorded in this part of the census, but only countries or provinces were given for the residents of the other sections of town. See U.S., Department of Commerce, Bureau of the Census, *Instructions to Enumerators* (Washington, D.C.: G.P.O., 1919), pp. 27–32.

them born in northern industrial states). Another 2.4% were Blacks, but in contrast to 1900, when most resident Blacks had been born in Michigan, 84.1% now came from the South, while only 15.9% were northern Blacks (see tables 13.1 and 13.2).

Among immigrant groups traditionally established in Detroit, many heads of households were now of the second generation, born in the United States of immigrant parents. German-headed households made up 15% of the sample, but only 6.1% of the sampled heads of households were immigrants, while 6.9% were native-born of German parents, and another 2.2% native-born of mixed German-American parentage. The Irish, who made up 3.5% of the sampled heads of households, were also better represented among the second generation, with 2% of the sampled heads native-born of Irish parents, 0.5% native-born of mixed Irish-American parentage, and only 1% Irish immigrants. In this census decade, then, the heads of households of the second generation German and Irish families outnumbered those of the first generation, for the first time.

Aside from the Germans and the Irish, all other groups, including the Anglo-Saxon groups, still had more immigrant heads of households than members of the second generation, although the latter were often well represented. The English-Canadian group made up 12% of Detroit's heads of households, including 8.6% immigrants. The British group (without Ireland) made up 5.5% of the sampled heads of households, still including 3.1% immigrants from Britain (counting a few declaring Scottish as a mother tongue). The other statistically important groups with few or no second-generation heads of households were all non–Anglo-Saxons, the most important of them being the Poles, who accounted for 9% of the sample, with 8% being immigrants from Poland—the single largest group of immigrants in the 1920 city. The other immigrant groups of importance in Detroit were Italians (1.3%), Austrians (1.4%), Hungarians (3.2%), and Russian Jews (1.5%) (see table 13.1).

All these groups accounted for 84% of the sampled heads of households. Heads of households of a score of smaller groups completed the sample: Czechoslovaks (some speaking Bohemian, some Slovak), Yugoslavians (some speaking Croatian and some Serbian), Swedes, Danes, Netherlanders, Belgians, French, Greeks, Orthodox Russians, Polish Jews, Lithuanians, Finns, Rumanians, as well as a variety of heads of households born in the United States but whose parents were of different origins, often a mix of Canadian and European origins.

Sorting heads of households by occupational status was also made somewhat easier with the 1920 census sample, because the census bureau, as it did for ethnic categories, again sought more detailed information.[4] Census takers now listed not only the occupational title of the individual worker but also the

4. Ibid., pp. 32–37.

TABLE 13.1

Ethnicity of heads of households, Detroit, 1920

Person		First Parent		Second Parent		Number in sample	Females (%)	City (%)
Mother tongue	Place of birth	Place of birth	Mother tongue	Place of birth	Mother tongue			
English	U.S. (White)[a]	U.S. (White)	English	U.S. (White)	English	1,437	8.52	29.62
English	U.S. (Black)[a]	U.S. (Black)	English	U.S. (Black)	English	121	.12	2.45
English	Canada	Canada	English	Canada	English	418	16.99	8.62
English	U.S.	Canada	English	Canada	English	67	10.45	1.38
English	U.S.	U.S.	English	Canada	English	96	11.46	1.98
English	Canada	Canada	English	Other[b]	Other	36	19.40	.74
French	Canada	Canada	French	Canada	French	25	12.00	.52
English	U.S.	Canada	French	Canada	French	17	-	.35
English	U.S.	U.S.	English	Canada	French	2	-	.04
English	Canada	Canada	French	Other[c]	Other	5	20.00	.10
Other[d]	Canada	Canada	Other	Canada	Other	19	10.50	.38
English	Canada	Canada	Other[e]	Canada	Other	4	-	.08
English	Great Britain	Great Britain	English	Great Britain	English	144	10.42	2.97
English	U.S.	Great Britain	English	Great Britain	English	67	12.50	1.38
English	U.S.	U.S.	English	Great Britain	English	53	20.75	1.09
Other[g]	Great Britain	Great Britain	English	Other[f]	Other	24	22.73	.49
English	Great Britain	Great Britain	Other[h]	Great Britain	Other	36	2.80	.74
English	U.S.	Great Britain	English	Great Britain	Other	15	20.00	.31
English	U.S.	U.S.	English	Great Britain	Other[i]	9	11.11	.18

Ireland	English	Ireland	English	Ireland	English	38	21.05	.78
U.S.	English	Ireland	English	Ireland	English	72	22.22	1.48
U.S.	English	U.S.	English	Ireland	English	28	3.57	.58
U.S.	English	Ireland	English	Other[j]	English	5	–	.10
Ireland	Irish	Ireland	Irish	Ireland	Irish	17	29.41	.35
U.S.	English	Ireland	Irish	Ireland	Irish	30	23.33	.62
U.S.	English	U.S.	English	U.S.	English	14	14.29	.29
U.S.	English	Ireland	Irish	Other[k]	Irish	4	25.00	.08
Netherlands	Dutch	Netherlands	Dutch	Netherlands	Dutch	19	5.56	.39
U.S.[l]	English	Netherlands	Dutch	Netherlands	Dutch	13	7.69	.27
Belgium	Flemish	Belgium	Flemish	Belgium	Flemish	36	–	.74
U.S.[m]	English	Belgium	Flemish	Belgium	Flemish	9	22.22	.18
France	French	France	French	France	French	14	21.43	.29
U.S.	English	France	French	France	French	34	8.82	.70
Germany	German	Germany	German	Germany	German	299	19.06	6.16
U.S.	English	Germany	German	Germany	German	335	9.85	6.90
U.S.	English	U.S.	English	Germany	German	98	5.21	2.02
U.S.	English	Germany	German	Other[n]	Other	25	16.00	.52
Austria	German	Austria	German	Austria	German	68	2.94	1.40
U.S.	English	Austria	German	Austria	German	3	–	.06
Hungary	Hungarian[o]	Hungary	Hungarian	Hungary	Hungarian	158	10.00	3.26
Czechoslovakia	Slovak[p]	Czechoslovakia	Slovak	Czechoslovakia	Slovak	23	–	.47
Switzerland	German[q]	Switzerland	German	Switzerland	German	8	25.00	.16

TABLE 13.1 (*Continued*)
Ethnicity of heads of households, Detroit, 1920

Person		First Parent		Second Parent		Number in sample	Females (%)	City (%)
Place of birth	Mother tongue	Place of birth	Mother tongue	Place of birth	Mother tongue			
Poland[r]	Polish	Poland	Polish	Poland	Polish	358	8.10	7.38
U.S.[s]	English	Poland	Polish	Poland	Polish	53	3.77	1.09
Russia[s]	Russian	Russia	Russian	Russia	Russian	53	1.89	1.09
U.S.	English	Russia	Russian	Russia	Russian	3	33.30	.06
Rumania	Rumanian	Rumania	Rumanian	Rumania	Rumanian	39	7.69	.80
Yugoslavia	Croatian	Yugoslavia	Croatian	Yugoslavia	Croatian	34	5.88	.70
Poland	Yiddish	Poland	Yiddish	Poland	Yiddish	21	4.76	.43
Austria	Yiddish	Austria	Yiddish	Austria	Yiddish	4	-	.08
Russia	Yiddish	Russia	Yiddish	Russia	Yiddish	73	5.48	1.50
Other[t]	Yiddish	Other	Yiddish	Other	Yiddish	9	-	.19
Italy	Italian	Italy	Italian	Italy	Italian	65	3.08	1.34
Greece	Greek	Greece	Greek	Greece	Greek	12	-	.25
Norway	Norwegian	Norway	Norwegian	Norway	Norwegian	6	-	.12
Sweden	Swedish	Sweden	Swedish	Sweden	Swedish	27	7.41	.56
Denmark	Danish	Denmark	Danish	Denmark	Danish	10	-	.21
Other foreign born[u]						70	1.43	1.44
Other U.S. born[v]						70	5.71	1.44
Missing data						12		
Total						4,864		

SOURCE: 1920 sample.

a. Including 6 Mulattoes, and 2 West Indians.

b. Including Great Britain (MT English and Scotch); Ireland (MT Englsih and Irish); Poland; France; Alsace-Lorraine (MT German); Papal States; and Cuba.

c. Including Great Britain; Germany; Switzerland (MT Swiss); and Canada (MT Dutch).

d. MT German: 8; Irish: 6; Scotch: 5.

e. MT Scotch: 3; German: 1.

f. Including Ireland (MT English and Irish); France; and Germany.

g. MT Scotch: 32, Welsh: 4.

h. MT Scotch: 9; Welsh: 4; German: 2.

i. MT Scotch: 5; Welsh: 4.

j. Including Ireland (MT Irish): 2; France; Belgium (MT Flemish); and Belgian Congo.

k. Including Canada (MT Irish); Ireland (MT Croatian); Switzerland (MT French); and Germany.

l. Including 1 case of mixed American and Netherlander parentage.

m. Including 4 cases of mixed American and Belgian parentage.

n. Including Switzerland (MT German and French); Alsace-Lorraine (MT German and French); Belgium (MT Flemish and German); Netherlands, Denmark; and Poland.

o. Or Magyar.

p. Or Moravian, Bohemian, Czech.

q. Or French, Italian.

r. Or born in Germany, Russia, Austria, Czechoslovakia, with MT Polish.

s. Or born in Poland (MT Russian or Ruthenian); in Austria (MT Russian); in Ukraine (MT Ukrainian).

t. Including 3 natives born of Polish or Russian parents; and immigrants from Germany, Rumania, Hungary, and Austria.

u. Including Lithuania: 26; Finland: 12; Armenia: 6; and China, Syria, Turkey, Japan, Korea, Australia, New South Wales, Mexico, Columbia, Malta, Bulgaria, and Luxembourg.

v. Of Swedish parents: 16; of Italian parents: 6; of Danish parents: 6; of Lithuanian (or mixed American-Lithuanian) parents: 11; of Czechoslovakian parents: 3; of Finnish (or mixed American-Finnish) parents: 5; and of a variety of other mixed parentage.

TABLE 13.2
Blacks' occupational status, by region, Detroit, 1920

Region of birth	Professionals		High white-collar		White-collar		Nonretail proprietors		Retailers		Craftsmen	
	(n)	(%)	(n)	(%)	(n)	(%)	(n)	(%)	(n)	(%)	(n)	(%)
North[a]	1	5.9	-	-	1	5.9	2	11.8	-	-	-	-
South[b]	1	1.1	-	-	-	-	5	5.6	2	2.2	1	1.1
All	2	1.9	-	-	1	.9	7	6.6	2	1.9	1	.9

SOURCE: 1920 sample.

a. New York: 2; Pennsylvania: 3; Ohio: 3; Indiana: 3; Illinois: 2; Michigan: 3; and one case from California and 2 from Kansas.

industry in which the individual worked and his or her class of worker: either employer, or wage worker, or working on one's own account. The census showed that Detroit in 1920 was overwhelmingly a city of factory workers: 52% of the sampled heads of households worked in factories, as skilled and semiskilled (39%) or unskilled (13%) wage laborers. After factory workers, the next largest category was that of white-collar office workers, comprising 19.25% of the sampled heads of households. Compared with these large groups, the other sampled heads of households were distributed in much smaller categories, including 7.65% as proprietors of manufactures or service enterprises (classified as nonretail proprietors) and 4% as proprietors of retail business. In stark contrast to the late nineteenth-century figures, only a handful (1.2%) of craftsmen were now self-employed in traditional trades, 3.4% in skilled service occupations, and another 7.4% in unskilled service occupations such as domestics, porters, sweepers, or stevedores, and a few (0.4%) in low-level retail jobs like peddlers (see table 13.3).

All ethnic groups of the city were heavily represented in the industrial labor force, but with important variations from one group to another. The groups with the largest percentage of factory workers were the immigrant Poles and the second-generation Poles (both with 81% of the household heads as factory workers), the Austrians (also 81%), and the Hungarians (77%). The remaining heads of households in these groups were generally distributed over all subsectors in small numbers, although virtually nobody in these groups held a high white-collar jobs (see table 13.3).

The Italians and Blacks had fewer of their members among the industrial force (55% and 52%, respectively), but were heavily represented in other lower-class occupations, such as unskilled service and peddling for the Italians (15%) and unskilled service occupations for the Blacks (28%). Each of these two

Skilled, semiskilled wage labor		Skilled, semiskilled service workers		Lower retailers		Unskilled wage labor		Unskilled service workers		Number in sample	Missing data	Percentage
(n)	(%)	(n)	(%)	(n)	(%)	(n)	(%)	(n)	(%)			
3	17.6	1	5.9	-	-	5	29.4	4	23.5	17	1	15.9
11	12.4	2	2.2	-	-	41	46.1	26	29.2	89	6	84.1
14	13.2	3	2.8	-	-	46	43.4	30	28.3	106	7	100.0

b. Georgia: 19; Alabama: 17; Tennessee: 14; Kentucky: 11; Virginia: 10; South Carolina: 4; Louisiana: 4; Mississippi: 3; Arkansas: 3; North Carolina: 3; Texas: 2; West Virginia: 2; Washington, D.C.: 1; Missouri: 1.

groups, like the preceding groups mostly represented in factory work, included a small number of white-collar office workers, a few professionals, some non-retail proprietors, as well as a variety of white-collar shopkeepers.

Still above the citywide figure of 52% of factory workers were second-generation English Canadians, British immigrants, German immigrants, and second-generation German heads of households. From 52% to 62% of the household heads in these groups were factory workers, but most of these groups also had a high percentage of white-collar office workers, 23% for the British immigrants, and 23% for the second-generation Germans.

Numbering below the city level of average factory work were the native white Americans (47%), the English Canadians (39%), the Irish immigrants (48%), the second-generation Irish (43%), and the second-generation British and the Jews, who had record low levels with 31% and 29% factory workers, respectively. All these groups were of course well represented in white-collar work, with 29% of the native white Americans so classified, 49% of the Jews, and 58% of the second-generation British. Only the Jews among this last set of groups were also well represented in unskilled service workers and peddling jobs, which accounted for 13% of their heads of households in the labor force.

With so many socioethnic groups distributed over such a wide territory, Detroit's changing socioethnic map was obviously quite complicated, but our fine-grain analysis at the block level helped order the complex interplay of the forces shaping the metropolis. Once again, I computed a series of indexes to measure population concentration at the block level.[5] One statistical series measures concentration patterns of white ethnic groups and the Blacks; the other serves to measure concentration of occupational groups. The standardized chi-

5. Same indexes as in chaps. 2 and 6.

TABLE 13.3
Ethnicity versus occupational status, Detroit, 1920

Ethnic group		Professionals	High white-collar	White-collar	Nonretail proprietors	Retailers	Craftsmen
				Occupational group			
Native white American[a]	(%)	3.0	.8	29.1	6.6	1.9	.8
Black	(%)	1.9	-	.9	6.6	1.9	.9
Canadian (English)	(%)	5.2	.9	30.7	8.3	4.3	.6
Canadian (English) American	(%)	3.3	-	21.7	5.0	1.7	-
British	(%)	1.7	-	23.3	9.2	-	1.7
British American	(%)	3.8	3.8	32.7	11.5	5.8	5.8
Irish	(%)	6.9	3.4	13.8	6.9	10.3	-
Irish American	(%)	5.2	-	27.6	12.1	-	-
German	(%)	1.8	.4	7.5	7.9	6.2	1.8
German American	(%)	.3	.3	23.5	8.7	3.4	1.3
Polish	(%)	.3	-	1.0	2.5	5.1	1.0
Polish American	(%)	-	-	4.2	2.1	6.3	-
Hungarian	(%)	-	.7	6.2	2.7	2.1	-
Austrian	(%)	-	-	4.8	6.3	3.2	3.2
Jewish	(%)	-	-	16.7	13.5	18.8	2.1
Italian	(%)	-	-	6.7	8.2	3.3	3.3
Citywide	(%)	2.1	.6	20.3	7.9	3.7	1.2

SOURCE: 1920 sample.

a. Born in the U.S. (MT English) of two U.S.-born parents (MT English); born in Canada (MT English) of two Canadian-born parents (MT English), etc.; see table 13.1.

squared measures (applied throughout this study to measure concentration patterns in the microenvironment of the city) are statistically complex, but interpretation of them is simple. Each series of measurement consists of computing two indexes. One index, computed for the city as a whole, indicates the existence of ethnic or occupational concentration. If the population were distributed at random and there were no ethnic or occupational concentrations, the overall citywide index would have a mean of zero and a standard deviation of one. The other index, computed for each block separately, usually shows an abnormal concentration of one group or of several groups if it has a value above 2.7. Such a value indicates that observed frequencies in the block significantly depart from expected frequencies against the hypothesis of randomness (see Appendix 4).

CLASS VERSUS ETHNICITY AND RACE

The city became increasingly segregated from 1880 to 1920. In 1880, only about 30% of the spatial units used to measure concentration had a significant

Skilled, semiskilled wage labor	Skilled, semiskilled service workers	Lower retailers	Unskilled wage labor	Unskilled service workers	Number in sample	Missing data	Percentage
42.1	4.4	-	5.1	6.1	1,307	130	29.62
13.2	2.8	-	43.4	28.3	106	15	2.45
32.7	4.3	-	6.6	6.6	349	69	8.62
46.7	5.0	-	15.0	1.7	60	7	1.38
50.0	.8	-	5.8	7.5	120	24	2.97
30.8	3.8	-	-	1.9	52	12	1.32
41.4	-	-	6.9	10.3	29	9	.78
36.2	6.9	-	5.2	6.9	58	14	1.48
40.5	2.2	.4	15.4	15.9	227	72	6.16
46.0	3.4	-	6.0	7.0	298	37	6.90
46.5	1.3	.3	34.7	7.6	314	44	7.38
50.0	2.1	-	31.3	4.2	48	5	1.09
35.6	2.7	.7	41.1	8.2	146	12	3.26
49.2	-	-	31.7	1.6	63	5	1.40
17.2	7.3	7.3	11.5	5.2	98	9	2.21
34.4	4.9	3.3	24.6	11.5	61	4	1.34
39.8	3.4	.4	13.3	7.4	4,297	555	100.00

index; many clusters were still so loosely populated that no ethnic group dominated them. Still, enough clusters were ethnically well defined to produce an overall index of 39 (or 39 standard deviations away from a hypothetical mean of zero if ethnicity did not play a statistically significant role in population distribution). More of the spatial units were also ethnically dominated in 1900, when the Poles began to take over entire blocks, a pattern of complete takeover which replaced the more subtle dominance pattern that had prevailed before. As a result, the overall index for 1900 rose to a value of 98. In 1920, over 75% of the blocks had a significant index value (above 2.7); not only the Poles, but also the Hungarians, Jews, and Blacks reached record levels of concentration in some blocks. As a result, the overall index for 1920 reached an amazing figure of 185. By then, the population of Detroit appeared to have been distributed at random in less than 25% of the city blocks.

But ethnicity, the dominant clustering force in 1880, slowly lost ground to class. In 1880 and 1900, ethnic affiliation was primarily responsible for the distribution of the population in the urban territory; large concentrations existed because members of the same ethnic group lived together in neighborhoods. Compared with ethnicity, social status played a much smaller role in forming spatial concentrations. In 1880, the overall index for ethnic concentration was 39 but that for occupational categories was only 9, still significant but a great deal lower than the ethnic index. Both indexes jumped for 1900, the ethnic index to 98, and the occupational index to 56. The rise in occupational index reflected important concentrations on the basis of social status, but still not as numerous and important as those due to ethnic affiliations. In 1920, however, the occupational index—which reached 181—caught up with the 185 value of the ethnic index. For the first time, there were as many blocks with significant concentrations of socioeconomic groups as blocks with significant concentrations of ethnic or racial groups (the ethnic index, when computed without Blacks, reaches a value of only 172, lower than that of the occupational index). And for the first time the concentrations of factory day laborers or of white-collar office workers were as dramatic as those of Poles, Jews, Blacks, or Hungarians. The ethnic bonds that had traditionally defined the city's spatial structures were still important, but now occupational bonds played an equal role in shaping the metropolitan territory.

The interaction pattern between ethnicity and social status at the microenvironment level also changed from the late nineteenth century to 1920. In 1880 and 1900, only a few areas were dominated by one homogeneous socioethnic group; more importantly, areas of high ethnic concentration often displayed a great occupational diversity. This strong tendency toward the inversion of concentration patterns tended to disappear in 1920. Now ethnic and occupational concentrations occurred more often in the same blocks, reflecting the cohesiveness of well-defined socioethnic groups such as native white American factory workers, or native white American white-collar office workers, or Polish factory laborers, and the like. Only in tight-knit communities like those of the Jews and also in the Black ghetto did a wide occupation range persist in ethnically dominated blocks.

DETROIT'S SOCIOETHNIC GEOGRAPHY

Drastic changes in the distribution of ethnic and occupational groups since 1900 overshadowed the continuities. Many trends overlapped: Anglo-Saxon middle-class and some working-class groups continued their expansion outward in blocks where they clustered along a narrower occupational range. Anglo-Saxon upper-class residents tended to leave a city which was becoming more and more working class; the Anglo-Saxon middle class consolidated its hold on some residential areas and developed new ones; in turn, the Anglo-Saxon working class moved closer to factories. In addition to these changes among Anglo-

Saxon groups, the concentrated character of the traditional Detroit Irish community—still thriving in the late nineteenth century—virtually disappeared. Similarly, the important and diversified German community lost its spatial cohesiveness, and only scattered German concentrations still existed in 1920.

An array of new ethnic groups and Blacks poured into sections of the east side and around newly built industrial sites elsewhere in the city. Each working-class ethnic group settled near factories, creating small ethnic mill towns in the city for the first time, with the Polish laborers in the east and the Hungarians in the west. Still other groups—such as the Jews and the Italians, with fewer factory workers among them—located closer to the city center in the old east side. In turn the Blacks, now a large group, took over large sections of the east side and other scattered concentrations.

Two maps, one showing ethnic clustering and one showing occupational clustering, help us understand the mosaic of the socioethnic groups that were shaping the urban territory. The maps show the blocks for which segregation indexes were statistically significant and which were inhabited by one dominant group (at least 60% of the heads of households in one ethnic or occupational category) or two dominant groups (if none reached 60%). Let us read these maps and examine the trends one by one, starting with the Anglo-Saxons on the west and north sides of town (see maps 13.2–13.3).

For several decades, native white Americans, English Canadians, and British immigrants had made up the bulk of the city's middle class. It is therefore not surprising to see these groups again associated in the middle-class areas of Detroit in 1920. What is new, however, is that the city had been slowly losing its upper-class residents who, year after year, abandoned the city for the suburbs, and few areas retained a strong and distinct upper-class tone. High white-collar managers, presidents, and high-level professionals, who accounted for 4.6% of Detroit's heads of households in 1900, accounted for only 2.8% of the heads of households twenty years later. Roderick McKenzie, one of the Chicago sociologists, studied this relative decline of prominent families within Detroit. McKenzie computed from *Who's Who in America* that the ratio of notables per 100,000 people was 22.1 for Detroit in 1910, but had dropped sharply to 16.2 in 1920. He also determined that in 1910, 51.8% of Detroit's substantial families (as listed in Dau's *Blue Book*) lived within the limits of Grand Boulevard, 38.5% from Grand Boulevard to the city limits, and only 9.7% outside the city limits. In 1920, only 20.3% of the prominent families lived within the boulevard, 57.2% from the boulevard to the city limits, and as many as 22.5% outside the city itself.[6]

6. Roderick D. McKenzie, *The Metropolitan Community* (New York: McGraw-Hill, 1933), pp. 123, 182–85.

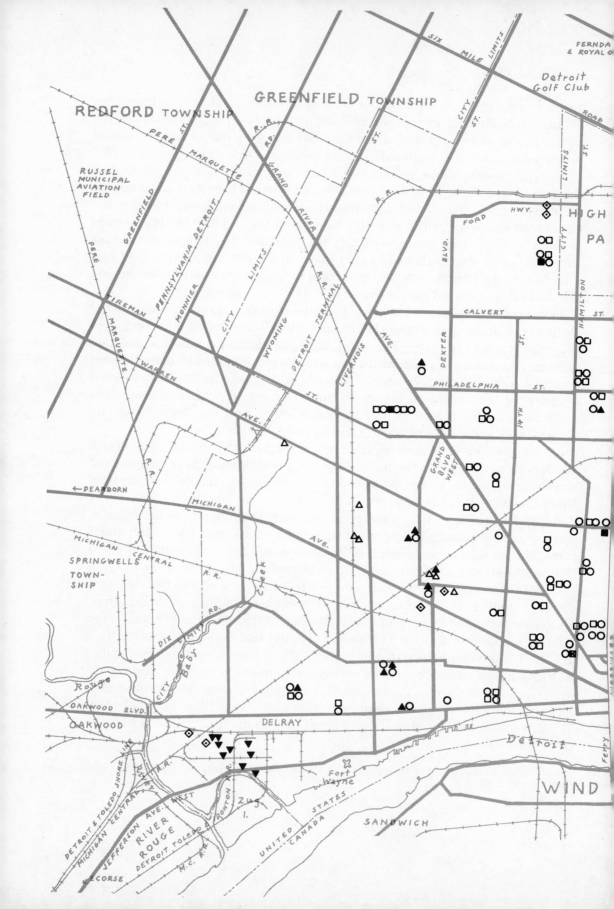

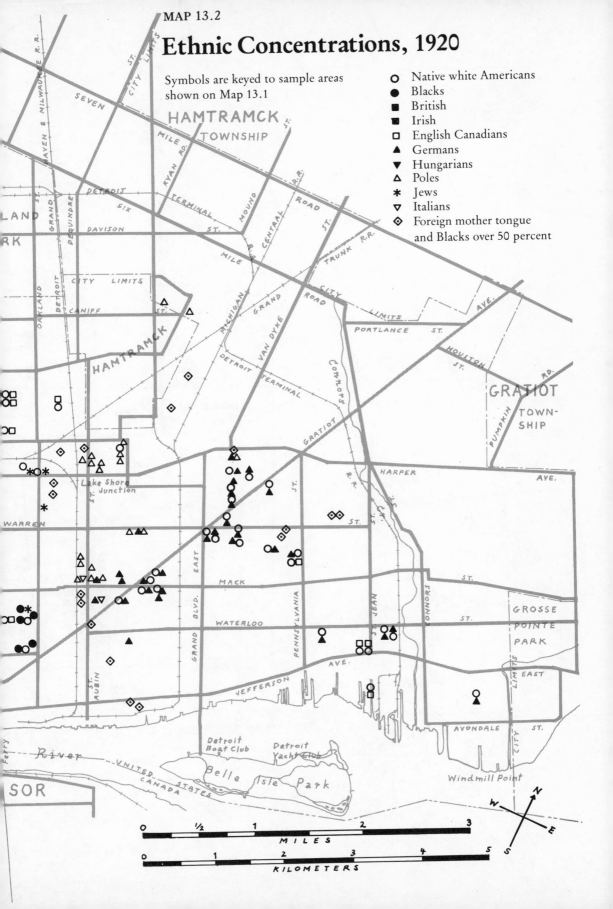

MAP 13.2

Ethnic Concentrations, 1920

Symbols are keyed to sample areas
shown on Map 13.1

○   Native white Americans
●   Blacks
■   British
▨   Irish
□   English Canadians
▲   Germans
▼   Hungarians
△   Poles
✳   Jews
▽   Italians
◈   Foreign mother tongue
     and Blacks over 50 percent

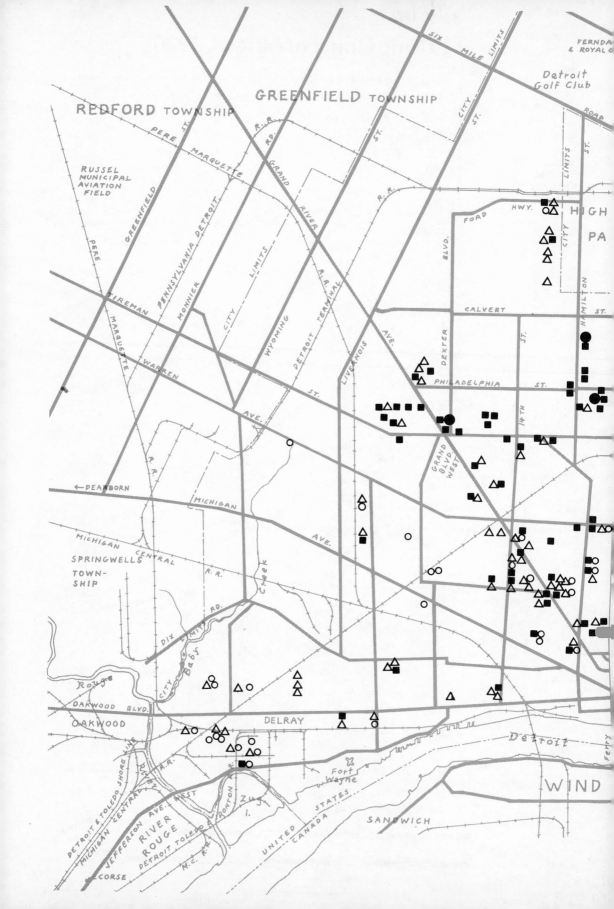

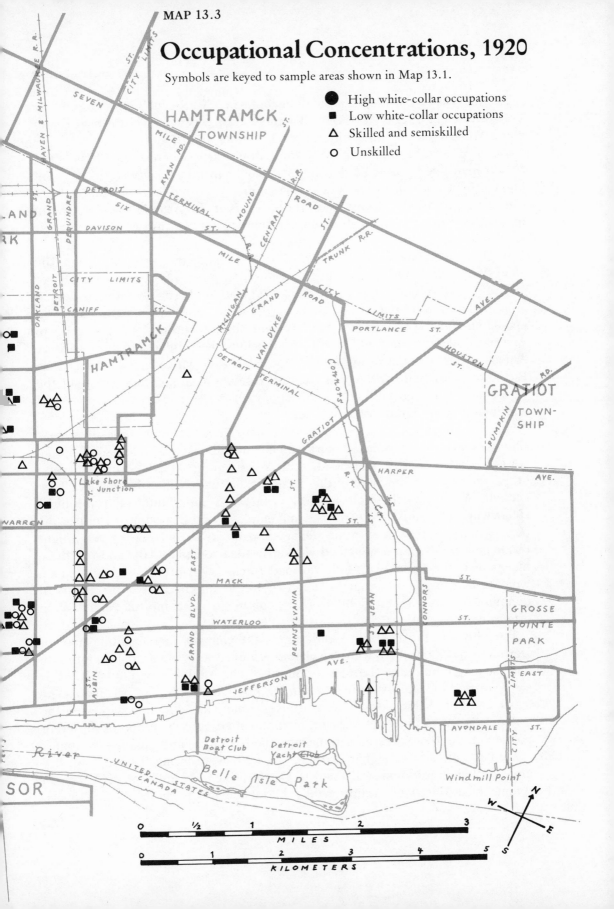

MAP 13.3

Occupational Concentrations, 1920

Symbols are keyed to sample areas shown in Map 13.1.

- ● High white-collar occupations
- ■ Low white-collar occupations
- △ Skilled and semiskilled
- ○ Unskilled

My analysis of the 1920 sample data confirmed McKenzie's observations: by 1920, the center of gravity of Detroit's upper class was no longer the near center along Woodward Avenue, but rather 3.5 miles to the north, near the new General Motors headquarters on Grand Boulevard, where some of the city's richest men lived. Some of the sampled blocks in this neighborhood were inhabited by presidents of manufacturing companies, high-level officials in large companies, attorneys-at-law, and other professionals. Around them a score of middle-level office white-collar workers and managers also established their residences.

Anglo-Saxon groups retained a grip on sections of the inner city, primarily along Woodward Avenue and in the traditional west side along Grand River and Michigan Avenue. But the main concentration of Anglo-Saxon residential areas had moved beyond Grand Boulevard, on the north between the boulevard and Highland Park on Woodward Avenue, and in the new west side up to Livernois street, where all recent subdivisions were inhabited primarily by Anglo-Saxons. Except for lots along the tracks of the Michigan Central and the Pere Marquette railroads which cut into residential areas, these areas of the west side, the larger west side, and the north side were exclusively residential and inhabited by white-collar workers.

As one approached the railroad tracks, these Anglo-Saxon middle-class areas slowly faded into Anglo-Saxon working-class neighborhoods. While some blocks were inhabited mostly by skilled, semiskilled, or unskilled factory workers, others retained a component of the Anglo-Saxon white-collar dominance. True enough, in many of these blocks close to factories both white-collar and blue-collar workers could have had the same employer; an inspector or clerk in the parts department or accounting department of an automobile factory might reside near a foreman or a skilled worker in the same plant. But most of these blocks near the upper west side railroad tracks were primarily Anglo-Saxon working-class areas, and many not shown on the map because of no clear dual dominance were inhabited by workers coming from a mix of Anglo-Saxon origins and generations.

Probably the most striking and significant changes in the ethnic map of Detroit from 1900 to 1920 were the virtual disappearance of the Irish community and the loosening of the German community. The Anglo-Saxon industrial leaders who tried to impress on recent immigrants that they had to become Americans, certainly belonged to a generation of Americans who had witnessed the gradual disappearance of ethnic concentration of groups which were, at different points in time, the two largest in the city: the Irish first, and then the Germans.

We have already seen that in 1900, the Irish were losing their grip on key areas of their traditional settlement in Detroit, like Corktown (along Michigan Avenue near Most Holy Trinity, which had its heyday in the 1850s and 1860s), and areas of the east-side riverfront, near docks and factories. But by 1920, there was hardly any trace in the city of Irish dominance; only one working-class block of the sample near Woodward Avenue turned out to be equally dominated by second-generation Irish workers and native white American workers; in the meantime Corktown had simply become a mixed Anglo-Saxon working-class neighborhood, where only a handful of second-generation Irish still lived. The Irish had not all disappeared from the city, but they had lost their residential cohesiveness.

Even more remarkable was the waning of the German east side. In the 1890s the Germans, the single largest foreign-born group in the city, dominated the city's east side, the most colorful and economically diversified area of Detroit. While acting as a port of entry for other ethnic groups, the Germans gave this area both its overall ethnic tone and its occupational diversity. By 1920 the situation was radically different. The Germans generally did not retain their hold over east-side institutions and houses, but had left the area to other groups. There were few German blocks left in the eastern part of the inner city (within the boulevard) and those that remained were generally a mixture of second-generation Germans and native white Americans. These blocks were primarily inhabited by factory workers and occasionally some white-collar business or factory employees.

Other blocks located farther east again mixed native white Americans with primarily second-generation Germans and skilled factory workers with some white-collar employees. These blocks were beyond Grand Boulevard East, between the Detroit, Grand Haven and Milwaukee Railroad and the Detroit Terminal Railroad, and also in the western peripheries, near the Michigan Central and the Pere Marquette Railroad. The move of the Germans toward the periphery was not new; I have documented it for the 1890s. What was new in 1920 was that this move was no longer associated with the creation of German-Polish working-class districts of unskilled laborers, but rather with communities of second-generation Germans and native white Americans employed in occupations at the junction of middle and working-class status. What we see here resembles the Chicago model of deconcentration from the center and settlement in peripheral cosmopolitan zones associated with generational change and increasing status. This German-American association and equation of social status is as close to a classic sociological pattern of assimilation as one can find in Detroit, although the rise of social status with distance from the city center did not follow a linear pattern because of the peculiar intrusion of Detroit's factory districts into peripheral residential zones.

The Poles, in contrast to the Germans, had become the most concentrated ethnic group of Detroit, with over 80% of the Polish population living in blocks which they dominated. The Poles had replaced the Germans as the dominant group in this large working-class east-side area, where they played the role of receiving group for the new arrivals. But in this giant working-class city, the new inhabitants of the old east side did not display the occupational variety of their predecessors but remained mostly factory workers. Already in the 1890s most of the Poles were factory workers; there were very few craftsmen, but the few professionals and shopkeepers of the community brought occupational diversity to some sections of the Polish neighborhood. By 1920, some Polish white-collar workers were still living with their fellow countrymen, but the disproportionate continuous inflow of factory workers—fostered by Detroit's industrial growth—had made the Polish neighborhoods look even more like working-class communities than ever before. As we can see on the map, Polish immigrants were located at the geographic center of the east side within the boulevard; there, just above Gratiot, was the older Polish church of Saint Albertus; and there too passed the tracks of the Detroit, Grand Haven and Milwaukee Railroad. While other groups located in residential areas as far from the railroad tracks as they could, the Poles, in contrast, settled close to the tracks and the factories. Still in the old east side, they also clustered at the Lake Shore Junction, the single most heavily industrial railroad junction of Detroit.

Poles also moved into newer industrial areas at the periphery of the city, on the northeast border of Hamtramck, an industrial town which became an extension of the Polish community, and on the west side, along the Pere Marquette Railroad. All these blocks were dominated by unskilled and also skilled factory workers, with occasional white-collar proprietors and retail merchants inhabiting these otherwise working-class blocks. With Detroit's transformation into a major industrial metropolis, and the Poles replacing the Germans as the most numerous immigrant group, the east side and other ethnic communities lost their occupational diversity and became blue-collar neighborhoods.

The next two groups of white immigrants who settled primarily in the east side composed two small communities: the Jews and the Italians. About 60% of Detroit's Jews lived in primarily Russian-Jewish blocks. As we have noted, the Jews were better represented in white-collar work and in unskilled service and peddling jobs than in factory work, and consequently their east side concentration was closer to the downtown area than to the new factory districts where many of the Poles had concentrated. The tiny Jewish community (originally lodged in the German east side of 1900) had grown to bigger proportions; in the Jewish east side—near offices and markets—lived the white-collar office worker, the peddler and street vendor, the community Talmud teacher, the factory worker, the tailor, the candy dealer, and the traveling salesman. The Jews were the only group that still displayed a real variety of jobs in their concentrated neighborhoods of 1920 Detroit. Only such a tight ethnic community resisted the impact of social class to divide previously socially diverse, ethnically concentrated communities into more socially stratified socioethnic groups.

Italians were far less concentrated than Jews and overall were a less important group in Detroit. The 1920 sample did not reveal blocks that Italians fully dominated but only some in which they shared dominance with either Poles or Germans. Many of these Italians were involved in unskilled service occupations and peddling and, like the Jews, clustered close to the city center.

Polish blocks, Jewish blocks, and some Italian blocks were the east-side primary colors of the new urban quilt, also inhabited by Blacks (on whom I shall expand later), and by a variety of smaller groups. In and around the various Polish settlements of the east side, recent immigrant workers of small groups concentrated heavily: Czechoslovakians (some Bohemians, some Slovaks), Yugoslavians (some Croatians, some Serbians), Rumanians, some Austrians, some Hungarians, a German or two, occasionally a Polish Jew, a Russian Jew, or a Black. These blocks, made up of heterogeneous small groups of foreign "new immigrant" workers, were numerous in the inner east side of 1920 and made up distinct areas of the east side. In between these primary colors, other blocks reflected transitional neighborhoods between Russian Jews and Polish Catholics, and between lower-class Jews of all origins and the growing Black ghetto.

The only large group of recent white immigrants that escaped the east side altogether and settled directly into the new factory districts of the west were the Hungarians, also a tightly concentrated group of industrial workers who settled in what was at one point Delray Village (before being integrated into Detroit in 1905), close to Solvay Process and close to the new River Rouge complex of factories. The Hungarians were as tightly concentrated an ethnic community as the Poles (with about 72% living in blocks that they dominated). Most of them were industrial workers, and only a handful held white-collar occupations, often as retailers serving the community. The creation of Hungarian Delray is a classic example of a mill town within the metropolis, like some Polish settlements in other parts of the city around large industrial sites. An ethnic community of factory workers, clustering away from other working-class groups of different ethnic origins, Delray exemplified the growing correspondence between ethnicity and social status.[7]

7. Malvina Hauk Abonyi and James A. Anderson, *Hungarians of Detroit* (Detroit: Center for Urban Studies, Wayne State University, 1977); Erdmann Doane Benyon, "Social Mobility and Social Distance among Hungarian-Immigrants in Detroit," *American Journal of Sociology* 61 (January 1936): 423–34.

THE BLACK GHETTO

The most complex transformation of Detroit's social geography, however, was due to the sudden and dramatic growth of the Black settlement, which rapidly became the prototype of the modern ghetto. Unlike Polish workers who, arriving in large numbers, expanded existing communities on which they initially relied, Black migrants disrupted the small existing Black community. Few in numbers before the great migration, Blacks lived in scattered concentrations on the east side. Rapidly, however, most Blacks clustered in one area which reached the highest population density in the city (see maps 12.1 and 13.2). While many southern Blacks had gained industrial employment, most settled in the old east side rather than in the new factory districts.

Before examining in detail the process by which the Black ghetto came to exist, it is important to recognize the areas in which the Blacks settled and to determine the occupational difference between the area of prime concentration and other scattered settlements. In 1917, George Haynes counted six areas of Black settlement in Detroit.[8] Three years later, Forrester B. Washington defined thirteen areas of concentration of Blacks.[9] Neither Haynes nor Washington provided population estimates for each area, a deficiency which I can partially correct from the figures of my 1920 sample of city blocks. According to Haynes, Blacks found their homes "largely in the crowded Negro district which had been formed before their influx," in the Old Saint Antoine Street district of the east side, where Black hotels, restaurants, barbershops, and other Black businesses were. As the population grew the Black district

> expanded north to about Rowena Street and south to about Macomb, within about twenty city blocks—some of the blocks are small compared with the size of a usual city block. They were overcrowded in this district. They overflowed toward the North beyond Brady Street, toward the south below Lafayette Street, toward the east beyond Rivard Street and toward the west to about Beaubien Street. They share the neighborhood with kindly Jews. Toward the north end of the district Jews predominate. Going toward the East they have pushed into an Italian neighborhood.[10]

Three years later, Washington reported that this relatively small core area had tripled in size, expanding eastward to Elmwood Cemetery, southward to

8. George Edmund Haynes, *Negro Newcomers in Detroit, Michigan: A Challenge to Christian Statesmanship, A Preliminary Survey* (New York: Home Missions Council, 1918; Arno Press and the New York Times, 1969), pp. 8–9.

9. Forrester B. Washington, "The Negro in Detroit: A Survey of the Conditions of a Negro Group in a Northern Industrial Center during the War Prosperity Period" (Detroit, 1920), part 1 of section, "The Environment of the Negro in Detroit: The Physical Environment," BHC.

10. Haynes, *Negro Newcomers in Detroit*, p. 9.

the river, and northward to Farnsworth (near Woodward), to Hale (at Chene Street), and to Waterloo Street (at Elmwood Cemetery).[11] A reasonable estimate is that about 70% of the Blacks living in Detroit in 1920 lived in this large east-side zone, but only 50% of Detroit's Blacks lived in blocks which they fully dominated, while the others shared blocks with Jews or Italians or with a variety of small east-side groups such as the Czechs, Yugoslavians, Rumanians, or Lithuanians. In fact, very few Blacks penetrated solid Polish blocks or solid Russian-Jewish blocks, or solid German or Italian blocks; rather, Blacks settled in those undefined blocks where foreign (mostly slavic) mother tongues were predominant but no single group dominated. Blacks expanded the ghetto area more easily in those transitional neighborhoods than in the more cohesive communities of the east side or in other sections of town.

Outside the main east-side area, Haynes had located five scattered concentrations in 1917: two on the west side (one bounded by Warren Avenue, Grand Trunk Railroad, Twenty-third Street, and McKinley Avenue, and one bounded by McGraw, Kirby, Fourteenth Street, and Stanton) no longer existed by the time Washington undertook his survey in 1920, attesting to the fragility of Black advances in some sections of the city. Washington, however, listed twelve small areas where in all about 30% of Detroit's Blacks lived scattered in small pockets: on both sides of Grand Boulevard west between Woodrow, Cobb, Merrick, and Scovel Place; in a northern section between the Detroit, Grand Haven and Milwaukee Railroad, the Detroit Terminal Railway, Conant, and Carpenter; in the North Russell Street area; at the Milwaukee Junction; on Porter Street between Twentieth and Twenty-fifth Street; on Harper Avenue near Warren; on Jefferson west near Fort; on Jefferson east in the Connor's Creek area; on Lumley Avenue in the Springwells district; in the village of River Rouge; in Highland Park; and in Hamtramck.[12]

The 1920 sample picked up a number of these scattered concentrations where Blacks often shared the blocks with representatives of the less homogeneous ethnic communities, especially those of low occupational status like the Blacks themselves. But even in these mixed blocks, there were scarcely more Black skilled workers or white-collar workers than there were in the east-side ghetto, because even the Blacks of higher socioeconomic status were drawn into the ghetto (see chap. 14). The east-side ghetto had 9% of Black white-collar workers, the scattered concentration only 12%. The solid Black blocks counted 12.7% skilled or semiskilled workers, the scattered concentrations only 19%.

11. Washington, "The Negro in Detroit," part 1 of section, "The Environment of the Negro in Detroit: The Physical Environment," BHC.

12. Haynes, *Negro Newcomers in Detroit*, pp. 8–9; Washington, "The Negro in Detroit," part 1 of section, "The Environment of the Negro in Detroit: The Physical Environment," BHC.

It seems, then, that two different patterns for developing residential zones were coinciding in 1920 Detroit. On the one hand, a few well-established, cohesive socioethnic neighborhoods, well adapted to the new urban and suburban subdivisions of residences and factories, were replacing the nineteenth-century cross-class ethnic neighborhoods. On the other, Blacks became increasingly segregated from whites, drawn into a ghetto solely on the basis of race and without regard to their social status.

DETROIT'S SUBURBS

If we turn now to satellite cities and suburban areas, we find again more evidence of the consolidation of class and ethnicity into cohesive socioethnic groups which I have already described for the city proper. Detroit contained two independent cities which the city proper encircled, Hamtramck and Highland Park. The first grew mainly around the Dodge Plant and the second around the Ford Motor Company.[13] Hamtramck had 61.3% of its work force in auto plants and Highland Park 58%, but apart from these similarities, the two cities were quite different. Hamtramck was a working-class community dominated by one ethnic group only: 65.8% of the city's heads of households were Poles and another 4% native-born Americans of Polish parents; 85% of them were factory workers, 43% skilled or semiskilled and 42% unskilled, leaving, then, only a handful in white-collar positions, mostly shopkeepers (table 13.4). In short, Hamtramck was a giant extension of the city's Polish neighborhood and showed the same limited occupational horizons as the Polish community.

Highland Park was completely different. Even though the Ford Motor Company employed many immigrants and more Blacks than any of the other auto companies, Highland Park was inhabited primarily by native white American and other Anglo-Saxon workers (see table 13.5). Of a sample of 202 heads of households, only two were Poles, one Hungarian, and one Black. In addition to the 60% skilled and unskilled workers, 42% of Highland Park families were headed by native white American or generally Anglo-Saxon white-collar workers. Parts of Highland Park, then, were made up of residences of an ethnically homogeneous group of workers, different from that of neighboring Hamtramck, and another part of it was a middle-class neighborhood.

The six other suburbs all reflected a complex array of industry, farmland, and residences. Some suburbs were primarily residential, others were production suburbs, but all, despite their varieties, reflected the new trend toward cohesive socioethnic residential patterns. These patterns are clear despite the

13. Arthur Evans Wood, *Hamtramck: A Sociological Study of a Polish-American Community* (New Haven, Conn.: College and University Press, 1955), pp. 46–47.

fact that our samples now reflect large suburban areas rather than the microenvironment of small neighborhoods.

The five Grosse Pointe villages, situated along the river at the eastern tip of the metropolitan district, were home to upper-class businessmen, industrialists, and professionals (9%), of middle-class white-collar workers (25%), but also of skilled (19%) and unskilled (14.7%) factory workers, and of farmers (5%) (table 13.6). Grosse Pointe Park Village in particular was highly exclusive, and had a large concentration of upper-class families. Many lived in mansions with separate buildings for domestics. As many as twenty-two of the 164 sampled heads of households were gardeners, chauffeurs, and chefs living in houses separated from the main mansion and thus recorded as independent heads of households in the 1920 census. Nowhere else did such a pattern occur in the Detroit area. Grosse Pointe was entirely white, about 40% native white American, with most other residents of Anglo-Saxon extraction. The sample included only seven Germans and one Pole, despite the relatively large working-class population of several of the villages.

The other suburbs—even the residential suburbs, free from large industrial concerns—reflected both Detroit's working-class composition and the suburbanization of workers and middle class alike. But primarily native white American and Anglo-Saxon workers lived in the residential suburbs, while immigrant workers populated production suburbs. Ferndale and Royal Oak townships north of Detroit made up such a residential suburban area. Only about 28% of the suburb was middle-class; the rest was built as working-class subdivisions (with 43.2% skilled workers and 22% unskilled, and about 5% of the population still employed as farmers). Of 209 heads of households sampled in this region, only one was Polish and only one was Black; it was, by and large, an Anglo-Saxon working-class residential suburb (with almost 70% of the heads of households either native white Americans or of British or English-Canadian extraction and only 11.6% either German immigrants or children of German immigrants; table 13.7).[14] Greenfield Township in the northwestern part of the city was similarly Anglo-Saxon, with only a handful of recent immigrants. Thirteen percent of the 146 sampled heads of households were still farmers in Greenfield; other sections of the township were middle class (30%), and yet others working class (34% skilled and 21% unskilled workers; table 13.8).

---

14. There were only twenty-eight Catholic families in Royal Oak, a stronghold of the Ku Klux Klan, when Father Coughlin became pastor of the first Catholic church in 1926; see Sheldon Marcus, *Father Coughlin: The Tumultuous Life of the Priest of the Little Flower* (Boston: Little, Brown, 1973), p. 22.

TABLE 13.4
Ethnicity versus occupational status, Hamtramck, 1920

Ethnic group		Professionals	High white-collar	White-collar	Nonretail proprietors	Retailers	Craftsmen
			Occupational group				
Polish	(%)	-	-	3.1	1.6	3.1	.8
Native white American	(%)	-	-	-	-	-	-
Russian[a]	(%)	-	-	-	-	-	-
Polish American	(%)	-	-	12.5	-	-	-
Austrian	(%)	-	-	20.0	-	20.0	-
Lithuanian	(%)	-	-	-	-	-	-
German	(%)	33.3	-	-	-	-	-
Czechoslovakian	(%)	-	-	-	-	-	-
German American	(%)	-	-	50.0	-	-	-
Jewish[b]	(%)	-	-	-	-	50.0	-
Hungarian	(%)	-	-	-	-	-	-
Other foreign-born[c]	(%)	-	-	-	-	-	-
Other native-born[d]	(%)	-	-	-	-	-	-
	n	1	-	7	2	6	1
	(%)	.5	-	3.6	1.0	3.1	.5

SOURCE: 1920 sample.
  a. Including 5 cases born in Ukraine (MT Ukrainian), Austria (MT Russian), and Poland (MT Ruthenian).
  b. One Austrian and one Russian.

It is only when we examine production suburbs with factories that we find immigrant, working-class suburban neighborhoods, located primarily on the southwestern border of the city. In Springwells, while farming still accounted for 6% of the 129 sampled heads of households, white-collar workers made up 19% of the population, skilled factory workers 26%, unskilled workers almost 50% of this suburban area, some working at the blast furnaces of the River Rouge complex, and others in the brick-making factories of the township (table 13.9). Fully 70% of Springwells' population was of non–Anglo-Saxon origin; immigrant Poles, Czechoslovakians, Yugoslavians, Austrians, Hungarians, Russians, Rumanians, and Armenians made up 32% of the population. Very similar were the villages of Oakwood, River Rouge, and Ecorse at the outer range of Detroit's industrial belt, populated mostly by skilled and unskilled factory workers (66%; table 13.10).

Immediately beyond this industrial belt, farmland arose again with almost 20% of the sampled heads being farmers in Dearborn. Dearborn, where the smaller Ford tractor plant was located, was perhaps the perfectly balanced combination of production suburb, residential suburb, and also farming area.

Skilled, semiskilled wage labor	Skilled, semiskilled service workers	Lower retailers	Unskilled wage labor	Unskilled service workers	Farm owners and laborers	Number in sample	Missing data	Per-centage
40.2	.8	-	45.7	4.7	-	127	4	65.8
53.3	-	-	40.0	6.7	-	15	-	7.5
42.9	-	-	57.1	-	-	14	-	7.0
50.0	-	-	37.5	-	-	8	-	4.0
60.0	-	-	-	-	-	5	-	2.5
40.0	-	-	40.0	20.0	-	5	-	2.5
-	-	-	66.7	-	-	3	-	1.5
100.0	-	-	-	-	-	3	1	2.0
50.0	-	-	-	-	-	2	1	1.5
50.0	-	-	-	-	-	2	-	1.0
-	-	-	50.0	50.0	-	2	-	1.0
75.0	-	-	-	25.0	-	4	-	2.0
66.6	-	-	33.3	-	-	3	-	1.5
84	1	-	81	10	-	193	6	100.0
43.5	.5	-	42.0	5.2	-	100.0		

c. Canada (MT English): 1; Yugoslavia (MT Croatian): 1; Sweden: 1; Italy: 1.
d. Black: 1; native born of British parents: 1; of mixed American and Irish parentage: 1.

But although 41% of the 154 sampled heads of households were industrial workers, Dearborn was an Anglo-Saxon suburb; there were only four Poles and one Russian Jew in the sample (table 13.11). Each section of metropolis now showed a clearer balance between ethnic and occupational clustering.

Such were the major shifts in Detroit's spatial cleavages. This cross-sectional analysis for 1920 has shown how social class now served to define urban space in terms stronger than ever before and equal to those of ethnicity. Social class became a more important factor in dividing Detroit, but not because the various groups of workers suddenly mixed to form a new cosmopolitan working class. Instead, most ethnic groups—adjusting separately to the new realities of factory life—fragmented along socioeconomic lines in a fashion unknown at the turn of the century. Several trends overlapped: old non–Anglo-Saxon groups like the Irish and the Germans tended now to mix residentially with native white Americans of the same social status. The German community, which was still a cross-class community in the 1890s, economically based on independent small enterprises, disappeared under the pressures of industrialization and of the ideological trauma associated with the First World War. In turn, even neigh-

TABLE 13.5
Ethnicity versus occupational status, Highland Park, 1920

Ethnic group		Professionals	High white-collar	White-collar	Nonretail proprietors	Retailers	Craftsmen
				Occupational group			
Native white American	(%)	2.5	1.3	32.5	2.5	6.3	-
British	(%)	5.9	-	17.6	-	-	-
Canadian (English)	(%)	7.7	-	23.1	-	-	-
Canadian (English) American[a]	(%)	-	-	30.8	15.4	-	-
German American[b]	(%)	11.1	-	11.1	11.1	-	-
British American[c]	(%)	-	-	42.9	14.3	-	-
Italian	(%)	-	-	-	-	-	-
Armenian	(%)	-	-	-	-	33.3	-
Canadian-British American	(%)	-	-	-	50.0	-	-
Irish American	(%)	33.3	-	-	-	-	-
Swiss American	(%)	-	-	66.7	-	-	-
German	(%)	-	50.0	-	-	50.0	-
Other foreign-born[d]	(%)	4.5	-	22.7	4.5	-	-
Other native-born[e]	(%)	-	-	20.0	-	20.0	-
	(n)	7	2	49	9	9	-
	(%)	3.7	1.0	25.7	4.7	4.7	-

SOURCE: 1920 sample.
   a. Including 5 cases of mixed American and English-Canadian parentage.
   b. Including 7 cases of mixed American and German parentage.
   c. Including 4 cases of mixed American and British parentage.
   d. Ireland (MT English): 3; Poland: 2; Sweden: 2; Austria: 2; Russia (MT Yiddish): 2; Turkey: 2; Canada (MT

borhoods of new immigrants were different in 1920 from those in the 1890s. Newcomers such as the Hungarians and the Poles made up a class of factory workers who took over large sections of the city generally near large plants. In the process, the Polish neighborhood of the 1890s, with its atmosphere of a compact village, its isolated institutional and social life (including an independent educational curriculum), and its ability to retain the more successful Poles as shopkeepers or professionals, had given way to the classic milltown of workers, retaining not most but only a handful of nonworkers within its ranks. Only the small Russian-Jewish community grew in the nineteenth-century "German" tradition of occupational diversity. And the Blacks—a special case, on which I will expand in the next chapter—were forced to concentrate in an increasingly dense ghetto, irrespective of their social status.

The 1920 maps, then, show not only a movement toward the blend of old ethnic groups into a new social order, but also a diversification and fragmen-

Skilled, semiskilled wage labor	Skilled, semiskilled service workers	Lower retailers	Unskilled wage labor	Unskilled service workers	Farm owners and laborers	Number in sample	Missing data	Per-centage
42.5	-	-	6.3	6.3	-	80	4	41.6
47.1	-	-	29.4	-	-	17	1	8.9
46.2	-	-	15.4	7.7	-	13	-	6.4
38.5	-	-	15.4	-	-	13	1	6.9
66.7	-	-	-	-	-	9	1	5.0
14.3	-	-	14.3	14.3	-	7	1	4.0
28.6	-	-	57.1	14.3	-	7	-	3.5
33.3	-	-	16.7	16.7	-	6	-	3.0
25.0	-	-	-	25.0	-	4	-	2.0
66.7	-	-	-	-	-	3	1	2.0
33.3	-	-	-	-	-	3	-	1.5
-	-	-	-	-	-	2	-	1.0
31.8	-	-	31.8	4.5	-	22	1	11.4
40.0	-	-	20.0	-	-	5	1	3.0
77	-	-	27	11	-	191	11	100.0
40.3	-	-	14.1	5.8	-	100.0		

French): 2; Yugoslavia (MT Serbian): 1; Hungary: 1; Russia (MT Russian): 1; Rumania: 1; Bulgaria: 1; New South Wales (MT English): 1; Australia: 1; South America (MT Spanish): 1.

e. Black: 1; native born of Belgian parents (MT Flemish): 2; 1 case of mixed British and English-Canadian parentage; 1 case of mixed Russian and German parentage; and 1 case of mixed British and Irish parentage.

tation of the society into a greater number of ethnically and racially isolated working-class groups. As a consequence, the intensity of ethnic affiliation became more susceptible to variation by class. Ethnicity remained an important force but lost its power to transcend other social cleavages.

TABLE 13.6
Ethnicity versus occupational status, Grosse Pointe, 1920

Ethnic group		Professionals	High white-collar	White-collar	Nonretail proprietors	Retailers	Craftsmen
				Occupational group			
Native white American	(%)	9.1	7.3	25.5	5.5	-	1.8
British	(%)	-	-	12.5	6.3	-	-
German American[a]	(%)	6.3	-	25.0	6.3	-	-
Belgian	(%)	-	-	-	-	-	6.7
German	(%)	-	-	14.3	-	14.3	-
Canadian (English) American	(%)	16.7	-	50.0	-	-	-
Irish American[b]	(%)	20.0	-	20.0	20.0	-	-
Irish	(%)	-	-	-	-	-	-
Canadian (French) American[c]	(%)	-	-	-	-	-	-
Belgian American[d]	(%)	-	-	33.3	-	-	-
Canadian (English)	(%)	-	-	50.0	-	-	-
British American	(%)	-	-	-	-	-	-
Other foreign-born[e]	(%)	-	-	-	-	-	33.3
Other native-born[f]	(%)	14.2	-	28.6	-	-	-
	n	9	4	29	6	1	3
	(%)	6.3	2.8	20.3	4.2	.7	2.1

SOURCE: 1920 sample.
   a. Including 6 cases of mixed American and German parentage.
   b. Including 4 cases of mixed American and Irish parentage.
   c. Including 3 cases of mixed American and French-Canadian parentage.

Skilled, semiskilled wage labor	Skilled, semiskilled service workers	Lower retailers	Unskilled wage labor	Unskilled service workers	Farm owners and laborers	Number in sample	Missing data	Percentage
14.5		-	16.4	20.0	-	55	15	42.7
6.3	-	-	-	62.5	12.5	16	-	9.8
31.3	-	-	12.5	12.5	6.3	16	-	9.8
33.3	-	-	33.3	6.7	20.0	15	2	10.4
-	-	-	57.1	14.3	-	7	-	4.3
-	-	-	-	33.3	-	6	1	4.3
-	-	-	20.0	20.0	-	5	1	3.7
33.3	-	-	-	66.7	-	3	1	2.4
66.7		-	33.3	-	-	3	1	2.4
33.3	-	-	-	-	33.3	3	-	1.8
-	-	-	-	50.0	-	2	-	1.2
100.0	-	-	-	-	-	2	-	1.2
33.3	33.3	-	-	-	-	3	-	1.8
28.6	-	-	-	28.6	-	7	-	3.7
28	1	-	21	34	7	143	21	100.0
19.6	.7	-	14.7	23.8	4.9	100.0		

d. Including 1 case of mixed American and Belgian (Flemish) parentage, and 1 native born of Dutch parents.

e. Canada (MT English): 1; Poland: 1; France: 1.

f. Native born of Polish parents: 1; of Danish parents: 1; of French parents: 1; 1 case of mixed French and German parentage; 1 of mixed English and Irish parentage; and 2 of mixed German and Irish parentage.

TABLE 13.7
Ethnicity versus occupational status, Ferndale and Royal Oak, 1920

Ethnic group		Professionals	High white-collar	White-collar	Nonretail proprietors	Retailers	Craftsmen
				Occupational group			
Native white American	(%)	5.3	-	29.3	5.3	-	-
Canadian (English)	(%)	-	-	9.1	13.6	-	-
British	(%)	-	-	11.1	-	5.6	5.6
German American[a]	(%)	8.3	-	-	8.3	-	-
British American[b]	(%)	-	-	33.3	-	-	-
Canadian (English) American[c]	(%)	22.2	-	22.2	11.1	-	-
German	(%)	-	-	-	-	12.5	-
Netherlander[d]	(%)	-	-	-	40.0	-	-
Irish Canadian	(%)	-	-	-	-	-	-
Irish American[e]	(%)	-	-	-	-	-	-
Canadian (Irish) American	(%)	-	-	-	-	-	-
Scandinavian[f]	(%)	-	33.3	-	33.3	-	33.3
Other foreign-born[g]	(%)	-	-	-	-	-	-
Other native-born[h]	(%)	-	10.0	-	10.0	-	-
	n	7	2	32	13	2	2
	(%)	3.6	1.0	16.7	6.8	1.0	1.0

SOURCE: 1920 sample.

  a. Including 2 cases of mixed American and German parentage.

  b. Including 9 cases of mixed American and British parentage.

  c. Including 6 cases of mixed American and English-Canadian parentage.

  d. Including 1 Belgian (MT Flemish).

  e. Including 2 cases of mixed American and Irish parentage.

  f. Denmark: 2; Sweden: 1.

Skilled, semiskilled wage labor	Skilled, semiskilled service workers	Lower retailers	Unskilled wage labor	Unskilled service workers	Farm owners and laborers	Number in sample	Missing data	Per-centage
41.3	-	-	14.7	1.3	2.7	75	2	37.0
31.8	-	-	45.5	-	-	22	2	11.5
55.6	5.6	-	16.7	-	-	18	3	10.1
50.0	8.3	-	16.7	8.3	-	12	1	6.3
33.3	8.3	-	8.3	-	16.7	12	-	5.8
11.1	-	-	22.2	-	11.1	9	-	4.3
62.5	-	-	12.5	-	12.5	8	3	5.3
60.0	-	-	-	-	-	5	-	2.4
75.0	-	-	-	25.0	-	4	-	1.9
33.3	-	-	-	33.3	33.3	3	-	1.4
100.0	-	-	-	-	-	3	1	1.9
-	-	-	-	-	-	3	-	1.4
25.0	-	-	50.0	12.5	12.5	8	3	5.3
40.0	-	-	10.0	20.0	10.0	10	2	5.8
80	3	-	35	7	9	192	17	100.0
41.7	1.6	-	18.2	3.6	4.7	100.0		

g. Ukraine (MT Ukranian): 2; Canada (MT French): 1; Canada (MT German): 1; Poland: 1; France: 1; Australia: 1; Yugoslavia (MT Serbian): 1; Italy: 1; Czechoslovakia (MT Bohemian): 1; Austria: 1.

h. Black: 1; native born of French-Canadian parents: 2; of Polish parents: 1; of Swedish parents: 1; of Swiss parents (MT German): 1; of French parents: 1; of mixed English-Canadian and British parentage: 1; of mixed German and Netherlander parentage: 1; of mixed American and French-Canadian parentage: 1; of mixed American and French parentage: 1; and one born at sea.

TABLE 13.8
Ethnicity versus occupational status, Greenfield, 1920

Ethnic group		Professionals	High white-collar	White-collar	Nonretail proprietors	Retailers	Craftsmen
				Occupational group			
Native white American	(%)	2.2	-	22.2	6.7	4.4	-
British	(%)	-	-	27.8	5.6	-	-
German American[a]	(%)	-	-	6.7	-	6.7	-
Canadian (English)	(%)	-	-	36.4	-	-	-
Canadian (English) American[b]	(%)	-	-	57.1	-	14.3	-
French[c]	(%)	-	-	20.0	20.0	-	-
Canadian (French)	(%)	-	-	-	-	-	-
German	(%)	-	-	50.0	25.0	-	-
British American[d]	(%)	-	-	33.3	-	33.3	-
Irish American	(%)	-	-	-	-	-	-
Dutch American	(%)	-	-	-	50.0	-	-
Other foreign-born[e]	(%)	11.1	-	-	-	-	-
Other native-born[f]	(%)	-	-	-	-	-	-
	(n)	2	-	28	7	5	-
	(%)	1.5	-	21.5	5.4	3.8	-

SOURCE: 1920 sample.

   a. Including 4 cases of mixed American and German parentage.

   b. Including 5 cases of mixed American and English-Canadian parentage.

   c. Including 5 cases of mixed American and French parentage.

   d. Including 3 cases of mixed American and British parentage.

Skilled, semiskilled wage labor	Skilled, semiskilled service workers	Lower retailers	Unskilled wage labor	Unskilled service workers	Farm owners and laborers	Number in sample	Missing data	Per-centage
28.9	4.4	-	13.3	8.9	8.9	45	1	31.5
33.3	-	-	22.2	11.1	-	18	1	13.0
20.0	-	-	-	13.3	53.3	15	4	13.0
36.4	9.1	-	-	9.1	9.1	11	-	7.5
-	-	-	-	28.6	-	7	-	4.8
20.0	-	-	20.0	-	20.0	5	4	6.2
25.0	-	-	50.0	-	25.0	4	-	2.7
-	25.0	-	-	-	-	4	2	4.1
-	33.3	-	-	-	-	3	4	4.8
50.0	-	-	-	50.0	-	2	-	1.4
-	-	-	50.0	-	-	2	-	1.4
66.7	-	-	11.1	11.1	-	9	-	6.2
80.0	-	-	-	-	20.0	5	-	3.4
39	5	-	15	12	17	130	16	100.0
30.0	3.8	-	11.5	9.2	13.1	100.0		

e. Canada (MT German): 1; Ireland (MT Irish): 1; Czechoslovakia (MT Bohemian): 1; Yugoslavia (MT Serbian): 1; Denmark: 1; Belgium (MT Flemish): 1; Austria: 1; Lithuania: 1; Spain: 1.

f. Native born of Danish parents: 1; of mixed German and Irish parentage: 1; of mixed German and French parentage: 1; of mixed British and Irish parentage: 2.

TABLE 13.9
Ethnicity versus occupational status, Springwells, 1920

Ethnic group		Professionals	High white-collar	White-collar	Nonretail proprietors	Retailers	Craftsmen
				Occupational group			
Native white American	(%)	-	-	16.1	6.5	-	-
German American[a]	(%)	-	-	9.1	27.3	-	-
Polish	(%)	-	-	-	-	-	-
Hungarian	(%)	-	-	-	-	20.0	-
German	(%)	11.1	-	-	11.1	-	-
Canadian (English)	(%)	-	-	14.3	14.3	-	-
Russian	(%)	-	-	-	-	-	-
Czechoslovakian	(%)	-	-	25.0	-	-	-
Rumanian	(%)	-	-	-	-	-	-
British	(%)	-	-	-	33.3	-	-
British American	(%)	-	-	-	-	-	-
Polish American[b]	(%)	-	-	-	-	-	-
Other foreign-born[c]	(%)	-	-	-	14.3	14.3	-
Other native-born[d]	(%)	-	-	-	11.1	-	-
	n	1	-	8	10	3	-
	(%)	.9	-	6.9	8.6	2.6	-

SOURCE: 1920 sample.
  a. Including 3 cases of mixed American and German parentage.
  b. Including 1 case of mixed American and Polish parentage.
  c. Austria: 2; Armenia: 2; Canada (MT French): 1; Canada (MT Irish): 1; Yugoslavia (MT Serbian): 1.

Skilled, semiskilled wage labor	Skilled, semiskilled service workers	Lower retailers	Unskilled wage labor	Unskilled service workers	Farm owners and laborers	Number in sample	Missing data	Per-centage
38.7	-	-	25.8	9.7	3.2	31	2	25.6
-	-	-	45.5	-	18.2	11	4	11.6
10.0	-	-	70.0	20.0	-	10	-	7.8
40.0	-	-	30.0	10.0	-	10	-	7.8
-	-	-	55.5	11.1	11.1	9	2	8.5
28.6	-	-	-	28.6	14.3	7	1	6.2
16.7	-	-	66.7	16.7	-	6	1	5.4
75.0	-	-	-	-	-	4	1	3.9
25.0	-	-	75.0	-	-	4	-	3.1
-	-	-	33.3	33.3	-	3	2	3.9
66.7	-	-	33.3	-	-	3	-	2.3
-	-	-	50.0	50.0	-	2	-	1.6
14.3	-	-	42.9	-	14.3	7	-	5.4
33.3	-	-	44.4	-	11.1	9	-	7.0
30	-	-	45	12	7	116	13	100.0
25.9	-	-	38.8	10.3	6.0	100.0		

d. Native born of French-Canadian parents: 1; of Irish parents: 1; of mixed American and Canadian (MT Irish) parentage: 1; of mixed American and French parentage: 1; and mixed British and English-Canadian parentage: 1; of mixed British and Irish parentage: 1; of mixed German and French parentage: 1; of mixed German and French-Canadian parentage: 1; of mixed English-Canadian and Rumanian parentage: 1.

TABLE 13.10

Ethnicity versus occupational status, Oakwood, River Rouge, and Ecorse, 1920

Ethnic group		Professionals	High white-collar	White-collar	Nonretail proprietors	Retailers	Craftsmen
				Occupational group			
Native white American	(%)	4.8	-	6.3	1.6	1.6	3.2
German American[a]	(%)	-	-	4.3	8.7	8.7	-
Hungarian	(%)	-	-	-	-	23.1	7.7
Polish	(%)	-	-	-	-	-	-
German	(%)	-	-	12.5	-	-	-
Canadian (French)	(%)	-	-	-	-	16.7	-
British	(%)	-	-	-	-	-	-
British American[b]	(%)	-	-	-	-	-	-
Canadian (French) American[c]	(%)	-	-	20.0	-	20.0	-
Canadian (English)[d]	(%)	-	-	20.0	-	-	20.0
Rumanian	(%)	-	-	-	25.0	-	-
Irish American[e]	(%)	-	-	75.0	-	-	-
Other foreign-born[f]	(%)	5.6	-	11.1	5.6	-	11.1
Other native-born[g]	(%)	-	-	33.3	-	-	-
	(n)	4	-	15	5	8	6
	(%)	2.2	-	8.3	2.8	4.4	3.3

SOURCE: 1920 sample.

  a. Including 3 cases of mixed American and German parentage.

  b. Including 2 cases of mixed American and British parentage.

  c. Including 2 cases of mixed American and French-Canadian parentage.

  d. Including 2 cases with mother tongue Scotch.

Skilled, semiskilled wage labor	Skilled, semiskilled service workers	Lower retailers	Unskilled wage labor	Unskilled service workers	Farm owners and laborers	Number in sample	Missing data	Per-centage
47.6	-	-	20.6	11.1	3.2	63	2	34.6
39.1	-	-	26.1	4.3	8.7	23	-	12.2
30.7	-	-	38.5		-	13	-	6.9
33.3	-	-	41.7	8.3	16.7	12	-	6.4
37.5	-	-	12.5	-	37.5	8	3	5.9
33.3	16.7	-	-	16.7	16.7	6	-	3.2
100.0	-	-	-	-	-	6	-	3.2
100.0	-	-	-	-	-	6	-	3.2
20.0	-	-	40.0	-	-	5	-	2.7
60.0	-	-	-	-	-	5	1	3.2
50.0	-	-	25.0	-	-	4	-	2.1
25.0	-	-	-	-	-	4	-	2.1
33.3	-	-	27.8	5.6	-	19	1	10.6
50.0	-	-	-	-	16.7	6	1	3.7
79	1	-	40	11	11	180	8	100.0
43.9	.6	-	22.2	6.1	6.1	100.0		

e. Including 2 cases of mixed American and Irish parentage.

f. Italy: 3; Austria: 3; Canada (MT German): 2; Ireland: 2; Finland: 2; Czechoslovakia (MT Bohemian): 2; Yugoslavian (MT Croatian): 1; Belgium (MT Flemish): 1; France: 1; Lithuania: 1; Canada (MT French): 1.

g. Native born of English-Canadian parents; 3; of Norwegian parents: 1; of Hungarian parents: 1; of Russian parents: 1; of mixed American and Canadian (MT German) parentage: 1.

TABLE 13.11
Ethnicity versus occupational status, Dearborn, 1920

Ethnic group		Professionals	High white-collar	White-collar	Nonretail proprietors	Retailers	Craftsmen
				Occupational group			
Native white American	(%)	5.5	-	29.1	5.5	3.6	1.8
German American[a]	(%)	5.6	-	11.1	-	5.6	-
German	(%)	-	-	-	-	10.0	10.0
British American[b]	(%)	-	-	33.3	-	-	-
British	(%)	12.5	-	25.0	-	-	-
Canadian (English) American[c]	(%)	-	-	12.5	12.5	-	-
Canadian (English)	(%)	-	-	20.0	-	-	-
Polish	(%)	-	-	-	-	-	-
Netherlander and Belgian[d]	(%)	-	-	-	-	-	-
Swiss American	(%)	-	-	50.0	-	-	-
Austrian	(%)	-	-	-	-	-	-
Russian	(%)	-	-	-	-	-	-
Other foreign-born[e]	(%)	-	-	-	-	-	-
Other native-born[f]	(%)	12.5	-	25.0	-	-	12.5
	(n)	6	-	29	4	4	3
	(%)	4.3	-	21.0	2.9	2.9	2.2

SOURCE: 1920 sample.

   a. Including 2 cases of mixed American and German parentage.

   b. Including 6 cases of mixed American and British parentage.

   c. Including 7 cases of mixed American and English-Canadian parentage.

   d. Netherlands (MT Dutch): 2; Belgium (MT Flemish): 1.

Skilled, semiskilled wage labor	Skilled, semiskilled service workers	Lower retailers	Unskilled wage labor	Unskilled service workers	Farm owners and laborers	Number in sample	Missing data	Per-centage
21.8	-	-	18.2	5.5	9.1	55	4	38.8
27.8	-	-	22.2	5.6	22.2	18	4	14.3
20.0	-	-	-	30.0	30.0	10	2	7.8
33.3	-	-	-	11.1	22.2	9	1	6.5
25.0	-	-	12.5	-	25.0	8	1	5.8
25.0	-	-	-	-	50.0	8	-	5.2
40.0	-	-	20.0	-	20.0	5	1	3.9
-	-	-	75.0	-	25.0	4	-	2.6
66.7	-	-	-	-	33.3	3	-	1.9
50.0	-	-	-	-	-	2	-	1.3
50.0	-	-	50.0	-	-	2	-	1.3
50.0	-	-	-	-	50.0	2	-	1.3
25.0	-	-	25.0	-	50.0	4	-	2.6
-	-	-	25.0	12.5	12.5	8	3	7.1
34	-	-	22	9	27	138	16	100.0
24.6	-	-	15.9	6.5	19.6	100.0		

e. Czechoslovakia (MT Bohemian): 2; Hungary: 1; Yugoslavia (MT Serbian): 1.

f. Native born of Irish parents: 3; of Czechoslovakian (MT Bohemian) parents: 1; of French-Canadian parents: 1; of mixed American and Norwegian parentage: 1; of mixed Swedish and Norwegian parentage: 1; of mixed English-Canadian and British parentage: 1; of mixed English-Canadian and Irish parentage: 2; of mixed German and French parentage: 1.

14

Black and White Newcomers in Working-Class Detroit

Plate 14. Black laundresses, c. 1910.
Courtesy of the Burton Historical Collection, Detroit Public Library.

As Blacks poured into Detroit during and after the First World War, they soon formed a large ghetto. Nothing quite like it had existed in Detroit before. Blacks competed with whites for jobs and houses, and the sheer number of new arrivals threatened the established racial composition of many neighborhoods. As a consequence, Blacks became the victims of many forms of terrorism designed to keep them in place, and the ghetto sprang up, in part, as a reaction to a xenophobic violence which no other group of migrants to the city had ever experienced. In many ways, the violent pressures of the white community upon Black newcomers worked as they were meant to, because white violence hit a community unable to defend itself and unprepared to fight back. Thus the Black ghetto was formed, as this latest group of newcomers to Detroit established a settlement process almost totally unlike that of the immigrant groups that had been pouring into the city since the 1870's.

VIOLENCE AND SEGREGATION

Although racial violence erupted often, Detroit was spared the large-scale riots that had plagued other cities since the turn of the century. In Springfield, Illinois, in 1908, for example, a riot contributed to the creation of the NAACP; in other cities, such as East Saint Louis in 1917 or Washington, D.C., and Chicago in 1919, mobs of angry whites—often middle-class members of ethnic athletic clubs, as in Chicago, or even uniformed soldiers, as in Washington, D.C.—chased small groups of Blacks, attacked them, and beat them, often to death.[1] In these cities, mobs sometimes attacked the fringes of Black residential areas, but most of the fighting took place in areas dominated by whites, either in central business districts or in transitional neighborhoods where whites outnumbered Blacks.

Violence often erupted in Detroit, too, but it was generally confined to a specific locality and rarely spread to large-scale rioting. Violent clashes occurred especially in the spring of 1919, when the postwar recession caused a rash of strikes in Detroit and stiff competition between Blacks and whites for jobs on the assembly line. During this period, violence often broke out at factory gates when Blacks were used as strikebreakers, and at least one Black man was killed.[2] There is evidence that some of the strikebreakers were provided to

1. August Meier and Elliott M. Rudwick, *From Plantation to Ghetto: An Interpretive History of American Negroes* (New York: Hill & Wang, 1966), pp. 167, 192–96; Guichard Parris and Lester Brooks, *Blacks in the City: A History of the National Urban League* (Boston: Little, Brown, 1971), pp. 145–51; Chicago Commission on Race Relations, *The Negro in Chicago: A Study of Race Relations and a Race Riot* (Chicago: University of Chicago Press, 1923), pp. 11–17, 55.

2. Forrester B. Washington, "The Negro in Detroit: A Survey of the Conditions of a Negro Group in a Northern Industrial Center during the War Prosperity Period" (Detroit, 1920), chap. 5 of section, "The Negro in the Industries of Detroit," BHC.

employers by the Urban League's Employment Bureau, the head of which received his salary from the Employer's Association—the very organization that successfully maintained an open shop in the auto industry.[3] The Black leadership had good reasons to side with management to maintain open shops, for they saw a number of industrial unions work toward the exclusion of Black workers. By 1920, for example, the Street Railway Men's Union had persuaded the Detroit United Railway to stop employing Blacks, and Blacks generally believed they were better off without unions.[4]

Racist impulses were expressed, however, in many other ways than killing Blacks on the street. Detroit's Black citizens did not confront citywide racial warfare as did Blacks in a few other cities, but they were not spared the continuous form of local discrimination that typically contributed to the formation of ghettos. To begin with, Blacks were constricted to one area of the city. They were generally prevented from entering white neighborhoods—not through racially exclusive zoning ordinances, which were declared unconstitutional in 1917—but through private real estate covenants in which white property owners agreed not to sell to Blacks.[5] When these covenants failed to prevent some Blacks from moving into white neighborhoods, white residents resorted to force to expel them. Bombing of houses inhabited by Blacks and expulsion of Black residents began as early as 1917, and by the 1920s became frequent incidents.[6] In one instance, the Urban League reported the ejection of fifty Blacks from a house at 202 Harper Avenue by a mob of two hundred whites. The landlord, a policeman, supposedly dissatisfied with the way his white tenants were caring for his property (although it is more likely that he wanted to increase his profit), rented the house to Blacks. But as soon as the Black families and their lodgers moved in, a crowd of whites forced entrance, moved the furniture out of the house into four waiting trucks, and dumped it down the street. The Black tenants appealed to a nearby policeman, who suggested it was best they leave and so avoid trouble. Someone in the crowd shouted: "before we will stand for these niggers staying there, we will turn this house upside down during the night." Not surprisingly, the mob consisted of

3. August Meier and Elliott M. Rudwick, *Black Detroit and the Rise of the UAW* (New York: Oxford University Press, 1979), pp. 18–19.

4. Washington, "The Negro in Detroit," chap. 5 of section, "The Negro in the Industries of Detroit," BHC.

5. David Allen Levine, *Internal Combustion: The Races in Detroit, 1915–1926* (Westport, Conn.: Greeenwood Press, 1976), pp. 72, 130–31; Meier and Rudwick, *From Plantation to Ghetto*, p. 198; Roger L. Rice, "Residential Segregation by Law, 1910–1917," *Journal of Southern History* 34 (May 1968): 179–99; *Buchanan* v. *Warley*, 245 U.S. 60 (1917).

6. Especially well documented for Chicago; see Thomas Lee Philpott, *The Slum and the Ghetto: Neighborhood Deterioration and Middle-Class Reform, Chicago, 1880–1930* (New York: Oxford University Press, 1978), pp. 146–80.

"respectable" whites, including a former alderman, resident of the neighborhood. Not surprisingly, Harper Avenue—formerly a middle-class neighborhood,
already run down and already partly inhabited by Blacks—was adjacent to the
Black community.[7]

White residents of border areas were attempting to check the process of ghetto
expansion, a process which resulted primarily from profiteering schemes and
rent hikes by greedy landlords. As F. B. Washington explained, "Negro and
white real estate sharks . . . are preying upon homeless colored people." They
expanded the Black zone by raising rents unduly: landlords forced white tenants
out, and Black tenants who could not find homes anywhere else had to give
in to the profiteering scheme and accept a home in the high rent areas bordering
the ghetto.[8] Washington reported, for example, that Jewish families moved out
of a house on Alfred Street, between Antoine and Hastings, because their rent
was raised to $38.00 per month; Blacks moved in and subsequently accepted
an additional increase which brought the rent to $50.00. Both Black and white
realtors were involved in this new profit-making business of ghetto expansion.
Some cases of profiteering were so blatantly dishonest that the county prosecutor
charged seven Black realtors in a six month period in 1920, often for having
accepted rent deposits from several customers and then disappearing. In one
case, a white man moved into a house claiming he was the new landlord; he
evicted the tenant while promising him another, mythical, house, for which he
received a deposit; at the same time, this fake landlord received a deposit from
a new would-be tenant of the house being vacated. It was only later, when the
real landlord appeared to collect the rent, that the imposture was discovered.
In another case, an older, semi-illiterate Black woman who lived on Winder
Street collected $5,000 in advance rent for new houses presumably being built
by "friendly Jews" in the neighborhood, but the woman had simply invented
the housing project in question. Not all cases were so dramatic as these, but
life in the ghetto meant that tenants from the lower economic class had to pay
an exorbitant price for a house or even a shack. Such rent profiteering provided
the only means for many home-hungry Blacks to find a shelter and thus caused
the ghetto to expand in size and density.[9]

A SLUM

The ghetto, then, was a limited area, expanded only through "the invasion
of white districts by negroes," to use the words of some contemporary realtors,

7. Report by Forrester B. Washington, Director, Detroit League on Urban Conditions among
Negroes, 25 August 1917, Executive Secretary's General File, DUL Papers.
8. Washington, "The Negro in Detroit," part, "Relation of Rents to Income," in section, "The
Housing of the Negro in Detroit," BHC.
9. Ibid.

or through the abandonment of dilapidated housing to newcomers, to use the Chicago sociologists' terminology.[10] This dual process of concentration and expansion made the ghetto the highest density area in the city. While sections of Detroit's white immigrant neighborhoods were slums, they never reached the degree of squalor and unhealthfulness that characterized most sections of the Black ghetto of the World War I years. The time when Robert DeForest and Laurence Veiller could conclude their 1900 exhibit on tenements in United States' cities by stating that there was no tenement problem in Detroit was definitely over.[11]

Admittedly, sections of Detroit still had a low building density and open spaces, traces of a time when Detroit's east side was still loosely populated. As Washington accurately remarked, crowding still happened more inside than outside:

> while there is a great over-crowding within the building . . . there is no such land density as in the case of Negro colonies in other cities. Scattered all over this East Side District in almost every block will be found many one-story frame buildings, in which a large portion of the Negro population live. Invariably these buildings are placed on the front or side of a lot which is large enough for the location of another building of the same size or larger. . . . In the rear of many of these one-story frame houses are spacious yards on which large out-buildings are built which are chiefly used for the storage of coal and wood. The majority of these homes were built in the days when the price of land was low and it was cheaper to build a shack in the rear than it was to build a cellar to store coal.[12]

But even if Detroit's ghetto was not so physically dense as sections of Harlem or the Chicago Black belt, it was the densest area of the city, with over 300 people per acre (see map 12.1), and the life that most Blacks lived there reflected the worst sanitary conditions in the city. In 1919 the death rate among Blacks in Detroit was 16.2 per 1,000 in contrast to 12 for whites; the infant mortality rate (counted as the number of deaths of children under one year of age per 1,000 births) was 150 among Blacks, but 95.3 among whites.[13] While these very high figures in fact represented a slight improvement over preceding years,

10. Washington, "The Negro in Detroit," part, "The Effect on Realty Values of Negro Invasion," in section, "The Housing of the Negro in Detroit," BHC.

11. Robert W. DeForest and Lawrence Veiller, eds., *The Tenement House Problem, Including the Report of the New York State Tenement House Commission of 1900,* 2 vols. (New York: Macmillan Co., 1903), 1:146–47.

12. Washington, "The Negro in Detroit," part, "The Prevailing Types of Negro Housing," in section, "The Housing of the Negro in Detroit," BHC.

13. Washington, "The Negro in Detroit," part, "Death Rate," in section, "The Health of the Negro in Detroit," BHC.

there was no improvement in the Black community from 1915 to 1919 in the high incidence of pneumonia, tuberculosis, and syphilis.[14]

All observers familiar with conditions in other cities reported intense crowding in Detroit. There were practically no vacant houses in the ghetto; three or four families to an apartment was the rule rather than the exception, and Washington reported that "75% of the Negro homes have so many lodgers that they are really hotels. Stables, garages and cellars have been converted into homes for Negroes. The pool-rooms and gambling houses are beginning to charge for the privilege of sleeping on pool-room tables over night."[15] These observations are corroborated by Haynes's descriptions of apartments "in the midst of saloons, gambling places or 'buffet flats,' " the buffet flat being "a sort of high-class combination of a gambling parlor, a 'blind tiger' and an apartment of prostitution."[16]

The crowding was so intense that often floors were partitioned into many windowless rooms, and generally the houses were in a state of appalling disrepair, both in the main Black ghetto and in other sections of town where Blacks had made inroads as well. Once again, Washington's firsthand observations provide us with vivid descriptions of the dilapidation of the ghetto, a condition undoubtedly aggravated by the continuous flow of new arrivals. Sanitary conditions were often disgusting; 25% of the homes which he and other social workers visited had only outside toilets, and worse, many of the homes had inside toilets located, without partition, either in a bedroom or in the kitchen. Washington reported instances such as "a shack of four rooms on Napoleon Street, for which a widow pays $30.00 per month" in which "the investigator, on a stormy day saw the rain, literally, pour through the ceiling onto the floor," or "a house on Wilkins Street, the walls and floors of which are so damp that the tenants have to keep their beds standing well away from the walls to avoid getting wet," or a house on Sherman Street where "the investigator has seen children stumbling over ice frozen on the floors," or again one house on Hastings Street in which "a baby died on account of exposure, resulting from the fact that the window in the front of the house was blown out by a storm, two months previous and had not been repaired. There was no heat in the house visited because the pipe connected with the hot water system had burst, and the

14. Washington, "The Negro in Detroit," part, "Diseases Which Prevail," in section, "The Health of the Negro in Detroit," BHC.

15. Washington, "The Negro in Detroit," part, "Housing," in section, "The Housing of the Negro in Detroit," BHC.

16. George Edmund Haynes, *Negro Newcomers in Detroit, Michigan: A Challenge to Christian Statesmanship, A Preliminary Study* (New York: Home Missions Council, 1918; Arno Press and the New York Times, 1969), p. 21.

landlord, although he was receiving $65.00 per month, would make no repairs."[17]

AN UNSUCCESSFUL GRAFT ONTO A DEMOGRAPHICALLY VULNERABLE COMMUNITY

These brutal facts of segregation had far-reaching implications in a Black community which was ill-equipped to grow and adapt itself to new Detroit. What is remarkable when we move back in time to examine conditions before the ghetto was formed is that northerners were so unprepared to receive southerners and that the Black community had none of the means of white immigrant communities to incorporate newcomers into its ranks. The tragedy of Blacks in Detroit is that (as we have seen in preceding chapters) they had the almost opposite experience to that of white ethnic groups.

The small Black elite—about seventy families—had succumbed to the pressures of the native white American world to a much greater extent than members of German or Polish elites. The late nineteenth-century Black elite, as David Katzman explained, interacted with at least some whites on "a regular and equal basis."[18] Instead of working for poor Blacks, "the physicians, dentists and attorneys had mostly white practices, and the managers and clerks worked for white businesses or were in government service."[19] Members of this very small Black elite were often congregants in white churches, and some belonged to the exclusive Republican Michigan Club. This small group of integrationist Blacks lived separated from the vast majority of nonelite Blacks. In contrast, white ethnic groups had developed independent neighborhoods and supported communitywide institutions (like the luxurious Polish churches built in the 1890s), in part through the cross-class nature of their communities.

Isolated from the small Black elite, the great majority of the Blacks already in the city before the Great Migration were dispersed in some of the worst houses in Detroit in scattered pockets within largely white neighborhoods. And they were employed in the most menial unskilled and semiskilled service jobs (see tables 1.5 and 9.1). In contrast, members of all-white immigrant groups were much more widely distributed across the economic spectrum and could experience upward mobility within their own community.

While immigrant families adopted family strategies of income pooling be-

17. Washington, "The Negro in Detroit," part, "Maintenance," in section, "The Housing of the Negro in Detroit," BHC.

18. David M. Katzman, *Before the Ghetto: Black Detroit in the Nineteenth Century* (Chicago: University of Illinois Press, 1973), p. 160.

19. Ibid., p. 158; see also Elizabeth H. Pleck, *Black Migration and Poverty: Boston, 1865–1900* (New York: Academic Press, 1979), pp. 92–119; Alan Spear, *Black Chicago: The Making of a Negro Ghetto, 1890–1920* (Chicago: University of Chicago Press, 1967), pp. 51–70.

tween the heads of households and teenaged children—strategies which helped
Germans, Poles, and other workers to support their institutions and to survive
difficult times, most Black families in late nineteenth-century Detroit had no
teenaged children to send to work and could not develop similar strategies. The
majority of Black nuclear families were either childless couples or single parents
with children, rather than complete families with the two parents and children
present. Estimates from the 1900 census showed that Black women had a low
child to woman ratio of 415 children under age five per 1,000 married women
between the ages of twenty and forty-nine (compared with 1,200 children for
each 1,000 Polish women!). There are good indications in this data that such
a low fertility ratio was due to disease-caused sterility and high infant mortality
rather than to effective birth control (see chap. 10).

When the war industrialization fostered the rapid growth of Detroit's Black
population, Urban League workers were quick to report the resentment of
southern Blacks by northern Blacks, but they failed to understand its real
historical dimensions. George Haynes and Forrester B. Washington directed
their attention only to the small Black elite and neglected the circumstances of
the majority of Detroit's prewar Blacks. They simply reduced the problem to
an unhappy, regretful, but inevitable clash between respectable northern
Blacks, "the old Detroiters," and a class of southern migrants, "the outlanders"
lacking the middle-class values of the established communities.[20] George
Haynes, for instance, contrasted pre-1915 Blacks, the well-integrated "families
of a high grade both in intelligence and well being", to the undesirable newcomers:

> During the earlier days in Detroit the old residents, enjoyed a large share
> in the general life and activity of the community. With the large increase
> in the number of Negroes and the coming of many of the less desirable
> type, there was a reaction of these older residents against a gradual tending
> toward the segregation of all Negroes. There was also a class feeling
> growing out of their more favorable conditions.[21]

Washington, in turn, provided many examples of who these undesirable Blacks
were and how they were brought to Detroit, pointing to the way many labor
agents, working for industrialists,

> endeavored to get the Negro laborer overnight. This was their first mistake.
> The most desirable class of men of any race cannot separate themselves
> from their family and their community in twenty-four hours. In the second

---

20. Washington, "The Negro in Detroit," part, "Social Classes among the Negroes of Detroit,"
in section, "The Identification of the Negro in Detroit," BHC.
21. Haynes, *Negro Newcomers in Detroit*, p. 10.

place the labor scouts presented the sorts of arguments which would appeal most to the least desirable men. They spoke of the ease with which liquor could be obtained in Detroit, of the city's many gambling houses, and in general pictured Detroit as a "wide-open town."[22]

What Haynes and Washington diagnosed as a malaise of Black "old Detroiters" against newcomers was in fact a sign of a more pervasive social problem, the basic inability of most Blacks to expand their community to make room for newcomers. In sharp contrast to their idealized view of the past, the majority of the Blacks in Detroit before the World War I migration were already living in such dismal conditions that they had no means to establish a strong chain migration process to receive newcomers. It was only because the Black community was so small—and posed no threat of growing—that the dismal conditions in which most Blacks had lived had gone relatively unnoticed; and the existence of a tiny elite integrated into the white institutional and residential environment served to mask the true lot of the Black community.[23] It is no surprise, then, that when full-scale industrialization brought many single Black workers from the South, the tremendous pressure of numbers simply overwhelmed an already vulnerable community. Southerners came to work. They found work, but for the most part they failed to become more than a floating labor force, a heap of unattached single workers living in shacks in a growing ghetto.

CONTRASTS

The way in which Black newcomers congregated in the growing ghetto and the ways in which their settlement differed from that of all other groups appear clearly when we follow the 1920 census takers in their enumeration of a few representative blocks. What follows is not an analysis of Detroit's entire Black community in 1920 but a comparison of the ghetto's core—the area described by Haynes and Washington—to concentrations of other recent immigrant groups: Poles, Hungarians, Russian Jews, and Italians. A few blocks (no more than three for each group studied) were selected from my larger 1920 sample for an intensive analysis of housing and demographic characteristics, chosen on the basis of their unusually high segregation indexes for recent migrants to the city. The white ethnic groups to which Blacks are compared were selected

22. Washington, "The Negro in Detroit," chap. 9, part C of section "The Negro in the Industries of Detroit," BHC.

23. As in other cities, the occupational status of Blacks in Detroit may have declined since the 1850s; see Stephan Thernstrom, ed., *Harvard Encyclopedia of American Ethnic Groups* (Cambridge, Mass.: Harvard University Press, 1980), p. 14; however, Katzman, *Before the Ghetto*, contains no indication of a decline.

because of the relative recentness of their arrival in Detroit and because the male to female ratio at the time of the 1920 census was almost 140 males for 100 females in all these groups. All groups, then—Blacks and whites alike— suffered from similar demographic imbalance caused by the recent migration of male factory workers.

I chose three aspects of family life for close scrutiny: the degree of crowding in houses and the relationships between owners and renters; household composition; and fertility. Many social scientists and historians of the family, focusing primarily on household composition, have emphasized the disorganization of the Black urban household. They point to the many Black female-headed households and to the large number of unrelated boarders sharing living quarters as evidence of endemic disintegration n Black households in the "city of destruction," to use Franklin Frazier's phrase.[24] Yet other historians, often using the same sources of information, have argued that the Black household was remarkably stable under the pressures of migration and urbanization. Instead of stressing signs of fragmentation, they point to positive factors such as the large number of "two-parent" households in the urban population. They also argue that Black migrants often depended on complex networks of alley life for their survival and that it is impossible to evaluate the remarkable adaptability of the Black family if one insists in locating everybody within the confines of a traditional nuclear household.[25]

To be sure, the listing of household members in a census enumeration tells very little about the complex texture and the varieties of family life. One way to overcome the impasse, however, is to move from the study of household composition to that of vital statistics. Theodore Hershberg, for example, recently argued that the large number of Black female-headed households in nineteenth-century Philadelphia was due more to the high mortality of Black males than to marital desertion, a typically Frazerian sign of family "pathology."[26] I have already argued (when studying the demography of ethnic neighborhoods; see

24. E. Franklin Frazier, *The Negro Family in the United States* (Chicago: University of Chicago Press, 1939), pp. 271–390.

25. The most forceful critique of Frazier is Herbert Gutman, "Persistent Myths about the Afro-American Family," *Journal of Interdisciplinary History* 6 (Autumn 1975): 181–210. Elizabeth H. Pleck originally adopted Gutman's position; see Pleck, "The Two-Parent Household: Black Family Structure in Late Nineteenth-Century Boston," *Journal of Social History*, 6 (Fall 1972): 3–36; she then reversed herself and presented a neo-Frazierian interpretation of the Black family; see Pleck, *Black Migration and Poverty: Boston, 1865–1900*, pp. 162–96. The most powerful, but exaggerated argument against the breakdown thesis of the Black migrant is in James Borchert, *Alley Life in Washington* (Urbana: University of Illinois Press, 1980), pp. 57–99.

26. Frank F. Furstenberg, Jr., Theodore Hershberg, and John Modell, "The Origins of the Female-Headed Black Family: The Impact of the Urban Experience," *Journal of Interdisciplinary History* 6 (Autumn 1975): 181–210.

chap. 3) that the study of household composition in itself is insufficient to isolate behavioral differences between groups and areas. I thus turn again to fertility to complement household composition data, so as to evaluate the degree of adaptability of Blacks in the ghetto. A measure of fertility based on a child to woman ratio—thus independent of the number of boarders or the type of household extension—will provide a good comparative test of the Blacks' ability to give birth and to keep their children alive in the sordid living conditions of the ghetto, conditions often aggravated by the rough and windy climate of Michigan winters.

I will first examine in detail two of the sampled blocks in the Saint Antoine district, the heart of the Black ghetto (see table 14.1 and map 13.1). There were 215 Blacks living in the first block (most born in the South and including 53 mulattoes), and 283 Blacks in the second block.

TABLE 14.1

Household relationships and male-female ratio, by ethnicity, for selected blocks, Detroit, 1920

Ethnic groups by block[a]	Population	Heads of household	Other kin-related members	Boarders (N)	Boarders (%)	Male-female ratio[b]
Block 9301						
Black[c]	162	34	43	85	52.5	179.3
Mulatto	53	8	19	26	49.1	120.8
Block 9704						
Black[d]	283	79	121	83	29.3	128.3
Block 9701						
Black[e]	120	32	49	39	32.5	135.3
Russian Jewish	45	15	27	3	6.7	114.1
Russian-American Jewish	36	-	36	-	-	49.9
Austrian-American Jewish[f]	36	-	36	-	-	200.0
Austrian Jewish	27	9	18	-	-	79.9
Canadian Jewish	15	3	12	-	-	66.7
British-American Jewish	9	-	9	-	-	-
Hungarian Jewish	6	-	3	3	50.0	-
Polish Jewish	3	3	-	-	-	-
Polish-American Jewish	3	-	3	-	-	-
Block 17205						
Russian Jewish	142	53	72	17	12.0	141.0
Russian-American Jewish[g]	109	3	104	2	1.8	72.4
Polish Jewish	103	30	59	14	13.6	119.3
Polish-American Jewish	54	2	52	-	-	107.9
Canadian Jewish	21	-	21	-	-	90.8
Austrian Jewish	6	1	3	2	33.3	-
British Jewish	2	1	1	-	-	-
Swedish Jewish	2	-	2	-	-	-

TABLE 14.1 (*Continued*)

Household relationships and male-female ratio, by ethnicity, for selected blocks, Detroit, 1920

Ethnic groups by block[a]	Population	Heads of household	Other kin-related members	Boarders (N)	(%)	Male-female ratio[b]
Hungarian Jewish	1	1	-	-	-	-
Rumanian Jewish	1	-	1	-	-	-
Rumanian-Canadian-American-Jewish	1	-	1	-	-	-
Australian Jewish	1	1	-	-	-	-
Jewish (born at sea)	1	-	1	-	-	-
Bulgarian	15	-	1	14	93.3	139.2
Yugoslavian	9	-	-	9	100.0	-
Native white American	5	-	5	-	-	-
Hungarian	4	-	3	1	25.0	-
Rumanian	4	-	-	4	100.0	-
Greek	3	-	-	3	100.0	-
Canadian (English)	2	-	1	1	50.0	-
Canadian American	2	-	2	-	-	-
German American	1	-	-	1	100.0	-
Polish American	1	-	-	-	100.0	-
Norwegian	1	-	-	1	100.0	-
Finnish	1	-	-	1	100.0	-
Lithuanian	1	-	1	-	-	-
Italian	1	-	-	1	100.0	-
Columbian	1	-	-	1	100.0	-
Block 28109						
German American	46	9	35	2	4.3	84.2
German	27	13	12	2	7.4	107.9
Italian	31	11	12	8	25.8	244.8
Italian American	19	-	19	-	-	216.5
Native white American	24	-	24	-	-	60.0
Swiss American	1	-	1	-	-	-
Italian-French American	1	-	1	-	-	-
Block 28307						
Italian[h]	50	13	27	10	20.0	194.1
Italian American[i]	22	-	21	1	4.5	119.8
Polish	16	8	8	-	-	166.7
Polish American	23	-	23	-	-	91.5
Block 28401						
Polish	91	44	38	9	9.9	116.5
Polish American[j]	156	5	151	-	-	122.7
Native white American	5	-	5	-	-	-
German American	1	-	1	-	-	-
Block 28906						
Polish	185	62	82	41	22.2	164.6
Polish American[k]	168	7	159	2	1.2	118.3
Native white American	10	-	10	-	-	100.0

(*continued on next page*)

TABLE 14.1 (*Continued*)
Household relationships and male-female ratio, by ethnicity, for selected blocks,
Detroit, 1920

Ethnic groups by block[a]	Population	Heads of household	Other kin-related members	Boarders (N)	Boarders (%)	Male-female ratio[b]
Block 40511						
Polish	27	12	12	3	11.1	170.3
Polish American	37	-	37	-	-	146.9
Unknown	3	-	3	-	-	-
Block 60911						
Hungarian	74	24	34	16	21.6	155.1
Hungarian American	46	-	46	-	-	109.2
Block 60912						
Hungarian	116	35	54	27	23.3	169.5
Hungarian American	79	-	76	3	3.9	79.5
Native white American	1	-	1	-	-	-
Polish	1	-	-	1	100.0	-

SOURCE: 1920 sample.

a. Native white American: born in the U.S. of two U.S.-born parents; Black: born in the U.S. of two U.S.-born Black parents; Polish-Jewish: born in Poland with mother tongue Hebrew or Yiddish of two Polish parents; Polish-American Jew: born in the U.S. of two Hebrew- or Yiddish-speaking Polish parents, etc. Exceptions are noted below.

b. Male-female ratio computed for 10 or more cases.

c. Includes 1 case born in the West Indies of two West Indian parents; 1 case born in Costa Rica of two Costa Rican parents; two cases of unknown parents.

d. Includes 8 cases born in Canada of two Black Canadian parents; 2 cases born in the West Indies of two West Indian parents.

e. Includes 3 cases born in the West Indies of two West Indian parents.

f. Includes 18 cases born in the U.S. of mixed Austrian and Hungarian parents.

g. Includes 9 cases born in the U.S. of mixed native-born American (speaking Yiddish), and Russian (speaking Yiddish), parentage; and 2 cases born in the U.S. of Russian-Jewish and Hungarian parents.

h. Includes 2 cases born in Great Britain (MT Italian); 1 case born in Canada (MT Italian).

i. Includes 4 cases born in the U.S. of Italian (MT Italian) and British parents.

j. Includes 9 cases born in the U.S of Polish and native white American parents.

k. Includes 6 cases born in the U.S. of Polish and native white American parents.

Home ownership in the ghetto was dismally low, with only 4.8% of the heads of households owning their homes in one block and 2.6% in the other (table 14.5). In one block most households (58.5%) lived in detached houses not divided into apartments, leaving only 24.4% of the households in two-family dwellings and the rest in three- and four-family dwellings. In the other block, only 19% of the houses were single-family dwellings and as many as 60.7% of the houses included three to seven households (table 14.5). Regardless of the structure of the dwellings, all Black households who rented their abode rented from absentee owners; in no case did the census takers find owner and renter living in the same house, a common combination in ethnic neighborhoods where renting part of one's house was an integral part of the process of acquiring a home.

The demographic characteristics of these two blocks are startling because they show an almost complete absence of nuclear family life; families in each block were very small (2.49 and 2.56 people on the average) and most often composed of childless adults, predominantly males (table 14.2). In the first

TABLE 14.2

Family and household sizes and marital fertility, by ethnicity, for selected blocks, Detroit, 1920

Ethnic group by block[a]	Number of households	Mean family size	Mean household size	Number of women aged 20–49[b]	Child-woman ratio[c]
Block 9301					
Black	42	2.56	5.23	33	110.85[g]
Block 9704					
Black	79	2.49	3.57	67	98.47[g]
Block 9701					
Black	32	2.36	3.63	24	0
Jewish	30	5.90	6.10	27	1,100.00
Block 17205					
Jewish	92	4.65	5.43	81	719.52
Block 28109					
German[d]	22	4.27	4.40	10	595.00
Italian	11	4.00	4.73	5	1,067.00
Block 28307					
Polish	8	4.88	4.88	6	1,306.61
Italian	13	4.62	5.46	8	696.53
Block 28401					
Polish[e]	49	5.08	5.16	28	950.83
Block 28906					
Polish[f]	69	5.05	5.72	63	750.28
Block 40515					
Polish	12	5.33	5.58	8	920.00
Block 60911					
Hungarian	24	3.20	5.00	22	748.33
Block 60912					
Hungarian	35	4.88	5.79	28	972.23

SOURCE: 1920 sample.

a. Ethnicity of heads of households, as described in table 14.1.

b. Married women with husbands present.

c. Standardized for age distribution.

d. Includes 9 heads of households born in the U.S of two German parents.

e. Includes 5 heads of households born in the U.S. of two Polish parents.

f. Includes 7 heads of households born in the U.S. of two Polish parents.

g. Overall fertility for block 9301 was 97.86 (38 cases) and for block 9704 was 106.7 (75 cases).

block, for example, only 16.7% of the families consisted of complete nuclear families (two parents and their children); as many as 28.7% of the families were in fact solitaries, and another 33.3% childless couples (table 14.6). Almost 70% of the inhabitants were between the ages of twenty-one and forty; 62% were males and 52.5% boarders (tables 14.1 and 14.3). Thirty-four of the forty-one households had boarders, and the large household sizes (5.23 on the average including boarders) contrasted to the smaller family sizes (2.56 when only the blood relatives are counted). In the other block, less than half of the households had boarders; but the households without boarders were also made up of small families (with 2.49 people on the average), also composed of childless adults, predominantly males (table 14.2). Most likely many of these small families of the second block, already packed in tiny apartments, could not possibly accommodate as many boarders as the families living in the larger houses of the first block.

TABLE 14.3
Age distribution for selected blocks, Detroit, 1920

Ethnic group by block[a]	Population	Under 20 (%)	21–40 (%)	41 and above (%)
Block 9301				
Black	215	19.1	66.0	14.9
Block 9704				
Black	283	19.6	68.4	12.0
Block 9701				
Black and Jewish	300	43.0	47.0	10.0
Block 17205				
Jewish	495	41.3	44.7	14.0
Block 28109				
German and Italian	149	41.6	32.9	25.5
Block 28307				
Polish and Italian	111	53.2	42.3	4.5
Block 28401				
Polish	253	49.8	31.6	18.6
Block 28906				
Polish	363	48.9	38.4	12.7
Block 40515				
Polish	67	59.7	32.8	7.5
Block 60911				
Hungarian	120	45.8	42.5	11.7
Block 60912				
Hungarian	197	48.2	35.0	16.8

SOURCE: 1920 sample.

a. Ethnicity of heads of households, as described in table 14.1.

Black women living in these blocks bore hardly any children. It may be that migrating parents had left some children with grandparents in the South, but once in Detroit couples had few new children. Only a handful of them survived birth and were registered in the 1920 census. The age-standardized child to woman ratio (the best estimate of fertility we can calculate from census data)—computed as the number of children under five per 1,000 married women aged twenty to forty-nine—was only 110 in one block and 98 in another, one of the lowest to be found in any block of the city. When computed with all women in these age groups, not only the married women, the ratio remains essentially at the same level, around 100 (see table 14.2). Fertility was extremely low, regardless of the nature of the bond between men and women.

Each block of the ghetto naturally reflected the occupational distribution of the Blacks in the labor force (see table 13.2), but more importantly—and in sharp contrast with the turn-of-the-century scattered concentrations of Blacks—Black businessmen and Black professionals now lived in the very heart of the ghetto. The Black elite, separated from the unskilled service workers who lived in east side blocks in 1900, now joined the other Blacks in the transformed city. In one block 49% of the heads of households and 51% of the boarders were day laborers. Other heads of households (5%) and boarders (8%) were domestics; still others were distributed in other service occupations at different levels of skill, ranging from elevator operator, delivery boy, chauffeur, laundress, or janitor to barber and tailor; some heads of households were in the building trades as electrician, plasterer, or sandblaster. The few working wives were domestics or maids and the handful of working children were also either laborers or unskilled service workers. Only among heads of households were there a few white-collar workers (one in government work as a postal clerk), two businessmen, and a physician. The second block of the intensive study tells the same story of most Blacks still clustered in traditional Black occupations in unskilled service or employed at unskilled industrial jobs and of the Black occupational elite now integrated into the ghetto. The second block had a few more skilled and semiskilled industrial workers among the heads of households (three machinists, one molder, one auto worker, one toolmaker), a few more city employees (one fireman, one patrolman, one policeman), a few more local businessmen (one pharmacist, one undertaker), and one minister.

The contrasts between the structure of the Black ghetto and that of all other concentrations of recent Detroit immigrant groups are startling. If we leave the Black ghetto and follow the 1920 census takers into areas of Polish, Hungarian, Russian-Jewish, and Italian concentrations, we find a very large proportion of homeowners, and a flourishing nuclear family life—the two missing components of life in the ghetto.

Poles had continued to migrate to the city continuously until 1916, when immigration was reduced to a trickle. Despite the fact that they were often single men with little knowledge of American ways, they quickly adopted proven Polish-American community traditions in settling in the larger city. If we single out three blocks of highly concentrated Polish settlement, the differences from the Black blocks far outweigh the similarities. Like the Black sections, these blocks were largely inhabited by unskilled factory workers of recent arrival: in one block, characteristic of the others, sixty of the sixty-seven Polish households were headed by an immigrant and the other seven by sons of immigrants; almost 40% of the newcomers had immigrated to the United States after 1911; 91% were still aliens (table 14.4). In all, 19% of the heads of households, 48% of the wives, and 52% of the boarders could not speak English; and 58% of the block's

TABLE 14.4

Date of arrival in the United States and inability to speak English, by ethnicity, for selected blocks, Detroit, 1920

Ethnic group by block[a]	Population	Prior to 1901 (%)	1901–1910 (%)	1911–1915 (%)	1916–1920 (%)	Do not speak English (n)	(%)
Blocks 9301, 9704							
Foreign-born Black	4	25.0	75.0	-	-	4	-
Block 9701							
Foreign-born Black	3	-	-	100.0	-	3	-
Foreign-born Jewish	96	10.7	42.8	46.4	-	81	-
Block 17205							
Foreign-born Jewish	274	13.1	46.7	33.6	6.6	268	5.6
Other foreign-born	41	2.4	22.0	70.7	4.9	40	5.0
Block 28109							
German	26	84.6	11.5	-	3.8	27	-
Italian	31	12.9	22.6	64.5	-	31	3.2
Block 28307							
Polish	16	25.0	37.5	37.5	-	16	25.0
Italian	47	12.7	31.9	44.7	10.6	37	2.7
Block 28401							
Polish	91	58.2	27.5	13.2	1.0	88	50.0
Block 28906							
Polish	182	7.6	51.7	39.0	1.6	184	38.5
Block 40515							
Polish	27	11.1	48.1	40.7	-	26	26.9
Block 60911							
Hungarian	68	5.9	51.4	42.6	-	70	44.3
Block 60912							
Hungarian	109	2.7	46.7	50.5	-	11	53.2

SOURCE: 1920 sample.

a. Ethnicity of heads of households, as described in table 14.1.

TABLE 14.5

Home ownership and home occupancy, by ethnicity, for selected blocks, Detroit, 1920

Ethnic group by block[a]	Population	Own free (%)	Own mortgaged (%)	Rent (%)	Population	One household per dwelling (%)	Two households per dwelling (%)	Three or more households per dwelling (%)
Block 9301								
Black	41	2.4	2.4	95.1	41	58.5	24.4	17.1
Block 9704								
Black	79	1.3	1.3	97.4	79	19.0	20.3	60.7
Block 9701								
Black	32	-	-	100.0	32	18.8	18.8	62.4
Jewish	30	27.3	-	72.7	32	3.1	18.8	78.1
Block 17205								
Jewish	91	-	26.4	73.6	92	34.1	15.4	50.5
Block 28109								
German[b]	22	4.5	36.4	59.1	22	45.5	36.4	18.2
Italian	10	-	50.0	50.0	11	54.4	36.4	9.1
Block 28307								
Polish	8	12.5	25.0	62.5	8	25.0	50.0	25.0
Italian	13	23.1	30.8	46.5	13	23.1	30.8	46.2
Block 28401								
Polish[c]	47	29.8	19.1	51.1	49	34.7	38.8	26.5
Block 28906								
Polish[d]	67	10.4	20.9	68.7	69	11.6	42.0	46.4
Block 40515								
Polish	12	16.7	58.3	25.0	12	41.7	58.3	-
Block 60911								
Hungarian	24	4.2	33.3	62.5	24	45.8	16.7	37.5
Block 60912								
Hungarian	34	5.9	29.4	64.7	35	17.6	61.8	20.6

SOURCE: 1920 sample.
a. Ethnicity of heads of households, as described in table 14.1.
b. Includes 9 heads of households born in the U.S of two German parents.
c. Includes 5 heads of households born in the U.S. of two Polish parents.
d. Includes 7 heads of households born in the U.S. of two Polish parents.

inhabitants were males. But the excess of male factory workers did not upset the fundamental balance of home ownership and family life in the Polish community. Boarders made up less than 12% of any block's population. In two blocks, 13% and 17% of the households had boarders, in another 30%. When Ford's inspectors visited the Polish neighborhoods and talked about discouraging the boarder evil which disrupted family life, they actually talked about a real, sizable, and rather recent process of household extension among the Poles, but nothing that had upset traditional family life in these neighborhoods.[27] Taking in boarders was simply the inevitable result of the general lack of housing in Detroit during the war years. Despite the relatively large number of boarders, the Polish blocks had still more children than adults; up to 75% of the families were nuclear families with both parents and the children present, and the child to woman ratio varied from one block to another from 750 to 950, much higher than the Black ratio of about 100 (tables 14.2 and 14.6).

To be sure, the Polish settlement was dense and the percentage of single-family dwellings was sometimes low, varying from 11% to 42% (table 14.5). But when Poles doubled up, the crowding was one of Polish owners and Polish renters together, not a crowding of tenants piled up in deteriorating houses by absentee landlords who had no real stake in maintaining the property as long as they could find renters. Many Poles, although recent immigrants, managed to buy their homes. Among the sample Polish blocks no fewer than 30% and as many as 75% of the household heads were homeowners.

In many ways, the Polish sections of town had changed considerably since the 1880s and the early days of the settlement; they had grown congested, and many sections were now little dormitory towns near Detroit's large plants. They had lost some of the independence and autonomy of the earlier immigrant working-class neighborhood, but they overcame the demographic pressures brought by the migration of single workers and continued to invest in the two key components of their economic stability: home and family. The geographic distance between them and the Blacks was small, but to enter the Polish section of town from the Black ghetto was to enter a sharply different world.

Hungarians, even more recent arrivals than Poles, had settled on the other side of town, in the former village of Delray. In one of the two blocks of my study, 50% of the residents had arrived in the United States between 1911 and 1915, but despite the newness of their community and despite the demographic pressure of an excess of adult male factory workers, the newly formed Hungarian community also developed a core of homeowners and a nuclear family life.

27. Jonathan Schwartz, "Henry Ford's Melting Pot," in *Ethnic Groups in the City: Culture, Institution and Power*, ed. Otto Feinstein (Lexington, Mass.: D. C. Heath & Co., 1971), pp. 193–94.

TABLE 14.6

Family structure (kin-related members only), by ethnicity, for selected blocks, Detroit, 1920

Ethnic group by block[a]	Population	Solitary and Coresidents (%)	Couple without children (%)	Head only with children (%)	Complete nuclear (%)	Extended[b] (%)	Multiple[c] (%)
Block 9301							
Black	42	28.7	33.3	2.4	16.7	11.9	7.1
Block 9704							
Black	76	11.8	47.4	2.6	23.7	6.6	7.9
Block 9701							
Black	32	-	36.4	27.3	36.4	-	-
Jew	30	-	20.0	20.0	50.0	10.0	-
Block 17205							
Jew	88	1.1	6.8	1.1	73.9	10.2	6.9
Block 28109							
German[d]	22	9.1	13.6	13.6	50.2	9.1	4.5
Italian	11	18.2	9.1	9.1	36.4	9.1	18.2
Block 28307							
Polish	8	-	12.5	12.5	62.5	12.5	-
Italian	12	-	8.3	25.0	58.3	8.3	-
Block 28401							
Polish[e]	48	4.2	2.1	16.7	60.4	4.2	12.5
Block 28906							
Polish[f]	63	1.6	7.9	6.3	65.1	9.5	9.5
Block 40515							
Polish	12	8.3	8.3	-	75.0	8.3	-
Block 60911							
Hungarian	24	-	8.3	4.2	70.8	12.5	4.2
Block 60912							
Hungarian	34	2.9	5.9	2.9	67.6	17.6	2.9

SOURCE: 1920 sample.

a. Ethnicity of heads of households, as described in table 14.1.

b. Extension of relatives up, across and down the family tree, without forming a second nucleus.

c. Extension leading to the formation of two or more nuclei in the same family (married children, married parents, etc.).

d. Includes 9 heads of household born in the U.S. of two German parents.

e. Includes 5 heads of household born in the U.S. of two Polish parents.

f. Includes 7 heads of household born in the U.S. of two Polish parents.

There, too, given the general crowding of Detroit, single-family dwellings were not always the rule: only 17.6% of the dwellings were single-family dwellings in one block and 45.8% in the other, but at least 32% of the heads of households were homeowners, and again, owners and renters lived in the same houses. No more than 29% of the households had boarders, and each family had many children since the child to woman ratio ranged from 748 to 972.

If we turn to a completely different community, the east-side Jews, who were generally not factory workers and who came from all horizons, we find again the two qualities the Black ghetto lacked: home ownership and nuclear family life. Of the 444 Jews living in one block selected for the intensive study, 142 came from Russia, 103 from Poland, 21 from Canada, 6 from Austria, 2 from Sweden, one from Hungary, one from Rumania, one from Australia, one from England, one from Scotland, and 164 were born in the United States of parents of different Jewish origins; there were as many different occupations represented on the block as there were jobs available in Detroit's east side. Despite the high population density, despite the recentness of most heads of households' arrival in the U.S. (87% had come since 1900), despite the large number of boarders (46% of the households had boarders), and despite the relatively central location of the Jewish community, 26.4% of the heads of households were homeowners; and 65% of the Jews who rented, rented from other Jews who lived on the premises. All these Jewish families had many children, with a high child to woman ratio of 719.

Actually, the best way to contrast the urban experience of new Black migrants to that of the other ethnic groups is to look at one of these transitional blocks where, as George Haynes put it, Blacks lived with "kindly Jews."[28] The 1920 sample revealed one such block at the northern junction of the Black ghetto, just where Haynes and Washington said that Blacks and Jews mixed. What is remarkable is that, despite their proximity, the demographic characteristics of the Blacks and the Jews were, once again, strikingly different. The population of the block was 40% Blacks and 60% Jews, but there were more Black households than Jewish households because many of the Black households were composed of solitaries or couples without children. Eighty-one percent of the Blacks lived in houses entirely occupied by Blacks, leaving only a few families in mixed dwellings. In the Jewish part of the block, 27.3% of the Jews owned a home; only 20% of the households had boarders (the mean Jewish family size being 5.9 and the mean Jewish household size 6.1), and the child to woman ratio was a high 1,100. In sharp contrast, none of the Blacks owned their homes, and the mean household size was 3.63, largely due to the number of boarders.

28. Haynes, *Negro Newcomers in Detroit*, p. 9.

There were no Black children; the child to woman ratio was zero. In this block, where it seems that Blacks were slowly replacing Jews (possibly through the usual rent profiteering scheme described by Washington), the contrast between Blacks and Jews was extreme.

As the Jews bordered the northern side of the ghetto, the Italians bordered its east side. There were few Italian concentrations in Detroit, but the sample did reveal some blocks shared by Italians with either Poles or Germans at the eastern fringe of the Black ghetto. Although Italians were all recent immigrants working at the bottom of the occupational ladder, in jobs such as helper, sewer digger and laborer, the census enumeration also reveals that 54% of them were homeowners and that the child to woman ratio was 696 in the block they shared with Poles; almost the same percentage, 50% of the Italians, were also home-owners in the block shared with the Germans, and there the child to woman ratio was as high as 1,065.

Decidedly, the Blacks were a unique case in Detroit, as they were in other cities. The brutal facts of segregation—racial violence combined with demographic pressure—greatly handicapped Black newcomers. In all other immigrant communities, family and economic autonomy were intimately related: a high birth rate within the nuclear family was the key to income pooling, which provided a degree of economic security, including the possibility of buying a home. Segregation, however, made home ownership impossible for most Blacks, and the practice of income pooling with boarders only helped to pay the exorbitant rents. In turn, Blacks in the ghetto remained childless, partly because of poor health and sterility caused by tuberculosis, partly because of high infant mortality. In the ghetto, where there were more deaths than births, adaptive strategies were just good enough to insure the survival of the newcomers, but not of their descendants. In such an environment, when newcomers began to pour in by the thousands—"not knowing what they would do when they got here, having no direction, not knowing where they would sleep, who they were going to see, or who would be interested in them," as John Dancy remembers the daily arrival of trains from Saint Louis and Cincinnati—they entered a Black community with little internal stability.[29] They were assaulted by segregation from all sides and the problems that had been plaguing the Black community for years grew to giant proportions.

A BLACK MIDDLE CLASS?

One of the most dramatic effect of ghetto formation was the reshaping of the Black middle class. Considering the squalid living conditions in the ghetto,

29. John C. Dancy, *Sand against the Wind: The Memoirs of John C. Dancy* (Detroit: Wayne State University Press, 1966), p. 55.

learning to live there was a traumatic experience for the few Black white-collar workers and professionals who had traditionally been associated with white groups and were now forced into the ghetto. The Black professional, doctor, or lawyer, educated at white institutions and expecting a spacious home in a white neighborhood, could no longer find it. He now had to live with peers whom he did not recognize as such. By 1920, the pressures of industrialization had cut deep into traditional ethnic autonomy; white ethnic neighborhoods had lost some of their cross-class character and become working-class neighborhoods. In contrast, the process of ghettoization consisted of putting together elements of the Black population which, had they been whites, would now have been kept separate. As a result, strong divisions rapidly developed within the ghetto on the basis of social class. These divisions were easily recognized, as Blacks were distributed among various religious denominations according to social status. There were "thirty-eight reputable Negro churches in Detroit," with 52% of the Blacks Baptists and another 25% belonging to one of the Methodist churches.[30] But according to F. B. Washington,

> the pseudo-aristocrats and intellectuals of the race are members of the Protestant Episcopal Churches. Secondly, one finds that the great mass of middle-class Negroes, the fairly well-paid workmen and businessmen, are located in the larger Baptist and Methodist churches. The laboring classes, the rough peasant type of Negroes, make up almost 100% of the memberships of the smaller Baptist and Methodist churches.[31]

Washington also reported that the Great Migration brought a tremendous increase in "frenzied" forms of religion. He clearly expressed his own resentment of such southern religious practices transplanted into the city, where

> services are given over to hysteria in all forms. These services are noisy and emotional. They are characterized by protracted singing, moaning and shouting. Long drawn out prayers which end only in exhaustion or fainting are typical of their regular meetings. Shaking of the body, jumping and rolling on the floor are frequent occurrences.[32]

Such practices, Washington admitted, served as safety valves for many people, men and women who "were it not for the existence of their kind of church,

30. Washington, "The Negro in Detroit," part, "The Number of Churches," in section, "The Religious Life of the Negro in Detroit," BHC.

31. Washington, "The Negro in Detroit," part, "Functions of the Negro Church in Detroit," in section "The Religious Life of the Negro in Detroit," BHC.

32. Washington, "The Negro in Detroit," part, "Religious Hysteria," in section "The Religious Life of the Negro in Detroit," BHC.

where they could go and scream and shout and jump—they would go crazy as a result of the wearisome toil and worry of their daily life."[33]

Despite their resentment of such religious practices, there was little that the Black elite could do to escape the ghetto. In fact, the elite shrank to ridiculously small proportions in the face of the constant growth of the ghetto. The number of Black doctors, for example, was extremely small for the area of Detroit with the highest rate of disease. In March 1918, J. H. Porter, chairman of the Good Citizenship League (a short-lived organization that challenged the Urban League's connection with the white establishment), pointed out that during a recent smallpox epidemic, only " 'broken down' white doctors and nurses with officers were forcibly vaccinating, poisoning quite a few arms."[34] Similarly, the number of lawyers was extremely limited in a community ridden with legal problems. Only a handful of cases could be handled by the newly created branch of the NAACP, cases of job discrimination primarily, while Urban League social workers solved daily problems of Blacks evicted by greedy landlords by offering ad hoc solutions for problems which never reached the courts. The 1920/21 city directory listed only nine "colored" physicians and five "colored" lawyers.[35] When Moses and Turner published their first directory of Detroit's Black community in 1924, the number of Blacks in the city had already doubled the 1920 figure of 40,000, but there were only 35 physicians and 24 lawyers listed in that "Black" directory, and only 24 dentists, 15 pharmacists, 8 social service workers, and 26 nurses. Other white-collar jobs or jobs in the various departments of the municipal, county, and federal governments were also rare in 1924, as the directory mentions only 2 accountants, 2 architects, 7 bookkeepers, 18 stenographers, 29 public school teachers, 25 postmen, 10 postal clerks, and 8 policemen. By 1924, Blacks had made no advance in white-collar jobs and professional jobs, although they had made some headway at developing small businesses catering to the Black community, such as employment agencies to place servants throughout the city, undertakers who were among the wealthiest in the community (the directory lists eleven), real estate dealers (the directory lists thirty-seven), and a score of small retail establishments of new or secondhand goods.[36]

33. Ibid.
34. J. H. Porter, Chairman, Good Citizenship League, to Officers and Members of Detroit Board of Commerce, 11 March 1918, Executive Secretary's General File, DUL Papers.
35. *Polk's Detroit City Directory* (Detroit: R. L. Polk & Co., 1921), pp. 2809–3064.
36. Arthur Turner and Earl R. Moses, *Colored Detroit: A Brief History of Detroit's Colored Population and a Directory of Their Businesses, Organizations, Professions, and Trades* (Detroit, 1924).

Ultimately, the ghetto created its own "middle class." After a long period of learning how to live together the "New Negro" emerged, and a different Black bourgeoisie developed, the members of which were all ghetto Blacks: Black doctors helping Black patients, Black lawyers taking the cases of Black defendants, Black office workers working for Black firms.[37] But the Black community was forced into this cross-class composition in Detroit. It took a long time—up to the 1930s—for it to emerge, a time of disarray during which the ghetto took shape.

In fact, even the Urban League claim that Black workers were experiencing real advancement by entering the industrial labor force was highly questionable and may merely reflect the high opinion that Urban League social workers had of their own work. The massive entry of Blacks into the labor force did constitute a significant turn in the history of race relations, but one that must be evaluated cautiously. Admittedly, Black factory workers made more money in a day in Detroit than in a week in the South, and there was little wage discrimination between Black and white factory workers. But employers were slow at integrating Blacks into the factories; Dodge, for example, did not employ Blacks before John Dancy made a personal appeal to John Dodge as late as 1919.[38] What could be claimed of the men could hardly be said of the women, who were still predominantly employed in personal services in 1920. And many of the men who did enter industrial jobs experienced a great deal of stress in trying to adjust to their new work environment. Washington himself cited cases of men who had always been employed in service occupations "around white folks" in the South and "washed dishes in restaurants about the city at a very low wage rather than go to work in a factory."[39]

About 52% of the Black male labor force was employed in factories, but only 12% at semiskilled or skilled occupations. Ford was the only employer in the city who initiated a new policy in 1919 of employing Blacks in all hourly-wage classifications, and the only employer to develop openly a hiring network among Blacks in Detroit through Reverend Bradby of the Second Baptist Church. But this new policy toward Blacks, spectacular as it might have appeared, had only a limited impact on the sociological composition of the Black community, since most other employers continued to employ Blacks in backbreaking jobs that

37. For a good discussion of the rise of the "new Negro," see Kenneth L. Kusmer, *A Ghetto Takes Shape: Black Cleveland, 1870–1930* (Urbana: University of Illinois Press, 1976), pp. 235–74.
38. Dancy, *Sand against the Wind*, pp. 128–29.
39. Washington, "The Negro in Detroit," chap. 8, part B of section, "The Negro in the Industries of Detroit," BHC.

the whites did not want, such as those in the metal trade industry where the work was hot and dirty.[40]

In the face of such barriers to the occupational advancement of the Blacks (and the simple result that Blacks were overwhelmingly employed in unskilled occupations either in factories or in personal services), the Black leaders themselves came to question the very notion of Black advancement that they otherwise openly advocated. In the most interesting piece of semantics in Forrester B. Washington's extensive survey of Black Detroit, Washington borrowed words from his famous namesake, Booker T. Washington, and shifted the meaning of Black advancement from occupational achievement—as commonly used when applied to white groups—to other qualities such as "thrift" and "industry."[41] The Blacks whom Forrester B. Washington finally singled out as middle-class Blacks were not the few white-collar Blacks or professional Blacks (although these were implicitly included), but rather those few factory workers who managed to escape the ghetto and its consequences, and who lived in a small section of the west side: there,

> in a district bounded by Woodrow, Twenty-fourth, Scovel Place and McGraw is found what may be called a developing Negro middle class. Over one-half of the Negroes in this section own their own homes. The majority of them are migrants who have been in Detroit over two years, who have worked in the factories of this city, earned good wages, saved a portion of them and who have emerged from the East Side District class into the "home owning group" of the West Side. This group is the most promising element in the Negro community of Detroit. They are the bone and sinew of the race. They are hard-working and thrifty. Because they love their own race they are able to cooperate.[42]

Washington's optimistic statistic of 50% Black home ownership outside the ghetto was not confirmed by my own estimates based on the larger 1920 sample, which yielded a figure of only 12%, significantly lower than Washington's but higher than the figure of 1.8% in the ghetto itself. It is only above this "middle class" that Washington recognized "the 'cream' of the classes based upon in-

40. David L. Lewis, "History of Negro Employment in Detroit Area Plants of Ford Motor Company, 1914–1941" (undergraduate paper, University of Michigan, 1954, available at WRL), p. 4; also on Blacks in industry in the 1920s and 1930s, see Glen E. Carlson, "The Negro in the Industries of Detroit" (Ph.D. diss., University of Michigan, 1929); Lloyd H. Bailer, "Negro Labor in the Automobile Industry" (Ph.D. diss., University of Michigan, 1943).

41. Washington, "The Negro in Detroit," part, "Social Classes among the Negroes of Detroit," in section, "The Identification of the Negro in Detroit," BHC; Katzman, *Before the Ghetto*, p. 169.

42. Washington, "The Negro in Detroit."

come," a few wealthy realtors, a few professionals and even some who made money in the underworld when Detroit was a "wide-open town."[43]

In 1920, then, Blacks were already faced with the dilemma that has haunted them throughout the twentieth century: either escape the oppressive system of the ghetto or learn to live in it. But evading the ghetto may have awarded a different status to a few Blacks—not on the basis of occupation but of residence—for only a short period of time, because many of these isolated spots of independent Black settlements were rapidly joined by an ever growing ghetto. Writing in the 1920s, Louis Wirth included the Blacks in his model of succession of immigrants, assuming that Blacks—the last large group to enter the American city—needed only to wait their turn to receive the well-earned fruits of their toil.[44] Many social observers after him shared the same view, but the Blacks in Detroit never confirmed it. Indeed, when we analyze the process of ghetto-making from the late nineteenth century to the early 1920s, not only do we see the intense segregation Blacks suffered from all corners of the white community, but we also see that, compared with white ethnic groups, Blacks lived history in reverse. When ethnic neighborhoods were flourishing cross-class communities providing opportunities to their members, Blacks were atomized and dispersed. With the formation of the large industrial working class, cross-class ethnic neighborhoods were transformed into primarily working-class ethnic areas, abandoned by upwardly mobile people dispersed throughout the metropolitan area. It was at the very time when occupational bonds began to replace ethnic bonds in the white community that Blacks were drawn into an ever growing ghetto, irrespective of their social status. With white ethnic groups more and more segmented along class lines in the many sections of the metropolis, the growth of the Black ghetto was a dramatic anachronism.

43. Ibid.
44. Louis Wirth, *The Ghetto* (Chicago: University of Chicago Press, 1928), p. 283; Wirth's position was revolutionary in his day.

Conclusion

The purpose of this study was to identify the social forces behind Detroit's shift from an ethnically divided city to a metropolis reorganized by ethnicity and class. I argue that such a transformation of Detroit accompanied its industrialization and can be fully understood only in the context of the city's changing dimensions and activities. It would be fascinating to pursue the investigation further at both ends of the chronological spectrum to identify the ways in which other major economic changes contributed to social change: the development of ethnic autonomy in the mid-nineteenth century commercial city, for example, or the growth of working-class consciousness through the Depression years, until the United Auto Workers succeeded in appealing to the mass of automobile workers.[1] Many conclusions of this study should also be tested in the history of Detroit's later growth, including the World War II economic boom, the violent segregation of the Blacks, the dispersion of most white ethnic groups throughout the metropolitan area, and the increasing demarcation between city and suburbs.

A social history project never ends. The more one digs into the complex web of social relations, the more one finds to explore. Yet I had to resist the temptation to widen my inquiry even further. I had initially conceived this study as a systematic attempt to use conflicts for space as an index of other, perhaps more profound social divisions. Along the way, I found it necessary to use many other analytic grids to observe a variety of phenomena through different lenses. Yet, my investigation was intentionally limited to one city and one time period—the forty years of Detroit's systematic industrial growth and ascent to national

1. Sidney Fine, *Sit Down: The General Motors Strike of 1936–1937* (Ann Arbor: University of Michigan Press, 1969), p. 340.

prominence—in order to circumscribe the universe better and to search through those records that permitted a reconstruction of group characteristics from individual data.

In order to understand Detroit's social mechanisms, I explored special circumstances of the city's political life, institutions, industries, land use, and population, and found, by combining this diverse evidence, that on the eve of Detroit's industrialization the primary colors of the urban quilt were ethnic and cultural, not socioeconomic. People's daily lives generally centered in the smaller communities within the larger city, where class divisions were often mediated by ethnic bonds. In contrast, living in 1920 Detroit was living in an overwhelmingly industrial landscape. By then industrialization had cut deep into ethnic autonomy: the German and Irish communities had virtually disappeared from the ethnic map; other neighborhoods had become as much working class as ethnic. At the inception of our now familiar industrial and metropolitan world, Detroit's space was becoming reorganized according to social class.

Although different characteristics may have prevailed in other cities or may have surfaced at other times, I hope to have identified trends valid not only for Detroit but also for the entire class of northeastern and midwestern industrial cities. It is no accident, I believe, that the Chicago sociologists' observations of the "zone of workingmen's homes" were first formulated around 1910, or that Bostonian social workers identified Anglo-Saxon working-class neighborhoods for the first time in that same period.[2] Indeed, what troubled Robert Woods and Albert Kennedy in Boston's "zone of emergence" was the existence of a working-class life distinctly lacking ethnic character. This struck them as both a new and important development in the metropolis but also one they were ill-equipped to understand. Change rather than continuity thus marked northern American industrial society from 1880 to 1920.

There were two phases in Detroit's industrialization: one lasted from approximately the 1870s through about 1910, when Detroit was only one of the cities of the industrial belt, and another when the automobile industry and war production made Detroit a major national industrial center. Ethnic autonomy withstood well the unifying pressures of the first phase of Detroit's industrialization, and ethnic communities continued to play a major role in the late nineteenth-century city-building process. The neighborhoods were growing eth-

2. The Burgess model was developed in the 1920s; see Ernest W. Burgess, "The Growth of the City," in *The City*, ed. Ernest W. Burgess and Roderick D. McKenzie (Chicago: University of Chicago Press, 1925), pp. 47–62. Some of these ideas, however, had already been formulated in Richard M. Hurd, *The Structure of Cities* (New York: Alexander Hamilton Institute, 1910). See also Robert A. Woods and Albert J. Kennedy, *The Zone of Emergence: Observations of the Lower Middle and Upper Working Class Communities of Boston, 1905–1914* (Cambridge, Mass.: M.I.T. Press, 1962).

nic communities with a sophisticated institutional life, symbolized by their lavish churches. That even starving Catholic or Jewish poor shunned Protestant charities in the 1890s is a good indication of the great social distance which separated the society's ethnoreligious segments.

But after 1910, in one way or another, everybody in Detroit was affected by the new economic order. All were pressured by its imperative demands during the years of heightened war production, all experienced its limits during recession periods. The nineteenth-century plural opportunity structure gave way to a new, single opportunity structure, characterized in Detroit by increasing competitiveness among industrial firms, and by the centralization of control (not only of factories, but also of other key facets of Detroit's industrial economy) in the hands of relatively few, predominantly native white American industrialists. As we have seen, during the period of rapid industrialization, few industrial leaders emerged from even the old, well-established Irish and German communities of Detroit. Physically, small mill towns replaced previously semi-autonomous ethnic neighborhoods in just about every section of the metropolitan territory. Numerically, the new factory system exerted an influence on a continuously growing number of workers and their families, imposing the same sets of constraints on all. And the separation of the rank and file from the elite was reinforced by working-class families' need to pull together to make ends meet.

Detroit evolved into what Roderick McKenzie called the "metropolitan community."[3] The city experienced an overall redefinition of public and private spaces, corresponding to a loosening of previously homogeneous ethnic communities and a more uniform social contract ordering people primarily by social status. It may be just a spatial image but in 1880, only the city center was clearly linked to class affiliation, while the rest of the city was either organized in ethnic neighborhoods or stood empty. Forty years later, Detroit's center had lost its residential attractiveness, and several exclusively business centers had developed. In the city's shift from a single nucleus to multiple nuclei, class affiliation had spread out from the residential center to the rest of the metropolitan territory.

The last large wave of immigrants brought many factory workers to Detroit who never experienced life in autonomous ethnic communities. Ironically, the importance of ethnicity began to vanish in the industrial city during the very peak of immigration in the United States, just when the tide of immigration brought the widest variety of people to the Atlantic shores. The decline of ethnicity antedated, then, the immigration restriction policies of the 1920s.

3. Roderick D. McKenzie, *The Metropolitan Community* (New York: McGraw-Hill Book Co., 1933).

Conversely, America's door was closed a decade after the industrial establishment had deeply corroded the ethnic mold. As early as 1914, Anglo-Saxon industrialists and ethnic leaders had joined efforts to promote a program of Americanization and had chosen an industrial image—the melting pot—to promote a new theory of social change. If these efforts were successful, it was not because of Henry Ford's influential personality, but because (as Ford's genius had led him to recognize) they corresponded to a new sociological reality.

Most intellectuals, Tocqueville as well as Marx, agree that there is no class without class consciousness. Yet a large working class had developed in Detroit before it recognized common concerns. Social stratification preceded class consciousness in Detroit, a rather unique development which can be accounted for not only by the relative openness of Detroit's social system, but also, and more readily, by another unique historical reality, the formation of a working class from independent segments. It appears that Detroit's modern class structure arose by default. Class gradually became a salient feature of urban life not because the social structure became suddenly more rigid, but because the traditional ethnic matrix for people's lives vanished. Inequality cut deeper into previously cross-class ethnic communities, which became increasingly segmented along class lines until they had to give way. On the one hand they were independent and autonomous, but on the other they were cut off from the society at large and suffered from isolation. The new economic structure, then, jeopardized the city's fragile balance of unity and diversity in relatively autonomous ethnic communities.

Much evidence points to a continuing pattern of working-class segmentation in the 1920s: a persistent fragmentation along ethnic lines as well as separation of the workers from the upper levels of society. The surprisingly large numbers of Detroiters who joined the Ku Klux Klan in the 1920s, for example, were primarily native white American factory workers who, confusedly and sometimes violently, fought for prohibition and 100 percent Americanism.[4] They felt threatened economically by their fellow workers and cut off culturally from their fellow Americans of a higher socioeconomic level; so, dramatically, they turned against Catholics, Jews, and Blacks.

The intense racism that sprang up in the northern industrial city at the same time was without doubt also related to the decline of ethnic homogeneity. The white immigrant worker, insecure about his own status in a changing socioethnic hierarchy and also at times threatened in his job by southern Blacks, made every effort to differentiate himself from those he considered to be the lumpenproletariat. The working-class immigrant was more likely to contribute to

4. Kenneth T. Jackson, *The Ku Klux Klan in the City, 1915–1930* (New York: Oxford University Press, 1967), pp. 127–43, 235–49.

the formation of the Black ghetto when he was cut off from his ethnic base and had only his status as unskilled day laborer in a factory to compare himself with the Blacks. With ethnic groups now segmented along class lines, and the successful immigrants parting from the working-class ethnic neighborhoods for a better life elsewhere in the new urban order, the formation of the ghetto— lumping Blacks of all status together—was a dramatic anachronism, but one which was there to stay.

Detroit came to symbolize most of the social extremes in the American industrial city: unprecedented wealth, but also the sifting and resifting of a multitude of individuals who tried their lots in the industrial universe. Inequality, translated into the city's space, took the many faces which I have tried to identify, from the largely self-imposed segregation of the nineteenth-century ethnic communities to the enforced segregation of Blacks in the twentieth-century ghetto. Today, as one drives on Detroit's intracity highways, one cannot avoid being struck by the many churches that stand alone at their intersections, without houses around them. They are the archaeological traces of Detroit's formerly tight ethnic communities. Large sections of the inner city—left empty since they were burned and looted in the 1967 riots—are in turn signs of the twentieth century's intense racial conflicts and of the abandonment of the old industrial city's core. Many in America and in other parts of the world are watching to see what the new Detroit will be. This book has shown how the first industrial Detroit came to exist and how it altered the social fabric. It has also shown that the industrial American city was the prime locus of immigrant assimilation into American society. To be sure, the city operated as a melting pot, not by an automatic absorption of minority into majority through some magically open social system, but because slowly, separately, each group took part in the challenges of industrial life. At one point, these challenges came to replace the group as the center of people's lives. Only then, immigrants and their children saw themselves as an integral part of a new industrial America, and the ensuing restructuring of social relations took place.

Appendixes

Appendices

Appendix 1

The 1880 and 1900 Samples

The cross-sectional study of Detroit in 1880 is based on a probability sample of the six-front clusters geographically distributed across the city, a sample which required a precise linkage of the street addresses listed in the manuscript schedules of the 1880 federal census to the addresses shown on the Robinson-Pidgeon atlas of Detroit.[1] A pilot study was conducted (with the collaboration of W. A. Ericson and D. J. Fox) to divide the city into density and land use zones for sampling purposes, to determine how well the population and land use sources could be matched, and to determine the feasibility of collecting data on individual respondents, as well as on households and on houses, in sampled fronts, blocks, and clusters. A description of the data collected in the pilot study as well as the computations that led us to believe that the two sources could be successfully matched has been published elsewhere.[2] My purpose here is simply to present the final design—a stratified sample, by atlas plate and block type, of clusters. The design insured that clusters were sampled in all parts of the city, but at different rates in different density and land use zones. The sampling was more intensive in densely populated areas, but vacant and non-residential areas were also included so that I could study their characteristics in 1900.

The Robinson-Pidgeon atlas covers the city of Detroit in twenty plates. For each block, parcels and buildings are designated; houses are numbered, and

---

1. Elisha Robinson and Roger H. Pidgeon, *Atlas of the City of Detroit and Suburbs Embracing Portions of Hamtramck, Springwells and Greenfield Townships* (New York, 1885); manuscript schedules of the 1880 population census for Detroit.

2. Olivier Zunz, William A. Ericson, and Daniel J. Fox, "Sampling for a Study of the Population and Land Use of Detroit in 1880–1885," *Social Science History* 1 (Spring 1977): 307–32.

the atlas contains many nonresidential buildings. The atlas contained sufficient detail so that each of the 1,540 city blocks could be placed in one of four classes:

R   Residential, i.e., Blocks containing almost all dwelling structures

NR   Nonresidential, blocks mainly occupied by industrial and commercial establishments

V   Vacant, blocks containing no structures, 90% or more vacant

O   All other blocks

For R and NR blocks, we treated the downtown area a little differently from the rest of the city in order to take into account the density decline from the center to the periphery. This decline was expected and indeed visible in the atlas. Plates 1, 2, 6, and 11 of the atlas roughly comprised all the area within one mile of the city center. In those plates, roughly 75% of the dwelling structures of a block had to be residential for that block to qualify for R, and 75% nonresidential to qualify for NR. Elsewhere only 66% was considered sufficient.

Estimates of the pilot sample (including a preliminary match of the census manuscript with the atlas) led us to divide the twenty atlas plates into three density classes. The peripheral plates (pls. 5, 10, 17–20) were all of areas more than two miles from the city center. They were almost vacant, with an average of 38 people per inhabited cluster. The remaining plates could be divided into two other groups on the basis of estimated population per cluster: plates 1, 3, 4, 8, 15, and 16 seemed to represent the most densely populated areas of the city with at least 139 people per cluster; the last group consisted of the remaining plates 2, 6, 7, 9, 11–14, with about 58 people per cluster. Given our analysis of population estimates and types of blocks, we felt that drawing at least 100 clusters, the primary block being classified either "residential" or "other," would yield tolerably small standard errors for estimating residential and population characteristics. Such a number would also keep the search in the census manuscripts to a manageable task. In order to estimate other city characteristics, we decided that 25 clusters would be selected from the nonresidential and vacant blocks. Estimating an average of 5 people per household, we expected that a sample of 100 clusters would yield 1,786 households, or 8,930 persons.

In the end, 102 R and O blocks were selected with their opposing frontages (see table A1.1). We sampled rather intensely in the most populated plates (Category 2), 9.4% of the R and O blocks, that is, 40 of the 425 such blocks. Applying the same ratio to Categories 1 and 3 would have yielded too many clusters, that is, more than were needed at too great expense at the time of the data collection. We therefore reduced it to roughly 6.8% or 12 blocks from among the 177 R and O blocks in Category 1—sparsely populated plates—and about 7.7% or 50 of the 650 blocks in Category 3—remaining plates. These

TABLE A1.1

Sample design, Detroit, 1880

Plate	Population Size				Sample Size			
	R	O	NR	V	R	O	NR	V
Group 1								
5	5	12	0	11	0	1	0	1
10	21	14	0	20	1	1	0	2
17	13	30	1	59	1	2	0	6
18	18	24	0	42	1	2	0	4
19	6	24	0	41	0	2	0	4
20	5	5	0	24	1	0	0	2
Total	68	109	1	197	4	8	0	19
Group 2								
1	29	28	15	0	3	3	1	0
3	68	0	0	0	6	0	0	0
4	35	30	0	3	4	3	0	0
8	85	25	0	4	8	2	0	0
15	42	18	3	1	4	1	0	0
16	49	16	0	2	5	1	0	0
Total	308	117	18	10	30	10	1	0
Group 3								
2	63	9	10	0	4	1	1	0
6	69	8	9	0	5	1	1	0
7	94	12	3	0	7	1	0	0
9	28	13	4	3	2	1	0	0
11	73	14	11	2	6	1	1	0
12	100	11	7	1	8	1	1	0
13	86	29	1	6	7	2	0	1
14	23	18	3	2	2	1	0	0
Total	536	114	48	14	41	9	4	1
Grand Total	912	340	67	221	75	27	5	20

ratios were applied separately to the R and O block categories. Also 25 or about 8.7% of the 288 NR and V blocks were sampled, yielding a total sample of 127 geographic units. The actual mechanics of drawing the sample were quite straightforward given table A1.1 and the tracings of the blocks as shown on the twenty plates of the atlas. The blocks of each type were serially numbered on the plate and, using random numbers, a simple random sample without replacement of blocks was selected for each of the four block categories within each plate. Once a block was selected and located on the atlas plate tracing, then the Rand table of random digits was used to choose one of the, usually four, block corners. The opposing frontages, usually two, were then included to make up the cluster. Based on an exhaustive search in the manuscript census, the final sample includes 12,185 people. This comprises 2,410 households on 721 frontages or 127 clusters. Of these, 353 frontages were actually inhabited.

THE STANDARD ERRORS OF ESTIMATES

Some aspects of the representativeness of the sample can be judged by checking to see how known population characteristics (from published census figures) are estimated from our sample. Many of these characteristics are proportions—for example, the proportion of inhabitants who were whites, the proportion born in Canada, the proportion of females in the working population. In each of these cases the estimated proportion is a ratio where both numerator and denominator are subject to sampling variability.

Suppose that the population proportion to be estimated from the sample is designated by

$$R = X/Y$$

where Y is the population number of all persons in the population and X is the number of those having the attribute. In such a case R is estimated by

$$r = x/y$$

where x and y are sample estimates of X and Y respectively.

For the sampling design used, x and y are given by

$$x = \sum_{h=1}^{H} w_h \sum_{a=1}^{a_h} x_{ha}$$

and

$$y = \sum_{h=1}^{H} w_h \sum_{a=1}^{a_h} y_{ha}$$

where H is the number of strata, a_h is the number of clusters in stratum h,[3] w_h is a weight associated with the h-th stratum and is proportional to N_h/n_h, the ratio of the population number of clusters to the sample number of clusters in the h-th stratum, and x_{ha} and y_{ha} are the sample totals for the a-th cluster within the h-th stratum.[4]

3. The stratum of a cluster is identified by its primary block.

4. In the original sample design there were eighty strata—twenty plates, each with four types of blocks. However, only four different sampling fractions were used, and thus there are only four different values of w_h. These correspond effectively to R and O blocks for each of the three groups of plates shown in Table 6 and to the NR and V blocks over all plates. The actual weights used were taken as being proportional to N_i/n_i where the constant of proportionality was chosen so that the weighted sum of the sample number of persons in each of these four categories reproduced the total sample size of 12,185 persons. Details are shown on the following chart:

Group	N_i	n_i	N_i/n_i	w_i	Sample Number of Persons
1	177	12	14.750	1.2162	433
2	425	40	10.625	0.8761	4,597
3	650	50	13.000	1.0719	6,823
4	288	25	11.520	0.9499	332

Owing to the stratification by plate of the atlas which permitted us to achieve geographic coverage, some plates have only one sampled cluster per stratum. In computing r, strata having one (or fewer) sampled cluster presented no difficulty. However, in estimating the variance of r (or its square root, the standard error of r), one needs two or more sample observations or clusters per stratum. In computing the standard error of r, denoted by SE(r), the 80 strata were reduced to 27 by combining similar strata so that each combined stratum had at least two sample clusters. In chapter 1, we compare the sample estimate, r, for each of ten population ratios, to the true population value from the published census. A range of two standard errors above and below the sample estimate is also indicated (see figure 1.2).[5]

5. The formula for the estimated variance of r is given by

$$\text{Var} (r) = \frac{1}{y^2}[\text{Var} (x) + r^2 \text{Var} (y) - 2r \text{Cov} (x,y)]$$

where

$$\text{Var} (y) = \sum_{h=1}^{H} \sum_{a=1}^{a_h} (y'_{ha} - \bar{y}'_h)^2,$$

$$\text{Var} (x) = \sum_{h=1}^{H} \sum_{a=1}^{a_h} (x'_{ha} - \bar{x}'_h)^2$$

and

$$\text{Cov} (x,y) = \sum_{h=1}^{H} \sum_{a=1}^{a_h} (x'_{ha} - \bar{x}'_h)(y'_{ha} - \bar{y}'_h)$$

Also,

$$x'_{ha} = w_h x_{ha},$$
$$y'_{ha} = w_h y_{ha}$$

and

$$\bar{y}'_h = \frac{1}{a_h} \sum_{a=1}^{a_h} y'_{ha},$$

$$\bar{x}'_h = \frac{1}{a_h} \sum_{a=1}^{a_h} x'_{ha}$$

Finally the standard error of r is given by

$$\text{SE} (r) = \sqrt{\text{Var} (r)}$$

See Leslie Kish, *Survey Sampling* (New York: John Wiley and Sons, Inc., 1965), pp. 182–216.

   The 1880 sample has been replicated for 1900, and enlarged to include a few clusters within the expanded city limits. The sample size accordingly grew from 127 to 178 clusters (including the added clusters and the clusters resulting from the subdivisions of large empty 1880 clusters). The 1897 Sanborn atlases of Detroit were used to prepare the list of addresses to be searched in the manuscript schedules of the 1900 federal census, yielding a final sample of 26,181 people.[6] This replication formed the base for a new cross-sectional analysis of Detroit in 1900, and a study of Detroit's evolution in the last twenty years of the nineteenth century.[7]

   6. Sanborn Map Company, *Insurance Maps of Detroit, Michigan,* 6 vols. (New York: Sanborn-Perris Map Co., 1897); manuscript schedules of the 1900 population census for Detroit.
   7. City-wide estimates with the 1900 sample are computed by weighing proportions at the plate level with the following formula

$$\hat{p}_j = \frac{\sum\limits_{i=1}^{20} \frac{N_i n_i^*}{n_i} p_{ij}}{\sum\limits_{i=1}^{20} \frac{N_i n_i^*}{n_i}} \, ,$$

where N_i = population in plate i,
         n_i^* = sample size in plate i in category studied,
         n_i = sample size in plate i
         p_{ij} = proportion for each category in plate i,
         $\hat{p}_j$ = estimated proportion for category j in the city;

to estimate a mean, we simply replace p_{ij} by $\bar{x}_{ij} = \frac{\Sigma x_{ij}}{n_i^*}$

Appendix 2

The 1920 Sample

While free, unrestricted access to the 1880 and 1900 census manuscripts is available, the seventy-two-year confidentiality rule still applies to the manuscript schedules of the 1920 census, which will be closed to researchers' inspections until 1992. In order to use these records—indispensable for analyzing Detroit in 1920—I worked out a contract with the U.S. Bureau of the Census, the repositor of the data, in which the bureau agreed to code a sample of Detroit's respondents following my elaborate geographic sampling design and to provide me with aggregate statistics at the block level. This contract, then, fulfilled both the confidentiality rule of the Census Bureau and the specific geographic requirements of this study.

The intent was again—as for 1880 and 1900—to represent the various sections of the metropolis and to estimate block characteristics (and occasionally enumeration districts' characteristics, and city characteristics, to complement the already extensive set of tables already available in the published census). The design consisted of stratifying the city by geographic areas (corresponding to stages of Detroit's growth), further stratifying each area by density zones, then drawing a sample of blocks and of heads of household in each sampled block. Following the equal probability of selection method, each head of household living in 1920 Detroit would have roughly the same probability of being selected.[1]

We first divided the city into eight broad geographic areas corresponding to Detroit's three rings of growth since 1880:

1. Two areas, east and west (of Woodward), within the 1880 city limits

1. I wish to thank William A. Ericson for his collaboration in designing the 1920 sample.

413

2. Three areas, east, center, and west, for the area added between 1880 and 1900

3. And three areas, east, center, and west, for the area added before 1920

We then conducted a survey of Detroit's blocks in the 1918 Baist atlas and of Detroit's 659 enumeration districts (including their exact boundaries, the number of households within them, and their population totals), in order to partition the city into land-use and density zones.[2] We drew maps of each of the 659 enumeration districts, and in each of them counted the number of

R   primarily residential blocks (⅔ or more)
NR   primarily nonresidential blocks (⅔ or more)
V   primarily vacant blocks (90%)
O1   blocks combining residence and another land use
O2   blocks combining vacant land and nonresidential uses

We then computed the area and population density of each enumeration district (ED), as well as an average corrected area and corrected density for the R and O1 blocks only, in order to divide each of the eight geographic areas into density zones: up to 50 people per acre, from 51 to 100, from 101 to 200, from 201 to 300, and above 300. The resulting twenty-four strata were subsequently reduced to nineteen to eliminate small strata (see table A2.1).

The next stage was to sample blocks within EDs and then heads of households within blocks. We knew from experience with the 1880 and 1900 samples that collecting data at the block level, following a sequence of street addresses in the manuscript census, is a long and costly process. Based on cost considerations, we decided to sample 100 EDs out of 659 (or 640 after eliminating EDs with only V, NR, or O2 blocks). This meant drawing 15.6%, or at least two, of the EDs within each stratum. After careful estimating procedures, we decided upon selecting 38% of R and O1 blocks within ED (and then one of every third head of household in the sampled blocks). Several considerations went into this decision.

1. The size of the estimated standard error of a proportion at the block level. The average block was estimated to comprise sixty heads of households, and with ⅓ sampling fraction the standard error of p would be approximately

$$\sqrt{2/3 \; \frac{.25}{60}} \; = \; .05$$

2. This estimated standard error had to be balanced with the estimated standard error at the ED level. The typical ED comprised about six blocks, and

2. G. William Baist, *Real Estate Atlas of Surveys of Detroit and Suburbs*, 2 vols. (Philadelphia, 1818); manuscript list of Detroit enumeration district, 1920 population census, available at the National Archives.

with our two-stage design, it was estimated that for the typical ED, the standard error of an ED level estimated proportion would be at most .12, this being a very conservative estimate.[3]

3. The last consideration was whether the sample size was sufficiently large for the X^2 statistic to detect ethnic clustering at the block level (see Appendix 4). Of course, the smaller the block the more concentrated it must be in order to have the X^2 statistic detect such clustering. Several hypothetical examples were considered and the ⅓ sampling fraction seemed satisfactory on this score.

It was expected that the overall design would result in 258 blocks sampled and 4,596 heads of households. We prepared a complete description of the sampled blocks, including their ED number (for easy location in the manuscript) and (using the atlas) the house numbers on each front (and when available on each alley) in the blocks. In addition to the Baist atlas, the 1920/21 city directory provided another tool for locating every house in sampled blocks.[4] Detroit changed its numbering system effective 1 January 1921, implementing a new incremental sequence of numbers per block. The directory for that year gave both 1920 number (as in the census) and 1921 number (identifying block location). We thus used the directory to include on our lists the house numbers of houses built on sampled fronts between 1918 and 1920.

The final count of heads of households came after the Bureau of the Census completed the indexing of the manuscript census for each sampled block. The sample actually yielded 4,864 heads of households in 272 blocks in 101 EDs (instead of 100 because of a correction in the boundaries of one ED). There were only two out of the 272 blocks for which the census bureau staff could not locate inhabitants in the manuscript census. For ten other blocks, there were

---

3. The variance of proportion, p, at the ED level is given approximately by

$$\frac{b\,(B\,-\,b)}{B\,-\,1}\, \mathrm{Var}\, \left\{ \frac{N_i\pi_i}{N} \right\} + \frac{b}{B} \sum_{i=1}^{B} \frac{N_i\,-\,n_i}{N}\, \frac{\pi_i(1\,-\,\pi_i)}{n_i}, \tag{1}$$

where b = sample number of blocks selected from an ED
     B = population number of blocks in that ED
     N_i = number of heads of households in i-th Block
     n_i = sample number of heads of households in i-th Block

$$N = \sum_{i=1}^{B} N_i$$

     π_i = population proportion in i-th Block

Taking B = 6, b = .38 (B), N_i = 60, N = 360, n_i = 1/3 (60) = 20, and using the fact that Var $(\pi_i) \leq .25$ and $\pi_i\,(1\,-\,\pi_i) \leq .25$ it is easily seen that (1) must be less than or equal to .0149 or the SE of p is at most $\sqrt{.0149}$ = .12.

4. *Detroit City Directory* (Detroit: R. L. Polk & Co., 1920).

TABLE A2.1
Sample design, Detroit, 1920

Stratum		Population	Heads of households	EDs	Populated EDs	Blocks
Within 1880 city limits						
East	1–50 people/acre	17,493	3,414	20	12	185
	51–100	14,002	3,087	13	13	90
	101–200	161,313	32,747	91	91	682
	201–300	70,478	13,625	33	33	236
	301+	18,322	3,443	10	10	40
West	1–50	60,552	13,128	59	55	449
	51–100	125,081	27,681	99	99	584
	101–200	31,405	7,126	22	22	113
Area added between 1880 and 1900						
East	1–50	42,471	9,566	33	32	262
	51–100	57,340	12,593	38	38	225
	101–200	2,661	485	1	1	8
Center	1–50	26,985	6,671	32	32	186
	51–100	28,996	6,748	25	25	111
	101–200	6,344	1,226	3	3	18
West	1–50	27,686	5,431	18	17	133
	51–100	46,515	9,509	26	26	163
	101–200	2,020	454	1	1	4
Area added between 1900 and 1920						
East	1–50	63,258	14,646	37	35	652
	51–100	17,094	4,068	12	12	47
	101–200	1,083	264	1	1	2
Center	1–50	63,687	14,399	31	28	1,693
	51–100	12,227	2,766	4	4	57
West	1–50	84,344	17,605	38	38	697
	51–100	19,689	4,589	12	12	77

less than five sampled heads of households; for those ten almost vacant blocks the bureau provided us with only the ethnic distribution in the block but no cross-tabulated data on such small samples. All other sampled blocks met with the rules concerning privacy and protection of census data and provided the basis for a full analysis.

Once the indexes of segregation revealed patterns of dominance in the sampled blocks (see chap. 13), it was simple to go back to selected blocks in a second stage and take a total enumeration of the characteristics of their entire population for a finer housing and demographic survey of key areas. For the blocks

Blocks/Ed	Nonvacant blocks	Nonvacant blocks/Ed	Heads of households/ED	Heads of households/ nonvacant block	Sample number of EDs
9.25	172	8.6	170.7	19.8	2
6.92	87	6.7	237.5	35.5	2
7.49	677	7.4	359.9	48.4	14
7.15	236	7.1	412.8	57.7	5
4.00	40	4.0	344.3	86.1	2
7.61	439	7.4	222.5	29.9	9
5.90	579	5.8	279.6	47.8	16
5.13	113	5.1	323.9	63.1	3
7.94	243	7.4	289.9	39.4	5
5.92	225	5.9	331.4	56.0	} 6
8.00	8	8.0	485.0	60.6	
5.81	169	5.3	208.5	39.5	5
4.44	109	4.4	269.9	61.9	} 4
6.00	18	6.0	408.7	68.1	
7.39	127	7.1	301.7	42.7	3
6.27	159	6.1	365.7	59.8	} 4
4.00	4	4.0	454.0	113.5	
17.62	258	7.0	395.8	56.8	5
3.92	46	3.8	339.0	88.4	} 2
2.00	2	2.0	264.0	132.0	
54.61	445	14.3	464.5	32.4	} 5
14.25	46	11.5	691.5	60.1	
18.34	497	13.1	463.3	35.4	6
6.41	75	6.3	382.4	61.2	2

described in chapter 14, the Bureau of the Census tallied all house numbers, dwelling numbers, and household numbers in order of visitation, as well as ethnicity for each head of household, computed an age profile of each block, and collected all census variables on all members of the households of the dominant group. (For example, if a second stage block comprised eleven Hungarian families and one native white American family, the block tally was done on all twelve households, but the census variables were collected only for the residents of Hungarian-dominated households, so that the resulting block-level statistics truly reflect the dominant composition of the block.)

THE SUBURBS

In addition to this equal probability sample of heads of households, we also drew independent samples of heads of households in eight selected suburban areas of Detroit. By 1920, suburbs were already so much a part of both industrial and residential landscapes that the representation of the metropolitan area as a whole would have been incomplete without a check of suburban areas. We did not, however, use the same block design constructed for the city but opted for simplicity. We took eight systematic samples of heads of households (the size of which varies from one suburb to another), all designed to produce estimates of proportions with a standard error of .035 (see table A2.2).[5] We knew that the

TABLE A2.2

Suburban sample, Detroit metropolitan district, 1920

Study area	Civil divisions reported in census	Population	Estimated number of heads of households	Estimated sample size	Number in sample
Grosse Pointe	Grosse Pointe village	2,084	1,348	177	164
	Grosse Pointe Farms village	1,649			
	Grosse Pointe Park village	1,355			
	Grosse Pointe Shores village (that part in Wayne County)	503			
	Grosse Pointe twp (excluding the above four villages)	477			
Ferndale/Royal Oak	Ferndale village	2,640	3,429	193	209
	Royal Oak village	6,007			
	Royal Oak twp (excluding the above two villages)	6,785			
Greenfield	Greenfield twp	2,643	587	152	146
Dearborn	Dearborn village	2,470	1,156	174	154
	Dearborn twp (excluding the village)	2,736			
Oakwood/River Rouge/Ecorse	Oakwood village	1,990	4,137	195	188
	River Rouge village	9,822			
	Ecorse village	4,394			
	Ecorse twp (excluding the above three villages *and* Ford village)	2,411			
Springwells	Springwells twp	2,466	548	149	129
Highland Park	Highland Park City	46,499	10,333	200	202
Hamtramck	Hamtramck village	48,615	9,172	200	199

5. W. G. Cochran, *Sampling Techniques* (New York: John Wiley & Sons, 1963); in addition the historian may wish to consult R. S. Schofield, "Sampling in Historical Research," in *Nineteenth Century Society*, ed. E. A. Wrigley (Cambridge: Cambridge University Press, 1972), pp. 146–190.

average number of people per household was 5.3 in Hamtramck and 4.5 in Highland Park.[6] We applied the city average of 4.5 to the other civil divisions surrounding Detroit for which no tabulations were available. In the end, we sampled 1,391 heads of households to represent suburbs and satellite cities around Detroit.

6. U.S., Department of Commerce, Bureau of the Census, *Fourteenth Census of the United States, 1920: Population*, 4 vols. (Washington, D.C.: G.P.O., 1921), 2:1269.

Appendix 3

Occupational Classification, 1880, 1900, 1920

Occupational titles constitute a very important piece of information in the census manuscript, one on which much important historical work has been based, despite difficulties of interpretation. Historians have frequently noticed that a census occupational title is often an inconsistent piece of information which give only a partial understanding of an individual's position in the social structure. Historians usually face two major, but solvable, problems.

1. The characteristic occupational mobility of individuals makes it difficult to determine someone's position in the social structure solely on the basis of his/ her occupation at one point in time. Michael Katz, for example, showed how Wilson Benson, a typical Irish immigrant in Ontario, worked at 30 different occupations from 1833 to 1873.[1] The movements from one profession to another were most often, however, movements within the same broad job category rather than between categories. The use of rather large categories seems warranted in order to avoid the danger of artificially placing people in too narrowly defined pigeonholes.

2. Occupations are often internally differentiated. As Edward Pessen once noted, knowing that someone is a "merchant" says very little about "the wide range in income, wealth and scope of enterprise that marked this heterogeneous class." Herbert Gutman made similar observations on the inconclusiveness of occupational titles to determine someone's position within the working class.[2]

1. Michael B. Katz, *The People of Hamilton, Canada West* (Cambridge, Mass.: Harvard University Press, 1975), p. 106.
2. Edward Pessen, "The Social Configuration of the Antebellum City: An Historical and Theoretical Inquiry," *Journal of Urban History* 2 (May 1976): 267–306; Herbert G. Gutman, *Work, Culture, and Society in Industrializing America* (New York: Alfred A. Knopf, 1976).

It is therefore important to use occupational titles, not in the abstract and not as the only piece of evidence, but—as I have done in this study—in relationship to many other variables.

The historian's most immediate task is to classify the thousands of census occupational titles into broader categories. The 1880 sample, for instance, included 741 different titles, the 1900 sample, 2,147, and the 1920 sample, 2,384 combinations of the three census variables used in that year. Enumerators received different instructions for each census year, and the increase in number of titles in part stems from the greater precision of the survey from one census to the next. The 1880 instructions, for example, required enumerators to state only "the kind of mill or factory" a laborer worked in without specifying the task performed. In 1900, however, it was stressed that "the kind of work done" was also a major consideration: "works in tobacco factory" became "tobacco-roller" or "tobacco-stripper"; in white-collar occupations, "agent" became "agent in barber supplies," or "advertising agent," and the like. Even greater detail was provided in the 1920 census when enumerators were instructed to describe not only the occupation of each respondent but also the industry he/she worked in, and his/her class of work (whether the person was an employer, a salary or wage worker, or worked on own account). An example of the evolution of census data would be the worker recorded as "works in iron works" in 1880, becoming "iron molder" in 1900, and "molder," "wage worker," in "iron works" in 1920.[3]

The increase in occupational titles is also due to the development of new occupations from 1880 to 1920, such as the sudden upsurge of office sector occupations in 1900 (cashiers, clerks of all types, bookkeepers, assistants in all categories) or the growth of new industries and service sector jobs (electricity, telephone, city jobs, etc.). The 1920 titles, of course, reflected the transformation of Detroit into the major automobile city in the country.

The code adopted for the 1880 and 1900 samples divides the occupation into four broad categories: high white-collar, low white-collar, skilled, and semis-killed and unskilled occupations. The occupations were distributed into one of the four categories on the basis of a broad agreement among historians who had already developed occupational coding schemes: Stephan Thernstrom's code for his study of Boston, Theodore Hershberg's vertical code for Philadelphia, and the five-city project coding scheme. These codes were in basic agree-

---

3. Carrol D. Wright, *The History and Growth of the United States Census* (Washington, D.C.: G.P.O., 1900), pp. 167–77; U.S., Department of the Interior, Census Office, *Instructions to Enumerators: Twelfth Census of the United States* (Washington, D.C.: G.P.O., 1900); U.S., Department of Commerce, Bureau of Census, *Instructions to Enumerators* (Washington, D.C.: G.P.O., 1919).

ment with each other as well as with Donald Treiman's standard occupational prestige scale for use with historical data (see table A3.1).[4]

Titles included in the Detroit samples but not in the other studies' codes were logically placed into one of the four categories. An ambiguous title was generally coded in the lower category unless the number of persons in the household, the person's age, or household relationship clearly suggested a higher classification. Table A3.2 displays the most frequent titles of the 1900 sample per ethnic group and occupational category.

In an effort to refine occupational data, some of the tables in chapter 9 were prepared by attaching income figures to occupational titles. We were able, using data from BLIS studies—surveys of workers in the 1890s listed in Appendix 7—to find income data for most members of 912 households from the 1900 sample. Occupations of the heads of households were distributed as follows:

White-collar occupations.—Bookkeeper, 14; teacher, 7; civil engineer, 1; marine engineer, 1.

Skilled occupations.—Carpenter, 83; painter, 33; machinist, 32; iron molder, 22; blacksmith, 20; stove molder, 20; dressmaker, 19; barber, 16; cabinetmaker, 13; butcher, 13; bricklayer, 12; printer, 12; cigar maker, 10; tailor, 9; baker, 9; engineer, 9; plumber, 8; shoemaker, 8; boiler maker, 7; stove molder, 6; electrician, 5; railroad conductor, 5; streetcar conductor, 5; stationary engineer, 3; nurse, 1.

Semiskilled and unskilled occupations.—Laborer, 460; teamster, 25; peddler, 9; watchman, 8; laundress, 5; janitor, 2.

Other household members, men, women, children, and boarders, were distributed over the same occupations, with an additional sixty-four job titles for which we could find income figures.

For males.—Bartender, brakeman, brass finisher, brass molder, broommaker, clerk, core maker, finisher, furniture finisher, ironworker, lithographer, lumber inspector, machine hand, molder, office boy, musician, paper hanger, patternmaker, polisher, pressman, shipping clerk, stamp worker, tinsmith, trunkmaker, upholsterer, wire worker.

For females.—Awning maker, bookbinder, box factory, box maker, bunch maker, candy dipper, candy maker, capsule maker, cigar maker, clerk, confectioner, corset maker, domestic, dry goods clerk, dry goods saleslady, forelady

4. Stephan Thernstrom, *The Other Bostonians* (Cambridge, Mass.: Harvard University Press, 1973), pp. 290–92; Theodore Hershberg and Robert Dockhorn, "Occupational Classification," *Historical Methods Newsletter* 9 (March–June 1976): 78–98; Theodore Hershberg, et al., "Occupation and Ethnicity in Five Nineteenth-Century Cities: A Collaborative Inquiry," *Historical Methods Newsletter* 7 (June 1973): 174–216; Donald J. Treiman, *Occupational Prestige in Comparative Perspective* (New York: Academic Press, 1977), pp. 235–60.

TABLE A3.1

Comparison of five occupational codes

Detroit		Boston		Five-city project		Philadelphia	Prestige scale
1	High white-collar	1	High white-collar; Professional	1	Professional & "well-off"	1	Professional, High white-collar	77.9 high 61.9 ave. 31.7 low
		2	High white-collar; Major proprietor; Manager; Official	2	(High) white-collar[a]	2	(Major) proprietor[a]	
2	Low white-collar	3	Low white-collar; Clerks; Salesmen	2	(Low) white-collar[a] Petty proprietors	2	(Petty) proprietor, Low white-collar[a]	57.9 high 42.7 ave. 21.9 low
		4	LWC–semiprofessionals					
		5	LWC–petty proprietors; Managers; Officials					
3	Blue-collar–skilled	6	Blue-collar–skilled	3	Skilled artisan	3	Skilled crafts	70.3 high 31.7 ave. 19.1 low
4	Blue-collar semiskilled & unskilled	7	Blue-collar semiskilled & service workers	4	Semiskilled specified & unskilled specified	4	Unskilled specified	41.7 high 27.8 ave. 14.4 low
		8	Blue-collar unskilled & menial service workers	5	Unspecified semiskilled & unskilled	5	Unskilled unspecified	
5	Other					6	Other unskilled	
						7	Ambiguous	
						8	No occupation	
						9	Unclassified	

SOURCES: See note 4.

a. Distinction made for the clarity of the comparison.

in capsule works, furrier, feeder, hatmaker, housework, knitter, laboratory helper, milliner, pill maker, pin machine worker, saleslady, seamstress, sewer, shirt maker, tobacco stamper, stenographer, tailoress, tobacco packer, tobacco roller, tobacco stripper, tobacco worker, washer, wrapper.

We matched these income figures from BLIS data—after indexing them to 1912 values—with census occupational titles for this subsample of households by further refining income figures. Income varied by age and by ethnic group, and different figures were attached to the corresponding individuals in the 1900

Most frequent occupations by ethnic group and occupational group, Detroit, 1900 sample[a]

Occupation	Native white American[b]	Black	Canadian (English)	Canadian (French)
High white-collar				
Physician	33	-	9	1
Lawyer	31	-	2	-
Dentist	13	-	3	-
Merchant	10	-	-	-
Architect	8	-	-	-
Low white-collar				
Clerk	85	1	12	-
Bookkeeper	77	1	21	1
Schoolteacher	60	-	5	-
Stenographer	45	-	9	1
Grocer	14	-	2	-
Salesman	23	1	4	-
Saloonkeeper	6	-	2	-
Traveling salesman	24	-	2	-
Insurance agent	17	-	3	-
Dry goods clerk	13	-	5	2
Shipping clerk	9	-	6	-
Grocery clerk	6	-	4	-
Music teacher	15	1	3	-
Druggist	18	-	1	-
Office clerk	13	-	5	-
Landlord	9	-	1	1
Commercial traveler	10	-	1	-
Saleslady	10	-	3	-
Teacher	10	-	1	-
Musician	6	1	1	-
Chemist	6	-	2	-
Railroad clerk	6	-	3	-
Hotel clerk	11	-	-	-
Hotel keeper	8	-	-	-
Traveling man	8	-	-	-
Telegraph operator	5	-	3	-
Photographer	7	-	1	-
Civil engineer	7	-	-	-
Cashier	6	-	1	-
Store clerk	5	-	3	-
Restaurant keeper	5	-	3	-
Drug clerk	5	1	1	-
Contractor	6	-	1	-
Draftsman	5	-	-	-
Artist	5	-	-	-
Post office clerk	5	-	-	-
Hardware clerk	5	-	-	-
Broker	5	-	-	-

(*continued on pages 426–27*)

British	Irish	German	Polish	Russian
1	1	1	-	-
1	1	2	-	-
1	-	1	-	1
1	-	1	-	-
-	-	-	-	-
7	2	6	-	3
8	-	3	-	1
1	1	3	1	-
2	-	1	-	-
4	1	15	4	4
2	-	4	1	-
-	2	19	4	-
3	-	3	-	-
2	1	5	-	-
3	-	2	-	-
3	1	4	1	-
5	2	5	1	-
2	-	1	-	-
1	-	1	-	-
2	-	-	-	-
2	1	3	2	-
3	-	1	-	-
-	1	1	-	-
-	-	3	-	-
-	-	6	-	-
2	-	2	-	-
1	1	1	-	-
-	-	-	-	-
1	-	2	-	-
-	-	3	-	-
-	-	2	-	-
-	-	1	-	-
-	1	1	-	-
1	-	1	-	-
-	1	-	-	-
1	-	-	-	-
1	-	-	-	-
-	-	1	-	-
1	-	1	-	-
1	-	-	-	-
-	-	1	-	-
1	-	-	-	-
-	-	-	-	-

Most frequent occupations by ethnic group and occupational group, Detroit, 1900 sample[a]

Occupation	Native white American[b]	Black	Canadian (English)	Canadian (French)
Skilled				
Pressmaker	93	12	27	1
Carpenter	24	-	12	3
Machinist	34	-	7	2
Painter	27	2	7	-
Tailor	9	1	4	-
Iron molder	7	-	4	3
Barber	17	14	5	1
Cigar maker	2	-	1	-
Shoemaker	6	-	1	5
Blacksmith	3	-	2	2
Baker	6	-	5	2
Nurse	20	-	6	-
Printer	20	1	7	-
Butcher	3	1	4	2
Plumber	18	-	2	2
Stove molder	2	-	2	3
Engineer	9	-	3	-
Milliner	16	-	3	1
Seamstress	13	-	1	-
House painter	5	-	3	2
Electrician	12	-	2	-
Bricklayer	4	-	-	-
Cabinetmaker	1	-	1	-
Tailoress	4	-	-	-
Station engineer	5	-	2	1
Molder	5	-	4	-
Brewer	1	-	-	-
Street-car conductor	6	-	1	-
Knitter	2	-	2	1
Home carpenter	2	-	-	1
Ladies tailor	5	-	-	-
Brass finisher	1	-	2	-
Ship's carpenter	-	-	-	6
Bookbinder	1	-	-	-
Stonecutter	1	-	-	1
Semiskilled and unskilled				
Day laborer	29	6	18	5
Servant	56	7	32	-
Laborer	23	15	-	10
Teamster	22	7	7	2
Housekeeper	21	-	7	1
Domestic	13	4	9	1
Housework	11	5	4	4
Cook	9	7	3	1
Peddler	-	1	1	-

(continued on pages 428–29)

British	Irish	German	Polish	Russian
7	5	20	6	1
14	2	64	15	1
11	2	13	5	-
6	2	11	5	3
1	2	28	6	8
2	2	24	10	-
1	-	7	-	1
-	-	22	14	7
4	2	23	4	-
6	-	20	10	-
5	-	21	3	-
9	4	2	-	-
2	1	7	1	-
6	2	18	4	1
3	4	4	1	-
-	1	9	13	-
4	1	8	1	-
1	-	2	-	1
1	2	5	-	1
6	1	3	1	-
2	1	2	-	-
2	-	9	4	-
1	-	14	1	-
-	1	11	1	1
8	1	1	-	-
3	-	3	3	-
-	-	10	-	-
1	2	1	-	-
1	-	5	-	-
-	-	6	-	-
-	-	2	-	2
-	-	5	-	-
1	-	-	-	-
-	1	5	-	-
5	-	-	-	-
9	21	227	215	1
9	14	54	1	2
7	15	57	17	1
4	6	23	5	-
6	8	4	-	-
2	8	11	-	-
3	5	9	-	2
7	12	6	3	-
-	1	5	4	21

TABLE A3.2 (*Continued*)

Most frequent occupations by ethnic group and occupational group, Detroit, 1900 sample[a]

Occupation	Native white American[b]	Black	Canadian (English)	Canadian (French)
Laundress	2	8	1	-
Sailor	8	2	7	1
Coachman	10	1	1	-
Bartender	9	-	5	-
Janitor	4	5	1	-
Policeman	7	-	2	-
Porter	6	5	1	-
Railroad laborer	-	-	-	-
Cook and maid	7	-	5	-
Waiter	3	9	1	-
Chambermaid	3	-	-	-
Watchman	-	-	1	-
Cigar roller	-	-	-	-
Machine hand	5	-	-	-
Messenger	6	2	-	-
Tobacco stripper	-	-	-	-
Housemaid	-	-	5	-
Office boy	5	-	-	1
Hotel waiter	-	6	-	-
Tailoring worker	-	-	-	-

a. At least five occurrences in one of the major ethnic groups; occcupations listed in decreasing number of occurrences for the combined groups.

sample. Stratifying income by age and ethnicity was always possible for the 439 occupational titles included in the BLIS surveys of individual workers for which the individual level data has been published (see surveys listed in Appendix 7), and sometimes possible for some occupations in other specialized reports on women's work (1892) and on children's work (1885 and 1887).

The refined census categories for 1920 allowed us to develop a new code for the 1920 sample with twelve occupational categories corresponding to the following criteria:

Professionals.—The traditional professions (medicine, religion, law) and professions such as engineering, architecture, and accounting when the person is employed by a firm specializing in that professional service.

High white-collar.—Corporate officers and major government officials; owners of firms requiring large investments of capital.

White-collar.—Employees of all types of firms whose jobs do not involve manual production or who do not render services with their hands (inspectors, salespeople, clerks, cashiers, buyers, agents, teachers, real estate salesmen, etc.).

Nonretail proprietors.—Persons self-employed or employing others in any

British	Irish	German	Polish	Russian
1	1	12	8	-
3	2	1	-	-
8	1	1	-	-
-	1	4	-	-
4	1	3	-	-
1	5	2	-	-
-	1	2	-	-
1	3	8	1	-
1	-	-	-	-
-	-	-	-	-
1	1	7	-	-
-	3	6	-	-
-	-	2	7	-
-	-	4	-	-
-	-	-	-	-
1	-	2	5	-
1	2	-	-	-
-	-	-	-	-
-	-	-	-	-
-	-	-	5	-

b. Born in the U.S. of two U.S.-born parents; born in English-speaking Canada of two Canadian parents, etc.

kind of nonretail enterprise including (service enterprises such as hotels and boardinghouses) that does not *obviously* require large capital investment.

Retailers.—Persons self-employed or employing others in an enterprise likely to carry on sale of goods at a regular location: a store in a permanent building.

Craftsmen.—Persons self-employed whose occupation is among traditional trades.

Skilled and semiskilled wage labor.—Persons who are involved in producing (with their hands, or by directly supervising or operating machinery) a *material good* from the sales of which the employee derives wages; included here are skilled railroad/street-railroad workers, though strictly interpreted their jobs do not involve production of a good.

Skilled and semiskilled service workers.—Persons deriving wages from services performed with their hands, when these services do not render a product, and whose job requires a degree of training and experience.

Lower retailers.—Owning or self-employed in a retail endeavor likely to do business from a temporary location on a day-to-day, week-to-week, or month-to-month basis; i.e., peddlers.

Unskilled service.—A person paid for rendering menial services with their hands: domestics of all sorts, porters, stevedores, sweepers, regardless of employer (firm or family).

Unskilled wage labor.—Persons paid for rendering menial work for a manufacturing firm of some kind: "laborers," "helpers"; does *not* include "sweepers," "truck driver," etc.

Farmers (for suburban areas)

Table A3.3 presents the most frequent combinations in the 1920 sample.

TABLE A3.3
Most frequent occupations, by occupational group, Detroit, 1920 sample[a]

Industry	Class[b]	Occupation	Number in sample
Professionals			
Medicine	OA	Physician	26
Law	OA	Attorney	13
White-collar			
Auto manufacturing	W	Inspector	42
Real estate	W	Salesman	28
Retail clothing	W	Salesman	22
Auto manufacturing	W	Clerk	15
City	W	Teacher	11
Auto manufacturing	W	Accountant	10
Auto manufacturing	W	Salesman	9
Food manufacturing	W	Salesman	9
Retail food	W	Salesman	9
Retail, other	W	Salesman	9
Motor manufacturing	W	Inspector	8
Retail furniture	W	Salesman	7
Retail unspecified	W	Salesman	7
Unidentified	W	Clerk	7
Auto manufacturing	W	Engineer	6
Auto manufacturing	W	Stock clerk	6
Unspecified factory	W	Salesman	6
Retail auto	W	Salesman	6
Restaurant, foodstand	W	Manager	6
Railroad	W	Clerk	6
Wholesale food	W	Salesman	5
Wholesale, other	W	Salesman	5
Retail food	W	Clerk	5
Retail clothing	W	Manager	5
Nonretail proprietors			
Real estate	OA	Salesman	23
Lodging	OA	Keeper	21
Restaurant, foodstand	OA	Proprietor	10
Lodging	OA	Landlady	9
Tailoring	OA	Tailor	8

TABLE A3.3 (*Continued*)

Most frequent occupations, by occupational group, Detroit, 1920 sample[a]

Industry	Class[b]	Occupation	Number in sample
Real estate	OA	Real estate	6
Lodging	OA	Housekeeper	6
Barbering	OA	Barber	6
Building trades	Em	Contractor	5
Restaurant, foodstand	Em	Proprietor	5
Domestic service	OA	Housekeeper	5
Retailers			
Retail food	OA	Proprietor	11
Retail food	OA	Retail merchant	9
Retail food	OA	Butcher	8
Retail food	OA	Grocer	7
Retail clothing	OA	Merchant	7
Retail food	OA	Merchant	5
Retail food	OA	Merchant	5
Craftsmen			
Building trades	OA	Carpenter	14
Clothing manufacturer	OA	Shoemaker	8
Skilled-semiskilled wage labor			
Auto manufacturing	W	Machinist	195
Building trades	W	Carpenter	99
Auto manufacturing	W	Foreman	66
Unspecified manufacturing	W	Machinist	57
Auto manufacturing	W	Toolmaker	53
Auto manufacturing	W	Painter	29
Auto manufacturing	W	Assembler	27
Unspecified manufacturing	W	Toolmaker	23
Motor manufacturing	W	Machinist	22
Auto manufacturing	W	Carpenter	18
Auto manufacturing	W	Millwright	18
Auto manufacturing	W	Mechanic	17
Auto manufacturing	W	Trimmer	17
Auto manufacturing	W	Repairman	16
Foundry	W	Molder	14
Unspecified manufacturing	W	Patternmaker	14
Auto manufacturing	W	Machine operator	13
Auto manufacturing	W	Electrician	12
Auto manufacturing	W	Woodworker	11
Building trades	W	Bricklayer	11
Unspecified manufacturing	W	Foreman	11
Unspecified manufacturing	W	Molder	11
Railroad	W	Switchman	11
Street railway	W	Motorman	11
Auto manufacturing	W	Auto body builder	10

Most frequent occupations, by occupational group, Detroit, 1920 sample[a]

Industry	Class[b]	Occupation	Number in sample
Hardware manufacturing	W	Machinist	10
Hardware manufacturing	W	Tool and die maker	10
Building trades	W	Plumber	10
Street railway	W	Conductor	10
Auto manufacturing	W	Auto body maker	9
Auto manufacturing	W	Finisher	9
Auto manufacturing	W	Steamfitter	9
Retail food	W	Butcher	9
Railroad	W	Engineer	9
Auto manufacturing	W	Grinder	8
Auto manufacturing	W	Molder	8
Stove manufacturing	W	Molder	8
Publishing	W	Printer	8
Motor manufacturing	W	Foreman	7
Retail food	W	Baker	7
Auto manufacturing	W	Blacksmith	6
Food manufacturing	W	Baker	6
Building trades	W	Plasterer	6
Unspecified manufacturing	W	Millwright	6
Electric utility	W	Electrician	6
Auto manufacturing	W	Motor assembler	5
Business machine manufacturing	W	Machinist	5
Foundry	W	Core maker	5
Iron works	W	Molder	5
Building trades	W	Painter	5
Unspecified manufacturing	W	Mechanic	5
Skilled, semiskilled service workers			
Barbering	W	Barber	18
Decorating	W	Painter	12
Tailoring	W	Tailor	11
Auto service	W	Repairman	11
Decorating	W	Decorator	7
Auto service	W	Auto repairs	6
Entertainment	W	Musician	5
City	W	Detective	5
Unskilled wage labor			
Auto manufacturing	W	Laborer	184
Unspecified manufacturing	W	Laborer	34
Chemical manufacturing	W	Laborer	23
Auto manufacturing	W	Machine hand	22
Foundry	W	Laborer	14
Auto manufacturing	W	Auto worker	12
Auto manufacturing	W	Sheet metal worker	12
Building trades	W	Laborer	11

Most frequent occupations, by occupational group, Detroit, 1920 sample[a]

Industry	Class[b]	Occupation	Number in sample
Ship manufacturing	W	Laborer	8
Motor manufacturing	W	Laborer	7
Brass works	W	Laborer	7
Food manufacturing	W	Laborer	6
Hardware manufacturing	W	Laborer	6
Blast works	W	Laborer	6
Lumber	W	Laborer	6
Street railway	W	Laborer	6
Tire manufacturing	W	Laborer	5
Railroad		Laborer	5
Unskilled service workers			
City	W	Laborer	17
City	W	Policeman	17
Restaurant, foodstand	W	Cook	10
Domestic service	W	Janitor	9
City	W	Foreman	8
Auto manufacturing	W	Watchman	6
Trucking and shipping	W	Driver	6
Food manufacturing	W	Driver	5
Domestic service	W	Chauffeur	5
City	W	Teamster	5

a. At least five occurrences of any unique combination of industry, class, and occupation. There were no more than one case per combination in the high white-collar category of presidents and vice-presidents of companies; and no more than three among the lower retailers (peddlers).

b. Em = employer

    W = salary or wage worker

    OA = working on own account

Appendix 4

Measuring Segregation

This appendix presents a chi-squared statistic approach for measuring and testing geographic clustering, as used in chapters 2, 6, and 13.[1] As is well-known, the usual chi-squared statistic, X^2, is a natural measure of the departure of observed from expected frequencies under various hypotheses. Recall that the X^2 statistic is defined as the sum of terms equal to the ratio of the square of the discrepancy between observed and expected frequencies to the expected frequency. While this statistic is an ideal measure of discrepancy between "expected" and "observed" values to test the hypothesis of the randomness of the different groups' geographic distributions within the city, it needs to be standardized before we can compare units of various sizes and different categories at different geographic levels of analysis.

METHODOLOGY AND FORMULAE

Suppose that each element in some population falls into one of K categories with respect to some attribute. For example, each person in the city of Detroit might be classified as belonging to one of K = 6 ethnic groups: American, Canadian, Irish, English, German and Polish. Let p_k be the proportion of the population elements which fall into the k-th of these K categories. Note that if N is the total population size and N_k is the number of these falling into the k-th category then

1. I wish to thank William A. Ericson and his students of the Department of Statistics, University of Michigan, who have contributed to the formulation of this approach. Readers interested in other approaches, including a brief but good overview of traditional segregation indexes, can consult Theodore Hershberg, Alan N. Burstein, and Susan M. Drobis, "The Historical Study of Urban Space," *Historical Methods Newsletter* 9 (March–June 1976): 99–136.

$$p_k = \frac{N_k}{N}, \; k = 1, 2, \ldots, K$$

Now, we are interested in the geographic distribution of this categorical attribute over the population or city and in determining whether such a distribution may be considered random or whether there are geographic clusterings or concentrations of the attribute. Suppose then that the population may be partitioned into B geographical sub regions and a sample of b of them is observed. These subregions could comprise block fronts, blocks, or other geographical units. Suppose n_i denotes the size or number of population elements located in the i-th geographical subregion. Also let n_{ik} denote the number of the n_i units which fall in category k of the attribute under study. Note that

$$n_i = n_{i1} + n_{i2} + \ldots + n_{iK}$$

for each i.

If the hypothesis that individual population elements distribute themselves at random among the B subregions is true then it can be shown that, given the n_i's and the p_k's, the n_{ik}'s have approximately a multinomial distribution within each of the b observed sample subregions. Furthermore, the n_{ik}'s among the b subregions will be approximately independent, especially if b is small relative to B.

In such a situation it is well-known that the mean or expected number of population elements in the i-th subregion which fall in category k will be equal to $n_i p_k$. Also, if n_i is large then the chi-squared statistic

$$X_i^2 = \sum_{k=1}^{K} \frac{(n_{ik} - n_i p_k)^2}{n_i p_k}, \; i = 1, \ldots, b$$

will have an approximate chi-squared distribution with $K - 1$ degrees of freedom. Thus, if the randomness hypothesis is true then the b observed values of X_i^2 should behave like a sample of b observations from a chi-squared distribution assuming that the n_i's are each large.

At this point one of the requisite assumptions for application of the standard chi-squared distribution to the Detroit data breaks down since the n_i's, i = 1, ..., b, are not large, especially at the front level of analysis, and they vary considerably among the geographic subregions.

To eliminate this difficulty, another approach was taken. First, it can be shown that the mean and variance of X_i^2 are given by $K - 1$ and

$$\frac{2(n_i - 1)(K - 1)}{n_i} - \frac{K^2}{n_i} + \frac{1}{n_i} \sum_{k=1}^{K} \frac{1}{p_k}$$

respectively.[2] Also, since the X_i^2's are independent an overall test of the randomness hypothesis may be based on the statistic

$$X^2 = \sum_{i=1}^{b} X_i^2 = \sum_{i=1}^{b} \sum_{k=1}^{K} \frac{(n_{ik} - n_i p_k)^2}{n_i p_k}$$

Note that X^2 has a mean of $b (K - 1)$ and a variance equal to

$$V(X^2) = \sum_{i=1}^{b} \left\{ \frac{2(n_i - 1)(K - 1)}{n_i} - \frac{K^2}{n_i} + \frac{1}{n_i} \sum_{k=1}^{K} \frac{1}{p_k} \right\}$$

It follows that if the randomness hypothesis is true and if b is not small, then the standardized value of X^2, given by

$$X_s^2 = \frac{X^2 - b(K - 1)}{\sqrt{V(X^2)}}$$

will, to a good approximation, have a standard normal distribution with mean zero and variance one $\mathcal{N}(0,1)$. The overall test of randomness is carried out by comparing the observed value of X_s^2 with appropriate percentage points of the standard normal distribution. Thus, for example, randomness is rejected using a 5% level of significance if X_s^2 exceeds 1.65.

In addition, specific clusterings may be singled out by examining the individual X_i^2 value for each subregion and by looking at how many standard deviations it is away from its mean, i.e., by looking at standardized values of X_i^2 using the mean and variance of X_i^2 given above. Even though the distribution of these individual X_i^2's is not normal, when a value of 3 or more occurs, we can reject the hypothesis of randomness at a .11 of significance or more likely lower. (According to Chebyshev's theory, if the random variable X has finite mean μ and finite standard deviation, σ, and k is any positive number, then the probability outside the closed interval $[\mu - k\sigma, \mu + k\sigma]$ is less than $1/h^2$.[3])

In carrying out this methodology for various characterisitics of the Detroit samples another difficulty was encountered. This problem arose because the population proportions, p_k, were not available. These had to be estimated from the sample. The sample estimates, denoted by $\hat{p}_k$, were obtained using the formula

$$\hat{p}_k = (\sum_{i=1}^{b} n_{ik}) / (\sum_{i=1}^{b} n_i)$$

2. Maurice G. Kendall, *The Advanced Theory of Statistics*, 2 vols. (London: C. Griffin, 1943–46), 2:462.

3. Frederick Mosteller, Robert E. K. Rourke, and George B. Thomas, *Probability with Statistical Applications* (Reading, Mass.: Addison Wesley, 1970), p. 228.

i.e., by using the overall sample proportion of elements falling in the k-th category. The methodology described above, assuming that the p_k were known, was carried out by substituting the estimated values, $\hat{p}_k$, for the p_k values everywhere.

One final problem arose in applying this analysis at the small neighborhood or cluster level because several of these clusters were overlapping, that is, they contained common frontages. This difficulty was eliminated by redefining the clusters by assigning any common frontages to one or the other cluster. This had little or no practical effect since the overlapping frontages were mostly vacant. This difficulty could also be overcome by incorporating covariance terms, arising from the common frontages, in the calculation of the variance of X^2.

Appendix 5

Other Statistical Measurements

All statistical measurements in this book not explained in Appendixes 1, 2, and 4 or in this appendix are explained in most introductory texts in statistics.[1] Such texts, however, do not cover the techniques of demographic analysis used in chapters 3, 10, and 14. The formulae for the computation of vital statistics are given in published articles, the references of which are in these chapters' footnotes.

The reader should also consult documentations of specialized computer programs which often provide important references to points of statistical theory. A variety of systems of statistical computing are available to the quantitative historian. Most of the analysis for this book (as well as data manipulation and data storage—see Appendix 7) was done with MIDAS, designed by Daniel J. Fox and maintained by the University of Michigan's Statistical Research Laboratory. I also used OSIRIS (maintained by the Inter-University Consortium for Political and Social Research, Institute for Social Research, Ann Arbor, Michigan) for one analysis described below. And I used a special demographic program of the University of Michigan's Population Studies Center for the mortality estimates in chapter 10. The analyses of the 1920 data were conducted at the U.S. Bureau of the Census with the Bureau's versions of SPSS and SAS.

The following formulae are important to understand the density graph of chapter 1, the log-linear regression of chapter 2, and the cluster analysis of chapter 4.

DENSITY DECLINE

The graph of density decline in chapter 1 represents the predicted values of the following quadratic regression:

1. Such as Hubert M. Blalock, Jr., *Social Statistics* rev. 2d ed. (New York: McGraw-Hill, 1979).

438

Ln Density = 3.4 + 1.35 Distance − .99 Distance^2 + ε;
R^2 = .92

The city was divided into 22 density gradients from the center to the periphery. Areal and population data were computed from the sample on each gradient.[2]

DICHOTOMOUS REGRESSION

The technique of dichotomous regression used in chapter 3 (to predict dichotomous variables such as living in the east or in the west) is documented in specialized articles and in OSIRIS IV under the program DREG.[3] The model used in DREG is a Logit model of the form:

Log P(Y = 1)/(1 − P(Y = 1)) = B$_0$ + B$_1$X$_1$ + . . .

This log-linear model is analogous to but different from ordinary regression. DREG uses maximum likelihood and not least square fits to the dependent variable to obtain regression coefficients, thus "allowing for the fact that the mean of a dichotomous variable is restricted and that its variance may not be constant across cases." As the documentation explains: "Rather than minimizing the residual sum of squares to obtain the regression coefficients, dichotomous regression minimizes the predictive error, π_e, defined as $\pi_e = 1 - \pi$, where π is the geometric mean of the fitted probabilities of the sample values of the dependent variable. . . . The larger P(Y$_1$) is the better the ith case fits the model (1 − P(Y$_1$) is like a residual), and the maximum likelihood algorithm chooses those regression coefficients which make the predictive power, π, largest and thus the predictive error, π_e, smallest. Dichotomous regression treats π_e just like least squares regression treats residual sums of squares. There are "due to regression" "error" and "total" π_e's and the ratio of the "due to regression" and "total" π_e is analogous to R^2, the fraction of variance explained by the regression."

CLUSTER ANALYSIS

The multivariate analysis in chapter 4 (with the cluster program in MIDAS) uses the following formula for the computation of the euclidean distance.

$$d(j, j') = \sqrt{\sum_{i=1}^{P} wi^*(vij - vij')^2},$$

where vij is the value taken by the jth unit on the ith variable with weight wi*.

2. A full treatment of mathematical models used to predict density will be found in Brian J. L. Berry and Frank E. Horton, *Geographic Perspectives on Urban Systems* (Englewood Cliffs, N.J.: Prentice-Hall, 1970), pp. 276–306; see note 5, p. 302 especially.

3. See William H. DuMouchel, "On the Analogy between Linear and Log-Linear Regression," (University of Michigan, Department of Statistics, Technical Report No. 67, March 1976).

Appendix 6

The Leaders of Detroit's Industrialization

This appendix includes biographical data on 115 industrialists in Detroit in 1900.[1]

The headings of columns in the table below—where industrialists are listed in alphabetical order—are as follows:

1. Name
2. President, Chairman, Senior Partner, or Owner
3. Firm and product
4. Number of employees
5. Place of birth
   5a. person
   5b. first parent
   5c. second parent
6. Year of birth
7. Age on arrival in Detroit
8. Age on becoming head of firm
9. Route to directing firm
10. Board member of other firms or banks
11. College
12. Religious affiliation
13. Political affiliation
14. Number of club memberships

The numbers below each name refer to specific publications and manuscript collections listed on page 460; the references following the colon complete the notes for each individual case.

1. For a guide to local biographical research, see Francis Loomis, comp., "Michigan Biography Index," 11 vols. (DPL, 1946). There were six presidents for whom no data could be found: Robert H. McCutcheon (United States Capsule Co.), Charles Scherer (Peerless Mfg. Co.), Frederick J. Foote (William Wright and Co.), George G. Clarkson (Detroit Screw Works), Benjamin F. Ray (Detroit Malleable), and George S. Sill (Detroit Can Co.).

1	2	3	4	5a	5b	5c
Anderson, William 6. 13: p. 32.	P	Anderson Carriage Co.	175	English Canada	-	-
Annis, Newton 6. 24: 5-10-31. 10-24-32.	O	Newton Annis Co. (furs)	250	Michigan	Great Britain	Great Britain
Armstrong, Edwin E. 4: vol. 5, p. 207. 6. 29.	SP	Armstrong and Graham (saddlery)	150	Detroit	Ireland	Ireland
Backus, Henry N. 23: 3-11-42.	P	A. Backus Jr. and Sons (box mfg.)	225	New York	-	-
Bagley, John N. 4: vol. 3, p. 372. 6.	P	Bagley and Co. (tobacco)	160	Detroit	New York	Iowa
Barbour, George H. 4: vol. 3, p. 98. 6.	P	Ireland and Matthews Mfg. Co. (brass works)	500	Connecticut	Connecticut	Connecticut
Barbour, William T. 3: vol. 3, p. 326–7. 4: vol. 5, p. 349. 6.	P	Detroit Stove Works	1,150	Detroit	Connecticut	New York
Berry, Joseph H. 3: vol. 3, p. 20–23. 29.	P	Berry Brothers (varnish)	150	New Jersey	England	England
Boyer, Joseph 3: vol. 3, p. 16–20. 6.	P	Boyer Machine (pneumatic tools)	190	English Canada	English Canada	English Canada
Brasie, William L. 4: vol. 5, p. 1089.	O	St. Clair Mfg. (furniture)	275	Michigan	England	New York
Briscoe, Benjamin 17: part 2, p. 112.	P	Detroit Galvanizing and Sheet Metal Works (stove and boilers)	100	Detroit	-	-
Brown, John H. 6. 24: 1-6-14. 29.	P	Brown Brothers (cigars)	675	Ohio	Ireland	Ireland
Buhl, Theodore D. 2: p. 328. 6. 29.	P	Parke, Davis and Co. (drugs)	1,350	Detroit	Pennsylvania	New York

6	7	8	9	10	11	12	13	14
1853	42	-	founder	-	yes	Episcopalian	Republican	1
1858	22	29	founder	-	-	Unitarian	-	1
1853	-	27	founder	-	-	Presbyterian	-	3
1855	12	-	founder	-	-	-	-	1
1860	-	23	inherited	yes	±	Unitarian	Republican	6
1844	28	-	cofounder	yes	-	-	Democrat	6
1877	-	20	inherited	yes	yes	Episcopalian	-	6
1839	16	19	founder	yes	-	Presbyterian	Prohibitionist	-
1848	52	-	founder	-	-	-	-	8
1871	-	-	-	yes	yes	-	Republican	1
1867	-	23	-	-	-	Episcopalian	-	2
1849	37	-	-	-	-	-	-	-
1844	-	31	investor	yes	-	-	Republican	2

	1	2	3	4	5a	5b	5c
" "		P	Buhl Stamping (tinware)	200	"	"	"
" "		P	Buhl Malleable Co. (casting)	500	"	"	"
Buick, David D. 15: p. 79. 22: 3-7-29. 24: 11-13-56.		P	Buick and Sherwood Mfg. Co. (iron and steel)	300	Scotland	Scotland	Scotland
Caille, Adolph 6. 14: p. 92. 29.		SP	Caille, Scheimer Co. (vending machines)	100	Detroit	Switzerland	Switzerland
Calvert, Thomas 3: vol. 3, p. 93. 29.		P	Calvert Lithographing	375	England	England	England
Carhartt, Hamilton 3: vol. 3, p. 695. 6.		O	Hamilton Carhartt and Sons (cotton mill)	535	New York	United States	United States
Chittenden, William 2: p. 326. 6.		P	Hargreaver Mfg. (lumber)	326	New York	United States	United States
" "		P	Michigan Wire Cloth	110	"	"	"
Clark, Emory W. 4: vol. 3, p. 22. 6.		P	Clark Can Co.	100	Detroit	-	-
Colburn, Henry C. 6. 9: vol. 2, p. 665.		P	Detroit Bridge and Iron Works	500	Vermont	United States	United States
Crawford, Andrew J. 6. 29.		P	The Grand Laundry	150	Michigan	Michigan	Michigan
Dailey, Elvin G. 29.		P	E. G. Dailey and Co. (food)	175	New York	New York	New York
Davies, William L. 2: p. 550. 6.		P	Acme White Lead and Color Works	200	Wales	Wales	Wales
Ducharme, George 6. 14: p. 157. 22: 5-20-45. 5-24-45.		P	U.S. Heater Co.	135	Detroit	French Canada	New York

6	7	8	9	10	11	12	13	14
"	"	-	"	"	"	"	"	
"	"	"	"	"	"	"	"	"
1854	2	30	founder	-	-	-	-	-
1863	-	-	founder	-	-	-	-	-
-	-	-	founder	-	-	-	-	-
1861	23	28	founder	-	-	Episcopalian	-	3
1835	18	29	investor	yes	-	Episcopalian	Republican	4
"	"	-	"	"	"	"	"	"
1868	-	-	-	-	-	-	-	6
1845	30	-	inherited	-	-	-	-	-
-	-	-	-	-	-	-	-	-
-	-	-	-	-	-	-	-	-
1858	14	26	cofounder	-	-	-	-	-
1860	-	-	-	-	-	-	Independent	6

	1	2	3	4	5a	5b	5c
DuPont, Charles 28. 29.		P	Banner Laundering Co.	125	Michigan	English Canada	Michigan
Dwyer, Jeremiah 3: vol. 5, p. 312. 6. 8: vol. 2, p. 1187. 29.		P	Michigan Stove	1,000	New York	Ireland	Ireland
Dyar, John B. 3: vol. 3, p. 144–48. 4: vol. 3, p. 228.		P	American Radiator	912	Michigan	Vermont	New Jersey
Falconer, R. C. 29.		P	Leland and Mfg. Co. (machinery)	251	Michigan	Vermont	New York
Ferry, Dexter M. 3: vol. 3, p. 8–12. 6. 8: vol. 2, p. 1143.		P	D. M. Ferry and Co. (grain wholesale)	900	New York	New York	Massachu- setts
Flinn, Elisha H. 3: vol. 3, p. 712. 6.		P	Farrand and Votey Organ Co.	225	New York	New York	New York
George, Henry 27. 29.		O	H. George and Sons (builders)	300	New York	New York	New York
" "		O	Henry George Co. (lumber)	100	"	"	"
Gillett, Rufus W. 6. 8: vol. 2, p. 1148.		P	Detroit Copper and Brass	500	Connecticut	Connecticut	Connecticut
Goldsmith, Charles 14: p. 191–2.		O	Charles Goldsmith Co. (clothing)	200	Germany	Germany	Germany
Gordon, Alexander 22: 11-14-17 29.		O	Alex Gordon Co. (tobacco)	150	English Canada	Scotland	English Canada
Graham, Burke M. 6. 14: p. 195. 29.		SP	Armstrong and Graham (saddlery)	150	New York	New York	New York
Gray, John S. 3: vol. 3, p. 108–111. 6.		P	Gray, Toynton, and Fox (candies)	250	Scotland	Scotland	Scotland

6	7	8	9	10	11	12	13	14
1868	-	-	investor	-	-	-	-	3
1837	1	49	founder	-	-	Roman Catholic	Democrat	-
1846	-	-	cofounder	-	yes	-	-	-
-	-	-	-	-	-	-	-	-
1833	19	46	cofounder	yes	-	Congregationalist	Republican	-
1843	22	-	-	yes	-	-	-	-
1838	12	-	founder	-	-	Episcopalian	-	4
"	"	"	"	"	"	"	"	"
1825	37	-	-	yes	-	-	Democrat	-
1858	16	41	founder	-	-	-	-	1
1841	25	36	-	-	-	-	-	3
1854	15	26	founder	-	-	-	-	3
1841	16	27	inherited	-	-	-	Independent	-

1	2	3	4	5a	5b	5c
Haberkorn, Christian H. 3: vol. 3, p. 116. 6.	O	C. H. Haberkorn and Co. (furniture)	125	Detroit	Germany	Germany
Hammond, Charles F. 4: vol. 3, p. 638. 6.	P	Hammond, Standish and Co. (meat packers)	130	Detroit	Massachusetts	Detroit
Hammond, George S. 6. 14: p. 218	P	Winn and Hammond (printing)	125	Ohio	-	-
Harvey, John 3: vol. 3, p. 580. 6.	P	A. Harvey and sons (valves)	200	Scotland	Scotland	Scotland
Hawley, Ransom 29.	SP	Thorp, Hawley and Co. (candies)	100	English Canada	English Canada	English Canada
Hecker, Frank 6. 14: p. 233. 29.	P	American Car and Foundry (railroad equipment)	2,200	Michigan	Germany	Germany
Hemmeter, John P. 14: p. 235. 19.	P	Hemmeter Cigar Co.	178	Michigan	Germany	Germany
Hodge, Harry S. 6. 8: vol. 2, p. 1192. 29.	P	Samuel F. Hodge and Co. (marine engines)	100	Michigan	England	England
Hodges, Henry Clay 3: vol. 5, p. 72–75.	P	Detroit Lubricator	200	Vermont	-	-
Holliday, William, P. 4: vol. 3, p. 672. 6.	O	W. P. Holliday Box Co.	352	Pennsylvania	Pennsylvania	Connecticut
Howard, Frank 6. 14: p. 239. 29.	P	Pearl Button Co.	240	Michigan	Ireland	Ireland
Howarth, John B. 2: p. 458. 6.	SP	Pingree and Smith (shoes)	700	Massachusetts	England	England
Hubel, Frederick A. 6. 8: vol. 2, p. 1193.	O	F. A. Hubel Gelatin Capsule Works	200	Germany	Germany	Germany
Jenks, Charles C. 6. 21: 10-29-23. 24: 10-24-24. 29.	P	Jenks and Muir Mfg. Co. (iron and steel)	150	Michigan	New York	New York

6	7	8	9	10	11	12	13	14
1856	-	22	founder	-	-	Congregationalist	-	5
1868	30	30	inherited	-	yes	Roman Catholic	-	7
1855	12	30	founder	-	yes	-	Republican	4
1840	-	-	inherited	-	yes	Presbyterian	-	-
1849	-	-	-	-	-	-	-	-
1847	-	-	cofounder	-	-	-	-	4
1862	35	31	founder	-	-	Lutheran	-	2
-	-	-	inherited	-	-	-	-	-
1828	27	-	investor	yes	-	-	Republican	1
1852	20	26	founder	-	-	-	Republican	7
1840	-	-	investor	yes	-	Roman Catholic	-	1
1858	17	25	rose through ranks	-	-	Episcopalian	Republican	1
1846	16	27	founder	-	yes	-	-	-
1854	21	39	cofounder	yes	-	-	-	-

1	2	3	4	5a	5b	5c
Johnson, Thomas L. 16: p. 63–73, 102–3. 130–32. 141–45.	O	Detroit Citizens St. Rwy (repair shop)	275	Kentucky	-	-
Keenan, James J. 6. 14: p. 277.	P	Detroit Cabinet Co.	100	English Canada	-	-
Kelly, Martin 3: vol. 3, p. 403. 6. 29.	P	Palace Laundry Co.	100	Ohio	New York	New York
Kempf, Rueben 6. 10: p. 555. 11: p. 561.	P	Globe Tobacco	260	Pennsylvania	-	-
Kirby, Frank E. 6. 14: p. 287. 29.	P	Detroit Boat Works	100	Ohio	Ohio	Ohio
Larned, Abner E. 3: vol. 3, p. 111–12. 6.	P	Larned and Carter and Co. (clothing mfg.)	125	Michigan	Michigan	Michigan
Laurense, Leonard 19. 29.	O	Leonard Laurense (molding mfg.)	100	Holland	Holland	Holland
Lee, James L. 3: vol. 4, p. 97–98. 6. 29.	SP	Strong, Lee and Co. (clothing mfg.)	100	Michigan	New York	New York
McMillan, James 2: p. 280. 6. 20.	C	American Car and Foundry (railroad equipment)	2,200	English Canada	Scotland	Scotland
" "	P	Seamless Steel and Tube Co. (iron and steel)	150	"	"	"
" "	P	Fulton Iron and Engine Works (machinery)	120	"	"	"
McMillan, Neil 2: p. 594. 6.	P	Art Stove Co.	170	Scotland	Scotland	Scotland

6	7	8	9	10	11	12	13	14
1854	40	40	investor	-	-	-	-	-
1840	24	33	-	-	-	Roman Catholic	Democrat	1
1857	38	-	investor	-	-	-	Republican	2
1835	-	-	-	-	-	-	Republican	1
1849	21	33	-	-	-	-	Republican	-
1871	19	-	cofounder	-	-	-	Republican	10
1841	-	-	-	-	-	-	-	2
1858	18	30	rose through ranks	yes	-	Presbyterian	Independent	4
1838	17	26	cofounder	yes	-	Presbyterian	Republican	-
"	"	"	investor	"	"	"	"	"
"	"	"	"	"	"	"	"	"
1852	300	35	cofounder	-	-	Methodist	Republican	3

1	2	3	4	5a	5b	5c
McMillan, William C. 2: p. 259. 6.	P	Michigan Malleable Iron Works	200	Detroit	English Canada	Detroit
McRae, William D. 6. 29.	SP	McRae and Roberts Co. (brass goods)	300	English Canada	Scotland	Scotland
McVittie, Alexander 6. 17: p. 768.	P	Detroit Shipbuilding	500	Scotland	Scotland	Scotland
Marvin, Frank W. 6. 29.	P	Michigan Lubricator Co. (iron and steel)	125	Detroit	New York	New York
Marx, Stephen 22: 4-5-01.	P	Michigan Optical	119	Germany	Germany	Germany
Mason, Lucia 29.	SP	Zacharias and Mason (clothing)	250	Michigan	Pennsylvania	Pennsylvania
Miller, Sherman 6. 14: p. 348. 29.	fO	Royal Mfg. (silverware)	175	New York	New York	New York
Miller, William H. 6. 14: p. 326.	O	William H. Miller and Co. (clothing)	100	Ohio	Germany	Ohio
Mills, Merrill B. 6. 15: p. 51. 22: 6-19-29. 29.	P	Banner Cigar	300	Detroit	Connecticut	Connecticut
Moebs, George 7: p. 267. 12: p. 131.	O	George Moebs & Co. (tobacco)	148	Germany	Germany	Germany
Moran, Frederick T. 2: p. 530.	P	Peninsular Stove Co.	800	Detroit	Detroit	Detroit
Morgan, Charles L. 3: vol. 5, p. 947.	P	Morgan and Whately (clothing)	110	Indiana	United States	United States
Murphy, Michael J. 6. 8: vol. 2, p. 1195.	P	Murphy, Wasey and Co. (furniture mfg.)	475	English Canada	Ireland	Ireland
Murphy, Thomas 26: vol. 8, p. 195. 29.	O	Murphy Iron Works	100	Ireland	Ireland	Ireland
Nelson, Edwin H. 2: p. 491. 6.	P	Nelson, Baker and Co. (drugs)	250	English Canada	Ireland	United States

6	7	8	9	10	11	12	13	14
1861	-	-	investor	yes	yes	-	Republican	-
1849	-	-	-	-	-	-	-	-
1842	25	-	rose through ranks	-	-	Methodist	Prohibitionist	-
1854	-	-	-	-	-	-	-	-
1823	23	-	-	yes	-	-	-	1
1848	-	-	-	-	-	-	-	-
1852	17	36	founder	yes	-	Congregationalist	Republican	3
1857	-	31	founder	-	yes	Congregationalist	Republican	2
1854	-	-	inherited	yes	yes	Episcopalian	Democrat	-
1833	21	37	founder	yes	-	-	-	-
1855	-	40	inherited	yes	yes	-	Independent	-
1865	6	31	founder	-	-	-	Democrat	1
1851	17	-	founder	yes	yes	-	-	-
-	-	-	founder	-	-	Congregationalist	-	1
1856	23	-	founder	yes	. yes	Episcopalian	Republican	2

1	2	3	4	5a	5b	5c
Newberry, Truman H. 4: vol. 3, p. 28. 6. 18: p. 1938–39.	P	Detroit Steel and Spring Co. (industrial hardware)	200	Detroit	New York	New York
Oades, Walter H. 14: p. 347. 29.	O	Walter Oades Co.	100	New York	England	New York
Olds, Ransom E. 4: vol. 2, p. 1357–59. 6. 18: p. 1896. 29.	P	Olds' Motor Works	165	Ohio	Ohio	Ohio
Peck, George 2: p. 255. 6.	SP	Pingree and Smith (shoes)	700	Connecticut	Connecticut	Connecticut
Pingree, Frank C. 3: vol. 4, p. 455. 6.	SP	Pingree and Smith (shoes)	700	Maine	New England	New England
Pingree, Hazen 3: vol. 13, p. 832. 4: vol. 5, p. 506. 6. 8: vol. 2, p. 1119.	SP	Pingree and Smith (shoes)	700	Maine	New England	New England
Posselius, Alphonse 4: vol. 4, p. 260.	SP	Posselius Brothers Furniture Mfg. Co.	125	Belgium	Belgium	Belgium
Posselius, John C. 4: vol. 4, p. 260.	SP	Posselius Brothers Furniture Mfg. Co.	125	Belgium	Belgium	Belgium
Pungs, William 3: vol. 3, p. 982. 6.	P	Pungs-Anderson (carriage mfg.)	100	France	France	France
Quinby, William E. 6. 8: vol. 2, p. 1096.	P	Detroit Free Press	250	Maine	Maine	Maine
Reese, Carl 14: p. 357. 29.	P	Modern Match Co.	160	Indiana	Germany	Michigan
Roberts, Dugald H. 14: p. 411. 22: 10-26-27. 24: 10-26-24.	SP	McRae and Roberts (brass goods)	300	English Canada	-	-
Rodgers, Fordyce H. 6. 8: vol. 2, p. 1202	P	Detroit White Lead Works (paint)	150	Detroit	Vermont	Detroit

6	7	8	9	10	11	12	13	14
1864	-	23	investor	yes	yes	Presbyterian	Republican	19
1849	-	-	inherited	-	-	-	-	1
1864	36	36	founder	-	-	Baptist	-	3
1834	23	-	investor	yes	-	Presbyterian	Republican	-
1848	20	35	inherited	yes	-	Congregationalist	Republican	2
1842	23	24	founder	-	-	Congregationalist	Republican	2
1844	12	27	inherited	-	-	-	-	-
1842	14	29	inherited	yes	-	-	-	-
1849	3	-	cofounder	-	-	-	Prohibitionist	-
1835	15	40	investor	-	yes	-	-	-
1861	29	-	-	-	-	-	Republican	1
1851	41	26	founder	-	-	Congregationalist	-	-
1840	-	40	investor	-	-	-	Republican	4

1	2	3	4	5a	5b	5c
Russel, George H. 2: p. 271. 6.	P	Russel Wheel and Foundry Co. (railroad equipment)	250	Detroit	Pennsylvania	United States
Schloss, Albert W. 4: vol. 3, p. 624. 6.	O	Schloss Brothers (clothing)	200	Detroit	Germany	Germany
Schloss, Emmanuel 6. 29.	O	E. Schloss and Sons and Co. (clothing)	200	Germany	Germany	Germany
Schmidt, Edward J. 3: vol. 3, p. 432. 6.	P	Traugott Schmidt (tanning)	115	Detroit	Germany	Germany
Scotten, Oren 3: vol. 5, p. 156. 6. 29.	P	Scotten, Dillon and Co. (tobacco)	125	New York	Scotland	-
Scotten, William 17: p. 273. 29.	P	Daniel Scotten Co. (tobacco)	976	Michigan	Great Britain	-
Scripps, James E. 6. 8: vol. 2, p. 1096	P	Evening News Assoc.	250	England	England	England
Sherwood, Theodore 5: p. 113.	P	The Norris Co. (clothing)	100	New York	New York	New York
Siegel, Jacob 3: vol. 5, p. 911. 6. 29.	O	American Lady Corset Co.	555	Germany	Germany	Germany
Smith, Frederick B. 3: vol. 5, p. 781–82. 6.	O	Woolverine Mfg. Co. (lumber)	350	Detroit	United States	United States
Snover, Edward J. 6. 29.	P	Novelty Knitting Co.	150	Michigan	New Jersey	New Jersey
Stanton, Marvin M. 6. 23: 6-6-08. 29.	SP	Stanton, Marvin and Co. (clothing)	300	New York	New York	New York
Stearns, Frederick K. 3: vol. 3, p. 809. 4: vol. 5, p. 402. 6.	P	Frederick Stearns and Co. (drugs)	400	New York	New York	New York

6	7	8	9	10	11	12	13	14
1847	-	-	founder	yes	-	Presbyterian	Democrat	1
1862	-	-	inherited	-	-	-	-	4
-	-	-	-	-	-	Jewish	-	-
1865	-	32	inherited	-	-	-	-	-
1850	16	25	cofounder	-	-	Baptist	-	1
1857	-	37	inherited	-	-	-	-	-
1835	24	38	founder	-	-	-	-	-
1839	15	-	investor	-	-	Episcopalian	Republican	1
1841	45	-	founder	-	-	-	-	-
1863	-	25	founder	-	-	-	Republican	9
-	-	-	-	-	-	-	-	-
1847	-	40	cofounder	-	yes	Presbyterian	-	5
1854	1	33	inherited	-	yes	-	Republican	8

1	2	3	4	5a	5b	5c
Stroh, Bernard 6. 22: 4-5-16. 24: 4-5-16.	P	Stroh Brewing Co.	110	Detroit	Germany	Germany
Strong, William H. 6. 29.	SP	Strong, Lee and Co. (clothing)	100	Connecticut	Connecticut	Connecticut
Swift, Edward Y. 22: 6-15-13. 29.	P	Michigan Bolt and Nut Works (industrial hardware)	270	Vermont	Connecticut	Connecticut
Thomas, Claudius W. 29.	P	Roe, Stephens Mfg. Co. (brass works)	200	Michigan	England	England
Thompson, Edwin L. 3: vol. 3, p. 488.	P	Delta Lumber Co.	160	Pennsylvania	Pennsylvania	Vermont
Thorp, Darius D. 6. 25: 8-15-31. 29.	SP	Thorp, Hawley and Co. (candies)	100	Indiana	Indiana	Indiana
Vinton, Warren G. 3: vol. 4, p. 74. 6. 29.	P	Vinton Co. (lumber)	250	New York	Connecticut	New York
Wadsworth, Thomas A. 2: p. 638. 6. 29.	O	Western Cigar Box Mfg.	100	Michigan	Connecticut	Connecticut
Webb, Albert H. 23: 10-5-14. 29.	P	Parker, Webb and Co. (meat packers)	175	England	England	England
Werneken, Frank S. 3: vol. 5, p. 453. 6.	P	John Brennan Co. (stove and boilers)	200	New Jersey	-	-
Williams, William H. 6. 22: 8-1-28. 27: vol. 1, p. 126.	O	Williams Bros. and Charbonneau (foods)	500	Wales	Wales	Wales
Wright, Charles 6. 15: p. 114–5. 24: 8-18-24.	P	Charles Wright and Co. (drugs)	100	New York	New York	Vermont
Wright, James N. 6. 24: 11-14-10.	P	Ideal Mfg. Co. (iron and steel)	1,100	Connecticut	Connecticut	Connecticut
Zacharias, Ida 29.	SP	Zacharias and Mason (clothing)	250	Michigan	Pennsylvania	Pennsylvania

6	7	8	9	10	11	12	13	14
-	-	-	inherited	yes	-	-	-	2
-	-	-	-	-	-	-	-	-
1827	29	-	-	yes	yes	-	-	-
1845	-	-	-	-	-	-	-	-
1845	35	45	founder	yes	-	-	-	-
1839	37	-	-	-	-	-	Republican	2
1830	-	28	founder	-	-	-	-	-
1844	2	23	founder	yes	-	-	Republican	1
1847	13	-	cofounder	yes	-	-	-	-
1850	10	40	inherited	-	yes	-	Republican	6
1849	14	-	-	-	-	-	-	-
1850	30	31	founder	-	yes	-	Republican	5
1839	55	-	-	yes	-	-	Republican	1
1854	-	-	-	-	-		-	-

Books

2. Clarence M. Burton, ed., *Compendium of History and Biography of the City of Detroit and Wayne County, Michigan* (Detroit: Henry Taylor & Co., 1909).

3. Clarence M. Burton, ed., *The City of Detroit, Michigan, 1701–1922*, 5 vols. (Detroit: S. J. Clarke Publishing Co., 1922).

4. Clarence M. Burton and M. Agnes Burton, eds., *History of Wayne County and the City of Detroit, Michigan*, 5 vols. (Chicago: S. J. Clarke, 1930).

5. *Detroit Illustrated* (Akron, Ohio: Harry Hook Co., 1891).

6. *The Detroit Society Address Book* (Detroit: Dau's Publishing Co., 1899); *The Detroit Society Address Book* (New York: Dau's Publishing Co., 1900–1901); *The Detroit Society Address Book* (New York: Dau's Publishing Co., 1901–1902).

7. Richard E. Edwards, *Industries of Michigan: City of Detroit* (New York: New York Historical Publishers, 1880).

8. Silas Farmer, *History of Detroit and Wayne County and Early Michigan*, 3d ed., rev. and enl., 2 vols. (Detroit: S. Farmer & Co. for Munrell & Co. [New York] 1890).

9. Paul Leake, *History of Detroit*, 2 vols. (New York: Lewis Publishing, 1912).

10. Michigan, *Legislative Manual and Official Directory of the State of Michigan for the Year 1885*, Harry A. Conant, Secretary of State (Lansing, Mich.: W. F. George & Co., 1885).

11. Michigan, *The Official Directory and Legislative Manual of the State of Michigan for the Years 1895 and 1896*, Washington Gardner, Secretary of State (Lansing, Mich.: Robert Smith & Co., 1895).

12. J. W. Leonard, *Industries of Detroit* (Detroit: J. M. Elstner & Co., 1887).

13. Albert Nelson Marquis, ed., *The Book of Detroiters* (Chicago: A. N. Marquis, 1908).

14. Albert Nelson Marquis, ed., *The Book of Detroiters* (Chicago: A. N. Marquis, 1914).

15. James J. Mitchell, *Detroit in History and Commerce* (Detroit: Rodgers & Thorpe, 1891).

16. Graeme O'Geran, *A History of the Detroit Street Railways* (Detroit: Conover Press, 1931).

17. Robert B. Ross and George B. Catlin, *Landmarks of Detroit: A History of the City* (Detroit: Evening News Co., 1898).

18. *Who's Who in America*, 20 (Chicago: A. N. Marquis & Co., 1938–1939).

Articles

19. "Detroit's Young Men," *YMCA Newsletter* 20 (September 21, 1922).

20. Elleine H. Stones, "The McMillan Papers," *Among Friends* 2, no. 4 (March–April, 1948) [quarterly news bulletin of the DPL].

Newspapers

21. *The Detroiter.*
22. *Detroit Free Press.*
23. *Detroit Journal.*
24. *Detroit News.*
25. *Detroit Saturday Night.*

Manuscripts

26. Clarence M. Burton, "Scrapbook," BHC, DPL.

27. Clarence M. Burton, Biographical File, undated obituary, BHC, DPL.

28. Grand Army of the Republic, Detroit Post 384, GAR, Necrology File, BHC, DPL.

29. Washington, D.C., National Archives, Bureau of the Census Records, Manuscript Schedules for the Twelfth Federal Census of Detroit, 1900, Record Group 29.

Appendix 7

Note on Sources

Most of the data coded from sources listed below was computerized and analyzed on the University of Michigan computer with the Michigan Interactive Data Analysis System. The computerized sources are indicated by the letter c, immediately following the reference; the letter i stands for individual level data and the number following it indicates the number of cases recorded in the computer file.

INTRODUCTION TO THE UNITED STATES CENSUS

Wright, Carroll D. *The History and Growth of the United States Census.* Washington, D.C.: G.P.O., 1900.

U.S. Department of the Interior. Census Office. *Instructions to Enumerators: Twelfth Census of the United States.* Washington, D.C.: G.P.O., 1900.

U.S. Department of Commerce. Bureau of Census. *Instructions to Enumerators.* Washington, D.C.: G.P.O., 1919.

PUBLISHED VOLUMES OF THE POPULATION CENSUS

U.S. Department of the Interior. Census Office. *Tenth Federal Census of the United States, 1880, Population.* Washington, D.C.: G.P.O., 1883.

U.S. Department of the Interior. Census Office. *Compendium of the Tenth Census, 1880.* Vol. 1, *Population.* Washington, D.C.: G.P.O., 1888.

U.S. Department of the Interior. Census Office. *Report on Vital and Social Statistics in the United States at the Eleventh Census: 1890.* 2 vols. Washington, D.C.: G.P.O., 1896.

U.S. Department of the Interior. Census Office. *Twelfth Census of the United States, 1900: Population.* 2 vols. Washington, D.C.: G.P.O., 1901.

U.S. Department of Commerce. Bureau of the Census. *Thirteenth Census of the United States, 1920: Population.* 2 vols. Washington, D.C.: G.P.O., 1911.
U.S. Department of Commerce. Bureau of the Census. *Fourteenth Census of the United States, 1920: Population.* 4 vols. Washington, D.C.: G.P.O., 1921.

MANUSCRIPT SCHEDULES OF THE POPULATION CENSUS

NA. Manuscript schedules of the 1880 population census for Detroit. (c, i, 12,185)
NA. Manuscript schedules of the 1900 population census for Detroit. (c, i, 26,181)
NA. 1920 population census. Manuscript list of Detroit enumeration districts.
U.S. Bureau of the Census. Manuscript schedules of the 1920 population census for Detroit and suburbs. (c, i, 6,055 heads of households)

PUBLISHED VOLUMES OF THE MANUFACTURING CENSUS

U.S. Department of the Interior. Census Office. *Compendium of the Tenth Census, 1880.* Vol. 2, *Manufactures.* Washington, D.C.: G.P.O., 1888.
U.S. Department of the Interior. Census Office. *Twelfth Census of the United States, 1900: Manufactures.* 4 vols. Washington, D.C.: G.P.O., 1902.
U.S. Department of Commerce and Labor. Bureau of the Census. *Census of Manufactures, 1904.* Washington, D.C.: G.P.O., 1905.

MANUSCRIPT SCHEDULES OF THE MANUFACTURING CENSUS

Michigan State Archives. Lansing, Michigan. Manuscript schedules of the 1880 nonpopulation census for Detroit: products of industry.

REPORTS OF THE MICHIGAN BUREAU OF LABOR AND INDUSTRIAL STATISTICS

Michigan. *Annual Report of the Bureau of Labor and Industrial Statistics.* Lansing, 1885–1901.
Surveys providing individual level data on the workers in specific industries:
   1890 Furniture workers. (c, i, 848)
   1891 Agricultural implements and iron works industry. (c, i, 3,899)
   1894 Railroad employees. (c, i, 839)
   1896 Owners of hack and bus lines. (c, i, 63)
   1896 Employees of hack and bus lines. (c, i, 147)
   1896 Street railway employees. (c, i, 600)
   1897 Vehicle manufacturing workers. (c, i, 402)
Factory Inspections: Appendixes to Reports for the years 1898–1901.

OTHER STATE DOCUMENTS

Michigan. *Local Acts of the Legislature of the State of Michigan.* Lansing, 1879, 1905, 1907, 1913, 1917, 1919.

Michigan. *State of Michigan Report on Building and Loan Associations.* Lansing, 1897.

LAND USE SURVEYS AND REPORTS ON HOUSING

Robinson, Elisha, and Pidgeon, Roger H. *Atlas of the City of Detroit and Suburbs Embracing Portions of Hamtramck, Springwells, and Greenfield Townships.* New York, 1885. (c, 720 fronts)

Sanborn Map Company. *Insurance Maps of Detroit, Michigan.* 6 vols. New York: Sanborn-Perris Map Co., 1897. (c, 8,132 parcels)

Baist, G. William. *Real Estate Atlas of Surveys of Detroit and Suburbs.* 2 vols. Philadelphia, 1918.

DeForest, Robert W., and Veiller, Lawrence, eds. *The Tenement House Problem, Including the Report of the New York State Tenement House Commission of 1900.* 2 vols. New York: Macmillan Co., 1903.

U.S. Congress. House. Industrial Commission. *Report of the Industrial Commission on the Relations and Conditions of Capital and Labor Employed in Manufactures and General Business.* H. Doc. 183, 57th Cong., 1st sess., 1901.

DIRECTORIES

J. W. Weeks & Co. *Detroit City Directory.* Detroit, 1880–84.

R. L. Polk & Co. *Detroit City Directory.* Detroit, 1885–1920. Title varies: 1885, *J. W. Weeks & Co.'s Detroit City Directory*; 1886, *Detroit City and Wayne County Directory.*

MHC. Smołczyński, Wincenty. *Przewodnik Adresowy i Historya Osady Polskiej w Detroit, Michigan.* Detroit, 1907.

BHC. Turner, Arthur, and Moses, Earl R. *Colored Detroit: A Brief History of Detroit's Colored Population and a Directory of Their Businesses, Organizations, Professions and Trades.* Detroit, 1924.

REAL ESTATE PUBLICATIONS

BHC. Hannah's Real Estate Exchange. *The Real Estate Advertiser.* Detroit, 1890.

BHC. Shelley and Simpson. *The Real Estate Review.* Detroit, 1892.

BHC. Hannan Real Estate Exchange. *W. W. Hannan's Real Estate Record.* Detroit, 1889.

CITY REPORTS

Detroit. *The Charter of the City of Detroit.* 1893.

Detroit. *The Charter of the City of Detroit.* 1918.

Detroit. *Annual Message of Mayor Hazen S. Pingree.* 1890–97. Title varies: 1893, *Annual Address of Hazen S. Pingree, Mayor of the City of Detroit.*

Detroit. *Annual Report of the Board of Poor Commissioners to the Common Council of the City of Detroit.* 1891–1900.

Detroit. *Annual Report of the Board of Public Works of the City of Detroit.* 1892–1900.

Detroit. *Annual Report of the Board of Water Commissioners of the City of Detroit.* 1892–1900.

Detroit. *Annual Report of the City Historiographer.* 1908.

Detroit. *Annual Report of the Fire Commissioner.* 1893–96, 1900.

Detroit. *Annual Report of the Public Lighting Commission.* 1897.

CITY ARCHIVES

BHC. Detroit. Department of Building and Safety. Fire Marshal Building Permits. 1881–1901.

COUNTY ARCHIVES

Wayne County, Michigan. Wayne County Clerk. Marriage Transcripts. 1887–1900. (c, i, 758 couples)

PUBLISHED REPORTS OF THE DETROIT ASSOCIATION OF CHARITIES

DAC. *Annual Report.* Detroit, 1882–83, 1885, 1889–93, 1896–98, 1901. Title varies: 1882, *Proceedings of the . . . Annual Meeting*; 1883, 1885, 1889, *Annual Report of the Central Council*; 1890–93, 1896–98, 1901, *Annual Report of the Board of Trustees.*

ARCHIVES OF THE DETROIT ASSOCIATION OF CHARITIES

WRL. DAC Case files. United Community Services Collection. 1891. (c, i, 342)

ARCHIVES OF THE YOUNG WOMAN'S HOME ASSOCIATION

MHC. Young Woman's Home Association. 1880 Employment Register. (c, i, 483)

PAPERS OF THE DETROIT URBAN LEAGUE

MHC. *Guide to the Microfilm Edition of the Detroit Urban League Papers.* Ann Arbor, 1974.

MHC. Detroit Urban League Papers. Board of Directors Minutes and Papers. 1916–50.

MHC. Detroit Urban League Papers. Board of Directors General File. Undated, 1945–50.

MHC. Detroit Urban League Papers. Executive Secretary's General File. Undated [June 1916–June 1927].

SURVEYS OF DETROIT'S BLACK COMMUNITY AFTER 1917

Haynes, George E. *Negro Newcomers in Detroit, Michigan: A Challenge to Christian Statesmanship, A Preliminary Survey.* New York: Home Missions Council, 1918; reprint ed., New York: Arno Press and the New York Times, 1969.

BHC. Washington, Forrester B. "The Negro in Detroit: A Survey of the Conditions of a Negro Group in a Northern Industrial Center during the War Prosperity Period." Detroit, 1920.

PAPERS OF THE AMERICANIZATION COMMITTEE OF DETROIT

MHC. Papers of Arthur J. Tuttle. Americanization Committee of Detroit Papers. 1914–31.

NEWSPAPERS

The Detroiter.
Detroit Evening News.
Detroit Free Press.
Detroit News.
Detroit Saturday Night.
Detroit Sunday News-Tribune.
Detroit Tribune.

BIOGRAPHIES

See Appendix 6.

GENERAL HISTORIES

Burton, Clarence M., ed. *The City of Detroit, Michigan, 1701–1922.* 5 vols. Detroit: S. J. Clarke Publishing Co., 1922.

Burton, Clarence M., and Burton, M. Agnes, eds. *History of Wayne County and Detroit, Michigan.* 5 vols. Chicago: S. J. Clarke, 1930.

Farmer, Silas. *The History of Detroit and Michigan.* Detroit: S. Farmer & Co., 1890; reprint ed., Detroit: Gale Research Co., 1969.

RECORD LINKAGE

Several hundred computer files were created from the master files for analysis. All were kept separately and all were matched with other files when needed for specific analyses (a simple operation with MIDAS's powerful "compute" command). It was easy, for example, to compute the number of people per house from a census file, and then, using house addresses as a matching variable, to transfer this result to a house level file containing data on houses collected in land use sources. With the matching done, we could then study population data in relationship to housing characteristics. Or it was possible to compute the different ethnic groups' fertility at the cluster level and use the results in conjunction with the already developed indexes of segregation computed at the same level. The same principle of data analysis served to compare the different points in time. Throughout the study, the main levels of data analysis were the individual, the household, the house, the front, the block, the cluster, and the city as a whole, and some intermediate levels such as the plate level for weighting purposes (see Appendix 1), or a combination of clusters. All the primary computer files for 1880 and 1900, as well as the most important derived files, are available at the Inter-University Consortium for Political and Social Research of the Institute for Social Research of the University of Michigan, together with computer dictionaries. The 1920 computer files which were created for this study but are still protected by the privacy act are kept at the Bureau of the Census.

Not all record linkage could be successfully handled by computer, however, especially when we had to use the twenty-year run of city directories (from 1880 to 1900) for special analysis or search individuals not in the initial sample through the manuscript schedules of the census. The most ambitious manual linkage of the study (in addition to the one linking occupation to income described in Appendix 3) consisted of linking building permits to our initial samples, and searching information on permit takers through city directories and manuscript censuses (chap. 6). Other manual linkages were conducted between sampled individuals and Wayne County marriage licences for the study of religious affiliations (chap. 5); between the sampled clusters and city directories for the study of residential persistence (chap. 7); between sampled clusters and city reports for the study of the geographic distribution of services (chaps. 5 and 6); and between sampled clusters and factory inspection for the study of work and residence patterns (chap. 7).

Index

DATE DUE

The Library Store   #47-0106